Audie Murphy's
Film and Television Co-Stars
From A to Z

David Alan Williams

© 2013 by David Alan Williams.

Self-published First Edition, 2014 updated Edition
All rights reserved. No part of this document may be reproduced or transmitted in any form or by any means, electronic, mechanical, photocopying, recording, or otherwise, without prior written permission of David Alan Williams.

All photos are used for illustration purposes only and are not meant to infringe on the rights of any party. This is a reference work intending to acknowledge the co-stars of Audie Murphy.

Cover photographs:
    Front - Audie Murphy from *Whispering Smith* 1961 (Revue Studios/ MCA TV)
    Back – Audie Murphy from *To Hell and Back* 1955 (Universal International)
    Covers designed by Deborah Ellen Williams

Manufactured in the United States of America
Printed by:
Razorback Printing Co.
405 West 4th Avenue
Pine Bluff, Arkansas 71601

ISBN-10:0615799914
ISBN-13: 978-0-615-79991-9

Dedication

This book is dedicated to my wife Deborah who has been my everything for more than a quarter of a century. Without her belief in me this project would never have been started, let alone finished. I love you most!

Acknowledgements

All thanks must first go to our Lord and Savior Jesus Christ, for without Him all are lost.

Many thanks to everyone involved in getting this book written. My sincere appreciation goes to Momma Sue (Sue Gossett), & Betty Tate who, without their consummate help, cooperation, ideas, and contacts, this book could never have been achieved.

Thanks to Dale Waldrop for his assistance with research.

Thanks to the Audie Murphy American Cotton Museum.

Thanks to all the 'Audie Murphy Days crew' who get together every year for our own 'family reunion' and those who make it as frequently as possible: Ken & Betty Tate, Teri Edge, Stan Smith, Sharon Lovell, Ann Joiner, Dave & Sue Gossett, Rowenia Ely, Jerry Lynch, Myrna Koska, Vic Mizzone, Larry Winters, Jimmy & Lori James, Bob Moore, Chet & Ann Lang, Wayne & Margie Cutshaw, Deanna Glause & family, Al & Vickie Lee, David Caraway, Gerald Bayer, and the rest that I am most likely forgetting.

Thanks to Dave Phillips who started the petition to get the Presidential Medal of Freedom for Audie Murphy.

Great big thanks to Richard Rodgers who created the wonderful website www.audiemurphy.com that gives so many honors to not only Audie Murphy, but to all veterans.

Thanks to the members of the Audie Murphy message board on Richard's site who share stories, interests, and loads of information about their hero, especially Christie Huard and the late Eva Dano.

To www.imdb.com, Wikipedia, www.findagrave.com, www.westernclippings.com, Universal-International, Columbia, Paramount, United Artists, 20th Century Fox, Allied Artists, American International, Metro-Goldwyn-Mayer, FIPCO Productions, and Revue Studios/ MCA TV for their information, photographs and films of Audie Murphy. .

Last, but certainly not least, to the most devoted Audie Murphy fan ever, Mary Ferguson.

Contents

Introduction	1
Foreword I by Michael Dante	3
Foreword II by Sue Gossett	4
Foreword III by Nadine Murphy Lokey	5
Foreword IV by Jan Merlin	6
Which Co-Star?	7
A	9
B	22
C	56
D	87
E	116
F	123
G	138
H	154
I	176
J	180
K	191
L	206
M	228
N	278
O	283
P	291
Q	304
R	306
S	332
T	378
U	398
V	399
W	407
Y	433
Z	435
Filmography	436
Television Episodes	437
Co-Stars Who Attended Audie Murphy Days	438
Alphabetical Index of Co-Stars	439
About the Author	442

I hope you enjoy learning about these folks as much as I did.
DW

Introduction

Audie Leon Murphy was born near Kingston, Texas June 20, 1925 and was an American actor and was also the most decorated United States soldier in American History.

The son of poor Texas sharecroppers, Audie Murphy became a national hero during World War II as the most decorated combat soldier of the war. Among his thirty-three awards was the Congressional Medal of Honor, the highest award for bravery that a soldier can receive. In addition, he was also decorated for bravery by the governments of France and Belgium, and was credited with killing over 240 German soldiers and wounding and capturing many more, all while he was still a teenager.

Murphy had tried to enlist in the army in his native Texas, but was rejected because he was too young. With his sister Corinne's help, he falsified his age to appear to be old enough, tried again and was accepted this time. After undergoing basic military training, he was sent to Europe, where he fought in nine major campaigns over three years and rose from the rank of private to a battlefield commission as a second lieutenant. Part of Murphy's appeal to many people was that he didn't fit the "image" most had of a war hero. He was a slight, almost fragile-looking, shy and soft-spoken young man, whose boyish appearance (something he never lost throughout his life; he always looked at least fifteen years younger than he actually was) often shocked people when they found out that, for example, during one battle he leaped on top of a burning tank, which was loaded with fuel and ammunition and could have exploded at any second, and used its machine gun to hold off waves of attacking German troops, killing dozens of them and saving his unit from certain destruction and the entire line from being overrun. In September 1945 Murphy was released from active duty and assigned to inactive status.

His story caught the interest of superstar James Cagney, who invited Murphy to Hollywood. Cagney Productions paid for acting and dancing lessons but was reluctantly forced to admit that Murphy, at least at that point in his career, didn't have what it took to become a movie star. For the next several years he struggled to make it as an actor, but jobs were few, specifically just two bit parts, in *Beyond Glory* (1948) and *Texas, Brooklyn & Heaven* (1948). He finally got a lead role in *Bad Boy* (1949), and starred in the trouble-plagued production of MGM's *The Red Badge of Courage* (1951), directed by John Huston. While this film is now considered a minor classic, the politics behind the production sparked an irreparable fissure within the ranks of the studio's upper management. Murphy proved adequate as an actor, but the film, with virtually no female presence (or appeal), bombed badly at the box office. Murphy, however, had already signed with Universal-International Pictures, which was putting him in a string of modestly budgeted Westerns, a genre that suited his easygoing image and Texas drawl.

Over the next few years he starred in many exciting westerns like his role as Billy the Kid in *The Kid from Texas* (1950), playing opposite his then wife Wanda Hendrix in *Sierra* (1950), playing Jesse James for the first time in *Kansas Raiders* (1950), outlaw Bill Doolin in *The Cimarron Kid* (1951), the Silver Kid in *The Duel at Silver Creek* (1952), *Gunsmoke* (1953), *Column South* (1953), *Tumbleweed* (1953), *Ride Clear of Diablo* (1954), *Drums Across the River* (1954), and the unforgettable *Destry* (1954).

He then starred in the film version of his autobiography, *To Hell and Back* (1955), which was a huge hit, setting a box-office record for Universal that wasn't broken for twenty years until it was finally surpassed by *Jaws* (1975).

He continued making interesting pictures such as *World in My Corner* (1956), *Walk the Proud Land* (1956), *The Guns of Fort Petticoat* (1957), and *Joe Butterfly* (1957).

One of his better pictures was *Night Passage* (1957), a Western in which he played the kid brother of James Stewart. More pictures followed with *The Quiet American* (1958), *The Gun Runners* (1958), *Ride a Crooked Trail* (1958), *No Name on the Bullet* (1959), *The Wild and the Innocent* (1959), *Cast a Long Shadow* (1959), and *Hell Bent for Leather* (1960).

He worked for Huston again on *The Unforgiven* (1960). The film also starred Audrey Hepburn, Doug McClure, Burt Lancaster, and Lillian Gish as their mother.

A few more films followed like *Seven Ways from Sundown* (1960), *Posse from Hell* (1961), and *Battle at Bloody Beach* (1961). He then starred in his own television series as the title character of *Whispering Smith* (1961) for twenty-six episodes.

Some more films continued with *Six Black Horses* (1962) and *Showdown* (1963), which was Universal-International's last film under the U-I name.

The studio system that Murphy grew into as an actor crumbled. Universal's new owners, MCA, dumped its "International" tag in 1962 and turned the studio's focus toward the more lucrative television industry. For theatrical productions, it dropped its roster of contract players and hired actors on a per-picture basis only. That cheap Westerns on the big screen were becoming a thing of the past bode no good for Murphy, either.

He appeared on screen as the opening narrator in *War is Hell* (1963). The film goes down in history as the film that was playing in the theater that Lee Harvey Oswald was captured in after he assassinated President Kennedy.

He appeared then in a number of independent films such as *Gunfight at Comanche Creek* (1963), *The Quick Gun* (1964), *Bullet for a Badman* (1964), *Apache Rifles* (1964), *Arizona Raiders* (1965), *Gunpoint* (1966), and *Trunk to Cairo* (1966) filmed entirely in Isreal.

The Texican (1966), his lone attempt at a new, European form of inexpensive horse opera, to be known as the Spaghetti Western, was unsuccessful.

He made *40 Guns to Apache Pass* (1967) before he filmed his last role, again playing outlaw Jesse James, in *A Time for Dying* (1969).

In addition to his acting career, he made a total of forty-five films; Murphy was also a successful rancher and businessman. He bred and raised thoroughbred horses and owned several ranches in Texas, Arizona, and California. He was also a songwriter and penned hits for such singers as Dean Martin, Eddy Arnold, Charley Pride, Jimmy Dean, Porter Waggoner, Roy Clark, Slim Whitman, and many others.

His postwar life wasn't all roses, however. He suffered from what is now called Post-Traumatic Stress Disorder (PTSD) but was then called "combat fatigue", and was known to have a hair-trigger temper. He had a short-lived marriage to actress Wanda Hendrix, but had a more successful marriage to Pamela Archer, which produced two sons, Terry and Skip.

In the 1960s his increasing bouts of insomnia and depression resulted in his becoming addicted to a particularly powerful sleeping pill called Placidyl, an addiction he eventually broke by locking himself in a motel room all alone until he was free of the addiction, a feat not many could accomplish, if anyone else even could.

He ran into a streak of bad financial luck and was forced to declare bankruptcy in 1968 after investing in some foreign oil wells. He eventually got his investment back.

Admirably, he campaigned vigorously for the government to spend more time and money on taking care of returning Vietnam War veterans, as he more than most others knew exactly what kinds of problems they were going to have on the home front.

On May 28, 1971, Murphy was aboard a private plane on his way to a business meeting when it ran into thick fog near Roanoke, Virginia, and crashed into the side of a mountain, killing all six aboard. He was buried with full military honors in Arlington National Cemetery. According to cemetery records, the only grave site visited by more people than Murphy's is that of assassinated President John F. Kennedy.

Audie Murphy Days is held each year in Greenville and Farmersville, Texas on or near his birthday in June. My family has been privileged to attend every one since the beginning in 1996. We were also honored to attend on October 29, 2013 the presentation of the Texas Legislative Medal of Honor awarded posthumously to Audie Murphy in Farmersville. The award was presented to Audie's sole surviving sibling Nadine Murphy-Lokey by Texas Governor Rick Perry to a crowd of thousands!

This book is a reference guide and a tip of the hat to all the wonderful actors and actresses who co-starred with Audie Murphy in forty-four of his movies and the twenty-nine episodes of television he made.

War is Hell (1963) is not included, as he only introduced the finished product and didn't actually act with the cast. Any co-star or supporting player omitted is purely the fault of the author.

Foreword I

It was the year 1964 when I co-starred in *Apache Rifles*, the first of two films I did with Audie Murphy; the other film in 1965, was entitled *Arizona Raiders*. I was very excited and looked forward to working with Audie and how proud I was to be working with the most decorated soldier in World War II, including a Congressional Medal of Honor recipient.

I enjoyed working with Audie, because he was a good actor, honest, sensitive, polite, soft-spoken, and subtle; always the consummate professional. He was a much better actor than he was given credit for. Audie was also a fine song writer and poet. If I had to describe his character in one word, it would be feline. He was like a cat; smooth, smart, and lightning fast.

In 2007, I had the honor of presenting *The Silver Spur Award*, posthumously, to Audie Murphy during a special ceremony at the Sportsman's Lodge in Studio City, California. I gave the award to his lovely wife Pamela, and two sons James and Terry. It was very nice seeing them throughout that memorable evening. They were a pleasure to be with. Audie was very proud of his family and they were proud of him.

My life has been enriched to have known Audie Murphy and to have had the distinct opportunity of co-starring in two films with one of America's greatest heroes, on screen and off.

Michael Dante
April 2012

Michael Dante, Sue Gossett, and David Williams 2012

Foreword II

Forewords are usually composed by people who know or knew the person about whom the book is being written. I never knew Audie Murphy in real life. Being a fan for most of my teenage years and my entire adult life meeting Audie Murphy was a dream of mine. Unfortunately, it was a dream which did not come true in the actual sense. But in a way I did meet him through his family, co-stars, stuntmen, and directors. They all said the same thing: Audie was a quiet man, a very generous person, a practical joker, and a friend. What I heard from them was of a man who had strong convictions. He did not make friends easily, but when he did, they were friends for life.

Many books have been written about Audie Murphy, mostly biographies regarding his military career. We have heroes today who perform tremendous acts of bravery. Audie did what he did to protect his men as our fearless men and women do now in the present conflicts. We all know of Audie's difficult growing up years and his military exploits of heroism and courage.

There have been a few books written about Audie's films, but this one is unique in that his co-stars are highlighted in depth and detail. Many of them had interesting and funny things to say as well as serious comments about him. He had a sense of humor that was just a bit different in that he loved playing practical jokes on people.

His friend, stuntman, and actor Neil Summers, put it very succinctly: "Audie was the real thing".

This work by David Williams will admirably fill a real gap.

Sue Gossett, Author of *The Films and Career of Audie Murphy* and *Audie Murphy Now Showing*.
April 2012

Sue Gossett and Jan Merlin 1998

Foreword III

In this book, you will read about some good, talented people who played in the movies with my brother Audie Murphy.

These men are just men, like every-day John's and Joe's, like we have for friends, family, and neighbors, except that they chose acting for a living.

It takes a lot of people to make a movie. We need to pay tribute to these hard-working folk who have brought many hours of good entertainment into our lives!

I'm honored that my friend David Williams, the author, asked me to express my opinion of these actors. My best to each one and many blessings on you all!

Nadine Murphy-Lokey
April 2012

David Williams, Nadine Murphy Lokey (sister), and the late Gene Murphy (brother) 2001

Foreword IV

A number of us got to be in battles with Audie during the last century, though ours were not lethal.

I had the pleasure of playing the heavy for the pilot episode "The Blind Gun" of Audie Murphy's television series, *Whispering Smith*.

We became instant friends and did two feature films afterwards. Again, I was the bad guy in *Hell Bent for Leather*, and he asked to have me play his good buddy in *Gunfight at Comanche Creek*.

We were hoping to do another film, but his tragic demise prevented that. He never discussed his war years against the Germans and I didn't talk about mine against the Japanese. We were simply actors, trying to do the best job we could.

He was a delight to work with and dedicated to his new profession. I'm humbly proud to have been a small part of his extraordinary life.

Jan Merlin
June 2012

Audie Murphy and Jan Merlin 1960

Which co-star..............

1. Raised pineapples in Guatemala?
2. Was Rod Serling's first choice to narrate *The Twilight Zone*, but couldn't because of contractual issues?
3. Was electrocuted while attempting to repair the garbage disposal unit in his kitchen sink?
4. Was tried and acquitted for attempted murder at age nine?
5. Made toy animals and pillows during the depression?
6. Was a successful dentist?
7. Died tragically, when he fell under a subway train at the Kensington High Street Station in London on May 25, 1971, the same week Audie Murphy died in the plane crash?
8. Had a street named after him in Stamford, Connecticut, in 2011?
9. Was found murdered, strangled in her West Hollywood apartment, on November 28, Thanksgiving Day, 1963, six days after the assassination of President Kennedy?
10. Was *Playboy* playmate of the month for October 1958?
11. Was *Playboy* playmate of the month for November 1958?
12. Posed for *Playboy* in the October 1959 issue?
13. Was *Playboy* playmate of the month for May 1967?
14. Posed for the August 1984 issue of *Playboy* at age 55?
15. Worked as an animator at Disney Studios on such classics as Fantasia and Bambi?
16. Joined the army at age fourteen and served with the expedition that pursued Pancho Villa into Mexico?
17. Worked as a receptionist...for Bugsy Siegel?
18. Wrote the unused lyrics to "The Fishin' Hole", the theme song for *The Andy Griffith Show*?
19. Died after slipping and falling through a glass shower door in his home July 30, 1980, at age 66?
20. Changed his professional name to that of his characters' name in his first movie?
21. Made the first appearance of an admiral in the original *Star Trek* series?
22. Used his engineering background to help create the original design for the Hollywood Walk Of Fame?
23. Formed the Los Angeles Smog Corporation to manufacture cans of 'Genuine Los Angeles Smog' for tourists to take back home?
24. Was killed by her own son?
25. Appeared in movies as Audie Murphy's and Elvis Presley's father?
26. Was a manager of the Bel Air Hotel in Los Angeles?
27. Died during the filming of the western *Comes a Horseman* as he was dragged to death behind a horse?
28. Never knew her real parents because during her infancy she was left outside the doors of a church with a note pinned to her?
29. Was the first person to win an Oscar, an Emmy, and a Tony Award?
30. Was the French voice of Warner Brothers cartoon character Tweetie Pie?
31. Had a son who was killed while serving time in a U.S. penitentiary?
32. Died twenty years before his final film appearance was released?
33. Was World Rodeo Champion for several years before turning to acting, directing, and stunt work?
34. Had the longest screen kiss in cinema history with Jane Wyman?
35. Body was stolen by carjackers when the hearse was stolen on the way to the mortuary, involved in a fender bender, and the car and the body were found shortly after.
36. Opened his own hamburger and malt shop in Hollywood before his big break, which he called Tiny's Patio?
37. Was bludgeoned to death in his Hollywood apartment following a grocery trip when he surprised a thief in his home?
38. Served as the live-action reference model for Cruella De Vil in Walt Disney's *One Hundred and One Dalmatians*?
39. Passed her bar exam in 1914, becoming at the age of 26 the first female attorney in her home state of Texas?
40. Played semi-pro basketball in a league that included the original Harlem Globetrotters?
41. Said "Good night, Dear" as the final words spoken in a very long career?

To find the fascinating answers to these exciting trivia questions, simply read the book.............

Lee Aaker

Audie Murphy and Lee Aaker in *Destry*

    Lee Aaker was born on September 25, 1943, in Los Angeles, where his mother owned a dance studio. As Rusty, the boy whose parents were killed by Indians and who was subsequently adopted by a cavalry unit at Fort Apache on the popular adventure *The Adventures of Rin Tin Tin* (1954), tyke actor Lee Aaker left a lasting mark in the early days of television, but he had in fact, appeared in several major films prior to this series.

    On TV almost from infancy, he started appearing in unbilled film bits at the age of eight in such classics as *The Greatest Show on Earth* (1952) and *High Noon* (1952). He quickly moved to featured status before year's end. He showed promise as the kidnapped Indian "Red Chief" in a segment of the film *Full House* (1952) and another kidnap victim as the son of scientist Gene Barry in *Atomic City* (1952). From there he co-starred in the John Wayne western classic *Hondo* (1953) as the inquisitive blond son of homesteader Geraldine Page, and appeared to good advantage in other movies such as the film noir thriller *Jeopardy* (1953) with Barbara Stanwyck, the horse opera drama *Arena* (1953) with Gig Young and the comedies *Mister Scoutmaster* (1953) with Clifton Webb and *Ricochet Romance* (1954) with Marjorie Main. He appeared in *Ride Clear of Diablo* (1954) and *Destry* (1954), two of Audie Murphy's most memorable movies.

    Stardom, however, was assured after nabbing the role of the famous dog's young master on the *Rin Tin Tin* series. After the show's demise, however, Aaker did not survive the transition into adult roles. He instead moved into the production end of the business, serving as an assistant to producer Herbert B. Leonard on the *Route 66* (1960) series, then later dropped out altogether to become a carpenter. He still attends nostalgia conventions and was recently a "Kids of the West" honoree at the 2005 Golden Boot Awards.

Rudolph Acosta

Rudolph Acosta with Audie Murphy in *Posse from Hell*

Born July 29, 1920, Mexican character actor Rodolfo Acosta achieved his greatest success in the US, primarily as a villain in westerns. He worked in Mexico in films of the great director Emilio Fernández, which led to a bit role in John Ford's film *The Fugitive* (1947). He came to the US and was signed by Universal for a small role in *One Way Street* (1950). He stayed in the US and his sharp, ruthless features led him to a long succession of roles as bandits, Indian warriors and outlaws. He played the role of Johnny Caddo in the Audie Murphy picture *Posse From Hell* (1961). In *The Tijuana Story* (1957), he actually had a sympathetic leading role, but in general he spent his career as a very familiar western bad guy. He died in 1974 at the age of 54 in Los Angeles.

Lillian Adams

Born May 13, 1922, she was an American stage and television actress with over 100 film and television roles to her credit. She appeared in such films as *Private Benjamin* (1980) and *Bruce Almighty* (2003), and television series as *Archie Bunker's Place* (1981), *The Twilight Zone* (1986), *Married... with Children* (1992) and *NYPD Blue* (1994). She appeared with Audie Murphy in *The Wild and the Innocent* (1959) as Kiri Hawks. She also appeared in commercials for CVS Pharmacy as mascot Super Saver Lillian.

Her last film project was *Tim and Eric's Billion Dollar Movie* (2012), released eight months after her death. She died May 25, 2011, in Los Angeles, California.

Mary Adams

Mary Adams was born in 1910 and made forty-three films and episodes of various television series from 1948 to 1973. Some of her other work incudes films such as *Night Has a Thousand Eyes* (1948), *Bugles in the Afternoon* (1952), *Executive Suite* (1954), *The Mountain* (1956), *Blood of Dracula* (1957), *Diary of a Madman* (1963), and *Doctors' Wives* (1971).

Her television appearances include *Craig Kennedy, Criminologist* (1952), *Medic* (1955), *Gunsmoke* (1956), *Have Gun - Will Travel* (1957), *Hawaiian Eye* (1959), *Twilight Zone* (1961), the final episode of *Whispering Smith* (1961) with Audie Murphy, *The Alfred Hitchcock Hour* (1963), and *My Three Sons* (1961-1964).

She died November 30, 1973, in Los Angeles, California.

Phil Adams

Although no biographical information could be found for Phil Adams, he has been a very busy actor and stunt man from 1950 to 2010, appearing in thirty-two films and television series.

Some of his acting appearances include *Darby's Rangers* (1958), *Lafayette Escadrille* (1958), the *Ford Startime* (1960) episode "The Man" with Audie Murphy, *Alfred Hitchcock Presents* (1961), *Kelly's Heroes* (1970), *The Poseidon Adventure* (1972), *Christmas Miracle in Caufield, U.S.A.* (1977), *C.H.O.M.P.S.* (1979), *Raw Deal* (1986), *Maximum Overdrive* (1986), *Xena: Warrior Princess* (1998), and *Being Eve* (2001).

He was also William Shatner's stunt double in several episodes of *Star Trek* (1966-1969).

Yvonne Adrian

Little is known about actress Yvonne Adams except she appeared in an episode of *Whispering Smith*, "Poet and Peasant Case" and an episode of *The Andy Griffith Show* "The Beauty Contest", both in 1961.

John Agar

John Agar was born in Chicago January 31, 1921, the eldest of four children. In World War II, Sgt. John Agar was a United States Army Air Force physical instructor. His 1945 marriage at the Wilshire Memorial Church to "America's Sweetheart" Shirley Temple put him in the public eye for the first time, and a movie contract with independent producer David O. Selznick quickly ensued.

Agar debuted opposite John Wayne, Henry Fonda, and Temple in John Ford's *Fort Apache* (1948), initial film in the famed director's "Cavalry Trilogy". His marriage to Shirley Temple ended in 1949, while his movie career continued, with ninety-four films and television episodes from 1948 to 2001, which include *She Wore a Yellow Ribbon* (1949), *Sands of Iwo Jima* (1949), *Along the Great Divide* (1951), *The Rocket Man* (1954), *Revenge of the Creature* (1955) which was the sequel to *The Creature From the Black Lagoon* (1954), *Tarantula* (1955), *The Mole People* (1956), *Joe Butterfly* (1957) with Audie Murphy, *Attack of the Puppet People* (1958), *Invisible Invaders* (1959), *Hand of Death* (1962), *Stage to Thunder Rock* (1964), *Zontar: The Thing from Venus* (1966), *Curse of the Swamp Creature* (1966), *Women of the Prehistoric Planet* (1966), *Night Fright* (1967), *The Undefeated* (1969), *Chisum* (1970), *Big Jake* (1971), *Charlie's Angels* (1976), *The Twilight Zone* (1986), and *Body Bags* (1993).

Popular with fans of Westerns and sci-fi flicks, Agar was a staple at film conventions and autograph shows. He died April 2, 2002 in Burbank, California.

Rico Alaniz

Americo Alaniz was born October 25, 1919 in Mexico and appeared in eighty-one films and television episodes starting in his first film *The Capture* (1950) in an uncredited role as 'policeman'. He appeared in numerous television programs, such as several episodes of *The Adventures of Kit Carson* (1951-1953), a couple episodes of *The Adventures of Rin Tin Tin* (1956), a couple *26 Men* (1957), two *Border Patrol* (1959), seventeen episodes of *The Life and Legend of Wyatt Earp* (1955-1960), two episodes of *Tales of Wells Fargo* (1957-1962), a couple *Rawhide* (1964-1965), two appearances on *The Fugitive* (1965-1967), three episodes of *Gunsmoke* (1963-1968), four of *Bonanza* (1962-1970), and five of *The High Chaparral* (1967-1970).

Some of his film roles were in movies such as *Column South* (1953) with Audie Murphy, *Drum Beat* (1954) and *Santiago* (1956) with Alan Ladd, *The Magnificent Seven* (1960) with Steve McQueen, and his last film *Final Analysis* (1992) with Richard Gere.

Eddie Albert

Audie Murphy and Eddie Albert in *Gunrunners*

Edward Albert Heimberger was born April 22, 1906 and known professionally as Eddie Albert, was an American actor and activist. Prior to World War II, and before his film career, Albert had toured Mexico as a clown and high-wire artist with the Escalante Brothers Circus, but secretly worked for U.S. Army intelligence, photographing German U-boats in Mexican harbors. On September 9, 1942, Albert enlisted in the United States Navy and was discharged in 1943 to accept an appointment as a lieutenant in the U.S. Naval Reserve. He was awarded the Bronze Star with Combat "V" for his actions during the invasion of Tarawa in November 1943, when, as the pilot of a U.S. Coast Guard landing craft, he rescued forty-seven Marines who were stranded offshore, and supervised the rescue of 30 others, while under heavy enemy machine-gun fire.

Since 1948, Albert enjoyed being character actor and guest-starred in nearly ninety TV series. He was nominated for the Academy Award for Best Supporting Actor in 1954 for his performance in *Roman Holiday*, and in 1973 for *The Heartbreak Kid*.

Other well-known screen roles of his include Bing Edwards in the *Brother Rat* films, as a villainous gun runner in a remake of "To Have and Have Not" based on an Ernest Hemingway short story, *The Gun Runners* (1958) with Audie Murphy as a fishing boat captain, unusual roles for both, traveling salesman Ali Hakim in the musical *Oklahoma!*, and as the corrupt prison warden in 1974s *The Longest Yard*. He starred as Oliver Wendell Douglas in the 1960s television situation comedy *Green Acres* (1965-1970), his most well known television role and as Frank MacBride in the crime drama *Switch* (1975-1978).

Albert suffered from Alzheimer's disease in his last years. His son put his acting career aside to care for his father. Despite his illness, Albert exercised regularly until shortly before his death. Eddie Albert died of pneumonia in 2005 at the age of ninety-nine at his home in Pacific Palisades. He was interred at Westwood Village Memorial Park Cemetery in Los Angeles, California, next to his wife Margo and his *Green Acres* co-star Eva Gabor.

John Alderson

John "Basher" Alderson was born August 4, 1906, and led a colorful life considering his origins in a mining village in the north of England. After spending all of two weeks as a miner, he lied about his age, joined the British

Army and attained the rank of Major. Leaving for the US, he married a General's secretary and got into the movies, often playing villains.

He played in 134 films and television episodes from 1951 to 1990, including *The Highwayman* (1951), *Plymouth Adventure* (1952), *City Detective* (1955), *To Catch a Thief* (1955), *Screen Directors Playhouse* (1956), *Shoot-Out at Medicine Bend* (1957), *Boots and Saddles* (1957-1958), *No Name on the Bullet* (1959) with Audie Murphy, *Wagon Train* (1960), *Romanoff and Juliet* (1961), *Donovan's Reef* (1963), *Strange Bedfellows* (1965), *Doctor Who* (1966), *Hellfighters* (1968), *Rod Serling's Night Gallery* (1972), *Hec Ramsey* (1973), *Blazing Saddles* (1974) as the gun chewer, *The Wild Geese* (1978), *Ragtime* (1981), *The American Way* (1986), and *Young Guns II* (1990).

He died April 10, 2006 in Woodland Hills, California.

Sara Allgood

Sara Allgood was born in Dublin, Ireland October 31, 1879 and started her acting career in her native country with the famed Abbey Theatre. From there she traveled to the English stage, where she played for many years before making her film debut in 1918. Her warm, open Irish face meant that she spent a lot of time playing Irish mothers, landladies, neighborhood gossips and the like, although she is best remembered for playing Mrs. Morgan, the mother of a family of Welsh miners, in *How Green Was My Valley* (1941), for which she was nominated for an Academy Award for Best Supporting Actress. Her sister Maire O'Neill was an actress in Ireland, and famed Irish poet William Butler Yeats was a family friend.

Some of her other film work includes *Just Peggy* (1918) as the title character, *The World, the Flesh, the Devil* (1932), *The Passing of the Third Floor Back* (1935), *The Fugitive* (1939), *Dr. Jekyll and Mr. Hyde* (1941), *Jane Eyre* (1943), *The Spiral Staircase* (1945), *The Fabulous Dorseys* (1947), and *Cheaper by the Dozen* (1950).

Sara Allgood died of a heart attack on September 13, 1950, shortly after making her last film, *Sierra* (1950) with Audie Murphy.

Merry Anders

Merry Anders with Audie Murphy in *The Quick Gun*

Merry Anders, born May 22, 1934, in Chicago, practically grew up in local bijous watching films and their accompanying stage shows with her movie-crazy mother and grandmother. The family relocated to Los Angeles in

1949 and, while attending John Burroughs Junior High School, Anders made the acquaintance of Rita La Roy, an old-time film actress who convinced her to take a modeling course.

Later, to help her with her modeling, she took dramatic lessons at the Ben Bard Playhouse and was "spotted" by a 20th Century-Fox talent scout in a Playhouse stage presentation. After several years at Fox, Anders turned freelancer, working in TV as well as starring in a string of modestly budgeted Western, science fiction, and horror films, including *Titanic* (1953), *How to Marry a Millionaire* (1953), *Three Coins in the Fountain* (1954), *All That Heaven Allows* (1955), *Desk Set* (1957), *The Dalton Girls* (1957), *How to Marry a Millionaire* (1957-1959), the television series based on the film of the same name that she also appeared in, *Richard Diamond, Private Detective* (1959), *Young Jesse James* (1960) as Belle Starr, *Beauty and the Beast* (1962), *The Quick Gun* (1964) with Audie Murphy, *Women of the Prehistoric Planet* (1966), *Airport* (1970), and *Gunsmoke* (1971).

Merry Anders died on October 28, 2012 in Encino, California. She was 78.

Clinton Anderson

Audie Murphy with Clinton Anderson in *The Quiet American*

Not much is known about actor Clinton Anderson other than he only appeared in one television episode of *Goodyear Playhouse* ''The Huntress'' (1954), and one movie *The Quiet American* (1958) with Audie Murphy.

Herbert Anderson

Herbert Anderson was born March 30, 1917, and was an American character actor from Oakland, California, probably best remembered for his part as Henry Mitchell in the classic television sitcom *Dennis The Menace*.

After a few minor roles in films for Warner Bros., Anderson got his big break in the 1941 picture *Navy Blues*, starring Martha Raye and Ann Sheridan. His other films include the 1949 World War II film *Battleground*, *Joe Butterfly* and *Night Passage*, both in 1958 and starring Audie Murphy. Anderson also acted extensively in Broadway shows, including the role of Dr. Bird in *The Caine Mutiny Court-Martial*. He was also in the film version of *The Caine Mutiny* (1954), with Humphrey Bogart; he was the only one of both casts to be both in the Broadway play and the movie. Anderson retired from acting in 1982 after having heart surgery. He died of complications from a stroke on June 11, 1994 in Palm Springs, California.

James Anderson

Audie Murphy with James Anderson in *Duel at Silver Creek*

Born July 13, 1921, James Anderson was a familiar face to movie audiences in the 1950s. James Anderson's rugged and somewhat sinister good looks made him a natural for westerns, and he appeared in many of them over the years, often as a gunman or hired killer but occasionally as a storekeeper or grizzled frontier scout. He turned in a very good performance as one of the survivors of a nuclear attack in *Five* (1951) and another as a redneck farmer in *To Kill a Mockingbird* (1962), but it's for his 137, mostly westerns, roles in films and on TV that Anderson is best known. He appeared in two Audie Murphy pictures, *Duel at Silver Creek* (1952) and *Drums Across the River* (1954).

He died at 48 in Billings, Montana, on September 14, 1969, before the release of his final two films, Sam Peckinpah's *The Ballad of Cable Hogue* (1970) and the Dustin Hoffman epic *Little Big Man* (1970).

Sara Anderson

Sara Anderson was born June 26, 1920 in Rosholt, Wisconsin and appeared in ten films and television programs from 1947 to 1965, including *The Philco-Goodyear Television Playhouse* (1949), *Sure As Fate* (1950), *State Trooper* (1957), *Bachelor Father* (1957), *Leave It to Beaver* (1959), *The Real McCoys* (1959), *Battle at Bloody Beach* (1961) with Audie Murphy, and *I Saw What You Did* (1965).

Cisco Andrade

Cisco Andrade was born in Los Angeles, California on January 25, 1930. Cisco Andrade was a boxer whose professional record was 'won 46 (KO 26) + lost 12 (KO 2) + drawn 1 = 59'. One of his managers was Frank Sinatra.

He appeared in one film *World in My Corner* (1956) with Audie Murphy, one two-part episode of *Mission Impossible* "The Contender" (1968), and one television movie *D.A.: Conspiracy to Kill* (1971) with Robert Conrad. He died in Compton, California on January 1, 1989 at the age of 58.

E.J Andre

E.J. Andre with Audie Murphy in *Whispering Smith*

E. J. Andre was born August 14, 1908, in Detroit, Michigan, and a familiar face among character actors, even if his name was not recognized. He appeared in eighty-six films and television programs starting with his first appearance in *The Ten Commandments* (1956), as the Sheik of Hazerath. He also appeared in *Battle at Bloody Beach* (1961), the *Whispering Smith* episode "Dark Circle" (1961), and *Showdown* (1963), all three with Audie Murphy.

Others he appeared in were *Perry Mason* (1964), *The Legend of Jesse James* (1966), *The Fugitive* (1966), *The Green Hornet* (1967) with Bruce Lee, *The Flying Nun* (1968), *The Shakiest Gun in the West* (1968), *Rod Serling's Night Gallery* (1970), *Papillon* (1973), *Harry O* (1974), *Starsky and Hutch* (1975), *Greatest Heroes of the Bible* (1979), *The Chisholms* (1980), *Nickel Mountain* (1984), and *Evil Town* (1987), which was released three years after his death on September 6, 1984 at age 76 in Hollywood, California.

Morris Ankrum

Morris Ankrum with Audie Murphy behind the scenes of *Drums Across the River*

Morris Winslow Ankrum was born on August 28, 1897, in Danville, Illinois. A graduate of the University Of Southern California School Of Law, Morris Ankrum was an attorney and an economics professor before switching careers and joining the theater.

He was a veteran stage actor by the time he entered the film industry in the 1930s, where he spent much time in westerns, playing everything from Indian chiefs to crooked town bankers. It was in the 1950s, though, that he hit his stride in the genre for which he is most fondly remembered, science-fiction films, where his gruff, no-nonsense demeanor and authoritative voice perfectly fit the role of the military officer helping scientists fight an outer-space menace, most memorably as Col. Fielding in the classic *Invaders from Mars* (1953).

Among his hundreds of films and television episodes, he appeared in *Drums Across the River* (1954) and *Walk the Proud Land* (1956), both with Audie Murphy. Toward the end of his career Ankrum had a recurring role as a judge on the *Perry Mason* (1957) TV series. He died September 2, 1964, at age 67 in Pasadena, California.

Art Aragon

Audie Murphy with Art Aragon in *World in my Corner*

Art Aragon was born November 13, 1927, in Belen, New Mexico. He was a professional lightweight boxer from 1944 to 1960. He had a career record of 90-20-6 though he never gained a championship. Known for his boxing apparel, he wore a gold robe and trunks.

He appeared in twenty films and television programs during and after his boxing career, including *To Hell and Back* (1955) and *World in My Corner* (1956), both with Audie Murphy. He died on March 25, 2008, in Northridge, California, of complications from a stroke.

John Archer

Born Ralph Bowman May 8, 1915, the future film and TV star moved to California with his family when he was five; he attended Hollywood High and the University of Southern California. He first set his sights on a job behind the camera, taking a cinematography course at USC, but then couldn't land an entry-level position.

He later drifted into acting, on stage at the Ben Bard Playhouse and in serials at Universal and Republic. He then entered a radio contest, "Jesse Lasky's Gateway to Hollywood", where aspiring actors competed for a studio contract. The top prize, an RKO contract made out in the name of "John Archer", was won by Bowman after thirteen weeks of competition (edging out Hugh Beaumont for the prize and the "Archer" name). The actor quips, "I went from being a Bowman to an Archer!"

He appeared in 139 films and television episodes, some of which were *Cheers for Miss Bishop* (1941), *Police Bullets* (1942), *Sherlock Holmes in Washington* (1943), *Colorado Territory* (1949), *Best of the Badmen* (1951), *Rock Around the Clock* (1956), *She Devil* (1957), *City of Fear* (1959), *Twilight Zone* (1961), *Blue Hawaii* (1961), *Apache Rifles* (1964) with Audie Murphy, *Batman* (1966-1967), *Mannix* (1969), *How to Frame a Figg* (1971), *Amelia Earhart* (1976), and *American Playhouse* (1986).

He had four children, two by his first wife Marjorie Lord (one of whom is actress Anne Archer) and two by his second wife Ann (whom he married in 1956). He died on December 3, 1999, at age 84.

Richard Arlen

Richard Arlen with Audie Murphy in *Kansas Raiders*

Richard Arlen was as born September 1, 1900. During World War I, Richard Arlen served in the Royal Canadian Flying Corps as a pilot, but he never saw combat. After the war he drifted around and eventually wound up in Los Angeles, where he got a job as a motorcycle messenger at a film laboratory. When he crashed into the gates of Paramount Pictures and suffered a broken leg, the studio provided prompt medical attention. Impressed by his good looks, executives also gave him a contract after he had recovered.

Starting as an extra in 1925, Arlen soon rose to credited roles, but the quality of his work left much to be desired. However, this was the silent era, which was more about looks than substance, and he continued on. His big break came when William A. Wellman cast him as a pilot in the silent film *Wings* (1927) with Charles 'Buddy' Rogers and Clara Bow. The story of fighter aces would win the Oscar for Best Picture and Arlen would continue to play the tough, cynical hero throughout his career. Arlen appeared in three more pictures directed by Wellman, *Beggars of Life* (1928), *Ladies of the Mob* (1928), and *The Man I Love* (1929). In *Wings* he had a scene with a young actor named Gary Cooper. In 1929, he again worked with Cooper in the western *The Virginian* (1929), only this time Cooper was the star and Arlen was the supporting actor. While Arlen moved easily into sound, his career just bumped along. By 1935 he was working in such "B" pictures as *Three Live Ghosts* (1936). It was in 1935 that he became a freelance actor and his freelance career soon waned. In 1939, he signed with Universal and began working in its action films. In 1941 he moved to the Pine-Thomas unit at Paramount, where he appeared in adventure films.

With the war on, most of his earlier films included war scenarios. By the end of the 1940s Arlen was becoming deaf and this seemed to signal the end of his career. However, he had an operation in 1949 that restored his hearing and he went on making a handful of adventures and westerns through the 1950s, including *Kansas Raiders* (1950) with Audie Murphy, and worked more in the 1960s. He made fifteen westerns for producer A.C. Lyles, who worked with the old western stars. Some more of his roles included *Hurricane Smith* (1952), *Hidden Guns* (1956), *Cavalry Command* (1958), *The Crawling Hand* (1963), *Apache Uprising* (1965), *Buckskin* (1968), *The Sky's the Limit* (1975), and *A Whale of a Tale* (1977).

He died March 28, 1976, of emphysema.

R.G. Armstrong

A golden career was reflected in his name. Robert Golden Armstrong was born in Birmingham, Alabama, on April 7, 1917. He attended the University of North Carolina at Chapel Hill. While there he was frequently performing on stage with the Carolina Playmakers. After graduating, R.G. headed to New York, where his acting career really took off.

In 1953 he, along with many of his Actors Studio buddies, was part of the cast of "End As a Man", this became the first play to go from off-Broadway to Broadway. The following year, R.G. got his first taste of movies, appearing in *Garden of Eden* (1954). However, he returned to New York and the live stage. He received great reviews for his portrayal of Big Daddy in the Broadway production of *Cat on a Hot Tin Roof* in 1955. In 1958 he took the plunge to Hollywood. He appeared in two movies, a TV series, and did numerous guest appearances on TV shows that year, usually in westerns such as *The Rifleman* (1958), *Have Gun, Will Travel* (1957) and *Zane Grey Theater* (1956), among others. He would go on to appear in eighty movies and three TV series in his career, and guest-starred in ninety TV series, many of them westerns, often as a tough sheriff or a rugged land baron. He appeared with Audie Murphy in *No Name on the Bullet* (1959).

R.G. was a regular cast member in the TV series *T.H.E. Cat* (1966), playing tough, one-handed Capt. MacAllister.

Even though he had a long, versatile career, the younger generation knows him as spooky Lewis Vandredi (pronounced VON-drah-dee), who just wouldn't let the main characters have a good night's sleep on the *Friday the 13th* (1987) TV series.

Finally retiring after six successful decades in show business, his last film appearance was *Purgatory* (1999). R.G. Armstrong died of natural causes July 27, 2012 in Studio City, California.

James Arness

James King Aurness was born May 26, 1923 and was an American leading man famed as the star of one of the longest-running shows in U.S. television history, *Gunsmoke* (1955). Born of Norwegian heritage (the family name, Aurness, had formerly been Aursness) in Minneapolis, Minnesota, James attended West High School in Minneapolis. Although he appeared in school plays, he had no interest in performing, and dreamed instead of going to sea. After high school, he attended one semester at Beloit College before receiving his draft notice in 1943. He entered the army and trained at Camp Wheeler, Georgia, before shipping out for North Africa. After landing at Casablanca, Arness joined the 3rd Infantry Division in time for the invasion of Anzio. Ten days after the invasion, Arness was severely wounded in the leg and foot by German machine-gun fire. His wounds, which plagued him the rest of his life, resulted in his medical discharge from the army.

While recuperating in a Clinton, Iowa, hospital, he was visited by his younger brother Peter (later to gain fame as actor Peter Graves), who suggested he take a radio course at the University of Minnesota. James did so, and a teacher recommended him for a job as an announcer at a Minneapolis radio station. Though seemingly headed for success in radio, he followed a boyhood friend's suggestion and went with the friend to Hollywood in hopes of getting work as film extras. He studied at the Bliss-Hayden Theatre School under actor Harry Hayden, and while appearing in a play there was spotted by agent Leon Lance. Lance got the actor a role as Loretta Young's brother in *The Farmer's Daughter* (1947). The director of that film, H.C. Potter, recommended that he drop the "u" from his last name and soon thereafter the actor was officially known as James Arness.

Little work followed this break, and Arness became something of a beach bum, living on the shore at San Onofre and spending his days surfing. He began taking his acting career more seriously when he began to receive fan mail following the release of the Young picture. He appeared in a production of "Candida" at the Pasadena Community Playhouse, and married his leading lady, Virginia Chapman. She pressed him to study acting and to work harder in pursuit of a career, but Arness has been consistent in ascribing his success to luck. He began to get small roles with frequency, often, due to his size, villainous characters. He played a character called 'Little Sam' in *Sierra* (1950) with Audie Murphy.

Most notable among these was that of the space alien in *The Thing from Another World* (1951). While playing a Greek warrior in a play, Arness was spotted by agent Charles K. Feldman, who represented John Wayne. Feldman introduced Arness to Wayne, who put the self-described 6' 6" actor under personal contract. Arness played several roles over the next few years for and with Wayne, whom he considered a mentor.

In 1955, Wayne recommended Arness for the lead role of Matt Dillon in the TV series *Gunsmoke* (1955). Arness at first declined, thinking a TV series could derail his growing film career, but Wayne argued for the show, and Arness accepted. His portrayal of stalwart marshal Dillon became an iconic figure in American television and the series, on the air for twenty seasons, is the longest-running dramatic series with continuing characters in U.S. television history. Arness became world-famous and years later reprised the character in a series of TV movies. After the surprising cancellation of *Gunsmoke* in 1975, Arness jumped immediately into another successful (though much shorter-lived) Western project, a TV-movie-miniseries-series combination known as *How the West Was Won* (1977). A brief modern police drama, *McClain's Law* (1981), followed, and Arness played his mentor John Wayne's role in *Red River* (1988) (TV), a remake of the Wayne classic. Following the aforementioned *Gunsmoke* TV movies, the last in 1994, when Arness was 71, Arness basically retired. James Arness died at the age of 88 on June 3, 2011 in Los Angeles, California.

Roscoe Ates

Roscoe Ates was born in the rural hamlet of Grange, Mississippi, on January 20, 1895, northwest of Hattiesburg. Grange is no longer included on road maps. Ates spent much of his childhood overcoming a severe stutter. He entered the entertainment medium as a concert violinist but found economic opportunities greater as a vaudeville comedian. He revived his long-gone stutter for humorous effect. Besides his early films, Ates starred in his own short subject series with RKO and Vitaphone.

His first film role was at the age of thirty-four in 1929 as a ship's cook in *South Sea Rose*. The next year he was cast as "Old Stuff" in the film *Billy the Kid* (1930) with Johnny Mack Brown (1904–1974) as Billy the Kid and Wallace Beery (1885–1949) as Deputy Sheriff Pat Garrett. From 1946-48, Ates appeared as the western character Soapy Jones in fifteen films, including *Colorado Serenade*, *Driftin' River* (with Shirley Patterson), *Stars Over Texas*, and *Tumbleweed Trail* (all 1946), *West to Glory*, *Shadow Valley*, and *Wild Country* (all 1947), and *Check Your Guns*, *Black Hills*, *Tornado Range*, *The Westward Trail*, and *The Tioga Kid* (all 1948). His Soapy Jones character is the sidekick to the "Singing Cowboy" portrayed by native Texan, Eddie Dean (1907–1999). Thereafter, George "Gabby" Hayes employed archival footage from many Soapy Jones films in his 1950s children's television series, *The Gabby Hayes Show*.

In 1950, Ates was cast in his first television role as Deputy Roscoe in the short-lived ABC series *The Marshal of Gunsight Pass*, which was broadcast live from a primitive studio lot in Los Angeles, California. Eddie Dean also appeared in this program, as did Jan Sterling (1921–2004) in the role of Roscoe's much younger girlfriend.

From 1959-1960, Ates appeared once as "Old Timer" and in seven episodes as Ike Jenkins in the John Russell and Peter Brown ABC western series *Lawman*, set in Laramie, Wyoming. During this same time frame as he appeared on *Lawman*, Ates guest starred as Renton in two episodes of Dale Robertson's *Tales of Wells Fargo* and four times on ABC's *Maverick* In 1960, he appeared as a bartender in the episode "The Rape of Red Sky" of NBC's *The Outlaws*. He appeared in Will Hutchins's ABC western, *Sugarfoot*, in the 1960 episode "The Man from Eudora".

Ates's last credited roles were in 1961 as a drunk in Robert Stack's ABC series *The Untouchables* and in *The Red Skelton Show* in an episode entitled "Candid Clem" and in "Three for One" of NBC's *Whispering Smith* starring Audie Murphy. His final screen appearance in Jerry Lewis's 1961 film *The Errand Boy* was uncredited.

He died of lung cancer on March 1, 1962.

Athena

Nothing is known about the actress who called herself Athena when she appeared as one of Mamie's girls in Audie Murphy's last film *A Time for Dying* (1969).

Malcolm Atterbury

Philadelphia native Malcolm Atterbury was born on February 20, 1907, into a wealthy family. His father was president of the Pennsylvania Railroad, but he himself had no desire to go into the family business. He had always wanted to be an actor, and to that end, he aquired a job managing a radio station. From there he went into vaudeville, then into stage work in both musicals and dramas, gaining a reputation as a solid and reliable stage actor. He made his film debut in *Dragnet* (1954).

Although he soon became a busy supporting actor in films, he still kept his hand in the theater world; he owned two theaters in upstate New York. A versatile actor, he could play anything from a priest to a senator to a hotel clerk to a gunfighter to a cranky, cantankerous old codger. He appeared with Audie Murphy in *Hell Bent for leather* (1960). He appeared in 148 films and television programs in his long career. His last film was *Emperor of the North* (1973). He died in Beverly Hills of natural causes August 16, 1992.

Barry Atwater

Garrett "Barry" Atwater was born May 16, 1918. He was an American character actor who appeared frequently on TV from the 1950s into the 1970s. He served as head of the UCLA Sound Department before he began his acting career. His work teaching audio techniques led to a role in the student film *A Time Out of War* (1954), a Civil War allegory that won the Oscar as best short film that same year.

By 1960, he had achieved enough stature to be named by host Rod Serling in the on-screen promo as one of the stars of the well-known *Twilight Zone* episode "The Monsters Are Due on Maple Street." This flourishing period of TV appearances coincided with some major supporting roles in low-budget movies; otherwise, film was an only occasionally fertile medium for him. Atwater also performed regularly on stage throughout his career.

He made a film appearance with Audie Murphy in *Battle at Bloody Beach* (1961).

In the mid-1960s, Atwater spent three years on the soap opera *General Hospital* while also working in prime-time appearances, billing himself as "G.B" Atwater from 1963 to 1965, during a period in which he (like many other actors who had thrived on 1950s anthology shows) was cast in supporting parts. By the mid-1970s, he was relegated to featured TV parts and small bits in movies, and he returned to UCLA to teach TV and film sound production

Atwater's role as vampire Janos Skorzeny in the acclaimed TV thriller *The Night Stalker* (1972) made him a popular guest at 1970s fan gatherings that capitalized on the resurgence of classic horror during that decade. The first series from the new FOX network was *Werewolf* (1987) and the head werewolf, played by Chuck Conners, was deliberately named 'Janos Skorzeny' as homage to the vampire Barry played in *The Night Stalker*.

Had he lived a little longer, his role as Surak in the original *Star Trek* (1969) series would have made him an even bigger attraction at the sci-fi conventions that were just taking off at the time of his death from a stroke in Los Angeles, California May 24, 1978.

Jim Backus

Audie Murphy with Jim Backus in *The Wild and the Innocent*

Jim Backus was one of the few actors to do it all: radio, Broadway, movies, television and cartoons. He was born James Gilmore Backus February 25, 1913, in Cleveland, Ohio. After attending prep school in his native Cleveland, Backus enrolled at the American Academy of Dramatic Art, to ply his trade. While waiting for parts, he did radio and became friends with such future notables as Garson Kanin and Keenan Wynn. Backus stuck it out and soon was doing motion pictures in addition to radio.

Some of his early roles include *The Truth About Youth* (1930), his first cartoon as Mr. Magoo *A-Lad-in His Lamp* (1948), *Ragtime Bear* (1949), *Ma and Pa Kettle Go to Town* (1950), *Hollywood Story* (1951), *Don't Bother to Knock* (1952), and ninety-eight episodes of *I Married Joan* (1952-1955).

He was typecast in roles as "rich types" but broke the mold when he portrayed James Dean's father in the classic *Rebel Without a Cause* (1955).

He had roles in *The Girl He Left Behind* (1956), *The Opposite Sex* (1956), *The Pied Piper of Hamelin* (1957), *Macabre* (1958), *The Wild and the Innocent* (1959) with Audie Murphy, *The Jim Backus Show* (1960-1961), *The Horizontal Lieutenant* (1962), *It's a Mad Mad Mad Mad World* (1963), as Thurston Howell III, in *Gilligan's Island* (1964), as Mr. Dithers in *Blondie* (1968-1969), *Cockeyed Cowboys of Calico County* (1970), *Now You See Him, Now You Don't* (1972), the cartoon sequel series *The New Adventures of Gilligan* (1974), *Harry O* (1975), *Kolchak: The Night Stalker* (1975), *Charlie's Angels* (1977), *Pete's Dragon* (1977), and as the hotel doorman with Chuck Norris in *Good Guys Wear Black* (1978).

He next appeared as Mr. Howell in *Rescue from Gilligan's Island* (1978), *The Castaways on Gilligan's Island* (1979), *The Harlem Globetrotters on Gilligan's Island* (1981), and *Gilligan's Planet* (1982).

He continued working through his Parkinson's disease in roles such as *Trapper John, M.D.* (1983), *Prince Jack* (1985), and as the voice of Smoky the Genie *The Bugs Bunny and Tweety Show* (1986).

He would voice Mr. Magoo off and on from 1949 through 1977. In the late 1980's, he reprised his role of Mr. Howell with Natalie Schafer as Mrs. Howell for the well-received Orville Redenbacher popcorn commercial.

He was the first castaway to pass away, on July 3, 1989.

Jimmy Baird

Jimmy Baird with Audie Murphy in *To Hell and Back*, and with the author in 2011

Jimmy Baird was born November 5, 1945 in Seattle, Washington and became the consummate child actor of the 1950s, appearing in fifty-six films and television programs from 1954 to 1965.

Some of those were *There's No Business Like Show Business* (1954), *The Seven Little Foy's* (1955) as Eddie Foy, Jr., he then played Audie Murphy's younger brother in *To Hell and Back* (1955), *Rebel Without a Cause* (1955), *My Friend Flicka* (1956), *The Lone Ranger* (1956), *Sheriff of Cochise* (1957), his best known role as Pee Wee Jenkins on *Fury* (1958), *The Return of Dracula* (1958), *The Black Orchid* (1958), *Maverick* (1959), *Lassie* (1960), *King of the Roaring 20's: The Story of Arnold Rothstein* (1961) as the younger version of Arnold Rothstein, *Twilight Zone* (1962), *The Travels of Jaimie McPheeters* (1963), and *The Donna Reed Show* (1965).

He later went to college to get his teaching credentials and became a high school English teacher. He has been teaching at the same high school since 1967. His older sister Sharon was one of the original *Mouseketeers*.

He is currently appearing at western film festivals around the country.

Walter Baldwin

Walter Baldwin with Audie Murphy in *Destry*

Walter Baldwin was born January 2, 1889, and became a prolific character actor whose career spanned five decades and 150 film and television roles, and numerous stage performances.

Baldwin, who was born Walter S. Baldwin Jr. in Lima, Ohio from a theatrical family, served in the First World War.

He was probably best known for playing the father of the handicapped sailor in *The Best Years of Our Lives* (1946). He was the first actor to portray "Floyd the Barber" on *The Andy Griffith Show* (1960).

Prior to his first film roles in 1939, Baldwin appeared in more than a dozen Broadway plays. He played Whit in the first Broadway production of *Of Mice and Men*, and also appeared in the original *Grand Hotel* in a small role, as well as serving as the production's stage manager. He originated the role of Bensinger, the prissy Chicago Tribune reporter, in the Broadway production of *The Front Page*.

In the 1960s he had small acting roles in television shows such as *Petticoat Junction* (1967) and *Green Acres* (1965). He continued to act in motion pictures, and one of his last roles was in *Rosemary's Baby* (1968).

Baldwin was known for playing solid middle class burghers, although sometimes he gave portrayals of eccentric characters. He played a customer seeking a prostitute in *The Lost Weekend* (1945), the rebellious prison trusty Orvy in *Cry of the City* (1948), and a poker player who gets cheated out of his farm in *Destry* (1954) with Audie Murphy.

Walter Baldwin died January 27, 1977 in at the age of 88 in Santa Monica, California.

Anne Bancroft

Anne Bancroft with Audie Murphy in *Walk the Proud Land*

Anne Bancroft was born September 17, 1931. She was an American actress associated with the method acting school, which she had studied under Lee Strasberg. Respected for her acting prowess and versatility, Bancroft was often acknowledged for her work in film, theatre and television. She won one Academy Award, three BAFTA Awards, two Golden Globes, two Tony Awards and two Emmy Awards, and several other awards and nominations.

She made her film debut in *Don't Bother to Knock* (1952) and, following a string of supporting film roles during the 1950s, including the role of Indian maiden "Tianey" in *Walk the Proud Land* (1956) with Audie Murphy, won an Academy Award for Best Actress for her performance in *The Miracle Worker* (1962), receiving subsequent nominations for her roles in *The Pumpkin Eater* (1964), *The Graduate* (1967), *The Turning Point* (1977), and *Agnes of God* (1985). Bancroft's other acclaimed movies as a lead actress include *Young Winston* (1972), *The Prisoner of Second Avenue* (1975), *To Be or Not to Be* (1983), and *84 Charing Cross Road* (1987).

Later in her career, she made the transition back to supporting roles in theatrical films such as *Point of No Return* (1993), *Home for the Holidays* (1995), *Great Expectations* (1998), *Antz* (1998), *Keeping the Faith* (2000), and *Heartbreakers* (2001). She also starred in seven television films, the last of which was *The Roman Spring of Mrs. Stone* (2003) for which she received Emmy and Screen Actors Guild Award nominations.

Bancroft died of uterine cancer on June 6, 2005 at the age of 73, in 2005. She was survived by her husband of forty years, Mel Brooks, and their son Max Brooks.

Holly Bane

Holly Bane was born Hollis Alan Bane February 18, 1918, in Los Angeles, California. He sometimes billed himself as Mike Ragan and was best known for specializing in playing a bad guy in B Western movies.

He made his first film appearance in *Wake Island* (1942), and then went on to be in many classic westerns. His western credits included *Hoppy's Holiday* (1947), *Song of the Wasteland* (1947), *Overland Trials* (1948), *Roaring Westward* (1949), *West of Wyoming* (1950), *Storm Over Wyoming* (1950), *The Dakota Kid* (1951), *Target* (1952), *Son of Belle Starr* (1953), *Bitter Creek* (1954), *Rage at Dawn* (1955), *Blackjack Ketchum, Desperado* (1956), *Tombstone Territory* (1957), *Frontier Gun* (1958), *Wanted: Dead or Alive* (1958-1960), *Stagecoach to Dancers' Rock* (1962), *4 for Texas* (1963), *The Legend of Jesse James* (1963), and *Three Guns for Texas* (1968).

He appeared in *Gunsmoke* (1953), *Ride Clear of Diablo*, (1954), *Hell Bent for Leather* (1960), and *Gunpoint* (1966) with Audie Murphy.

After he left films he became a makeup director and worked on several 1970s television series.

He died August 25, 1995 at age 77 in Los Angeles, California.

Roy Barcroft

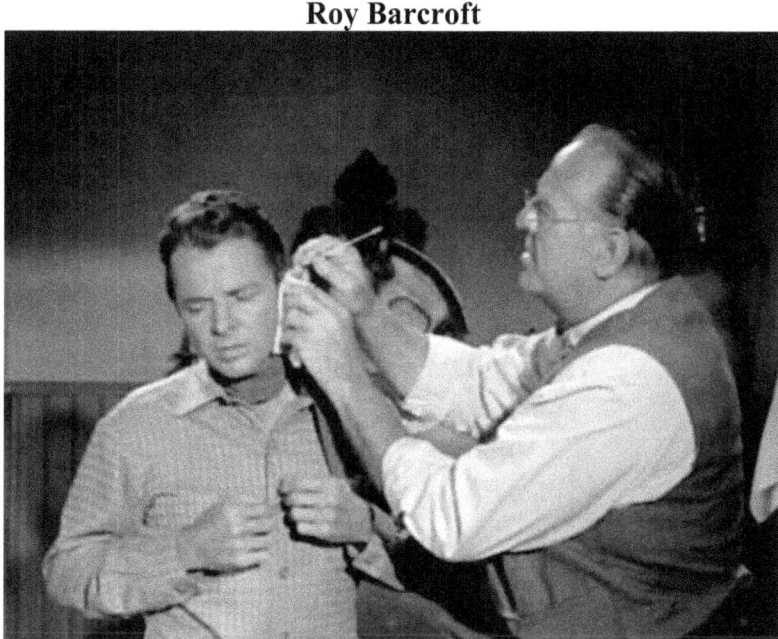

Audie Murphy with Roy Barcroft in *Six Black Horses*

Roy Barcroft was born September 7, 1902. He was an American character actor famous for playing villains in B-Westerns and other genres. Noted film critic Leonard Maltin acclaimed Barcroft as "Republic Pictures' number one bad guy".

Barcroft was born Howard Harold Ravenscroft to a farming family in Nebraska. In 1917 he joined up with the United States Army to fight in France in World War I, where he was wounded in action. After leaving the army he drifted through several jobs (including ranch hand, roughneck, railroad worker, and seaman) before re-enlisting and being stationed in Hawaii.

In 1929, he moved to California and worked as an extra and a salesman. He was discovered while acting in an amateur theatre production (a hobby he took up to improve his speaking voice as a salesman) and cast in the serial *S.O.S. Coast Guard* (1937). He worked for many studios in the years that followed until 1943 when he signed an exclusive ten-year contract with Republic. Under this contract, he starred in almost 150 films and serials, becoming instantly recognizable as the villain to the audiences of the day.

His career slowed with the decline of B-Westerns but he found work in television and B-Movies during the 1950s and 1960s. From 1955–1957, he became familiar to a new generation of youthful audiences, not as a villain but as "Col. Jim Logan", the kindly owner of the Triple-R boys' ranch in the hit television serials *Spin and Marty* (1955*).* He appeared in *Six Black Horses* (1962) with Audie Murphy.

In marked contrast to his villainous movie persona, Barcroft off-screen "had a reputation as one of the nicest guys in Hollywood," said Leonard Maltin in 2005. Barcroft died of kidney cancer at the Motion Picture Country Hospital on November 28, 1969, survived by his wife, Vera Thompson, and his three children. His remains were donated to medical science.

Trevor Bardette

Trevor Bardette was born November 19, 1902, in Nashville, Arkansas. He was an American film actor. He made over 172 movies and seventy-two TV appearances in his career. Bardette appeared in several memorable episodes in *Adventures of Superman* (1953). In the episode, "The Human Bomb", he played the sinister title character. In the 1954 episode, "Great Caesar's Ghost", he was a member of a criminal gang trying to drive Editor Perry White insane by making him think the subject of his oft-heard epithet had materialized.

He had a short, but memorable role as Sheriff Joe Bailey in *Destry* (1954) with Audie Murphy. He was a regular on *The Life and Legend of Wyatt Earp* (1961), playing Old Man Clanton. More of his roles included *The Rawhide Years* (1955), *Red Sundown,* (1956), *Dragoon Wells Massacre* (1957), *The Mating Game* (1959), *Twilight Zone* (1962), *Papa's Delicate Condition* (1963), *My Favorite Martian* (1966), and numerous episodes of *Gunsmoke* (1959-1970).

He died in Los Angeles, California, on November 28, 1977.

Griff Barnett

Audie Murphy with Griff Barnett in *Sierra*

Griff Barnett was born Manley Griffith November 12, 1884, was an American actor in Blue Ridge, Texas. He played the role of the family druggist on the *The Phil Harris-Alice Faye Show* on radio in the late 1940s and early 1950s. He was noted for his solid supporting film and television roles most often as judges or doctors.

He made his screen debut in The *Lone Ranger* (1938) and went on to appear in over eighty films. His credits included *Arizona* (1940), *Danger Woman* (1946), *To Each His Own* (1946), *Possessed* (1947), *Apartment for Peggy* (1948), *Tap Roots* (1948), *Crossfire* (1949), *Pinky* (1949), and *Sierra* (1950) with Audie Murphy.

He died at home in El Monte, California on January 12, 1958, survived by his wife Lara, two children, and three grandchildren

Robert Barrat

Born in New York July 10, 1889, Robert Barrat's theatrical debut was in a stock company in Springfield, Massachusetts. He later acted on Broadway and went into films, acting in some one-hundred fifty films from 1915 through 1964, an incredible fifty years.

He appeared in seven pictures with James Cagney during the 1930s. Two of his most noted roles were as the murder victim Archer Coe in Michael Curtiz's *The Kennel Murder Case* (1933) and as the treacherous Major Ferdinand Walsin Esterhazy in the 1937 Warner Bros. Academy Award winning film, *The Life of Emile Zola*. He also played Ingrid Bergman's father in *Joan of Arc* (1948), though his role was so brief that when an edited version of the film was released in 1950, Barrat's role had actually been eliminated. (The film has since been restored to its full length.) He also appeared in *The Kid From Texas* (1950) with Audie Murphy.

He played several other historical characters as well, among them Davy Crockett in *Man of Conquest* (1939), Zachary Taylor in *Distant Drums* (1951), Abraham Lincoln in *Trailin' West* (1936), Cornelius Van Horne in *Canadian Pacific* (1949) and General Douglas MacArthur in *American Guerrilla in the Philippines* (1950). He was also seen as the Native American Chief Chingachgook, in the 1936 film version of *The Last of the Mohicans*.

By 1954, he turned to TV playhouse roles, off and on until 1964. He died January 7, 1970, at age 80 in Hollywood, California. He was buried at Green Hill Cemetery in Martinsburg, West Virginia.

Gregg Barton

Gregg Barton was born in Oswego, New York, June 5, 1912. He is possibly best known for his role as Stan Richter in TV series *The Gene Autry Show* (1950-1955). He also played Clay Wagner in the TV western *The Range Rider* (1953). Barton played guest roles in serials such as *Adventures of Superman* (1953), *The Cisco Kid* (1954), *Steve Donovan, Western Marshal* (1956), *Bonanza* (1960) and Seven episodes of *The Lone Ranger* (1950-1957), as well as movies such as *Flying Tigers* (1942) with John Wayne.

Barker enlisted as a Marine while working on *Flying Tigers* (1942). He was still filming his part as his reporting date approached, but the crew worked overtime to finish shooting his scenes. Shooting wrapped at 12:30 a.m., and he was with the Marines in San Diego seven-and-a-half hours later. On February 25, 1945, he earned a Silver Star leading a platoon of the 5th Tank Battalion, 5th Marine Division on Iwo Jima.

He appeared in many other movies after the war, like *The Three Musketeers* (1948), *The Man from Laramie* (1955), *China Doll* (1958) with Victor Mature and *Morituri* (1965) with Marlon Brando. He appeared in four movies with Audie Murphy, such as *The Red Badge of Courage* (1951), *Gunsmoke* (1953), *Tumbleweed* (1953), and *Drums across the River* (1954).

He died November 28, 2000, in Fallbrook, California.

William Bassett

William Bassett was born on December 28, 1935, in Evanston, Illinois. He has acted in films and television since 1960, such as Audie Murphy's final film *A Time for Dying* (1969), *The Karate Kid* (1984), and *House of 1000 Corpses* (2003).

Some of the television shows he has appeared in are *Arrested Development* (2005), *Reno 911!* (2005), *Scrubs* (2004), *The Invisible Man* (2000), *Dharma & Greg* (1999), *Days of Our Lives* (1977), *Dallas* (1979-1982), and *The Young and the Restless* (1982-1983).

He has also been the gravelly-voiced pitchman who mixed subtle humor with a slight Texas twang to promote the Whataburger experience on television and radio for the nine years. He is still active and also voices characters in video games.

Florence Bates

Audie Murphy with Florence Bates behind the scenes of *Texas, Brooklyn, and Heaven*

The American character actress, born Florence Rabe on April 15, 1888, was the daughter of an antique store owner. She gained a degree in Mathematics from the University of Texas in 1906 and went on to a career in teaching and social work. She changed course after being persuaded by a friend to study law, and, passing her bar exam in 1914, becoming at the age of 26 the first female attorney in her home state.

When her parents died, she took over the business and travelled abroad extensively to acquire stock; all the while adding to her knowledge of foreign languages (she was, for instance, a fluent Spanish speaker).

After the Wall Street crash of 1929, Florence sold the antique store and married Texan oilman William F. Jacoby. Jacoby eventually went bankrupt and the couple moved to California in the late 1930's, briefly becoming proprietors of a bakery.

At this time, Florence, a heavy-set woman of matronly appearance and well into her middle age, developed an interest in acting and auditioned for the part of Miss Bates in the Pasadena Playhouse production of Jane Austen's 'Emma'. This proved to be a momentous career choice. Her popularity became such that she went on to leading roles with the same company, changing her name to Florence Bates as a nod to her perceived good fortune.

In 1939, at the age of 51, she screen tested for Alfred Hitchcock, who was sufficiently impressed to cast her as the demanding, imperious dowager Mrs. Edythe Van Hopper in Rebecca (1940). Her excellent performance was the first in a gallery of memorable characters: wealthy socialites, irritable, henpecking wives, hotel managers, such as *The Moon and Sixpence* (1942), a theatre owner in *Tonight and Every Night* (1945) and an unctuous, gossipy landlady in *Portrait of Jennie* (1948). She was equally adept at comedy, appearing to great effect in *Heaven Can Wait* (1943) and *Lullaby of Broadway* (1951), with frequent co-star S.Z. Sakall, aka 'Cuddles'. She was enjoyably larger-than-life as Danny Kaye's prospective mother-in-law in *The Secret Life of Walter Mitty* (1947) and as Vera-Ellen's inebriated Russian dance teacher, Madame Dilyovska, in *On the Town* (1949). Bates even essayed a murderess in *The Brasher Doubloon* (1947). She appeared in the Audie Murphy film *Texas, Brooklyn, and Heaven* (1948).

Destined never to win any awards, Florence Bates continued in films and television until her death on January 31, 1954. She was pre-deceased by her sister, her only daughter, and her husband.

Hugh Beaumont

Eugene Hugh Beaumont was born February 16, 1909, and was an American actor and television director. He was also licensed to preach by the Methodist church. Beaumont is best known for his portrayal of Ward Cleaver, the husband of June Cleaver (Barbara Billingsley) and the father of Wally (Tony Dow) and Beaver (Jerry Mathers) on the television series, *Leave It to Beaver* (1957–1963).

His parents were Ethel Adaline Whitney and Edward H. Beaumont, a traveling salesman whose profession kept the family on the move. After graduating from Baylor School, in Chattanooga, Tennessee, he attended the University of Chattanooga, where he played football. He later studied at the University of Southern California and graduated with a Master of Theology degree in 1946. He married Kathryn Adams Doty in 1942, and the pair had three children. They divorced in 1974.

Beaumont began his career in show business in 1931 by performing in theaters, nightclubs and on the radio. He began acting in motion pictures in 1940, appearing in over three dozen films (many roles not credited; he was credited along with another future TV dad-William Bendix, who would star in *The Life of Riley* in the 1946 film *The Blue Dahlia* which starred Alan Ladd) before taking his best-known role as the archetypal philosophy-dispensing suburban father, Ward Cleaver, on the popular sitcom television series *Leave It to Beaver*. Beaumont starred in five films as private detective Michael Shayne, such as *Murder is My Business* (1946), *Larceny in Her Heart* (1946), *Blonde For a Day* (1946), *Three on a Ticket* (1947), and *Too Many Winners* (1947), taking over the role from Lloyd Nolan.

Local legend in Chattanooga says that the fictional town of Mayfield where the Cleavers lived actually came from Mayfield Dairy, for which Beaumont had worked for while attending school in Chattanooga.

A precursor to his role as the kindly father figure came in *Adventures of Superman* (1953). In an episode called "The Big Squeeze", he played an ex-convict with a wife and son whose trust he must win back after an apparent return to his criminal past. He later appeared with Audie Murphy and James Stewart in *Night Passage* (1957).

Beaumont not only acted in *Leave It to Beaver*, he also wrote and directed several episodes, including the final, retrospective episode, "Family Scrapbook" (1963). His portrayal as head of the Cleaver household ranked #28 in *TV Guide's* list of the "50 Greatest TV Dads of All Time" in the June 20, 2004, issue.

Beaumont did not like the role of the patient Ward Cleaver much at all, which he believed had unfairly typecast him and overshadowed his many other roles in film and on television.

After *Leave It to Beaver* ended production and went into syndication in the fall of 1963, Beaumont appeared in many community theater productions and did a few guest roles on other television series.

Beaumont retired from show business in the late 1960s, launching a second career as a Christmas-tree farmer in Grand Rapids, Minnesota. His wife at the time, Kathryn Adams Doty, was born in New Ulm, Minnesota. He was forced to retire in 1972 after suffering a stroke from which he never fully recovered. On May 14, 1982, Beaumont died of a heart attack while visiting his son, a psychology professor, in Munich, Germany. His ashes were scattered on the then family-owned island on Lake Wabana, Minnesota, near Grand Rapids.

James Beck

Next to nothing is known of actor James (Jim) Beck except he appeared in numerous films and television programs from 1958 to 1967, like *Paratroop Command* (1957), *The Outsider* (1961), and *40 Guns to Apache Pass* (1967) with Audie Murphy.

He had the recurring role of Burt Alvord in several episodes of the television series *Texas John Slaughter* (1961), and Sgt Highton in the television series *Hondo* (1967), based on the John Wayne movie of the same name, which was based on a story by highly acclaimed western author Louis L'amour.

Noah Beery

Noah Beery, Jr. was born in New York City, New York, August 10, 1913, where his father was working as a stage actor. The family moved to California in 1915 when his father began acting in motion pictures. After attending school in Los Angeles, they moved to a ranch in the San Fernando Valley, a style of living he would maintain for the rest of his life.

At the age of seven, he appeared with his father in *The Mark of Zorro* (1920) and like his father, who immediately began billing himself as "Noah Beery, Sr.," he went on to become a respected character actor. His uncle, Oscar-winning screen phenomenon Wallace Beery, became the world's highest-paid actor by 1932, and while neither Noah nor his father ever approached that level, both had extremely long and memorable film careers. All three acting Beery's physically resembled each other rather closely, but Noah, Jr. lacked a thrillingly powerful voice like his father's and uncle's (which is ironic, since both older Beery's made major careers as supporting actors in silent movies).

Noah Beery, Jr. appeared in dozens of films, including a large early role as John Wayne's action partner in *The Trail Beyond* (1934), *20 Mule Team* (1940) with his uncle, and *Red River* (1948) with Wayne, and played noted outlaw Bob Dalton in *The Cimarron Kid* (1952) with Audie Murphy, but is best known for his role as Joseph "Rocky" Rockford, the father of Jim Rockford, James Garner's character on the popular television series *The Rockford Files* (1974–1980).

Beery's television work also included a weekly stint as a clown in *Circus Boy* (1956-1957) with Mickey Dolenz. In 1960, he replaced Burt Reynolds in the co-starring role in *Riverboat,* an NBC western series starring Darren McGavin. He appeared three times on the long running TV western *The Virginian* in the 1960s. He played Buffalo Baker in the series *Hondo* (1967). The role was originally played by Ward Bond in the movie of the same name fourteen years earlier.

Noah Beery, Jr. died November 1, 1994 in Tehachapi, California, of a cerebral thrombosis and was interred in the Forest Lawn Hollywood Hills Cemetery with his father and mother, Margarite Lindsey. His uncle, Wallace Beery is interred at Forest Lawn Memorial Park in Glendale, California. His first wife was Maxine Jones, the only child of Western star Buck Jones. His second wife was Lisa Thorman, from 1968 until his death. He was survived by his wife, Lisa; two daughters, Muffett and Melissa; a son, actor Bucklind Beery; and three step children, Page, Sean, and Lorena. His television star on the Hollywood Walk of Fame is at 7021 Hollywood Blvd.

James Bell

Audie Murphy with James Bell in *Posse from Hell*

James Harlee Bell was born December 1, 1891, in Suffolk, Virginia, and was an American character actor and bit player. His first film role was in *I Am a Fugitive from a Chain Gang* (1932). He went on to play roles in movies such as *So Proudly We Hail* (1943) with Veronica Lake, *Blood on the Sun* (1945) and *Tribute to a Bad Man* (1956) with James Cagney, *Flying Leathernecks* (1951) with John Wayne, *Red Mountain* (1951) with Alan Ladd, *Riding Shotgun* (1954) and *A Lawless Street* (1955) with Randolph Scott, *Stranger on Horseback* (1955) with Joel McCrea, and *Posse From Hell* (1961) with Audie Murphy.

He amassed an impressive 150 films and television roles through 1964. He died October 26, 1973, in Kents Store, Virginia.

Russ Bender

Audie Murphy with Russ Bender in *No Name on the Bullet*

He was born Russell Richard Bender, Jr. January 1, 1910, in New York City. Over his fourteen-year film career, starting in 1950, actor Russ Bender appeared almost exclusively in low-budget horror films like *The Amazing Colossal Man* (1957), *Invasion of the Saucer Men* (1957), *It Conquered the World* (1957), *Navy vs. the Night Monsters* (1965).

Some of his bigger projects include *War of the Worlds* (1953), *Man of a Thousand Faces* (1957), *I Bury the Living* (1958), and *No Name on the Bullet* (1959) with Audie Murphy.

A few of his televisions programs are *Broken Arrow* (1957-1958), *Maverick* (1958), *The Life and Legend of Wyatt Earp* (1956-1958), *Richard Diamond, Private Detective* (1959), *Black Saddle* (1959-1960), *Wanted, Dead or*

Alive (1958-1960), *Rawhide* (1959-1961), *Have Gun, Will Travel* (1958-1962), *Perry Mason* (1959-1962), *The Twilight Zone* (1960-1963), *The Virginian* (1962-1965), *The Fugitive* (1965), and *Bonanza* (1963-1969).

Russ Bender is also listed as screenwriter *Voodoo Woman* (1957). He died August 16, 1969, in Hollywood, California.

Val Benedict

No biographical information could be found for character actor Val Benedict. Of his nineteen film and television roles from 1957 to 1962, only two are films: *Bernardine* (1957), his first role, and *The Wild and the Innocent* (1959) with Audie Murphy. Some of his seventeen television roles include *Have Gun, Will Travel* (1958), *Gunsmoke* (1958), *Maverick* (1958), *Bronco* (1958), *Bat Masterson* (1959), *Yancy Derringer* (1959), *Cheyenne* (1959), and *Rawhide* (1962).

James Best

James Best with Audie Murphy in *The Cimarron Kid*

James Best was born July 26, 1926, and is an American actor best known for his role as bumbling Sheriff Rosco P. Coltrane in the CBS television series *The Dukes of Hazzard* (1979-1985). He has also worked as an acting coach, artist, and musician. Best was born as Jules Guy in Powderly in Muhlenberg County, Kentucky. His mother was the sister of Ike Everly, the father of the pop group the Everly Brothers.

After his mother died in 1929, the three-year-old was sent to live in an orphanage. He was later adopted by Armen and Essa Best and went to live with them in Corydon, Indiana.

He began his acting career with an uncredited role in the 1950 western *One Way Street*.

Best would portray a wide variety of characters in a wide spectrum of film genres. Some of his more notable roles include Jason Brown in the historical drama *Seven Angry Men* (1955), Kit Caswell in the western *Cole Younger, Gunfighter* (1958), Private Rhidges in the film adaptation of Norman Mailer's *The Naked and the Dead*

(1958), the vicious outlaw Billy John in *Ride Lonesome* (1959), Dr. Ben Mizer in the comedy *Three on a Couch* (1966), the cross dressing Dewey Barksdale in the 1976 drama *Ode to Billy Joe* (1976), and the gunman Drew in *Firecreek* (1968), with James Stewart and Henry Fonda.

He co-starred with Audie Murphy in five films: *Kansas Raiders* (1950), *The Cimarron Kid* (1952), *Column South* (1953), *Cast a Long Shadow* (1959), and *The Quick Gun* (1964). He also guest starred in the Audie Murphy *Whispering Smith* television series as the title character in the episode "The Hemp Reeger Case'' (1961).

Best has guest starred more than 280 times in numerous television programs.

Fans of *The Andy Griffith Show* will remember Best for his portrayal of the young guitar player Jim Lindsey in two episodes.

Best played Sheriff Rosco P. Coltrane on *The Dukes of Hazzard* from the show's debut in 1979 until the series ended in 1985, and this role was Best's most visible success. He later revealed that the caricature-like persona of Sheriff Rosco P. Coltrane was developed from a voice he used when he would play with his young children. In 1991, in contrast to the comic Coltrane of *Dukes of Hazzard*, Best appeared in an episode of the NBC crime drama *In the Heat of the Night*. He won the Crystal Reel Award for *Best Actor* for his portrayal of Nathan Bedford in the episode "Sweet, Sweet Blues". In the episode, directed by Vincent McEveety and written by William James Royce, Best plays a repentant killer who has to come to terms with his crime.

He later moved to Florida and taught at the University of Central Florida. Now semi-retired, Best runs a production company and takes occasional acting roles. He has also earned a name for himself as an artist and painter.

A highly respected acting coach, he taught drama and acting techniques for over twenty-five years in Los Angeles. His acting school listed some of the top names in Hollywood as pupils. He also served as artist-in-residence and taught drama at the University of Mississippi for two years prior to his stint on *The Dukes of Hazzard*.

Best married Jobee Ayers, in 1959. They had two daughters, Janeen and Jojami. They divorced in 1977. Best also has a son, Gary, from a previous marriage.

He married his current wife, Dorothy Best, in 1986. Best is also the father-in-law of actor-singer Michael Damian. James Best is currently a resident of Hickory, North Carolina.

He currently frequents western film festivals and I talked with him in detail about Audie Murphy at the Memphis Film Festival in June of 2013. He had some great stories and recollections and you could tell he really liked and admired Audie.

Lyle Bettger

Lyle Bettger with Audie Murphy in *Destry*

Lyle S. Bettger was born February 13, 1915 and was a character actor known most for his Hollywood roles from the 1950s, typically portraying villains. He is perhaps most recognizable as the wrathfully jealous elephant handler Klaus from the Oscar winning film *The Greatest Show on Earth* (1952).

Born in Philadelphia, Pennsylvania, Lyle was the son of Frank Bettger, who was an infielder for the St Louis Cardinals. An enthusiastic fan of cinema, Lyle left school in his late teens with the ambition of becoming an actor.

Bettger graduated from the American Academy of Dramatic Arts in New York. His theatrical debut was in *Brother Rat* at the *Biltmore Theatre* in New York City in 1936. After a period languishing in small-time theatre he landed the lead role in the Broadway production of *The Flying Gerardos* in 1940. When Paramount sent a talent scout to see the show, Bettger was signed on a three-year contract.

Bettger's movie career began when he was cast as the lead in the film noir *No Man of Her Own* (1950). He soon became a regular on the set of Westerns such as *Denver and Rio Grande* (1952), *The Great Sioux Uprising* (1953), *Drums Across the River* (1954), *Destry* (1954), *The Lone Ranger* (1956), and *Gunfight at the O.K. Corral* (1957). Lyle developed a reputation for playing the bad guy and excelled in villainous roles such as the menacing Joe Beacom in *Union Station* (1950) and the cold-blooded Nazi Chief Officer Kirchner in *The Sea Chase* (1955). He also appeared in *Guns of the Timberland* (1960) with Alan Ladd. The movie was based on a novel by Louis L'amour.

Bettger also made many appearances in dramatic roles on television, starring in the 1957 series *The Court of Last Resort* as well as guesting on *Hawaii Five-O* (1969-1980), *Rawhide* (1960-1964), *The Rifleman* (1959-1962), *Bonanza* (1962-1966), and *The Time Tunnel* (1966).

He was a regular on *The Grand Jury* (1960) and *The Court of Last Resort* (1957).

Lyle was married to Mary Rolfe (1940–1996) until her death. They had three children: Lyle Jr., Frank, and Paula. He was also survived by a sister, Lee Morgan.

Lyle Bettger died on September 24, 2003 in San Luis Obispo County, California.

Clem Bevans

Born October 16, 1879, Clem Bevans spent most of his performing career on the stage. First appearing in 1900 in a vaudeville act with Grace Emmett as a boy and girl act, he would move on to burlesque and eventually make the move to Broadway and even opera productions.

His first screen appearance did not come until 1935, when at the age of 55 he was cast as toothless old codger Doc Wiggins in *Way Down East* (1935). So good was his performance that he would become pigeonholed into "old codger" roles for his entire movie career.

Occasionally he would be given the opportunity to play something out of character, such as a voyeuristic millionaire with a fetish for women's knees in *Happy Go Lucky* (1943) and a Nazi spy in Alfred Hitchcock's *Saboteur* (1942), and Captain Bjorn in *Texas, Brooklyn, and Heaven* (1948) with Audie Murphy. He would go on to to play variations of his "old coot" role until the day he died on August 11, 1965.

Charles Bickford

Charles Bickford was born January 1, 1891, and was an American actor best known for his supporting roles. He was nominated three times for the Academy Award for Best Supporting Actor, for *The Song of Bernadette* (1943), *The Farmer's Daughter* (1947), and *Johnny Belinda* (1948). Other notable roles include *Whirlpool* (1948), *A Star is Born* (1954) and *The Big Country* (1958).

Bickford was born in Cambridge, Massachusetts, during the first minute of 1891. The fifth of seven children, he was a very independent and unruly child who was tried and acquitted at nine years old of the attempted murder of a trolley motorman who had callously driven over and killed his dog. In his late teens he drifted aimlessly around the United States for a time. Before breaking into acting he worked as a lumberjack, investment promoter, and for a short time, ran a pest extermination business. He was a stoker and fireman in the United States Navy when a friend dared him to get a job in Burlesque. He did and remained on stage for the next sixteen years

Bickford had intended to attend the Massachusetts Institute of Technology to earn an engineering degree, but while wandering the country, he became friends with the manager of a burlesque show, who convinced Bickford to take a role in the show. He debuted in Oakland, California in 1911. Bickford enjoyed himself so much that he abandoned his plans to attend M.I.T. He made his legitimate stage debut with the John Craig Stock Company at the Castle Square Theatre in Boston in 1912. Bickford eventually joined a road company and traveled throughout the United States for more than a decade, appearing in various productions. In 1925, while working in a Broadway play called *Outside Looking In*, he and co-star James Cagney (in his first Broadway role) received rave reviews. He was offered a role in Herbert Brenon's 1926 film of *Beau Geste*, but anxious not to give up his new-found Broadway stardom, turned it down. Following his appearance in the critically-praised but unsuccessful Maxwell Anderson-Harold Hickerson drama about the Sacco and Vanzetti case, *Gods of the Lightning* (Bickford was the Sacco character), Bickford was contacted by filmmaker Cecil B. DeMille and offered a contract with MGM studios to star in DeMille's first talking picture, *Dynamite*. He soon began working with MGM head Louis B. Mayer on a number of projects.

He became a star after playing Greta Garbo's lover in *Anna Christie* (1930), but never developed into a romantic lead. Always of independent mind, strong-willed and quick with his fists, Bickford would frequently argue and nearly come to blows with Mayer. During the production of DeMille's *Dynamite*, he punched out his director. He rejected numerous scripts and made no secret of his disdain for much of the material he was offered. His association with MGM was short-lived, and Bickford asked for and received a release from his contract, but found himself blacklisted at other studios. He became an independent actor for several years. Bickford was mauled by a lion and nearly died while filming *East of Java* (1935). While he recovered, he lost his contract with Fox as well as his leading man status due to extensive neck scarring coupled with his advancing age. Much preferring the character roles that now became his forte, Bickford appeared in many notable films including *The Unforgiven* (1960) with Audie Murphy.

Bickford found his greatest success playing character actor roles, both in films and later in television. He became highly sought after; his burly frame and craggy, intense features, coupled with a gruff, powerful voice lent themselves to a wide variety of roles. Most often he played lovable father figures, stern businessmen, heavies, ship captains or authority figures of some sort.

Bickford played rancher John Grainger, owner of the Shiloh Ranch on NBC's *The Virginian* (1962-1967) western series.

In 1965, he published his autobiography, *Bulls, Balls, Bicycles, & Actors*.

He continued to act in generally prestigious projects right up until his death. He died in Los Angeles November 9, 1967, of a blood infection at the age of seventy-six, just days after filming a 1967 *Virginian* episode.

Claudia Barrett

Claudia Barrett was born Imagene Williams in Los Angeles, California, June 20, 1923, and was a very busy actress on television and in B-movies of the 1950s. Alas, she is remembered best today for the one leading role that she would likely wish viewers could forget, as the heroine in Phil Tucker's notorious low-budget sci-fi thriller *Robot Monster* (1953).

She grew up in Sherman Oaks and trained at the Pasadena Playhouse during the 1940s. She was spotted by a Warner Brothers talent scout who signed her up and changed her name to Claudia Barrett, and her screen career began well enough, with a small, uncredited role in Raoul Walsh's classic thriller *White Heat* (1949), starring James Cagney. She played small roles in a string of subsequent pictures, and then started freelancing, which resulted in her getting a few larger parts at Republic Pictures during the waning days of the B-studio's production history. It was in 1953 that Barrett was contracted to play the female lead in Phil Tucker's alien invasion fantasy *Robot Monster*, playing opposite young leading man George Nader as the hero, and George Barrows as "Ro-Man," an invader from outer space (essentially a man in a gorilla suit with a diving helmet). Shot in less than a week, from a script that reads as though it didn't take much longer than that to write, and on a budget of less than $30,000, *Robot Monster* was a notoriously bad movie in the judgment of nearly all viewers and critics. It ended up becoming a kind of camp classic, grouped with such so-bad-they're-entertaining pictures as *Plan 9 From Outer Space*, although in the 1960s and early 1970s, before such ironic sensibilities took hold on programmers, it was frequently shown as a straight horror/sci-fi film, in the company of perfectly respectable entries in the field such as *Kronos* (1957) and *Invisible Invaders* (1959).

She turned to television around this same time and became a downright ubiquitous presence on the small-screen, primarily (though not entirely) in westerns. She could be seen in episodes of *The Cisco Kid* (1953-1955), *Hopalong Cassidy* (1952), *The Lone Ranger* (1953-1954), *Wild Bill Hickok* (1955), and *The Roy Rogers Show* (1955), as well as the later wave of somewhat more mature oaters such as *Death Valley Days* (1954-1959), *Tales of Wells Fargo* (1957), *Shotgun Slade* (1961), and *Trackdown* (1958).

Her most accessible television work, however, was in a pair of episodes of *The Abbott & Costello Show* (1953), which were seen in syndication for close to 30 years and have been reissued twice on DVD, as well as VHS.

She still continued in films and appeared in *Seven Ways from Sundown* (1960) with Audie Murphy, and her final film was an adaptation of a Louis L'amour novel *Taggart* (1964).

Barrett gave up acting in the early '60s and subsequently went to work for the Academy of Motion Picture Arts and Sciences. She has busied herself as a successful artist since the 1980s. As most of the 1950s Republic library has disappeared from distribution, and her work at Warner Brothers was confined to small roles, Barrett's most widely seen role in the twenty-first century remains that of Alice, the petulant, headstrong heroine in *Robot Monster*.

Paul Birch

Paul Birch with Audie Murphy in *The Gunrunners*

Paul Birch was born Paul Smith January 13, 1912, in Atmore, Alabama, and was an American actor of stage and film. He entered motion pictures via small roles in several westerns in the late 40s and early 50s. He appeared in two Audie Murphy movies such as *Ride Clear of Diablo* (1954) and *The Gun Runners* (1958).

He was a veteran of thirty-nine movies, fifty stage dramas and a number of television shows including the *Hallmark Hall of Fame* (1951). In the late 1950s he starred, along with William Campbell, in the syndicated Canadian series *Cannonball* (1958), a half-hour drama/adventure show about truckers. He was the original "Marlboro Man" in TV commercials and played both Union General Ulysses S. Grant and Confederate General Robert E. Lee in several historical plays. He enjoyed playing the roles of Lee and Grant and once remarked, "There were times when I was switching those two roles so fast I could have surrendered to myself."

He started out as the first of the original members of the Pasadena Playhouse and his stage work included *The Caine Mutiny*. He also had a recurring role as Captain Carpenter, the boss of Lt. Phillip Gerard in *The Fugitive* (1963-1967) starring David Janssen. He starred in some low-budget science-fiction films in the 1950s, including *The Beast with a Million Eyes* (1955), *Day the World Ended* (1955), *Not of This Earth* (1957) and the cult classic *Queen of Outer Space* (1958). Birch also had small roles in *It's a Mad, Mad, Mad, Mad World* (1963), and *Dead Heat on a Merry-Go-Round (1967)*. He died May 24, 1969, St. George's, Grenada.

Whit Bissell

Whitner Nutting Bissell was born October 25, 1909 in New York City. He was the son of prominent surgeon Dr. J. Dougal Bissell. He trained with the Carolina Playmakers, a theatrical organization associated with the University of North Carolina at Chapel Hill. He had a number of roles in Broadway theatre, including the Air Force show *Winged Victory*, when he was a private.

In a career that began in 1943 with the film *Holy Matrimony*, Bissell appeared in literally hundreds of films and television series episodes, including *Sheriff of Cochise* (1957) and Rod Cameron's syndicated *City Detective* (1955), *The Brothers Brannagan* (1960), and *The DuPont Show with June Allyson* (also 1960), and two Audie Murphy westerns like *The Red Badge of Courage* (1951) and *No Name on the Bullet* (1959)..

Viewers of 1950s low-budget science fiction, horror films and B movies know him as one of "those actors" (perhaps *the* actor) that always shows up somewhere in such movies. Some of the most well-known of these roles were as a mad scientist in the film *I Was a Teenage Werewolf* (1957), as well as Professor Frankenstein in *I Was a Teenage Frankenstein* (1957). He also played the doctor who treats Kevin McCarthy's character in the classic *Invasion of the Body Snatchers* (1956) and in the original *Creature from the Black Lagoon (*1954).

In 1960, he appeared in George Pal's production of *The Time Machine*, as Walter Kemp, one of the Time Traveler's dining friends. Thirty-three years later, in 1993 the documentary film *Time Machine: The Journey Back*, reunited Bissell with Rod Taylor and Alan Young from the original, he recreated his role as Walter in the opening sequence. It was Bissell's last acting performance. In 1957, he appeared in "The Man on the 35th Floor" of *Fireside Theater*, hosted by Jane Wyman, with fellow guest stars Macdonald Carey and Phyllis Avery.

Bissell was a regular for the third and fourth seasons of the television series *Bachelor Father* (1959–1961), costarring John Forsythe, Noreen Corcoran, and Sammee Tong. He appeared as a guest star in practically every dramatic television series that aired between the early 1950s and the mid 1970s, with more sporadic appearances after that. In 1959, he appeared on NBC's science fiction series *The Man and the Challenge*. In 1961, he guest starred in the episode "A Fool for a Client" on James Whitmore's *The Law and Mr. Jones* legal drama on ABC. He appeared three times on the long running TV western *The Virginian* in the 1960s.

His most prominent television role came when he co-starred as General Heywood Kirk in the science-fiction television series *The Time Tunnel* (1966-1967). He often played silver-haired figures of authority, here as in many other roles (as described by Allmovie), "instantly establishing his standard screen characterization of fussy officiousness," leavened in many instances with a military bearing.

Bissell appeared in the classic episode "The Trouble with Tribbles" of *Star Trek* (1967), footage of which was re-used in *Star Trek: Deep Space Nine'*s (1996) "Trials and Tribble-ations".

In 1978 and 1980, Bissell appeared in episodes of *The Incredible Hulk*, first in the second season episode "Kindred Spirits", and next (and lastly) in the second part of the fourth season two-parter "Prometheus". He played a different professor in both episodes.

Bissell's most-screened motion picture role is as the undertaker (who sees every man, no matter his race, as "just another future customer") in *The Magnificent Seven* (1960).

Bissell received a life career award from the Academy of Science Fiction, Fantasy & Horror Films in 1994. He also served for many years on the board of directors of the Screen Actors Guild, as well as representing the actors' branch of the Academy of Motion Picture Arts and Sciences board of governors.

Bissell died March 5, 1996 in Woodland Hills, California, from the effects of Parkinson's disease. He was interred in the Westwood Village Memorial Park Cemetery in Los Angeles.

Mari Blanchard

Audie Murphy with Mari Blanchard in Destry

Petite, attractive Mari Blanchard was born April 13, 1923. The daughter of an oil tycoon and a psychotherapist, she suffered from severe poliomyelitis from the age of nine, which denied her a hoped-for dancing career. For several years, she worked hard to rehabilitate her limbs from paralysis, swimming and later even performing on the trapeze at Cole Brothers Circus. At the urging of her parents, she then attended the University of Southern California from where she graduated with a degree in international law. This was not to lead to a career, either. Sometime in the late 1940's, she joined the Conover Agency as an advertising model and, at the same time, was promoted by famed cartoonist and writer Al Capp, becoming the inspiration for one of his "L'il Abner" characters.

As the result of an advertisement on the back page of the Hollywood Reporter, Mari was spotted by Paramount and signed to a contract. However, her early experience in the movie business proved an unhappy one, most of her roles being walk-ons and bit parts. *Ten Tall Men* (1951), for example, limited her to a token stroll down a street, twirling a parasol and smiling seductively at members of the Foreign Legion. It wasn't until Mari joined Universal that her fortunes improved somewhat, with a co-starring role (opposite Victor Mature) in *The Veils of Bagdad* (1953).

After that, Burt Lancaster, co-producer and star with Gary Cooper of the excellent A-grade western *Vera Cruz* (1954), had requested Mari as his leading lady, but Universal refused her release to United Artists and forbade her to accept the lucrative role (Denise Darcel ended up getting the part). Mari then lost the lead in a much lesser picture, *Saskatchewan* (1954), to Shelley Winters. Instead, she was cast as Venusian Queen Allura in one of the least exciting outings by Universal's leading comic duo, *Abbott and Costello Go to Mars* (1953).

Mari did end up with a respectable starring role in the western *Destry* (1954), opposite Audie Murphy. A remake of the classic *Destry Rides Again* (1939), she was cast in the Marlene Dietrich part and took great pains to affect a totally different look, darkening her hair, so as not to be compared to the great star. Even the name of her character was changed from 'Frenchy' to 'Brandy'. *Destry* was not all smooth sailing. There was tension between her and director George Marshall (who had also directed the original version) and Mari suffered a facial injury as the result of a fight scene. The film was critically well received. Unfortunately, Universal failed to renew their contract with Miss Blanchard, and her career then went into free-fall.

Free-lancing for lesser studios, she played a TB victim injected with a serum turning her into a Mr. Hyde-like killer in the lurid *She Devil* (1957) (during filming she nearly died of acute appendicitis). Mari then appeared for Republic in the eminently forgettable *No Place to Land* (1958), before briefly starring in her own short-lived adventure series *Klondike* (1960). Her last role of note was as the cheerful and likeable town madam in the rollicking John Wayne western comedy *McLintock!* (1963). Sometime that year, Mari Blanchard developed the cancer which was to claim her life in May 10, 1970 at the age of just 47.

Michael Blodgett

Audie Murphy with Michael Blodgett in *40 Guns to Apache Pass*

The handsome and engaging Michael Blodgett was born on January 1, 1940, in Minneapolis, Minnesota. Blodgett attended the University of Minnesota and began his acting career in his hometown of Minneapolis. Michael earned a law degree in political science from Cal State Los Angeles and attended Loyola Law School for a year. In the summer of 1967, Blodgett was the emcee on *Groovy*, a weekly TV program of beach party music that was broadcast on Los Angeles' Channel 9. That same year he appeared with Audie Murphy in *40 Guns to Apache Pass* (1967).

In 1968, Michael subsequently switched to Channel 11 and went on to serve as the host for *The Michael Blodgett Show*, a 90 minute talk show in which he interviewed such guests as Connie Stevens, Agnes Moorehead, Pat Paulsen and Henry Mancini. Blodgett achieved his greatest enduring cult popularity with his excellent portrayal of blithely decadent and hedonistic playboy "Lance Rocke" in Russ Meyer's outrageously campy treat *Beyond the Valley of the Dolls* (1970).

Other memorable movie roles include brash young prisoner "Coy Cavendish" in *There Was a Crooked Man* (1970), free-spirited hippie "Lee Ritter" in the offbeat fright feature *The Velvet Vampire* (1971), and abusive masseur "Roger Hudson" in *The Carey Treatment* (1972). Blodgett had a recurring role on the short-lived TV series *Never Too Young* (1965).

Among the TV shows Michael did guest spots on are *McHale's Navy* (1962), *The Alfred Hitchcock Hour* (1962), *The Munsters* (1964), *Daniel Boone* (1964), *Rod Serling's Night Gallery* (1969), *Ironside* (1967), *Barnaby Jones* (1973) and *Barbary Coast* (1975).

Blodgett quit acting in the late 70s and became a successful novelist and screenwriter. He penned the novels *Captain Blood*, *Hero and the Terror,* and *The White Raven*. In addition, he either wrote or co-wrote the scripts for the Chuck Norris action vehicle *Hero and the Terror* (1988) in which Michael also makes an uncredited cameo appearance in this particular picture, the hit comedy *Turner & Hooch* (1989), *Rent-a-Cop* (1987), *Run* (1991), the made-for-TV thriller *Revenge on the Highway* (1992) and *The White Raven* (1998). Michael Blodgett died at age 67 from a heart attack in Los Angeles on November 14, 2007.

Willis Bouchey

Willis Ben Bouchey was born May 24, 1907 and was an American character actor who appeared in almost 150 films and television shows over a 30-year period from 1951 to 1979. He was born in Vernon, Michigan, but reared by his mother and stepfather in Washington State.

Bouchey may be best known for his appearances in *The Horse Soldiers* (1959), *The Long Gray Line* (1955), *The Man Who Shot Liberty Valance* (1962), *The Big Heat* (1953), and *No Name on the Bullet* (1959) with Audie Murphy. Bouchey appeared twice as Joe Carr in the 1960-1961 ABC sitcom, *Harrigan and Son*, starring Pat O'Brien and Roger Perry. He played the judge in twenty-three episodes of Perry Mason and again with Raymond Burr in an episode of *Ironside* (1969).

He also appeared with James Garner in both *Support Your Local Sheriff* (1969) and *Support Your Local Gunfighter* (1971).

Throughout his career, he worked in twelve different productions for director John Ford and was one of the more frequently-used members of the John Ford Stock Company. In *The Man Who Shot Liberty Valance* he delivered the line, *"Nothing's too good for the man who shot Liberty Valance."*

He was one of those wonderful character actors who would be a crooked judge in one film and a humorous cavalry officer in another. His longevity resulted, in part, due to his professionalism and acting ability. He always provided a fine performance no matter how small or insignificant the role. He died September 27, 1977, in Burbank, California.

Lane Bradford

Lane Bradford was born August 29, 1922, in Yonkers, New York. He has appeared in many television series and b western movies. On stage, he co-starred in *Desperadoes' Outpost* (1952), *The Great Sioux Uprising* (1953), *Apache Warrior* (1957).

He appeared with Audie Murphy in *Ride Clear of Diablo* (1954) and *Drums Across the River* (1954).

In the 1950s, 1960s, and 1970s, Bradford guest-starred in nearly all TV western-series such as *Hopalong Cassidy (1952-1953)*, *The Cisco Kid (1954-1956)*, *The Lone Ranger* (1949-1957) fifteen episodes, *Buffalo Bill Jr.* (1955-1956) six episodes, *The Adventures of Rin Tin Tin* (1954-1957) five episodes, *The Life and Legend of Wyatt Earp* (1955-1960) five episodes, *Cheyenne* (1956-1962) seven episodes, *Wagon Train* (1958-1965) eight episodes, *The High Chaparral* (1967-1968) two episodes, *The Restless Gun* (1958-1959) four episodes, *Bonanza* (1959-1971) fourteen episodes, *Gunsmoke* (1959-1972) thirteen episodes, and many more.

His last appearance was in *Cannon* (1973) with William Conrad. He died June 7, 1973 in Honolulu, Hawaii, at age 50.

Scott Brady

He had the manly good looks and rugged appeal to make it to top stardom in Hollywood and succeeded quite well as a sturdy leading man of standard action on film and TV. Born in Brooklyn on September 13, 1924, Irish-American Scott Brady was christened Gerard Kenneth Tierney (called Jerry) by parents Lawrence and Maria Tierney. His father, chief of New York's aqueduct police force, had always had show business intentions and later did print work after retiring from the force. Both Scott's older and younger brothers, Lawrence Tierney and Edward Tierney went on to become actors as well.

Scott grew up in Westchester County and attended Roosevelt and St. Michael's High Schools. Like his older brother Lawrence, Scott he was an all-round athlete in school and earned letters for basketball, football, and track and expressed early designs on becoming a football coach or radio announcer. Instead he enlisted before graduating from high school and served as a naval aviation mechanic overseas. During his term of duty he earned a light heavyweight boxing medal. He was discharged in 1946 and decided to head for Los Angeles where his older brother Lawrence was making encouraging strides as an actor.

Toiling in menial jobs as a cabbie and day-time laborer, the handsome, blue-eyed looker was noticed having lunch in a café by producer Hal B. Wallis and offered a screen test. The test did not fare well but, not giving up, he enrolled in the Bliss-Hayden drama school under his G.I. Bill, studied acting, and managed to rid himself of his thick Brooklyn accent.

He signed with a minor league studio, Eagle-Lion, and made his debut of sorts in the poverty-row programmer *In This Corner* (1948) utilizing his boxing skills from his early days in the service. He showed more promise with his second and third films *Canon City* (1948) and *He Walked by Night* (1948), the latter as a detective who aids in nabbing psychotic killer Richard Basehart.

Scott switched over to higher-grade action stories for Fox and Universal over time. Westerns and crime stories would be his bread-winning genres with *The Gal Who Took the West* (1949) opposite Yvonne De Carlo and John Russell and *Undertow* (1949), with Russell again, being prime examples. He frequently switched from hero to heavy during his peak years. In one film he would romance a Jeanne Crain in *The Model and the Marriage Broker* (1951) or a Mitzi Gaynor in *Bloodhounds of Broadway* (1952), while in the next beat Shelley Winters to a pulp in *Untamed Frontier* (1952). He even played outlaw Bloody Bill Anderson in the Audie Murphy film *Kansas Raiders* (1950).

A favorite pin-up hunk in his early years, he hit minor cult status as a bad hombre, *The Dancin' Kid* (1954), in the offbeat western *Johnny Guitar*. He and the other manly men, however, were somewhat overshadowed in the movie by the Freudian-tinged gunplay between Joan Crawford and Mercedes McCambridge. Other roles had him sturdily handling the action scenes while giving the glance over to such diverting female costars as Barbara Stanwyck, Mala Powers and Anne Bancroft.

Scott would mark the same territory in TV, westerns, and crime stories, finding steadier work on the smaller screen into the 1960s. He starred as the title hero in the western series *Shotgun Slade* (1959).

The seemingly one-time confirmed bachelor decided to settle down after meeting and marrying Mary Tirony in 1967 at age 43. Prior to this he had been linked with such luminous beauties as Gwen Verdon and Dorothy Malone. The couple had two sons. Parts dwindled down in size in later years and he gained considerable weight as he grew older and balder, but he still appeared here-and-there as an occasional character heavy or hard-ass cop in less-important movies such as *Doctors' Wives* (1971), *$* (1971), *The Loners* (1972) and *Wicked, Wicked* (1973).

He had a memorable role in the *Police Story* (1977) episode "Trigger Point" with David Janssen. Minor TV roles in mini-movies also came his way at a fair pace. Towards the end he was seen in such high-profile big-screen movies as *The China Syndrome* (1979) and his last screen appearance in *Gremlins* (1984).

Scott had a collapse in 1981 and was diagnosed with pulmonary fibrosis, a progressive respiratory disease. He later relied on an oxygen tank. He died of the disease four years later on April 16, 1985 at age 60 and was interred at the Holy Cross Cemetery in Culver City, California.

William Bramley

Audie Murphy with William Bramley in *Gunpoint*

William Bramley was born April 18, 1928 in Runnemede, New Jersey. He was a character actor who appeared in nearly 100 movies and television programs.

Some of those include *The Aquanauts* (1961), *West Side Story* (1961), *Laramie* (1962-1963), *Destry* (1964), *The Outer Limits* (1965), *Lost in Space* (1965-1966), *Gunpoint* (1966) with Audie Murphy, *The Fugitive* (1966), *The Monkees* (1967), *Star Trek* (1968), *Suppose They Gave a War and Nobody Came?* (1970), *O'Hara, U.S. Treasury* (1972), *Get Christie Love!* (1974), *Adam-12* (1968-1974), *Revenge of the Cheerleaders* (1976), *How the West Was Won* (1979), *The Dukes of Hazzard* (1982), and *The Wild Life* (1984).

He died October 27, 1985, at age 57 in Los Angeles County, California.

Henry Brandon

Henry Brandon with Audie Murphy in *Suspicion*

Henry Brandon was born June 8, 1912, and was an American character actor in over 100 films, famous for playing Indian, Arab, Persian, Turkish, Native American and East Asian roles, usually villains.

Born Heinrich von Kleinbach in Berlin, Germany, his parents immigrated to the United States while he was still an infant. A stage actor, he performed on Broadway and continued to act on stage periodically throughout his acting career. He made his motion picture debut in 1932.

In 1940, Brandon appeared in the title role of the famous Republic serial *Drums of Fu Manchu*. He also played a French army captain in Robert Aldrich's *Vera Cruz* (1954), and "Officer Chaney" in John Carpenter's 1976 film, *Assault on Precinct 13*. Many people will remember him for his role as "Silas Barnaby", the evil character in the Laurel & Hardy 1934 classic *Babes in Toyland* later retitled *March of the Wooden Soldiers*. He was also the nasty opera manager who signed Alfalfa to an unbreakable contract singing "The Barber of Seville" in the *Little Rascals/Our Gang* short ''Our Gang Follies of 1938''. He was memorable as the foreign spy Derek in a 1965 two-part episode of *Mister Ed*. In the 1960s TV series *The Outer Limits*, Brandon played General Crawford in the episode "The Chameleon" starring Robert Duvall. He is perhaps best remembered for his role as Acacius Page in the 1958 film *Auntie Mame*.

His most famous acting roles were as "Chief Cicatrice" (Scar) in John Ford's *The Searchers* (1956) and "Chief Quanah Parker" in Ford's *Two Rode Together* (1961). Also in 1961, he appeared in the episode "The Mortal Coil" of Audie Murphy's *Whispering Smith* television series.

Brandon died in February 15, 1990, at age 77 from a heart attack. He was cremated.

Peter Breck

Audie Murphy with Peter Breck in *The Wild and the innocent*

Primarily remembered as Barbara Stanwyck's rugged middle son, Nick Barkley, the handsome and strapping "loose cannon" on the popular action-driven TV western *The Big Valley* (1965), actor Peter Breck is a survivor who has gone through the ups and downs of not only his own personal life, but this tough business they call acting. Like Nick, Peter has maintained a strong, positive outlook and still shows the fighter in him in a career that has touched on five decades.

He was born Joseph Peter Breck, the son of a jazz musician, also named Joseph (nicknamed "Jobie"). Over time, his father worked with such legendary greats as Fats Waller, Bix Beiderbecke, Paul Whiteman and Billie Holiday. Peter nicknamed "Buddy", was on the road with his parents for much of his early life. Realizing the need for stability in young Peter's life, his parents sent him to live with his grandparents in Haverhill, Massachusetts. His parents eventually divorced and young Peter returned to Rochester to live with his mother and her new husband, Al Weber, who was a sports editor of the *Rochester - Times Union*.

Following his schooling at John Marshall High School in Rochester, Peter served in the United States Navy. He then turned his attention back to education and studied English and drama at the University of Texas in Houston. While performing in college plays, he started to apprentice at Houston's Alley Theatre, where he appeared in such productions as "Stalag 17", among others. He also had a talent for singing and performed in several clubs around the Houston area.

Peter extended his stage resume at Washington D.C.'s Arena Theatre. While performing there in a 1957 production of George Bernard Shaw's "The Man of Destiny", he was 'discovered' by Robert Mitchum, who cast him in an unbilled role in the film *Thunder Road* (1958), which Mitchum himself produced, co-wrote and starred in. Mitchum invited the young tenderfoot to Los Angeles and helped set him up out there. While Peter struggled trying to establish himself in films (he played a local thug called Chip in *The Wild and the Innocent* (1959) with Audie Murphy and a juvenile delinquent in the movie *The Beatniks* (1960)), it seemed that rugged TV roles came easier to him. He found his first series lead as Clay Culhane in the western *Black Saddle* (1959), the story of a gunfighter (Breck) who switches guns for law books and tries to tame the West through reason. The series co-starred Russell Johnson (later the "Professor" on *Gilligan's Island* (1964)) who plays a suspicious U.S. Marshal, the series was canceled after a single season.

A Warner Brothers studio contract, however, did come out of this...and a new visibility. Tall, dark and handsome at 6'2", Breck guest-starred on all the top Warner Brothers television shows of the day like *The Roaring Twenties* (1960), *Sugarfoot* (1957), *Surfside 6* (1960), *Bronco* (1958), *Hawaiian Eye* (1959), *77 Sunset Strip* (1958), *Cheyenne* (1955) and played a recurring "Doc Holliday" in the popular series *Maverick* (1957).

He returned to the movies as well, but this time in stronger leads or co-leads. Handed a choice co-starring assignment in *Portrait of a Mobster* (1961) opposite star Vic Morrow, who played the infamous "Dutch Schultz", Peter also managed to show a rare, gentler side in the outdoor family drama *Ladd: A Dog* (1962).

He left Warners after only a few years but managed to score the leads in two low-budget cult thrillers in its wake: *Shock Corridor* (1963) and *The Crawling Hand* (1963), along with a very dismal lead in the musical outing

Hootenanny Hoot (1963), in which he was given no songs to perform despite his singing capabilities. Again, TV came to the rescue after winning the brotherly co-lead on *The Big Valley* (1965). Despite a uniformly strong ensemble cast that included oldest brother Richard Long, youngest brother Lee Majors, and sister Linda Evans, Stanwyck was the only performer on the show who was nominated for an Emmy during its four-season run (she was nominated twice and won once).

Following this TV peak, Peter abruptly left Hollywood and focused on the theater both in the U.S. and Canada throughout the 1970s, appearing in such showcase vehicles as "The Gazebo", "A Thousand Clowns", "The Rainmaker" and "Mister Roberts". Married to former dancer Diana Bourne since 1960, the couple settled in Vancouver, Canada, with their son Christopher, where Peter checked out the film scene. He also set up a full-time acting academy school, The Breck Academy, which ran for ten years. Tragically, it was during this time that their son, Christopher, was diagnosed with acute myeloid leukemia and died (two years later).

Peter decided to lay back following this traumatic period, but still managed to perform in films and TV from time to time. As he grew older, he joined the cast of some very offbeat "B" films (shot either in Canada or the U.S.) that hardly reflected his image created during the 60s: *Terminal City Ricochet* (1990) and *Highway 61* (1991). His more recent "B" movies have included *Decoy* (1995), *Enemy Action* (1999) and *Jiminy Glick in Lalawood* (2004).

His last television performance was on an episode of *John Doe* in 2002. In June 2010, Breck's wife Diane announced on his website that the actor has been suffering from dementia and can no longer sign autographs for fans, although he still read and enjoyed their letters. Despite this diagnosis, she said he was still physically healthy and did not require medication.

According to his wife Diane, Breck was hospitalized on January 10, 2012. On February 6, 2012, Peter Breck died from his illness at age 82.

Walter Brennan

Audie Murphy and Walter Brennan in *Drums Across the River*

Walter Andrew Brennan was born July 25, 1894, in Lynn, Massachusetts, less than two miles from his family's home in Swampscott. He was the second of three children born to Irish immigrants William John Brennan and Margaret Elizabeth Flanagan. The elder Brennan was an engineer and inventor, and young Walter studied engineering at Rindge Technical High School in Cambridge, Massachusetts.

While in school, Brennan became interested in acting, and began to perform in vaudeville. While working as a bank clerk, he enlisted in the U.S. Army and served as a private with the 101st Field Artillery Regiment in France during World War I. Following the war, he moved to Guatemala and raised pineapples, before settling in Los Angeles. During the 1920s, he became involved in the real estate market, where he made a fortune. Unfortunately, he lost most of his money when the market took a sudden downturn due to the Great Depression.

Finding himself broke, he began taking extra parts in 1929 and then bit parts in as many films as he could, including *The Invisible Man* (1933), the Three Stooges short *Woman Haters* (1934), and *Bride of Frankenstein* (1935), and also worked as a stunt man. In the 1930s, he began appearing in higher-quality films and received more substantial roles as his talent was recognized. This culminated with his receiving the very first Academy Award for Best Supporting Actor for his role as Swan Bostrom in the period film *Come and Get It* (1936) with Joel McCrea. Two years later he portrayed town drunk and accused murderer Muff Potter in *The Adventures of Tom Sawyer* (1938).

Throughout his career, Brennan was frequently called upon to play characters considerably older than he was in real life. The loss of many teeth in a 1932 accident, rapidly thinning hair, thin build, and gravelly voice all made him seem older than he really was. He used these physical features to great effect. In many of his film roles, Brennan wore dentures; in *Northwest Passage* (1940), a film set in the late 18th century, when most people had bad teeth, he wore a special dental prosthesis which made him appear to have rotting and broken teeth.

Director Jean Renoir gave the character actor a leading role in 1941: Brennan played the top-billed lead in *Swamp Water*, a drama directed by Renoir and featuring Walter Huston.

In *Sergeant York* (1941), he played a sympathetic preacher and dry goods store owner who advised the title character played by Gary Cooper. He was particularly skilled in playing the hero's sidekick or as the "grumpy old man" in a picture. Though he was hardly ever cast as the villain, notable exceptions were his roles as Old Man Clanton in the 1946 film *My Darling Clementine* opposite Henry Fonda, the 1962 Cinerama production *How the West Was Won* as the murderous Colonel Jeb Hawkins, and as Judge Roy Bean in *The Westerner*, for which he won his third best supporting actor Academy Award, in 1940. He appeared as Audie Murphy's kindly father in *Drums Across the River* (1954) in the sympathetic-to-Indians film, unusual for its time.

From 1957-1963, he starred in the ABC television series *The Real McCoys*, which costarred Richard Crenna, and Kathleen Nolan. The comedy about a poor West Virginia family that relocated to a farm in southern California ran on ABC from 1957 to 1962 before switching to CBS for a final season as simply *The McCoys*. In the last season, Janet De Gore and Butch Patrick joined the cast as a widow and son; she being the new romantic interest of the recently widowed Luke McCoy, played by Richard Crenna. The revised format of *The McCoys* was no match in the ratings for NBC's powerhouse western series, *Bonanza* (1959-1973). Brennan joined with the series creator, Irving Pincus, to form Brennan-Westgate-Marterto Productions. The series was filmed during its six-year run at Desilu Studios.

Brennan appeared as himself as a musical judge in the 1953-1954 ABC series *Jukebox Jury*. On May 30, 1957, he guest starred on NBC's *The Ford Show, Starring Tennessee Ernie Ford*. He also made a few recordings, the most popular being "Old Rivers" about an eccentric but much-beloved farmer; it was released as a single in 1962 by Liberty Records with "The Epic Ride Of John H. Glenn" on the flip side, and peaked at number five in the U.S. Billboard charts. In his music, Brennan sometimes worked with Allen "Puddler" Harris, a Louisiana native who was a member of the original Ricky Nelson Band. He also co-starred with James Garner in the 1969 *Support Your Local Sheriff!*, playing the head of the Danby Family.

Brennan starred as wealthy executive Walter Andrews in the short-lived 1964-1965 series *The Tycoon*, with Van Williams. In 1967, he starred in another series, *The Guns of Will Sonnett*, in which he played a man in search of his gunfighter son, James, with his grandson, Jeff, played by Dack Rambo. After the series went off the air in 1969, Brennan continued working in both television and feature films. He received top billing over Pat O'Brien in the TV-movie *The Over-the-Hill Gang* in 1969 and Fred Astaire in *The Over-the-Hill Gang Rides Again* the following year. From 1970 to 1971, he was a regular on the show *To Rome With Love*, which was his last TV show as a member of the permanent cast.

Film historians and critics have long regarded Brennan as one of the finest character actors in motion picture history. While the roles he was adept at playing were extremely diverse, he is probably best remembered for his portrayals in movie Westerns, such as trail hand Nadine Groot in *Red River* (1948) and Deputy Stumpy in *Rio Bravo* (1959) both directed by Howard Hawks. He was the first actor to win three Academy Awards. He remains the only person to have won three Best Supporting Actor awards. However, even he remained somewhat embarrassed as to how he won the awards. In the early years of the Academy Awards, extras were given the right to vote. Brennan was extremely popular with the Union of Film Extras and since their numbers were overwhelming, each time he was nominated, he won. Though never described as undeserving of the awards he won, his third win was one of the catalysts leading to the disenfranchisement of the Extras Union from Oscar voting.

Unlike many actors, Brennan's career never really went into decline. As the years went on, he was able to find work in dozens of high quality films, and later television appearances throughout the 1950s and 60s. As he grew older, he simply became a more familiar, almost comforting film figure whose performances continued to endear him to new generations of fans. In all, he would appear in more than 230 film and television roles in a career spanning nearly five decades.

For his contribution to the television industry, Walter Brennan has a star on the Hollywood Walk of Fame at 6501 Hollywood Blvd. In 1970, he was inducted into the Western Performers Hall of Fame at the National Cowboy & Western Heritage Museum in Oklahoma City, Oklahoma, where his photograph adorns a wall.

Upon his death from emphysema at the age of eighty September 21, 1974 in Oxnard in Ventura County, Brennan's remains were interred at San Fernando Mission Cemetery in Los Angeles. Brennan was married to the former Ruth Wells (December 8, 1897 – January 12, 1997), whom he married in 1920. The Brennan's had a daughter and two sons.

Peter Brocco

Peter Brocco was born January 16, 1903, and was an American film and TV character actor for nearly sixty years. He appeared as a criminal type in several episodes of *Adventures of Superman* (1952-1956). He holds the distinction of having been killed off in two of them, a relative rarity for villains in the series. In the first, "The Secret of Superman", he deduces that Kent is Superman, but is killed in a police shootout soon after. In "The Clown Who Cried", he falls off a building and Superman is unable to save him. He also appeared as The Spector in "The Phantom Ring", where the criminals developed a machine that can make them invisible. Finally, in that episode, he survives.

He appeared in two episodes of *The Twilight Zone* (1960-1962). He played Doctor Appleby in *The Three Stooges in Orbit* (1962) and was in Audie Murphy's final film *A Time for Dying* (1969).

He appeared as an Organian council member in the *Star Trek* (1967) episode "Errand of Mercy" which established the uneasy treaty of peace between the United Federation of Planets and the Klingon Empire.

For fans of those two series, it is noteworthy that he and Jeff Corey appeared in both series, and that both men were blacklisted for a while during the red scare of the early 1950s.

Brocco played Colonel Matterson, a patient suffering from dementia, in the Academy Award-winning *One Flew Over the Cuckoo's Nest* (1975).

He lived for some forty years in Laurel Canyon, and died in Los Angeles, California, from a heart attack on December 20, 1992, aged 89.

Kevin Brodie

Audie Murphy with Kevin Brodie in *Battle at Bloody Beach*

Kevin Brodie was born May 31, 1952, and is a film director, screenwriter, and former child actor. He is the son of the actors Steve Brodie and Lois Andrews.

As a child, Brodie had small roles in such films as *Some Came Running* (1958), *The Five Pennies* (1959) and *Battle at Bloody Beach* (1961) with Audie Murphy. He appeared with Audie Murphy a second time in *Showdown* (1963).

His first major role was in *The Night of the Grizzly* (1966), playing he son of Clint Walker. In the following year he appeared in the comedy *Eight on the Lam* (1967). During the same period he also made guest appearances on such popular television shows as *Cheyenne* (1961), *Ben Casey* (1962), *Death Valley Days* (1964-1965), *My Three Sons* (1964-1969), and *Mannix* (1973).

In 1975 he was one of the leads in the low budget sci-fi thriller *The Giant Spider Invasion*, appearing with his father, Steve Brodie.

In the 1970s he moved into production, working as an assistant director, line producer and writer. He has written and directed a small number of films in genres ranging from exploitation comedy such as *Delta Pi*, also known as *Mugsy's Girls*, (1985) to thrillers like *Treacherous*, (1993) and family fare films like *A Dog of Flanders*, (1999).

Sheila Bromley

Sheila Bromley was born October 31, 1911, in San Francisco, California, and was an American television and film actress. She was a blue-eyed beauty, a former Miss California. She studied at Berkeley and entered films at the age of twenty-six. She had the curious habit of frequently changing her surname, making appearances as Sheila Fulton, Sheila Mannors (or Manners) or Sheila Manners-Bromley.

She is best known for her roles in B-movies, mostly westerns of the era.

She began her career in the 1930s on contract with Monogram Pictures, she was first billed as Sheila LeGay starring in 1930 westerns alongside Tom Tyler. She frequently co-starred with Ken Maynard, Hoot Gibson, Johnny Mack Brown, Bill Cody, and Dick Foran. She first starred alongside Bill Cody in the western *Land of Wanted Men* (1932). She starred opposite John Wayne in the 1935 films *Westward Ho & Lawless Range* and the film *Idol of the Crowds* (1937). In 1944 Bromley appeared in the touring production of *Good Night Ladies*. She also appeared with Audie Murphy in *World in My Corner* (1956). In 1960 she appeared as a central character Mrs. Spencer alongside Paul Brinegar's character Wishbone in the *Rawhide* episode "Incident of the Deserter".

During World War II she worked often for the USO, continuing that service until the war ended in 1945. There she met her husband Jairus Bellamy.

She is credited with seventy-five films in her career, of which seventeen were westerns, for which she is best known. Her last appearance was on cop drama *Adam-12* (1975)

Bromley retired from films and lived in the Greater Los Angeles Area until her death at 91 on July 23, 2003.

Lillian Bronson

Lillian Bronson was born in Lockport, New York, October 21, 1902. Over her long career, Lillian Bronson played numerous small character roles in a wide variety of films. Miss Bronson was educated at Bryn Mawr and the University of Michigan.

During the Depression, Miss Bronson and her late sister, Dorothy, opened the Bronson Studio in New York, designing and making toy animals and pillows. She began her career on Broadway, appearing in "Camille" with Lillian Gish and "Lean Harvest" with Leslie Banks.

The New York City native made her screen debut in *The Happy Land* (1943) starring Don Ameche.

After many film appearances, she branched out into television, working as a regular on shows like *Kings Row*, where she played Grandma from 1955 to 1956, and *Date with the Angels* between 1957 and 1958.

Lillian Bronson was also famous as the model for the controversial mural near the four-level interchange in Downtown Los Angeles called "Old Woman of the Freeway". Artist Kent Twitchell painted the mural, featuring white-haired Miss Bronson wearing an afghan spinning off into a night sky, in 1974 as part of a Los Angeles County art program funded by the National Endowment for the Arts.

His canvas was the twenty-five room Prince Hotel at 125 W. Temple St., selected for its visibility from the Hollywood Freeway. But in a controversy with building owners that led to litigation, the mural was painted over with a billboard in 1986. Many people believed that the model for the mural was Twitchell's grandmother. But he said he selected Miss Bronson from a Screen Actors Guild catalogue, partly for her stately bearing and partly because she resembled two of his great-grandmothers.

In Hollywood, Miss Bronson played society matrons and influential aides or relatives like Clark Gable's secretary in the 1947 film *The Hucksters*, Claudette Colbert's sister in the 1948 *Family Honeymoon*, and Henry Fonda's mother in the 1963 Spencer's Mountain. She even appeared with Audie Murphy in *Battle at Bloody Beach* (1961).

On television, Miss Bronson played a judge on several episodes of the *Perry Mason* series and her final appearance was as 'Fonzie's', the Henry Winkler character's, motorcycle-riding grandmother on *Happy Days* (1975).

Lillian Bronson died Aug. 1, 1995, at age 93 in Los Angeles, California of natural causes.

Rand Brooks

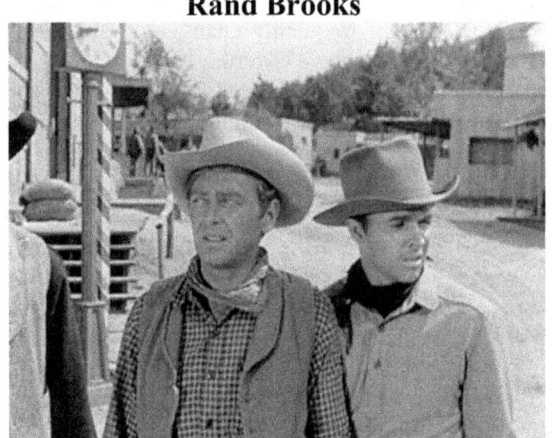

Rand Brooks with Audie Murphy in *The Cimarron Kid*

Rand Brooks was born in St Louis, Missouri, September 21, 1918, and was an American film actor. Brooks was the son of a travelling jewellery salesman who later settled in Los Angeles. After leaving school, he managed to get a screen test at MGM, and was given a bit part in *Love Finds Andy Hardy* (1938).

He was better known as the actor who played opposite Vivien Leigh as Scarlett O'Hara's ill-fated first husband in *Gone with the Wind* (1938) and as the first actor who gave Marilyn Monroe her first on-screen kiss in her first starring role in the Columbia Pictures movie *Ladies of the Chorus* (1948).

After *Gone With the Wind*, he had relatively small parts in other movies, then a regular role as Lucky in the *Hopalong Cassidy* series of westerns starring William Boyd in the mid to late 1940s.

He appeared in *The Cimarron Kid* (1952) with Audie Murphy and then in two of Audie Murphy's four movies with 'Hell' in the title: he was Audie Murphy's commanding officer in *To Hell and Back* (1955) and again with Audie Murphy in *Posse From Hell* (1961). The other two 'Hell' movies are *Hell Bent for Leather* (1960) and *War is Hell* (1962).

Television brought new opportunities, again often in westerns. He played Cpl. Randy Boone in the thirty-seven episodes of the television series *The Adventures of Rin Tin Tin* (1954-1958). Mr. Brooks had guest roles in other 1950s western series, including *The Adventures of Wild Bill Hickok* (1951-1954), *The Lone Ranger* (1949-1957), and *Maverick* (1957-1959).

He guest starred in other series such as *Perry Mason* (1963-1965), *Rocky Jones, Space Ranger* (1954), *The Munsters* (1964), *The Green Hornet* (1966) with Bruce Lee, and *Adam-12* (1970).

After he left show business, he ran an ambulance service that became the largest private ambulance provider in Los Angeles County. He sold the company in 1994 and retired to the Santa Ynez Valley where he bred champion Andalusian horses.

Brooks died at his ranch September 1, 2003 in Santa Inez, where he had retired to raise horses. He is survived by his second wife, Hermine (his first wife Lois Laurel, was Stan Laurel's daughter) and he had four children.

Robert Brubaker

Audie Murphy with Robert Brubaker in *Apache Rifles*

Robert Brubaker was born in Robinson, Illinois, on October 9, 1916, and was an American character actor best known for his roles in television and movie westerns, including twenty-nine episodes of *Gunsmoke* and two Audie Murphy movies *Apache Rifles* (1964) and *40 Guns to Apache Pass* (1967).

Brubaker was the only actor to have two recurring roles on the television series, *Gunsmoke*, portraying both a bartender named Floyd and a stagecoach driver named Jim Buck.

Bob attended Robinson Township High School, which was where he became interested in theatrics. Bob started as a freshman, appearing in every production that was at the high school. When a lot of kids are growing up they want to be a soldier or a fireman; Bob had always wanted to be an actor. While in high school Bob was captain of the debating team and won the State Oratory contest. He had a public speaking teacher who was the one that really urged him about continuing his ambition as an actor. As a result of her urgings and her talking and her pushing, she suggested that Bob go to Northwestern University in Evanston, Illinois, at the Annie Mae Swift School of Speech. Bob's freshman year was in September of 1934 and he decided they were trying to teach him to be a teacher instead of how to be an actor. While there he did a show, which was a revival of a musical comedy called "Good News", in which he played the comedy lead, and it was a tremendous success. He got reviews in the *Chicago Tribune* where the critic stated he liked Bob's characterization of "Bobby" better than that of Jack Haley, which Bob felt was quite an accomplishment. After two years, Bob decided to leave school and learn his profession on the job.

Martin Burton, who had, in conjunction with George Condoff, become producers of the first musical ever done by the Federal Theater, had seen Bob's work in "Good News", and offered him a great opportunity. The Federal Theater was the only time that this government had ever subsidized the theater. That was during the Works Progress Administration when Franklin D. Roosevelt was President. In the summer of 1936, Bob went to work in the Federal Theater in a show called "Oh Say Can You Sing, Dance or Act". One of the people in that show who went on to become very famous was a young seventeen-year old kid who did a tap dancing number with a pair of drumsticks. His name was Buddy Rich. That was Bob's first professional show and he worked in that until September 1937.

Then, he had to make a decision. There was two ways he could go: he could go to New York or go to Hollywood, but was much more drawn to Hollywood than he was to New York.

The first thing Bob did when he arrived in Hollywood was to go back to school. He went to a dramatic school by the name of "Bards". There are some well-known alumni from "Bards" that were in school when he was there: Alan Ladd, Jack Carson and Gig Young. Bob was with "Bards" off and on for over two years and finally became a teacher there to help pay for his tuition. In addition to attending "Bards", Bob worked on a number of radio shows at the original KMPC out on Wilshire Boulevard opposite the Beverly Hotel. At that time, Clete Roberts was staff announcer and William Conrad was one of the staff actors.

While at "Bards", Bob was brought to the attention of a man who was at that time head of Paramount Studios on the West Coast. They used to have a talent show every so often at "Bards" and all the major talent scouts and casting directors and hierarchy of the production side of the studios that Ben Bard could get into the theater would come to see these talent shows. They did original skits and also scenes from plays and motion pictures.

When Bob first came to Hollywood, he was told he was not a leading man. He was told by studio executives they wanted Bob to be Paramount's answer to John Garfield, because that was sort of a breakthrough in that they were accepting a man that looked like that as a possible leading man. All these contracts were drawn up and sent back to be consummated by the head office in New York, and then there was a big rollover in the studio and all the people that were in the top echelon were all gone and nothing ever came of it. This was one of Bob's first 'almosts' that didn't happen.

Bob was involved in a radio program called *Gateway to Hollywood* in 1939. The producer of the show was a man from RKO named Jesse L. Lasky, and Bob appeared with guest stars such as Merle Oberon and Sir Cedric Hardwicke. It was a talent search and Bob made his way to the finals of that particular show. The first prize was a year contract for RKO. "Josephine Cottle" won the female prize and was given the name of Gale Storm; the fellow who won was Lee Bonnell, who later married Gale Storm. After leaving "Bards", Bob became involved with the Bliss-Hayden Theater for a time and then had the opportunity to go to New York and landed the male lead in a play called "Days of Our Youth" that was being done for the opening of The New School of Social Research, which was off-Broadway. That was in 1941. It was directed by John Baird who had been one of Bob's teachers at Northwestern. They had outstanding critical reviews from the major critics in the New York area, so much so that there were a couple of guys who were looking to invest some money. Their names were Olsen and Johnson, well-known comics who wanted to bring the show to Broadway. They didn't think it was necessary to go out of town, so what they did was post an Equity Bond and got a theater lined up on Broadway. The show closed at The New School of Social Research and went into rehearsals for uptown, or Broadway, and, during this time, December seventh came along. The Japanese bombed Pearl Harbor, and they paid off the Equity Bond and that was the end of that.

Bob eventually returned to Hollywood in the early part of 1942, and subsequently volunteered for the US Army Air Force, was selected, went into the cadet program and became a pilot. He was an instructor and then became an aircraft commander in B-24's. His group was selected to go overseas two different times. They got as far as San Francisco and, both times, they canceled their orders and they ended the war at Gowen Field up in Boise, Idaho.

Bob was discharged from the service on December 15, 1945, and returned to Hollywood, and had to start all over again. When you're gone for any period of time, memory is very short in Hollywood or in New York. He did some more radio work and performed on some of the major radio shows of that period. Then, Bob decided to return to New York, where he was a Hollywood actor in New York, and, at that time, they didn't have much use for Hollywood actors in New York, so he went to work in the men's section for Lord and Taylor Department Store to survive. Then, Bob was recalled into the service. Anybody who was a pilot at the end of World War II and in physically good health was not discharged, just given separation papers from active duty but kept on active reserve. Bob was recalled to fly the airlift in 1949 on what they called a contract and was supposed to be in the service for eighteen months. He was to serve six months on the airlift, and then spend a year in the training command as an instructor. Bob did his six months on the airlift, flying one hundred and thirty missions into Berlin.

When he returned home at the end of his six months, he was greeted by General Curtis LeMay, who was the Commanding General of the Strategic Air Command. General LeMay put out an emergency requisition letter saying that all four-engine pilots returning from the Berlin Airlift with bombardment experience would be assigned to the Strategic Air Command. So, instead of going into the training command for a year, Bob went into the Strategic Air Command and, instead of getting out in a year, he finally got out in February of 1954. During his second tour in the Air Force, Bob flew B-29's and was involved in the Korean War.

He flew almost one hundred missions over Korea during the nine months he was over there. When he got out of the service, he came back to Hollywood and started his career all over again. He still had some friends who were active in the business. One was a woman by the name of Eve McVeagh. She had an agent that she steered him to by the name of Leon O. Lance (aka Leo Lance). Bob was very fortunate as he started working almost immediately in television. One of the very first shows that he was involved with was Reed Hadley's show, *The Public Defender* (1954). Bob went on to work on *Gunsmoke* (1955). The first five years, off and on, he played Jim Buck, the stagecoach driver; then from the fifth year to the nineteenth year he did a lot of *Gunsmoke* as a guest; and then when Glenn Strange, who played Sam the bartender, died, Bob took over that job as Floyd.

He died on April 15, 2010, in Riverside, California, at the age of 93.

Edgar Buchanan

Edgar Buchanan with Audie Murphy in *Destry*

William Edgar Buchanan was born March 20, 1903, in Humansville, Missouri, and was an American actor with a long career in both film and television, most familiar today as Uncle Joe Carson from the *Petticoat Junction(1963-1970)*, *Green Acres* (1965-1969), and *The Beverly Hillbillies* (1968) television sitcoms of the 1960s. As Uncle Joe, he took over as proprietor of the Shady Rest Hotel following the death of Bea Benaderet, who had played Kate Bradley.

Like his father before him, he was a successful dentist. He and his wife Mildred were married in 1928. In 1939, they moved from Eugene, Oregon, to Altadena, California. He joined the Pasadena Playhouse as an actor. He appeared in his first film *My Son is Guilty* in 1939, at the age of thirty-six, after which he turned his dentistry practice over to his wife. He was a member of Theta Chi Fraternity and a Freemason

Buchanan appeared in more than 100 movies, including *Penny Serenade* (1941) with Cary Grant, *Tombstone, the Town Too Tough to Die* (1942), *The Talk of the Town* (1942) with Ronald Colman and Jean Arthur, *The Man from Colorado* (1948), *Cheaper by the Dozen* (1950), *Shane* (1953) with Alan Ladd, *Destry* (1954) and *Gunpoint* (1966) with Audie Murphy, (1954), *Ride the High Country* (1962) with Randolph Scott and Joel McCrea, *McLintock!* (1963) with John Wayne, *Move Over, Darling* (1963) with Doris Day and James Garner, and *Benji* (1974).

Television series in which he appeared included *Hopalong Cassidy* (1952-1954), *Judge Roy Bean* (1956-1957) in which he played the lead, Texas Justice of the Peace Judge Roy Bean, and numerous other series. He appeared in all 222 episodes of *Petticoat Junction*, as well as in seventeen episodes of *Green Acres*, and three episodes of *The Beverly Hillbillies*, always as the character Uncle Joe Carson. From 1960-1962, he appeared four times as Cletus McBain on the NBC western series *Laramie*, with John Smith and Robert Fuller.

Buchanan and another star from *Petticoat Junction* appeared together in the movie *Benji* (1974): the other "star" being Higgins, the unnamed "dog" from the sitcom, who portrayed the title role in the film. Higgins had been found in an animal shelter and trained by Frank Inn, who also trained Arnold Ziffel (the pig) and all the other animals used on *The Beverly Hillbillies, Petticoat Junction,* and *Green Acres* sitcoms.

Buchanan died from a stroke complicated by pneumonia April 4, 1979, in Palm Desert, California, and was interred in the Forest Lawn Hollywood Hills Cemetery in Los Angeles, California.

Sam Buffington

Sam Buffington with Audie Murphy in *Whispering Smith*

Sam Buffington was born on October 12, 1931, in Massachusetts. Sam Buffington's first role was in the television series *The Gray Ghost* (1957) and appeared in numerous films and series non-stop until his death by his own hand. He has performed in movies such as *The Rawhide Trail* (1958), in which he portrayed James Willard, *Damn Citizen* (1958) and *Unwed Mother* (1958).

He is perhaps best known as Chief Richards in Audie Murphy's television series *Whispering Smith* (1961). The series was filmed in 1959, but not aired until 1961, after Sam Buffington's death. His character of Chief Richards was Audie Murphy's elder senior officer, as Buffington was balding and rotund and looked older than Audie. In actuality, Murphy was more than six years older than Buffington.

He died May 15th, 1960, at the age of twenty-eight in Los Angeles, California, United States.

Donald Buka

Donald Buka was born August 17, 1920, in Cleveland, Ohio, and was a veteran stage actor who toured with the Lunts and acted opposite the likes of Helen Hayes and Bette Davis.

His first Broadway stage credit was in 1940 and it was a doozy: The Theatre Guild's revival of *The Taming of the Shrew*, starring Alfred Lunt and Lynn Fontanne in their sole attempt at Shakespeare. By the end of the year he was in the ensemble of a *Twelfth Night* in which Helen Hayes, as Viola, was directed by Margaret Webster. In 1944, he was cast in no less than three Broadway productions, beginning with *Bright Boy*, one of the first shows produced by David Merrick, and followed by the short-lived *Helen Goes to Troy* and *Sophie*.

After one more flop, 1945's *Live It Again*, the darkly handsome actor began concentrating on television and film. His first film role was perhaps his best known, playing the son of Bette Davis in the 1943 film adaptation of Lillian Hellman's *Watch on the Rhine*.

A few notable film noirs followed: *Vendetta* (1950), produced by Howard Hughes, who had Mr. Buka under contract for a time, *The Street With No Name* (1948) as Richard Widmark's evil under-boss, and *Between Midnight and Dawn* (1950) in which he played a cop-killing gangster. He played a rare lead role in *Stolen Identity* (1953), portraying a refugee taxi driver working illegally in Vienna who switches identities with a passenger who is murdered soon after leaving his cab.

He also took roles in many of the notable television programs of the next two decades, including *Kraft Television Theatre (1950)*, *The Philco-Goodyear Television Playhouse* (1951), *Dragnet* (1957), *M Squad* (1959), *Alfred Hitchcock Presents* (1960), *77 Sunset Strip* (1959-1961), Audie Murphy's *Whispering Smith* (1961), *Perry Mason* (1964), *Ironside* (1967), and *The Barbara Stanwyck Show* (1961).

He returned to Broadway one in the 1960s, for *Those That Play the Clowns*; one in the 1970s, *A Texas Trilogy*; and three times in the 1980s, for revivals of *Major Barbara, The Corn Is Green* and *Design for Living*. Off-Broadway theatre credits included *The Adding Machine* with the Phoenix Theatre, and a *Hamlet* starring Siobhan McKenna. Mr. Buka also taught acting classes on the Upper West Side for years. His final appearance was on the daytime soap opera *All My Children* (1987).

Mr. Buka was married three times. The first two unions ended in divorce. His third marriage, to artist Suzanne Sinaiko, lasted from 1992 until her 1998, her death. Donald Buka died July 21, 2009, at age 88 in Reading, Massachusetts.

James Burke

James Burke was born September 24, 1886, and was an American actor born in New York City. He made his stage debut in New York around 1912 and went to Hollywood in 1933. He made over 200 film appearances during his career, which ranged from 1932 to 1964. He appeared in *The Maltese Falcon (1941)*, *Lone Star (1952)*, and many others, including *Bombshell* (1933) and *The Girl From Missouri* (1934), both with Jean Harlow, and *Great Guy* (1936) as James Cagney's partner Patrick James Aloysius 'Pat' Haley.

He appeared in Audie Murphy's first, second, and fourth movies: *Texas, Brooklyn, and Heaven* (1948), *Beyond Glory* (1948), and *The Kid From Texas* (1950).

In the early 1950s, Burke appeared with Tom Conway in the ABC detective drama series then called *Inspector Mark Saber, Homicide Detective,* (1951-1954), later renamed, reformatted, and switched to NBC under the title *Saber of London*. From 1960-1961, Burke appeared in the role of Zeke Bonner in seven episodes of the ABC western television series *Stagecoach West*.

Burke suffered from a heart condition, which took his life May 23, 1968 at the age of eighty-one.

Robert Easton Burke

Audie Murphy with Robert Easton Burke in *The Red Badge of Courage*

Robert Easton, was born Robert Easton Burke November 23, 1930, in Milwaukee, Wisconsin. He was a character actor turned accent coach to the stars, who transformed Drew Barrymore into Amy Fisher, Ben Kingsley into Meyer Lansky and Gregory Peck first into Josef Mengele and later into Abraham Lincoln, among other feats of articulatory alchemy.

His parents divorced when he was about seven, and he moved with his mother to San Antonio, giving him his first awareness of regional dialect. As a young man, he legally changed his surname from Burke to Easton to distinguish himself from his father. A childhood stutter also made him attuned to the minutiae of speech. "When you have a big problem like that you overcompensate", Mr. Easton told The New York Times in 1998. "I found it easier to do voices other than my own".

At fourteen, he appeared on the popular radio show *The Quiz Kids*. This led to dramatic roles on hundreds of other radio programs and from there to small parts in films, including T*he Red Badge of Courage* (1951) with Audie Murphy, and bigger parts on numerous television shows. But there was a problem. The accent Mr. Easton had absorbed in Texas was confining him, as he told Newsday in 1989, to roles of the "dopey deputy and halfwit hayseed" variety. He soon mastered other dialects. After his marriage in 1961 to June Grimstead, an Englishwoman, he lived for several years in England, where he studied phonetics at University College London. He returned to Hollywood thoroughly linguistically armed and hung out his shingle.

For more than forty years Mr. Easton reigned as the entertainment industry's dean of dialects, sought after by actors needing to lose an accent, or gain one, sometimes in the few frantic hours before a critical audition. 'The Henry Higgins of Hollywood', he called himself, and the description was apt: Mr. Easton could get his own larynx around at least 200 different accents, such as ethnic, historical, regional, sociological, with little to no study.

His profession was not for the faint of heart. A few years ago he was awakened in the dead of night by a series of long-distance telephone calls; through the line came the menacing voice of Idi Amin. But the caller was merely Forest Whitaker, Mr. Easton's pupil, who was phoning, in character, for some last-minute instruction while filming *The Last King of Scotland* (2006) in Uganda.

Besides Ms. Barrymore, who starred as the Long Island temptress in the TV movie *The Amy Fisher Story (*1993), Mr. Kingsley, who played Lansky in *Bugsy* (1991) and Mr. Peck, Mengele in *The Boys from Brazil* (1978), and Lincoln in the mini-series *The Blue and the Gray (*1982), Mr. Easton's clients included Al Pacino, Cuban in *Scarface* (1983), Laurence Olivier, Michigander in *The Betsy* (1978), Liam Neeson, Kentuckian in *Next of Kin* (1989), and Natasha Richardson, whom he turned into the title character of *Patty Hearst* (1988).

Without doubt, Mr. Easton's greatest triumph came when a student, the Japanese actress Yoko Shimada, won a Golden Globe for her nuanced English-language performance in the 1980 mini-series *Shogun*, despite the fact that she did not actually know a word of English.

Mr. Easton wrote the screenplay for *The Giant Spider Invasion,* a 1975 film in which he also appeared. He continued acting and appeared in *Star Trek VI: The Undiscovered Country* (1991) in which he played a Klingon judge

For all his skill at aural surgery, there was one actor, a master of dialect, for whom he could not take credit. As United Press International reported in 1986, nearly every time Meryl Streep made a movie, at least one of Mr. Easton's friends would congratulate him on the fine job he had done with her accent. And, Mr. Easton said, he would have to apologize and say: "No, it wasn't me. But I wish it was".

He died December 16, 2011, at age 81 in Toluca Lake, Los Angeles, California.

Monte Burkhart

Monte Burkhart was born August 31, 1931. No biographical information can be found, but he appeared in three films and three television programs from 1960 to 1962.

The television programs he appeared in were episodes in *One Step Beyond* (1960), "Gypsy", the *Whispering Smith* (1961) episode "Swift Justice" with Audie Murphy, and the *Dr. Kildare* (1961) episode "Breakdown".

The films he appeared in were *North to Alaska* (1960) with John Wayne, *Flaming Star* (1960) with Elvis Presley, and *Gun Fight* (1961) with Gregg Palmer.

Monte Burkhart died just days before his 45th birthday in August of 1976.

Michael Burns

Michael Burns with Audie Murphy in *40 Guns to Apache Pass*

Michael Burns was born December 30, 1947, in Mineola, Long Island, New York, and is a former child actor who went on to a distinguished career as a historian, writer, and college professor.

He was familiar to television audiences of the early 1960s as the teenage character, 'Barnaby West', on the popular *Wagon Train* (1960-1965) series. He appeared in numerous episodes of *The Virginian* (1966-1971). He had a substantial role in *40 Guns to Apache Pass* (1967) with Audie Murphy.

After other TV and film credits in his late teens and early twenties, including his final acting appearance in *Police Woman* (1977), Burns left acting to pursue his interest in history, graduating from the University of California. He earned a Ph. D. from Yale University in 1977 and wrote an acclaimed history book, *Dreyfus*, about the Dreyfus Affair.

From 1980 to 2002, Burns was a professor of history at Mount Holyoke College in Massachusetts. He is now retired and raising thoroughbred horses in Kentucky.

Robert Burton

American actor Robert Burton was born August 13, 1895. His film roles were confined to such stock parts as the crooked politician, the unfeeling physician, the self-absorbed scientist, the crooked attorney, the weakling politician, the hidden killer, or the surly fellow whom the heroine shouldn't have married. Burton's movies seldom made the "classic" category; while he appeared in several "A" films like *The Big Heat* (1953), *Compulsion* (1959), and *The Manchurian Candidate* (1962), appearing in the latter as the convention chairman in the climactic assassination sequence, most of his movies were along the lines of *I Was a Teenage Frankenstein* (1957) and *Invasion of the Animal People* (1962) for which he was top-billed.

He appearedin Lou Costello's final film *30 Foot Bride of Candy Rock* (1959) and with Audie Murphy in *Seven Ways From Sundown* (1960).

His final film *The Slime People* (1963) was released after his death. He died September 29, 1962, in Woodland Hills, Los Angeles, California at age 67.

Viola Burwick

Viola Burwick was born January 11, 1907, and no biographical information can be found. She only appeared in five episodes of television programs from 1953 to 1961. The television series she appeared in were *The Bennetts* (1953), *A Time to Live* (1954), *Johnny Midnight* (1960), *Coronado 9* (1961), and her final appearance was with Audie Murphy in the *Whispering Smith* (1961) episode "Hired to Die". She died January 13, 1988.

Bruce Cabot

Bruce Cabot with Audie Murphy in *The Quiet American*

Bruce Cabot was born Etienne Pelissier Jacques de Bujac in Carlsbad, New Mexico, April 20, 1904, and was an American film actor, best remembered as Jack Driscoll in *King Kong* (1933).

Cabot was born to French Army Colonel Etienne de Bujac and his wife Julia Armandine Graves, who died shortly after giving birth to him. Leaving the University of the South in Sewanee, Tennessee, without graduating, Cabot worked at a many jobs, including as a sailor, an insurance salesman, oil worker, surveyor, prize fighter, sold cars, handled real estate, and also worked at a slaughterhouse.

Cabot appeared in nearly one hundred feature films. He made his debut in 1931 in *Heroes of the Flames*. He tested for the lead role of The Ringo Kid in John Ford's western *Stagecoach* (1939), but John Wayne got the part.

He played a soldier who seduced a naive woman (portrayed by Irene Dunne) and got her pregnant as he left for the war, in the 1933 production *Ann Vickers*. He then starred in the 1933 blockbuster *King Kong*, which became an enormous success and established Cabot as a star.

Cabot also played villains, appearing as a gangster boss in *Let 'Em Have It* (1936) and as the Huron warrior Magua opposite Randolph Scott in *The Last of the Mohicans* (1936). He starred with Spencer Tracy, playing the leader of a lynch mob in Fritz Lang's first Hollywood film, *Fury* (1936), and with Errol Flynn in Michael Curtiz's epic Western *Dodge City* (1939), which became one of Warner Brother's biggest hits. A consistent box office draw, Cabot appeared in many movies at many studios before leaving Hollywood to serve in World War II.

Cabot was a first lieutenant in the U.S. Army Air Forces and was as an Air Transport Command operations officer in Tunis.

Cabot returned to Hollywood after his discharge. He met John Wayne on the set of *Angel and the Badman* (1947) and they became close friends. Cabot played supporting roles in many of Wayne's movies. They appeared together in ten additional films: *The Comancheros* (1961), *Hatari!* (1962), *McLintock!* (1963), *In Harm's Way* (1965), *The War Wagon* (1967), *The Green Berets* (1968), *Hellfighters* (1968), *The Undefeated* (1969), *Chisum* (1970), and *Big Jake* (1971).

Bruce Cabot had one of the few American roles in *The Quiet American* (1958) with Audie Murphy.

Cabot's final screen appearance was in the 1971 James Bond film *Diamonds Are Forever*.

Bruce Cabot died in May 3, 1972, in Woodland Hills, California, from lung cancer and was buried in his hometown, Carlsbad, New Mexico.

Susan Cabot

Susan Cabot with Audie Murphy in *Gunsmoke*

Susan Cabot was born Harriet Shapiro to a Russian Jewish family in Boston, Massachusetts, July 9, 1927, and was an American actress.

Cabot's early life was one of turmoil, and she was raised in eight different foster homes. She completed her education in New York, New York, and found employment as an illustrator. She supplemented her income by working as a singer, and also worked in theater. She made her film debut in 1947, by chance when *Kiss of Death* was filmed in New York, and she played a bit part. She expanded her acting work into television and was seen by a Hollywood talent scout who took her to Hollywood to work for Columbia Pictures. This brief period was not successful, and she moved to Universal Studios where she was signed to an exclusive contract.

After a series of roles which Cabot played mainly in "B" western films, she was in several mainstream movies with Audie Murphy like *Duel at Silver Creek* (1952), *Gunsmoke* (1953), and *Ride Clear of Diablo* (1954), playing Audie's love interest in all three.

She grew frustrated and asked to be released from her contract. She moved back to New York, where she resumed her stage career with a role in *A Stone for Danny Fisher*. She was invited to return to Hollywood and appeared in a few more films, including *The Wasp Woman* in 1959, her final film role. She did appear one more time on television in an episode of *Bracken's World* (1970).

Cabot first married in 1944 to Martin Sacker. They divorced in 1951. In 1959, she began a relationship with King Hussein of Jordan. The couple was engaged, but broke up after King Hussein discovered that Cabot was Jewish.

In 1968, she married second husband Michael Roman with whom she had one son, Timothy Scott Roman, before divorcing in 1983. Another contemporary actor, Christopher Jones, also claims paternity of her son.

On December 10, 1986, Cabot's son, Timothy Scott Roman, who suffered from dwarfism and psychological problems, bludgeoned her to death in her home in Encino, California, with a weight lifting bar. He was subsequently charged with involuntary manslaughter and received a three-year suspended sentence.

Director Stephan Elliott is in development to make a biopic about Cabot entitled *Black Oasis* with actress Rose McGowan portraying her.

Joseph Campenella

Joseph Campenella was born November 21, 1927, in Lewistown, Pennsylvania and is an American character actor who has appeared in over 200 TV and film roles since 1955, including such shows as *The Eleventh Hour* (1964), *The Fugitive* (1964-1967), *Mission: Impossible (1967-1968), Gunsmoke (1968-1962), Rod Serling's Night Gallery* (1970-1971), *The Golden Girls* (1987), and *Mama's Family* (1987-1988).

One of his early roles had him appearing in a live television drama with Audie Murphy in the Ford *Startime* (1960) episode "The Man". He also had a role in 1967 as Lew Wickersham in the television series *Mannix* as Joe Mannix's boss and friend, before the P.I. went solo and started his own firm. Campanella would go on to appear as attorney Brian Darrell from 1969 to 1972 in *The Bold Ones: The Lawyers*. He played Ann Romano's ex-husband, Ed Cooper, in seven episodes of *One Day at a Time* (1975–1984) and Barbara Stanwyck's love interest in the first season (1985–1986) of the Aaron Spelling's short-lived *Dynasty* spinoff, *The Colbys*.

The actor had a prominent role as Harper Deveraux on the soap opera *Days of Our Lives* from 1987 to 1988 and from 1990 to 1992, had a recurring role on *The Bold and the Beautiful* from 1996 to 2005. He is the brother of actor Frank Campanella, who died in December 2006.

He voiced the role of Dr. Conners, also known as the 'Lizard' in the animated *Spiderman* series from 1994-1997, and appeared in *Walker, Texas Ranger* (1996). He also had a bit part in the cowboy episode of *CSI: Crime Scene Investigation* (2008). Campanella also hosted the Canadian educational program *Science International* between 1976 and 1979; the show aired on Nickelodeon as *What Will They Think Of Next?* He played an endearing character in the independent comedy *For Heaven's Sake* (2008).

Campanella formerly provided the voiceover for BMW commercials in the United States, intoning, "BMW... the ultimate driving machine." He also narrated the Discover Magazine science series on the Disney Channel from 1992-1994.

Two of Campanella's sons, Rob and Dominic, play in the L.A. psychedelic-rock band The Quarter After.

Colin Campbell

Colin Campbell was born March 20, 1883 in Falkirk, Scotland. He entered films in 1915, first appearing in *Tillie's Tomato Surprise*. He had numerous roles in films and televisions programs over the next fifty years.

He appeared with Audie Murphy in *Texas, Brooklyn, and Heaven* (1948), with Bud and Lou in *Abbott and Costello Meet the Keystone Kops* (1955), and with Moe, Larry, and Curly Joe in *The Three Stooges Go Around the World in a Daze* (1963).

He was in such television programs as *Adventures of Superman* (1953), *The Many Loves of Dobie Gillis (*1959), *The Jack Benny Program* (1955-1950), and *The Twilight Zone* (1963).

His final appearance was in *My Fair Lady* (1964). He died March 25, 1966, in Woodland Hills, California.

Harry Carey, Jr.

Harry Carey, Jr. was born on May 16, 1921, at the ranch of his parents, actors Olive Carey and Harry Carey. His father gave him the nickname "Dobe" shortly after his birth because the baby's red hair reminded him of the adobe soil at the ranch. Dobe went to school in the Newhall Public Schools, and then went to the Black Foxe Military Institute in Hollywood.

The young Dobe's dream was to become a classical singer like the opera singer/movie star Lawrence Tibbett, and he moved to New York City to study voice. In 1939 Dobe got his first paying job as a performer at the New York World's Fair, as a horse-rider in the show "Railroads on Parade." He became a page at the National Broadcasting Co. in 1941, but with the declaration of war he joined the Navy. In his three years as a sailor he served as a medical corpsman before being transferred to director John Ford's photographic unit, which was part of the Navy, but also worked for the Office of Strategic Services (OSS), the predecessor of the CIA. Ford had been the director on many Dobe's father's silent westerns and was close to his parents. Dobe protested against the transfer, but it was made nonetheless.

Dobe married Marilyn Fix, the daughter of the actor Paul Fix, in 1944 while he was on leave from the Navy. They remained married for over 60 years, and had four children and three grandchildren.

After being discharged from the Navy at the end of the war, Carey followed his father into acting in 1946 by accepting a role in *Rolling Home* (1946), and then following it up with a featured role in Raoul Walsh's *Pursued* (1947). Carey's long association with John Wayne began in Howard Hawks's classic western *Red River* (1948), and his long-time acting association with Ford began with his role as "The Abilene Kid" in *3 Godfathers* (1948), a movie that was dedicated to his father, who had passed away in 1947. Ford had been the director of the original version of this movie in 1919, which had starred Carey's father. John Wayne was Carey's co-star, and the pair acted together in nine more movies.

Carey became a member in good standing of John Ford's stock company of actors. He appeared in the Ford/Wayne films *She Wore a Yellow Ribbon* (1949), *Rio Grande* (1950) and *The Searchers* (1956), and with Ford but without Wayne in *Wagon Master* (1950) and *The Long Gray Line* (1955). Carey also appeared in *Mister Roberts* (1955) which was begun by Ford but completed by Mervyn LeRoy after a couple of weeks of filming. He worked with Ford again in *Two Rode Together* (1961), and in *Cheyenne Autumn* (1964) without Wayne. Other movies filmed in which he worked with Wayne, but not Ford, were *Island in the Sky* (1953), *Rio Bravo* (1959), *The Undefeated* (1969), *Big Jake* (1971) and *Cahill U.S. Marshal* (1973). In total, Harry Carey, Jr. appeared in nearly 100 movies and almost 100 television programs, mostly westerns, including *Whispering Smith* (1961) with Audie Murphy.

Carey has also made two film documentaries, *John Ford's America* (1989) (TV) and *Legends of the West* (1992), and wrote the book *Company of Heroes: My Life As An Actor In the John Ford Stock Company*. Carey appeared with his father, Harry Carey, Sr. in just one film, *Red River* (1948), although the two Careys did not have any scenes together. Dobe was cast in two movies with his mother, Olive Carey: *The Searchers* (1956) and *Two Rode Together* (1961).

In 1987 Dobe was awarded a Golden Boot by the Motion Picture & Television Fund Foundation, and in 2003 he won a Silver Spur Award from Reel Cowboys. He has a star on the Hollywood Walk of Fame; awarded for his television activities, located at 6363 Hollywood Blvd.

Harry Carey, Jr. died peacefully of natural causes December 27, 2012 at age 91 in the seaside town of Santa Barbara, California, surrounded by family members, said his daughter, Melinda Carey. "No cancer or nothing, he just got old," she said of her father, who is survived by his wife of 68 years, Marilyn, and three adult children.

Olive Carey

Olive Carey was born Olive Fuller Golden on January 31, 1896. Olive was eighteen when she appeared in her first motion picture, a silent entitled, *Tess of the Storm Country* (1914). After she made *A Knight of the Range* (1916), she retired from films. In 1916, she married actor Harry Carey who was eighteen years older. They had two children, one of whom was Harry Carey, Jr. who was a very good actor in his own right. Olive briefly returned to the screen in 1931 in a film called *Trader Horn* (1931).

After 1935's *Naughty Marietta* (1935) Olive again stepped away from the cameras. But in 1947, her husband passed away, and she, once more, stepped into films. This time her stay was a bit longer. Her first film following Harry's death was *Air Hostess* (1949). She was cast in two movies with her son, Harry Carey, Jr.: *The Searchers* (1956) and *Two Rode Together* (1961). She appeared with Audie Murphy and James Stewart in *Night Passage* (1957) as Miss Vittles, the mule riding guide. She continued to act in films off and on until age 70 when she appeared for the last time in 1966's *Billy the Kid vs. Dracula* (1966). On March 13, 1988, Olive died in Carpinteria, California, at the age of 92.

Marty Carrizosa

No biographical information could be found for Marty Carrizosa, but he appeared in only two films: *Walk the Proud Land* (1956) with Audie Murphy, and *The Restless Breed* (1957) with Scott Brady. He appeared in only one television program called *Cavalcade of America* (1957).

Paul Carr

Paul Carr was born February 1, 1934, and was a character actor who was born in New Orleans, Louisiana. Carr acted for some fifty years in television, in film, and on stage.

Carr grew up in the town of Marrero, in Jefferson Parish, Louisiana. As a teenager, he had an interest in music as well as acting. After a short stint in the United States Marine Corps during his late teens, his acting career began with a role in a New Orleans production of *Billy Budd*. By the mid-1950s, he was working on live television in New York City, including appearances on the popular *Studio One* (1957) and *Kraft Television Theater* (1956), while continuing theatrical work in stock companies in Ohio and Michigan; including roles such as 'Peter Quilpe' in *The Cocktail Party*, 'Haemon' in *Antigone*, 'Jack' in *The Rose Tattoo*, and 'Hal Carter' in *Picnic*. He also toured in summer stock with Chico Marx in *Fifth Season*.

Carr made his film debut in 1955 with a small uncredited role in Alfred Hitchcock's fact-based thriller *The Wrong Man*.

That same year, he portrayed a prisoner of war in the New York Theatre Guild production of *Time Limit* on Broadway. His film career continued with a much larger role in Alfred Werker's *The Young Don't Cry* (1957) starring James Whitmore and Sal Mineo; and that same year he appeared in the Warner Brothers rock and roll jukebox movie *Jamboree* as Pete Porter. He appeared in *Posse from Hell* (1961) with Audie Murphy.

He worked steadily on television in the late 1950s and early 1960s with guest spots and supporting roles in many Western series such as *Trackdown* (1959), *Rawhide* (1961-1964), *The Rifleman* (1959-1960), and *The Virginian* (1963-1969). Later he appeared in detective, medical, and war dramas, including *77 Sunset Strip* (1961), *Dr. Kildare* (1962), *The Fugitive* (1963-1964), and *Twelve O'Clock High* (1964-1966). Other television appearances included *The Green Hornet* (1966) with Bruce Lee and Van Williams, and dozens of other shows in the middle of the decade.

In 1965, Carr won the role of 'Bill Horton', the physician son of protagonist Dr. Tom Horton on *Days of our Lives*. He was later a regular on *General Hospital* (1994).

Carr went on to work in dozens of other television shows in the intervening years like Adam-12 (1968-1969), *Get Smart* (1969), *Mannix* (1969-1974), O'Hara, U.S. Treasury (1971), Hec Ramsey (1972), S.W.A.T. (1972), *The Rockford Files* (1975-1978), and *Murphy Brown* (1992).

He may be remembered best, however, for his various appearances on science fiction shows over the years. In 1964/1965, he had the recurring role of the uptight crewman 'Casey Clark' on *Voyage to the Bottom of the Sea*. In 1966, he played the role of 'Lt. Lee Kelso', the affable *USS Enterprise* helmsman who is strangled psychokinetically by the ship's rapidly mutating navigator, 'Lt. Commander Gary Mitchell', in the second *Star Trek* pilot episode, "Where No Man Has Gone Before", giving him the dubious honor of technically being the first dead Red Shirt (technically peachy red since the uniforms in the pilots were made of a different material from that in the other episodes) in *Star Trek* history. In 1981, he joined the cast of *Buck Rogers in the 25th Century* as 'Lt. Devlin', one of the officers on the Earth Starship *Searcher*.

He died from cancer February 17, 2006, in Los Angeles, California.

Jimmy Carter

No biographical information could be found for actor Jimmy Carter. He appeared in twelve television programs from 1958 to 1963, in such series as *The Alaskans* (1960), *Bonanza* (1960), *Route 66* (1960), *Whispering Smith* (1961) with Audie Murphy, *Leave it to Beaver* (1961-1962), and *The Rifleman* (1962). His final appearance was in *The Travels of Jaimie McPheeters* (1963).

Anthony Caruso

Anthony Caruso with Audie Murphy in *Walk the Proud Land*

Anthony Caruso was born April 7, 1916, in Frankfort, Indiana, and was an American character actor in over 100 American films, usually playing villains, including the First Season of Walt Disney's *Zorro* as Captain Juan Ortega. He trained at the Pasadena Playhouse where he befriended actor Alan Ladd, who got him work in twelve of his films, like *Lucky Jordan* (1942), *And Now Tomorrow* (1945), *The Blue Dahlia* (1946), *Wild Harvest* (1947), *The Iron Mistress* (1952), *Desert Legion* (1953), *Saskatchewan* (1954), *Drum Beat* (1954), *Hell on Frisco Bay* (1955), and *The Big Land* (1957).

Caruso also had early television roles, some playing sympathetic characters, like "Ash," on an early episode of *Gunsmoke* (1957). He guest starred on two of Rod Cameron's syndicated series, *City Detective* (1954) and *Coronado 9* (1960). In 1954, Caruso played Tiburcio Vasquez in an episode of Jim Davis's syndicated western series, *Stories of the Century*. Also, the same year he appeared in *Walk the Proud Land* (1954) with Audie Murphy.

At Christmas 1957, Caruso appeared as a Roman Catholic priest in the episode "The Child" of NBC's *The Restless Gun*, starring John Payne, and also guest starring Dan Blocker and James Gleason.

In 1966, Caruso guest starred in the Barry Sullivan western series *The Road West*, set in Kansas, in the episode entitled "This Dry and Thirsty Land". From 1966 to 1970 he guest starred on the long running western *The Virginian* three times.

Some of his more memorable roles were that of the alien gangster "Bela Oxmyx" in the classic *Star Trek* (1968) episode "A Piece of the Action", Chief Blackfish on the television series *Daniel Boone*, Mongo in the film *Tarzan and the Leopard Woman* (1946), Sengo in *Tarzan and the Slave Girl* (1950) and Louis Ciavelli in *The Asphalt Jungle* (1950*)*. Caruso played the comical character of the Native American "Red Cloud" on the 1965 *Get Smart* episode "Washington 4, Indians 3".

Caruso died three days before his 87th birthday April 4, 2003, in Brentwood, California. His ashes were scattered into the Pacific Ocean.

Antonio Casas

Antonio Casas with Audie Murphy in *The Texican*

Antonio Casas was born November 11, 1911, in A Coruña, Galicia, Spain, and was a Spanish footballer turned film actor who appeared in film between 1941 and his death in 1982.

Casas originally began as a footballer for Atlético Madrid, but entered film in 1941 and made nearly 170 appearances in film and television, mostly Italian productions, between then and 1982.

He appeared in *A Pistol for Ringo* (1965) and Sergio Leone's Spaghetti Western the *The Good, the Bad and the Ugly* (1966), a film that has consistently been voted one of the greatest of all time. He also appeared in *The Texican* (1966) with Audie Murphy.

In the early 1970s he worked in television but returned to film after 1975 until his death at age 70 February 14, 1982 in Madrid, Spain.

Mary Castle

Audie Murphy with Mary Castle in *Gunsmoke*

Mary Ann Castle was born January 22, 1931, and was an American actress of early film and television. Her best known role was as female detective Frankie Adams in the syndicated western series, *Stories of the Century*, which aired from 1954 to 1955.

Castle was born as Mary Ann Noblett to Erby G. Noblett, Sr. and Myrtle A. Noblett in Pampa. Her mother was one-sixteenth Quapaw Indian. The Nobletts moved to Fort Worth, Texas, then Phillips, subsequently a ghost town in Hutchinson County, Texas, prior to relocating to Long Beach, California. At the age of nine, Castle contracted pneumonia. Her brother, Erby Noblett, Jr. (1927–1992), taught her trick riding and later became a police officer in Long Beach.

At nineteen, Castle was a model for a bathing suit company. A studio scout became interested in her after seeing her photograph in a magazine. In August 1950, she was dubbed the "lady who looks more like Hayworth than Hayworth does."

Her first contract was said to have been granted solely on the basis that the red-haired Castle indeed resembled Hayworth. Harry Cohn, boss of Columbia Pictures, was said to have envisioned Castle as a replacement for Hayworth, who had married Prince Aly Khan and was rearing a family.

Castle's first credited role was as Flo in the 1950 film *The Tougher They Come*. Columbia plotted Castle's career as they had for Rita Hayworth when she had first signed with Columbia: frequent exposure and seasoning in the studio's low-budget films. Most of Mary Castle's early Columbia's were Westerns. Her appearance in *Criminal Lawyer* (1951) didn't free her from the Western mold; in 1953, she appeared in the Western features *The Lawless Breed* with Rock Hudson and *Gunsmoke* with Audie Murphy. The most frequently revived Mary Castle feature is probably her least prestigious: she played a gold-digging femme fatale opposite Huntz Hall and The Bowery Boys in the low-budget comedy *Crashing Las Vegas* (1956).

Mary Castle's first television appearance occurred in 1952 as Marcia Thorne in the episode "One Angle Too Many" of the detective series *Racket Squad*. She appeared with Jim Davis in twenty-six of the thirty-nine episodes of *Stories of the Century* (1954), the first western to win an Emmy Award. The series focuses upon the capture of such western outlaws as Billy the Kid, the Dalton Brothers, the Younger Brothers, and Sam Bass. When Castle left the series, she was replaced for the final thirteen episodes by Kristine Miller.

In 1956, she appeared on *The Bob Cummings Show* in the episode "The Trouble with Henry". In 1957, she guest starred on ABC's *The Adventures of Ozzie and Harriet*, in "The Case of the Baited Hook" on CBS's *Perry Mason*, and in "Test of Courage" of ABC's *Cheyenne* (1957), starring Clint Walker. In 1959, she appeared on Rex Allen's *Frontier Doctor* series. In 1960, Castle appeared in the episode "The Chinese Pendant" of CBS's crime drama *Tightrope* starring Mike Connors. Castle's last television appearance was as an unnamed saloon girl in the 1962 episode "Collie's Free" of James Arness's long-running CBS western *Gunsmoke*.

Castle spent her later years in Lodi, California. She died of lung cancer April 29, 1998 at the age of 67 in Palm Springs, California.

Richard Castle

Richard Castle with Audie Murphy in *To Hell and Back*

No biographical information can be found for Richard Castle, though he did appear in three films and three television programs. The films he appeared in were *Six Bridges to Cross* (1955), *To Hell and Back* (1955) as the character Kovak in Audie Murphy's platoon, and *Running Wild* (1955).

The television programs he appeared in were *Man Against Crime* (1953), two episodes of *Cisco Kid* (1955), and an episode of *Ben Casey* (1965).

Jack Catron

No biographical information could be found for Jack (Jerry) Catron. He appeared in thirty two films and television programs from 1960 to 1970. His first appearance was in the episode "The Last Flight" of *The Twilight Zone* (1960).

He appeared three times with Audie Murphy, first in *Posse From Hell* (1961), then two episodes of *Whispering Smith* (1961) titled "Swift Justice" and "Poet and Peasant Case".

He appeared in three episodes of *Voyage to the Bottom of the Sea* (1966-1967), two episodes of *Batman* (1967), three episodes of *Big Valley* (1967), two episodes of *Star Trek* (1967), and two episodes of *The Guns of Will Sonnett* (1967-1968).

His final appearance was in the film *WUSA* in 1970.

Richard Chamberlain

Audie Murphy with Richard Chamberlain in *Whispering Smith*

Actor Richard Chamberlain was THE leading TV heartthrob of the early 1960s. As Dr. Kildare, the slim butter-haired hunk with the near-perfect Ivy-League good looks and polite, charming demeanor became a huge celebrity and had all the girls fawning over him.

Born George Richard Chamberlain in Beverly Hills on March 31, 1934, he was the second son of salesman Charles and homemaker Elsa Chamberlain. Richard experienced a profoundly unhappy childhood and did not enjoy school at all, making up for it somewhat by excelling in track and becoming a four-year letterman in high school and college. He also developed a strong interest and enjoyment in acting while attending Pomona College. He lost an initial chance to sign up with Paramount Pictures, which became interested in him right after graduation, because he had to serve his military obligation in Korea for sixteen months.

He headed for Hollywood soon after his discharge, and in just a couple of years had worked up a decent resumé with a number of visible guest spots on such series as *Gunsmoke* (1955) and *Mr. Lucky* (1959). He appeared in the episode "Stain of Justice" of *Whispering Smith* with Audie Murphy three months before he appeared on television as Dr. Kildare.

It was as the star of the medical series *Dr. Kildare* (1961), however, that he became an "overnight" sensation, a huge pin-up favorite, and a source of idol-worship for teenagers everywhere (it also sparked a brief singing career for the actor). The attention Richard received was phenomenal. He subsequently advanced into the usual soap-style leads on film befitting his image, but *Twilight of Honor* (1963) with Joey Heatherton and *Joy in the Morning* (1965) opposite Yvette Mimieux did not bring him the screen fame they were expected to. Crossover stardom is elusive, and at the time he was considered strictly a TV commodity with a glossy "Prince Charming" image to shoulder on top of that.

An important role in director Richard Lester's *Petulia* (1968) led Richard to England, where he dared to test his acting prowess on the classical stage. His bravura performances as *Hamlet* (1969) and *Richard II* (1971), as well as his triumph in *The Lady's Not for Burning* (1972), won over the not-so-easy-to-impress British audiences. On the classier film front he portrayed Octavius Caesar opposite Charlton Heston's *Julius Caesar* (1970) and Jason Robards' Brutus; composer Pyotr Ilyich Tchaikovsky in Ken Russell's grandiose *The Music Lovers* (1970) opposite Glenda Jackson; and Lord Byron alongside Sarah Miles' *Lady Caroline Lamb* (1973). While none of these three films were critical favorites by any measure, they helped to reshape Richard's image as a sturdy and reliable actor.

Richard felt ready to return again to America. While he made a triumphant Broadway debut as Reverend Shannon in *The Night of the Iguana* (1975), he enjoyed modest box-office popularity with the action-driven adventure movies *The Three Musketeers* (1973) as Aramis and a villainous role in *The Towering Inferno* (1974) opposite Steve McQueen and Paul Newman, and earned cult status for the Aussie film *The Last Wave* (1977). It was television that made him a TV idol all over again as the "King of 80s Mini-Movies". The epic storytelling of *The Count of Monte-Cristo* (1975), *Shogun* (1980), and *The Thorn Birds* (1983), all of which earned him Emmy nominations, placed Richard solidly on the star list again. He won Golden Globe awards for his starring roles in the latter two miniseries.

In later years he devoted a great deal of his time to musical stage tours as Henry Higgins in "My Fair Lady", Captain Von Trapp in "The Sound of Music" and Ebenezer Scrooge in "Scrooge: The Musical". Enormously private, Richard moved to Hawaii quite some time ago and at age 69 decided to "come out" with a tell-all biography entitled *Shattered Love*, in which he quite candidly discussed the anguish of hiding his homosexuality to protect his enduring matinée idol image. He has shown himself to be a good sport, appearing in the gay-themed comedy film *I Now Pronounce You Chuck & Larry* (2007) and in TV episodes of *Will & Grace* (1998) and *Desperate Housewives* (2004).

Richard Chamberlain is still very active professionally and is most recently starring in the film *Forbidden Love* (2012).

Phil Chambers

Phil Chambers was born June 16, 1916, and was an American character actor. Born in California, Phil Chambers was known for his role as Sgt. Myles Magruder in the TV series *The Gray Ghost*. He appeared in exactly 100 films and television programs from 1953 to 1982.

He appeared with Audie Murphy in *Tumbleweed* (1953) and *Drums Across the River* (1954). He was in numerous television series, including *Big Valley* (1967), *Bonanza* (1962-1969), *The F.B.I.* (1965-1971), and *Gunsmoke* (1960-1975).

He died January 16, 1993, in Los Angeles, California.

George Chandler

George Chandler was born June 30, 1898, was an American actor best known for playing the character of "Uncle Petrie" on the television series *Lassie* (1956-1959). He was born in Waukegan, Illinois. After military service during the First World War, Chandler studied at the University of Illinois, financing his studies by playing jazz violin in a band.

During the early 1920's, he returned to the vaudeville circuit and began in films from 1928. Most of his early efforts were short one- and two-reel comedies, arguably his best being *The Fatal Glass of Beer* (1933) with W.C. Fields. While he mostly appeared in comedy and had countless bit parts, he later proved that he could handle meatier assignments, such as the simple-minded husband of Ginger Rogers, Amos, in *Roxie Hart* (1942). George was a protege of director William A. Wellman, who used him in twenty of his films. He appeared in Kansas Raiders (1950) with Audie Murphy.

Chandler appeared six times in Bill Williams's western series *The Adventures of Kit Carson* (1951–1955) in episodes entitled "Law of Boot Hill", "Lost Treasure of the Panamints", "Trails Westward", "The Wrong Man", "Trail to Bordertown", and "Gunsmoke Justice". He appeared as the character Ames in the two-part episode "King of the Dakotas" in the 1955 NBC western anthology series *Frontier*. In the 1954-1955 season, he appeared as a milkman in two episodes of the NBC sitcom *It's a Great Life*, co-starring Frances Bavier and James Dunn.

In 1961-1962 television, Chandler co-starred with Robert Sterling, Reta Shaw, Jimmy Hawkins, Burt Mustin, and Christine White in CBS's comedy series, *Ichabod and Me*. He played the former newspaper editor of a small New England town and the current traffic commissioner.

He continued to work in films and television in series such as six episodes of *Alias Smith and Jones* (1971-1972), and *Kolchak, The Night Stalker* (1975) with Darren McGavin, He appeared with Clint Eastwood in *Every Which Way but Loose* (1978). His last appearance was in the series *Lou Grant* (1979).

He died June 10, 1985 and died in Panorama City, California, at the age of eighty-six.

Marguerite Chapman

Marguerite Chapman with Audie Murphy in *Kansas Raiders*

Marguerite Chapman was born March 9, 1918, in Chatham, New York and was an American actress.

She was working as a telephone switchboard operator in White Plains, New York, when her good looks brought about the opportunity to pursue a career in modeling. Signed by the prestigious John Robert Powers Agency in New York City, the publicity she earned modeling brought an offer from 20th Century Fox film studios in Hollywood.

She made her film debut in 1940, working for the next two years in small roles. In 1942, her big break came with Republic Pictures when she was cast in the leading female role in the twelve-part adventure film serial *Spy Smasher*, a production that is considered by many as one of the best serials ever made. As a result, Chapman soon began receiving offers for more leading roles and appeared opposite important stars such as Edward G. Robinson and George Sanders. With America's entry in World War II, she entertained the troops, worked for the War bond drive and at the Hollywood Canteen.

During the 1950s Chapman continued to perform mostly in film roles, like *Kansas Raiders* (1950) with Audie Murphy, and in Marilyn Monroe's 1955 hit *The Seven Year Itch*. However, with the advent of television she kept busy into the early 1960s with guest appearances in a number of different shows including *Richard Diamond, Private Detective* (1958), *Rawhide (1959)*, *Perry Mason (1960)*, and *Four Star Playhouse (1954)*.

Chapman was reportedly initially selected to play the role of "Old Rose" Dawson-Calvert in the 1997 James Cameron epic *Titanic* but poor health prevented her from accepting the offer.

For her contribution to the motion picture industry, Marguerite Chapman has a star on the Hollywood Walk of Fame at 6290 Hollywood Blvd.

Marguerite Chapman died in August 31, 1999 at age 81 and was interred in Holy Cross Cemetery, in Culver City, California.

Kim Charney

Kim Charney was born August 2, 1945 in San Diego, California, and appeared in thirty-seven films and television programs from 1952 to 1963. He was in such TV fare as *The Adventures of Superman* (1953), *Dragnet* (1957), *Zane Grey Theatre* (1957), *Tales of the Texas Rangers* (1955-1957), *Wagon Train* (1957), *The Rifleman* (1959), and *Leave it to Beaver* (1962-1963).

He appeared in films like *The Werewolf* (1956), *The Guns of Ft Petticoat* (1957) with Audie Murphy, *Quantrill's Raiders* (1958), and *How the West Was Won* (1962).

Frank Chase

Audie Murphy with Frank Chase in *Night Passage*

Frank Chase was born February 22, 1923, in Potsdam, New York. He was an actor/writer from 1950 to 1981. He appeared with Audie Murphy in *Walk the Proud Land* (1956), *Joe Butterfly* (1957), *Night Passage* (1957), and *Ride a Crooked Trail* (1958).

He appeared in other films such as *Winchester '73* (1950), *The Creature walks Among Us* (1956), *Showdown at Abilene* (1956), and *Attack of the 50 Foot Woman* (1958).

He wrote episodes of such western series as *The Rebel* (1960-1961), *Branded* (1965-1966), *Hondo* (1967), *Bonanza* (1961-1969), *The Virginian* (1963-1970), *High Chaparral* (1967-1970), and *Chips* (1979-1981).

He died July 2, 2004, at age 81 in Los Angeles, California.

Stephen Chase

Audie Murphy with Stephen Chase in *Bad Boy*

Stephen Chase was born Guy Alden Chase April 11, 1902, in Huntington, Long Island, New York. He appeared in 140 films and television programs from his first with Joel McCrea in *Chance at Heaven* (1933) to his last appearance with Tim Conway in an episode of *Rango* (1967). In between those performances he appeared in movies such as *Les Misérables* (1935), *Under Western Stars* (1938), *Buried Alive* (1939), *The Green Hornet Strikes Again!* (1940), *They Met in Bombay* (1941), *Bad Boy* (1949) with Audie Murphy, *Cavalry Scout* (1951), *The Great Sioux Uprising* (1953), and *The Blob* (1958) with Steve McQueen.

He started appearing on television in *The Marshal of Trail City* (1950) and continued appearing in television programs like *The Cisco Kid* (1950-1951), *Craig Kennedy, Criminologist* (1952), *The Lone Ranger* (1950-1953), *Space Patrol* (1952-1953), *Richard Diamond, Private Detective* (1958-1960), *77 Sunset Strip* (1959-1963).

He died April 1, 1982 at the age of 79 in Santa Monica, California.

Michael Chekhov

Michael Chekhov was a Russian actor of Moscow Art Theatre who immigrated to America and made a career in Hollywood earning himself an Oscar nomination.

He was born Mikhail Aleksandrovich Chekhov in St. Petersburg, Russia in 1891. His mother, Natalya Golden, was Jewish, and his father, Aleksandr Chekhov, was a brother of writer Anton Chekhov, who wrote of his nephew in

1895, "I believe that he has a growing talent." From 1907 to 1911 he studied classic drama and comedy at Suvorin Theater School in St. Petersburg, graduating with honors as an actor. In St. Petersburg he met Konstantin Stanislavski who invited him to join the Moscow Art Theater. The two became good friends and partners in propelling the Moscow Art Theater to international fame. Later Stanislavsky wrote that Michael Chekhov was a genius.

His film career began in 1913 with a role in *Tryokhsotletie tsarstvovaniya doma Romanovykh* (1913) also known as *Tercentenary of the Romanov Dynasty*, followed by a few more roles in Russian silent films. During the Russian Revolution of 1917 his beloved first wife, Olga Tschechowa, divorced him, and he was devastated and suffered from depression and alcoholism for the rest of his life.

Between 1922 and 1928 he led the second Moscow Art Theater, earning himself a reputation as teacher, actor, and director who brought innovations experimenting with symbolism and acmeist poetry. Chekhov updated the Stanislavsky's acting method, by blending it with yoga, theosophy, psychology and physiology, and adding his own ideas of transformation of actor's consciousness through psychological gesture and movement techniques for entering a special state of subconscious creativity. His idea of using an actor's own intuition and creative imagination was a departure from the original method of his teacher, Stanislavsky.

Meanwhile Chekhov ignored the communist regime and was attacked by the Soviets for joining the anthroposophic society. In 1928 he was fired from the Moscow Art Theatre and eventually emigrated from Russia. In Europe he taught his acting method and also made a big success in German films, co-starring with his ex-wife Olga Tschechowa, who was then living in Germany with her second husband. In 1931 he founded the Chekhov Theatre, with support from Rachmaninov, Bohner and Morgenstern, and in 1935 he brought the Chekhov Theatre on tour to New York. He taught acting in France, Austria, Latvia, Lithuania, and in England, before WWII. In 1938 he moved to the United States, where he started his own school, and also successfully directed Dostoyevsky's *Demons* on Broadway. Then he was introduced to Hollywood by Sergei Rachmaninoff.

In 1945 Chekhov played his best known film role, psychiatrist Brulov in *Spellbound* (1945). He received an Academy Award nomination for the role and became a member of the American Film Academy in 1946. At that time he taught his method in Hollywood. He appeared in *Texas, Brooklyn, and Heaven* with Audie Murphy (1948). In 1953 he published a book about his method, *To The Actor*, with preface written by Yul Brynner. His students included Gregory Peck, Marilyn Monroe, Gary Cooper, Ingrid Bergman, Anthony Quinn, Jack Palance, Feodor Chaliapin Jr., Elia Kazan, Clint Eastwood, and many other Hollywood actors and directors.

At the end of his life Chekhov reunited with his daughter Ada Tschechowa in California. He died in 1955 in Beverly Hills, and was laid to rest in the Forest Lawn Cemetery in Los Angeles.

Ken Christy

Ken Christy was born in Greenville, Pennsylvania, November 23, 1894, and was an American television and film character actor. Christy appeared in 144 films and television programs between 1940 and 1962 and many of his films list him as uncredited. His first acting role was in the film *Foreign Correspondent* (1940) with Joel McCrea and his career ended with the television series *Shannon* (1962).

Christy's film credits include *Burma Convoy* (1941), *Tarzan's New York Adventure* (1942), *Cheaper by the Dozen* (1950), *A Place in the Sun* (1951), *Abbott and Costello Go to Mars* (1953), *Inside Detroit* (1956), and *Utah Blaine* (1957).

His television credits include *Gang Busters* (1952), *Meet Corliss Archer* (1954), *Death Valley Days* (1955), *I Love Lucy* (1954–56), *Celebrity Playhouse* (1956), *Dragnet* (1957), *Wagon Train* (1958), *General Electric Theater* (1959), *M Squad* (1960), *My Three Sons* (1961), and *Whispering Smith* (1961) with Audie Murphy.

Ken Christy died November 23, 1962.

Fred Clark

Fred Clark with Audie Murphy in *Joe Butterfly*

Fred Clark was born March 19, 1914, in Lincoln, California. This popular, baggy-eyed, bald-domed, big lug of a character actor had few peers when called upon to display that special "slow burn" style of comedy few others perfected. But perfect he did on stage, film and TV. In fact, he pretty much cornered the market during the 50s and 60s as the dour, ill-tempered guy you loved to hate.

Born Frederick Leonard Clark, the son of Frederick Clark, a county agriculture commissioner, and Stella Clark, Fred's initial interest was in medicine and he pursued his pre-med studies at Stanford University. A chance role in the college play "Yellow Jack" changed the course of his destiny. Earning a scholarship to the American Academy of Dramatic Arts, he paid his dues performing in local community theater and summer stock. By May of 1938, at age 24, he was making his Broadway debut with the short-lived comedy play "Schoolhouse on the Lot". He then returned to Broadway a few months later to appear in the melodrama "Ringside Seat", which also closed early.

Fred's career was interrupted when America entered World War II. He served as a Navy pilot in 1942 but later joined the Army and spent nearly two years with the Third Army in Europe. Clark returned to acting and during the post-war years broke into films via Hungarian film director Michael Curtiz who cast him in the noir classic *The Unsuspected* (1947). Able to provide cold-hearted villainy in crime drama as well as dyspeptic humor to slapstick comedy, film work came to Fred in no short order. *Ride the Pink Horse* (1947), *Cry of the City* (1948), *Flamingo Road* (1949), *White Heat* (1949), *Alias Nick Beal* (1949), *Sunset Blvd.* (1950), *The Jackpot* (1950), *The Lemon Drop Kid* (1951) and *Meet Me After the Show* (1951) all made the most of Fred's sour skills. In 1952, he married actress Benay Venuta, whom he met while both were performing on stage in *Light Up the Sky* (1950). The popular couple continued to work together from time to time, which included a 1956 stage production of *Bus Stop* at the La Jolla Playhouse.

Well-established on film by this point, Fred set his sights on TV and earned raves providing weekly bombastic support to George Burns and Gracie Allen on their popular sitcom *The George Burns and Gracie Allen Show* (1950). Joining the cast into its second season (his role had already been played by two other actors), Fred made the role of neighbor/realtor Harry Morton his own, becoming the first definitive Harry on the show. Investing his character with an amusing, child-like grumpiness, he was ideally paired with comedienne Bea Benaderet (as wife Blanche). Together they provided perfect foursome chemistry with Burns and Allen, much in the same way Vivian Vance and William Frawley did for Lucille Ball and Desi Arnaz on *I Love Lucy* (1949). Clark, however, would leave the show in the fall of 1953 following a salary dispute, and was replaced by a fourth Harry Morton, Larry Keating, who managed to keep the role until the end in 1958. Fred would find steady but lesser success on TV after this.

With his trademark cigar, scowl, shiny baldness and pencil-thin mustache, Fred continued to be high in demand in film, usually playing some high-ranking military officer, gang boss, shifty politician or executive skinflint. The Martin & Lewis comedy *The Caddy* (1953), Marilyn Monroe's *How to Marry a Millionaire* (1953), *Abbott and Costello Meet the Keystone Kops* (1955), *The Solid Gold Cadillac* (1956), *Don't Go Near the Water* (1957), *Joe Butterfly* (1958) with Audie Murphy, *The Mating Game* (1959), *Bells Are Ringing* (1960), *Visit to a Small Planet* (1960), *Boys' Night Out* (1962) and *Move Over, Darling* (1963), all displayed Clark at his blustery best. He also received some attention pushing potato chips in commercials.

Fred made a successful stage debut in London with 1963's *Never Too Late* co-starring Joan Bennett and Samantha Eggar, as a cranky middle-aged father-to-be. He would also return infrequently to Broadway with prime roles in *Romanoff and Juliet* (1957), *Viva Madison Avenue!* (1960), and *Absence of a Cello* (1964). On a sad note, many of Fred's final years were spent in inferior films. Movies such as *Dr. Goldfoot and the Bikini Machine* (1965),

I Sailed to Tahiti with an All Girl Crew (1968) and the notorious bomb *Skidoo* (1968), which was directed by Otto Preminger and starred Jackie Gleason and Carol Channing, were undeserving of his talents.

Divorced from Ms. Venuta in August of 1962, Fred subsequently married a model, Gloria Glaser, in 1966. Fred's sudden death of liver disease two years later on December 5, 1968, at the untimely age of 54, had Hollywood mourning one of its finest comic heavies, gone way before his time.

Stanley Clements

Stanley Clements with Audie Murphy in *Bad Boy*

Stanley Clements was born Stanislaw Klimowicz in Long Island, New York, July 16, 1926, and was an American actor and comedian.

Young Stan realized that he wanted a show-business career while he was in grammar school, and when he graduated from college he toured in vaudeville for two years. He then joined the touring company of the *Major Bowes Amateur Hour*. In 1941, he was signed to a contract by 20th Century Fox and appeared in several B films for the studio.

After a short stint with the East Side Kids, he set out on his own again, this time landing roles in more prestigious pictures. He was featured in the Bing Crosby hit *Going My Way* (1944), and scored a great success as a jockey in the Alan Ladd feature *Salty O'Rourke* (1945). His career was interrupted by military service in World War II, and when he returned, he began appearing in lower-budgeted films, including *Johnny Holiday* (1949), cast against type as a psychopath. He starred in a series of action/detective pictures at Allied Artists for producer Ben Schwalb and director Edward Bernds. He also appeared with Audie Murphy in *Bad Boy* (1949).

Schwalb soon became staff producer for The Bowery Boys, and when he needed a replacement for Leo Gorcey in 1956, he asked Clements to step in. Clements comfortably settled into the role of Huntz Hall's sidekick, beginning with *Fighting Trouble* (1956), and co-starred in the final seven Bowery Boys comedies.

The series finally ended in 1958, and Clements went on to a steady career of supporting roles in film and television, including a guest starring role in *Whispering Smith* (1961), his second appearance with Audie Murphy.

One of his last jobs was an appearance in a nationally advertised commercial for Pringle's potato chips. He died from emphysema October 16, 1981, in Pasadena, California.

John Cliff

John Cliff was born Jack Clifford on a minstrel show on November 26, 1918, in Swainsboro, Georgia. His father owned Clifford's Carolina Minstrels. Later his father had a booth called the Grease Store where he sold hotdogs and hamburgers in the Tom Mix Circus, the Hildebrand Circus and various state fairs and rodeos. John handled the soda pop and beer concession for his father. John's dad also had a stable of prize fighters, so John started at one time to be a fighter. However, before he got going he had a double hernia and the doctors told him to lay off for a year.

John decided to leave carnival life when his father and brother realized the old days were coming to an end and leased out their carnival. Relocating in California, John started working labor at the movie studios.

Falling in love with aviation, he learned to fly and got a commercial instructor's license. With very little money he bought out a small company and ended up with five airplanes, fully intending to go into the flight instruction business. His timing couldn't have been worse. Within a few weeks it was December 7, 1941, and all private planes were grounded.

John joined the service and spent his time 'flying the hump'—the Himalayas. Coming out of the service a Captain, he wanted to fly commercial airlines but was not qualified due to not having a college degree, even with all his experience.

John decided to get an agent and try for a career in the movies. Luckily, he signed with a respected agent, Mitch Hamilburg, and his perennial scowl found work on *The Lone Ranger* (1950-1957), *Range Rider* (1951), *Rin Tin Tin* (1955-1957), *Cisco Kid* (1956), *My Friend Flicka* (1955), *Whispering Smith* (1961) with Audie Murphy, and many other television programs right away. Naturally, he was cast as a heavy.

John also was cast in small roles with *Abbott and Costello In the Foreign Legion* (1950), Gene Autry's *Beyond the Purple Hills* (1950), Audie Murphy's *Red Badge of Courage* (1951), *The Three Stooges Meet Hercules* (1962), among others. In 1951 his fledgling career was interrupted by Korea. He'd remained in the reserves and 'got sucked into Korea'. Returning in 1953, John lost no time getting back to film work.

Becoming established, the parts got better in westerns with Tim Holt, Dale Robertson, John Payne, Scott Brady and others, as well as on television series like *Cheyenne* (1956-1961), *Superman* (1956-1957), *Perry Mason* (1957-1965), *Wyatt Earp* (1957-1958), *Maverick* (1957-1961), *Twilight Zone* (1964), and dozens more.

Retiring from acting after a bit in an episode of *Kung Fu* (1972), John relocated to northern California and went into real estate. Retiring from real estate in 1986, he spent his time traveling and golfing. He was honored at western film festivals in Sonora, California, and Charlotte, North Carolina, in his later years.

A very warm-hearted heavy died at 82 of cancer May 12, 2001, in Hayward, California.

Don Collier

Don Collier and with author in 2013

Donald Collier was born in Santa Monica, California, October 17, 1928 and is an American radio personality and a former actor, particularly known for his role in television westerns during the 1960s. He played U.S. Marshal Will Foreman in the 1960-1962 NBC series *Outlaws*, with Barton MacLane, Jock Gaynor, and Bruce Yarnell. He appeared as a deputy marshal to MacLane in the first season of *Outlaws* and was promoted to full marshal in the second season, with Yarnell as the new deputy. MacLane left the series after the first season.

His only sibling, a sister, died when she was thirteen. After graduation from high school, Collier joined the United States Navy at the end of World War II. Upon his return to California, Collier obtained a part in the 1948 film *Massacre River*. The recipient of a football scholarship, he entered Hardin-Simmons University, a Baptist-affiliated institution in Abilene in Taylor County in West Texas. He transferred to Mormon-affiliated Brigham Young University in Provo, Utah, where he also played football.

Collier has made more than seventy film and television appearances. He starred with John Wayne, Robert Mitchum, Anthony Quinn, Dean Martin, Tom Selleck, James Arness, and Elvis Presley. After *Massacre River*, he acquired roles in *Fort Apache* (1948) and *Davy Crockett, Indian Scout* (1950).

Prior to his lead role in *Outlaws*, Collier appeared in the first seasons of both CBS's long-running *Gunsmoke* (1955) and NBC's powerhouse western *Bonanza* (1959). He guest starred in 1957 in NBC's *Wagon Train* with Ward

Bond during its first year on the air. One of his earliest television appearances was in 1952 in the syndicated *Death Valley Days* anthology series later hosted by Ronald W. Reagan. He was in *Seven Ways from Sundown* (1960) with Audie Murphy. He appeared in Chuck Connors' NBC western series *Branded* (1965).

From 1967-1971, he was cast as Sam Butler, the ranch foreman, in sixty-two episodes of NBC's *The High Chaparral*, a David Dortort series with Leif Erickson, Linda Cristal, Cameron Mitchell, Mark Slade, and Henry Darrow. In 1972, he appeared in George Peppard's NBC series *Banacek* and in CBS's family drama, *The Waltons*. In 1974, he guest starred in the initial season of Michael Landon's NBC family western drama, *Little House on the Prairie*. A decade later, he starred in the first season of Landon's other NBC series, *Highway to Heaven*, with co-star Victor French.

Collier's cowboy image enabled him to win the designation of the 'Gum Fighter' for Hubba Bubba bubble gum. In 1989, he accepted the recurring role of William Tompkins in ABC's *The Young Riders*, based loosely on the Pony Express (1860–1861). He has also been a sidekick of Fred Imus, younger brother of Don Imus, on Sirius Satellite Radio's weekly program, *Fred's Trailer Park Bash*. He has been working on a western radio drama, *West of the Story*.

Collier is married to the former Holly Hire, a casting director, and is the father of six children.

Ray Collins

Ray Collins with Audie Murphy in Column South

Ray Bidwell Collins was born December 10, 1889, in Sacramento, California, to Lillie Bidwell and William C. Collins, a newspaper reporter and dramatic editor on the *Sacramento Bee*. He was an American actor in film, stage, radio, and television.

He started acting on stage at the age of fourteen. In 1922, he was part of a stock company called Vancouver's Popular Players which enacted plays at the original Orpheum Theatre in Vancouver, B.C. In the mid 1930s, now an established stage and radio actor, Collins began working with Orson Welles' Mercury Theatre leading to some of his most memorable roles. Having already appeared on radio with Welles on *The Shadow*, a regular as Commissioner Weston, and in Welles' serial adaptation of *Les Misérables* from 1937, Collins became a regular on *The Mercury Theatre on the Air*; through the run of the series. He played many roles in literary adaptations, from Squire Livesey from *Treasure Island* and Dr. Watson to Mr. Pickwick in an adaptation of *Pickwick Papers*. Collins' best known (albeit uncredited) work on this series, however, was in the infamous *The War of the Worlds* (1938) broadcast, playing three roles, including Mr. Wilmuth, on whose farm the Martian craft lands, and the newscaster who describes the destruction of New York.

Along with other Mercury Theatre players, Collins made his first notable screen appearance in *Citizen Kane* (1941), as ruthless Boss Jim Gettys. He also played key roles in Welles's *The Magnificent Ambersons* (1942) and *Touch of Evil* (1958). Collins appeared in more than ninety films in all, including *Leave Her to Heaven* (1945), *The Best Years of Our Lives* and *Crack-Up* (1946), *A Double Life* (1947), two entries in the Ma and Pa Kettle series, as in-law Jonathan Parker, and the 1953 version of *The Desert Song*, in which he played the non-singing role of Kathryn Grayson's father. He displayed comic ability in *The Bachelor and the Bobby-Soxer* (1947), and *The Man from Colorado* (1948). He also played in *Column South* (1953) with Audie Murphy.

He may be best remembered for his work on television, playing Lieutenant Tragg for 236 episodes on *Perry Mason* (1957-1965). He was also a regular as John Merriweather on the television version of *The Halls of Ivy* (1954-1955) starring Ronald Colman.

Ray Collins died July 11, 1965 in Santa Monica, California.

Miriam Colon

Audie Murphy with Miriam Colon in *Battle at Bloody Beach*

Míriam Colón was born Míriam Colón Valle August 20, 1936, in Ponce, Puerto Ricois, and is a Puerto Rican actress and the founder and director of the Puerto Rican Traveling Theater in New York City.

She was a young girl in the 1940s when her recently divorced mother moved the family to a public housing project called 'Residencial Las Casas', located in Barrio Obrero, San Juan. She attended the Ramon Baldorioty de Castro High School in Old San Juan, where she actively participated in the school's plays. Her first drama teacher, Marcos Colón, no relation, believed that she was very talented and with his help she was permitted to observe the students in the Drama Department of the University of Puerto Rico.

She was a good student in high school and was awarded scholarships that enabled her to enroll in the Dramatic Workshop and Technical Institute and also in The Lee Strasburg Acting Studio in New York City.

In 1953, Colón debuted as an actress in *Peloteros* (*Baseball Players*), starring Ramón (Diplo) Rivero, a film produced in Puerto Rico, and in which she played a character called 'Lolita'.

In 1954, Colón moved to New York City, where she worked in theater and later landed a role on the soap opera *Guiding Light* (1999-2002). On one occasion she attended a performance of Rene Marques' *La Carreta* (*The Oxcart*). That presentation motivated her to form the first Hispanic theater group, with the help of *La Carreta's* producer, Roberto Rodríguez, called El Circuito Dramatico.

In 1954 she appeared on stage in *In The Summer House* at the Play House in New York City. Between 1954 and 1974, Colón made guest appearances in numerous television shows, mostly in westerns. In 1961, Colón appeared in *One-eyed Jacks* (1961) as 'the Redhead'. The same year she appeared in *Battle at Bloody Beach* (1961) with Audie Murphy.

In 1979, she starred alongside fellow Puerto Rican actors José Ferrer, Raúl Juliá, and Henry Darrow in *Life of Sin*, a film in which she portrayed Isabel la Negra, a real-life Puerto Rican brothel owner. In 1983, she played the mother of Tony Montana, played by Al Pacino, in *Scarface*. She was also cast as 'María' in the 1999 film *Gloria*, which starred Sharon Stone.

She continues to take acting jobs, having four films not yet released, including *Unhallowed* (2013) she is currently filming.

Tommy Cook

Audie Murphy with Tommy Cook in *Night Passage*

Tommy Cook was born July 5, 1930, in Duluth, Minnesota. A spry, curly-haired, dark-complexioned child, his most famous roles happened during his career were in serial adventures. He came on the feature film scene auspiciously in the role of young Indian boy Little Beaver alongside western good guy 'Don 'Red' Barry' in the *Adventures of Red Ryder* (1940), and followed that portraying Kimbu, the young jungle boy, alongside Frances Gifford's heroine Nyoka in *Jungle Girl* (1941).

Tommy's father was stricken with Bright's disease, a kidney ailment, which forced the family (which included a sister and grandmother) to seek warmer climate. In California, his mother inspired him toward theatrics and he gained entry at the Pasadena Playhouse where he stayed for seven years. Naturally talented, radio jobs soon cropped up for the youngster.

After appearing in a couple of short films for MGM and RKO, Tommy auditioned for and won the role of Little Beaver in the twelve-chapter *Red Ryder* (1940) cliffhanger at Republic. He also played the role on radio.

On screen Tommy had to learn to ride a horse bareback. While these first two roles were prominent parts that could have insured youthful stardom, it didn't. Tommy continued in films in both highly visible and unbilled parts. The former included active roles in *Good Luck, Mr. Yates* (1943), *Hi, Buddy* (1943), as Kimba, the Leopard Boy in *Tarzan and the Leopard Woman* (1946) with Johnny Weissmuller and Brenda Joyce, a juvenile delinquent in *Bad Boy* (1949) with Audie Murphy, a Filipino in *American Guerrilla in the Philippines* (1950) starring Tyrone Power, and lead delinquent in the sub-par propaganda film *Teen-Age Crime Wave* (1955). He appeared again with Audie Murphy in *Night Passage* (1957) also starring James Stewart.

More or less typed in exotic parts, his characters' names were usually dead giveaways: Paco, Salim, Ponca, Mario, Chito, Pablo, Little Elk, and Keoga among them. His transition from child to adult actor was rocky and eventually his career dissipated. A brawny, good-looking man, his short stature may have figured into the problem.

Tommy's days as a standout junior tennis player on the Southern California circuit eventually led to an entirely new existence in mid-life as a respected organizer (emcee/producer/director) of celebrity gala/charity events.

Ben Cooper

Ben Cooper with Audie Murphy in *Arizona Raiders*

Ben Cooper was born September 30, 1933, and is a retired American actor of film and television, who won a Golden Boot award in 2005 for his work in westerns.

Cooper's earliest credited screen appearance was as an eighteen-year-old in 1952–1953 on the *Armstrong Circle Theatre*, then on NBC, in the two episodes "The Commandant's Clock" and "Changing Dream." Thereafter, he appeared in numerous films: *Thunderbirds* (1952) as Calvin Jones, *Women They Almost Lynched* (1953) as Jesse James Dingus, *A Perilous Journey* (1953) as Sam, *Flight Nurse* (1953) as Private First Class Marvin Judd, *Sea of Lost Ships* (1954) as a crewman, *Johnny Guitar* (1954) as Turkey Ralston, *The Outcast* (1954) as The Kid, *Duel at Apache Wells* (1957) as Johnny Shattuck (or the Durango Kid).

Starting in 1959, Cooper began appearing on dozens of television westerns, including a guest starring role on Don Durant's CBS series *Johnny Ringo* (1960), a spinoff of *Dick Powell's Zane Grey Theater* (1956-1960), on which Cooper appeared five times between 1956 and 1960. Cooper appeared on another *Zane Grey* spinoff, *Stagecoach West* (1960), starring Wayne Rogers and Robert Bray; he portrayed the title guest role in the episode "The Saga of Jeremy Boone."

Other westerns followed: NBC's *The Westerner* (1960) as Cal in "Hand on the Gun", ABC's *The Rifleman* (1961) as Simon Lee in the episode "Face of Yesterday," NBC's *Bonanza* (1960) as Sam Kirby in "Showdown", and as Johnny Lightly in "The Horse Breaker" (1961). In 1962, Cooper appeared in two episodes of NBC's *Laramie* as Sandy Catlin in "The Runt" and as Johnny Hartley in "Gun Duel."

Cooper appeared three times on CBS's *Gunsmoke*: as Breck Taylor in the two 1965 episodes "Breckinridge" and "Two Tall Men" and as Pitt Campbell in "Apprentice Doc" in 1961. He appeared on CBS's *Rawhide* (1964) as Clell

Miller in the episode "The Photographer". In 1967, Cooper appeared as Lieutenant Drake in the film *Red Tomahawk*. In 1969, he starred in the syndicated series *Death Valley Days* as Jason Tugwell in the episode "Biscuits and Billy the Kid." He then appeared twice with Audie Murphy: *Gunfight at Comanche Creek* (1963) and *Arizona Raiders* (1965).

In 1970, Cooper appeared in the episode "With Love, Bullets, and Valentines" of the long-running NBC series *The Virginian* starring James Drury and Doug McClure. In 1971, Cooper appeared in the role of "Colorado" in the James Garner film *Support Your Local Gunfighter*. In 1974, Cooper guest starred as Goodnight in the episode "The Cenotaph: Part 2" of ABC's *Kung Fu* starring David Carradine. Twenty-one years later in 1995, Cooper appeared as Sheriff Dowd in the episode "The Promise" of another *Kung Fu* series, *Kung Fu: The Legend Continues*.

Cooper also made many appearances in television drama. In 1961, he appeared as Dauger in the American Civil War episode, "Still Valley" of CBS's *The Twilight Zone* created by Rod Serling. In 1965, he appeared as Sam Grayson in the episode "Won't It Ever Be Morning?" of NBC"s *Kraft Suspense Theatre*. He guest starred in five episodes of CBS' s legal drama *Perry Mason* starring Raymond Burr.

On September 16, 1966, he appeared, along with Larry Ward, James T. Callahan, and Warren Stevens, in the ABC science fiction series *The Time Tunnel* in the role of Nazarro, an astronaut, in the episode "One Way To The Moon." In 1969, he portrayed "Pete" in the episode "The Playground" of Mike Connors's CBS detective series *Mannix*. The next year, he appeared again as Pete in the *Mannix* episode "To Cage a Seagull" and also as Officer Brinkman in the episode "Log 95: Purse Snatcher" of Jack Webb's NBC police drama *Adam-12*, starring Martin Milner and Kent McCord, and as Larry Adams in "Sea of Security" on Robert Young's ABC medical drama *Marcus Welby, M.D.*

From 1981 to 1983, he appeared as the stunt scene director in seven episodes of ABC's *The Fall Guy* starring Lee Majors. Among Cooper's last television roles were as Mr. Parrish in two 1985 episodes, "Dead Ends" and "Terms of Estrangement," of CBS's prime time soap opera *Dallas* and as a bureaucrat in the *Dallas* spinoff, *Knots Landing* in the 1986 episode "His Brother's Keeper."

Cooper's last film roles were as in *Lightning Jack* (1994) and in the 1996 television production, *Joan Crawford: Always the Star*.

Ben Cooper is a regular fixture at Western Film Star gatherings around the country, including three years at Audie Murphy Days in Greenville, Texas.

Ellen Corby

Ellen Corby was born Ellen Hansen on June 3, 1911, in Racine, Wisconsin. She began her career as a bit player in the film *Speed Limited* (1935). Ellen would not be seen on the big screen again until 1945 in *Cornered* (1945). In 1946, she appeared in fourteen films, although mostly in small, minor roles. One of them was in the Christmas classic *It's a Wonderful Life* (1946).

One of the highlights of her career came about in 1948 in *I Remember Mama* (1948) as Aunt Trina. Ellen garnered a nomination for Best Supporting Actress, which was ultimately won by Claire Trevor in *Key Largo* (1948). The Oscar nomination didn't send her to the heights she had hoped. This wonderful actress continued in roles that were mostly minor compared to some of her contemporaries. She appeared in *Night Passage* (1957) with Audie Murphy and James Stewart.

However, it was television where she would receive the acclaim that had eluded her on the screen. Time after time she played parts that were absolutely outstanding. One of the funniest was as Myrt "Hubcaps" Lesh in *The*

Andy Griffith Show (1960). She was the ringleader of a gang that stole cars and then sold them, and she sold Barney Fife a stolen car that turned out to be a real lemon. The series that brought her worldwide recognition, though, was the highly acclaimed *The Waltons* (1971) as Esther "Grandma" Walton. The role got her Emmy awards in 1973, 1974, and 1975. Although a stroke in 1977 slowed her down, Ellen still made appearances on the series.

Her last TV appearance was in 1997 in the TV movie *A Walton Easter* (1997). On April 14, 1999, Ellen died at the Motion Picture & Television Hospital in Woodland Hills, California. She was 87 years old.

Hugh Corcoran

Hugh Corcoran with Audie Murphy in *No Name on the Bullet*

Hugh Corcoran was born July 28, 1947 in Santa Monica, California, and is the brother of acting siblings Donna Corcoran, Noreen Corcoran, Kevin Corcoran, Brian Corcoran, and Kelly Corcoran.

Hugh Corcoran appeared in seventeen films and television programs from 1953 to 1980. Some of those credits include *Half a Hero* (1953), *It's a Great Life* (1954), *World Without End* (1956), *The Search for Bridey Murphy* (1956), *Cat on a Hot Tin Roof* (1958), *No Name on the Bullet* (1959) with Audie Murphy, *Caged Heat* (1974), *The Manitou* (1978), and *Don't Answer the Phone!* (1980).

Mara Corday

Mara Corday with Audie Murphy in *Drums Across the River*

Mara Corday was born Marilyn Joan Watts on January 3, 1930 in Santa Monica, California, and is a showgirl, model, actress, *Playboy* Playmate and a 1950s cult figure.

Wanting a career in films, Mara Corday came to Hollywood while still in her teens and found work as a showgirl at the Earl Carroll Theatre on Sunset Boulevard. Her physical beauty brought jobs as a photographer's model that led to a bit part as a showgirl in the 1951 film *Two Tickets to Broadway*. She signed on as a Universal International Pictures contract player where she met actor Clint Eastwood with whom she would remain lifelong friends. With UI, Corday was given small roles in various B-movies and television series.

She appeared with Audie Murphy in *Drums Across the River* (1954). In 1954 on the set of *Playgirl* she met actor Richard Long. Following the death of Long's wife, the two began dating and married in 1957.

Her roles were small until 1955 when she was cast opposite John Agar in *Tarantula*, a Sci-Fi B-movie that proved a modest success. She had another successful co-starring role in that genre *The Black Scorpion* (1957), as well as in a number of Western films. Respected film critic Leonard Maltin said that Mara Corday had "more acting ability than she was permitted to exhibit."

Mara Corday appeared as a pinup girl in numerous men's magazines during the 1950s and was the Playmate of the month for October 1958 issue of *Playboy*, together with famous model and showgirl Pat Sheehan. In 1956, she had a recurring role in the ABC television series *Combat Sergeant*.

From 1959 to early 1961, Corday worked exclusively doing guest spots on various television series. She then gave up her career to devote her time to raising a family. During her seventeen-year marriage to Richard Long she had three children.

A few years after her husband's death in 1974, Corday's friend Clint Eastwood offered her a chance to return to filmmaking with a role in his 1977 film *The Gauntlet*. She acted with him again in *Sudden Impact* (1983), *Pink Cadillac* (1989), and in her last film to date, 1990's *The Rookie*.

George Coulouris

George Coulouris was born October 1, 1903, in Manchester, England. He was the son of a Greek immigrant father and an English mother. He was educated at England's Manchester Grammar School. As an actor he was quite adept at playing villains, particularly wealthy businessmen, but he was just as suitable at playing nobler roles. A member of Orson Welles' famed Mercury Theater players, he appeared in such films as *Citizen Kane* (1941), *For Whom the Bell Tolls* (1943), *Papillon* (1973) and *Murder on the Orient Express* (1974). The film that established him as an interesting and reliable heavy, with his massive shoulders and hooded eyes, was *Watch on the Rhine* (1943).

Coulouris studied with Elsie Fogerty at London's Central School of Speech and Drama. His London stage debut came in 1925 with "Henry V" at the Old Vic. He was soon playing the Yank at the first British staging of Eugene O'Neill's "The Hairy Ape". By 1929 he had reached Broadway, via a modern dress version of "Measure for Measure". His role as Tallant in *The Late Christopher Bean* took him to Hollywood in 1933 for MGM's film of the play.

The next milestone in his burgeoning career occurred when he was playing in *Ten Million Ghosts* and met Orson Welles. They got on well and Coulouris joined Welles' Mercury Theatre, playing Mark Antony in the famous modern dress production of *Julius Caesar* (1937). When Welles went to Hollywood to make *Citizen Kane* (1941), Coulouris climbed into movie history in the part of Walter Parks Thatcher, the Kane family's crotchety lawyer and business manager. By that time his future as a cinema actor was assured and he went on to play character parts in a long string of Hollywood productions throughout the 1940s, including *Beyond Glory* (1948) with Audie Murphy and Alan Ladd.

At the end of the 1940s Coulouris returned to England, joining the Bristol Old Vic where he was notable as Tartuffe, transferring to London. In the 1950s and 1960s he remained a stalwart stage actor in spite of his movie reputation. He liked nothing better than to grapple with Henrik Ibsen, George Bernard Shaw, August Strindberg, Molière or William Shakespeare. During these years he tackled Dr. Stockman in Ibsen's *An Enemy of the People*, Patrick Flynn in Sean O'Casey's *The Plough and the Stars*, the father in Jean-Paul Sartre's *Altona*, Edgar in Strindberg's *The Dance of Death* and Big Daddy in Tennessee Williams' *Cat on a Hot Tin Roof*.

All of these are parts to swell a scene and Coulouris had the flourish to fill them, sometimes to overflowing, always compellingly. In Britain his film parts tended towards the mundane, though he rose to the occasion as the native Babalatchi in Carol Reed's *Outcast of the Islands* (1951) and seized rare chances to play comedy in *Doctor in the House* (1954), *Doctor at Sea* (1955) and the Frankie Howerd vehicle *The Runaway Bus* (1954).

Towards the end of his life he tried his hand at writing and produced some charming memoirs describing his early life in Manchester and his early stage experiences, as yet unpublished except for a vivid excerpt published in the Guardian newspaper in February 1986. He died April 25, 1989, in London, England.

Bruce Cowling

Audie Murphy with Bruce Cowling in *To Hell and Back*

Bruce Cowling was born October 30, 1919, and was a film and television actor in the 1940s and 1950s. The Coweta, Oklahoma-born actor appeared in twenty films including *The Beginning or the End* (1947), *The Stratton Story* (1949), *Battleground* (1949), *Cause for Alarm!* (1951), *The Painted Hills* (1951), *The Battle at Apache Pass* (1952), as Virgil Earp in *Gun Belt* (1953), as Wyatt Earp in *Masterson of Kansas* (1954), and his last film *To Hell and Back* (1955) with Audie Murphy.

Among his television work, he appeared in several episodes of *The Lone Ranger* (1953-1955), *Perry Mason* (1957), *Zane Gray Theatre* (1958), *Have Gun, Will Travel* (1958), and his last television appearance in *The Texan* (1959).

He died August 22, 1986, in Los Angeles, California.

Buster Crabbe

Audie Murphy with Buster Crabbe in *Arizona Raiders*

Buster Crabbe was born as Clarence Linden Crabbe II to Lucy Agnes McNamara and Edward Clinton Simmons Crabbe on February 7, 1908, in Oakland, California. His father was born in Nevada and his paternal grandfather, Clarence Linden Crabbe I (1861–1941), was born in Hawaii. Buster had a brother, Edward Clinton Simmons Crabbe II (1909–1972), who was known as "Buddy". In 1910 the family was living in a boarding house in Oakland and Edward senior was working as a real estate broker.

Buster Crabbe graduated from the University of Southern California. In 1931, while working on *That's My Boy* (1932) for Columbia Pictures, he was tested by MGM for Tarzan and rejected. Paramount Pictures put him in *King of the Jungle* (1933) as Kaspa, the Lion Man (after a book of that title but clearly a copy of the Tarzan stories). Publicity for this film emphasized his having won the 1932 Olympic 400-meter freestyle swimming championship and suggested a rivalry with Johnny Weissmuller. Producer Sol Lesser wanted Crabbe for an independent *Tarzan the Fearless* (1933), though he first had to get James Pierce to waive rights to the part already promised to him by his father-in-law, Edgar Rice Burroughs.

The film was released as both a feature and a serial; most houses showed only the first serial episode, which critics panned as a badly organized feature. Just prior to the film's release, Crabbe married his college sweetheart and gave himself one year to either make it as an actor or start law school at USC. Paramount put him in a number of Zane Grey westerns, then Universal Pictures gave him the lead him in very successful sci-fi serials like *Flash Gordon* and *Buck Rogers* from 1936-40.

Buster began a string of Billy the Kid westerns for low-budget (very low-budget) studio PRC in 1940. After World War II, he devoted much of his time to his swimming pool corporation and operation of a boys' camp in New York. He then made the serials *Pirates of the High Seas* (1950) and then *King of the Congo* (1952). In addition, he was very active on television in the 1950s. In 1953, he hosted a local show in New York City that featured his serials. He played the title role of the adventure series, *Captain Gallant of the Foreign Legion* (1955).

He later returned to western features to play Wyatt Earp in *Badman's Country* (1958), and gave a stellar performance in *Arizona Raiders* (1965) as the head of the Arizona Rangers who recruits Audie Murphy and Ben Cooper.

Buster Crabbe died at age 75 of a heart attack on April 23, 1983, in Scottsdale, Arizona.

Richard Crane

Richard Crane was born June 6, 1918, in San Fernando Valley, California, and was a veteran character actor whose career spanned three decades in films and television. His early career included many uncredited performances in feature films made in the 1940's. He is best remembered for his portrayal of the title role in the TV science fiction series *Rocky Jones, Space Ranger*, which ran for two seasons starting in 1954.

Of notable athletic ability, Crane also appeared in the outer-space adventure serial *Commando Cody: Sky Marshal of the Universe* (1953), as Cody's semi-comical sidekick, and was the hero of the 1951 serial based loosely on Jules Verne's *Mysterious Island*.

He later made numerous appearances in many popular TV shows including *Gang Busters* (1952), on which he played gangster John Dillinger and associate Homer Van Meter. He also made an appearance on *Whispering Smith* (1961) with Audie Murphy.

He died March 9, 1969 of a heart attack at the age of 50. He is buried in Valhalla Memorial Park Cemetery.

Broderick Crawford

Audie Murphy with Broderick Crawford in *The Texican*

He was born William Broderick Crawford on December 9, 1911, in Philadelphia, Pennsylvania, to Lester Crawford and Helen Broderick, two vaudeville performers. His mother eventually had a small movie career acting in comedies shot in Hollywood. Her son, the large and burly Broderick Crawford, was no one's idea of a leading man due to his rough-and-tumble looks, but he broke through as an actor playing John Steinbeck's simple-minded giant Lenny in the Broadway adaptation of Steinbeck's novella *Of Mice and Men*.

After his Broadway success, Crawford moved to Hollywood and made his cinema debut in the comedy *Woman Chases Man* (1937), in a supporting role to stars Joel McCrea and Miriam Hopkins. When producer-director Lewis Milestone was casting the movie version of Steinbeck's classic *Of Mice and Men* (1939), he passed over Crawford and chose Lon Chaney Jr. to play Lenny. Chaney gave a wonderful performance, and Crawford was in peril of being overlooked, as there were not many good roles for a man with his hulking bulk and gravelly voice.

After many supporting roles, including a memorable turn as a big but kind-hearted lug in the comedy *Larceny, Inc.* (1942), and a stint in the military during World War II, Crawford had his breakthrough role in Robert Rossen's adaptation of Robert Penn Warren's Pulitzer Prize-winning novel, *All the King's Men* (1949). Crawford gave a masterful performance as the Southern politician modeled on Louisiana's Huey Long. In addition to the Oscar, he also won the New York Film Critics' Award as Best Actor. *All the King's Men* was a hit, as was *Born Yesterday* (1950). However, he was unable to keep up his career due to typecasting as a crude, boorish brute.

Five years after copping the Academy Award, TV producer Frederick W. Ziv hired Crawford to play the lead role in his syndicated police drama, *Highway Patrol* (1955-1959). The show ran for four seasons, and imprinted Crawford's character of Dan Matthews into a generation of Baby Boomers' minds in its first and subsequent runs in syndication on the television. After being moribund in the early 1950s, Crawford's career was revived, and he generally eschewed making movies for TV for the rest of his life.

One of his films from the 1950s that stood out above the rest was *Between Heaven and Hell* (1956) as Captain Waco Grimes, Robert Wagner's superior officer. Another memorable role had him as the bad guy against good guy Audie Murphy in the Italian spaghetti western *The Texican* (1966).

Broderick Crawford continued to act almost up until his death in Rancho Mirage, California, on April 26, 1986. He passed away at the age of 74, after a series of strokes.

Dani Crayne

Dani Crayne with Audie Murphy in *World in My Corner*

Dani Crayne was born Darlyne Danielle Swanson December 25, 1934 in Minneapolis, Minnesota. She was spotted by a Universal-International talent scout while she gave Mambo lessons at a Hollywood dance school. She was offered a Universal stock contract in 1955. After performing the usual starlet duties of leg art and bit parts, including a role in *World in my Corner* (1956) with Audie Murphy, she landed the role of Helen of Troy in *The Story of Mankind* (1957). Unfortunately, the star-studded but low-budget 'epic' became a notorious failure and Crayne spent the remainder of her brief career in television Westerns.

She married actor David Janssen October 4, 1975, and the marriage lasted until his death February 30, 1980.

Gary Crosby

Audie Murphy with Gary Crosby in *Battle at Bloody Beach*

Gary Evan Crosby was born in Los Angeles, California, June 27, 1933, and was an American singer and actor. He may have become better known for writing a revealing memoir of his father, entertainment legend Bing Crosby, than for his own music and acting work. His mother was singer/actress Dixie Lee, Bing Crosby's first wife.

He attended Stanford University but dropped out, then fell into following in his father's footsteps in the entertainment business. He performed in a harmony singing group, The Crosby Boys, with his three brothers, Philip, Lindsay, and Dennis, during the 1940s, 1950s, and 1960s.

As an actor, Crosby was briefly under contract to 20th Century-Fox, where he appeared in *Battle at Bloody Beach* (1961) and his character gets eaten by a shark while helping Audie Murphy, but is perhaps best-remembered for his recurring role as Officer Ed Wells on NBC's *Adam-12* from 1968 to 1975, as well as appearances on several other shows produced by Jack Webb's Mark VII Limited.

He also appeared in the 1965 film *Girl Happy* (1965), with Elvis Presley, and "Come Wander With Me," an episode of *The Twilight Zone* in 1964.

Later in the 1970s, Crosby appeared occasionally on such game shows as *Match Game* and *Tattletales* as a guest panelist.

In 1983, six years after Bing's death, Crosby published his autobiography, *Going My Own Way*.

Gary Crosby died of lung cancer in Burbank, California, August 24, 1995, and was interred in the Forest Lawn - Hollywood Hills Cemetery in Los Angeles.

Kathleen Crowley

Audie Murphy with Kathleen Crowley in *Showdown*

Betty Jane Kathleen Crowley was born December 26, 1931, in Green Bank, New Jersey, is an American actress and was Miss New Jersey in 1949 and a contestant for Miss America in the same year (she came in sixth). After the pageants, she became an actress who specialized in being phenomenally seductive in TV series and movies. Most well known for playing a variety of sirens in TV's *Maverick* (1957-1962) opposite James Garner, Jack Kelly, and Roger Moore, she appears in eight episodes, a series record for leading ladies: "The Jeweled Gun" (with Jack Kelly), "Maverick Springs" (with James Garner and Jack Kelly), "The Misfortune Teller" (with James Garner), "A Bullet for the Teacher" and "Kiz" (with Roger Moore), and "Dade City Dodge," "The Troubled Heir," and "One of Our Trains Is Missing" (with Jack Kelly).

Crowley made eighty-one television appearances on various series and appeared in twenty movies between 1951 and 1970, including *Showdown* (1963) with Audie Murphy. One of her last movie roles was in *Downhill Racer* (1969) with Robert Redford.

Pat Crowley

Audie Murphy with Pat Crowley in *Walk the Proud Land*

Patricia Crowley was born September 17, 1933, in Olyphant, Pennsylvania. A very pleasing and thoroughly enjoyable vision on 1950s film and 1960s TV, Patricia Crowley effortlessly lit up her surroundings with a warm, inviting personality and fresh-faced attractiveness that she still carries today.

It was her older sister Ann Crowley (born October 17, 1929) who triggered Pat's interest in performing when, during Ann's appearance in a Chicago musical production, the ten-year-old Pat was given a walk-on part. Ann Crowley would go on to have a promising musical career appearing in such late 1940s/early 1950s N.Y. shows as *Carousel*, *Oklahoma!* and *Paint Your Wagon*.

By age 11, Patricia had become a photographer's model and subsequently attended New York's High School of Performing Arts. She won her first major TV part scarcely out of high school and seemed destined to become an important teen star as the bobbysoxer lead in the Saturday morning TV series *A Date with Judy* (1952), which was adapted from the highly popular radio series of the 1940s. When the series moved to prime time, however, another actress replaced her.

Like her sister, Patricia was also musically inclined and appeared in a few tuneful stage shows such as Tovarich and Kiss Me Kate (as Bianca). Billed as 'Pat Crowley', she made an auspicious Broadway debut with the relatively short-lived comedy play 'Southern Exposure' in 1950, earning the 1951 Theatre World Award for 'promising personality'. She followed this with another short run (one day) in the comedy 'Four Twelve's Are 48'.

After a number of early 1950s TV assignments, Pat was brought out to Hollywood to co-star with Dean Martin and Jerry Lewis in one of the pair's typical slapstick outings *Money from Home* (1953). In it, she played a feisty lady veterinarian. She then moved engagingly into the show business comedy *Forever Female* (1953) co-starring William Holden and Ginger Rogers. As the young aspirant who is vying with the long-in-the-tooth Rogers for a prime Broadway ingénue role, Pat made the most of her role and earned a Golden Globe award for 'best promising female newcomer'. From there, she played the second female lead in the musical *Red Garters* (1954), but crooning headliners Rosemary Clooney and Guy Mitchell got most of the songs. Pat did have a dance number, however, opposite Mitchell with the tune "Meet a Happy Guy".

While much of her work came from dramatic TV showcases, Pat continued in movie roles co-starring as the girlfriend of Tony Curtis in the boxing yarn *The Square Jungle* (1955), appearing as the female ingénue in the sudsy drama *There's Always Tomorrow* (1956) opposite veterans Barbara Stanwyck, Fred MacMurray and Joan Bennett, and reuniting with Martin & Lewis in their very last film *Hollywood or Bust* (1956) before the pair's professional breakup. The same year she appeared as Audie Murphy's wife in *Walk the Proud Land* (1956).

At her peak she courted top TV stardom in the mid-1960s as the beleaguered wife and mom on the successful series *Please Don't Eat the Daisies* (1965) and easily made the original Doris Day film role her own. Both she and TV husband Mark Miller made a handsome couple and the series deserved more than its two-season run. Perhaps audience taste, which was changing rapidly with the counterculture era taking over, triggered its somewhat quick demise.

Since then, Patricia has continued to maintain a strong visibility especially on TV, although she was not given the star-making opportunities like this again. Crowley is best known to a later generation of viewers for her regular roles on daytime's *Generations* (1989-1990), *Port Charles* (1997-2003), and *The Bold and the Beautiful* (1987-2005).

A guest on such sitcoms as *Frasier* (1993), *Roseanne* (1988), and *Friends* (1994), recurring roles on *Joe Forrester* (1975) (perfectly paired with Lloyd Bridges), *Dynasty* (1981), and *Beverly Hills, 90210* (1990) also showed Pat to good advantage. More recently, she has graced episodes of *The Closer* (2005) and *Cold Case* (2003).

In 1958 Patricia married Ed Hookstratten, a successful attorney for top entertainment and sports icons. They had a son, Jon, and a daughter, Ann, named after her sister. After their two-decade marriage ended, she went on to marry producer Andy Friendly in 1986. While many understandably agree that Patricia Crowley's talents deserved perhaps a better serving in Hollywood, particularly on film, she has nevertheless proved herself a lovely, lively and still ingratiating presence.

Donald Curtis

Too often overlooked as a heavy in 1940s Columbia B-westerns, Donald Curtis went from bad man to ordained minister.

Born Curtis Donald Rudolf February 27, 1915, in Cheney, Washington, Curtis won a scholarship then obtained a B.S. and M.A. in dramatic production from the School of Speech at Northwestern University in Evanston, IL. He worked as an associate professor of dramatic Art at Duquesne University in Pittsburgh, PA, then won a Rockefeller Fellowship and used it to study acting.

After making his screen debut uncredited as an ambulance intern in *Emergency Squad* (1940), which starred Bill Henry, Curtis' next role as Ronal, one of Prince Barin's trusted officers, in Universal's third (and final) Flash Gordon serial, *Flash Gordon Conquers the Universe* (1940), established him further. A small role as a thug in another Universal serial, *Junior G-Men* (1940), followed the same year.

Roles in a dozen B-westerns in the 1940s opposite Tex Ritter, Bill Elliott, Charles Starrett, Russell Hayden and the 3 Mesquiteers, led to a contract at prestigious MGM from 1943-1946.

Freelancing again in the late 1940s and 1950s, Curtis appeared in a few more westerns like *Stampede* (1949) with Rod Cameron, *7th Cavalry* (1956) with Randolph Scott, and made a sci-fi thriller that he called his favorite, *It Came From Beneath the Sea* (1955), because "it was the only time I got the girl at the end of the picture."

In 1953 Curtis changed his life. He went to Santa Barbara and was ordained a minister in the Church of Religious Science. He made a few more pictures and television episodes then retired after *Night Passage* (1957) with Audie Murphy and James Stewart.

He did go back into acting briefly in the 1960s and had a role with David Janssen in *Warning Shot* (1967).

For well over 20 years Curtis and his wife, Dorothy, lived in Dallas, TX, where they were known not for his film career, but as Reverend Donald Curtis and Reverend Dorothy Curtis, pastors of Unity Church on Forest Lane. He established and recorded the five-times-per-week program, *Five Minutes That Will Change Your Life* on WRR radio. The program was also in syndication. Curtis was the author of thirty books on self improvement, metaphysics and New Thought. He traveled throughout the world giving classes and seminars on meditation and higher dimensions of human potential. He appeared on *Oprah Winfrey* in 1987 discussing true meaning of the new age.

Curtis was honored at the Memphis Film Festival in 1989 and a few years later retired to Desert Hot Springs, California, where, at 82, he died on May 22, 1997, of unknown causes.

Tony Curtis

Tony Curtis with Audie Murphy in *Kansas Raiders*

Tony Curtis was born Bernard Schwartz; June 3, 1925 in Bronx, New York and was an American film actor whose career spanned six decades, but had his greatest popularity during the 1950s and early 1960s. He acted in more than 100 films in roles covering a wide range of genres, from light comedy to serious drama. In his later years, Curtis made numerous television appearances.

He was one of three sons of Emanuel Schwartz and Helen Klein. His parents were Hungarian Jewish immigrants from Mátészalka, Hungary. Hungarian was Curtis' only language until he was five or six. His father was a tailor and the family lived in the back of the shop; the parents in one corner and Curtis and his brothers Julius and Robert in another.

When Curtis was eight, he and his brother Julius were placed in an orphanage for a month because their parents could not afford to feed them. Four years later, Julius was struck and killed by a truck. Curtis joined a neighborhood gang whose main crimes were playing hooky from school and minor pilfering at the local dime store. Aged 11, a friendly neighbor saved him from what he felt would have led to a life of delinquency by sending him to a Boy Scout camp where he was able to work off his energy and settle down. He attended Seward Park High School. At 16, he had his first small acting part in a school stage play.

Curtis enlisted in the United States Navy after the attack on Pearl Harbor and war was declared. After being inspired by Cary Grant's role in *Destination Tokyo* (1943) and Tyrone Power in *Crash Dive* (1943), he joined the Pacific submarine force. Curtis served aboard a submarine tender, the USS *Proteus* until the end of the Second World War. On September 2, 1945, Curtis witnessed the Japanese surrender in Tokyo Bay from his ship's signal bridge about a mile away. Following his discharge from US Navy, Curtis attended City College of New York as a result of the G.I. Bill. He then studied acting at the The New School in Greenwich Village under the influential German stage director Erwin Piscator. Fellow contemporaries included Elaine Stritch, Walter Matthau, Bea Arthur, and Rod Steiger. While still at college, Curtis was discovered by Joyce Selznick, the notable talent agent, casting director, and niece of film producer David O. Selznick. He later claimed it was because he "was the handsomest of the boys."

In 1948, Curtis arrived in Hollywood aged 23. When he was placed under contract at Universal Pictures, he changed his name from Bernard Schwartz to Tony Curtis. The first name was from the novel *Anthony Adverse* and "Kurtz" from a surname in his mother's family. Although Universal Pictures taught him fencing and riding, in keeping with the cinematic themes of the era, Curtis admitted he was at first only interested in girls and money. Neither was he hopeful of his chances of becoming a major star.

Although his early film roles were partly the result of his good looks, by the latter half of the 1950s he became a notable and strong screen presence. He began proving himself to be a "fine dramatic actor," having the range to act in numerous dramatic and comedy roles. In his earliest parts he acted in a string of "mediocre" films, including swashbucklers, westerns, light comedies, sports films, and a musical. One of his first films was as outlaw Kit Dalton in *Kansas Raiders* (1950) with Audie Murphy and with Audie Murphy again in *Sierra* (1950). However, by the time he starred in *Houdini* (1953) with his wife Janet Leigh, "his first clear success," notes critic David Thomson, his acting had progressed immensely.

He won his first serious recognition as a skilled dramatic actor in *Sweet Smell of Success* (1957) with co-star Burt Lancaster. The following year he was nominated for an Oscar for Best Actor in another drama, *The Defiant Ones*

(1958). Curtis then gave what many believe was his best acting, in a completely different role, the comedy *Some Like It Hot* (1959). Thomson calls it an "outrageous film," and it was voted the number one funniest film in history from a survey done by the American Film Institute. It costarred Jack Lemmon and Marilyn Monroe, and was directed by Billy Wilder. That was followed by Blake Edwards' comedy *Operation Petticoat* (1959) with Cary Grant. They were both "frantic comedies," and displayed "his impeccable comic timing." He often collaborated with Edwards on later films.

His most significant serious part came in 1968 when he starred in the true-life drama *The Boston Strangler*, which some consider his "last major film role." The part reinforced his reputation as a serious actor with his "chilling portrayal" of serial killer Albert DeSalvo. He gained thirty pounds and had his face "rebuilt" with a false nose to look like the real DeSalvo.

One of his better television roles was as casino owner Phillip Roth on *Vega$* (1978-1981) with Robert Urich.

Curtis was the father of actresses Jamie Lee Curtis and Kelly Curtis by his first wife, actress Janet Leigh.

He was the host of *Hollywood Babylon* (1992), a half-hour documentary/gossip program where he also told about his early years in Hollywood.

Curtis nearly died when he contracted pneumonia in December 2006 and was in a coma for several days. As a result he used a wheelchair and could only walk short distances.

On July 8, 2010, Curtis, who suffered from chronic obstructive pulmonary disease (COPD), was hospitalized in Las Vegas after suffering an asthma attack during a book signing engagement in Henderson, Nevada at Costco.

Curtis died at his Henderson, Nevada home on September 29, 2010, of a cardiac arrest. In a release to the Associated Press, his daughter, actress Jamie Lee Curtis, stated:

"My father leaves behind a legacy of great performances in movies and in his paintings and assemblages. He leaves behind children and their families who loved him and respected him and a wife and in-laws who were devoted to him. He also leaves behind fans all over the world. He will be greatly missed".

Richard Cutting

Richard Cutting with Audie Murphy in *Whispering Smith*

Richard Cutting was born October 31, 1912, in Arlington, Massachusetts, and was an American character actor. He appeared in ninety-nine films and television programs from 1953 to 1967.

In the 1950s Richard Cutting derived fame as "Manners," a tiny butler in a Bowler derby hat in a series of commercials for Kleenex Napkins. By trick photography he appeared to be about only inches in height and would manifest under a dinner table in a traditional butler's cutaway. A paper napkin was always slipping off the lap of a diner, giving Manners the opportunity, after a polite "ahem," to inform the guest of the non-slip benefit of the Kleenex napkin.

Some of his non-commercial roles were *Law and Order* (1953), *The Great Jesse James Raid* (1953), *The Man from the Alamo* (1953), *Hopalong Cassidy* (1954), *Shotgun* (1955), *The Private War of Major Benson* (1955), *The Fastest Gun Alive* (1956), *Showdown at Abilene* (1956), *Attack of the Crab Monsters* (1957), *South Pacific* (1958), as Banker Curtis in *Ride a Crooked Trail* (1958) with Audie Murphy, *The Horse Soldiers* (1959), *Wichita Town* (1960), as Banker Gallager in *Whispering Smith* (1961) again with Audie Murphy, *The Legend of Jesse James* (1965-1966), *The Green Hornet* (1966), and *Ride to Hangman's Tree* (1967).

He died March 7, 1972, at age 59 in Woodland Hills, Los Angeles, California.

Audrey Dalton

Audrey Dalton was born January 21, 1934, in Dublin, Ireland. She knew right from childhood that she wanted to be an actress: She appeared in school plays and after the family's move to London applied to the Royal Academy of Dramatic Art. While Dalton was at RADA, a London-based Paramount executive saw her in a play and asked her to audition for the upcoming film *The Girls of Pleasure Island* (1953).

Winning the part (and a Paramount contract), Dalton arrived in the U.S. in 1952 and co-starred in *The Girls of Pleasure Island*; the studio loaned her out to 20th Century-Fox for *My Cousin Rachel* (1952) and *Titanic* (1953).

Dalton later freelanced, working in films and on TV, such as *Drum Beat* (1954) with Alan Ladd, *The Monster That Challenged the World* (1957), *Bat Masterson* (1958-1961), *Whispering Smith* (1961) with Audie Murphy, *Thriller* (1960-1962), *Gunsmoke* (1963), *Wagon Train* (1958-1964), *The Big Valley* (1965-1966), *Family Affair*, (1967), and *Police Woman* (1974-1978).

Her first husband was assistant director James H. Brown, who is the father of her five children; she is now married to a retired engineer.

Royal Dano

Audie Murphy and Royal Dano in *Posse from Hell*

Royal Edward Dano was born November 16, 1922, and was an American film and television character actor. Dano was born in New York City to Mary Josephine, an Irish immigrant, and Caleb Edward Dano, a printer for newspapers. He left home at the age of twelve and at various intervals, lived in Florida, Texas, and California. After reaching an agreement with his father, he agreed to continue his education, on the condition that he be allowed to travel. He was a Mason and a member of Al Malaikah Shrine in Los Angeles, Ca. Dano is remembered for his supporting roles in a number of 1950s westerns and mystery films. In "Mr. Lincoln", a five-part TV episode appearing in 1952-53 on *Omnibus*, Royal Dano very convincingly portrayed Lincoln.

He often worked with Anthony Mann and James Stewart. He played Elijah in John Huston's film version of *Moby Dick*, memorably intoning to Richard Basehart as Ishmael. In *The 7 Faces of Dr. Lao* (1964), he portrayed Carey.

He appeared with Audie Murphy in *The Red Badge of Courage* (1951), *Posse From Hell* (1961), and *Gunpoint* (1966).

Over the years, Dano made many television appearances, specializing in bizarre, macabre roles.

On December 2, 1957, Dano appeared as Wilbur English, a fearful man who kills a fellow gang member to collect the reward in the episode "Cheyenne Express" of John Payne's *The Restless Gun*. Ultimately, his cowardice causes Wilbur's own accidental death.

In the MGM Technicolor widescreen religious epic *King of Kings* (1961), Dano played the role of Simon Peter.

In 1962, he guest starred on the CBS anthology series *The Lloyd Bridges Show*. In the 1965-1966 season, he guest starred on ABC's western series *The Legend of Jesse James*. Dano also played an ex-con who became Northfork's pastor in a 1961 episode of *The Rifleman*, an ABC Western series. He appeared on the series five times. Dano was also a frequent guest star on *Gunsmoke*, with a total of thirteen appearances.

Dano was the voice of Abraham Lincoln for Walt Disney's "Great Moments with Mr. Lincoln" program, first presented at the 1964 World's Fair. Disney personally selected Dano, because he felt the actor came closest to the historical descriptions of Lincoln's voice. The "Great Moments" program was moved to Disneyland in 1965, and Dano's vocals continued to be a part of the program until 2001. In 1971, Dano's voice was also used for a revised Lincoln speech in the new "Hall Of Presidents" program at Walt Disney World in Florida, which ran to 1993. In 2009, Dano's vocals were returned to "Great Moments with Mr. Lincoln" at Disneyland in a revised version of the show.

He had a memorable (if short) role as the coroner in *Electra Glide in Blue* (1973), who gets into a loud shouting match with Robert Blake's character. With no spoken dialogue (only one solo song), Dano was memorable as the saddened, unnamed preacher in *The Right Stuff* (1983). Dano is remembered for his comedic performance as the undead gold prospector, Gramps, in the horror/suspense/comedy/Aztec adventure *House II: The Second Story* (1987).

His final roles include Wrenchmuller in 1993's *Spaced Invaders* and Judge Clinton Sternwood in the TV series *Twin Peaks*. His very last role was as Digger Holt in the Stephen King Horror movie *The Dark Half* (1993).

At age 71, Dano died of a heart attack May 15, 1994, following a car accident. He was buried in the Los Angeles National Cemetery. He is the father of actor Rick Dano and grandfather of Disney Channel star Hutch Dano.

Michael Dante

Audie Murphy with Michael Dante in Arizona Raiders, and Michael with David Williams in 2011

Michael Dante was born Ralph Vitti September 2, 1931, in Stamford, Connecticut, and is an American award winning actor of television, films, and stage, and a former professional baseball player who went to spring training with the Washington Senators baseball club in 1955.

As a boy growing up on the West Side neighborhood of the city, he used to sneak into a local movie theater with his friends and watch westerns.

"I grew up wanting to be the sidekick of the Lone Ranger and wanting to follow my heroes," he told a reporter in 2006.

He was a shortstop on the Stamford High School baseball team, and then played for "The Advocate All-Stars" team which won a 1949 New England baseball championship. He signed a bonus contract with the Boston Braves out of high school. His $6,000 bonus went to buy his family a four-door Buick with whitewalls.

During spring training with the Washington Senators, later to become the Texas Rangers, he took drama classes at the University of Miami in Florida. Bandleader Tommy Dorsey arranged a screen test at Metro-Goldwyn-Mayer soon after. His first movie was *Somebody up There Likes Me* (1956) with Steve McQueen and Paul Newman.

He changed his name at the urging of Jack Warner, who thought "Vitti" wouldn't look good on movie marquees. Warner suggested some first names, from which the actor picked "Michael." He chose the last name "Dante" because it had been used by some relatives.

Dante has appeared in thirty films and 150 television shows. He is also notable for spending several years under contract to three major studios: MGM, Warner Brothers and Twentieth Century Fox.

He considers his best performances the role he played in "Killer Instinct" on the television program *Desilu Playhouse* (1959), along with his roles in the movies *Westbound* (1959), *Winterhawk* (1975) for which he played the title character, and *Seven Thieves* (1960).

He appeared with Audie Murphy in *Apache Rifles* (1964) and *Arizona Raiders* (1965) and was in talks to make a third movie with Audie Murphy when Audie died in 1971. The film was to be called *Perfect Target* with Audie Murphy playing a meek corporal in the Salvation Army in the 19th century.

His 1967 performance in the "Friday's Child" episode of *Star Trek* as a member of an alien race, has garnered him invitations to *Star Trek* conventions. He also had a recurring role as the Sioux Chief Crazy Horse in the short-lived ABC military western series *Custer* (1967) starring Wayne Maunder in the title role of Lieutenant Colonel George Armstrong Custer.

In the 1970s, Dante met John Wayne, whom he watched on screen as a child. Wayne had seen Dante in *Winterhawk* and asked him to co-host a charity event in Newport Beach, California, for Wayne's favorite charity Child Abuse. That started a friendship between the two actors, and they co-hosted many more events together for the rest of Wayne's life. Wayne had a film project planned for himself and Michael Dante, but Wayne's health declined and he died in 1979, ending the project before it could get started.

Michael Dante is currently the host of a syndicated radio talk show, *On Deck*, previously known as the *Michael Dante Celebrity Talk Show* on which he interviews some of Hollywood's biggest stars. Guests on the program have included Milton Berle, Tony Curtis, and Bryant Gumbel.

An avid golfer, he once hosted the annual Michael Dante Celebrity Golf Tournament, a charitable fund-raiser held annually in Palm Springs, California, beginning in 1991.

In 2012, he told this author that he had written a script for a sequel to *Winterhawk* and was in the final stages of trying to get funding for the movie to be filmed in Canada. The title will be *Winterhawk's Land*.

He is the recipient of the Golden Boot Award, the Oscar of Westerns, in August, 2003, in recognition of his starring and co-starring in film and television Westerns throughout his illustrious career. The award was presented by Dawn Wells, his co-star and love interest in *Winterhawk*.

Michael received the Southern California Motion Picture Council Award in 2003 for the 'best of the best' in the entertainment industry and the performing arts.

Michael Dante received the 'Silver Spur Award' in 2006 for best career achievement in acting from the Western Film Industry.

He was honored with his own street, MICHAEL DANTE WAY in his hometown of Stamford, Connecticut, on Oct. 7, 2011.

Dante and his wife Mary Jane make their home in Rancho Mirage, California. He is a frequent guest at western film festivals around the country. He is currently penning his autobiography.

The January 2012 issue of *Classic Images* magazine Number 439 features Michael Dante in a very impressive article spanning numerous pages with loads of pictures.

He was the most recent Audie Murphy co-star to attend Audie Murphy Days in Greenville, Texas, in April, 2012.

He released his own memoirs entitled *From Hollywood to Michael Dante Way* in 2014.

Claude Dauphin

Claude Dauphin was born August 19, 1903, and was a French actor. He appeared in over 130 films between 1930 and 1978. He was born in Corbeil-Essonnes, Essonne. His father was Maurice Étienne Legrand, a poet who wrote as Franc-Nohain, and who was the librettist for Maurice Ravel's opera *L'heure espagnole*.

Dauphin married American actress Norma Eberhardt in 1955. The couple divided their time between Paris, Los Angeles, New York City, and Ocean Township, New Jersey.

Most of his films were French, but he did make numerous American films and television shows such as *Suspense* (1952-1953), *Studio One in Hollywood* (1951-1955), *Schlitz Playhouse* (1954-1955), *The Quiet American* (1958) with Audie Murphy, *The United States Steel Hour* (1953-1960), *Naked City* (1962), and as the President of Earth in *Barbarella* (1968).

Claude Dauphin died in Paris November 16, 1978.

Jim Davis

Audie Murphy with Jim Davis in *Whispering Smith*

Jim Davis was born as Marlin Davis August 26, 1909, in Edgerton, Missouri. His first major screen role was opposite Bette Davis in the 1948 melodrama *Winter Meeting*, a lavish failure for which he was lambasted in the press as being too inexperienced to play the part properly.

His subsequent film career consisted of mostly B movies, many of them westerns, although he made an impression as a U.S. senator in the Warren Beatty conspiracy thriller *The Parallax View* (1974).

From 1954-55, Davis starred and narrated the syndicated western television series *Stories of the Century*. He portrayed Matt Clark, a detective for the Southwestern Railroad who works to bring notorious gunfighters to justice. His costars were Mary Castle and Kristine Miller. *Stories of the Century* was the first western series to win an Emmy Award. Among the historical figures featured were John Wesley Hardin, Sam Bass, Doc Holliday, the Dalton Brothers, the Younger Brothers, Belle Starr, L.H. Musgrove, and Clay Allison.

From 1958-1960, Davis starred as Wes Cameron opposite Lang Jeffries in the role of Skip Johnson in the syndicated adventure series *Rescue 8*.

He appeared with Audie Murphy in an episode of *Whispering Smith* (1961).

He was cast in numerous films with John Wayne; among them were *El Dorado* (1966), *Rio Lobo* (1970), and *Big Jake* (1971).

After years of relatively low profile roles, he was cast as family patriarch Jock Ewing in the *Dallas* TV series, which began in 1978.

During season three, he was diagnosed with multiple myeloma, but continued to film the show as long as he could. In many scenes as the season progressed, he was shown seated. He wore a wig to cover the hair he lost from chemotherapy. A season three storyline regarding the Takapa development and his separation from Miss Ellie was ended abruptly at the end of season three. The writers had the couple leave to go on an extended second honeymoon (their departure in a limousine in the episode "New Beginnings" was Davis's only scene in that episode and his final appearance on the show) when it became obvious that Davis could no longer continue to work. He died of complications from his illness April 26, 1981 at age 74, while season three was on the air.

The show's writers made the decision not to write his death into the storyline right away. Initially, plans were made to replace him with another actor, but were dropped because of audience awareness, and that no suitable actor could be found for the role to be successfully recast. His character was kept alive for 13 episodes after his death with the storyline that he was in South America drilling for oil after taking care of Ewing Oil-related legislative business in Washington. The episode "The Search" confirmed the character's death in a helicopter crash was broadcast on January 8, 1982. A portrait of Davis in his role as Jock Ewing often appeared as a memorial on *Dallas* after his death.

He married his wife, Blanche Davis (1918-2009) in 1945; their only child, daughter Tara Diane Davis, was killed in a car crash in 1970.

From the late 1970s until his death, Davis was also a voice actor, in the commercials for the American Beef Council, voicing the slogan "Beef: It's what's for dinner". He was replaced by actor Robert Mitchum.

Davis was interred in Forest Lawn Memorial Park Cemetery. For his contribution to the television industry, Jim Davis has a star on the Hollywood Walk of Fame at 6290 Hollywood Blvd.

Rosemary Day

Rosemary Day was born February 17, 1934. She made no films, but appeared in eight television programs from 1955 to 1964. They are *I Led 3 Lives* (1955), *Lock Up* (1959), *M Squad* (1959), *Tallahassee 7000* (1961), *Whispering Smith* (1961) with Audie Murphy, *Hawaiian Eye* (1961), *Perry Mason* (1961-1962), and *The New Phil Silvers Show* (1964).

Edgar Dearing

Edgar Dearing was born May 4, 1893, and was an American actor who became heavily type cast as a motorcycle cop in Hollywood films.

He started in silent comedy shorts for Hal Roach, including several with Laurel and Hardy, notably in their classic *Two Tars* (1928) as the motorcycle cop, probably his best ever screen role. It's been said Dearing was a motorcycle cop in real life before he started acting. Some other Laurel and hardy pictures he appeared in were *Why Girls Love Sailors* (1927), *The Second 100 Years* (1927), *Call of the Cuckoo* (1927), *Leave 'Em Laughing* (1928), *A-Haunting We Will Go* (1942), and *The Big Noise* (1944).

Other non-Laurel and Hardy roles included *The Painted Desert* (1931), *The Lost Squadron* (1932), *The Plainsman* (1936), *The First Hundred Years* (1938), *Blondie* (1938), *Nick Carter, Master Detective* (1939), *Primrose Path* (1940), *Knute Rockne All American* (1940), *One Night in the Tropics* (1940) with Abbott and Costello, *Hold That Ghost* (1941) again with Bud & Lou, *Star Spangled Rhythm* (1942), *Ghost Catchers* (1944), *Bud Abbott and Lou Costello in Hollywood* (1945), *Wild Harvest* (1947), *The Paleface* (1948), *Samson and Delilah* (1949), *The Range Rider* (1951-1952), *The Abbott and Costello Show* (1953), *It Came from Outer Space* (1953), *Hopalong Cassidy* (1952-1953), *Tarantula* (1955), *Sergeant Preston of the Yukon* (1956-1958), *No Name on the Bullet* (1959) with Audie Murphy, *Tales of Wells Fargo* (1961), *The Tall Man* (1962), and his last appearance as the first resurrected man in the *Twilight Zone* (1964) episode "Mr. Garrity and the Graves".

He was still active in films and TV until he retired in 1964. He died August 17, 1974, from lung cancer and was buried at Chapel of the Pines Crematory.

Suzette DeCarlo

No biographical information could be found for Suzette DeCarlo. She only appeared in one film: *A Time for Dying* (1969) with Audie Murphy. She appeared as one of Mamie's saloon girls.

Ted DeCorsia

Ted DeCorsia with Audie Murphy in *The Quick Gun*

Ted de Corsia was born September 29, 1903, in Brooklyn, New York and was a radio and movie actor. He is probably best remembered for his role as a gangster turned state's evidence in *The Enforcer* (1951). In radio, he voiced roles on many radio shows including *The March of Time*, *The Shadow*, and *Mike Hammer*.

He made his movie debut in Orson Welles' *The Lady from Shanghai* (1947) and went on to make a career playing villains and gangsters in 1940s and 1950s films including *The Naked City* (1948), *The Big Combo* (1955), *The Killing* (1956), *Baby Face Nelson*, and *Slightly Scarlet* (1956). He appeared as Shanghia Peirce in *Gunfight at the O.K. Corral* (1957).

In the 1960s, he appeared in a number of television series, including five episodes of *Steve Canyon* (1959-1960) as Police Chief Hagedorn.

He also appeared with Audie Murphy in *The Quick Gun* (1964).

In his last film, *The Outside Man* (1972) with Ann-Margret and Angie Dickinson, his character, the mobster Victor, is killed off early in the film, but he later appears as his embalmed corpse, posed in a chair, holding a cigar.

He died April 11, 1973, at the age of 69 in Encino, California from a heart attack. His body was donated to medical science upon his death.

Sandra Dee

Sandra Dee with Audie Murphy in *The Wild and the Innocent*

Sandra Dee was born Alexandra Zuck April 23, 1942, in Bayonne, New Jersey. She was an American actress. Dee began her career as a model and progressed to film. Best known for her portrayal of ingénues, Dee won a Golden Globe Award in 1959 as one of the year's most promising newcomers, and over several years her films were popular. By the late 1960s her career had started to decline, and a highly publicized marriage to Bobby Darin ended in divorce.

Her parents, Mary and John Zuck, met as teenagers at a Russian Orthodox Church dance. They married shortly after, but divorced before she was five. She was of Polish and Carpatho-Russian ancestry and was raised in the Russian Orthodox Church. Her son Dodd Darin wrote in his biographical book about his parents *Dream Lovers* that Dee's mother, Mary Cymboliak, and her sister Olga "were first generation daughters of a working class Russian Orthodox couple." Dee herself recalled, "We belonged to a Russian Orthodox Church, and there was dancing at the social events."

Alexandra would soon take the name Sandra Dee. She became a professional model by the age of four and subsequently progressed to television commercials.

After having studied at Hollywood Professional School, she graduated from University High, Los Angeles, California, in June 1958.

In a 1959 interview, Dee recalled that she "grew up fast", surrounded mostly by older people, and was "never held back in anything [she] wanted to do."

Ending her modeling career, Dee moved from New York to Hollywood in 1957. There, she made her first film, *Until They Sail*, in 1957, and the following year, she won a Golden Globe Award for New Star Of The Year - Actress, along with Carolyn Jones and Diane Varsi.

She became known for her wholesome ingénue roles in such films as *The Reluctant Debutante* (1958), *Gidget* (1959), *Imitation of Life* (1959).

An interesting side note on *Imitation of Life:* Sandra Dee's character told John Gavin's character "You ride like Audie Murphy", and her character also had pictures of Audie Murphy in her bedroom. Sandra's next picture after *Imitation of Life* was with Audie Murphy in *The Wild and the Innocent* (1959). Also, John Gavin would portray the son of Audie Murphy's Tom Destry character from *Destry* (1954) in the 1964 television series *Destry*.

She later played "Tammy" in two Universal sequels to *Tammy and the Bachelor* (1957) in the role created by Debbie Reynolds.

Her marriage to Bobby Darin in 1960 kept her in the public eye for much of the decade. They met while making the film *Come September* (released in 1961) together. She was under contract to Universal Studios, which tried to develop Dee into a mature actress, and the films she made as an adult—including a few with Darin—were moderately successful. On December16, 1961, they had one son, Dodd Mitchell Darin (also known as Morgan Mitchell Darin). She and Darin divorced in 1967 and Darin died in 1973.

In 1994, Dee's son Dodd Darin published a book about his parents, *Dream Lovers: The Magnificent Shattered Lives of Bobby Darin and Sandra Dee*, in which he chronicled his mother's anorexia, drug and alcohol problems and her disclosure that she had been sexually abused as a child by her stepfather, Eugene Douvan.

In 2000 it was reported that she had been diagnosed with several ailments, including throat cancer and kidney disease. Complications from kidney disease led to her death on February 20, 2005, at the Los Robles Hospital & Medical Center in Thousand Oaks, California.

John Dehner

John Dehner with Audie Murphy in *Cast a Long Shadow*

John Dehner Forkum was born November 23, 1915, and was an American actor in radio, television, and films, playing countless roles, often as a droll villain. Between 1941 and 1988, he appeared in over 260 films and television programs. Prior to acting, Dehner had worked as an animator at Walt Disney Studios on such classics as *Fantasia* (1940) and *Bambi* (1942), and later became a radio disc jockey. He was also a professional pianist.

Dehner had an extensive career as a radio actor, appearing as a lead or supporting player in such series as *Gunsmoke* and *Philip Marlowe*. He starred as Paladin in the radio version of *Have Gun — Will Travel*, one of the few times a show began on television and then was later adapted for radio. On CBS radio in 1958, he starred in *Frontier Gentleman*, a radio Western series that opened with a trumpet theme by Jerry Goldsmith and this introduction:

> "Herewith, an Englishman's account of life and death in the West. As a reporter for *The Times*, he writes his colorful and unusual accounts. But as a man with a gun, he lives and becomes a part of the violent years in the new territories. Now, starring John Dehner, this is the story of J. B. Kendall, Frontier Gentleman..."

Written and directed by Antony Ellis, the short-lived series followed the adventures of journalist Kendall as he roamed the Western United States in search of stories for *The Times*.

Dehner appeared with Maudie Prickett in the 1953 episode "Bad Men of Marysville" of the syndicated Western television series *The Adventures of Kit Carson*, starring Bill Williams. He guest starred on the 1955-1956 NBC Western anthology series, *Frontier* and in the CBS Cold War drama, *Crusader*, starring Brian Keith. He played Sheriff Henry Plummer in an episode of the 1954-1955 syndicated *Stories of the Century*, starring Jim Davis as Matt Clark, the fictitious detective of the Southwestern Railroad. In 1966 he played assassin 'Iron Man' Torres in the "Night of the Steel Assassin" episode of *The Wild, Wild West* starring Robert Conrad.

He delivered two memorable performances on ABC's *Maverick* (1957) opposite James Garner in the episodes "Shady Deal at Sunny Acres" ("...if you can't trust your banker, whom can you trust?") and "Greenbacks, Unlimited." Dehner appeared in *Scaramouche* (1952) as Doutreval of Dijon, and he played the non-singing role of Mr. Bascombe, the mill owner and intended robbery victim, in the 1956 film version of Rodgers and Hammerstein's *Carousel*.

He appeared as Audie Murphy's father in *Cast a long Shadow* (1959). It was revealed near the end of the movie, as Audie's character thought someone else was his father. Sorry, no spoiler alerts here.

Dehner appeared in three episodes of *The Twilight Zone*: as Captain Allenby in the 1959 episode "The Lonely"; a 1961 episode, "The Jungle", as an engineer who receives an African curse; and "Mr. Garrity and the Graves" in the series' fifth and final season.

He guest starred in the episode "Three" of the syndicated crime drama *The Brothers Brannagan*, starring Stephen Dunne and Mark Roberts as well as playing Arvid Lacey in the *Rawhide* episode "Incident at Sulphar Creek" in 1960.

He also guest-starred in NBC's *The Wide Country*, a drama about rodeo performers which aired in 1962-63. In 1966, he guest starred in the episode "Power of Fear" of Barry Sullivan's NBC western series *The Road West* and played the recurring role of Morgan Starr on *The Virginian* (1963-1969). In 1970, he appeared in *The Cheyenne Social Club* with James Stewart and Henry Fonda.

From 1971-73 he was Cy Bennett, Doris Martin's overbearing boss on *The Doris Day Show*. He starred as Enos Straight's boss in the *Dukes of Hazard* (1979-1985) spinoff series *Enos* (1980-1981). In 1983, he starred in the short-lived NBC prime time soap opera *Bare Essence* as Hadden Marshall.

Dehner also portrayed a number of historical figures, including Pat Garrett in the 1957 western film *The Left Handed Gun*; Jean Lafitte in the 1964 episode "The Gentleman from New Orleans" of the series *Bonanza*; Thomas Jefferson in the 1964 episode "Plague" of the anthology series *The Great Adventure*; Dean Acheson in the 1974 TV-movie *The Missiles of October*; Lafayette C. Baker in the 1977 film *The Lincoln Conspiracy*; John Muir in the 1979 TV movie *Guardian of the Wilderness* (also known as *Mountain Man*); Henry Luce in the 1983 film *The Right Stuff*; and Admiral Ernest J. King in the 1988 TV miniseries *War and Remembrance*, his last appearance.

He died February 4, 1992 of emphysema and diabetes at the age of 76 in Santa Barbara, California. His interment is at Carpinteria, California's cemetery.

Albert Dekkar

Audie Murphy with Albert Dekkar in *The Kid From Texas*

Albert Dekkar was born Albert Van Dekker December 20, 1905, in Brooklyn, New York. He was a stage actor from 1927; Albert Dekker was an established Broadway star when he made his film debut ten years later. Tall and with rugged good looks, Dekker often played aggressive character roles, and was memorable as the double-crossing gang leader in the classic *The Killers* (1946).

Dekker's off screen preoccupation with politics led to his winning a California State Assembly seat in 1944. During the McCarthy era, Dekker became an outspoken critic of the Wisconsin senator's tactics, and as a result the actor found it hard to get work in Hollywood.

He appeared in *The Kid from Texas* with Audie Murphy (1950) as Alexander Kain, who has Audie's boss killed, then betrays Audie's character of Billy the Kid. .

As he got older, Dekker, unlike many actors, turned to the stage rather than television, and achieved great success there and on the college lecture circuit.

Dekker's last role, in *The Wild Bunch* (1969), was one of his most memorable: the tough railroad detective Harrigan, who hires a murderous group of bounty hunters to track down and kill a gang of outlaws who've been robbing his company's trains.

On May 5, 1968, at age 62 he was found dead in his Hollywood, California, home. While the particulars of the case were never officially explained, it was finally ruled that Albert Dekker had died of accidental asphyxiation.

Charles Delaney

Charles Delaney was born August 9, 1892, in New York, New York, and was an American actor. He appeared in ninety-four films between 1913 and 1960.

He was originally a motor mechanic and having learned to fly during World War I, he started doing flying vaudeville acts on his return to civilian life before entering pictures.

Through the silent era, the dark-haired and handsome Delaney starred in, produced, and sometimes even wrote scores of low-budget action melodramas, usually portraying a happy-go-lucky entrepreneur ridding society of various ills.

Never a major box office attraction but always a welcome name on a neighborhood theater marquee, Delaney belonged in the same category as Johnnie Walker, Glenn Tryon, and Richard Talmadge. All suffered a decline after the changeover to sound but Delaney hung in there and appeared in another 200 feature films, most often in bit roles, like *Kansas Raiders* (1950) with Audie Murphy and *The Bounty Hunter* (1954) with Randolph Scott.

In the 1950s the now veteran performer added a host of television appearances to his growing resumé, like *The Abbott and Costello Show* (1953) and *The Adventures of Falcon* (1955).

His last appearance was in *The Beatniks* (1960) with Peter Breck.

He died August 31, 1959, in Hollywood, California.

Oscar Del Campo

Oscar Rodrigues de Campos was born Delio Sanoja. He appeared in three films from 1950 through 1966. They were *Caiçara* (1950), *Nadando em Dinheiro* (1952), and *The Texican* (1966) with Audie Murphy.

His role in *The Texican* was memorable as the guitar player who basically sings the movie's theme song while warning Audie's character not to get in the poker game.

No other information can be found for Oscar.

Cyril Delevanti

Audie Murphy with Cyril Delevanti in *Whispering Smith*

Cyril Delevanti was born in London, as Harry Cyril Delevanti, February 23, 1889, sometimes credited as Syril Delevanti, and was a character actor with a long career in American films.

His first film appearance was in *Devotion* (1931). In 1938, he appeared in *Red Barry* for director Ford Beebe who would become his son-in-law. From the 1940s, he appeared in countless small roles, frequently uncredited, in films such as *Phantom of the Opera* (1943), *Confidential Agent* (1945), *Deception* (1946), *Monsieur Verdoux* (1947), *Forever Amber* (1947), *David and Bathsheba* (1951), *Limelight* (1952), *Les Girls* (1957).

In the 1950s and 1960s, he was a fixture of many television series and films including *David and Bathsheba* (1951), *D-Day the Sixth of June* (1956), *Trooper Hook* (1957), *Sabu and the Magic Ring* (1957), *I Bury the Living* (1958), *Jefferson Drum* (1958), *Alcoa Presents: One Step Beyond* (1960), *Whispering Smith* (1961) with Audie Murphy, *Twilight Zone* (1961-1963), *My Favorite Martian* (1964), *The Night of the Iguana* (1964), *The Fugitive* (1964), *The Greatest Story Ever Told* (1965), *Mission: Impossible* (1966), *The Killing of Sister George* (1968), *Macho Callahan* (1970), *Rod Serling's Night Gallery* (1972), *Soylent Green* (1973), and *Black Eye* (1974).

He was nominated for a Golden Globe Award as Best Supporting Actor in *The Night of the Iguana* (1964).

He died December 13, 1975, in Hollywood, California, of lung cancer. His interment was in Glendale's Forest Lawn Memorial Park Cemetery.

Pilar Del Ray

Pilar Del Ray was born Pilar Bouzas May 26, 1929, in Fort Worth, Texas. She attended M. G. Ellis Elementary School and J. P. Elder Jr. High in Fort Worth, Texas. She was eleven when she and her parents left Fort Worth for Hollywood. She attended Hollywood High School, before getting the acting bug and she made her first appearance at the age of twenty in *Illegal Entry* (1949).

A year later she appeared with Audie Murphy in *The Kid from Texas* (1950) as Marguarita.

She continued getting roles in films like *Border River* (1954) and *Black Horse Canyon* (1954) with Joel McCrea.

She appeared in such television programs as *The Adventures of Kit Carson* (1951-1953), *Hopalong Cassidy* (1953), *Have Gun - Will Travel* (1959), *Dragnet* (1968-1969), *Marcus Welby, M.D.* (1973-1974), and *Hart to Hart* (1984).

Her last appearance was in *The Forbidden dance* (1990).

Terence DeMarney

Terence DeMarney with Audie Murphy in *Whispering Smith*

Terence DeMarney was born March 1, 1908, in London, England. He was a gaunt, emaciated-looking British character actor, who enjoyed a lengthy career on the stage, both as an actor and as a director. By the age of 19, he was already a noted writer and producer of plays.

De Marney made his theatrical debut in London in 1923. His first major role was as Jim Hawkins in "Treasure Island". For the next eight years, he went on tour with "The Last of Mrs. Cheyney", "Journey's End" and "The Lady of the Camelias". In 1931, he started to direct plays at the Connaught Theatre in Worthing and in the following year, co-founded the Independent Theatre Club (formerly the Kingsway Theatre) with his brother, Derrick De Marney, as an outlet for works banned for various reasons by the Lord Chamberlain. His next important part was that of Tybalt in "Romeo and Juliet" at the Open Air Theatre in 1934, which marked the beginning of a tendency towards villainous or, at least, antagonistic portrayals.

In the 1930's, he acted in a variety of thrillers and Victorian mysteries, ranging from Agatha Christie's "Dear Murderer" to Daphne Du Maurier's "Trilby". He also co-wrote (in conjunction with Percy Robinson) several mystery plays, the most successful of which, "The Crime of Margaret Foley", ran for 210 performances at the Comedy Theatre in 1947 (with De Marney himself in the cast). Another, *Wanted for Murder* (1946), was later filmed, starring Eric Portman and Dulcie Gray. De Marney was also the very first actor to portray 'the Saint' (Simon Templar) in a radio serial of 1940.

After one of his plays flopped in 1953, De Marney went to Hollywood to try his luck on the screen. By the time he returned to England in 1962, he had notched up an impressive portfolio of credits as a TV guest star. This even included a recurring role in the western series *Johnny Ringo* (1959-1960).

For the better part of his remaining years, however, De Marney relished the sinister and the macabre. Some of these include the *Pharaoh's Curse* (1957) and the H.P. Lovecraft adaptation, *Die, Monster, Die!* (1965). On the other side of the ledger is the excellent B-production, *The Hand of Night* (1968), a vampire tale shot on location in Morocco. The film has style and atmosphere to boot and De Marney's performance as the maniacal Omar (henchman to the vampire queen Aliza Gur) is highly memorable.

He appeared in numerous television programs such as *Whispering Smith* (1961), *Maverick* (1957-1962), *The Twilight Zone* (1962), and *Lorna Doone* (1963).

Terence De Marney died tragically, when he fell under a subway train at the Kensington High Street Station in London on May 25 1971, the same week Audie Murphy died in the plane crash. Though he had always looked considerably older than his years, he was only 63.

Nick Dennis

Nick Dennis with Audie Murphy in *Gunpoint*

Nick Dennis was born April 26, 1904, in Thessaly, Greece. The supporting actor, who began in films in 1947, was known for playing ethnic types (usually Greek) in films such as *Kiss Me Deadly* (1955) and the Humphrey Bogart film *Sirocco* (1951), and in *Gunpoint* (1966) with Audie Murphy.

Dennis, who spoke Greek fluently, appeared in a number of television programs in the 1950's, 1960s, and 1970s including *Richard Diamond, Private Detective* (1957), *The Adventures of Ozzie & Harriet* (1960), *Ben Casey* (1961-1965), and *Kojak* (1974-1978). He died November 14, 1980, in Los Angeles, California.

Maria Desti

No biographical information can be found for Maria Desti, except she only appeared in one film and one television program. The one film was with Audie Murphy in *A Time for Dying* (1969) as one of Mamie's girls. The single television episode she appeared in was "The Biggest Little Post Office in the World", of the *Death Valley* (1970) series. She played a character named 'Clara'.

Andy Devine

Andrew Vabre "Andy" Devine was born October 7, 1905 in Flagstaff, Arizona, and was an American character actor and comic cowboy sidekick known for his distinctive raspy voice.

Andy Devine grew up in nearby Kingman, where his family moved when he was a year old. His father was Thomas Devine, Jr., born in 1869 in Kalamazoo County, Michigan. Andy's grandfather, Thomas Devine Sr., was born in 1842 in County Tipperary, Ireland, and immigrated to the United States in 1852. Andy's mother was Amy Ward, the granddaughter of Commander James H. Ward, the first officer of the United States Navy killed during the Civil War.

He attended St. Mary and St. Benedict's College, Northern Arizona State Teacher's College (now Northern Arizona University), and was a star football player at Santa Clara University. He also played semi-professional football under the pseudonym "Jeremiah Schwartz", it was *not* his birth name as has been erroneously reported elsewhere. His football experience led to his first sizable film role, in the 1931 *The Spirit of Notre Dame*.

He had acting ambitions, so after college, he went to Hollywood, where he marked time working as a lifeguard at Venice Beach, within easy distance of the studios. It was in 1933 on a film, *Doctor Bull*, directed by John Ford at Fox Studios, that Andy met his wife-to-be, Dorothy House. They were married on October 28, 1933, in Las Vegas, Nevada, and remained united until his death on February 18, 1977.

Although it was first thought that his peculiar voice would prevent him from moving to the talkies, it became his trademark. Devine told people that his speech resulted from a childhood accident. (He said that he had been running with a curtain rod in his mouth at the Beale Hotel in Kingman, and when he fell, it pierced the roof of his mouth. When he was able to speak, he had a wheezing, duo-tone voice.) However, a biographer explains that this wasn't true, but was one of several stories about his voice fabricated by Devine. Devine's son Tad told an Encore Westerns Channel interviewer (Jim Beaver, reporting from 2007 Newport Beach Film Festival) that the accident had indeed happened, but that Devine was uncertain whether it was the cause of his unique voice. When asked if he had strange nodes on his vocal cords, Devine replied, "I've got the same nodes as Bing Crosby, but his are in tune."

He appeared in more than 400 films and shared with Walter Brennan, another character actor, the rare ability to move with ease from "B" Westerns to "A" pictures. His notable roles included ten films as sidekick "Cookie" to Roy Rogers, a role in *Romeo and Juliet* (1936), and "Danny" in *A Star Is Born* (1937). He made several appearances in films with John Wayne, including *Stagecoach* (1939), *Island in the Sky* (1953), and as the frightened marshal in *The Man Who Shot Liberty Valance* (1962). While most of his characters were reluctant to get involved in the action, he played the hero in *Island in the Sky,* as an expert pilot who leads his fellow aviators through the arduous search for a missing airplane. Although Devine was known generally for his comic roles, Jack Webb cast him as a police detective in *Pete Kelly's Blues* (1955); Devine lowered his voice and was more serious than usual.

He appeared in the classic movie *The Red Badge of Courage* (1951) with Audie Murphy.

He also worked in radio. He is well-remembered for his role as "Jingles", Guy Madison's sidekick in *The Adventures of Wild Bill Hickok*, which Devine and Madison reprised on television from 1951 through 1958. He appeared over seventy-five times on Jack Benny's radio show between 1936 and 1942, often appearing in Benny's semi-regular western series of sketches "Buck Benny Rides Again". Benny frequently referred to Devine as "the mayor of Van Nuys." In fact Devine served as honorary mayor of that city, where he lived preferring to be away from the bustle of Hollywood, from May 18, 1938 to 1957, when he moved to Newport Beach.

He hosted a children's TV show, *Andy's Gang* on NBC from 1955 to 1960. He played "Hap" on the TV series *Flipper* (1964-1965), also on NBC. He starred in a *Twilight Zone* episode called "Hocus-Pocus and Frisby" as "Frisby", a talkative fibster faced with an alien invasion. He was also a frequent guest star on many television shows throughout the 1950s and 1960s, including the role of Jake Sloan in the 1961 episode "Big Jake" of the acclaimed

NBC anthology series *The Barbara Stanwyck Show*, He was Honest John Denton in the episode "A Horse of a Different Cutter" of the short-lived ABC series *The Rounders* (1966).

Devine also cameoed as Santa Claus during one of Batman and Robin's famous Batrope climbs on the 1960s live-action *Batman* TV series. The episode was originally broadcast on December 22, 1966, just three days before Christmas. During the appearance he directly addresses the viewers wishing them a Merry Christmas.

Finally, Devine performed voice parts in animated films, including "Friar Tuck" in Disney's *Robin Hood* (1973). He also provided the voice of Cornelius the Rooster in several Kellogg's Corn Flakes TV commercials.

He continued to be active in films until his death February 18, 1977 in Orange, California.

Richard Devon

Audie Murphy with Richard Devon in *Whispering Smith*

Richard Devon was born December 11, 1926, in Glendale, California, and was an American character actor best known for his roles in television and film.

Richard Devon wanted to be an actor from the time he was in first grade and played a small part in a school production. After finishing high school he answered a small ad in a Los Angeles newspaper for a school that offered training to the novice actor. This drama school, "Stage Eight", allowed him to work his way through, as he hadn't the money for tuition. He painted walls, built sets, waxed floors and strung lights.

It was during this time that he made his first live television appearance for the experimental TV station W6XAO, atop Mt. Lee in the Hollywood Hills. Amidst much additional work in TV, Devon also played a recurring character in the kiddie-oriented tele-series *Space Patrol* (1950) (when Devon asked for a pay hike, his character was put into permanent suspended animation).

He made his first film *Scorching Fury* (1952) and found steady work until he retired in 1991.

Richard Devon's film credits included the 1957 horror film *The Undead* (1957) as Satan, *Battle of Blood Island* (1960), and *The Three Stooges Go Around the World in a Daze* (1963).

He found even more work in television in programs such as *Sergeant Preston of the Yukon* (1957), *The Life and Legend of Wyatt Earp* (1957-1968), *Yancy Derringer* (1958-1959), *Richard Diamond, Private Detective* (1957-1960), *Whispering Smith* (1961) with Audie Murphy, *Gunsmoke* (1963), *The Fugitive* (1965), *The Big Valley* (1965-1968), *Get Smart* (1968), *Planet of the Apes* (1974), *Matt Houston* (1985), and his last appearance on *Midnight Caller* (1991).

Richard Devon died of vascular disease on February 26, 2010 in Mill Valley, California.

Brandon DeWilde

Brandon DeWilde with Audie Murphy behind the scenes of *Night Passage*

Andre Brandon DeWilde was born April 9, 1942, and was an American theatre and film actor. He was born into a theatrical family in Brooklyn. Debuting on Broadway at the age of seven, DeWilde became a national phenomenon by the time he completed his 492 performances for *The Member of the Wedding* and was considered a child prodigy. Before the age of twelve he had become the first child actor awarded the Donaldson Award, filmed his role in *The Member of the Wedding* (1952), starred in his most memorable film role as Joey Starrett in the film *Shane* (1953), been nominated for an Academy Award for Best Supporting Actor, starred in his own sitcom television series *Jamie* (1953-1954) on ABC and became a household name making numerous radio and television appearances before being featured on the cover of *Life* magazine on March 10, 1952, for his second Broadway outing *Mrs. McThing*.

Into adulthood, additional plays, movies, and TV appearances followed before his death at age 30 in a motor vehicle accident in Colorado, on July 6, 1972.

In 1952, DeWilde acted in the film *Shane* as Joey Starrett and was nominated for an Academy Award for Best Supporting Actor for his performance. He had the lead role in his own television series, *Jamie* (1953–1954), which, although popular, was cancelled due to a contract dispute. In 1956 he was featured with Walter Brennan, Phil Harris, and Sidney Poitier in the coming-of-age Batjac movie production of *Good-bye, My Lady*, adapted from James Street's book. This movie showcased the then-rare dog breed Basenji, the African barkless dog, to American audiences.

DeWilde's soft-spoken manner of speech in his early roles was more akin to a Southern drawl. In 1956, at the age of 14, DeWilde narrated classical music works *Peter and The Wolf* by Sergei Prokofiev and the *Young Person's Guide To The Orchestra* by Benjamin Britten. He also, with his *Good-bye, My Lady* co-star Walter Brennan, did a Huckleberry Finn reading in the album *The Stories of Mark Twain*. All three have been released as MP3 downloads.

DeWilde shared an on-screen camaraderie with both James Stewart and Audie Murphy in the western *Night Passage* (1957). In 1958 DeWilde continued his career starring in *The Missouri Traveler* sharing lead billing with Lee Marvin in another coming-of-age film, this one set in the early 1900s. He made a mark onscreen at age seventeen as an adolescent father in the 1959 drama *Blue Denim*, co-starring Carol Lynley, with the then mature theme of abortion, even though the word is never used in the film.

In 1961, Brandon DeWilde filmed an episode for the *Alfred Hitchcock Presents* TV series. "The Sorcerer's Apprentice" had De Wilde playing escaped retarded youth Hugo, who cannot separate fact from fantasy, receiving the aid of kindly magician Victor Sadini at a carnival playing in Toledo, Ohio. The episode never aired on the NBC network because the finale, by 1960s standards, was deemed "too gruesome", but it was included in *Alfred Hitchcock Presents* syndication and thrives in public-domain VHS, DVD and video on demand releases.

He appeared in *All Fall Down* (1962), opposite Warren Beatty and Eva Marie Saint, and in Martin Ritt's *Hud* (1963) co-starring with Paul Newman, Patricia Neal and Melvyn Douglas. Although the only lead actor not to be Oscar-nominated for *Hud*, DeWilde accepted the Best Supporting Actor trophy on behalf of co-star Melvyn Douglas (who was in Israel at the time). That same year, he appeared on Jack Palance's ABC circus drama, *The Greatest Show on Earth* (1964).

DeWilde did a 2-picture deal with Disney in 1964-1965. He first starred in *The Tenderfoot*, a three-part comedy Western for Walt Disney's *Wonderful World of Color* TV show with Brian Keith. The following year he and Keith did *Those Calloways* for theatrical release, reuniting DeWilde with his *Good-bye, My Lady* star, Walter Brennan. Also in 1965, DeWilde filmed a performance as Jere Torry, the screen son of John Wayne in *In Harm's Way* (1965). His character gets killed in battle. After that point, much of his roles were limited to television guest appearances, like a memorable role in *Rod Serling's Night Gallery* (1971). "Being small for his age and a bit too pretty...in his favor as a child...worked against him as an adult", wrote author Linda Ashcroft after talking with DeWilde at a party. "He spoke of giving up movies until he could come back as a forty-year-old character actor".

DeWilde's final western role was in Dino De Laurentis' 1971 spaghetti western *The Deserter*, one year before his death. He played adjutant Lieutenant Ferguson who meets with an untimely end. In a career spanning the years 1950 to 1972 (including five Broadway plays and thirteen movies), Brandon DeWilde made his last screen appearance in *Wild in the Sky* (1972).

On July 7, 1972, the day after his death, *The New York Times* wrote, "The professionals he worked with praised him for unpretentiousness that many found a surprising quality in one so celebrated from his earliest years".

Bobby Diamond

Bobby Diamond, and with David Williams in 2011

Bobby Diamond was born Robert Leroy Diamond August 23, 1943, in Los Angeles, and is a California civil and criminal law attorney who was a child star and young-adult actor, mostly in the 1950s and 1960s. In 1955, he was spotted by a talent-scout and was subsequently cast as Joey Clark Newton on Fury, for which he is best remembered after nearly a half-century, which ran on NBC with from October 15, 1955 through March 19, 1960.

In *Fury*, Diamond's character Joey, who had run afoul of the law, befriended a handsome wild black stallion and lived on the Broken Wheel Ranch in California with his widowed and presumably adopted father, Jim Newton, played by the late Peter Graves, later known for his role on *Mission: Impossible*. Newton's wife and son had been killed by a drunk driver. Joey called Jim by his first name, but in time looked upon him as a father. The late character actor William Fawcett played the housekeeper and top ranch hand Pete Wilkey. Roger Mobley also had a recurring role as Homer "Packy" Lambert and Jimmy Baird as PeeWee Jenks, friends of Joey's. The popular program originally ran after school hours during the week, but moved to Saturday mornings, and was subtitled: "The Story of a Horse and the Boy Who Loves Him." *Fury* reruns continued on the network until September 3, 1966, and later in syndication under the title the *Black Stallion* and as *Brave Stallion*.

The same year he started *Fury*, he portrayed Audie Murphy's brother Gene Murphy in *To Hell and Back* (1955).

In 1961, Diamond appeared as "Buddy" in NBC's situation comedy *The Nanette Fabray Show*. He was thereafter cast in 1962-1963 as Dobie Gillis's cousin, Duncan "Dunky" Gillis, for seven episodes of the final season of CBS's *The Many Loves of Dobie Gillis*, starring Dwayne Hickman and Bob Denver of *Gilligan's Island*, who played Maynard G. Krebs (the "G" stood for "Walter".)

Also in 1963, Diamond appeared briefly as "Pvt. Pip" in an episode of *Rod Serling's Twilight Zone*, titled "In Praise of Pip". He was credited as "Robert Diamond". Billy Mumy and Jack Klugman also appeared in that episode.

In 1964, Diamond graduated from Ulysses S. Grant High School in the San Fernando Valley, then located in Van Nuys but now in Valley Glen. His interest in the law was spurred by his efforts to procure a student draft deferment during the Vietnam War. He obtained his Bachelor of Arts degree from California State University, Northridge, previously known as San Fernando Valley State College. He received his Juris Doctor degree from the University of West Los Angeles, then known as the San Fernando Valley College of Law in Woodland Hills. On January 5, 1972, Diamond was admitted to the California bar and soon commenced the practice of law in Los Angeles. He resides in Woodland Hills.

In an attempt to graduate to more mature and serious roles, as well as break onto the silver screen, Diamond starred in the film *Airborne* (1962) as Eddie Slocome a naive, young, country boy who wants to join the US Airborne Division. The film which follows the course of his training to become a paratrooper was moderately well-received by the public upon release. It was critically panned because of its highly predictable story line and is today almost unknown.

Over the years, Diamond appeared in dozens of television series, including *The Fugitive* (1967) with the late David Janssen and *The Rebel* (1961) starring the late Nick Adams, both on ABC. He also appeared in episodes of NBC's *Wagon Train* (1960-1964) starring the late Ward Bond, *The Andy Griffith Show* (1965), and *Mr. Ed* (1965-1966). He starred with Robert Bray of *Stagecoach* fame, who portrayed U.S. Forest Ranger Corey Stuart, in three episodes of CBS's *Lassie* between 1965 and 1967. Diamond's last role was in Gary Cole's *Midnight Caller* program on NBC in 1990.

On October 21, 2000, Diamond was among the honorees at Iverson's Movie Ranch near Chatsworth in the San Fernando Valley, where he left his signature, handprints, and bootprints in the courtyard. Iverson's is dedicated to preserving the history of film and television Westerns.

Bobby Diamond currently appears at western film festivals throughout the country.

Douglas Dick

Audie Murphy with Douglas Dick in *The Red Badge of Courage*

Douglas Dick was born November 20, 1920, in Charleston, West Virginia and is a retired American actor. He is best known for his role as Carl Herrick in the television series *Waterfront* (1954–1955), and as Kenneth Lawrence in the Alfred Hitchcock film *Rope* (1948).

He appeared in his first movie *The Searching Wind* (1946) and worked steadily in films and television for the next twenty-five years. He appeared in films such as *Saigon* (1948) and *The Iron Mistress* (1952) with Alan Ladd, *The Red Badge of Courage* (1951) with Audie Murphy, *The Oklahoman* (1957) with Joel McCrea, *North to Alaska* (1960) with John Wayne, and *Flaming Star* (1960) with Elvis Presley.

Some of the television programs he appeared in were *The Man Behind the Badge* (1955), *Navy Log* (1955-1957), *Richard Diamond, Private Detective* (1958), *The Life and Legend of Wyatt Earp* (1957-1959), *Hawaiian Eye* (1959), *Sea Hunt* (1958-1960), *Adventures in Paradise* (1959-1961), *77 Sunset Strip* (1958-1963), *Perry Mason* (1957-1965), and *Mannix* (1971) with Mike Connors.

He was married to Ronnie Cowan until their 1960 divorce and to television screenwriter Peggy Chantler from 1963 until her death in 2001. Dick retired from acting and became a psychiatrist.

John Dierkes

Audie Murphy with John Dierkes in *The Red Badge of Courage*

John Dierkes was born February 10, 1905, in Cincinnati, Ohio. He was a tall and gaunt American character actor prominent in a number of classic American films. He attended Brown University and subsequently went to work as an economist for the United States Department of State.

In 1941, he joined the American Red Cross and served in Great Britain during the war. There he met director John Huston, who took a liking to Dierkes and recommended that he try Hollywood after the war.

Instead, Dierkes went to work for the U.S. Treasury Department, which, coincidentally, sent him to Hollywood to function as technical adviser on the film *To the Ends of the Earth* (1948). Orson Welles cast him as Ross in his adaptation of *Macbeth* (1948). Dierkes returned to the Treasury Department, but two years later, Huston called on him to play The Tall Soldier in *The Red Badge of Courage (*1951) with Audie Murphy.

Dierkes took a leave of absence from his job, a leave which lasted for the rest of Dierkes's life. His quiet dignity and distinctive appearance led him to dozens of roles in film and on television. Some of his film roles were in movies such as *The Thing from Another World* (1951), *Shane* (1953) with Alan Ladd, *Abbott and Costello Meet Dr. Jekyll and Mr. Hyde* (1953), *The Fastest Gun Alive* (1956), *The Guns of Fort Petticoat* (1957) again with Audie Murphy, *The Left Handed Gun* (1958), *The Alamo* (1960), *The Comancheros* (1961), *The Raven* (1963), and *The Omega Man* (1971).

In John Wayne's *The Alamo*, Dierkes plays a Scot, "Jocko Robertson", named after Dierkes's own maternal grandfather.

Among his numerous television roles, he appeared numerous times on *Gunsmoke* from 1956 to 1973.

He died January 8, 1975, in Los Angeles, California, from emphysema.

Ivan Dixon

Ivan Dixon was born Ivan Nathaniel Dixon III April 6, 1931, and was an American actor, director, and producer best known for his series role in the sitcom *Hogan's Heroes* (1965-1970), for his role in the telefilm *The Final War of Olly Winter* (1967), and for directing hundreds of episodes of television series. Active in the Civil Rights Movement, he served as a president of Negro Actors for Action.

When he was young, Dixon lived in the brownstone at 518 W. 150th St. in Harlem. Living on the same block were Josh White, Ralph Ellison and the Hines brothers (Gregory and Maurice). He graduated from the Lincoln Academy in Gaston County, North Carolina, and went on to earn a drama degree from North Carolina Central University in 1954, where the theater troupe is now known as the Ivan Dixon Players.

In 1957, he appeared on Broadway in the William Saroyan play *Cave Dwellers*. In 1958, he was a stunt double for Sidney Poitier in *The Defiant Ones*. In 1959, he co-starred in Lorraine Hansberry's groundbreaking drama *Raisin in the Sun*, the first produced Broadway play by a black woman.

He also appeared with Audie Murphy in *Battle at Bloody Beach* (1961) as Tiger Blair.

Dixon went on to television roles on *The Twilight Zone* in the episodes "The Big Tall Wish" (1960) and "I Am the Night—Color Me Black" (1964), and many other series. In 1964, he starred in the independent film *Nothing But a Man*, written and directed by Michael Roemer.

In his best-known role, Dixon appeared as POW Staff Sergeant Ivan Kinchloe in the ensemble of the hit television program *Hogan's Heroes*. "Kinch" was the communications specialist and default third (behind Sergeant-first-class Andrew Carter) in command to Colonel Hogan (portrayed by Bob Crane). Dixon played Kinchloe from 1965 to 1970, making him the only original actor on *Hogan's Heroes* not to remain for the entire series. *Hogan's Heroes* ended in 1971, by which time Kenneth Washington had succeeded Dixon.

From 1970 to 1993, Dixon worked primarily as a television director on such series as *Trouble Man* (1972), *The Waltons* (1974-1975), *The Rockford Files* (1975-1979), *The Bionic Woman* (1978), *The Greatest American Hero* (1981-1983), *Magnum, P.I.* (1982-1986), and *The A-Team* (1984).

He also directed the controversial 1973 feature film *The Spook Who Sat by the Door* based on a novel by Sam Greenlee, about the first black CIA agent, who takes his espionage knowledge and uses it to lead a black guerrilla operation in Chicago, Illinois.

Occasionally returning to acting, he played a doctor and leader of a guerrilla movement in the controversial 1987 ABC miniseries *Amerika*, set in post-Soviet invasion Nebraska.

After his career as an actor and director, Dixon was the owner-operator of radio station KONI (FM) in Maui. In 2001, he left Hawaii for health reasons and sold the radio station in 2002.

Ivan Dixon died on March 16, 2008, aged 76, at Presbyterian Hospital in Charlotte, North Carolina, of complications from kidney failure.

Faith Domergue

Audie Murphy with Faith Domergue in *Duel at Silver Creek*

Faith Marie Domergue was born June 16, 1924, and was an American television and film actress. Born in New Orleans, Domergue was adopted by Adabelle Wemet when she was six weeks old. When Faith was eighteen months old, Adabelle married Leo Domergue. The family moved to California in 1928 where Domergue attended Beverly Hills Catholic School and St. Monica's Convent School. While still in high school, she was signed to a Warner Brothers contract, and made her first on-screen appearance in *Blues in the Night* (1941).

After graduating in 1942, Domergue continued to pursue a career in acting, but after sustaining injuries in a near-fatal car accident, her plans were put on hold. While recuperating from the accident, she attended a party aboard Howard Hughes's yacht. Hughes was taken by her, so he bought out her contract with Warner, and signed her to a three-picture contract with RKO. Domergue then began an on-off relationship with Howard Hughes. After she discovered that Hughes was also seeing Ava Gardner, Rita Hayworth, and Lana Turner, the couple broke up in 1943. She later wrote a book about her relationship with Hughes entitled *My Life with Howard Hughes* (1972).

She later freelanced in a number of films, including film noir *Where Danger Lives* (1950) as a femme fatale opposite Robert Mitchum, with Audie Murphy in *The Duel at Silver Creek* (1952) as a wicked seductress named Opal Lacy, *Santa Fe Passage* (1955) and also in 1955, three sci-fi/monster films *It Came from Beneath the Sea*, *This Island Earth* and *Cult of the Cobra*.

She later made films in the United Kingdom and Italy, and a last sci-fi foray in the Russian film *Voyage to a Prehistoric Planet*, in 1965. In the late 1950s and 1960s she made many appearances on popular television series.

By the late 1960s, Domergue had lost interest in acting as a career, and her last acting appearances were mainly in low-budget 'B' horror movies. She traveled to Rome, Italy in 1952, and lived there for extended periods of time. She moved there permanently in 1968, and remained an expatriate in Rome, Geneva, Switzerland, and Marbella, Spain until the death of her Roman husband, Paolo in 1991. She then moved to Santa Barbara until her death.

In 1946, Domergue married bandleader Teddy Stauffer. The marriage lasted six months, ending in 1947. That same year, she married director Hugo Fregonese with whom she had two children, Diana Maria and John Anthony. The couple divorced in 1958. In 1966, she married Paolo Cossa.

On April 4, 1999, Faith Domergue died in Santa Barbara, California, from cancer, at age 74.

In the 2004 Howard Hughes biopic film *The Aviator*, Faith Domergue was played by Kelli Garner.

Vincent Donahue

Vincent Donahue was born March 21, 1918, in Portland, Maine. He had a very brief career in films in 1948. He appeared in three movies that one year. They were *The Street with No Name* with Richard Widmark, *Beyond Glory* with Alan Ladd and Audie Murphy, and *Joan of Arc* with Ingrid Bergman.

He died February 10, 1976 in New York City, New York, at the age of 57.

King Donovan

King Donovan was born January 25, 1918, and was an American film, stage, and television actor, as well as a film and television director.

His film acting work includes Mack the wrangler in *Tumbleweed* (1953) with Audie Murphy, Jack in the original *Invasion of the Body Snatchers* (1956); a role later reprised by Jeff Goldblum in the 1978 version, Solly in *The Defiant Ones* (1958), Joe Capper in *Cowboy* (1958), Major Collins in *The Perfect Furlough* (1958), and an uncredited but recognizable role in *Singin' in the Rain* (1952) as Rod (head of the Publicity Department).

Notable television roles include Jake Clampett (a deadbeat who mooches off the Clampetts) for two episodes of CBS's *The Beverly Hillbillies* (1963-1967), Blanche Morton's (Bea Benaderet's) brother Roger Baker on eight episodes of *The Burns and Allen Show* (1954-1956), and Harvey Helm in a seventeen-episode stint on NBC's *The Bob Cummings Show* (1955-1958). Donovan also appeared in six episodes as Chris Norman of *It's a Great Life*, a sitcom with Frances Bavier, James Dunn and Michael O'Shea, which aired on NBC from 1954 to 1956.

In 1963 Donovan directed the film *Promises! Promises!*, which received attention as the first sound film to feature a mainstream film star (Jayne Mansfield) nude. Later the same year Donovan directed two episodes of *Grindl*, which starred his wife Imogene Coca and two more the next year.

Donovan married comedienne Imogene Coca in 1960 and remained married to her until his death June 30, 1987 at age 69 in Hartford, Connecticut.

Brian Donlevy

Audie Murphy with Brian Donlevy in *Kansas Raiders*

Waldo Brian Donlevy was born in Portadown, County Armagh, Ireland February 9, 1901, and was an American film actor, noted for playing tough guys from the 1930s to the 1960s. He usually appeared in supporting roles. Among his best known films are *Beau Geste* (1939) and *The Great McGinty* (1940). For his role as Sergeant Markoff in *Beau Geste* he was nominated for the Academy Award for Best Supporting Actor.

When he was ten months old his parents moved to Racine, Wisconsin. When he was nine years old, his family moved to Cleveland, Ohio. He lied about his age (he was actually fourteen) in 1916 so he could join the army. When Mexican rebels under Villa's command raided Columbus, NM, and killed eighteen American soldiers and civilians, Gen. John J. Pershing sent American troops to invade Mexico in pursuit of Pancho Villa. Donlevy served with that expedition.

Donlevy began his acting career in New York in the early 1920s, appearing in many theater productions and also winning an increasing number of silent film parts. Previously, he had modeled for the illustrator J.C. Leyendecker, who produced illustrations for the famous Arrow Collar advertisements. His Broadway credits included *Hit the Deck* and *Life Begins at 8:40*.

Donlevy's break came in 1935, when he was cast in the Edward G. Robinson film *Barbary Coast*. A large amount of film work followed, with several important parts. In 1939, he played the lead villain in *Destry Rides Again* and was nominated for an Academy Award for Best Supporting Actor for his role as the ruthless Sergeant Markoff in *Beau Geste* (1939), although the Oscar went to Thomas Mitchell for *Stagecoach* (1939).

The following year, he played the role for which he is perhaps best remembered, that of McGinty in *The Great McGinty* (1940), a role he reprised four years later in *The Miracle of Morgan's Creek* (1944). In 1942, Donlevy starred in *Wake Island* and *The Glass Key*. In 1946 he portrayed Richard Henry Dana in *Two Years Before the Mast* opposite Alan Ladd, with whom he starred in *The Glass Key* with. He played the role of Col. William Clarke Quantrill opposite Audie Murphy's Jesse James in *Kansas Raiders* (1950).

In 1955, he played the lead in the British science-fiction horror film *The Quatermass Xperiment* (called *The Creeping Unknown* in the US) for the Hammer Films company, playing the lead role of Professor Bernard Quatermass. The film was based on a 1953 BBC Television serial of the same name. The character had been British, but Hammer cast Donlevy, who was born in County Armagh, Ireland, and raised in the United States, in an attempt to help sell the film to North American audiences. Quatermass creator Nigel Kneale disliked Donlevy's portrayal, referring to Donlevy as *"a former Hollywood heavy gone to seed"*. Nonetheless, the film version was a success and Donlevy returned for the sequel, *Quatermass 2* (*Enemy From Space* in the US), in 1957, also based on a BBC television serial. This made Donlevy the only man ever to play the famous scientist on screen twice, although later Scottish actor Andrew Keir would play him two times, once on film and later on the radio.

Throughout his film career, Donlevy also did several radio shows, including a reprise of *The Great McGinty*. He played the lead character in *Dangerous Assignment* between 1949 and 1954, taking the series to TV in 1952. He featured in a number of films over the following years until his death. He also appeared in a variety of television series from the late 1940s until the mid-1960s. In 1957, he appeared in a CBS production of the A. J. Cronin's *Beyond This Place*. In 1960, he appeared as John Ridges in the episode "Escape" of CBS's anthology series *The DuPont Show with June Allyson*, with Sylvia Sidney portraying his wife. His last film role was in *The Winner*, released in 1969.

Donlevy was married three times: first to Yvonne Grey from 1928–36, then to actress Marjorie Lane from 1936–1947, and finally to Lillian Arch Lugosi (the ex-wife of Bela Lugosi, famous for playing Dracula) from 1966 until his death in 1972.

Donlevy died from throat cancer on April 5, 1972 at the Motion Picture Country Hospital in Woodland Hills, California. He was survived by his wife and a daughter, Judy Donlevy, by his second wife. His ashes were scattered over Santa Monica Bay.

His obituary in *The Times* newspaper in the United Kingdom stated that "any consideration of the American 'film noir' of the 1940s would be incomplete without him".

Jeff Donnell

Jeff Donnell was born Jean Marie Donnell July 10, 1921, in South Windham, Maine. A reliable featured player and occasional co-star, she was born in a boy's reformatory. The younger of two daughters, her father (Howard) was a penologist and mother (Mildred) a schoolteacher. Raised in Maryland, she took piano and dance lessons while growing up. It was during her upbringing that she fixated on the popular "Mutt and Jeff" cartoon strip and gave herself the nickname "Jeff".

Studying at one time at the Yale School of Drama and performing briefly in summer stock, Jeff met her first husband, Bill Anderson, a drama teacher from her old Boston alma mater Leland Powers Drama School, and quickly married him at the young age of ninteen. Together they started the Farragut Playhouse in Rye, New Hampshire. Almost immediately she was noticed in a play there by a Columbia Studios talent scout and was signed.

Whisked to Los Angeles, Jeff made her first appearance in the war-era movie *My Sister Eileen* (1942) while husband Bill was hired on as a dialogue director. Hardly the chic, glamour girl type, Jeff possessed a perky, unpretentious, tomboyish quality that worked comfortably in unchallenging "B" escapism. usually the breezy girlfriend or spirited bobbysoxer. Typical of her movie load at the time were the fun but innocuous *Doughboys in Ireland* (1943), *What's Buzzin', Cousin?* (1943), *Nine Girls* (1944), *A Thousand and One Nights* (1945), *Carolina Blues* (1944) and *Eadie Was a Lady* (1945). She also enlivened a number of musical westerns that prominently featured Ken Curtis, Festus of *Gunsmoke* (1959-1975).

On a rare occasion, Jeff found herself in "A" pictures, most notably the Bogart film noir classic *In a Lonely Place* (1950), but more often than not she played the obliging or supportive friend of the leading lady. Unable to break away from her established "B" ranking, she later tried a move to RKO Studios but fared no better or worse. She did make a successful move to TV in the early 1950s and was seen in a number of comedy and dramatic parts.

Long separated from and finally divorcing her first husband in 1953, she married actor Aldo Ray, who was an up-and-rising film star at the time, in 1954 but the marriage crumbled within two years, beset by drinking problems. She also suffered a miscarriage during that marriage. Jeff went on to marry and divorce two more times.

As the 1950s rolled on she earned steady work in films, like *The Guns of Fort Petticoat* (1957) with Audie Murphy, and on TV bringing to life comedian George Gobel's often-mentioned wife Alice on the sitcom *The George Gobel Show* (1954) for four seasons. She also had the opportunity to play Gidget's mom in a couple of the popular lightweight movies of the early 1960s: *Gidget Goes Hawaiian* (1961) and *Gidget Goes to Rome* (1963).

Most daytime fans will remember Jeff's long-running stint on the soap drama General Hospital (1980-1988) as Stella Fields, the Quartermain housekeeper. Dogged by ill health in later years (including a serious bout with Addison's disease), Jeff died peacefully of a heart attack in her sleep April 11, 1988, in Hollywood, California, at age 66.

Ann Doran

Ann Lee Doran was born July 28, 1911, in Amarillo, Texas, and was an American character actress. She began acting at the age of four. She appeared in hundreds of silent films under assumed names to keep her father's family from finding out about her work. Rarely in a featured role, with the exceptions of Jean Andrews in *Rio Grande* (1938) and James Dean's dominating mother in *Rebel Without a Cause* (1955), Doran appeared in more than 500 motion pictures and 1,000 episodes of television shows.

Doran worked as a stand-in, then bit player, then incidental supporting player. By 1938 she was under contract to Columbia Pictures, where the company policy was to use the members of its stock company as often as possible. Thus, Doran appears in Columbia's serials, such as *The Spider's Web* (1938) and *Flying G-Men* (1939), short subjects including those of The Three Stooges, Charley Chase, Andy Clyde, and Harry Langdon, B features including the *Blondie*, *Five Little Peppers*, and *Ellery Queen* series, and major feature films. She became a favorite of Columbia director Frank Capra and appears in many of his productions. Most of these appearances were supporting roles, although she did play leads in Columbia's Charley Chase comedies of 1938-40.

When Columbia launched the boy-and-his-dog *Rusty* series in 1945, Doran was cast and prominently featured. Although the actor playing the boy's father changed several times, Doran continued constant as the boy's mother. Her steady, sensible maternal roles led to her being cast as James Dean's mother in *Rebel Without a Cause*.

She also appeared as Ma Calvert in *Cast a Long Shadow* (1959) with Audie Murphy.

In 1960, she was cast as Martha Brown, the mother of horse rider Velvet Brown (played by Lori Martin) in the NBC family drama *National Velvet*. Several years later, she appeared in the 1965-66 season of the thirty-four-episode ABC western series *The Legend of Jesse James* as Zerelda James Samuel, the mother of Jesse and Frank James.

Doran continued to work in movies and television until shortly before her death of natural causes September 19, 2000, at the age of 89.

John Doucette

Audie Murphy with John Doucette in *Destry*

John Doucette was born January 21, 1921, in Brockton, Massachusetts, and was a film character actor. He was a balding, husky man remembered for playing mob muscle and western bad guys in movies. He appeared in some 260 movies and television programs, with about sixty early appearances being uncredited.

Doucette progressed to dramatic roles including a small part as an architect in *The Fountainhead* in (1949) and the 1970 epic *Patton* when he played 3rd Infantry Division Commander Maj. Gen. Lucian K. Truscott.

His other notable performances included bit parts in *Sierra* (1950) and *Destry* (1954) both with Audie Murphy, *High Noon* (1952), *The Robe* (1953), and the mega-budget *Cleopatra* (1963). More familiarly, Doucette appeared in the John Wayne films *True Grit* (1969), *The Sons of Katie Elder* (1965), and *Big Jake* (1971).

Many baby boomers first saw John Doucette as the bad guy in several episodes of *The Lone Ranger* (1949-1955), a natural role considering his rough looks, commanding presence, and skill with a gun. He was considered by many to be one of the fastest draws in Hollywood. His roles, however, went well beyond that stereotype.

Twice Doucette played the Apache Chief Geronimo: (1) the 1958 episode "Geronimo" of the Pat Conway western series *Tombstone Territory*, and (2) in the 1961 episode "Gamble with Death" of the western anthology, *Death Valley Days*. In both programs, his co-star was the character actor Tom Greenway.

He had roles in other memorable films such as *Winchester '73* (1950), *Broken Arrow* (1950), *The Texas Rangers* (1951, *Carbine Williams* (1952), *The San Francisco Story* (1952), *The Wild One* (1953), *River of No Return* (1954), *The Far Country* (1954), *The Fastest Gun Alive* (1956), *The Burning Hills* (1956), *The Big Land* (1957), *Paradise, Hawaiian Style* (1966), *Nevada Smith* (1966), and *The Fastest Guitar Alive* (1967).

Some more of his appearances in television programs include *The Range Rider* (1951-1953), *The Gene Autry Show* (1950-1953), *The Adventures of Kit Carson* (1953), *The Cisco Kid* (1953), *The Roy Rogers Show* (1952-1954), *The Lone Wolf* (1954-1955), *Four Star Playhouse* (1954-1955), *Annie Oakley* (1954-1955), *Adventures of Superman* (1952-1955), *Science Fiction Theatre* (1955-1956), *Schlitz Playhouse* (1955-1957), *Richard Diamond, Private Detective* (1957), *Have Gun - Will Travel* (1958-1959), *The Adventures of Ozzie & Harriet* (1958-1959), seventy-eight episodes of *Lock Up* (1959-1961), *Tales of Wells Fargo* (1957-1962), *Wagon Train* (1961-1965), *The Wild Wild West* (1966-1967), *Get Smart* (1968-1969), *The Virginian* (1965-1969), twenty episodes of *The Partners* (1971-1972), *Harry O* (1974), *Kolchak: The Night Stalker* (1974), and *How the West Was Won* (1977).

John Doucette died August 16, 1994, at age 73 in Banning, California. His mausoleum is in Culver City, California's Holy Cross Cemetery.

Johnny Downs

Johnny Downs was born John Morey Downs in Brooklyn, New York, October 10, 1913, and was an American actor. Son of a naval aviator, he was taken to Hollywood in 1921 when his father was transferred to the San Diego naval base. He began his career as a child actor, most notably playing Johnny in the *Our Gang* short series from 1923 to 1926. He remained active in films, television, and theatre up through the early 1960s.

Following his stint with *Our Gang*, Downs stayed with the short-subject series until 1927, appearing in twenty-four two-reelers in various roles. He honed his dancing and singing skills on the vaudeville stage, working prominently on Broadway until returning to Hollywood in 1934.

Downs became a fixture of the "college musical" movie cycle of the late 1930s, usually cast as a team captain or a cheerleader. His movie career declined just after he returned to Hal Roach to star in a forty-five minute streamliner feature, *All-American Co-Ed* (1941).

From then on he mainly walked the boards in vaudeville, summer stock, and one solid Broadway hit "Are You With It". One of his outstanding cameo appearances is his performance in *Rhapsody in Blue* (1945) where he dances to Robert Alda's piano playing of "Swanee".

Downs made a short comeback in doing bit parts in the early 1950s, such as *Column South* (1953) with Audie Murphy. Despite never making it big, he has almost 100 movie credits to his name.

In the 1950s and early 1960s he hosted a local, after-school kids' television show, *The Johnny Downs Show* on Channel 10 "KOGO" in San Diego, California (KOGO was KFSD prior to 1961). The theme started out as an airport hangar with Downs playing a former World War II, "Johnny Jet". In between reruns of *The Little Rascals*, Downs entertained and informed his studio audiences and his viewers. After that, it was trains, and he could be seen getting off or on a locomotive at the start and end of a show. As the show changed to feature more *Popeye* cartoons, his theme changed from being a train engineer to being a boat captain at the San Diego harbor. Regardless of the theme, Johnny Downs was always a big star to the kids of the area and was always a draw when he appeared at contests, festivals, parades, or other events.

Johnny Downs died June 6, 1994, in Coronado, California, at age 80.

Charles Drake

Audie Murphy with Charles Drake

Charles Drake was born Charles Rupert October 2, 1917, in New York City, New York. He graduated from Nichols College in 1937 and initially became a salesman before switching to acting in 1939 and appearing in little theater productions. He changed his stage name to the more suitable Charles Drake and in the late 1930s managed to snag a contract with Warner Brothers.

Drake started apprenticing in small, often unbilled roles in what would become enduring WWII-era classics: *The Hunchback of Notre Dame* (1939), *The Maltese Falcon* (1941), *The Man Who Came to Dinner* (1942), *Now, Voyager* (1942), *Sergeant York* (1941), *I Wanted Wings* (1941) with Veronica Lake, and *Yankee Doodle Dandy* (1942), but did not rise suitably in billing rank during that time. Military service interrupted his career in 1943, but he returned to Hollywood within a couple of years sans his Warner's contract.

Following a slight lull in the freelancing department, he was finally picked up by Universal and actually found better work in still somewhat standardized roles. He played Dr. Sanderson in *Harvey* (1950), the hero in *You Never Can Tell* (1951), and Shelley Winters' cowardly boyfriend in *Winchester '73* (1950), among others.

He also became a top supporting player in the westerns and war pictures of Audie Murphy, who became a good friend offstage. The Audie Murphy films he appeared in were *Gunsmoke* (1953), *To Hell and Back* (1955), *Walk the Proud Land* (1956), *No Name on the Bullet* (1959), and *Showdown* (1963).

Other memorable films roles continued in movies such as the town sheriff in the superb cult classic *It Came from Outer Space* (1953), *The Lone Hand* (1953), *Four Guns to the Border* (1954), *All That Heaven Allows* (1955), *Tammy Tell Me True* (1961), and *Valley of the Dolls* (1967).

In 1955, Drake turned to television as one of the stock-company players on *Robert Montgomery Presents* (1950) and several years later became the host of the weekly British TV espionage series *Rendezvous* (1957).

He portrayed Commodore Stocker in the memorable episode "The Deadly Years" of *Star Trek* (1967) where he took command of the *Enterprise* when Captain Kirk, Spock, Scotty, Bones, etc. rapidly aged.

Although he played in over eighty films (mostly dramatic fare) between the years 1939 and 1975, he did not become a star. He continued on as a rather unobtrusive character actor in the 1960s while showing up occasionally as assorted high-rankers in such films as *The Arrangement* (1969) and *The Seven Minutes* (1971). He finished off his career on TV before retiring.

Charles Drake died September 10, 1994, in East Lyme, Connecticut, at age 76.

Joanna Dru

Joanna Dru with Audie Murphy in *The Wild and the Innocent*

Joanne Dru was born Joan Letitia LaCock in Logan, West Virginia January 31, 1922, and was an American film and television actress. She came to New York City in 1940 at the age of eighteen. After finding employment as a model, she was chosen by Al Jolson to appear in the cast of his Broadway show *Hold Onto Your Hats*. When the show closed in 1941, she married popular singer Dick Haymes and went with him to Hollywood. When she got to Hollywood, she found work in the theater. Dru was spotted by a talent scout and made her first film appearance in *Abie's Irish Rose* (1946).

Over the next decade, Dru appeared frequently in films and on television. She was cast often in western films such as Howard Hawks's *Red River* (1948), and John Ford's *She Wore a Yellow Ribbon* (1949), and *Wagon Master* (1950).

She gave a well-received performance in the dramatic film *All the King's Men* (1949) and co-starred with Dan Dailey in *The Pride of St. Louis* (1952) about major-league baseball pitcher Jerome "Dizzy" Dean.

She appeared in the James Stewart drama *Thunder Bay* in 1953 and then a Martin and Lewis comedy *3 Ring Circus* (1954). She appeared as a madam in *The Wild and the Innocent* (1959) with Audie Murphy.

Her film career petered out by the end of the 1950s, but she continued working frequently in television, most notably as "Babs Wooten" on the 1960-61 sitcom, *Guestward, Ho!*

After *Guestward, Ho!*, she appeared sporadically for the rest of the 1960s and the first half of the 1970s, in such programs as *The Green Hornet* (1967) with Bruce Lee, and *Marcus Welby, M.D.* (1975). She made her last appearance in *Super Fuzz (*1980).

She was the elder sister of Peter Marshall, an actor and singer best-known as the original host of the game show *Hollywood Squares*.

Divorced from Haymes in 1949, Dru married *Red River* co-star John Ireland less than a month later. The pair divorced in 1957.

She died in Los Angeles, California in September 10, 1996, at, age 74, from lymphedema. Her ashes were scattered into the Pacific Ocean.

Tom Dugan

Tom Dugan was born Thomas J. Dugan January 1, 1889, in Dublin, Ireland and was an Irish film actor. He appeared in over 260 films between 1927 and 1955. At an early age his family moved to Philadelphia, Pennsylvania, where he was educated at the Philadelphia High School.

After leaving school he tried three trades (shoe cutting, neck tie cutting and paper hanging) in quick succession but having a good tenor voice he decided on show business, in a travelling "medicine show", then a minstrel troupe before going on stage.

He was a headliner for the *Keith Circuit in America* for several years. He also played in musical comedies in New York and in Earl Carroll's *Vanities*. He eventually became a Broadway comedian.

He started a film career with his first role in *The Kid Sister* (1927) and amassed an amazing 276 roles through 1955. Some of his roles included *Wife vs. Secretary* (1936) with Jean Harlow, *Pick a Star* (1937) with Laurel and Hardy, *The Fighting 69th* (1940), *Captains of the Clouds* (1942), and *Yankee Doodle Dandy* (1942) with James Cagney, *The Glass Key* (1942) and *Star Spangled Rhythm* (1942) with Alan Ladd, *Texas, Brooklyn & Heaven* (1948) with Audie Murphy, and *The Story of Will Rogers* (1952).

He started appearing in television programs in 1952 and made his last appearance in an episode of *Studio 57* (1955).

He died March 7, 1955, in Redlands, California.

Yvette Dugay

Yvette Dugay with Audie Murphy in *The Cimarron Kid*

Yvette Dugay was born Yvette Duguay June 24, 1932, in Paterson, New Jersey. A child model from the age of six months, her parents brought her to Hollywood when she was two and, at twelve, she played Maria Montez as a child in *Ali Baba and the Forty Thieves* (1943).

The exotic-looking child actress, who later took to spelling her name Dugay, proved one of the few to also enjoy an adult career. She co-starred with Vince Edwards as *Minnehaha in Hiawatha* (1952), she portrayed Cimarron Rose Adams in *The Cimarron Kid* (1952) with Audie Murphy, and was an Indian squaw in *Cattle Queen of Montana* (1954), her most visible performance due to its public domain status.

She went on to appear in numerous television programs, mostly westerns, until seeming to leave performing behind to raise a family, following a 1960 episode of television's *Cheyenne.*

She died October 14, 1986 at age 54 in Los Angeles County, California.

Craig Duncan

No biographical information could be found for Craig Duncan, though he appeared in seventy-eight films and programs from 1947 to 1967. Some of his films were *Code of the Saddle* (1947), *Strange Lady in Town* (1955), *Blood of Dracula* (1957), and *Al Capone* (1959).

Most of the rest of his career was exclusively in television in programs such as *Captain Midnight* (1955), *Lone Ranger* (1955), *Tales of the Texas Rangers* (1955), *My Friend Flicka* (1955-1956), *Sergeant Preston of the Yukon* (1955-1957), *Richard Diamond, Private Detective* (1958) with David Janssen, *Mackenzie's Raiders* (1959), *Zane Grey Theater* (1959-1960), *Johnny Ringo* (1959-1960), *Wanted: Dead or Alive* (1961) with Steve McQueen, *Whispering Smith* (1961) with Audie Murphy, *The Untouchables* (1961-1962), *The Fugitive* (1964) with David Janssen, and *Death Valley Days* (1966).

His last appearance was in an episode of *Lost in Space* (1967).

Pamela Duncan

Pamela Duncan was born December 28, 1924, in Brooklyn, New York. Pert and pretty actress Pamela Duncan made brief movie news in the 1950s as a "B" level performer and would be best remembered for her damsel-in-distress participation in two of Roger Corman's cult turkeys: *Attack of the Crab Monsters* (1957) and *The Undead* (1957), both co-starring Richard Garland. She played a dual role in the latter.

Known for her exceptional fresh-faced beauty, she won several local pageants as a bobbysoxer on her way up. Deciding to pursue a movie career, she made her debut in *Whistling Hills* (1951) and appeared in small bits for the most part. In addition to her two prime sci-fi roles, she also enacted the role of Mike Hammer's secretary in the low-budget film whodunit *My Gun Is Quick* (1957)

Pamela was also a decorative presence on many major TV programs, especially westerns, such as *Adventures of Wild Bill Hickok* (1951), *The Roy Rogers Show* (1951), *The Adventures of Rin Tin Tin* (1954), *Colt .45* (1957), *Laramie* (1959), *Death Valley Days* (1952), *Maverick* (1957), and *Whispering Smith* (1961) with Audie Murphy.

She also provided pleasant distraction on crime-solving dramas including *Perry Mason* (1957), *Peter Gunn* (1958), *Mr. Lucky* (1959), *The Detectives* (1959), and *The Bill Dana Show* (1964).

Out of touch for decades, she appeared out of nowhere in the Oscar-nominated documentary *Curtain Call* (2000), a documentary that focused on the lives and careers of the residents of the Lillian Booth Actors' Fund of America Home in Englewood, New Jersey. She lived there for the last ten years of her life. The 80-year-old Pamela suffered a stroke and died at the home on November 11, 2005.

James Dunn

James Howard Dunn was born in New York City November 2, 1901, and was an American film actor. He was the son of a Wall Street stockbroker. He joined his father in his business for three years.

Dunn started his entertainment career in vaudeville before progressing to films at Paramount's Astoria studios in the late 1920s starting as an extra. After a gap where he appeared in stock companies, he returned to films. He was signed by Fox in 1931, making twenty-two films and several more on loan-out.

Dunn made a strong first impression with his first big role, in *Bad Girl* (1931). He went on to make several formula films, including *Society Girl* (1932) with Peggy Shannon and *Hello, Sister!* (1933) with Boots Mallory and ZaSu Pitts. Dunn's other early successes included four Shirley Temple films in 1934, *Baby Take a Bow*, *Stand Up and Cheer!*, *Change of Heart*, and *Bright Eyes*.

The roles that followed did nothing to further his career, and during the late 1930s his prospects were further diminished by a battle with alcoholism. In 1945 his performance in *A Tree Grows in Brooklyn* earned him an Academy Award for Best Supporting Actor, playing an alcoholic, but good-natured Irish father, a dreamer whose presence brought joy to those around him even though he was never a success in the traditional sense.

He then made an appearance in *Texas, Brooklyn & Heaven* (1948) with Audie Murphy. After 1950, he appeared in only three feature films, but continued working in television until his death.

From 1954 to 1956, he appeared as Earl Morgan, the deadbeat brother, always concocting "get-rich-quick" shemes, of the character Amy Morgan, played by Frances Bavier, in the NBC sitcom *It's a Great Life*.

Dunn was married three times. His first, to Edna O'Lier, ended in divorce. He was married to the actress Frances Gifford from 1938 until 1942. He married his third wife, Edna Rush in 1945, who survived him at his death on September 1, 1967 at the age of 65 from complications following stomach surgery in Santa Monica, California.

Tim Durant

Tim Durant was born Thomas Wells Durant October 18, 1899, in Waterbury, Connecticut. He only made four films, his first being the part of the General in *The Red Badge of Courage* (1951) with Audie Murphy. His second film was *Limelight* (1952) as 'music hall patron'. His third movie was *Return to Peyton Place* (1961) as John Smith. His fourth and final film appearance was in *The List of Adrian Messenger* (1963) as Hunt secretary.

He Died December 7, 1984 at age 85 in Santa Monica, California.

Dan Duryea

Audie Murphy with Dan Duryea

Dan Duryea was born January 23, 1907, and was an American actor, known for roles in film, stage and television. Born and raised in White Plains, New York, Duryea graduated from White Plains Senior High School in 1924 and Cornell University in 1928. While at Cornell, Duryea was elected into the Sphinx Head Society. He worked in the advertising business before pursuing his career as an actor. He made his name on Broadway in the play *Dead End*, followed by *The Little Foxes*, in which he portrayed Leo Hubbard.

Duryea moved to Hollywood in 1940 to appear in the film version of *The Little Foxes*. He continued to establish himself with supporting & secondary roles in films such as *The Pride of the Yankees* (1942) and *None But the Lonely Heart* (1944). As the 1940s progressed, he found his niche as the "sniveling, deliberately taunting" antagonist in a number of films noir like *Scarlet Street* (1945), *The Woman in the Window* (1944), *Criss Cross* (1949), *Too Late for Tears* (1949), though he was sometimes cast in more objective roles such as *Black Angel* (1946), *Ministry of Fear* (1944), and *One Way Street* (1950).

Dan Duryea give riveting performances in *Winchester '73* (1950) and its television remake in 1967.

Dan Duryea became this author's favorite frequent co-star of Audie Murphy's for his performances in *Ride Clear of Diablo* (1954) as Whitey Kincade (who died protecting Audie's character), *Night Passage* (1957) as Whitey Harbin (who died after killing Audie's character), and in *Six Black Horses* (1962) as Frank Jesse (who died by being shot by Audie's character).

Duryea starred as the lead character China Smith in the *China Smith* television series from 1952 to 1953; and "The New Adventures of China Smith" from 1954 to 1955. In 1959, Duryea appeared as an alcoholic gunfighter in a third season episode of *The Twilight Zone*, "Mr. Denton on Doomsday". He guest starred on NBC's anthology series *The Barbara Stanwyck Show*, and, in 1963, portrayed Dr. Ben Lorrigan on the NBC's *The Eleventh Hour*.

Other great western film roles came his way in films such as in Louis L'amour's *Taggart* (1964) and *The Bounty Killer* (1965).

From 1967 to 1968, Duryea appeared as Eddie Jacks on the soap opera *Peyton Place*. The last film performance was in *The Bamboo Saucer* (1968).

When interviewed by Hedda Hopper in the early 1950s, Duryea spoke of career goals and his preparation for roles: "Well, first of all, let's set the stage or goal I set for myself when I decided to become an actor... not just 'an actor', but a successful one. I looked in the mirror and knew with my "puss" and 155-pound weakling body, I couldn't pass for a leading man, and I had to be different. And I sure had to be courageous, so I chose to be the meanest s.o.b. in the movies... strictly against my mild nature, as I'm an ordinary, peace-loving husband and father. Inasmuch, as I admired fine actors like Richard Widmark, Victor Mature, Robert Mitchum, and others who had made their early marks in the dark, sordid, and guilt-ridden world of film noir; here, indeed, was a market for my talents. I thought the meaner I presented myself, the tougher I was with women, slapping them around in well produced films where evil and death seem to lurk in every nightmare alley and behind every venetian blind in every seedy apartment, I could find a market for my screen characters."

"At first it was very hard as I am a very even-tempered guy, but I used my past life experiences to motivate me as I thought about some of the people I hated in my early as well as later life... like the school bully who used to try and beat the hell out of me at least once a week... a sadistic family doctor that believed feeling pain when he treated you was the birthright of every man inasmuch as women suffered giving birth... little incidents with trade-people who enjoyed acting superior because they owned their business, overcharging you. Then the one I used when I had to slap a woman around was easy! I was slapping the over-bearing teacher who would fail you in their 'holier-than-thou' class and enjoy it! And especially the experiences I had dealing with the unbelievable pompous 'know-it-all-experts' that I dealt with during my advertising agency days ... almost going 'nuts' trying to please these 'corporate heads' until I finally got out of that racket!"

Duryea was married for thirty-five years to his wife, Helen, until her death in January 1967. The couple had two sons: Peter (who worked for a time as an actor), and Richard.

Dan Duryea died of cancer June 7, 1968, at the age of sixty-one. His remains are interred in Forest Lawn - Hollywood Hills Cemetery in Los Angeles, California.

Richard Egan

Richard Egan was born in San Francisco, California, July 29, 1921, and was an American actor. Egan served in the United States Army as a judo instructor during World War II. A graduate of the University of San Francisco (B.A.) and Stanford University (M.A.), he studied and taught at Northwestern University in Evanston, Illinois, for a time. Having studied theatre, he took a bit role in the 1949 Hollywood film *The Story of Molly X*.

This start would lead to his signing of a contract with 20th Century Fox where his talent, rugged physique and good looks made him a favorite and respected leading man.

One of his earliest appearances was in *Kansas Raiders* (1950) with Audie Murphy. In 1956, he starred as Elvis Presley's older brother in Presley's first film, *Love Me Tender,* and in 1959 was the male lead opposite Dorothy McGuire in *A Summer Place*. In 1960, Egan appeared with Jane Wyman and Hayley Mills in *Pollyanna*. He also starred with Joan Collins in *Esther and the King*. Other noteworthy films include *Undercover Girl* (1950), *Split Second* (1953), *A View from Pompey's Head* (1955), *Slaughter on 10th Avenue* (1957), *Voice In The Mirror* (1958), about the man who started Alcoholics Anonymous, *The 300 Spartans* (1962), *The Big Cube* (1969), and *Moonfire* (1970).

Egan was Rod Serling's first choice to narrate *The Twilight Zone*, because of his distinctive voice. However, contractual issues got in the way, and Serling narrated instead, rather than select any other actor than his first choice.

During the decade of the 1960s, Egan worked extensively in television, starring in the NBC western dramatic series, *Empire*, which aired from September 25, 1962 to December 31, 1963. In the shortened second season, the program was renamed *Redigo* after Egan's character, ranch manager Jim Redigo.

After his series ended, he made guest appearances on other television shows and acted in several motion pictures for the big screen plus in films made specifically for television. In 1982 he joined the cast for the new daytime television political drama *Capitol*.

Egan was a devout Roman Catholic, with a brother who was a Jesuit priest. He met his wife, the former Patricia Hardy, in 1956. The couple married in June 1958 and remained together for almost thirty years until his death. They had five children, including son Rich Egan, the founder of Vagrant Records, daughter Maureen Egan, a writer and director, as well as Patricia, Kathleen, and Colleen.

Egan was respected within the acting community for having helped a number of young actors get their first break in the film industry. One of these young actors was Ryan O'Neal. He worked out at the same gym as Egan, who got him credited work in four episodes of *Empire*.

Richard Egan died in Los Angeles, California, on July 20, 1987, of prostate cancer, nine days before his 66th birthday, and was buried in Culver City's Holy Cross Cemetery.

Jack Elam

Audie Murphy with Jack Elam in *Ride Clear of Diablo*

William Scott "Jack" Elam was born November 13, 1920, and was an American film actor best known for his numerous roles as villains in Western films and, later in his career, comedies (sometimes spoofing his villainous image). Elam was born in Miami, Arizona, to Millard Elam and Alice Amelia Kirby. Kirby died in 1924, when young Jack was not quite four years old. By 1930, he was once again living with his father, older sister Mildred, and their stepmother, Flossie (Varney).

He grew up picking cotton. He lost the sight in his left eye during a boyhood accident when he was stabbed with a pencil at a Boy Scout meeting. He was a student of both Miami High School in Gila County and Phoenix Union High School in Maricopa County and graduated from the latter in the late 1930s.

He attended Santa Monica Junior College in California and subsequently became an accountant in Hollywood; one of his clients was movie mogul Samuel Goldwyn. At one time, he was the manager of the Bel Air Hotel in Los Angeles. In 1949, Elam made his debut in *She Shoulda Said No!*, an exploitation film where a chorus girl's marijuana smoking ruins her career and drives her brother to suicide.

Some of his roles were in films like *Quicksand* (1950), *A Ticket to Tomahawk* (1950), *The Texan Meets Calamity Jane* (1950), *Bird of Paradise* (1951), *The Battle at Apache Pass* (1952), *High Noon* (1952), *Appointment in Honduras* (1953), *The Far Country* (1954), *Tarzan's Hidden Jungle* (1955), *Man Without a Star* (1955), *Wichita* (1955), *Gunfight at the O.K. Corral* (1957), *Baby Face Nelson* (1957), *Edge of Eternity* (1959), *The Slowest Gun in the West* (1960), *The Comancheros* (1961), *4 for Texas* (1963) with the Three Stooges, *The Night of the Grizzly* (1966), *Firecreek* (1968), *Once Upon a Time in the West* (1968), *Support Your Local Sheriff!* (1969), *Cockeyed Cowboys of Calico County* (1970), *Support Your Local Gunfighter* (1971), *Hannie Caulder* (1971), *Creature from Black Lake* (1976), *The Sacketts* (1979), *The Cannonball Run* (1981), and its sequel *The Cannonball Run II* (1984) as Doctor Nikolas Van Helsing, *Down the Long Hills* (1986), *Once Upon a Texas Train* (1988), *Suburban Commando* (1991), *Bonanza: The Return* (1993), and its sequel *Bonanza: Under Attack* (1995).

Jack Elam appeared in *Ride Clear of Diablo* (1954), *Night Passage* (1957), and *The Gun Runners* (1958) with Audie Murphy. The two became close pals off-screen.

In 1961, Elam played a slightly crazed character in an episode of *The Twilight Zone*, "Will the Real Martian Please Stand Up?"

In 1963, he got a rare chance to play the good guy when he played the part of Deputy Marshal J.D. Smith in *The Dakotas*, a TV western that ran for only nineteen episodes. He then appeared in *Temple Houston* (1963-1964) as George Taggart for twenty-six episodes.

Some of his other television work includes *Richard Diamond, Private Detective* (1958-1959), *F Troop* (1965), *The Wild Wild West* (1967), *Hondo* (1967), *Alias Smith and Jones* (1972), fifteen episodes of *Gunsmoke* (1959-1972), *Kung Fu* (1973), eight episodes of *The Texas Wheelers* (1974-1975) as Zack Wheeler, *How the West Was*

Won (1977), *The Life and Times of Grizzly Adams* (1978), *Fantasy Island* (1978-1981), *Webster* (1985), twenty-two episodes of *Easy Street* (1986-1987) with Loni Anderson, and *Home Improvement* (1992).

He had a hilarious role in the short lived series *Struck by Lightning* (1979). He played caretaker Frank of an old New England inn. His character was actually the original Frankenstein's monster! A pity the series didn't last long.

In 1985 Elam played as Charlie in *The Aurora Encounter*. During this film Elam made a lifelong relationship with an eleven year old boy named Mickey Hays, who suffered from progeria. As shown in the documentary *I Am Not A Freak* (1987) viewers see how close Elam and Hays really were. Elam said, "You know I've met a lot of people, but I've never met anybody that got next to me like Mickey."

In 1994, Elam was inducted into the Hall of Great Western Performers of the National Cowboy and Western Heritage Museum.

Elam classified the stages of a moderately successful actor's life, as defined by the way a film director refers to the actor suggested for a part. (He said this on a George Plimpton ABC documentary about the making of *Rio Lobo*.)
Stage 1: "Who is Jack Elam?"
Stage 2: "Get me Jack Elam."
Stage 3: "I want a Jack Elam type."
Stage 4: "I want a younger Jack Elam."
Stage 5: "Who is Jack Elam?"

He was married twice, and had two daughters, Jeri Elam and Jacqueline Elam and a son, Scott Elam. Elam died October 20, 2003, in Ashland, Oregon, of congestive heart failure.

George Eldredge

George Eldredge was born George Edwin Eldredge in San Francisco, California September 10, 1898, and was an American character actor. Although he never became a major performer, Eldredge played in over 180 movies during a career that stretched from the 1930s to the early 1960s. He also had a prolific television career during the '50's. He was the older brother of character actor John Dornin Eldredge.

His father, Rev. George Granville Eldredge was a Presbyterian minister in San Francisco. His mother was Julia Dornin Eldredge the daughter of George D. Dornin, a California legislator and noted Daguerrotypist, and Sarah Baldwin Dornin. In 1922, he married Phyllis Harms, and they had two children, George Granville Eldredge (1924–1998) and Helene Eldredge (1931-).

He was a photographer for the Berkeley, California Police Department, and prior to embarking on a film career, auditioned for and performed with the San Francisco Opera Company for two seasons in various supporting roles as a baritone.

Between 1936 and 1963 Eldredge appeared in 182 films beginning with his role as an English spy in *Till We Meet Again* (1936). He was typically cast as authority figures such as army generals, doctors, and innumerable police officers. However, Eldredge sometimes was cast against type, as in his role as the traitorous Dr. Tobor in the 'B' Movie, *Captain Video: Master of the Stratosphere* (1951).

Arguably his best known film role came in the 1945 cult exploitation film *Mom and Dad* where Eldredge portrayed Dan Blake, the father of a teenage girl who accidentally becomes pregnant because her parents withhold knowledge about sex from her. Although the mores of the time prevented most advertising for this film, it still became the number two moneymaker for 1945. In 2005 it received a National Film Preservation award from the Library of Congress.

Some of his other film work includes *They Died with Their Boots On* (1941), *The Ghost of Frankenstein* (1942), *Sherlock Holmes and the Secret Weapon* (1943), *The Strange Death of Adolf Hitler* (1943), *Raiders of Ghost City* (1944), *Cry of the Werewolf* (1944), *Secret Agent X-9* (1945), *The Bandit of Sherwood Forest* (1946), *The Babe Ruth Story* (1948), *Samson and Delilah* (1949) as The Lord, *Counterspy Meets Scotland Yard* (1950), *The Duel at Silver*

Creek (1952) and *Gunsmoke* (1953) with Audie Murphy, *It Came from Outer Space* (1953), *Demetrius and the Gladiators* (1954), *Spin and Marty: The Movie* (1955), *The Killer Is Loose* (1956), *Gang War* (1958), and *Psycho* (1960).

Throughout the 1950s Eldredge also had a prolific television career, appearing on such programs as *Peter Gunn* (1960), *The Adventures of Superman* (1955-1958), *Alfred Hitchcock Presents* (1958), and *Perry Mason* (1957).

Although he worked steadily for several decades George Eldredge never became a major star. Many of his roles were small and his name was often unlisted in the credits of the films he played in.

His final role was an uncredited part in the 1963 film *Johnny Cool*. He died in Los Angeles, California, March 12, 1977.

Rosemary Eliot

No biographical information could be found for Rosemary Eliot, but she did appear in two films, two television films, and six television series. Her first film was as a dancehall girl in *The Wild and the Innocent* (1959) with Audie Murphy.

She then appeared in television programs as *The Danny Thomas Show* (1959), *Perry Mason* (1961), *Accidental Family* (1967), *The Guns of Will Sonnett* (1967), *I Spy* (1968), and *Bewitched* (1969).

She appeared in two television movies *Three's a Crowd* (1969) and *Run, Simon, Run* (1970).

Her last appearance was only her second film *Mad Magazine's Up the Academy* (1980).

Ross Elliott

Ross Elliott with Audie Murphy in *Tumbleweed*

Ross Elliott was born in Bronx, New York, June 18, 1917, and was an American television and film character actor. He began his acting career with Orson Welles in Mercury Theatre, where he performed in Welles' famed radio program *The War of the Worlds*.

119

Some of his films were *Streets of San Francisco* (1949), *Last of the Buccaneers* (1950), *The Living Christ Series* (1951), *Affair in Trinidad* (1952), *Tumbleweed* (1953) with Audie Murphy, *Ma and Pa Kettle at Home* (1954), *Tarantula* (1955), *Indestructible Man* (1956), *Monster on the Campus* (1958), *Tammy Tell Me True* (1961), *The Crawling Hand* (1963), *Day of the Evil Gun* (1968), *Kelly's Heroes* (1970), *The Towering Inferno* (1974), *Gable and Lombard* (1976), and *Scorpion* (1986).

Throughout his career, he appeared in more than one hundred television programs, including the recurring role of crewman Cort Ryker on *The Blue Angels* (1960–1961), starring Dennis Cross and Don Gordon. Elliott appeared fifty-nine times in a recurring role as Sheriff Abbott on *The Virginian* (1962-1971). He also appeared on *Mr. & Mrs. North* (1954), *City Detective* (1953-1955), seven episodes of *The George Burns and Gracie Allen Show* (1954-1956), *The Gray Ghost* (1957), *State Trooper* (1958), *Richard Diamond, Private Detective* (1957-1959), *Alcoa Presents: One Step Beyond* (1959-1960), *Wanted: Dead or Alive* (1958-1961), six episodes of *Sea Hunt* (1960-1961), four episodes of *Sam Benedict* (1962-1963), *Twilight Zone* (1963), *The Fugitive* (1965), *I Spy* (1968), *Adam-12* (1970), *O'Hara, U.S. Treasury* (1971), *SWAT* (1975), *The New Adventures of Wonder Woman* (1977), *The Dukes of Hazzard* (1980), *Dallas* (1981), and *The A Team* (1983).

He may be best remembered, however, as playing the TV director in the classic 1952 "Vitameatavegamin" episode of *I Love Lucy*, in which Lucy does a commercial for a tonic that is 23% alcohol.

He died August 12, 1999, Los Angeles, California.

Steve Ellis

No biographical information could be found for Steve Ellis, but he did appear in five films from 1956 to 1959, including *World in my Corner (*1956) with Audie Murphy, *Four Girls in Town* (1957), *The Tarnished Angels* (1957), *High School Confidential!* (1958), and *The Big Operator* (1959).

He died February 16, 1966 in New York.

Isobel Elsom

Isobel Elsom was born Isobel Jeannette Reed in Cambridge, England, March 16, 1893, and was an English screen, stage, and television actress.

Elsom usually was cast as an aristocratic lady of the upper class. Over the course of three decades she appeared in seventeen Broadway productions, beginning with *The Ghost Train* in 1926. Her best-known stage role was the wealthy murder victim in *Ladies in Retirement* (1939), a role she repeated in the 1941 film version. Her other theatre credits included *The Innocents* and *Romeo and Juliet*. Elsom made her first screen appearance during the silent film era (she frequently co-starred with Owen Nares) and appeared in nearly 100 films throughout her career.

She met her first husband, director Maurice Elvey, when he cast her in his 1919 film *Quinneys*. He went on to direct her in eight more films before they divorced. Elsom's other screen credits included *The White Cliffs of Dover* (1944), *The Unseen* (1945), *Of Human Bondage* (1946), *The Ghost and Mrs. Muir* (1947), *Monsieur Verdoux*, *The Paradine Case*, and *The Two Mrs. Carrolls* (all 1947), *The Secret Garden* (1949), *Love Is a Many-Splendored Thing* (1955), *Lust for Life* and *23 Paces to Baker Street* (both 1956), *The Guns of Fort Petticoat* (1957) with Audie Murphy, and *The Pleasure Seekers* and *My Fair Lady* (both 1964). She appeared opposite Jerry Lewis in four of his late 1950s/early 1960s films.

Elsom's television credits included *Robert Montgomery Presents* (1951-1954), *Lux Video Theatre* (1951-1957), *Alfred Hitchcock Presents* (1956-1957), *Bourbon Street Beat* (1959-1960), *Hawaiian Eye* (1961-1962), and *Dr. Kildare* (1963-1964). She died January 12, 1981, in Woodland Hills, California, aged 87.

Hope Emerson

Hope Emerson with Audie Murphy in *Guns of Fort Petticoat*

Hope Emerson was born in Hawarden, Iowa, October 29, 1897 and was an American actress. Following her graduation from West High School in Des Moines in 1916, she moved to New York City, where she performed in vaudeville.

Emerson made her Broadway debut in *Lysistrata* in 1930. She made her film debut in *Smiling Faces* (1932) but then returned to theater work. In the 1940s, Emerson was well known as the voice of Elsie the Cow in Borden Milk commercials on radio.

Standing 6 ft 2 in, Emerson's most memorable roles were as a circus strongwoman in *Adam's Rib* (1949) who lifts Spencer Tracy up in the air, a larcenous conspirator in the noirish *Cry of the City* (1948), and a mail-order bride in *Westward the Women* (1952). Her most famous role, as sadistic prison matron Evelyn Harper, in *Caged* (1950) garnered her an Academy Award nomination for Best Supporting Actress. She appeared as Hannah Lacy in *The Guns of Fort Petticoat* (1957) with Audie Murphy. She helped Audie's character train the rest of the women to defend the fort.

On television, Emerson guest starred on the series finale ("The Housekeeper") of the sitcom, *It's a Great Life* (1956), playing a bossy housekeeper who temporarily takes charge while Amy Morgan, played by Frances Bavier, goes on vacation. She also had a regular role as Mother in *Peter Gunn* (1958), for which she received an Emmy nomination, and thirty-two episodes of the sitcom *The Dennis O'Keefe Show* (1959).

Emerson died of liver disease in April 25, 1960, at age 62, in Hollywood, California. She was interred in Grace Hill Cemetery in her hometown of Hawarden, Iowa. She never married nor had children.

Charles Evans

Charles Evans was born 1900 was an American character actor and bit player, active from 1944 through 1968, most often seen as doctors, policemen, judges and generals.

No other biographical information could be found even with his 145 acting credits, which include parts in *Pride of the Marines* (1945), *Without Reservations* (1946), *Beyond Glory* (1948) with Audie Murphy, *Samson and Delilah* (1949), *Colt .45* (1950), *The Day the Earth Stood Still* (1951), *Singin' in the Rain* (1952), *China Smith* (1952), *The Amos 'n Andy Show* (1953), *Jesse James vs. the Daltons* (1954), *Stories of the Century* (1955), *Earth vs. the Flying Saucers* (1956), *The Night the World Exploded* (1957), *King Creole* (1958) and *Fun in Acapulco* (1963) both with Elvis Presley, *Cyborg 2087* (1966), and *Skidoo* (1968). He died in 1968 at the age of 68.

Joan Evans

Joan Evans with Audie Murphy in *No Name on the Bullet*

Joan Evans was born Joan Eunson July 18, 1934, in New York City, New York, and is an American film actress who appeared in three movies with actor Farley Granger. Her first film with him was as the title role in *Roseanna McCoy* (1949), based on the real-life romance between two members of the Hatfield-McCoy feud. She gained the role after producer Samuel Goldwyn conducted a national talent search. She was only fourteen years old when she started work on *Roseanna McCoy,* and her parents added two years to her age so she could claim to be sixteen when the film was released.

Her parents were Hollywood writers Dale Eunson and Katherine Albert. Her father wrote the book *The Day They Gave Babies Away,* which was made into the movie *All Mine to Give* (1957).

She was named after actress Joan Crawford, her godmother. When Evans was seventeen years old, she announced that she would marry a car salesman named Kirby Weatherly. Her parents asked Crawford to dissuade her from marrying, since she was so young. But Crawford, not only gave the couple her blessing, but also had the wedding ceremony performed right in her own house without having the parents present. Evans's marriage to Weatherly lasted, but the friendship between Evans's parents and Crawford ended. In 1984, Joan Evans and her husband signed a tribute to Crawford in *Daily Variety*.

Evans continued to act in films such as *Column South* (1953) with Audie Murphy, *A Strange Adventure* (1956), *No Name on the Bullet* (1959) again with Audie Murphy, and *The Walking Target* (1960).

Some of her television work included *The Millionaire* (1956), *Cheyenne* (1958), four episodes of *Zorro* (1959) as Leonor, *Tales of Wells Fargo* (1961), and *Laramie* (1961).

She retired from acting in 1961.

Leif Erickson

Audie Murphy with Leif Erickson in *The Cimarron Kid*

Leif Erickson was born William Y. Wycliffe Anderson Alameda, California, October 27, 1911, and was an American film and television actor.

He worked as a soloist in a band as vocalist and trombone player and played in Max Reinhardt's productions, then gained a small amount of stage experience in a comedy Vaudeville act. Initially billed by Paramount Pictures as Glenn Erickson, he began his screen career as a leading man in Westerns.

Erickson made his film debut in two 1933 band films with Betty Grable before starting a string of Buster Crabbe Westerns based on Zane Grey novels. Erickson took four years off to serve in the Navy during World War II as a combat photographer. Erickson served as an instructor, was shot down twice in the Pacific, and was twice wounded.

Erickson appeared in films such as *College Holiday* (1937), *Conquest* (1937), *Ride a Crooked Mile* (1938), *Sorry, Wrong Number* (1948), *The Snake Pit* (1948), *Fourteen Hours* (1951), *The Cimarron Kid* (1952) with Audie Murphy, *Abbott and Costello Meet Captain Kidd* (1952), *Invaders from Mars* (1953), *On the Waterfront* (1954), *The Fastest Gun Alive* (1956), *Twilight for the Gods* (1958), *A Gathering of Eagles* (1963), *Roustabout* (1964) and *The Carpetbaggers* (1964).

Perhaps his most notable role was as Deborah Kerr's macho husband in the stage and film versions of *Tea and Sympathy*. He also played the role of Pete, the vindictive boat engineer, in the 1951 screen remake of the famed musical *Show Boat*. Erickson appeared frequently on television, having been cast with Bette Davis and Sandy Descher in the 1959 episode "Dark Morning" of CBS's anthology series *The DuPont Show with June Allyson*. He had a lead role as patriarch Big John Cannon in the television series *The High Chaparral* from 1967 until 1971.

Erickson was married to actress Frances Farmer from 1936 until 1942. The same day his divorce from Farmer was finalized, June 12, 1942, he married actress Margaret Hayes, however, they divorced a month later. He married Ann Diamond in 1945. They had two children, William (Bill) Leif (1946) and Susan Irene (1950). His son Bill died in a car accident in 1971. Leif Erickson died from cancer in Pensacola, Florida, on January 29, 1986, at age 74.

Felicia Farr

Audie Murphy with Felicia Farr behind the scenes of *Hell Bent for Leather*

Felicia Farr was born Olive Dines in Westchester County, New York, October 4, 1932, and is a former American actress and model. Felicia Farr appeared in several modeling photo shoots and advertisements during the 1950s and 1960s. Her earliest screen appearances date from the mid-fifties and included the Westerns *Jubal* (1956) and *3:10 to Yuma* (1957), both starring Glenn Ford.

Some of her other films include *The First Texan* (1956) with Joel McCrea, *Hell Bent for Leather* (1960) with Audie Murphy, *Kiss Me Stupid* (1964), *The Venetian Affair* (1967), and *That's Life!* (1986).

Lee Farr was her first husband, a liasion which produced a daughter, Denise Farr Gordon, (Denise Gordon is the wife of actor Don Gordon.) Farr's second husband was the film star Jack Lemmon; they married in 1962 (while Lemmon was filming the comedy *Irma La Douce* in Paris), and remained so until his death in 2001.

Her later films include the bawdy Billy Wilder farce *Kiss Me, Stupid* (1964) with Dean Martin and Ray Walston (as her husband, a role originally intended for Lemmon), Matthau's daughter-in-law in *Kotch* (1971, Lemmon's only film as director), the Don Siegel bank-heist caper *Charley Varrick* (1973) with Walter Matthau.

She had more than thirty television series appearances on programs like *The Lone Wolf (1954), Zane Grey Theater* (1960), *Wagon Train* (1961), *Bonanza* (1963), and *Harry O* (1975).

After her marriage to Jack Lemmon, Farr gave birth to a daughter, Courtney, in 1966. She is also the stepmother of Lemmon's son, actor and author Chris Lemmon.

William Fawcett

Audie Murphy with William Fawcett in *The Quick Gun*

William "Bill" Fawcett was born September 8, 1894, and was a character actor in Hollywood B-films and in television. His career extended from 1946 until the early 1970s. He is probably best remembered for his role as the cantankerous, rusty-voiced Pete Wilkey of the Broken Wheel Ranch on the NBC series *Fury* (1955-1960), co-starring Peter Graves, Bobby Diamond, and Roger Mobley. He was one of the few actors to have earned a Ph.D. degree.

Fawcett was born as William Fawcett Thompson in High Forest in Olmsted County near Rochester in southeastern Minnesota. The name "Fawcett" came from the physician who delivered him. His father, William Eaton Lawrence Thompson, was a Methodist pastor who encouraged young Bill to enter the ministry. On September 5, 1916, three days before his twenty-second birthday, Fawcett was licensed to preach by the Hamline Quarterly Conference of the Methodist Episcopal Church of Minnesota.

During World War I, Fawcett served as an ambulance driver. He graduated from Methodist-affiliated Hamline University in Saint Paul, Minnesota. Fawcett was decorated by the French government with the Légion d'honneur for his care of the wounded. After his military service, he went into acting, instead of the ministry, first in Canada and then in the United States. He had performed in church dramas and acted so convincingly that his mother would sometimes cry over his characterizations. He performed in repertory theater and stock companies during the 1920s and 1930s.

In 1936, Fawcett procured his Ph.D. in Elizabethan drama from the University of Nebraska at Lincoln. He then became a professor of theater arts at Michigan State University in East Lansing, Michigan.

In 1942, he left Michigan State to audition in Hollywood as an actor himself. He sought a part as a college professor but was turned down on the false grounds that he did not fit the part. Fawcett was a thin, wiry man and filled the bill for the ornery, cantankerous, but fiercely loyal, old coot. Fawcett adopted his stage name when he found that there were several other actors already using the name "William Thompson".

His first film credit came at the age of fifty-two, when he portrayed Judge Smith in *Stars Over Texas* (1946). The following year, 1947, he starred as Nat in *Green Dophin Street* and as Andre the beachcomber in *The Sea Hound*. That same year, he was Uncle Bob in *Pioneer Justice*. In 1948, Fawcett portrayed Judge Hammond in *Check Your Guns* and as a news hawker in *Superman*.

Fawcett's roles continued in 1949 as Professor (He finally got to portray his previous occupational role). He played Hammond, a scientist and inventor, in *Batman and Robin* and as Merlin the Magician in *Adventures of Sir Galahad*. He played Ezra Fielding that same year in *Barbary Pirate* and a judge in *Ride, Ryder, Ride!*

In 1950, Fawcett was cast as Zeke in *Chain Gang*, as Ezra in *Cody of the Pony Express*, and as Wharton in *Pirates of the High Seas*.

In 1951, one of his busiest years, he was Mr. Tuttle in *The Mating Season*, Mr. Jackson in *Mysterious Island*, Old Mountain Man in *Comin' Round the Mountain* with Abbott & Costello, Alkalai in *Cattle Queen*, and Alpha in *Captain Video: Master of the Stratosphere*. He had a good role as Washoe, a ranch cook in *Hills of Utah*.

In 1952, Fawcett played Weatherbee in *Kansas Territory*, the High Priest in *King of the Congo*, Caretaker in *Has Anybody Seen My Gal?*, and was Dr. Rolph in *Blackhawk*, a serial. He had some excellent scenes as cattle rancher Uncle John in *Barbed Wire*.

In 1953, Fawcett continued as Dr. Fairchild in *Neanderthal Man* and as Orin Hadley in *Run for the Hills*. In 1954, he was Rocky Ford in *Riding with Buffalo Bill* and as Old Pickup Driver in *Gang Busters*. In 1955, Fawcett was Cubby Crouch in *Seminole Uprising*. In 1956, he portrayed Jergens in *Canyon River*, Matthew Barnes in *Dakota Incident*, and "Pa" to Andy Griffith in *No Time for Sergeants*. He was also featured in archival footage on the children's program, *The Gabby Hayes Show*.

In 1958, Fawcett was a farmer in *Good Day for a Hanging*. From 1957-1959, Fawcett appeared as Sam Miller, the hanged publisher of the *Wilcox Clarion* newspaper in Willcox (later spelling), Arizona, in the premiere episode of the syndicated western series *26 Men*, stories about the Arizona Rangers, starring Tristram Coffin. He also appeared in the series in various roles on four other occasions.

In the 1960s, the roles in film grew fewer. He was Lester Lonnergan in Meredith Willson's *The Music Man* in 1962. He appeared as Steinmetz in *King Rat* (1965) and as Jensen the Pharmacist in *Jesse James Meets Frankenstein's Daughter* (1966). He was Ollie Jensen in *Hostile Guns* in 1967. He played Tax Man in *Blackbeard's Ghost* in 1968. In 1969 and 1970, Fawcett appeared, respectively, in two Disney films, *The Computer Wore Tennis Shoes* (starring the teenaged Kurt Russell) and *Menace on the Mountain*. In 1969, Fawcett played the key supporting role as Old Man Warner in the film version of Shirley Jackson's famous short story *The Lottery*.

Fury aired on Saturday mornings from 1955-1960. Fawcett played the housekeeper and general ranch hand to Jim Newton (Peter Graves) and Jim's adopted son, Joey Clark Newton (Bobby Diamond).

Fawcett guest starred on dozens of television series. He appeared as "Grampa" seven times between 1953 and 1956 in the syndicated series *The Cisco Kid*, starring Duncan Renaldo and Leo Carrillo.

He also appeared in *The Kid From Texas* (1950), *Gunsmoke* (1953), *The Wild and The Innocent* (1959), and *The Quick Gun* (1964), all with Audie Murphy.

His final appearance was in *The Manhunter* (1972), a made-for-television movie.

On August 18, 1925, Fawcett married the former Helene Krag in Minnetonka, a suburb of Minneapolis in Hennepin County. The union lasted until his death. The couple was childless. Fawcett died January 25, 1974 of cardiovascular disease at the age of seventy-nine in Sherman Oaks, California. He and Helene, who died on June 17, 1997, are interred in Roselawn Cemetery in Roseville, north of St. Paul.

Frank Ferguson

Audie Murphy with Frank Ferguson in *The Cimarron Kid*

Frank Ferguson was born December 25, 1899, in Ferndale, California and was an American character actor with hundreds of appearances in both film and television. His first appearance was in *Gambling on the High Seas* (1940).

Some of his other films include *They Died with Their Boots On* (1941), *Reap the Wild Wind* (1942), *This Gun for Hire* (1942) with Alan Ladd, *The Meanest Man in the World* (1943), *O.S.S.* (1946) again with Alan Ladd, *Fort Apache* (1948), *Bud Abbott and Lou Costello Meet Frankenstein* (1948) as Mr. McDougal, owner of the house of horrors, *Frenchie* (1950) with Joel McCrea, *The Cimarron Kid* (1952) with Audie Murphy, *House of Wax* (1953), *Riding Shotgun* (1954) with Randolph Scott, *The McConnell Story* (1955) and yet again with Alan Ladd, *The Iron Sheriff* (1957), and *The Quick Gun* (1964) again with Audie Murphy.

Perhaps his best known role was as the ranch handyman, Gus Broeberg, on the CBS television series, *My Friend Flicka* (1955-1956), based on a novel of the same name. He appeared with Gene Evans, Johnny Washbrook, and Anita Louise. At the time, Ferguson also portrayed the Calverton veterinarian in the first several seasons of CBS's *Lassie* (1954-1964).

Ferguson also appeared in the television programs *Hopalong Cassidy* (1952), *Topper* (1953-1954), *The Pride of the Family* (1953-1954), *The Lone Ranger* (1954-1955), *State Trooper* (1957), *Zane Grey Theater* (1957-1958), *Richard Diamond, Private Detective* (1959), *Wichita Town* (1959-1960) with Joel McCrea, *Maverick* (1958-1962), *Twilight Zone* (1964), *Destry* (1964), *Petticoat Junction* (1964-1970), *O'Hara, U.S. Treasury* (1971), and *How the West Was Won* (1977).

He also played the role of Eli Carson in the primetime serial *Peyton Place* (1964-1969) and reprised the role in the later daytime version *Return to Peyton Place* (1972-1974).

He died September 12, 1978, in Los Angeles, California.

Margaret Field

Margaret Field with Audie Murphy in a deleted scene from *Beyond Glory*

Margaret Field was born Margaret Morlan May 10, 1922 in Houston, Texas, and was an American film actress.

She was discovered by talent scout Milton Lewis for Paramount Pictures. Following a successful screen test, she was offered an eighteen-month contract. She then attended Pasadena Junior College, studying voice training and acting.

She first appeared in *The Little Witch* (1945), and then landed roles in *Beyond Glory* (1948) with Audie Murphy and Alan Ladd, *Riding High* (1950) with Bing Crosby and Oliver Hardy, *The Man from Planet X* (1951), *The Range Rider* (1951-1953), *The Gene Autry Show* (1954), *Blackjack Ketchum, Desperado* (1956), *Yancy Derringer* (1958), *Twilight Zone* (1963), *Adam-12* (1968), *To Rome with Love* (1971), and her last performance in *The Stranger* (1973).

She married Richard Dryden Field, an Army officer, and had two children by him: future actress Sally Field and Richard Field. The Fields divorced in 1950, and Margaret married actor Jock Mahoney, thereafter acting as Maggie Mahoney. She and Mahoney had a daughter, Princess. Margaret Field and Jock Mahoney divorced in June 1968. When her elder daughter Sally turned 13, Margaret virtually ended her acting career to focus on her family.

She died aged 89, on November 6, 2011, which was her daughter Sally Field's 65th birthday.

Mary Field

Audie Murphy with Mary Field in *Ride a Crooked Trail*

Mary Field was born in New York City, New York, June 10, 1909, and was an American film actress who primarily appeared in supporting roles. As a child she never knew her biological parents. During her infancy she was left outside the doors of a church with a note pinned to her saying that her name was "Olivia Rockefeller". She would later be adopted.

In 1937, she was signed under contract to Warner Bros. Studios and made her film debut in *The Prince and the Pauper* (1937). Her other screen credits include parts in such films as *Jezebel* (1938), *Cowboy from Brooklyn* (1938), *The Amazing Dr. Clitterhouse* (1938), *Eternally Yours* (1939), *When Tomorrow Comes* (1939), *Broadway Melody of 1940*, *Ball of Fire* (1941), *How Green Was My Valley* (1941), *Mrs. Miniver* (1942), *Out of the Past* (1947), and *Life With Father* (1947). During her time in Hollywood she starred in approximately 103 films.

She appeared as Audie Murphy's mother in *To Hell and Back* (1955) and with Audie Murphy in two of his other films like *Ride Clear of Diablo* (1954), and *Seven Ways From Sundown* (1960).

Her TV credits include parts in *Topper* (1953-1954), *City Detective* (1954), *The Loretta Young Show* (1954-1955), *Bachelor Father* (1957), *Death Valley Days* (1958), *Walt Disney's Wonderful World of Color* (1959-1960), *Gunsmoke* (1960-1962). In 1963, she had her last acting role playing a Roman Catholic nun in a television series modeled after the 1944 film *Going My Way* which starred Bing Crosby.

Following her 1963 retirement she was still married to her husband James Madison Walters and lived in Laguna Niguel, California. She also devoted her time to her family.

On June 12, 1996, just two days after her 87th birthday, Mary Fields died at her house in Fairfax, Virginia, from stroke complications where she lived with her daughter, Susana Kerstein and Son-in-Law, Bob Kerstein. She had two grandchildren, Sky Kerstein and Kendall Kerstein.

Eddie Firestone

Audie Murphy with Eddie Firestone in *Joe Butterfly*

Eddie Firestone was born December 11, 1920, and was an American radio, television, and film actor.

An early success was in the title role of radio's *That Brewster Boy*, which he left in 1943, during World War II, to join the U.S. Marine Corps. At the time, he was billed as Eddie Firestone, Jr.

He appeared in hundreds of television shows and films and is best remembered by many for his recurring role as 'Hap' in the television series *Gunsmoke* (1966-1974). After making his movie debut with a minor role in the 1950 picture *The Jackpot,* he had memorable performances in the films *Good Morning, Miss Dove* (1955), *The Great Locomotive Chase* (1956), *Joe Butterfly* (1957) with Audie Murphy, *The Mountain Road* (1960), *Two for the Seesaw* (1962), *Panic in the City* (1968), *Suppose They Gave a War and Nobody Came?* (1970), *Duel* (1971) and *The Stone Killer* (1973).

His other notable television credits include *Dragnet* (1952-1953), *Mike Hammer* (1956), *Telephone Time* (1957), *Black Saddle* (1959-1960), *The Untouchables* (1959-1963), *The Fugitive* (1965), *Cimarron Strip* (1967), *The Big Valley* (1967-1968), *Bonanza* (1961-1969), *The Virginian* (1971), *Kung Fu* (1973), *Mannix* (1967-1974), *Kolchak: The Night Stalker* (1975), The *Rockford Files* (1975-1976), *Charlie's Angels* (1978), *Buck Rogers in the 25th Century* (1979), *Galactica 1980* (1980), *Knight Rider* (1982), and *Dallas* (1985-1990).

He died from heart and respiratory failure March 1, 2007, at age 86 in Sherman Oaks, California. He is buried in Valhalla Memorial Park Cemetery in Hollywood, California.

Paul Fix

Peter Paul Fix was born March 13, 1901, in Dobbs Ferry, New York and was an American film and television character actor, best known for his work in Westerns. Fix appeared in more than a hundred movies and dozens of television shows over a fifty-six-year career spanning from 1925 to 1981. In the 1950s, Fix was best known for portraying Marshal Micah Torrance alongside Chuck Connors in *The Rifleman* (1958-1963).

A veteran of the United States Navy during World War I, Fix became an incredibly busy character actor who got his start in local productions around his New York home. By the 1920s he had moved to Hollywood and performed in the first of almost 350 movie and television appearances. In the 1930s, he became friends with John Wayne, coaching him acting, and eventually appearing as a featured player in about twenty-seven of his films. Fix co-wrote the screenplay for the John Wayne film *Tall in the Saddle* (1944).

Fix worked in early films such as *Lucky Star* (1929) and *Ladies Love Brutes* (1930), and became a regular performer for the film's director, Frank Borzage, on a further eight occasions. Fix later appeared as Richard Bravo in the 1950s cult classic, *The Bad Seed* (1955), and in George Stevens' *Giant* (1956), playing Elizabeth Taylor's father. He appeared as Mr. Feeney in *Night Passage* (1957) with Audie Murphy and James Stewart.

He played Dr. Mark Piper, Dr. Leonard McCoy's predecessor in the second pilot episode of *Star Trek* (1966), "Where No Man Has Gone Before". When NBC picked up *Star Trek* as a series in 1966, Fix was replaced as the *Enterprise* medical officer by DeForest Kelley as Dr. Leonard "Bones" McCoy.

Fix appeared as the presiding judge in *To Kill a Mockingbird* (1962). He played the sheriff in *The Sons of Katie Elder*. In 1966 he appeared in the film *El Dorado*. In 1972 he appeared in the film *Night of the Lepus*.

Fix appeared regularly as District Attorney Hale on *Perry Mason* (1957–1963). He guest starred on such television series as *The Twilight Zone* (1964), *The F.B.I.* (1965–1973), *Voyage to the Bottom of the Sea* (1966), *The Time Tunnel* (1966), *The Wild Wild West* (1966–1967), *Daniel Boone* (1969), *Owen Marshall: Counselor at Law* (1971), and *The Rockford Files* (1978). His last performance was in an episode of *Quincy M.E.* (1981).

His daughter Marilyn married actor Harry Carey, Jr. in 1944.

Fix died of renal failure October 14, 1983, in Los Angeles, at age 82.

James Flavin

James William Flavin, Jr. was born May 14, 1906, in Portland, Maine, and was an American character actor whose career lasted nearly half a century.

Flavin was the son of a hotel waiter of Canadian-English extraction and a mother, Katherine, whose father was an Anglo - Irish immigrant. Thus Flavin, well-known in Hollywood as an "Irish" type, was only one-quarter Irish. Flavin was born and raised in Portland, Maine, a fact that may have enriched his later working relationship with director John Ford, also a Portland native.

He attended the United States Military Academy at West Point but, contrary to some sources, did not graduate. Instead he dropped out and returned to Portland and drove a taxi. When the summer stock companies flocked to Maine in 1929 Flavin was asked to fill in for an actor. He did well with the part and the company manager offered him $150 per week to accompany the troupe back to New York. Flavin accepted and by the spring of 1930 was living in a rooming house at 108 W. 87th Street in Manhattan. Flavin didn't manage to crack Broadway at this time; his Broadway debut would not occur for another thirty-nine years, in the 1971 revival of *The Front Page*, in which he played Murphy and briefly took over the lead role of Walter Burns from star Robert Ryan.

Flavin worked his way across the country in stock productions and tours, arriving in Los Angeles around 1932. He quickly made the transition to movies, landing the lead role in his very first film, a Universal serial, *The Airmail Mystery* (1932). He also landed his leading lady, marrying the serial's female star Lucile Browne that same year. However, the serial marked virtually the last time that Flavin would play the lead in a film. Thereafter, he was restricted almost exclusively to supporting characters, many of them without as much as a name. He specialized in uniformed cops and hard-bitten detectives, but played chauffeurs, cabbies, and even a 16th-century palace guard with aplomb. Flavin appeared in nearly 400 films between 1932 and 1971.

Some of his roles were in such films and television shows as *The Most Dangerous Game* (1932) with Joel McCrea, *King Kong* (1933), *G Men* (1935), *Blondie* (1938), *Each Dawn I Die* (1938), *The Fighting 69th* (1940), *Buck Privates* (1941) with Abbott & Costello, *Great Guns* (1941) with Laurel & Hardy, *Yankee Doodle Dandy* (1942), *It Ain't Hey* (1943) again with Abbott & Costello, *Four Jills in a Jeep* (1944), *The Big Sleep* (1946), *The Noose Hangs High* (1948) and again with Abbott & Costello, *Mighty Joe Young* (1949), *Abbott and Costello Meet the Killer, Boris Karloff* (1949), *Operation Pacific* (1951), *Sky King* (1952), *The Abbott and Costello Show* (1953), *Abbott and Costello Go to Mars* (1953), *Ma and Pa Kettle at Home* (1954), *City Detective* (1955), *Mister Roberts* (1955), *So You Want to Be a Policeman* (1955), *Francis in the Haunted House* (1956), *The Gale Storm Show* (1957), *Night Passage* (1957) with Audie Murphy, *Richard Diamond, Private Detective* (1958), eight episodes as Lt. Donovan in *Man with a Camera* (1959-1960), *Twilight Zone* (1960-1961), thirty-three episodes of *The Roaring 20's* (1960-1962), *It's a Mad Mad Mad Mad World* (1963) with The Three Stooges, *The Addams Family* (1965), *In Cold Blood* (1967) with Robert Blake, *It Takes a Thief* (1968), and *Law and Order* (1976).

He appeared in almost 100 television episodes before his final appearance, as President Dwight D. Eisenhower in *Francis Gary Powers: The True Story of the U-2 Spy Incident* (1976).

Flavin died of a heart ailment at Cedars-Sinai Medical Center in Los Angeles, California on April 23, 1976, three weeks before his 70th birthday. His widow Lucile died 17 days later. They were survived by their son, William James Flavin, subsequently a professor at the United States Army War College. James and Lucile Browne Flavin were buried at Holy Cross Cemetery in Culver City, California.

Jay C. Flippen

Jay C. Flippen with Audie Murphy in *Night Passage*

Jay C. Flippen was born March 6, 1899, in Little Rock, Arkansas, and was American character actor who often played police officers or weary criminals in many films of the 1940s and 1950s.

Flippen was an established and respected vaudeville singer and stage actor before his film career. He'd been discovered by famed African-American comedian Bert Williams in the 1920s. He called himself "The Ham What Am," and performed occasionally in blackface. Flippen attained the most coveted booking in vaudeville, headlining at the Palace Theater in New York, not once but six times between March 1926 and February 1931.

At one time he was also a radio announcer for New York Yankees games and was one of the first game show announcers. Between 1924 and 1929, Flippen recorded over 30 songs for Columbia, Perfect and Brunswick.

His first film, the 1928 Warner Brothers short subject *The Ham What Am,* captures his vaudeville performance, and there are other shorts in the 1930s, but his film career started in earnest in 1947, with performances in such films as *Brute Force* (1947), *Winchester '73* (1950), *Bend of the River* (1952), *East of Sumatra* (1953), *The Far Country* (1954), *Man Without a Star* (1955), *Night Passage* (1957) with Audie Murphy, *From Hell to Texas* (1958), *The Plunderers* (1960), *How the West Was Won* (1962), *Cat Ballou* (1965), *Firecreek* (1968), *Hellfighters* (1968), and *The Seven Minutes* (1971).

Flippen also appeared on television, notably as Chief Petty Officer Homer Nelson on the 1962–1963 sitcom *Ensign O'Toole*. He also guest starred on *Climax!* (1955-1957), *Wanted: Dead or Alive* (1958), *Johnny Ringo* (1960), *Stagecoach West* (1961), *Burke's Law* (1963-1964), *Rawhide* (1959-1965), *Ironside* (1967), *The Virginian* (1966-1969), and *Here Come the Brides* (1970).

Later in life, Flippen continued acting although he used a wheelchair after an amputation. He was married for 25 years to screenwriter Ruth Brooks Flippen.

Jay C. Flippen died February 3, 1971, during surgery from an aneurysm caused by a swollen artery, one month before his 72nd birthday. He was interred in a crypt in the Corridor of Memories section at Westwood Village Memorial Park Cemetery in Los Angeles, near Marilyn Monroe.

Paul Ford

Paul Ford with Audie Murphy in *The Kid from Texas*

Paul Ford was born Paul Ford Weaver, November 2, 1901, in Baltimore, Maryland, and was an American character actor who came to specialize in authority figures whose ineptitude and pompous demeanor were played for comic effect. At a young age, he showed an adept talent for performance, but was discouraged when directors thought he was tone-deaf. However, in later years, he made his hollow, reverberating voice one of the most recognized of his era. His success was long in the making, and he did little acting, but instead raised his family during the Great Depression.

Franklin Delano Roosevelt's Public Works programs provided Ford with work, and to the day he died, he was a passionate Democrat. Ford auditioned for a play under his birth name, but did not get the part. Later, he dropped his surname and was known professionally as Paul Ford.

Ford became an "overnight" success at age 54 when he played Colonel Hall opposite Phil Silvers on Silvers' *Sergeant Bilko* (1955-1959) television show. His signature role may well be the part of Mayor George Shinn, a befuddled politico in the film adaptation of the Broadway show *The Music Man* (1962). Ford played the role straight and received glowing reviews.

Some of his other roles were in films such as *The Kid from Texas* (1950) with Audie Murphy, *The Teahouse of the August Moon* (1956), *The Matchmaker* (1958), *It's a Mad Mad Mad Mad World* (1963), *The Russians Are Coming the Russians Are Coming* (1966), *The Comedians* (1967), *Lola* (1970), *Richard* (1972), and *Journey Back to Oz* (1974).

He appeared in the 1962–1963 season in the CBS anthology *The Lloyd Bridges Show*. He starred in *The Baileys of Balboa*, which lasted only one season (1964–1965).

Most actors who worked with Ford claimed he was a kindly and very funny man. He was known for his quotes about the Depression in later years, including, "My kids used to think everyone lived on peanut butter sandwiches."

Paul Ford died April 12, 1976, at the age of 74 after suffering a massive heart attack at his home in Mineola, New York in 1976. His remains were cremated.

Wallace Ford

Wallace Ford with Audie Murphy in *Destry*

Wallace Ford was born Samuel Jones Grundy on February 12, 1898, in Bolton, Lancashire, England. Somehow as an infant he was separated from his parents and ended up in an orphanage and, while still quite young, was sent to its branch in Toronto. From then until 1909 he lived in an astonishing seventeen foster homes until, still just an eleven-year-old boy, he ran away and joined a Canadian vaudeville troupe called the Winnipeg Kiddies, with whom he stayed for three years.

Tragedy had not completely left his life yet, however. Samuel Jones Grundy, still just a young adolescent, joined a friend to ride the rails in America. It was perhaps an adventure to the two young hobos, but it was dangerous as well. His friend was crushed to death by a railroad car. His friend's name was Wallace Ford, and Grundy honored him by taking his name as he embarked on his career in the United States. The newcomer's fresh face and energetic talent helped him find work, in theatrical troupes, repertory companies, and vaudeville.

Ford made it to Broadway in 1921. He appeared in such plays as *Abraham Lincoln*, *Abie's Irish Rose*, and *Bad Girl*. More important, in 1922 he wed Martha Harworth. Their marriage would last for the rest of their lives. The couple had one child, their daughter, Patricia.

Then, in 1932, Ford signed a contract with MGM and had his film debut in *Possessed* with Joan Crawford. Also in 1932, he appeared in the movie for which many young film fans, especially horror aficionados, remember him: *Freaks*.

Ford was to act in quite a few chillers, several with Bela Lugosi, but for the most part he played the lead in a number of B pictures in the thirties many of them light mysteries and "old dark house" scares. He was never the handsome, debonair lead, but rather a quick-witted, wise-cracking, average-looking guy.

Thirteen of his films were directed by John Ford. When John Ford liked an actor, he cast him over and over in his films. Witness John Wayne. For example, in 1934 Wallace Ford appeared in *The Lost Patrol* with Victor McLaglen, Boris Karloff, and the Irish immigrant actor J.M. Kerrigan, who would be a life-long friend. Interestingly, while filming *The Lost Patrol* in the Arizona desert, Wallace Ford clobbered a cook who had refused to serve a black laborer. Then in 1935, John Ford cast him (again with McLaglen and Kerrigan) in the highly-respected film *The Informer*.

Another remarkable event occurred in Wallace Ford's life in the mid-1930s. He searched for his long-lost natural parents in England, a search that drew worldwide headlines and, amazingly, ended successfully.

In the 1940s Ford continued to make films steadily. By then he had settled into character parts, no more leads, but still a featured player. He had a wonderful reputation in the film community. Everyone who knew Ford seemed to agree he was a nice guy, with a breezy personality, always quick with a joke, who kept things light and fun on the set.

By 1950 Ford had put on enough weight to be called, generously, "stocky." His face had softened, his wavy hair had turned white, and he now had a white mustache and often a white beard or at least whiskers. Most of his remaining films would be Westerns, many of them highly-regarded.

He had a wonderful part as Doc Curtis in *Destry* with Audie Murphy. Two of his best-known films are *The Man from Laramie* (1955) with James Stewart and *Warlock* with Henry Fonda and Richard Widmark. In the latter he plays a hobbled townsman who, near the end of the film, irritates Fonda's character so much he kicks the crutch away from Ford, toppling him to the floor. In real life, Ford and Fonda were friends and appeared together in the 1959-1960 television series *The Deputy*.

One major non-Western Ford made in the 1950s was *The Matchmaker* (1958) in which he again got a chance to play comedy.

The only chance for an acting award Ford ever got was when he was nominated (but did not win) a Golden Laurel as best supporting actor for *A Patch of Blue* in 1965. It was his last film, and in it he looks gaunt and haggard, no doubt due to his failing heart.

Martha, his wife of forty-four years died in 1966. A short time later, on June 11, 1966, at the Motion Picture Country House in Woodland Hills, California, Wallace Ford's heart gave out. He is buried in Holy Cross Cemetery in Culver City.

Dianne Foster

Audie Murphy with Dianne Foster in *Night Passage*

Dianne Foster was born Olga Helen Laruska October 31, 1928, in Edmonton, Alberta, Canada. She began her career at the age of 13 in a stage adaptation of James Barrie's *What Every Woman Knows*. At fourteen she began a radio career, subsequently moved to Toronto, and became one of Canada's top radio stars. For a holiday in 1951 she traveled to London, England, where she met, and later married, Andrew Allen, drama supervisor for the Canadian Broadcasting Corporation.

In London that same year she appeared onstage in Agatha Christie's *The Hollow* and Orson Welles's *Othello*. In March 1952 her husband returned to Canada while she stayed in London to honor her five-year contract with a British film company. In 1953 she co-starred alongside Charlton Heston and Lizabeth Scott in the middling *Bad for Each Other*. In 1954 she was signed by Columbia Pictures and relocated to Hollywood, where her first appearance proper that year was with Mickey Rooney in the well-received *Drive a Crooked Road*.

Foster's marriage to Allen effectively was over before she left for the United States. In 1954 she married Joel A. Murcott, a Hollywood radio-television scriptwriter, during location filming for *The Kentuckian*.

1955 was a big year for Foster. She appeared on the cover of Picturegoer, and co-starred in two big films, Glenn Ford's *The Bandits* and Burt Lancaster's *The Kentuckian*.

On February 14, 1956, she gave birth to twins: a son, Jason, and a daughter, Jodi. Although her film career continued, it was not on the same upward trajectory as before.

In 1957 she co-starred in the biopic *Monkey on My Back* about boxer, Barney Ross, *Night Passage* with Audie Murphy and James Stewart and *The Brothers Rico* with Richard Conte. In 1958 she starred with Alan Ladd in *The Deep Six*, and that same year she appeared alongside Jack Hawkins in *Gideon of Scotland Yard* before her last really big picture, *The Last Hurrah*. It featured an all-star cast that included Spencer Tracy, Pat O'Brien, and Basil Rathbone, and was nominated for two BAFTA awards.

In 1960 Foster was the title guest star in the episode "Lawyer in Petticoats" on the short-lived NBC western series *Overland Trail* starring William Bendix and Doug McClure. Her fellow guest stars were Barton MacLane and Denver Pyle. There was a three-year absence before she next returned to the screen in *King of the Roaring 20's - The Story of Arnold Rothstein* (1961).

After her divorce from Murcott she married Dr. Harold Rowe, a Van Nuys dentist. On November 14, 1963, her son, Dustin Louis Rowe, was born in Los Angeles. In the same year she made her last film appearance, in the Dean Martin vehicle *Who's Been Sleeping in My Bed?* (1963).

Foster continued to appear in television programs, such as CBS's *The Lloyd Bridges Show* (1962–1963) and the ABC medical drama *Breaking Point* (1963–1964).

She retired from show business in 1966 to concentrate on rearing her three children. She still lives in California and is an accomplished pianist and painter.

Rachel Foulger

Audie Murphy with Rachel Foulger in *Whispering Smith*

Absolutely no information could be found for Rachel Foulger. Her only appearance on television was as the title character of Jody Tyler in the episode "The Jody Tyler Story" of Audie Murphy's television series *Whispering Smith* (1961).

Arthur Franz

Audie Murphy with Arthur Franz in *Whispering Smith*

Arthur Franz was born February 29, 1920, in Perth Amboy, New Jersey, and was a B-movie actor whose most notable role was as Lieutenant, Junior Grade H. Paynter, Jr. in *The Caine Mutiny* (1954). Franz's interest in acting developed when he was a high school student.

During World War II, Franz served as a B-24 Liberator navigator in the United States Army Air Forces. He was shot down over Romania and incarcerated in a POW camp, from which he escaped.

He also appeared in *Roseanna McCoy* (1949), *Invaders from Mars* (1953), *Abbott and Costello Meet the Invisible Man* (1951) as the invisible man, and *The Unholy Wife* (1957), among others. In *The Sniper* (1952), he played a rare movie lead in the film's title role as a tormented killer.

Some of his other film roles include *Sands of Iwo Jima* (1949), *Flight to Mars* (1951), *Bad for Each Other* (1953), *Bobby Ware Is Missing* (1955), *Hellcats of the Navy* (1957), *The Young Lions* (1958), *Monster on the Campus* (1958), *The Carpetbaggers* (1964), *Anzio* (1968), *Dream No Evil* (1970), *The 'Human' Factor* (1975), *Sisters of Death* (1977), and *That Championship Season* (1982).

In addition to films, Franz was a familiar face on American television, appearing on dozen of television programs including *Fireside Theatre* (1953-1955), *Celebrity Playhouse* (1956), *Science Fiction Theatre* (1955-1956), *Zane Grey Theater* (1958), *Men Into Space* (1959), *Wanted: Dead or Alive* (1960), *Gunsmoke* (1960), *Whispering Smith* (1961) with Audie Murphy, *Bonanza* (1962), *Lassie* (1964), *The Fugitive* (1965), *Tarzan* (1967), *The Invaders* (1968), *Lancer* (1969), *Mannix* (1971), *Cannon* (1972), *Police Story* (1974), *The Quest* (1976), and *The Walton's*.

Franz died June 17, 2006, in Oxnard, California at the age of 86 from emphysema and heart disease.

William Frawley

William Clement Frawley was born February 26, 1887, and was an American stage entertainer, screen and television actor. Although Frawley acted in over 100 films, he achieved his greatest fame playing landlord Fred Mertz for the situation comedy *I Love Lucy*.

William was born to Michael A. Frawley and Mary E. Brady in Burlington, Iowa. As a young boy, Bill (as he was commonly called) attended Roman Catholic school and sang with the St. Paul's Church choir. As he got older, he loved playing bit roles in local theater productions, as well as performing in amateur shows. However, his mother, a religious woman, discouraged the idea.

William did two years of office work at Union Pacific Railroad in Omaha, Nebraska. He later relocated to Chicago and found a job as a court reporter. Soon thereafter, against his mother's wishes, Frawley obtained a singing part in the musical comedy *The Flirting Princess*. To appease his mother, Bill relocated to St. Louis, Missouri, to work for another railroad company.

Unhappy with his railroad job, Frawley longed to be an actor. He finally decided he couldn't resist and formed a vaudeville act with his younger brother, Paul. Six months later, Frawley's mother told Paul to return to Iowa. It was during this period that William Frawley wrote a script titled, *Fun in a Vaudeville Agency*. He earned more than five hundred dollars for his efforts. After this, he decided to relocate to the West, settling in Denver, Colorado.

Frawley was hired as a singer at a café and teamed with pianist Franz Rath. The two men relocated to San Francisco with their act, "A Man, a Piano, and a Nut." During his vaudeville career, Frawley introduced and helped popularize the songs, "My Mammy," "My Melancholy Baby" and "Carolina in the Morning." In 1958, he recorded many of his old stage songs on the LP, *Bill Frawley Sings the Old Ones*.

In 1914, Frawley married fellow vaudevillian Edna Louise Broedt (1892–1927). They developed an act, "Frawley and Louise," which they performed all across the country. Their act was described as "light comedy, with singing, dancing, and patter." The couple separated in 1921 (later divorcing in 1927). They did not have any children.

Frawley began performing in a Broadway theater. His first such show was the musical comedy, *Merry, Merry*, in 1925. Frawley made his first dramatic role in 1932, playing press agent Owen O'Malley in the original production of Ben Hecht and Charles MacArthur's *Twentieth Century*. He continued to be a dramatic actor at various locales until 1933.

Frawley appeared in two short subject silent films during 1916. He performed subsequently in three other short films. It wasn't until 1933 that he decided to develop a cinematic career beginning with short comedy films, and the feature musical *Moonlight and Pretzels* (1933). He relocated to Los Angeles and signed a seven-year contract with Paramount Pictures. Finding much work as a character actor, he had roles in many different genres of films — comedies, dramas, musicals, westerns and romances. Frawley had a notable performance in the 1947 holiday favorite, *Miracle on 34th Street*, as Judge Harper's political adviser (who warns his client in great detail the dire political consequences if he rules that there is not any Santa Claus).

Some of his other memorable film roles were as the baseball manager in Joe E. Brown's, *Alibi Ike* (1935), and as the wedding host in Charlie Chaplin's, *Monsieur Verdoux* (1947).

By 1951 the 64-year-old Frawley had appeared in over 100 movies, including *Texas, Brooklyn, and Heaven* (1948) with Audie Murphy and *Abbott and Costello Meet the Invisible Man* (1951), but was starting to find film role offers becoming fewer. When he heard that Desi Arnaz and Lucille Ball were casting a new television situation comedy, he applied eagerly to play the role of the cantankerous, miserly landlord Fred Mertz.

One evening, Frawley telephoned Lucille Ball, asking her what his chances were. Ball was surprised to hear from him, a man she barely knew. Both Ball and Arnaz agreed that it would be great to have Frawley, a motion picture veteran, appear as Fred Mertz. Less enthusiastic were CBS executives, who warned of Bill's frequent drinking and instability. Arnaz immediately told Frawley about the network's concerns, telling him that if he was late to work, arrived drunk, or was unable to perform because of something other than legitimate illness more than once, he would be written out of the show. To the contrary, Frawley never arrived at work drunk, and in fact mastered his lines after only one reading. Arnaz eventually became one of the misanthropic Frawley's few close friends.

I Love Lucy debuted October 15, 1951, on CBS and was a huge success. The series was broadcast for six years as half-hour episodes, later changing to hour-long specials from 1957 to 1960 titled *The Lucille Ball-Desi Arnaz Show* (later retitled *The Lucy-Desi Comedy Hour*). Vivian Vance played Ethel Mertz, Frawley's on-screen wife. Although the two actors worked well together, they greatly disliked each other. Most attribute their mutual hatred to Vance's vocal resentment of having to play wife to a man 22 years her senior. Frawley reportedly overheard Vance complaining; he took offense and never forgave her. "She's one of the finest girls to come out of Kansas," he once observed, "But I often wish she'd go back there."

An avid New York Yankees baseball fan, Frawley had it written into his *I Love Lucy* contract that he did not have to work during the World Series if the Yankees were playing. The Yankees were in every World Series during that time except for 1954 and 1959. He missed two episodes of the show as a result.

For his work on the show, Frawley was Emmy-nominated five times (for 1953, 1954, 1955, 1956 and 1957) for "Outstanding Supporting Actor" in a comedy series.

During 1960, Ball and Arnaz gave Frawley and Vance the opportunity to have their own "Fred and Ethel" spin-off series for Desilu Studios. Despite his animosity towards her, Frawley saw a lucrative opportunity and accepted. Vance, however, refused the offer, having no desire to work with Frawley again. Afterward, and for the remainder of Frawley's life, he and Vance had very little contact with each other.

Frawley next performed for the ABC (later CBS) situation comedy *My Three Sons* (1960-1965), playing live-in grandfather/housekeeper Michael Francis "Bub" O'Casey beginning in 1960. Featuring Fred MacMurray as main actor, the series was about a widower raising his three sons.

Frawley reportedly never felt comfortable with the out-of-sequence filming method used for *My Three Sons* after doing *I Love Lucy* in sequence for years. Each season's episodes were arranged so that main actor Fred MacMurray could film all of his scenes during two separate intensive blocks of filming for a total of sixty-five working days on the set; Frawley and the other actors worked around the absent MacMurray for the remainder of the year's production schedule.

While appearing on *My Three Sons*, Frawley was the subject of *This Is Your Life* in January 1961. He received a lifetime baseball pass from the Angels' Fred Haney.

Poor health forced Frawley's retirement from the show after five years. He was dropped from *My Three Sons* after the studio could no longer obtain insurance for him. He was replaced as live-in housekeeper by actor William Demarest, who played Bub's brother, Uncle Charley. According to the book *Meet the Mertzes*, Frawley often would visit the studio after his retirement. He did not hide his resentment of Demarest and was eventually asked not to return to the set.

Frawley made two final on-screen appearances before his death. An appearance on *I've Got a Secret* consisted of contestants guessing Frawley's, "secret," which was that he was the first performer ever to sing "My Melancholy Baby," in 1912. He then performed the song one last time.

His final on-camera performance was in October 1965, a brief cameo appearance in Lucille Ball's second television sitcom *The Lucy Show* with Frawley playing a horse trainer and Lucy commenting, "He reminds me of someone I used to know." (Vivian Vance, who by then had left *The Lucy Show* except for an occasional guest appearance, does not appear in that episode.)

On March 3, 1966, Frawley collapsed of a heart attack while walking down Hollywood Boulevard after seeing a movie, *Inside Daisy Clover*. He was dragged to the nearby Knickerbocker Hotel, where he had previously lived for many years, by his male nurse, a constant companion since his prostate cancer operation more than a year before. He was then rushed to the nearby Hollywood Receiving Hospital (now the Hollywood LAPD Precinct) on Wilcox Ave, where he was pronounced dead.

Soon after his death, Desi Arnaz paid for a full-page advertisement in the newspaper *Hollywood Reporter*. It had a picture of Frawley, surrounded in black, the dates of his birth and death, and the caption, "Buenas Noches, Amigo!" ("Good Night, Friend!"). Arnaz, Frawley's *My Three Sons* co-star Fred MacMurray, and executive producer Don Fedderson were pallbearers at Frawley's funeral.

Lucille Ball issued the statement: "I've lost one of my dearest friends and show business has lost one of the greatest character actors of all time. Those of us who knew him and loved him will miss him".

Kathleen Freeman

Kathleen Freeman was born in Chicago, Illinois, February 17, 1919, and was an American film, television, and stage actress. In a career that spanned more than 50 years, she portrayed tart maids, secretaries, teachers, busybodies, nurses, and battle-axe neighbors, almost invariably to comic effect.

She began her career as a child, dancing in her parents' vaudeville act. After a stint studying music at UCLA, she went into acting full time, working on the stage, and finally entering films in 1948. She was a founding member, in 1946, of the Circle Players at The Circle Theatre, now known as El Centro Theatre.

Freeman's most notable early role was an uncredited part in the 1952 musical *Singin' in the Rain*, as Jean Hagen's articulate diction coach Phoebe Dinsmore. In 1954, Freeman played receptionist Miss Seely for lawyer Adam Calhorn Shaw (Edmund Purdom) in *Athena*. Beginning with the 1955 film *Artists and Models*,

Freeman became a favorite foil of Jerry Lewis, playing opposite him in 11 films. These included most of Lewis's better known comedies, including *The Disorderly Orderly* (1964) as Nurse Higgins, *The Errand Boy* (1961) as the studio boss's wife, and especially *The Nutty Professor* (1963) as Millie Lemon. Over 30 years later, she made a small cameo appearance in *Nutty Professor II: The Klumps* (2000), a sequel to the remake of the Lewis film.

Still other film roles included appearances in *The Missouri Traveler* (1958), the horror film *The Fly* (1958), the Western spoofs *Support Your Local Sheriff!* (1969) and *Support Your Local Gunfighter* (1971), and appearances in a spate of comedies in the 1980s and 1990s. Freeman played Sister Mary Stigmata (referred to as The Penguin) in John Landis' *The Blues Brothers* (1980) and *Blues Brothers 2000* (1998), had cameos in Joe Dante's *Innerspace* (1987) and *Gremlins 2: The New Batch* (1990) as tipsy cooking host Microwave Marge, and a Ma Barker type gangster mother in *Naked Gun 33⅓: The Final Insult* (1994).

In addition to teaching acting classes in Los Angeles, Freeman was also a familiar presence on television. She appeared from the 1950s until her death in regular or recurring roles on many sitcoms, including *Topper* ((1953-1954) as Katie the maid, *Father Knows Best* (1956), *Tombstone Territory* (1958), *Buckskin* (1958-1959), *Whispering Smith* (1961) with Audie Murphy, *Rawhide* (1962), *Ben Casey* (1964), *The Alfred Hitchcock Hour* (1963-1965), *Laredo* (1967), *Batman* (1968), *Lancer* (1969), *Cannon* (1972), *Kolchak: The Night Stalker* (1975), *Kojak* (1977), *Chips* (1980), *Mama's Family* (1987), *The Facts of Life* (1988), *ALF* (1988), *Head of the Class* (1990), *Tales from the Crypt* (1991), *Renegade* (1995), *ER* (1996), *Home Improvement* (1998), *Honey, I Shrunk the Kids: The TV Show* (1999), and *As Told by Ginger* (2000-2003).

Freeman remained active in her last two years, including a voice bit in the animated feature film *Shrek*, and, most notably, scoring a Tony Award nomination and a Theatre World Award for her role of accompanist Jeannette Burmeister in the Broadway musical version of *The Full Monty*.

In her final episode of *As Told By Ginger*, Season 2's "No Hope For Courtney", Freeman's character, Mrs. Gordon, retires from her teaching job though two of her students try convincing her to return to work. The script was originally written to have Mrs. Gordon come back to work, but Freeman died before the episode was finished. The script was then re-written to make her character die as well. The episode was dedicated in her memory.

Weakened by illness, Freeman reluctantly left Broadway's *Full Monty* cast on August 18, 2001. Five days later, she died of lung cancer August 23, 2001, at age 82. Her ashes are inurned in a niche at Hollywood Forever Cemetery in Hollywood, California.

Bruce Frichtl

Audie Murphy with Bruce Frichtl in *To Hell and Back*

No biographical information can be found for Bruce Frichtl, but he did appear in one television program and one film. The program was *The Pepsi-Cola Playhouse* (1955) episode "The Boy and the Coach", and as Audie Murphy's brother Richard Murphy in *To Hell and Back* (1955).

Rad Fulton

Rad Fulton with Audie Murphy in *Hell Bent for Leather*

Rad Fulton was born James Westmoreland November 25, 1935 in Dearborn, Michigan. He first came to Hollywood in 1954. In his early career he was represented by agent Henry Willson, who made Rock Hudson a star, who gave him the marquee name of "Rad Fulton". Westmoreland returned to using his original birth name after the two severed their business relationship in 1966.

It didn't take him long to get his first acting role in *Come Next Spring* (1956). He found steady work in films like *No Time for Sergeants* (1958), *The Young Philadelphians* (1959), *Hell Bent for Leather* (1960) with Audie Murphy, *The Last Sunset* (1961), and *Don't Answer the Phone!* (1980).

About filming *Hell Bent for Leather* he said "At the beginning of the shoot, I introduced myself to Audie and said how proud I was to be working with a man of his bravery and talent. He thanked me and we got along well on the set. Audie was a shy man, but I liked him".

He had a good many roles in television programs like *Alfred Hitchcock Presents* (1958-1959), *The Restless Gun* (1959), *Bronco* (1960), *Route 66* (1962), *The Wild, Wild West* (1966), *The Monroes* (1966-1967), *Emergency!* (1977), *T.J. Hooker* (1984), and *The New Mike Hamm*er (1987).

Since then he decided to move back to the desert where he worked and finished two novels, and is presently finishing a screenplay.

John Gallaudet

John Gallaudet was born John Beury Gallaudet August 23, 1903, in Philadelphia, Pennsylvania. The son of an Episcopal priest, John Gallaudet commenced his professional acting career after graduating from Williams College.

He appeared on both Broadway and in stock opposite actors ranging from Fred Astaire to Helen Hayes. The slight, thinnish-haired Gallaudet spent several years in the 1930s as the resident character star of Columbia Pictures' "B" unit, playing everything from kindhearted doctors to serpent-like crooks. Some of those movies include *Pennies from Heaven* (1936), and *I'll Take Romance* (1937).

He owns the distinction of being one the few actors to ever "murder" Rita Hayworth, dispatching the lovely young actress with a poisoned baseball glove in the 1937 potboiler *Girls Can Play*.

More roles followed in films and television programs such as *Code of the Secret Service* (1939), *Knute Rockne All American* (1940), *The Bride Came C.O.D.* (1941), *Captains of the Clouds* (1942), *Lost City of the Jungle* (1946), *Texas, Brooklyn & Heaven* (1948) with Audie Murphy, *Mighty Joe Young* (1949), *Angels in the Outfield* (1951), *Mayor of the Town* (1954), *Terror at Midnight* (1956), *The George Burns and Gracie Allen Show* (1953-1957), *Richard Diamond, Private Detective* (1959), *Go Naked in the World* (1961), *Leave It to Beaver* (1961-1963), twenty-one episodes of *Perry Mason* (1959-1966), *In Cold Blood* (1967), thirteen episodes of *My Three Sons* (1960-1972), and *Adam-12* (1970-1974).

John Gallaudet was well known and highly regarded throughout the film community for his off-camera vocation as a champion golfer. He died November 5, 1983, at age 80 in Los Angeles, California.

Lisa Gaye

Lisa Gaye with Audie Murphy in Drums Across the River

Lisa Gaye was born Leslie Gaye Griffin in Denver, Colorado, March 6, 1935, and was an American actress, singer and dancer until her retirement.

The family moved from Denver to Los Angeles in the 1930s to be close to the developing film industry. Her mother, actress Margaret Griffin, was determined that Gaye and her siblings would make their careers in show business. Gaye's sisters Judith (Teala Loring) and Debralee (Debra Paget), and her brother Frank (Ruell Shayne) each entered the business as either cast or crew.

She made her first professional appearance at age seven. She began her acting career in 1954 with *The Glenn Miller Story* and was a popular leading lady during the 1950s and 1960s, in other roles such as *Drums Across the River* (1954) with Audie Murphy, *Shake, Rattle & Rock!* (1956), *Ten Thousand Bedrooms* (1957), *Northwest Passage* (1958), *The Bob Cummings Show* (1955-1959), *How to Marry a Millionaire* (1958-1959), *Wanted: Dead or Alive* (1960), *Night of Evil* (1962), *Castle of Evil* (1966), *Get Smart* (1967), *The Flying Nun* (1969), and *Mod Squad* (1970).

She retired in 1970 to raise a family. She was married to Bently C. Ware in 1955 until his death in 1977; they had one child.

Martin Garralaga

Audie Murphy with Martin Garralaga in *The Kid From Texas*

Martin Garralaga was born November 10, 1894, Barcelona, Cataluña, Spain, and was a Spanish-born film and television actor who portrayed more than 200 roles in film and television.

He is probably best known for his portrayal as "Pancho" in the early *Cisco Kid* movies. Other roles he appeared in included *George White's 1935 Scandals* (1935), *Lawless Border* (1935), *The Charge of the Light Brigade* (1936), *Starlight Over Texas* (1938), *Another Thin Man* (1939), *Wagon Train* (1940), *Casablanca* (1942), *West of the Pecos* (1945), *The Virginian* (1946), *Ride the Pink Horse* (1947), *The Treasure of the Sierra Madre* (1948), *Four Faces West* (1948), *Streets of San Francisco* (1949), *The Kid from Texas* (1950) with Audie Murphy, *Branded* (1950), *Bela Lugosi Meets a Brooklyn Gorilla* (1952), *Border River* (1954), *Blackjack Ketchum, Desperado* (1956), *Gunsight Ridge* (1957), *Lonely Are the Brave* (1962), *Fun in Acapulco* (1963), *The Fugitive* (1964-1966), *Gunsmoke* (1968), *What Ever Happened to Aunt Alice?* (1969), and *It Takes a Thief* (1970).

He died on June 12, 1981, in Woodland Hills, Los Angeles, California.

Gordon Gebert

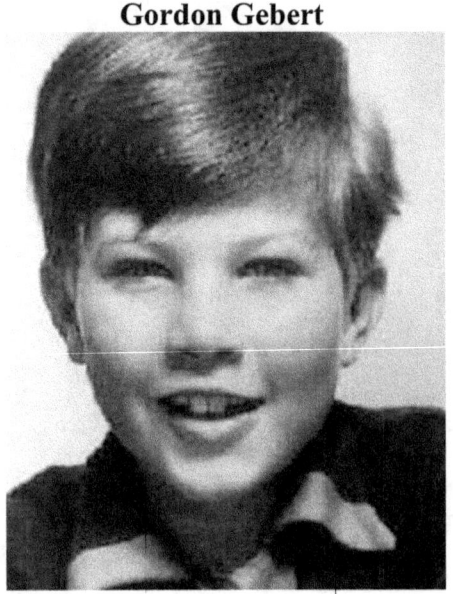

Gordon Alan Gebert was born in Des Moines, Iowa, October 17, 1941, and was a child actor who is predominantly known for having smaller roles, in such films as *Holiday Affair* (1949). He later turned away from acting and became a college professor.

His father, Gordon Gebert, Sr., was a salesman for Freuhauf Trailer Co. and eventually handled Iowa truck and bus fleet sales for Ford Motor Co. He was a "frustrated actor" who performed in theatre productions and plays, but never had a huge break.

In 1946, a boy was needed for a play and Gebert took the role, taking acting lessons through the theatre to be able to play it. In the spring of 1948, near the end of first grade, the family took off for Los Angeles and almost immediately young Gordon found himself performing in a Pasadena Playhouse production of *Life With Father*. Agent Lola Moore saw and signed him, and he soon had a small part in *Come to the Stable* (1949).

His break was *Holiday Affair* in 1949. He appeared with well-known stars and stood out, being written about in editorials and reviews. It got him spots on radio programs and in television work, such as *Cavalcade of America* (1955), *Gunsmoke* (1956) and *Pursuit* (1958). He continued his acting career in *The Flame and the Arrow* (1950) and *The Flying Leathernecks* (1951), but never passed the part of a son.

Eventually, in 1955, he got the coveted role as the World War II hero Audie Murphy as a boy, in *To Hell and Back*.

His last movie was *Summer Love* (1958) and his last television appearance was in *Bachelor Father* (1960). His adult acting career never left the ground. Instead, he found an interest in architecture; he enrolled at UCLA, switched to USC and eventually went to MIT for a bachelor's degree. He now is a professor of architecture at New York's City College School of Architecture.

Gebert met Lizabeth Paravisini, a professor of Spanish and Hispanic culture at Vassar College in 1986 while both were waiting for a flight to Cuba, to fill educational speaking engagements. They married and have a son, Gordon Jr. (born.1992); he has two grown daughters from an earlier marriage.

Will Geer

Will Geer with Audie Murphy in *The Kid From Texas*

Will Geer was born William Aughe Ghere; March 9, 1902, and was an American actor and social activist. He is known for his portrayal of Grandpa Zebulon Tyler Walton in the TV series, *The Waltons* (1972-1978).

Geer was born in Frankfort, Indiana, the son of Katherine (née Aughe), a teacher, and A. Roy Ghere, a postal worker. He was deeply influenced by his grandfather, who taught him the botanical names of the plants in his native state. Geer started out to become a botanist, studying the subject and obtaining a master's degree at the University of Chicago. While at Chicago he also became a member of Lambda Chi Alpha Fraternity.

He began his acting career touring in tent shows and on river boats.

Geer was also the lover of gay activist Harry Hay. In 1934, Hay met Geer at the Tony Pastor Theatre, where Geer worked as an actor. They became lovers, and Hay credited Geer as his political mentor. Hay and Geer participated in a milk strike in Los Angeles, where Hay was first exposed to radical gay activism in the person of "Clarabelle," a drag queen who held court in the Bunker Hill neighborhood, who hid Hay from police. Later that year, Hay and Geer performed in support of the San Francisco General Strike.

Geer made his Broadway debut as Pistol in a 1928 production of *Much Ado About Nothing*, created the role of Mr. Mister in Marc Blitzstein's *The Cradle Will Rock*, played Candy in John Steinbeck's theatrical adaptation of his novella *Of Mice and Men*, and appeared in numerous plays and revues throughout the 1940s. From 1948 to 1951, he appeared in more than a dozen movies, including *Winchester '73* (1950), *Broken Arrow* (1950), *The Kid From Texas* (1950) with Audie Murphy, and *Bright Victory* (1951).

Geer became a member of the Communist Party of the United States in 1934. Geer was also influential in introducing Harry Hay to organizing in the Communist Party. In 1934, Geer and Hay gave support to a labor strike of the port of San Francisco; the 1934 West Coast waterfront strike lasted eighty-three days. Though marred by violence, it was an organizing triumph, one that became a model for future union strikes.

Geer became a dedicated activist, touring government work camps in the 1930s with folk singers like Burl Ives and Woody Guthrie. In 1956, the duo released an album together on Folkways Records, titled *Bound for Glory: Songs and Stories of Woody Guthrie*. In his autobiography, fellow organizer and gay rights pioneer Harry Hay described Geer's activism and outlined their activities while organizing for the strike. Geer is credited with introducing Guthrie to Pete Seeger at the 'Grapes of Wrath' benefit Geer organized in 1940 for migrant farm workers.

Geer was blacklisted in the early 1950s for refusing to testify before the House Committee on Un-American Activities. In 1951 he founded the Will Geer Theatricum Botanicum in Topanga, California, with his wife, Herta Ware. He combined his acting and botanical careers at the Theatricum, by making sure that every plant mentioned in Shakespeare was grown there. In the late 1950s and early 1960s he played several seasons at the American Shakespeare Festival in Stratford, Connecticut, where he created a second "Shakespeare Garden" on the theater's grounds. By this time he was also working sporadically on Broadway. In 1964 he was nominated for the Tony Award for Best Featured Actor in a Musical for *110 in the Shade*.

In 1972, he played the part of "Bear Claw" in *Jeremiah Johnson* along with Robert Redford. In 1972, he was cast as Zebulon Walton, the family patriarch on *The Waltons,* a role he took over from Edgar Bergen, who played the character in the pilot. His last appearance was in *A Woman Called Moses* (1978).

Geer maintained a garden at his vacation home, called Geer-Gore Gardens, in Nichols, Connecticut. He visited often and attended the local Fourth of July fireworks celebrations, sometimes wearing a black top hat or straw hat and always his trademark denim overalls with only one suspender hooked.

When Geer died, shortly after completing the sixth season of *The Waltons*, the death of his character was written into the show's script as well.

His ex-wife, actress Herta Ware, was best known for her performance as the wife of Jack Gilford in the film *Cocoon* (1985). Although they eventually divorced, they remained close throughout the rest of their lives. Geer and Ware had three children, Kate Geer, Thad Geer, and actress Ellen Geer. Ware also had a daughter, actress Melora Marshall, from a previous marriage.

As Will Geer was dying on April 22, 1978, of respiratory failure at the age of 76, his family sang Guthrie's "This Land Is Your Land" and recited poems by Robert Frost at his deathbed. Geer's remains were cremated; his ashes are buried at the *Theatricum Botanicum* in the "Shakespeare Garden" in Topanga Canyon, near Santa Monica, California.

Ted Gehring

Ted Gehring with Audie Murphy in *40 Guns to Apache Pass*

Ted Gehring was born Theodore Edwin Gehring April 6, 1929, in Bisbee, Arizona. He was an American character actor 1965 to 1988.

Some of the roles he had included *The Big Valley* (1965), *Get Smart* (1966), *The Fugitive* (1965-1966), *40 Guns to Apache Pass* (1967) with Audie Murphy, *Star Trek* (1968), *The Thomas Crown Affair* (1969), *Wake Me When the War Is Over* (1969), *Monte Walsh* (1970), *Adam-12* (1970), *Dan August* (1971), *Deadhead Miles* (1972), *The Culpepper Cattle Co.* (1972), *The Whiz Kid and the Mystery at Riverton* (1974), *The Story of Pretty Boy Floyd* (1974), *Airport 1975* (1974), *Who Is the Black Dahlia?* (1975), *Captains and the Kings* (1976), *The Feather and Father Gang* (1977), *Three's Company* (1978), *M*A*S*H* (1973-1978), *Battlestar Galactica* (1978), *Galactica 1980* (1980), *Dallas* (1980-1981), *The Legend of the Lone Ranger* (1981), *T.J. Hooker* (1982), *The Best Little Whorehouse in Texas* (1982), *The Greatest American Hero* (1982-1983), *The Dukes of Hazzard* (1980-1983), *Murphy's Romance* (1985), *U.S. Marshals: Waco & Rhinehart* (1987), and *Too Good to Be True* (1988).

He died September 28, 2000, at age 71 in Steelville, Missouri.

Helga Genth

Helga Genth with Audie Murphy in *The Texican*

Helga Genth was born December 18, 1934. No other biographical information could be found. Her only film appearance was as Maria Banta in *The Texican* (1966) with Audie Murphy.

Frank Gerstle

Frank Gerstle was born Francis M. Gerstle September 27, 1915, in New York City, New York. Tall, stony-faced, white-maned Frank Gerstle is most familiar to the baby-boomer generation for his many TV commercial appearances. In films from 1950 through 1967, Gerstle was generally cast as military officers, no-nonsense doctors and plainclothes detectives.

His screen roles include Dr. MacDonald in *DOA* (1950), *I Was a Communist for the FBI* (1951), *Blackhawk: Fearless Champion of Freedom* (1952), *The Long, Long Trailer* (1953), *Drum Beat* (1954) with Alan Ladd, "machine" politician Dave Dietz in *Slightly Scarlet* (1954), *The McConnell Story* (1955) with Alan Ladd again, *The Proud Ones* (1956), *Between Heaven and Hell* (1956), *I Mobster* (1958), *Ambush at Cimarron Pass* (1958), *The Four Skulls of Jonathan Drake* (1959), *Hell to Eternity* (1960), *13 West Street* (1962) yet again with Alan Ladd, *Kid Galahad* (1962) with Elvis Presley, *The Quick Gun* (1964) with Audie Murphy, *The Silencers* (1966), *Murderers' Row* (1966), *Bullitt* (1968) with Steve McQueen, and *The Christine Jorgensen Story* (1970).

Some of his more sizeable film assignments could be found in the realm of science fiction, like *Killers From Space* (1953), *The Magnetic Monster* (1953), *Wasp Woman* (1960), *Monstrosity* (1963), and *The Bamboo Saucer* (1968).

He also appeared in many television programs such as *Racket Squad* (1952), *Dick Tracy* (1953), *The Amos 'n Andy Show* (1955), *The New Adventures of Charlie Chan* (1957), *Mike Hammer* (1959), *Richard Diamond, Private Detective* (1959), *Bourbon Street Beat* (1960), *Wanted: Dead or Alive* (1961), *Branded* (1966), *Laredo* (1966), *The Green Hornet* (1966), *The Banana Splits Adventure Hour* (1969), and *Mannix* (1970).

A prolific voiceover artist, Frank Gerstle also pitched dozens of products in hundreds of TV and radio ads.

He died February 23, 1970, at age 54 in Santa Monica, California.

Jody Gilbert

Jody Gilbert was born March 18, 1916, in Fort Worth, Texas. One time concert singer, Gilbert gave a recital at Carnegie Hall at the age of 19. By 1934, she was attending the Pasadena Playhouse and her first big screen appearance was in *Ninotchka* (1939) with Greta Garbo.

143

More of her roles included *Star Dust* (1940), *Sergeant York* (1941), *Never Give a Sucker an Even Break* (1941), *Hellzapoppin'* (1941), *Ride 'Em Cowboy* (1942) with Abbott and Costello, *Lost in a Harem* (1944) again with Bud & Lou, *Christmas in Connecticut* (1945), *Life with Blondie* (1945), *Blondie's Holiday* (1947), *Texas, Brooklyn & Heaven* (1948) with Audie Murphy, *Knock on Any Door* (1949), *My Friend Irma Goes West* (1950), *Houdini* (1953), *Butch Cassidy and the Sundance Kid* (1969), *Willard* (1971), *Rod Serling's Night Gallery* (1971), *Lifeguard* (1976), *Starsky and Hutch* (1977), and *Switch* (1978).

She died February 3, 1979, at age 62 in Los Angeles, California.

Lillian Gish

Lillian Gish with Audie Murphy in *The Unforgiven*

Lillian Diana Gish was born in Springfield, Ohio, October 14, 1893, and was an American stage, screen and television actress whose film acting career spanned seventy-five years, from 1912 to 1987. The longevity of her career earned her the nickname "The First Lady of American Cinema".

She was a prominent film star of the 1910s and 1920s, particularly associated with the films of director D.W. Griffith, including her leading role in Griffith's seminal *Birth of a Nation* (1915). Her sound-era film appearances were sporadic, but included memorable roles in the controversial western *Duel in the Sun* (1946) and the offbeat thriller *Night of the Hunter* (1955). She did considerable television work from the early 1950s into the 1980s, and closed her career playing, for the first time, opposite Bette Davis in the 1987 film *The Whales of August*.

The American Film Institute (AFI) named Gish seventeenth among the greatest female stars of all time. She was awarded an Honorary Academy Award in 1971, and in 1984 she received an AFI Life Achievement Award.

She was the daughter of Mary Robinson McConnell and James Leigh Gish. Gish's father left the family before she was old enough to remember him; her mother then took up acting to support the family. She had a younger sister, Dorothy. When Lillian and Dorothy were old enough, they joined the theatre, often traveling separately in different productions. They also took modeling jobs.

In 1912, their friend Mary Pickford introduced the sisters to D. W. Griffith who helped them get contracts with Biograph Studios. Lillian Gish would soon become one of America's best-loved actresses. Although she was already nineteen, she gave her age as sixteen to the studio.

The sisters debuted in Griffith's short film *An Unseen Enemy* (1912). Lillian went on to star in many of Griffith's most acclaimed films, including *The Birth of a Nation* (1915), *Intolerance* (1916), *Broken Blossoms* (1919), *Way Down East* (1920) and *Orphans of the Storm* (1921). One of the enduring images of Gish's silent film years is the climax of the melodramatic *Way Down East*, in which Gish's character floats unconscious on an ice floe towards a raging waterfall, her long hair trailing in the water.

Having appeared in over twenty-five short films and features in her first two years as a movie actress, Lillian became a major star, becoming known as "The First Lady of the Silent Screen" and appearing in lavish productions, frequently of literary works such as *The Scarlet Letter* (1926). MGM released her from her contract after the failure of *The Wind* (1928), now recognized by many as among her finest performances and one of the most distinguished works of the late silent period.

She directed one film, *Remodeling Her Husband* (1920), when D. W. Griffith took his unit on location; he told Gish that he thought the crew would work harder for a girl. Gish never directed again, telling reporters at the time that directing was a man's job.

With her debut in talkies only moderately successful, she acted on the stage for the most part in the 1930s and early 1940s, appearing in roles as varied as Ophelia in Guthrie McClintic's landmark 1936 production of *Hamlet* and Marguerite in a limited run of *La Dame aux Camélias*. Of the former, she said with pride, "I played a *lewd* Ophelia!"

Returning to movies, Gish was nominated for the Academy Award for Best Supporting Actress in 1946 for *Duel in the Sun*. The scenes of her character's illness and death late in that film seemed intended to evoke the memory of some of her silent film performances.

She appeared in films from time to time for the rest of her life, notably in *Night of the Hunter* (1955) as a rural guardian angel protecting her charges from a murderous preacher played by Robert Mitchum.

Another great role for her was as Mattilda Zackary, mother of Audie Murphy, Burt Lancaster, Doug McClure, and Audrey Hepburn in *The Unforgiven* (1960).

Gish made numerous television appearances from the early 1950s into the late 1980s. Her most acclaimed television work was starring in the original production of *The Trip to Bountiful* in 1953. She appeared as Dowager Empress Maria Feodorovna in the short-lived 1965 Broadway musical *Anya*. In addition to her later acting appearances, Gish became one of the leading advocates on the lost art of the silent film, often giving speeches and touring to screenings of classic works. In 1975, she hosted *The Silent Years*, a PBS film program of silent films.

Gish received a Special Academy Award in 1971 'For superlative artistry and for distinguished contribution to the progress of motion pictures'. In 1979, she was awarded the Women in film Crystal Award. In 1984, she received an American Film Institute Lifetime Achievement Award, becoming only the second female recipient (preceded by Bette Davis in 1977), and the only recipient who was a major figure in the silent era.

Her last film role was in *The Whales of August* in 1987 at the age of 93, with Vincent Price, Bette Davis and Ann Sothern, in which she and Davis starred as elderly sisters in Maine. Her final professional appearance was a cameo on the 1988 studio recording of Jerome Kern's *Show Boat*, starring Frederica von Stade and Jerry Hadley, in which she affectingly spoke the few lines of *The Old Lady on the Levee* in the final scene. The last words of her long career were, "Good night, Dear". Some in the entertainment industry were angry that Gish did not receive an Oscar nomination for her role in *The Whales of August*. Gish herself was more complacent, remarking that it saved her the trouble of "losing to Cher" (who did, in fact, win for her performance in *Moonstruck*).

Gish never married nor had children. The association between Gish and D. W. Griffith was so close that some suspected a romantic connection, an issue never acknowledged by Gish, although several of their associates were certain they were at least briefly involved. For the remainder of her life, she always referred to him as "Mr. Griffith".

During the period of political turmoil in the United States that lasted from the outbreak of World War II in Europe until the attack on Pearl Harbor, she maintained an outspoken non-interventionist stance. She was an active member of the America First Committee, an anti-intervention organization founded by retired General Robert E. Wood with aviation pioneer Charles Lindbergh as its leading spokesman. She said she was blacklisted by the film and theater industries until she signed a contract in which she promised to cease her anti-interventionist activities and never disclose the fact that she had agreed to do so.

She maintained a very close relationship with her sister Dorothy, as well as with Mary Pickford, for her entire life. Another of her closest friends was actress Helen Hayes; Gish was the godmother of Hayes' son James MacArthur.

She died in her sleep of natural causes on February 27, 1993, at age 99 and is interred beside her sister Dorothy at Saint Bartholomew's Episcopal Church in New York City. Her estate, which she left to Hayes, who ironically died one month later, was valued at several million dollars, and went to provide prizes for artistic excellence. It was called The Dorothy and Lillian Gish Prize, one of the richest prizes in the arts, given annually to 'a man or woman who has made an outstanding contribution to the beauty of the world and to mankind's enjoyment and understanding of life'.

James Gleason

James Gleason with Audie Murphy in *Bad Boy*

James Austin Gleason was born May 23, 1882, and was an American actor born in New York City. He was also a playwright and screenwriter.

Coming from theatrical stock, as a schoolboy he made stage appearances while on holiday. He began earning his living at the age of thirteen, being a messenger boy, printer's devil, assistant in an electrical store and a lift boy. He enlisted in the army at age sixteen and served three years in the Philippines.

On discharge, he began his stage career, later taking it up professionally. He played in London for two years and following his return to the United States, he began in films by writing dialogue for comedies. He also wrote several plays. His first film acting was in the film *The Count of Ten* (1927) by Universal.

Balding and slender with a craggy voice and a master of the double-take, Gleason portrayed tough but warm-hearted characters, usually with a New York background. He appeared in several movies with his wife Lucille.

Gleason co-wrote *The Broadway Melody* (1929), the second film to win the Academy Award for Best Picture, and had a small uncredited role in it. Gleason also co-wrote and briefly appeared as a hot dog vendor in the 1934 Janet Gaynor vehicle *Change of Heart*. He played a milk cart driver who gives lessons in marriage to Judy Garland and Robert Walker in the 1945 film *The Clock*, while Lucille played his wife. In the same year, he played the bartender in the film adaptation of *A Tree Grows in Brooklyn*.

Gleason also is remembered for playing police inspector Oscar Piper in a series of six Hildegarde Withers mystery films during the 1930s, starting with *Penguin Pool Murder* (1932).

He was nominated for an Academy Award for Best Supporting Actor for his performance as boxing manager Max 'Pop' Corkle in the 1941 film *Here Comes Mr. Jordan*. He played Lt. Rooney in *Arsenic and Old Lace* (1944). He appeared as the 'Chief' in *Bad Boy* (1949) with Audie Murphy.

Gleason also appeared on television, including the *The Life of Riley* (1953-1955), *Cheyenne* (1956), *Leave It to Beaver* (1957), and *The Real McCoys* (1958).

He made his last appearance was in *Money, Women and Guns* (1958).

James and Lucille Gleason had a son, actor Russell Gleason (1908-1945), who died after falling from the window ledge of a hotel in midtown Manhattan, on Christmas night in 1945. His untimely death happened just before his army regiment was due to leave for a posting in Europe, several months after the end of the hostilities of war. His death has been variously described both as suicidal and as accidental. Russell's most prominent role had been as Muller in the Academy Award-winning version of *All Quiet on the Western Front* (1930). Russell Gleason was married to Cynthia Lindsay, a former Busby Berkeley chorus girl who later wrote a biography of family friend Boris Karloff.

James Gleason died April 12, 1959, in Woodland Hills, Los Angeles, California, and was interred in the Holy Cross Cemetery in Culver City, California.

Louise Glenn

No biographical information could be found for Louise Glenn, but she did appear in twenty-five films and television programs from 1957 to 1974. Some of those roles included *Funny Face* (1957), *Shirley Temple Theatre* (1958), *The Wild and the Innocent* (1959) with Audie Murphy, thirty episodes as Gladys in *The Roaring 20's* (1960-1962), *It's a Mad Mad Mad Mad World* (1963), *The Munsters* (1966), *Bewitched* (1968), *Mayberry R.F.D.* (1970), and *The New Temperatures Rising Show* (1974).

Harold Goodwin

Audie Murphy with Harold Goodwin in *The Kid From Texas*

Harold Goodwin was born in Peoria, Illinois, December 1, 1902, and was an American film actor who performed in over 225 films.

Goodwin began his film career while still in his teens in the 1915 film short *Mike's Elopement*. One of his most popular roles of the silent era was that of Jeff Brown in the 1927 Buster Keaton Comedy *College*. Goodwin followed up with a role in another Keaton film *The Cameraman* in 1928 opposite Keaton and actress Marceline Day.

He worked steadily through the silent film era and transitioned into the talkie era as a popular character actor. One of his most notable roles of the era was that of Detering in the 1930 Lewis Milestone directed World War I drama *All Quiet on the Western Front*.

In his later years, Goodwin mainly acted in the Western film genre and often worked as a stuntman for film studios.

Some of his other roles included *Strawberry Roan* (1933), *Robin Hood of El Dorado* (1936), *Island in the Sky* (1938), *Union Pacific* (1939), *Great Guns* (1941) with Laurel and Hardy, *The Misadventures of Buster Keaton* (1950), *The Buster Keaton Show* (1950), *Life with Buster Keaton* (1951), *Cattle Drive* (1951) with Joel McCrea, *Hopalong Cassidy* (1952), *Black Horse Canyon* (1954) again with Joel McCrea, *Ma and Pa Kettle at Waikiki* (1955), *Showdown at Abilene* (1956), *Spartacus* (1960), and *Fate Is the Hunter* (1964).

He appeared in five movies with Abbott and Costello such as *Buck Privates* (1941), *Abbott and Costello meet the Invisible Man* (1951), *Comin' Round the Mountain* (1951), *Abbott and Costello go to Mars* (1953), and *Abbott and Costello meet the Keystone Kops* (1955).

He also had roles in seven movies and one television episode with Audie Murphy such as *Bad Boy* (1949), *The Kid from Texas* (1950), *Ride Clear of Diablo* (1954), *Walk the Proud Land* (1956), *Joe Butterfly* (1957), *Night Passage* (1957), *No Name on the Bullet* (1959), and *Whispering Smith* (1961).

Goodwin made eight guest appearances of the NBC television series *Daniel Boone* (1965-1968) starring Fess Parker and Ed Ames.

Goodwin made his last film appearance in the low-budget horror film *The Boy Who Cried Werewolf* before retiring from the film industry. He died July 12, 1987 in Woodland Hills, California.

Leo Gordon

Leo Vincent Gordon was born in Brooklyn, New York, December 2, 1922, and was an American movie and television character actor as well as a screenplay writer and novelist. He specialized in playing brutish bad guys during more than forty years in film and television.

He was raised by his father in dire poverty and grew up during the Great Depression. At the outset of World War II he joined the army.

Gordon took advantage of the benefits accorded him as part of the G.I. Bill and began taking acting lessons at the American Academy of Dramatic Arts. During his time at the academy, Gordon was enrolled with several future screen legends including Grace Kelly and Anne Bancroft. For a time, Jason Robards, who later became a two-time Academy Award winner was Gordon's instructor. It was here that he also met his future wife, Lynn Cartwright, who would have a sporadic but lengthy career as a character actress, mainly in television. They were married in 1950 and remained together until his death a half century later. They had one child, a daughter named Tara.

Gordon started his career on the stage and worked with such stars as Edward G. Robinson and Tyrone Power. He was soon discovered by a Hollywood agent in a Los Angeles production of *Darkness at Noon*. Over the course of his career, he would appear in more than 170 film and television productions from the early 1950s to the mid 1990s.

Gordon was often cast to make the most of his large size, intense features, deep menacing voice, and icy stare as Gordon had radiant light blue eyes. One of his earliest films was *Hondo* (1953) with John Wayne. His next film was *Riot in Cell Block 11* (1954), which was filmed at San Quentin.

Gordon may be most noted for his recurring character 'Big Mike McComb' on the *Maverick* television series from 1957 to 1960, working alongside James Garner and Jack Kelly, including an appearance in the famous "Shady Deal at Sunny Acres" episode. Garner later recalled in his videotaped interview for the Archive of American Television that Gordon purposely punched him for real in one of their first scenes together and that Garner hit him back when filming the next scene. Garner and Gordon reunited in the 1970s when Gordon appeared as a dimwitted bodyguard on four episodes of *The Rockford Files* (1978-1979).

He also appeared with Audie Murphy in one film and one television episode; *Ride a Crooked Trail* (1958) and *Whispering Smith* (1961).

One of his best remembered television appearances was a spoof of *High Noon*, playing an ex-convict who seemingly wants revenge against Andy Taylor in the episode "High Noon in Mayberry" on *The Andy Griffith Show* (1963).

Perhaps Gordon's single most memorable film scene occurred in *McLintock!* (1963), during which John Wayne knocks him down a long mudslide after uttering the famous line "Somebody oughta belt you but I won't! I won't! The hell I won't."

Another notable role was in the 1966 western *The Night of the Grizzly* opposite Clint Walker, one of the very few actors who could match Gordon's intense screen presence regarding physical size and strength. Gordon played bounty hunter Cass Dowdy, who would, as one character said: "...hunt anything for a price, man or animal.", but who had a soft spot for his enemy's son. Somehow, Gordon managed to make his character as sympathetic as he was frightening, and his final scene, giving his life to save the boy, is a classic.

Gordon portrayed sympathetic parts when called upon to do so, including his performances in the western *Black Patch* (1957), a film which he wrote, and in Roger Corman's civil rights drama *The Intruder* (1962), opposite a young William Shatner.

Gordon's final role was as Wyatt Earp in a 1994 episode of the television series *The Young Indiana Jones Chronicles*. He also appeared in *Maverick* earlier that same year with Mel Gibson, Jodie Foster and James Garner.

Gordon also wrote scripts for television episodes and movies, sometimes writing himself a good role. Frequently billed as "Leo V. Gordon," he wrote dozens of scripts that would later become movies or television episodes. His first successful film script, *The Cry Baby Killer* (1958), featured a young and unknown Jack Nicholson.

Among the most notable feature films he wrote were *You Can't Win 'Em All* (1970) starring Tony Curtis and Charles Bronson and *Tobruk* (1967) starring Rock Hudson and George Peppard and directed by Arthur Hiller, in which he appeared as Sergeant Krug.

In addition to film and television scripts, Gordon also wrote several novels, including the historical Western *Powderkeg*.

As a screen writer, he wrote nearly fifty scripts apiece for *Bonanza* (1963-1965) and *Cheyenne* (1956) as well as episodes for *Maverick* (1961-1961), in which he had a recurring role during the first two seasons in episodes he did not write. In the 1970s he would frequently appear on the popular police drama *Adam-12* (1971-1975), another show he often scripted.

In contrast to his screen persona, Gordon was a quiet, thoughtful and intelligent man who generally avoided the Hollywood spotlight. He was widely regarded by his fellow actors and his directors as a well-prepared professional.

In 1997, he received the "Golden Boot Award" for his many years of work in Westerns. In accepting the award, the actor simply flashed a smile for his fans and remarked "Thank God for typecasting!".

After struggling with a brief illness, Gordon died December 26, 2000, in his sleep at age 78 at his Los Angeles home from cardiac failure. He and his wife's ashes are interred at the Hollywood Forever Cemetery in Los Angeles.

Annette Gorman

Annette Gorman was born September 5, 1947 in New York City, New York. She appeared in seven films and television programs from 1959 to 1969.

Those include seven episodes as Addie Slaughter in *Texas John Slaughter* (1959-1961), five episodes as B.B. Preston of the *Moochie* series for *Walt Disney Presents* (1959-1960), *Five Finger Exercise* (1962), *Mister Ed* (1962), *The Many Loves of Dobie Gillis* (1962), *Leave It to Beaver* (1962), *Karen* (1964), and she played Mamie's new girl in her last film *A Time for Dying* (1969), which was Audie Murphy's last film, also.

Fred Graham

Audie Murphy with Fred Graham in *Arizona Raiders*

Fred Graham was born Charles Frederick Graham October 26, 1908, in Springer, New Mexico. Baseball gave burly Fred Graham his start in motion pictures. In 1928 he was working for the MGM sound department and also playing semi-pro baseball on the side. The studio was making a murder mystery called *Death on the Diamond* (1934), starring Robert Young and Nat Pendleton. Graham was hired to tutor Young and Pendleton in the fine points of the game, and doubled Pendleton in the catching scenes. This started him on a more than 40-year career as a stuntman and actor. While at the studio he doubled Clark Gable, Nelson Eddy and Charles Bickford.

He went over to Warner Brothers in 1938, and his initial assignment was to double Basil Rathbone in *The Adventures of Robin Hood* (1938). In 1941 he moved to Republic Pictures and worked on the studio's famed westerns and serials, and was a major part of the team of stunt experts, including such aces as David Sharpe and Tom Steele, responsible for the reputation that Republic enjoyed as having the best stunt department in the business.

Graham met John Wayne there and stunted for him in many of the films Wayne made at the studio. He also appeared in many films as an actor, usually playing truck drivers, cops, soldiers, crooks, etc.

Some of his acting roles were in *Libeled Lady* (1936) with Jean Harlow, *Dodge City* (1939), *The Roaring Twenties* (1939), *Reap the Wild Wind* (1942), *Buffalo Bill* (1944), *My Pal Trigger* (1946), *Buffalo Bill Rides Again* (1947), *Fort Apache* (1948), *The Fighting Kentuckian* (1949), *Flying Leathernecks* (1951), *The San Francisco Story* (1952), *The War of the Worlds* (1953), *20,000 Leagues Under the Sea* (1954), *Seven Men from Now* (1956), *The Restless Gun* (1957-1958), *Wanted: Dead or Alive* (1958), *The Giant Gila Monster* (1959), *Seven Ways from Sundown* (1960) with Audie Murphy, as William Clarke Quantrill in *Arizona Raiders* (1965) again with Audie Murphy, *Death Valley Days* (1966-1968), and *Guns of a Stranger* (1973).

In 1968 he went to work for Arizona's Department of Economic Planning and Development of Motion Pictures, and had more to do with bringing filming to the state of Arizona than anyone else. In Arizona they have the "Carefree at Southwest Studios", which was formerly known as "The Graham Studio".

On October 10, 1979, at age 70 in Scottsdale, Arizona, "Slugger", a nickname he got in his Republic days, passed away.

Kathryn Grant

Kathryn Grant with Audie Murphy in *Guns of Fort Petticoat*

Kathryn Grant was born Olive Kathryn Grandstaff November 25, 1933, in Houston, Texas. A pert, vivacious, and absolutely stunning brunette, the former Kathryn Grant is now known publicly as Kathryn Crosby. She was born in the Deep South and appeared on stage from age 3.

A graduate of the University of Texas and a student nurse at one point, she found her way into films via the beauty pageant circuit. The fresh-faced hopeful soon rose through the standard starlet ranks from unbilled parts to chipper "sis" types and decorative love interests alongside filmdom's top male stars.

She appeared opposite Richard Kiley in *The Phenix City Story* (1955), Tony Curtis in *Mister Cory* (1957), Jack Lemmon in *Operation Mad Ball* (1957), Audie Murphy in *Guns of Fort Petticoat* (1957), James Stewart in *Anatomy of a Murder* (1959) and Victor Mature in *The Big Circus* (1959), among others.

Her best known role, however, was as the princess-in-distress in the special effects-laden epic fantasy *The 7th Voyage of Sinbad* (1958), which has since reached semi-cult status.

For the most part, however, Kathryn was unchallenged as an actress and she retired rather uneventfully after marrying singer Bing Crosby in 1957.

They had three children, including actress Mary Crosby of *Dallas* (1978) fame. Seemingly content with family life, she, along with her children, dutifully appeared opposite her husband singing and lightly joking in his many popular Christmas-special presentations and even hosted a couple of syndicated TV series, but that was about it.

After Bing's death in 1977, however, she slowly involved herself in acting again, appearing every now and then on stage in such productions as *Same Time, Next Year*, *Charley's Aunt,* and a revival of the musical *State Fair* in 1996. She also appeared in the film *Queen of the Lot* (2010) as the mother of Mary Crosby's character.

In addition to authoring two sets of memoirs *Bing and Other Things* and *My Life with Bing*, Kathryn annually hosts the Crosby Gold Tournament in Winston-Salem, North Carolina.

Steve Gravers

Steve Gravers was born Solomon Gottlieb April 8, 1922 in New York, and was an American character actor who appeared in numerous television shows and also in several movies in a twenty-seven year career.

Some of his roles included *The Hunter* (1952), *Have Gun - Will Travel* (1959), *Hell Bent for Leather* (1960) with Audie Murphy, *The Detectives* (1961), *The Untouchables* (1959-1963), *Combat!* (1964), *The Loner* (1965), *Gunsmoke* (1966), *Get Smart* (1967), *Blood Sabbath* (1972), *Kojak* (1973-1974), *Future Cop* (1977), *Charlie's Angels* (1978), and *The Critical List* (1978).

He Died August 26, 1978, at age 56 in Studio City, California.

Dabbs Greer

Robert William "Dabbs" Greer was born April 2, 1917, and was an American actor who performed many diverse supporting roles in film and television for some fifty years. His distinctive, southern-accented voice fitted well in shows featuring rustic characters, such as westerns. However, he is probably best remembered as Reverend Alden in *Little House on the Prairie* (1974-1983).

Greer was born in Fairview, Missouri, the son of Bernice Irene (née Dabbs), a speech teacher, and Randall Alexander Greer, a druggist. Greer moved to Anderson as an infant with his family. He was eight when he began acting in children's theater productions. He attended Drury University, where he was a member of Theta Kappa Nu.

He made his film debut as an extra in the 1938 movie *Jesse James*, which was filmed mainly in Pineville. "They were paying $5 a day – a day! – to local people for being extras. That was really good money in those days, more money than we had seen in a long time", he told the Neosho Daily News in 2002.

Greer was recognizable to fans of *The Adventures of Superman* (1952-1958), as he appeared in three separate episodes on that show, including the series' inaugural entry, *Superman on Earth* (1952) where he played the first person to ever be saved by Superman. He was the major guest star, as a man framed for capital murder in *Five Minutes to Doom* (1954), and as an eccentric millionaire in *The Superman Silver Mine* (1958).

He appeared in many more films and television programs, including *Father's Little Dividend* (1951), *House of Wax* (1953), *Stranger on Horseback* (1955), *The McConnell Story* (1955) with Alan Ladd, *Invasion of the Body Snatchers* (1956), *The First Texan* (1956) with Joel McCrea, *The Vampire* (1957), *It! The Terror from Beyond Space* (1958), *Last Train from Gun Hill* (1959), *Wanted: Dead or Alive* (1958-1959) with Steve McQueen, *Richard Diamond, Private Detective* (1959) with David Janssen, *Wichita Town* (1959) again with Joel McCrea, *The Rifleman* (1959), *Twilight Zone* (1962-1963), *Showdown* (1963) with Audie Murphy, *Destry* (1964), *Roustabout* (1964) with Elvis Presley, *The Fugitive* (1963-1967) again with David Janssen, *The Ghost & Mrs. Muir* (1968-1969), *O'Hara, U.S. Treasury* (1971) yet again with David Janssen, *Adam-12* (1973), forty-two episodes of *Gunsmoke* (1955-1974),

Shazam! (1975), *The Incredible Hulk* (1978), *The Greatest American Hero* (1982), *Werewolf* (1987) with John J. York, *Sundown: The Vampire in Retreat* (1990), *Maybe It's Me* (2001-2002), and *Lizzie McGuire* (2003).

Greer had a prominent continuing role in the NBC series *Little House on the Prairie* as Reverend Robert Alden from 1974 to 1983. Often cast as a minister, he performed the marriages of Rob and Laura Petrie on *The Dick Van Dyke Show* (1962) and of Mike and Carol Brady on *The Brady Bunch* (1969), and he tended to the spiritual needs of the town folk in fictional Rome, Wisconsin, as Reverend Henry Novotny in *Picket Fences* (1992-1996).

In the 1958 film *I Want to Live!* he played the San Quentin captain who finished strapping down Barbara Graham in the gas chamber prior to her execution and was the last person to speak to her. He had a similar role in the 1999 film *The Green Mile*, in which he played the elderly version of Tom Hanks' Death Row officer Paul Edgecomb.

Most of his work was in supporting roles, but Greer told the Albany, N.Y., Times Union in 2000: "Every character actor, in their own little sphere, is the lead".

Greer died April 28, 2007, at age 90 at Huntington Hospital in Pasadena, California, after a battle with renal failure and heart disease. Greer never married and had no survivors.

Virginia Grey

Virginia Grey was born in Los Angeles, California, March 22, 1917, and was an American actress.

Her father, Ray Grey , was an actor. He was one of the Keystone Kops and a director for Mack Sennett and appeared on the silent screen with Mabel Normand, Dorothy Gish, and Ben Turpin, among others. He died while Virginia was still a child.

One of her early babysitters was movie star Gloria Swanson. Grey debuted at the age of ten in the silent film *Uncle Tom's Cabin* (1927) as Little Eva. She continued acting for a few more years, but then left movies in order to finish her education.

Grey returned to films in the 1930s with bit parts and extra work, but she eventually signed a contract with Metro-Goldwyn-Mayer and appeared in such MGM movies as *Another Thin Man* (1939), *Hullabaloo* (1940), *The Big Store* (1941), and *The Hardys Ride High* (1939) with Mickey Rooney.

She left MGM in 1942, and signed with several different studios over the years, working steadily. During the 1950s and 1960s, producer Ross Hunter frequently included Grey in his popular soap melodramas, such as *All That Heaven Allows* (1955), *Back Street* (1961), and *Madame X* (1966).

She had an on again/off again relationship with Clark Gable in the 1940s. After his wife Carole Lombard died and he returned from military service, Clark and Virginia were often seen at restaurants and nightclubs together. Many, including Virginia herself, expected him to marry her. The tabloids were all expecting the wedding announcement. It was a great surprise when he hastily married Lady Sylvia Ashley in 1949. Virginia was heartbroken. They divorced in 1952, but much to Virginia's dismay their brief romance was never rekindled. Her friends say that her hoping and waiting for Clark was the reason she never married.

She was a regular in films and n television in the 1950s and 1960s, appearing on *The Ford Television Theatre* (1953), *The Lone Wolf* (1954), *Trackdown* (1955), *No Name on the Bullet* (1959) with Audie Murphy, *Wagon Train* (1958-1961), *The Red Skelton Hour* (1955-1966), *Airport* (1970), *Marcus Welby, M.D.* (1970), *Love, American Style* (1973), *The Lives of Jenny Dolan* (1975), and *Arthur Hailey's the Moneychangers* (1976).

She retired from acting and died July 31, 2004, at age 87 in Woodland Hills, Los Angeles, California.

James Griffith

Audie Murphy with James Griffith in *Guns of Fort Petticoat*

James Griffith was born in Los Angeles, California, February 13, 1916, and was an American character actor, musician and screenwriter.

Griffith aspired to be a musician rather than an actor. Instead, he managed to find work in little theatres around Los Angeles, where the budding musician eased into a dual career of acting. He found success in the production *They Can't Get You Down* in 1939, but put his career on hold during World War II to serve with the U.S. military.

Following the war, Griffith switched from the stage to films when he appeared in the 1948 film noir picture *Blonde Ice*. From then on, he enjoyed a lengthy career of supporting and bit roles (sometimes uncredited) in westerns and detective films.

Though Griffith was generally cast as the outlaw in Western pictures, he managed to garner a few memorable "good guy" roles over his many years in Hollywood such as Abraham Lincoln in both 1950's *Stage to Tucson* and 1955's *Apache Ambush*, sheriff Pat Garrett in 1954's *The Law vs. Billy the Kid*, John Wesley Hardin in a 1959 television episode of *Maverick* entitled "Duel at Sundown" featuring Clint Eastwood, and Davy Crockett in 1956's *The First Texan*. In the role of Aaron Adams, he appeared in twelve episodes in 1958 on the Robert Culp western series *Trackdown*, which aired on CBS from 1957 to 1959. He also had a recurring role in the syndicated series, *Sheriff of Cochise* (1956-1957) starring John Bromfield.

Some of his other roles include *Indian Territory* (1950), *Al Jennings of Oklahoma* (1951), *Hopalong Cassidy* (1952), *Ride Clear of Diablo* (1954) with Audie Murphy, as Bob Dalton in *Jesse James vs. the Daltons* (1954), *Tribute to a Bad Man* (1956) with James Cagney, as Davey Crockett in *The First Texan* (1956) with Joel McCrea, *The Guns of Fort Petticoat* (1957) again with Audie Murphy, *Wichita Town* (1959) again with Joel McCrea, *How the West Was Won* (1962), *The Fugitive* (1964-1965), *The Monkees* (1967), *Heaven with a Gun* (1969), *Hec Ramsey* (1972), *Kolchak: The Night Stalker* (1974), *S.W.A.T.* (1975), *The Life and Times of Grizzly Adams* (1977), *Hart to Hart* (1981), *Dallas* (1982), and *Trapper John, M.D.* (1984).

As a somewhat "extra" activity, Griffith played the Reverend in Black and the opening, closing, and a few in the middle scenes in the 1964 Russ Meyer film *Lorna*, starring Lorna Maitland in one of Meyer's black-and-white 'skin' movies before the height of his career with *Beyond the Valley of the Dolls* in 1968.

Throughout his acting career, Griffith continued to practice his original love of music, having performed the Spike Jones band. He composed music for the 1958 film *Bullwhip* and the 1964 picture, *Lorna,* in which he also had a role and served as screenwriter).

He died September 17, 1993, at age 77 in Avila Beach, California.

Clu Gulager

Clu Gulager was born November 16, 1928, and is an American television and film actor and director. He is particularly noted for his co-starring role as William H. Bonney (Billy The Kid) in the 1960–62 NBC TV series *The Tall Man* and for his role in the NBC series *The Virginian* (1963-1968).

Gulager was born William Martin Gulager in Holdenville, Oklahoma, the son of John Gulager, a cowboy entertainer. His first cousin was Will Rogers through his paternal grandmother.

Gulager served in the United States Marine Corps from 1946 to 1948. He has Cherokee Native American ancestry. His nickname was given to him by his father for the clu-clu birds (known in English as Martins, like his middle name) that were nesting at the Gulager home at the time Clu was born. He attended NSU (Northeastern State University in Tahlequah, OK), then transferred to Baylor University.

In 1958, Clu Gulager appeared as Roy Carter in the episode "The Return of Roy Carter" (written by Gene Roddenberry of *Star Trek* fame) in the western television series *Have Gun-Will Travel* starring Richard Boone. In the spring of 1959, Gulager appeared as Tommy Pavlock in the episode "The Immigrant" of NBC's series *The Lawless Years*, a 1920s crime drama.

In the fall of 1959, he appeared in the episode "The Temple of the Swinging Doll" of NBC's short-lived espionage drama, *Five Fingers*, starring David Hedison. On October 11, 1959, he appeared as a U.S. Navy sailor in the "Appointment at Eleven" episode of *Alfred Hitchcock Presents* and again as an escaped convict in the episode "Pen Pal" on November 1, 1960. On *The Untouchables* (1959), he essayed the role of vicious mob killer Vincent "Mad Dog" Coll and turned in an utterly chilling performance as the psychopathic Coll.

He then played Billy the Kid in the 1960–62 NBC series *The Tall Man* opposite Barry Sullivan as Pat Garrett, and succeeded in portraying Billy as a sympathetic character without resorting to the "misunderstood young man" portrayal so often used in such films as *The Outlaw* and *The Left Handed Gun*.

In 1961, he guest starred on the NBC western *Whispering Smith*, Audie Murphy's only attempt at series television. Gulager portrayed "Emmett Ryker" from 1964 to 1968 on another NBC series *The Virginian* starring with James Drury, Doug McClure, Lee J. Cobb, Roberta Shore, Randy Boone, Gary Clarke and Diane Roter. He starred with Lee Marvin, Ronald Reagan and Angie Dickinson in the 1964 version of *The Killers*.

Some of his other roles include *Wanted: Dead or Alive* (1959), *Dr. Kildare* (1964), *San Francisco International Airport* (1970), *The Last Picture Show* (1971), *McQ* (1974) with John Wayne, *Smile Jenny, You're Dead* (1974), *Shaft* (1974), *Get Christie Love!* (1974), *The Other Side of Midnight* (1977), *A Force of One* (1979) with Chuck Norris, *Kenny Rogers as The Gambler* (1980), *Automan* (1983), *Cover Up* (1984) with Jon-Erik Hexum, *The Return of the Living Dead* (1985), *A Nightmare on Elm Street Part 2: Freddy's Revenge* (1985), *North and South, Book II* (1986), *I'm Gonna Git You Sucka* (1988), *Kung Fu: The Legend Continues* (1995), *Walker, Texas Ranger* (1995) again with Chuck Norris, *Dr. Quinn, Medicine Woman* (1996), and *Gunfighter* (1999).

Gulager is the father of film director John Gulager, contest winner in third season of *Project Greenlight* (2001), and is the widower of the actress Miriam Byrd-Nethery who died in 2003.

He appeared in his son John Gulager's *Feast* (2005-2009) series of films as a shotgun-toting bartender and currently will have a role in *Piranha 3DD* (2012).

Don Haggerty

Don Haggerty with Audie Murphy in *The Kid From Texas* and Don's son Dan Haggerty with author in 2013

Don Haggerty was born July 3, 1914, in Poughkeepsie, New York, and was an American film actor appearing in films in the 1940s and 1950s.

Before entering films in 1947, Haggerty was a Brown University athlete and served in the U.S. military. Usually cast as tough policemen or cowboys, he appeared in a number of memorable films including *Sands of Iwo Jima* (1949), *The Asphalt Jungle* (1951), *Angels in the Outfield* (1951) and *The Narrow Margin* (1952).

The B-movie actor continued to appear in films and television until the early 1980s. Some of those roles included *USS VD: Ship of Shame* (1942), *Gun Smugglers* (1948), *The Kid from Texas* (1950) with Audie Murphy, *Hopalong Cassidy* (1952), as Eddie Drake in *The Cases of Eddie Drake* (1952), *Strategic Air Command* (1955), as Sheriff Elder in Rod Cameron's syndicated western-themed crime drama, *State Trooper* (1956-1957), *26 Men* about the Arizona Rangers (1957-1958), *Behind Closed Doors* (1959), *Richard Diamond, Private Detective* (1959) with David Janssen, *Dan Raven* (1960), *Seven Ways from Sundown* (1960) again with Audie Murphy, twenty-one episodes as Marsh Murdoch in *The Life and Legend of Wyatt Earp* (1955-1961), *Hell Is for Heroes* (1962), *Gunsmoke* (1963), *Destry* (1964), *The Munsters* (1965), *Harlow* (1965), *My Favorite Martian* (1964-1965), *The Night of the Grizzly* (1966), *Dirty Harry* (1971), *O'Hara, U.S. Treasury* (1972) yet again with David Janssen, *Harry O* (1975) and again with David Janssen, *Baretta* (1977), and *California Gold Rush* (1981).

Don's son, actor Dan Haggerty of *Grizzly Adams* (1977-1978) has the dubious distinction of being the only actor to ever have his name removed from the Hollywood Walk of Fame. The Hollywood Chamber of Commerce chairman mistakenly spelled "Dan Haggerty" on the plaque when the honor was supposed to have gone to Don Haggerty. Dan later was honored with his own star.

Don Haggerty died August 19, 1988, in Cocoa Beach, Florida.

Alan Hale, Jr

Alan Hale with Audie Murphy in *Whispering Smith*

Alan Hale, Jr. was born Alan Hale Mackahan in Los Angeles, California, March 8, 1921, was an American film and television actor, best known for his role as Skipper (Jonas Grumby) on the popular sitcom *Gilligan's Island* (1964-1967).

His father was character actor Alan Hale, Sr. and his mother was Gretchen Hartman (1897–1979), a silent film actress. His father (whom junior greatly resembled) had an extremely successful career in movies both as a leading man in silent films and as a supporting actor in sound movies, appearing in many Errol Flynn films, acting in 235 movies altogether, and playing Little John in Robin Hood films three times over a 28-year span, beginning with the silent Douglas Fairbanks version. While his father was adapting to sound films, Hale, Jr., began his career while still a baby. After the death of his father in 1950, Alan stopped using "Junior".

Hale, Jr. enlisted in the United States Coast Guard during the Second World War. After his stint in the Coast Guard, Hale's first important roles were as a member of Gene Autry's recurring cast of players. During the late 1940s and early 1950s, he frequently appeared in Autry movies and *The Gene Autry Show* (1950-1952) on television. He starred in a television series, such as the CBS Cold War espionage program from 1952–1953, *Biff Baker, U.S.A.*, with co-star Randy Stuart, as his wife, Louise Baker.

He appeared as cattleman Jack Larson in *Destry* (1954) with Audie Murphy. He later appeared in the classic CBS western series *Wanted: Dead or Alive* (1958) opposite Steve McQueen, and played the titular lead in the television series *Casey Jones* (1957-1958). He played Scully in seven episodes of *The Texan* (1958-1960), *Wichita Town* (1960) with Joel McCrea, and again he appeared in Audie Murphy's short-lived NBC western detective series, *Whispering Smith* (1961), as the witness to a murder.

In 1962, Hale also appeared on *The Andy Griffith Show* as Jeff Pruitt, a rough, back-woods bachelor who comes to Mayberry to find a bride. In the episode, he refers to Barney Fife more than once as "little buddy," a nickname he would later use in his most famous and beloved role, that of the Skipper on *Gilligan's Island*, which ran from 1964 to 1967. He appeared in an episode of CBS's *The New Phil Silvers Show* in the 1963–1964 season. In 1967, he appeared in the *Batman* episode titled "The Ogg and I part 1" where he played a bartender named "Gilligan".

He starred with Bob Denver (Hale's *Gilligan* co-star) in *The Good Guys* (1968–70).

Hale also made an appearance on the television western *The Wild, Wild West* (1969), joining Robert Conrad as Secret Service agent Ned Brown. At the end of the episode, character James West asks Brown what he planned to do next. "I'm going to make a big dream come true. And do you know what my big dream is? I'm going to spend my vacation all alone... on a desert island", after which the first few notes of the theme from *Gilligan's Island* can be heard in the background. Fellow *Gilligan's Island* castaway Jim Backus also appears in the episode as Fabian Swanson.

The Skipper on *Gilligan's Island* (1964–1967) proved to be the most prominent role for Hale, as the show continued to be popular for later generations of viewers due to syndicated re-runs. The popularity of the show typecast its actors, making it difficult for them to successfully pursue diversified acting opportunities. They received no substantial residual payments for their roles, and the difficulty in finding roles often created financial hardship and resentment. However, Hale often said he did not mind being so closely identified with the Skipper. He co-owned a restaurant in the West Hollywood area (Alan Hale's Lobster Barrel) and would often greet customers in his "Skipper" hat.

During the weekends from 1974 to 1977, a new generation enjoyed the cartoon version of *The New Adventures of Gilligan*, and by 1978, they brought back the original crew for a TV film named *Rescue from Gilligan's Island*. Hale also portrayed the Skipper in two more TV reunion films *The Castaways on Gilligan's Island* (1979) and *The Harlem Globetrotters on Gilligan's Island* (1981), and participated in numerous reunions with the cast throughout the 1980s.

His final appearances as the Skipper were on a 1987 episode of the sitcom *ALF*, and for several 1989 clips promoting *Gilligan's Island* reruns on TBS (TV network), both alongside his old friend Bob Denver. He also made a cameo appearance with Denver in the 1987 film *Back to the Beach*.

Hale was known for his great love of children. When he was dying of cancer, he learned there was a sick child in the same hospital who loved the *Gilligan's Island* show. He went to see the boy and said "The Skipper's here, son, everything is going to be all right." The child, having noticed all the weight Hale had lost due to cancer, inquired about it. Hale made up a story on the spot about how there was a new version of the show in the works, and he was going to play Gilligan.

A resident of Hollywood, California, in the final years, Hale died of thyroid cancer at St. Vincent Medical Center in Los Angeles January 2, 1990, at aged 68. He was cremated, and his ashes were scattered at sea.

Gita Hall

Gita Hall with Audie Murphy in *The Gunrunners*

Gita Hall was born Birgitta Wetterhall September 6, 1933, in Sweden. She only made two films early in her career. The first was *The Gunrunners* (1958) with Audie Murphy and Eddie Albert, and the other was *Wolf Larsen* (1958) with Barry Sullivan.

She married actor Barry Sullivan in July of 1958, between the filming and the release of *The Gun Runners*. She had one daughter by Barry Sullivan before their divorce in 1961. She married Mitchell May III and stayed happily married to him until his death in 2000. She had two daughters with Mitchell.

She became a United States citizen in 1960.

She had retired from acting after *Wolf Larsen*, but returned as herself in the film *The Still Life* (2007) with friend Terry Moore, and the television show *Old Skool with Terry and Gita* (2008). The show is described "Terry Moore and Gita Hall hit the streets to discover what's hip amongst today's youth". Some of the guest stars were Mickey Rooney, Robert Wagner, and Gary Busey.

Brett Halsey

Brett Halsey was born Charles Oliver Hand June 20, 1933, in Santa Ana, California, and is an American film actor, sometimes credited as Montgomery Ford.

He is known for a prolific career in B pictures and in European made feature films as well as being the original John Abbott on the soap opera *The Young and the Restless*, a role he held from May 1980 to March 1981, before being replaced by Jerry Douglas. He is the great nephew of Admiral Bull Halsey; Universal Pictures selected his acting name from the Admiral.

Interested in acting since he was a child, Brett was employed as a page at CBS Television studios. Whilst there he met Jack Benny and his wife Mary Livingstone who introduced him to the head of Universal Pictures who placed him in a school with other aspiring actors for the studio.

His first film was *All I Desire* (1953). More of his films included *Ma and Pa Kettle at Home* (1954), *Revenge of the Creature* (1955), *To Hell and Back* (1955) with Audie Murphy, *The Girl He Left Behind* (1956), *Lafayette Escadrille* (1958), and *Gunman's Walk* (1958).

In 1958, Halsey guest starred in the episode "The Imposter" of Richard Carlson's syndicated western television series *Mackenzie's Raiders*, a fictional account of cavalry Colonel Mackenzie. Also in 1958, Halsey had the lead role of a life-saving sailor in an episode of *Highway Patrol*. In 1959, he had a co-starring role in the science-fiction film *The Atomic Submarine* with Arthur Franz and Dick Foran. Halsey guest starred in the episode "Thin Ice" in 1959 of Paluzzi's NBC espionage series, *Five Fingers*, starring David Hedison.

From 1961–1962, Halsey starred with Barry Coe and Gary Lockwood in the ABC television series *Follow the Sun*, a story of two magazine free-lance writers living in Honolulu, Hawaii.

In 1961, Halsey won the Golden Globe Award for "New Star of the Year". His *Follow the Sun* co-star, Barry Coe, had won the same honor in 1960. The award was discontinued in 1983.

Halsey played supporting and co-starring roles in Hollywood, having appeared in such films as *Return of the Fly* (1959) with Vincent Price. By the early 1960s, he relocated to Italy where he found himself in high demand in a score of adventurous films such as *The Avenger of Venice (1964)*, being often cast as a swashbuckling hero. He also appeared in a few Spaghetti Westerns and Eurospy films.

He returned to the United States in the early 1970s and worked in film and television. He made many appearances in such serials as *General Hospital* (1967) and *Love Is a Many Splendored Thing* (1972-1973), but also made supporting appearances in higher-profile films such as *The Godfather Part III* (1990).

He also appeared as the captain of a luxury space liner in the *Buck Rogers in the 25th Century* (1979) episode "Cruise Ship to the Stars", the episode to feature doomed Playboy Playmate Dorothy Stratten as Miss Cosmos.

In 1954, he married Miss Germany 1952 and actress Renate Hoy. They had two children, son Charles Oliver Hand (a.k.a. Rock Bottom of the notorious L.A. punk band Rock Bottom and the Spys) and daughter Tracy Leigh. They divorced in 1959.

From 1960 to 1962, he was married to Italian actress Luciana Paluzzi. They had one son, Christian, and co-starred in 1961 as a newlywed couple in *Return to Peyton Place* (1961).

In 1964, Halsey married the popular German actress and singer Heidi Brühl. They had two children, son Clayton Alexander Siegfried and daughter Nicole. They divorced in 1976.

Toward the end of the 1990s Halsey moved to Costa Rica to teach acting for camera in San Jose. Currently Halsey resides in Laguna Hills, California, with his wife Victoria Korda (granddaughter of Alexander Korda) where he spends most of his time writing and making the occasional film appearance. On August 10, 2005 his son Rock Halsey was killed while serving time in a U.S. penitentiary.

Kipp Hamilton

Audie Murphy with Kipp Hamilton in *The Unforgiven*

Kipp Hamilton was born Rita Marie Hamilton in Los Angeles, California August 16, 1935, and was an American actress. She was the sister of producer Joe Hamilton and the sister-in-law of Carol Burnett.

Hamilton was a beauty pageant contestant winning the title of "Miss Optometry" in New York in March 1953. In October 1955, she was named "Deb Star of 1955" along with Cathy Crosby, Anita Ekberg, Lilian Montevecchi, Jody Lawrence, Mara Corday, Lori Nelson, Tracey Morgan, Marisa Pavan, and Gloria Thomas. With little acting experience, she managed to make her debut in the 1955 movie, *Good Morning Miss Dove*, playing Jincey Baker.

Throughout the late 1950s and 1960s, Hamilton would go on to land roles on shows and films like *Richard Diamond, Private Detective* (1958) with David Janssen, *The Life and Legend of Wyatt Earp* (1958), *Never so Few* (1959) with Steve McQueen, *The Unforgiven* (1960) with Audie Murphy, and *Westinghouse Playhouse* (1961).

In 1965, she landed her most notable acting role as Pleasure O' Riley in *Bewitched*. More roles include *Harlow* (1965), *The Wild Wild West* (1965), and *Dragnet 1967* (1967).

Her next role was in *War of the Gargantuas* (1968). She was recommended for the part by her brother Joe. The director auditioned her, and she was hired for the part of a singer in the film. After filming, *War of the Gargantuas*, she appeared onscreen for the last time in an episode of *The Virginian* (1967).

Hamilton dated Frank Sinatra, actors Eric Fleming and Chris Robinson. She was also linked to screenwriter/producer Sy Bartlett and Efrem Zimbalist, Jr.

Hamilton married director David Geisel with whom she had a daughter, Marie, in 1963. The couple divorced in October 1965. In February 1968, Hamilton married Beverly Hills lawyer Donald Thorman Rosenfeld. Together they had a daughter, Dana, later that same year.

Hamilton died at the age of 45 on January 29, 1981, in Los Angeles, California.

Alvin Hammer

Alvin Hammer was born Irving Dratler January 2, 1915 in New York City, New York. He was an American character actor who performed in vaudeville, on stage, in nightclubs, on television, and in many films between the 1940s and the late 1980s.

Some of his roles included *Greenwich Village* (1944), *Miracle on 34th Street* (1947), *The Noose Hangs High* (1948) with Abbott and Costello, *Texas, Brooklyn & Heaven* (1948) with Audie Murphy, *Ma and Pa Kettle* (1949),

The Killer That Stalked New York (1950), *Mark Saber* (1952), *Peter Gunn* (1959), *Gomer Pyle, U.S.M.C.* (1969), *Adam-12* (1969), *Planet of the Apes* (1974), *Chico and the Man* (1977), *Trapper John, M.D.* (1980-1981), *Scrooged* (1988), and *The Ben Stiller Show* (1992).

He died October 31, 1993, at age 78 in Hollywood, California.

John Harding

Audie Murphy with John Harding in *The Gunrunners*

No biographical information could be found for John Harding but he was in thirty-three films and television programs from 1955 to 1978.

Some of those credits included *Love Me or Leave Me* (1955), *The Joker Is Wild* (1957), *The Gun Runners* (1958) with Audie Murphy, *Please Don't Eat the Daisies* (1960), *The New Breed* (1962), *The Man from U.N.C.L.E.* (1964), *Hawaii* (1966), *Get Smart* (1969), *The Wild Wild West* (1969), *Nichols* (1971-1972), *Hustle* (1975), and *The Next Step Beyond* (1978).

Betty Harford

Betty Harford was born in 1927, and is an American actress, highly active on television.

Her credits include *Alfred Hitchcock Presents* (1955-1957), *The Wild and the Innocent* (1959) with Audie Murphy, *Gunsmoke* (1960), *Dr. Kildare* (1963), *The Twilight Zone* (1962), *The Big Valley* (1966), and *Bud & Lou* (1978).

She also was well known for her performance in *The Paper Chase* as Mrs. Nottingham, the ever efficient secretary to Professor Charles Kingsfield. She performed this role during the first season in 1978-1979 and then later reprised it when the show was brought back by Showtime in 1983.

She is possibly best known for her recurring role in the soap opera *Dynasty* as cook Hilda Gunnerson. Harford appeared in the series throughout its nine-year run from 1981 to 1989, reprising the part for *Dynasty: The Reunion* in 1991.

John Harmon

Audie Murphy with John Harmon in *Whispering Smith*

John Harmon was born June 30, 1905, and was an American actor. Harmon was a very prolific bit actor.

His career spanned over six decades and almost 300 movie and television roles in a wide variety of genres. Many of his earlier appearances are uncredited. His first major screen credit was in *I Was Framed* (1942).

Some of his roles included *Buck Rogers* (1939), *The Green Hornet* (1940), *The Shepherd of the Hills* (1941), *Lucky Jordan* (1942) with Alan Ladd, *O.S.S.* (1946) again with Alan Ladd, *Fear in the Night* (1947) with DeForest Kelley (twenty years later he would steal DeForest Kelley's 'Phaser' in the *Star Trek* (1967) episode "The City on the Edge of Forever" and accidently disintegrate himself), *Streets of San Francisco* (1949), *Tales of Robin Hood* (1951), *Duffy's Tavern* (1954), *The Hardy Boys: The Mystery of the Ghost Farm* (1957), *Badman's Country* (1958), *Richard Diamond, Private Detective* (1959), *Wanted: Dead or Alive* (1958-1960), *Whispering Smith* (1961) with Audie Murphy, numerous episodes as hotel clerk Eddie Halstead in *The Rifleman* (1958-1962), *Twilight Zone* (1962-1963), *No Time for Sergeants* (1964), *Honey West* (1966), *The Fugitive* (1964-1966), *Texas Across the River* (1966), *Land of the Giants* (1969), *Adam-12* (1970), *O'Hara, U.S. Treasury* (1971), *Dirty Sally* (1974), *Hitch Hike to Hell* (1977), *Malibu High* (1979), and *Microwave Massacre* (1983).

The movie in which he made his last screen appearance was filmed shortly before he died, *The Naked Monster* (2005), but was not was released for twenty years after his death.

In his later years, Harmon became a used books dealer in Los Angeles. He collected first editions of Mark Twain. He suffered a stroke about a year before he died August 6, 1985, at age 80 in Los Angeles, California, from heart failure.

Berkeley Harris

Berkeley Harris with Audie Murphy in *Bullet for a Badman*

Berkeley Harris was born Elliott Berkeley Harris and was an American character actor. His first role was in *The Dick Powell Theatre* (1962). He continued acting in such television programs and films as *Route 66* (1963), *The Greatest Show on Earth* (1963), *Bullet for a Badman* (1964) with Audie Murphy, *Shenandoah* (1965), *Lassie* (1968), *Love Is a Many Splendored Thing* (1971), *O'Hara, U.S. Treasury* (1971), *Marcus Welby, M.D.* (1972), *The Groove Tube* (1974), *A Secret Space* (77), and *Texas* (1981-1982).

He marries actress Susan Harris in 1965 and had one son. He divorced her in 1969 and married actress Beverlee McKinsey in 1971 and it lasted until his death on September 17, 1984.

H. Tommy Hart

H. Tommy Hart with Audie Murphy in *To Hell and Back*

No biographical information can be found for Harold Tommy Hart. He has appeared in sixteen films and television programs from 1952 through 1962. Most of those have been with Audie Murphy, such as *Tumbleweed* (1953), *To Hell and Back* (1955), *World in My Corner* (1956), *Night Passage* (1957), *The Wild and the Innocent* (1959), and *Whispering Smith* (1961).

His non-Audie Murphy roles were *Gang Busters* (1952), *Miss Sadie Thompson* (1953), *Tennessee Champ* (1954), *Rails Into Laramie* (1954), *The Man with the Golden Arm* (1955), *Gunsmoke* (1956), *Never Steal Anything Small* (1959) with James Cagney, *Some Like It Hot* (1959), *The Silent Call* (1961), and *Kid Galahad* (1962) with Elvis Presley.

Harry Harvey

Harry Harvey with Audie Murphy in *The Cimarron Kid*

Harry Harvey, Sr. was born January 10, 1901, in Indian Territory, which is now Oklahoma. He was a film character actor and has more than 300 appearances in television series and movies.

His first role was in Tom Mix's version of *Destry Rides Again* (1932). He continued to get roles in such fare as *Manhattan Moon* (1935), *Gold Diggers of 1937* (1936), *Kid Galahad* (1937), *The Secret of Treasure Island* (1938), *Blondie Takes a Vacation* (1939), *Redskins and Redheads* (1941), *Mexican Spitfire's Elephant* (1942), *It Ain't Hay* (1943) with Abbott and Costello, *Badman's Territory* (1946), *Dick Tracy's Dilemma* (1947), *Belle Starr's Daughter* (1948), *Calamity Jane and Sam Bass* (1949), *The Cimarron Kid* (1952) with Audie Murphy, *The Duel at Silver Creek* (1952) as Audie Murphy's father, *Tumbleweed* (1953) a third time with Audie Murphy, *20,000 Leagues Under the Sea* (1954), *Richard Diamond, Private Detective* (1957-1958), *Wanted: Dead or Alive* (1958), *It's a*

Man's World (1962-1963), *Cat Ballou* (1965), *Lost in Space* (1965), *Doctor, You've Got to Be Kidding!* (1967), *Stay Away, Joe* (1968) with Elvis Presley, *Airport* (1970), and *Hec Ramsey* (1972-1974).

Harvey is best known for playing the role of Sheriff Tom Blodgett, in the series *The Roy Rogers Show* in fifty-three episodes (1951–57), and the series *Man Without a Gun* as Mayor George Dixon, in twenty-one episodes (1957–59). His last appearance was in *Adam-12* (1974) with Martin Milner and Kent McCord.

Harry's son, Harry Harvey Jr. (1929–1978) was also an actor.

Harry Harvey died November 27, 1985, at age 84 in Sylmar, California.

Raymond Hatton

Raymond William Hatton was born in Red Oak, Iowa, July 7, 1887, and was an American movie actor who appeared in almost five hundred movies, including a stint of being paired in 1920s comedies with Wallace Beery.

Although Hatton enjoyed a successful silent film career, sound helped to boost Hatton's career and making him best remembered as the tobacco-chewing, rip snorting Rusty Joslin in *The Three Mesquiteers* (1933) series.

Some of his roles included *Tragic Love* (1909), *The Wild Goose Chase* (1915), as the Artful Dodger in *Oliver Twist* (1916), *Officer 666* (1920), *The Hunchback of Notre Dame* (1923), *The Thundering Herd* (1925), *Fireman, Save My Child* (1927), *The Silver Horde* (1930) with Joel McCrea, *'G' Men* (1935), *The Arizona Raiders* (1936), *Tom Sawyer, Detective* (1938), as Jim Bridger in *Kit Carson* (1940), *Reap the Wild Wind* (1942), *Gun Smoke* (1945), *Marshal of Heldorado* (1950), *Skipalong Rosenbloom* (1951), *The Abbott and Costello Show* (1953), *Hopalong Cassidy* (1954), *Treasure of Ruby Hills* (1955), *Day the World Ended* (1955), *Shake, Rattle & Rock!* (1956), *Invasion of the Saucer Men* (1957), *Tales of the Texas Rangers* (1958), *Maverick* (1958-1960), *Wanted: Dead or Alive* (1960), *Whispering Smith* (1961) with Audie Murphy, *Destry* (1964), *The Quick Gun* (1964) again with Audie Murphy, and *In Cold Blood* (1967) with Robert Blake.

He died October 21, 1971, at age 84 in Palmdale, California.

Joe Haworth

Joe Haworth was born October 21, 1914, in Cleveland, Ohio. He comes from a theatrical family. His father William Haworth was a famous playwright; his uncle, Joe Haworth, was a top actor of the American stage in the last century, working with such greats as Edwin Booth. His brother-in-law was character actor Wallace Ford, and a brother, Ted Haworth, was an Academy Award-winning Art Director.

Joe made his first stage appearance as "Tiny Tim" in his grammar school play of *A Christmas Carol*, and later appeared on the New York stage, as well as operating his own theatre in Nyack, New York.

He came to Hollywood and made his film debut in *Gung Ho!: The Story of Carlson's Makin Island Raiders* (1943). When actor Addison Randall (aka Jack Randall) was killed on the first day of filming *The Royal Mounted Rides Again* (1945), it was Joe who replaced him.

More of his film roles included *Without Reservations* (1946), *I Was a Male War Bride* (1949), *The Red Badge of Courage* (1951) with Audie Murphy, *The Abbott and Costello Show* (1953), *The Spoilers* (1955), *3:10 to Yuma* (1957), *Richard Diamond, Private Detective* (1958), *The Badlanders* (1958), *Twilight Zone* (1960), *Spartacus* (1960), *Showdown* (1963), *Do Not Fold, Spindle, or Mutilate* (1971), *The Flight of the Grey Wolf* (1976), and *The Six Million Dollar Man* (1976).

In addition to his acting, Joe was a noted photographer in Hollywood for publicity shots of both the stars and for the movies.

He died July 2, 2000 at age 85 in Santa Cruz, California.

Jim Hayward

Jim Hayward with Audie Murphy in *Whispering Smith*

Jim Hayward was born in 1923 in West Bridgewater, Massachusetts. He appeared in 132 films and television programs from 1949 through 1967.

Some of those include *Coyote Canyon* (1949), *The Kid from Texas* (1950) with Audie Murphy, *Saddle Tramp* (1950) with Joel McCrea, *The Red Badge of Courage* (1951) again with Audie Murphy, *Ghost Buster* (1952), *Gang Busters* (1952), *The Lone Ranger* (1953), *The Roy Rogers Show* (1953-1954), *All That Heaven Allows* (1955), *Naked Gun* (1956), *Decision at Sundown* (1957), *Wanted: Dead or Alive* (1960), two episodes as Cyrus Gratch in *Whispering Smith* (1961) yet again with Audie Murphy, *Terror at Black Falls* (1962), *The Virginian* (1963), *Petticoat Junction* (1965-1966), and *The Beverly Hillbillies* (1967).

He died July 12, 1981, at age 57.

Myron Healey

Myron Daniel Healey was born in Petaluma, California, June 8, 1923, and was an American actor. He began his Hollywood career during the early 1940s in bit parts and minor supporting roles at various studios.

Healey served in World War II as an Air Corps navigator and bombardier, flying in B-26 Martin Marauders in the European Theatre. He continued that military duty, retiring in the early 1960s as a captain in the United States Air Force Reserve.

Returning to film work after the war, Healey played villains and henchmen in low budget western films. In the post-war period, he was often seen in Monogram studio films, which starred Johnny Mack Brown, Jimmy Wakely and Whip Wilson.

Some of his roles were in such films and television programs as *I Dood It* (1943), *The Time of Their Lives* (1946) with Abbott and Costello, *Blondie's Big Moment* (1947), *Buck Privates Come Home* (1947) again with Bud & Lou, *Wake of the Red Witch* (1948) with John Wayne, *Batman and Robin* (1949), *The Fuller Brush Girl* (1950), *Al Jennings of Oklahoma* (1951) with Dan Duryea, as John Dillinger in *Gang Busters* (1952), *Hopalong Cassidy* (1953), *Cattle Queen of Montana* (1954), as John Reno in *Rage at Dawn* (1955) with Randolph Scott, *Ma and Pa Kettle at Waikiki* (1955), *The First Texan* (1956) with Joel McCrea, *Quantrill's Raiders* (1958), *Apache Territory* (1958) with Rory Calhoun, and *Tombstone Territory* (1958-1959).

For the 1958-59 season, Healey replaced Douglas Fowley as Doc Holliday in the popular western TV series *The Life and Legend of Wyatt Earp*.

From 1959 to 1961, he played Maj./Col. Peter Horry, top aide to Leslie Nielsen in the *Swamp Fox* episodes of *Walt Disney Presents*, based on the American Revolutionary War hero Francis Marion.

More roles followed in *Rio Bravo* (1959), *Ma Barker's Killer Brood* (1960), *Assignment: Underwater* (1961), *Whispering Smith* (1961) with Audie Murphy, *Destry* (1964), *Harlow* (1965), *Gunfight in Abilene* (1967), *The Shakiest Gun in the West* (1968), *True Grit* (1969), *The Cheyenne Social Club* (1970), *Adam-12* (1969-1973), *Kolchak: The Night Stalker* (1975), *The Amazing Spider-Man* (1979), *V* (1983), *The New Mike Hammer* (1984), *RoboCop* (1994), and *Little Giants* (1994).

In 2005, Healey broke his hip in a fall and never recovered. He died December 21, 2005, at age 82 in Burbank, California, at the age of 82.

Wanda Hendrix

Wanda Hendrix with Audie Murphy

Dixie Wanda Hendrix was born November 3, 1928, in Jacksonville, Florida to a logging camp boss (Max Sylvester Hendrix) and his wife (Mary Bailley).

Wholesome, green-eyed, dark-haired Wanda Hendrix was involved in her hometown's little theater group when she was "discovered" by a passing talent agent and signed up for starlet roles in Warner Brothers films. Her family then moved to California.

Foregoing bit parts, the petite and lovely up-and-comer was immediately cast in featured roles in both *Confidential Agent* (1945) and *Nora Prentiss* (1947) for Warner Brothers and *Welcome Stranger* (1947) for Paramount.

Signing up with Paramount, she earned one of her best film roles with *Ride the Pink Horse* (1947), in which there was talk of an Oscar nomination, and appeared elsewhere in the light comedy *Miss Tatlock's Millions* (1948) and the melodrama *My Own True Love* (1949).

After appearing on the cover of Coronet magazine, decorated WWII hero-turned-Universal star Audie Murphy took notice and arranged a meeting with her. They married on February 8, 1949, and she co-starred with him a year later in one of his western vehicles, *Sierra* (1950). The marriage didn't last, though. The divorce became official on April 14, 1950.

After the divorce and after a few standard oaters and war yarns, the more notable ones being *Captain Carey, U.S.A.* (1950) co-starring Alan Ladd, *Saddle Tramp* (1950) with Joel McCrea, *The Highwayman* (1951) with Charles Coburn, and Roger Corman's *Highway Dragnet* (1954) with Richard Conte, her career waned.

The actress retired completely from pictures in 1954 to marry millionaire playboy and sportsman James L. Stack, Jr., brother of actor Robert Stack. She earlier appeared with her famous brother-in-law in the films *Miss Tatlock's Millions* (1948) and *My Outlaw Brother* (1951).

The career sacrifice did little to help the marriage and the couple divorced in 1958. Returning to acting, she made a comeback on stage, film, and television with roles in *Boy Who Caught a Crook* (1961), *The Lloyd Bridges Show* (1963), *Johnny Cool* (1963), *Stage to Thunder Rock* (1964), *My Three Sons* (1969), and *Bewitched* (1971), but experienced little progression.

Overlooked in her three 1960s films, her last film roles were filmed in the early 1970s. *Mystic Mountain Massacre*, co-starring Ray Danton, was never released, and the Civil War horror *One Minute Before Death* (1972), based on a short story The Oval Portrait by Edgar Allan Poe, in which she co-starred with Barry Coe and Gisele MacKenzie, died a quicker death than even the title suggests. Her last role was in the episode "World Full of Hurt" of *Police Story* (1974).

In 1969, she married a third and last time, to oil company executive Steve La Monte in Las Vegas.

At one point, she considered collaborating with author Douglas Warren on an autobiography of her first husband, Audie Murphy, but it never came to fruition. Divorced from her third husband in 1980, Wanda died shortly thereafter on February 1, 1981, in Burbank, California, at age 52 of double pneumonia. She had no children.

Thomas Browne Henry

Audie Murphy with Thomas Browne Henry in *Gunfight at Comanche Creek*

Thomas Browne Henry was born November 7, 1907 in Los Angeles, California, and was an American actor. If you've ever seen a war picture, sci-fi epic, or western from the 1940s or 1950s, then you've seen Thomas Browne Henry, and more than once.

Along with Morris Ankrum, Henry is probably the army officer most responsible for helping Earth drive off hordes of invading outer-space monsters, aliens, and other unwelcome intruders. His stocky build, sharply etched face, commanding voice and no-nonsense, get-down-to-business style were just right for the scores of generals, colonels, bankers, political leaders and other authority figures he played over his long and prolific career.

He had a very successful career as a stage actor and director, and was closely associated with the renowned Pasadena Playhouse, before breaking into films in 1948 and played a succession of cops, sheriffs, district attorneys, professors and, of course, army officers over the next 20+ years.

Some of those credits included *He Walked by Night* (1948), *Tulsa* (1949), *Captain Carey, U.S.A.* (1950), *The Asphalt Jungle* (1950), *Saddle Tramp* (1950), *Deadline - U.S.A.* (1952), *Space Patrol* (1952-1953), *Rocky Jones, Space Ranger* (1954), *D-Day the Sixth of June* (1956), *Earth vs. the Flying Saucers* (1956), *Hellcats of the Navy*

(1957), *Blood of Dracula* (1957), *Richard Diamond, Private Detective* (1957-1958), *The Thing That Couldn't Die* (1958), *Space Master X-7* (1958), *Alcoa Presents: One Step Beyond* (1959), *Wanted: Dead or Alive* (1960), *Gunfight at Comanche Creek* (1963) with Audie Murphy, *The Addams Family* (1965), *I Spy* (1967), *Green Acres* (1968), and *Airport* (1970).

He finally retired in 1970 and went back to his first love, the theater, again back to the Pasadena Playhouse. He died June 30, 1980, at age 72 in La Mesa, California.

Audrey Hepburn

Audrey Hepburn with Audie Murphy in *The Unforgiven*

Audrey Hepburn was born Audrey Kathleen Ruston on May 4, 1929 in Brussels, Belgium. She really was blue-blood from the beginning with her father, a wealthy English banker, and her mother, a Dutch baroness.

After her parents divorced, Audrey went to London with her mother where she went to a private girl's school. Later, when her mother moved back to the Netherlands, she attended private schools as well. While vacationing with her mother in Arnhem, Holland, Hitler's army took over the town. It was here that she fell on hard times during the Nazi occupation. Audrey suffered from depression and malnutrition.

After the liberation, Audrey went to a ballet school in London on a scholarship and later began a modeling career. As a model, she was graceful and, it seemed, she had found her niche in life, until the film producers came calling.

After being spotted modeling by a producer, she was signed to a bit part in the European film *Dutch in Seven Lessons* (1948). Later, she had a speaking role in the 1951 film, *Young Wives' Tale* (1951) as Eve Lester. The part still wasn't much, so she headed to America to try her luck there.

Audrey gained immediate prominence in the US with her role in *Roman Holiday* (1953). This film turned out to be a smashing success as she won an Oscar as Best Actress. This gained her enormous popularity and more plum roles.

One of the reasons for her popularity was the fact that she was so elf-like and had class, unlike the sex-goddesses of the time. *Roman Holiday* (1953) was followed by another similarly wonderful performance in the classic *Funny Face* (1957). *Sabrina* (1954), for which she received another Academy nomination, and *Love in the Afternoon* (1957), also garnered rave reviews.

She received yet another nomination for her role in *The Nun's Story* (1959). She then played the part of Rachel Zackary in *The Unforgiven* (1960) with Audie Murphy.

Audrey reached the pinnacle of her career when she played Holly Golightly in the delightful film *Breakfast at Tiffany's* (1961). For this she received another nomination. She scored commercial success again in the espionage caper *Charade* (1963).

One of Audrey's most radiant roles was in the fine production of *My Fair Lady* (1964). Her co-star, Rex Harrison, once was asked to identify his favorite leading lady. Without hesitation, he replied, "Audrey Hepburn in *My Fair Lady*".

After a couple of other movies, most notably *Two for the Road* (1967), she hit pay dirt and another nomination in *Wait Until Dark* (1967).

From time to time, she would appear on the silver screen. One film of note was *Robin and Marian* (1976), with Sean Connery. She then played in *They all Laughed* (1981) with John Ritter and Dorothy Stratten.

In 1988, Audrey became a special ambassador to the United Nations UNICEF fund helping children in Latin America and Africa, a position she retained until 1993.

She was named to People's magazine as one of the 50 most beautiful people in the world. Her last film was *Always* (1989)

At a cocktail party hosted by Gregory Peck, Hepburn met American actor Mel Ferrer. After meeting, working together and falling in love, the pair married September 25, 1954. Before having their only son, Hepburn had two miscarriages in March 1955 and in 1959. The latter occurred when filming *The Unforgiven* (1960) where breaking her back after falling off a horse and onto a rock resulted in a hospital stay and miscarriage induced by physical and mental stress. Hepburn, therefore, took a year off work in order to successfully have a child. Sean Hepburn Ferrer, their son, whose godfather was the novelist A. J. Cronin who resided near Hepburn in Lucerne, was born on 17 July 1960.

After a fourteen year marriage, the couple divorced on December 5, 1968. She later met Italian psychiatrist Andrea Dotti on a cruise and fell in love with him on a trip to Greek ruins. She believed she would have more children, and possibly stop working. She married him on January 18, 1969, at age 40. She gave birth to their son Luca Dotti on February 8, 1970. When pregnant with Luca in 1969, Hepburn was more careful, resting for months and passing the time by painting before delivering him by caesarean section. Hepburn had her final miscarriage in 1974. She divorced Dotti in 1982.

From then until her death, Hepburn lived and was romantically involved with Dutch actor Robert Wolders the widower of actress Merle Oberon. Wolders played Erik Hunter in the second and last season of Laredo (1966-1967).

She met Wolders through a friend in the later stage of her marriage to Dotti. The divorce from Dotti finalized, Wolders and Hepburn started their lives together, although they never married. In 1989, she called the nine years she had spent with him the happiest years of her life. "Took me long enough," she said in an interview with American journalist Barbara Walters. Walters then asked why they never married; Hepburn replied that they were married, just not formally.

I met Robert Wolders at the Memphis Film Festival in June of 2011 and we discussed his wife having worked in the *Unforgiven* with Audie Murphy.

Audrey Hepburn died on January 20, 1993 in Tolochnaz, Switzerland, from appendicular cancer. She had made a total of thiry-one high quality movies. Her elegance and style will always be remembered in film history as evidenced by her being named in Empire magazine's "The Top 100 Movie Stars of All Time."

William Hickey

William Hickey with Audie Murphy in *Ford Startime*

William Edward Hickey was born September 19, 1927, and was an American actor. He was best known for his Oscar-nominated role as Don Corrado Prizzi in the John Huston 1985 film *Prizzi's Honor*, as well as the voice of Dr. Finklestein in Tim Burton's *The Nightmare Before Christmas* (1993).

Hickey was born in Brooklyn, New York, the son of Nora and Edward Hickey, both of Irish descent. Hickey began acting on radio in 1938. Hickey had a long, distinguished career in film, television, and the stage. He began his career as a child actor on the variety stage and made his Broadway debut as a walk-on in George Bernard Shaw's *Saint Joan* (1951).

He performed often during the golden age of television, including appearances on *Studio One* (1956-1957) and *The DuPont Show of the Month* (1959). He also played The Bowling Man in *The Man* episode of Ford Startime (1960) with Audie Murphy.

Other acting credits include *Invitation to a Gunfighter* (1964), *Androcles and the Lion* (1967), *The Boston Strangler* (1968), as the historian in *Little Big Man* (1970), *92 in the Shade* (1975), *Wise Blood* (1979), *Remo Williams: The Adventure Begins* (1985), *The Name of the Rose* (1986), *Tales from the Darkside* (1986), *Moonlighting* (1987), *Miami Vice* (1989), *Christmas Vacation* (1989), *Tales from the Crypt* (1990), *Tales from the*

Darkside: The Movie (1990), *Wings* (1992-1994), *The Outer Limits* (1995), and *Mousehunt* (1997), which is also dedicated to his memory. His final movie *Knocking on Death's Door* (1999), in which he plays the town sheriff was released nearly two years after his death.

His most important contribution to the arts, however, remains his teaching career at the HB Studio in Greenwich Village, founded by Hagen and Herbert Berghof. George Segal, Sandy Dennis, and Barbra Streisand all studied under him.

Hickey died from emphysema and bronchitis June 29, 1997. He is interred in the Cemetery of the Evergreens in Brooklyn, New York. He died during the filming of Uzo's *Better Than Ever* (1997) and his role was played by the producer in a pickup shot depicting his character in the hospital.

Darryl Hickman

Darryl Hickman with Audie Murphy in *G.E. Theatre*

Darryl Gerard Hickman was born July 28, 1931, and is an American film and television actor, former television executive. Hickman first gained fame as a child actor during the late 1930s and 1940s, appearing in *The Grapes of Wrath* (1940), *Men of Boys Town* (1941), *The Human Comedy* (1943), *And Now Tomorrow* (1944), *Salty O'Rourke* (1945), and *Leave Her to Heaven* (1945), among many others. He also made a featured appearance in the 1942 *Our Gang* comedy *Going to Press*.

By the time he was 21, Hickman had appeared in over 100 motion pictures. After spending his entire childhood as an actor, Hickman retired from entertainment to enter a monastery in 1951, only to return to Hollywood just over a year later. He continued acting, but received fewer roles than he had in the peak of his career.

In 1954, he appeared as Chet Sterling in the "Annie Gets Her Man" episode of syndicated western television series *Annie Oakley*, with Gail Davis. In 1957, he appeared in the episode "Copper Wire" of the syndicated western-themed crime drama *Sheriff of Cochise*. Hickman appeared four times in the 1957-1958 syndicated drama series, *Men of Annapolis*, about Midshipmen at the United States Naval Academy in Annapolis, Maryland.

He appeared in the *G.E Theater* episode "The Incident" with Audie Murphy. It is the most sought-after Audie Murphy appearance. In 1959, Hickman appeared with his younger brother, Dwayne Hickman, on the latter's CBS-TV sitcom, *The Many Loves of Dobie Gillis*, playing his older brother, Davey. In 1959, Darryl Hickman also appeared in an episode of *Wanted: Dead or Alive* with Steve McQueen, titled "Rope Law."

In 1960, he guest starred as Donald in the 1960 episode "Moment of Fear" of CBS's *The DuPont Show with June Allyson*, also featuring Edgar Bergen. He also guest starred on NBC's science fiction series, *The Man and the Challenge*. During the Civil War Centennial, Hickman played a young Union soldier in the short-lived series, *The Americans* (1961), and as an officer in Disney's *Johnny Shiloh* (1963).

He had a key role in the 1981 film *Sharky's Machine*, directed by and starring Burt Reynolds, as a corrupt cop. Hickman eventually became a television executive and an acting coach, as well as a voice actor for Hanna-Barbera Productions towards the end of a five-decade career in the entertainment industry. Some of his notable voice-overs were Wags in *The Biskitts (1983)* and Derek from *The Greatest Adventure: Stories from the Bible* (1990-1992).

His book, *The Unconscious Actor: Out of Control, In Full Command*, was published in April 2007.

Hickman married actress Pamela Lincoln in 1959; the couple has since divorced. They had met on the set of the film *The Tingler* (1959) in which they both appear. Darryl and Pamela had two sons. Their younger son, Justin Hickman, was nineteen years old when he committed suicide in 1985.

Reiko Higa

No biographical information can be found for Reiko Higa. She was a Chinese actress who only appeared in two films. She appeared as the false Tokyo Rose in *Joe Butterfly* (1957) with Audie Murphy, and as Haruko in *The Big Wave* (1961).

Ed Hinton

Ed Hinton with Audie Murphy in *Walk the Proud Land*

Edgar Latimer Hinton, Jr. was born in Wilmington, North Carolina, March 26, 1919, and was an American actor known particularly for guest-starring roles on television westerns. He was the son of Edgar Latimer Hinton II, Sr. (1868–1934), the owner of the Seashore Hotel with one of the first steel piers for entertaining over the ocean in Wrightsville N.C. and the town's only laundry businesses as well as being a community actor in Wilmington.

His first appearance was in *Spring Madness* (1938). His next role was ten years later in *Harpoon* (1948). He continued to act another ten years until his death.

Hinton had uncredited roles in the films *Samson and Delilah* (1949) and in two 1951 productions, *The Red Badge of Courage* with Audie Murphy and *I Was a Communist for the FBI*, as agent Jim Broderick. The latter film inspired the syndicated television series, *I Led Three Lives*, in which Hinton appeared, apparently in only one episode, "Relatives" (1955), as Special Agent Henderson. Richard Carlson starred as informant Herbert Philbrick.

In 1954, Hinton appeared in some of his first television roles with an appearance on the CBS series *Captain Midnight*, starring Richard Webb. Other roles included *Tales of the Texas Rangers* (1955), *Adventures of Superman* (1955-1956), *Walk the Proud Land* (1956) again with Audie Murphy, *Tension at Table Rock* (1956), *The Ten Commandments* (1956), *Shoot-Out at Medicine Bend* (1957), *Circus Boy* (1956-1957), *The Dalton Girls* (1957), *The Fiend Who Walked the West* (1958), *The Life and Legend of Wyatt Earp* (1955-1958), and *Good Day for a Hanging* (1959).

Hinton and his wife, Marilynn Hinton had three children, Daryn Hinton, Darcy Hinton Cook, and Darby Hinton, who co-starred from 1964-1970 on NBC's western series, *Daniel Boone*, with Fess Parker in the title role.

I met and talked with Darby Hinton at the Memphis Film Festival in 2012 while he was there for the *Daniel Boone* reunion.

Ed Hinton perished in an airplane crash October 12, 1958, on Santa Catalina Island off the California coast. Mrs. Hinton never remarried after Ed's death.

Dennis Hoey

Dennis Hoey was born Samuel David Hyams March 30, 1893 in London, England, and was a British film and stage actor, best known for playing Inspector Lestrade in Universal's *Sherlock Holmes series* (1943-1946).

After a career as a singer, Hoey moved to acting on the stage in 1918 and later to films. In 1931, he moved to the United States and began appearing in Hollywood films. Some of his roles include *Tiptoes* (1927), *I Spy* (1934), *Brewster's Millions* (1935), *Son of Fury: The Story of Benjamin Blake* (1942), *Sherlock Holmes and the Secret Weapon* (1943), *Frankenstein Meets the Wolf Man* (1943), *Sherlock Holmes Faces Death* (1943), *The Spider Woman* (1944), *The Pearl of Death* (1944), *The House of Fear* (1945), *Terror by Night* (1946), *Golden Earrings* (1947), *Wake of the Red Witch* (1948), *The Kid from Texas* (1950) with Audie Murphy, *David and Bathsheba* (1951), *Caribbean* (1952), and *Plymouth Adventure* (1952).

He died July 25, 1960, at age 67 in Palm Beach, Florida.

Issue #45 of *Films of the Golden Age* magazine features an interview with Hoey's son Michael A. Hoey, who extensively discusses Dennis Hoey's early life, career, marriages and death. In his book, *Elvis, Sherlock and Me: How I Survived Growing Up in Hollywood* he discusses his father's career and their relationship.

Dick Hogan

Dick Hogan was born November 27, 1917 in Little Rock, Arkansas, and was an American character actor. He served in the armed forces during World War II. He began his career singing in clubs and sang with Glenn Miller's orchestra before turning to films.

Some of his roles include *Blazing Barriers* (1937), *Charlie Chan in Reno* (1939), *Mexican Spitfire Out West* (1940), *Gang Busters* (1942), *The Mummy's Tomb* (1942), *Action in the North Atlantic* (1943), *So Proudly We Hail!* (1943), *Blaze of Noon* (1947), *Beyond Glory* (1948) with Audie Murphy, and his last role in *Rope* (1948).

After quitting the movies, he returned to Arkansas and became an insurance agent. He died August 18, 1995, at age 77 in Little Rock, Arkansas.

Rex Holman

Audie Murphy with Rex Holman in *The Quick Gun*

Rex Holman was born Rexford George Holman November 19, 1928, in Denver, Colorado, and is a very recognizable character actor, mostly as heavies.

His first role was in *The Millionaire* (1959) and worked steadily through the mid 1980's. He had more roles in such films and television programs as *Ma Barker's Killer Brood* (1960), *Twilight Zone* (1961), *Tales of Wells Fargo* (1962), *The Rifleman* (1962-1963), *The Quick Gun* (1964) with Audie Murphy, *The Outer Limits* (1964), *Your Cheatin' Heart* (1964), a comedic turn as The Sunstroke Kid in the Three Stooges film *The Outlaws Is Coming* (1965), *Laredo* (1965-1966), *The Monkees* (1967), as Morgan Earp in the "Spectre of the Gun" episode of *Star Trek* (1968), *The Wrecking Crew* (1969), *The Over-the-Hill Gang* (1969), *Mission: Impossible* (1971), *Mannix* (1972), *Police Story* (1973), *The Rookies* (1974), sixteen episodes of *Gunsmoke* (1960-1974), *S.W.A.T.* (1975), *The Legend of the Golden Gun* (1979), *The Apple Dumpling Gang Rides Again* (1979), *Charlie's Angels* (1981), *The Wild Women of Chastity Gulch* (1982), *The Fall Guy* (1984), *Wildside* (1985), and his last appearance in *Star Trek V: The Final Frontier* (1989).

In 1970, Holman recorded an album on the Pentagram label called *Here in the Land of Victory*. It featured a mix of country, blues, and eastern influenced folk. It's a very good album, and the songs are all very fragile, floating acoustic type of songs, with sitar, Tablas and other exotic instrumentation scattered liberally throughout. The production credits "Schmitt-Douglas", and the album was recorded at Dimension Sounds. The album cover is a montage featuring Holman super-imposed over scenes of down and out street people.

Skip Homeier

Skip Homeier with Audie Murphy in *Bullet for a Badman*

Skip Homeier was born as George Vincent Homeier in Chicago, Illinois, on October 5, 1930. Homeier began acting as Skippy Homeier at the age of six, on the radio show *Portia Faces Life*. From 1943 until 1944 he played the role of Emil in the Broadway play, *Tomorrow the World*. Cast as a child indoctrinated into Nazism, who is brought to the United States from Germany following the death of his parents, Homeier was praised for his performance. He played the troubled youngster in the 1944 film adaptation and received good reviews playing opposite Fredric March and Betty Field as his American uncle and aunt.

Although Homeier worked frequently throughout his childhood and adolescence, playing wayward youths with no chance of redemption, he did not become a major star, but was able to make a transition from child actor to adult, especially in a range of roles as delinquent youths, common in Hollywood films of the 1950s.

At the age of twenty, Homeier played the young gunfighter who badgered and shot down Gregory Peck in *The Gunfighter* (1950). He then appeared in the Westerns *The Burning Hills* (1956) and with Randolph Scott in Budd Boetticher's, *The Tall T* (1957) and *Comanche Station* (1960).

Some of his television roles included *Wanted: Dead or Alive* (1958) with Steve McQueen, and *Wichita Town* (1959) with Joel McCrea. From 1960 to 1961, Homeier starred in the title role in *Dan Raven*, a crime drama on NBC set on the famous Sunset Strip of West Hollywood, California, with a number of celebrities appearing in guest roles as themselves. More roles followed such as *Stark Fear* (1962), *Showdown* (1963) with Audie Murphy, *Bullet for a Badman* (1964) again with Audie Murphy, *The Addams Family* (1965), and *Branded* (1965), *The Ghost and Mr. Chicken* (1966) with Don Knotts, *Star Trek* (1968-1969), and *Then Came Bronson* (1970).

In the 1970–1971 season, Homeier, at forty, co-starred as Dr. Hugh Jacoby in another series, *The Interns*, which was based on a film of the same name and aired on CBS. His costars were Broderick Crawford as the hospital administrator, Christopher Stone as Dr. Jim Hardin, and a pre-M*A*S*H Mike Farrell as Dr. Sam Marsh.

He continued to get roles in such fare as *Longstreet* (1971), *Starbird and Sweet William* (1973), *Movin' On* (1975), *Helter Skelter* (1976), *Washington: Behind Closed Doors* (1977), *The Six Million Dollar Man* (1977), *The Bionic Woman* (1976-1978), *How the West Was Won* (1979), *The Incredible Hulk* (1979), *The Wild Wild West Revisited* (1979), *Fantasy Island* (1979-1980), and *Quincy M.E.* (1979-1982).

Skip phased out his career following the 1970s decade (at the relatively young age of 50) and retired completely, remaining purposely out of the limelight. According to his son, Michael Homeier, Skip has not yet been tempted by film festivals or nostalgia conventions.

Charles Horvath

Charles Horvath was born October 27, 1920, in Upper Macungie Township, Pennsylvania. Horvath entered films in the immediate postwar years as a stunt man. From 1951 onward, Horvath began receiving speaking roles, most often in westerns.

Some of his roles include *Johnny Belinda* (1948), *Colorado Territory* (1949), *Dallas* (1950), as the Genie in *Aladdin and His Lamp* (1952), *The Lawless Breed* (1953), *Border River* (1954), *Phantom of the Rue Morgue* (1954), *Seven Brides for Seven Brothers* (1954), *Sheena: Queen of the Jungle* (1955), *Chief Crazy Horse* (1955), *Creature with the Atom Brain* (1955), *Blackjack Ketchum, Desperado* (1956), *Francis in the Haunted House* (1956), *The Werewolf* (1956), *Around the World in Eighty Days* (1956), *Richard Diamond, Private Detective* (1958), *The Thing That Couldn't Die* (1958), *The Gunfight at Dodge City* (1959), *Twilight Zone* (1960), *Elmer Gantry* (1960), *Spartacus* (1960), *Flaming Star* (1960), *The Wild Westerners* (1962), *McLintock!* (1963), *Destry* (1964), *Cat Ballou* (1965), *Johnny Reno* (1966), *Get Smart* (1965-1966), *Laredo* (1966), *The Andy Griffith Show* (1967-1968), *The Shakiest Gun in the West* (1968), *A Woman Under the Influence* (1974), *Medical Center* (1975), *Baretta* (1976), and *Another Man, Another Chance* (1977).

He appeared in five films with Audie Murphy, such as *The Guns of Fort Petticoat* (1957), *Seven Ways from Sundown* (1960), *Posse from Hell* (1961), *Showdown* (1963), and *Bullet for a Badman* (1964).

He worked up until he died on July 23, 1978, at age 57 in Woodland Hills, Los Angeles, California.

Robert Hoy

Robert Francis "Bobby" Hoy was born April 3, 1927, and was an actor, stuntman, and director. Hoy was born and raised in New York. He joined the Marines and served in World War II.

Bobby Hoy's career spanned fifty-five years as first a stuntman, then an actor and director. He doubled for stars such as Tony Curtis, Charles Bronson, Audie Murphy, Tyrone Power, David Janssen, Telly Savalas, and Jay Silverheels.

He appeared in more than sixty-seven films including *Ambush* (1950), *The Man from the Alamo* (1953), *Border River* (1954), *Four Guns to the Border* (1954), *Revenge of the Creature* (1955), *To Hell and Back* (1955) with Audie Murphy, *The Mole People* (1956), *No Time for Sergeants* (1958), *Operation Petticoat* (1959), *Spartacus* (1960), *Harlow* (1965), *Tickle Me* (1965), *5 Card Stud* (1968), *The Love Bug* (1968), *Scream Blacula, Scream* (1973), *Bite the Bullet* (1975), *The Outlaw Josey Wales* (1976), *The Enforcer* (1976), *Bronco Billy* (1980), *The Legend of the Lone Ranger* (1981), *Deadly Stranger* (1990), and *Hollywood, It's a Dog's Life* (2004).

On television, Hoy acted in more than seventy-five television programs including *The High Chaparral*, where he portrayed Joe Butler in sixty-two episodes from 1967 to 1971. Other credits include *Have Gun - Will Travel* (1958), *Wanted: Dead or Alive* (1960), *The Untouchables* (1962), *The Man from U.N.C.L.E.* (1965-1966), *The Green Hornet* (1966), *Laredo* (1965-1967), as the Horta creature in the episode "The Devil in the Dark" of *Star Trek* (1967), *Rod Serling's Night Gallery* (1971), *Hec Ramsey* (1972), *The New Perry Mason* (1973), *The Magician* (1974), *The Streets of San Francisco* (1973-1975), *The Six Million Dollar Man* (1974-1978), *The New Adventures of Wonder Woman* (1978-1979), *240-Robert* (1979), *Enos* (1981), *Dallas* (1978-1982), *Kenny Rogers as The Gambler: The Adventure Continues* (1983), *The Fall Guy* (1982-1985), *Magnum, P.I.* (1981-1986), *Houston: The Legend of Texas* (1986), *Desperado* (1987), *The Return of the Six-Million-Dollar Man and the Bionic Woman* (1987), as Cliff in *Our House* (1986-1988), *Bonanza: The Next Generation* (1988), *Walker, Texas Ranger* (1995), *Detective* (2005), and *NCIS* (2007).

He was the lead stunt man who doubled Tony Curtis in *The Defiant Ones* (1958). He also trained Sidney Poitier's stunt double, Ivan Dixon, in his first movie job. In 1961, he became a co-founding member of The Stuntman's Association of Motion Pictures. Director and lifelong friend Raymond Austin put Hoy behind the camera as second unit director and stunt coordinator in Spain for the TV series *Zorro* (1990-1992).

He appeared as the celebrity guest at Audie Murphy Days in Greenville, Texas, in June of 2008. On January 28, 2010, Hoy was honored with a Golden Boot by the Motion Picture & Television Fund, commemorating his contribution to the genre of Western television and movies in all three award categories: acting, stunt work and directing. It was presented to him in the penthouse suite of Northridge Hospital, the first time a Golden Boot has ever been given to an honoree in the hospital.

Bobby Hoy died on February 8, 2010, at Northridge Hospital after a six-month battle with cancer. He was 82. He is survived by his wife of 22 years, Kiva, and a son, Christopher.

John Hoyt

John Hoyt was born John McArthur Hoysradt in Bronxville, New York, October 5, 1905, and was an American film, stage, and television actor. Before becoming an actor with Orson Welles's Mercury Theatre, the Yale University graduate worked as a history instructor, acting teacher and even (under his birth name) a nightclub comedian. In the latter activity, Hoyt performed impressions of famous entertainers. His impersonation of Noël Coward was so remarkable that he was hired for the original cast of the Broadway comedy *The Man Who Came to Dinner*, in which he played Beverley Carlton. Hoyt soon shortened his surname when he began his movie career.

Hoyt had a number of memorable roles such as *O.S.S.* (1946), *The Lawless* (1950), *When Worlds Collide* (1951), *China Smith* (1952), *Julius Caesar* (1953), *The Purple Mask* (1955), *The Conqueror* (1956), *Wetbacks* (1956), *God*

Is My Partner (1957), *Attack of the Puppet People* (1958), *Richard Diamond, Private Detective* (1958-1959), *Never So Few* (1959), *Spartacus* (1960), *Twilight Zone* (1960-1961), *Cleopatra* (1963), *Destry* (1964), *The Outer Limits* (1964), as Doctor Boyce in the pilot for *Star Trek* (1964), *Two on a Guillotine* (1965), *Gunpoint* (1966) with Audie Murphy, *Winchester 73* (1967), *Get Smart* (1965-1968), *Hogan's Heroes* (1967-1971), *Planet of the Apes* (1974), *Kolchak: The Night Stalker* (1975), *Battlestar Galactica* (1979), and *Desperately Seeking Susan* (1985). His last screen role was as Grandpa in seventy-eight episodes of Nell Carter's television series *Gimme a Break!* (1982-1987).

He was one of a long list of actors and crew who worked on the film *The Conqueror* (1956). This movie is notorious for being shot in the deserts of Utah, almost ten years after the United States Army conducted nuclear bomb testing there. Of the 220 people involved in the film, 91 would die of cancer, including John Wayne, director Dick Powell, and every leading supporting cast member: Agnes Moorehead, Susan Hayward, along with John Hoyt. Another star, Pedro Armendáriz would also be diagnosed of cancer, but committed suicide after hearing the news. The number does not include the extras and other people involved in filming. Numerous American Indians who served as Mongolian warriors contracted cancer in later years, and even John Wayne's son Michael died in 2003 of cancer, after visiting his father on the set at age twenty-two. What is also even more mind-boggling is the fact that after principle shooting was finished in Utah, the production company had 60 tons of radioactive dirt shipped to Hollywood so filming could be finished on sound stages. Whatever became of this dirt is unknown; it's probably been used as filler in a back-lot by now.

He married Dorothy Oltman Haveman September 4, 1961, and it lasted until his death Septemebr 15, 1991, at age 85 in Santa Cruz, California.

John Hubbard

Audie Murphy with John Hubbard in *The Cimarron Kid*

John Hubbard was born in East Chicago, Indiana, April 14, 1914, and was an American television and film actor. Hubbard took acting lessons as a teen at the Goodman Theatre in Chicago, where he attracted attention and movie offers. He was signed by Paramount in 1937, but his contract was sold to MGM a year later. At MGM, Hubbard played a leading role opposite Luise Rainer in 1938's *Dramatic School*, which lead to a four-picture deal with Hal Roach, who used Hubbard in comedies such as *The Housekeeper's Daughter* (1939), *Turnabout* (1940), and *Road Show* (1941). Hubbard did a dramatic turn in *Whispering Footsteps* in 1943, but returned to comedy afterwards, usually in supporting roles.

Hubbard's film career was interrupted between 1944 and 1947 by military service. He continued to make films afterwards, but after 1950 he turned up more often on television. As a supporting actor, he played in *One Million B.C.* (1940), *The Mummy's Tomb* (1942), *Mexican Hayride* (1948), *The Cimarron Kid* (1952) with Audie Murphy, *The Mickey Rooney Show* (1954-1955), *The Tall T* (1957), *Maverick* (1957-1959), *Richard Diamond, Private Detective* (1960), *Don't Call Me Charlie* (1962-1963), *Gunfight at Comanche Creek* (1963) again with Audie Murphy, *Soldier in the Rain* (1963), *The Munsters* (1964), *The Green Hornet* (1966), *The Love God?* (1969), *Adam-12* (1970), and *Justin Morgan Had a Horse* (1972).

Between acting roles, Hubbard worked as an automobile salesman and the manager of a restaurant. He retired from acting in 1974 after a character role in *Herbie Rides Again*, although he made one more appearance in a television movie *OHMS* (1980).

Hubbard was married to his high school sweetheart, Lois, for nearly fifty years. The couple had three children together; Lois, Jane, and John. On November 6, 1988, Hubbard died at the age of 74 in a convalescent home in Camarillo, California.

John Hudson

John C. Hudson was born January 24, 1919 in Gilroy, California, and is the twin brother of actor William Hudson. His first film appearance was in *Hue and Cry* (1947), and worked steadily for the next twenty-five years in such fare as *Bright Victory* (1951), as Dynamite Dick Dalton *The Cimarron Kid* (1952) with Audie Murphy, *Biff Baker, U.S.A.* (1952), *Fort Yuma* (1955), as Virgil Earp in *Gunfight at the O.K. Corral* (1957), *Pete Kelly's Blues* (1959), *G.I. Blues* (1960), *Gunsmoke* (1964), *Dragnet 1967* (1968-1967), *Adam-12* (1970), and *Cannon* (1972),

He died April 8, 1996, at age 77 in Los Angeles, California.

Arthur Hunnicutt

Arthur Lee Hunnicutt was born in Gravelly, Arkansas, in February 17, 1910, and was an American actor known for his portrayal of wise, grizzled, old rural characters. In one of his last movies, *Moonrunners* (1975) which was the precursor to *The Dukes of Hazzard* (1979-1985), he played the original Uncle Jesse.

Hunnicutt attended Arkansas State Teachers College but dropped out during his junior year when he ran out of money. He moved to Martha's Vineyard, Massachusetts, where he joined up with a theatre company before moving to New York where he quickly found himself landing roles in Broadway productions. While touring as the lead actor in *Tobacco Road*, he developed the country character he would later be typecast as throughout his career. Hunnicutt often found himself cast as a character much older than his actual age.

Hunnicutt appeared in a number of films in the early 1940s like *Wildcat* (1942), *Abroad with Two Yanks* (1944), and *You Can't Take It with You* (1945), before returning to the stage for a short time. In 1949 he moved back to Hollywood and resumed his acting career. He played a long string of supporting role characters like sympathetic, wise rural types, as in *Stars in My Crown* (1950), *The Red Badge of Courage* (1951) with Audie Murphy, *The Lusty Men* (1952), as Davy Crockett in *The Last Command* (1955), *The Kettles in the Ozarks* (1956), *The Tall T* (1957), *A Tiger Walks* (1964), as Butch Cassidy in *Cat Ballou* (1965), *Apache Uprising* (1965), *El Dorado* (1966), *The Million Dollar Duck* (1971), *The Revengers* (1972), *Harry and Tonto* (1974), and *The Daughters of Joshua Cabe Return* (1975).

In 1952, he earned an Oscar nomination for Supporting Actor in the Howard Hawks western *The Big Sky*.

Throughout the 1950s, 1960s, and 1970s, Hunnicutt made nearly forty guest appearances on American television programs such as *Cheyenne* (1956), *Wanted: Dead or Alive* (1959), *The Andy Griffith Show* (1960), *Twilight Zone* (1962), *Perry Mason* (1963), *The Outer Limits* (1964), *Laredo* (1965), *The Wild Wild West* (1967), *Adam-12* (1970), and *Gunsmoke* (1971),

In his later years, Hunnicutt served as Honorary Mayor of Northridge, California. He died in September 26, 1979 at age 69 in Woodland Hills, Los Angeles, California, from tongue cancer and is buried in the Coop Prairie Cemetery in Mansfield, Arkansas.

Henry Hunter

Henry Hunter was born Frederick Arthur Jacobson Jr. October 9, 1907, in Rahway, New Jersey. He was a character actor who appeared in over one hundred films and television programs from 1936 to 1987.

Some of his appearances included *Nobody's Fool* (1936), *The Man Who Cried Wolf* (1937), *Calling Dr. Kildare* (1939), *Lux Video Theatre* (1955), *Mike Hammer* (1958), *Tales of Wells Fargo* (1959), *Bachelor Father* (1959-1960), *My Sister Eileen* (1961), *Twilight Zone* (1961), *Whispering Smith* (1961) with Audie Murphy, *Son of Flubber* (1963), *The Munsters* (1964-1965), *The Wild Wild West* (1965), *Hazel* (1961-1965), *Munster, Go Home!* (1966), *The Green Hornet* (1966), *Laredo* (1967), *Get Smart* (1967), *The Bold Ones: The New Doctors* (1969), *The Doris Day Show* (1970-1972), and *Florida Straits* (1987).

He died May 25, 1985, at age 77 in Los Angeles, California.

Eugene Iglesias

Eugene Iglesias with Audie Murphy in *Apache Rifles*

Eugene Iglesias was born December 3, 1926, in San Juan, Puerto Rico, and is the first Latino actor to be nominated for a Foreign Press Award.

He started acting in films in 1951, playing mostly Spanish or Indian roles in such movies as *The Brave Bulls* (1951), *Indian Uprising* (1952), *East of Sumatra* (1953), *Taza, Son of Cochise* (1954), *The Naked Dawn* (1955), *Domino Kid* (1957), *Cowboy* (1958), *Rio Bravo* (1959), *Frontier Uprising* (1961), and *Harper* (1966). He also had roles in *Dual at Silver Creek* (1952), *Tumbleweed* (1953), *Walk the Proud Land* (1956), and *Apache Rifles* (1964), all with Audie Murphy.

Some of his television roles were in programs such as *Dragnet* (1954), *Cheyenne* (1955), *The Loretta Young Show* (1956), *Tales of the 77th Bengal Lancers* (1957), *Broken Arrow* (1956-1957), *Maverick* (1958), *Lawman* (1959), *Sugarfoot* (1960), *Peter Gunn* (1961), *Rawhide* (1962), *The Untouchables* (1959-1962), *Bonanza* (1965), *The Fugitive* (1966), *Hondo* (1967), *The Wild Wild West* (1966-1967), and his last acting performance before retiring was in *The Flying Nun* (1970).

Jack Ingram

Jack Ingram was born John Samuel Ingram in Frankfort, Illinois, November 15, 1902, and was an American film actor. He appeared in over 300 films between 1935 and 1966.

A WWI veteran who later studied law at the University of Texas, tough-looking Jack Ingram began his long show business career as a minstrel player and later reportedly toured with Mae West. He began turning up playing scruffy henchmen and assorted other B-Western villains in the mid-'30s and was later the featured heavy in *Columbia* serials.

Ingram would go on to appear in a total of 200 Westerns and approximately fifty serials in a career that later included appearances on many television programs. Many of his later films and almost all his television westerns, were filmed on Ingram's own 200-acre ranch on Mulholland Drive in the Santa Monica Mountains overlooking Woodland Hills, which he had purchased from Charles Chaplin in 1944 and which remains a wilderness today.

He first appeared in *Westward Ho* (1935), and then worked steadily in films like *Winds of the Wasteland* (1936), *Gunsmoke Ranch* (1937), *The Arizona Kid* (1939), *The Green Archer* (1940), *West of Texas* (1943), *Ghost Guns* (1944), *Superman* (1948), *Atom Man vs. Superman* (1950), *Lost in Alaska* (1952) with Abbott & Costello, *Man Without a Star* (1955), *Utah Blaine* (1957), and *A Big Hand for the Little Lady* (1966).

He also had roles in *The Kid From Texas* (1950), *Sierra* (1950), *The Cimarron Kid* (1952), and *Column South* (1953), all with Audie Murphy.

Some of his television appearances were in *The Range Rider* (1951-1953), *The Adventures of Kit Carson* (1951-1953), *The Lone Ranger* (1950-1953), *Hopalong Cassidy* (1954), *The Cisco Kid* (1950-1954), *Buffalo Bill, Jr.* (1955), and *Tales of Wells Fargo* (1958).

He died February 20, 1969, in Canoga Park, California of a heart attack. He is interred in the Oakwood Memorial Park Cemetery in Chatsworth, California.

Dale Ishimoto

Dale Ishimoto with Audie Murphy in *Battle at Bloody Beach*

Dale Ishimoto was born April 3, 1923 in Delta, Colorado, and was an American actor of Japanese descent. He was raised in Guadalupe, California.

Ishimoto volunteered to fight in World War II after being sent to the Gila River internment camp in Arizona where he joined the 442nd Regimental Combat Team. Two years later, he was awarded a Purple Heart and given a medical discharge.

After starting a business in Chicago, he moved back to California, where he grew up, and started his acting career by acting at the Altadena Playhouse. He became a "familiar figure" for playing "villainous Japanese soldiers".

Over the course of his career, he acted in a wide variety of television programs and movies, such as *The Wackiest Ship in the Army* (1960), *Wanted: Dead or Alive* (1961), *Battle at Bloody Beach* (1961) with Audie Murphy, *Twilight Zone* (1961), *McHale's Navy* (1962-1963), *I Spy* (1965-1966), a Korean doctor in *M*A*S*H* (1970), *The Odd Couple* (1972), *Kung Fu* (1973-1975), as Vice Admiral Boshiro Hosogaya in *Midway* (1976), *Black Sheep Squadron* (1976), *Enter the Ninja* (1981), *Cannonball Run II* (1984), *Ninja III: The Domination* (1984), *The A-Team* (1986), *Morton & Hayes* (1991), *Dark Skies* (1996), and *Beverly Hills Ninja* (1997).

He became famous in the late 1990s for his appearances in television commercials for Nissan in which he portrayed Mr. K, supposedly Yutaka Katayama, the company's former president.

Ishimoto married Miiko Taka in Baltimore in 1944, and they had one son and one daughter. They divorced in 1958. He died at the age of 80 in Culver City, California, March 4, 2004.

Victor Israel

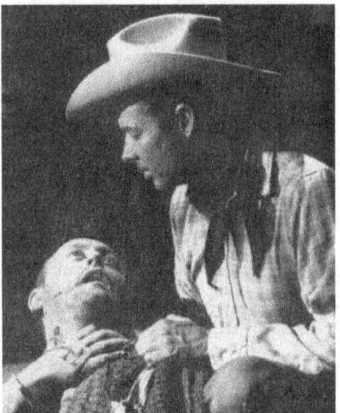

Victor Isreal with Audie Murphy in *The Texican*

Victor Israel was born Josep Maria Soler Vilanova June 13, 1929, in Barcelona, Catalonia, Spain. He was one of the most prolific and ubiquitous, yet anonymous, often overlooked, and hence underrated character actors in Spanish film history.

He attended the Escuela de actores de la Ciudad Condal. He began acting in films in the early 1960s. Short and dumpy, with a plain, round, pudgy face, thinning hair, medium height and build, snaggle teeth, a benign, humble, unassuming demeanor, and wide, moist, dark saucer eyes, Israel frequently portrayed ordinary working class types, timid cowards, men of the cloth, and meek victims.

He soon began making frequent appearances in rugged action films and gritty Italian spaghetti Westerns; he has an especially memorable uncredited part as a weary sergeant at a rundown Confederate fort who Lee Van Cleef talks to in Sergio Leone's magnificent *The Good, the Bad and the Ugly* (1966). He also appeared as the station master in *The Texican* (1966) with Audie Murphy.

From the late 1960s until the mid 1980s, Israel acted in an enjoyable slew of spooky horror features and entertainingly trashy exploitation films. Among his more notable roles are a creepy handyman in *The House That Screamed* (1969), a slimy, greedy, unctuous cemetery caretaker in *The Butcher of Binbrook* (1971), a craven coachman in *Murders in the Rue Morgue* (1971), a whistling train baggage handler in the fantastic *Horror Express* (1972), a near deaf, vaguely menacing innkeeper in *El Monte de las brujas* (1972), a despicable and untrustworthy sniveling wimp nightclub owner in the splendidly sleazy *Ricco* (1973), a scruffy, spineless mountain trail guide in the outrageous *Night of the Howling Beast* (1975), a zombie priest in *Hell of the Living Dead* (1980), and a boozy dock night watchman in the laughably lousy *The Sea Serpent* (1984).

Israel continued to act in both movies and television shows alike well into his 70s. He died at age 80 from natural causes on September 19, 2009, in Spain.

Burl Ives

Burl Ives with Audie Murphy in *Sierra*

Burl Ives was born Burle Icle Ivanhoe Ives June 14, 1909, in Hunt City, Illinois, and was one of six children born to a Scottish-Irish farming family. He first sang in public for a soldiers' reunion at age 4. In high school, he learned the banjo and played fullback, intending to become a football coach when he enrolled at Eastern Illinois State Teacher's College in 1927. He dropped out in 1930 and wandered, hitching rides, doing odd jobs, street singing.

Summer stock in the late 1930s led to a job with CBS radio in 1940; through his "Wayfaring Stranger" he popularized many of the folksongs he had collected in his travels. By the 1960s, he had hits on both popular and country charts. He recorded over 30 albums for Decca and another dozen for Columbia. In 1964 he was singer-narrator of *Rudolph, the Red-Nosed Reindeer* (1964), an often-repeated Christmas television special. His Broadway debut was in 1938, though he is best remembered for creating the role of Big Daddy in *Cat on a Hot Tin Roof* when it ran on Broadway.

His four-decade, movie career began with Ives playing a singing cowboy in *Smoky* (1946). He continued with roles such as Lonesome in *Sierra* (1950) with Audie Murphy, *East of Eden* (1955), and his career reached its peak as he reprised his role as Big Daddy in the movie version of *Cat on a Hot Tin Roof* (1958) and winning an Oscar for best supporting actor in *The Big Country* (1958), both in 1958. Other roles followed in *Our Man in Havana* (1959), *Ensign Pulver* (1964), *O.K. Crackerby!* (1965-1966), *Daniel Boone* (1969), *The Bold Ones: The Lawyers* (1969-1972), *Alias Smith and Jones* (1971-1972), Rod Serling's *Night Gallery* (1972), *Roots* (1977), *Uphill All the Way* (1986), and *Two Moon Junction* (1988).

Ives officially retired from show business on his 80th birthday in 1989 and settled in Anacortes, Washington, although he continued to do frequent benefit performances at his own request. Burl Ives died in 1995.

Richard Jaeckel

Richard Jaeckel with Audie Murphy in *The Gunrunners*

Richard Hanley Jaeckel was born in Long Beach, New York, October 10, 1926, and was an American actor of film and television. A short, but tough guy, he played a variety of characters during his fifty years in movies and television and became one of Hollywood's best known character actors. Jaeckel got his start in the business at the age of seventeen while working as a mail boy at 20th Century Fox studios in Hollywood. A casting director auditioned him for a key role in the 1943 film *Guadalcanal Diary*. Jaeckel won the role and settled into a lengthy career in supporting parts.

He served in the United States Merchant Marine from 1944 to 1949 then starred in two of the most remembered war films of 1949: *Battleground* and *Sands of Iwo Jima* with John Wayne. One of Jaeckel's shortest film roles was in *The Gunfighter*, in which his character is killed by Gregory Peck's character in the opening scene. He also played the role of Turk, the roomer's boyfriend, in the Oscar-winning 1952 film *Come Back, Little Sheba*, co-starring with Shirley Booth, Burt Lancaster, and Terry Moore.

Other roles included *Apache Ambush* (1955), *3:10 to Yuma* (1957), *The Naked and the Dead* (1958), *The Gun Runners* (1958) with Audie Murphy, *The Gallant Hours* (1960), *Flaming Star* (1960) with Elvis Presley, as Tony Gentry in twenty-six episodes of *Frontier Circus* (1961-1962), *4 for Texas* (1963), *The Outer Limits* (1964), *Town Tamer* (1965), and *The Wild Wild West* (1966-1967). He played Lee Marvin's able second-in-command in *The Dirty Dozen* (1967) for director Robert Aldrich. He had a great starring role in *The Green Slime* (1968) about a space station overcome with Sigmund the Sea Monster-looking aliens. He played Jess Evans in John Wayne's *Chisum* (1970). More roles followed in *O'Hara, U.S. Treasury* (1971), *Banyon* (1972-1973), and *Pat Garrett & Billy the Kid* (1973).

In 1972, Jaeckel received an Academy Award nomination for Best Supporting Actor for his role in *Sometimes a Great Notion*. He played Hank Myers in fourteen episodes of *Firehouse* (1973-1974). More roles continued like *Walking Tall Part II* (1975), *Joe Forrester* (1976), *Baretta* (1976), *Grizzly* (1976), *Black Sheep Squadron* (1978), *Centennial* (1978), *Salvage 1* (1979), *Herbie Goes Bananas* (1980), *McClain's Law* (1982) with James Arness, *Airplane II: The Sequel* (1982), *At Ease* (1983), *The Dirty Dozen: Next Mission* (1985), *Spenser: For Hire* (1985-1987), *Delta Force 2: The Colombian Connection* (1990) with Chuck Norris, and *Baywatch* (1989-1994).

Jaeckel died June 14, 1997, at the age of seventy after a three-year battle with melanoma, at the Motion Picture and Television Hospital in Woodland Hills, California. His son, Barry, is a professional golfer who has won on the PGA Tour.

Ted Jacques

Audie Murphy with Ted Jacques in *The Gunrunners*

Ted Jacques was born Theodore Emery Jacques May 11, 1912 in St. Paul, Minnesota, and was an American actor. He appeared in forty-two films and television programs from 1943 to 1968.

Some of those credits included *Action in the North Atlantic* (1943), *The Verdict* (1946), *Powder River Rustlers* (1949), *Western Pacific Agent* (1950), *I Led 3 Lives* (1955), *Black Patch* (1957), *The Gun Runners* (1958) with Audie Murphy, *Bat Masterson* (1959-1960), *Flaming Star* (1960) with Elvis Presley, *Gunsmoke* (1962), *Twilight Zone* (1964), *The Killers* (1964), *Beau Geste* (1966), and *Coogan's Bluff* (1968) with Clint Eastwood.

He died April 4, 1984, at age 71 in Los Angeles, California.

Dean Jagger

Dean Jagger with Audie Murphy in *Sierra*

Ira Dean Jagger was born in Columbus Grove, Ohio, November 7, 1903, and was film actor who received an Academy Award for his role in Henry King's *Twelve O'Clock High* (1949). He dropped out of school several times before finally attending Wabash College. While at Wabash he was a member of Lambda Chi Alpha fraternity. He worked as a teacher before studying acting at Chicago's Lyceum Art Conservatory. Prior to making his first movie in 1929, Jagger had worked in stock, vaudeville, and radio.

Jagger made his film debut in *The Woman from Hell* (1929) with Mary Astor. He became a successful character actor, without becoming a major star, and appeared in almost 100 films in a career that lasted until shortly before his death. He made his breakthrough to major roles in film with his portrayal of Brigham Young in *Brigham Young* (1940). According to George D. Pyper, a technical consultant on the film who had personally known Brigham Young, said that Jagger not only resembled Young, he also spoke like him and had many of his mannerisms. He then played prominent roles in *Western Union* (1941), *Sister Kenny* (1946), and Raoul Walsh's Western neo-noir *Pursued* (1947).

He received an Academy Award for Best Supporting Actor for his role in *Twelve O'Clock High* (1949). In the film he played the middle-aged adjutant Major Stovall, who acts as an advisor to the commander General Savage (Gregory Peck), and is tasked with writing letters to the next of kin of slain airmen.

Jagger next showed up in *Sierra* (1950) as Audie Murphy's father who was falsely accused of a crime that kept them hiding out for many years.

He appeared in the biblical epic *The Robe* (1953) as the weaver Justus of Cana, "whose words were like his work: simple, lasting, and strong," as Marcellus Gallio (Richard Burton) put it later in the film. He then played the retired general honored by Bing Crosby and Danny Kaye in the musical *White Christmas* (1954) and a helpless sheriff in the iconic *Bad Day at Black Rock* (1955) directed by John Eliot Sturges. For the 1956 British science-fiction film *X the Unknown*, there was controversy when Dean Jagger refused to work with director Joseph Losey on this film because Losey was on the Hollywood blacklist. Losey was removed from the project after a few days shooting and replaced with Les Norman. Jagger portrayed the father of Elvis Presley in 1958's *King Creole*. He was the traveling manager for an evangelist played by Jean Simmons in the acclaimed 1960 drama *Elmer Gantry*, which won three Academy Awards. In 1969 Jagger played "The Highwayman" in John Huston's *The Kremlin Letter*. In 1971's *Vanishing Point*, the actor made a brief but memorable appearance as a prospector in the desert with a knack for handling rattlesnakes. Jagger also achieved success in the television series *Mr. Novak*, receiving Emmy Award nominations for his role, in 1964 and 1965.

In later years, Jagger appeared in the made-for-TV movie in *The Glass House* (1972) which also starred Alan Alda and Vic Morrow. The screenplay was partially based on a story by Truman Capote. Jagger played state prison Warden Auerbach. In 1973, he was in another TV movie, a pilot for a proposed series called *The Stranger*, a science fiction film starring Glenn Corbett as an astronaut stranded on an alien planet, with Jagger as a leader of a corrupt deceptive government known as "The Perfect Order". Lew Ayres and Cameron Mitchell also starred. None of the major U.S. networks picked it up as a weekly series.

He appeared in *The Game of Death* (1978) playing Dr. Land who was the nemesis of Bruce Lee. Most of the movie was filmed five years after Bruce Lee's death, adding footage to what was shot years earlier. Bruce Lee had filmed the footage before he started work on *Enter the Dragon* (1973). The remaining footage that was shot in 1978 was of a Bruce Lee double or card board cut-outs of Bruce Lee taped to a mirror! He won a Daytime Emmy award for a guest appearance in the religious series *This Is the Life* (1980). His final role was playing Doctor Schaeffer In *Evil Town* (1987).

Jagger died February 5, 1991, from heart disease at age 87 in Santa Monica, and was buried in the small town of Hughson, California, at Lakewood Memorial Park. His widow, Etta Mae Norton Jagger, joined him there in death just eleven months later, in January 17, 1992. She was 67.

Conrad Janis

Audie Murphy with Conrad Janis in *Beyond Glory*

Conrad Janis was born February 11, 1928 and is an American jazz musician (trombone) and also a theatre, film, and television actor. Janis was born in New York City, New York, the son of Harriet, a writer, and Sidney Janis, an art dealer and writer. A New York-based radio actor from childhood, Conrad Janis was sixteen when he made his first Broadway appearance in Junior Miss. Janis went on to star in the 1945 film comedy *Snafu* and then played supporting roles in such 20th Century-Fox productions as *Margie* (1946) and *The Brasher Doubloon* (1947), as a teenaged murderer. His subsequent Broadway credits include *The Brass Ring* (for which he won a Theatre World Award), *Time Out for Ginger*, and *Visit to a Small Planet*.

He also appeared in *Beyond Glory* (1948) with Audie Murphy and Alan Ladd as the cause of all the problems.

Premature baldness compelled him to switch from leading-man assignments to character roles. A veteran of hundreds of film and television appearances, Janis was seen on such films and programs as *Suspense* (1950-1952), *Kraft Theatre* (1951-1955), *Zane Grey Theater* (1956), *The Untouchables* (1960), *Stoney Burke* (1962), *Get Smart* (1965), *My Favorite Martian* (1966), *Banacek* (1972), *Airport 1975* (1974), *Baretta* (1975), Police Story (1976), and *Kojak* (1978).

He was also seen on a regular weekly basis as Otto Palindrome on the 1978 sci-fi spoof *Quark*, and as Mindy McConnell's dad Fred on the Robin Williams sitcom *Mork and Mindy* (1978-1982). Dropped from *Mork and Mindy* after the 1978-79 seasons when the producers decided to retool the program, Janis was rehired in 1980, this time at a much heftier salary.

He continued to find work in such films and shows as *The Buddy Holly Story* (1978), *Oh, God! Book II* (1980), *Trapper John, M.D.* (1983), *V* (1985), *The Gods Must Be Crazy IV* (1993), *The Cable Guy* (1996), *Addams Family Reunion* (1998), and *Maneater* (2009). He also made a brief appearance as himself in the jazz bar scene from *Nothing in Common* (1986). Conrad Janis not only starred in *Bad Blood* (1986), and its sequel *Bad Blood...The Hunger* (2009), he produced, directed, and edited them.

In addition, Janis is the owner operator of a prominent avant-garde art gallery, and is in charge of his own production company, MiraCom.

Though justifiably proud of his acting accomplishments, Janis reportedly is prouder still of his activities as a jazz musician, fronting such prestigious musical aggregations as The Tailgaters and the Beverly Hills Unlisted Jazz Band. This latter group served as the subject of a lively PBS documentary.

David Janssen

Audie Murphy with David Janssen in *To Hell and Back*

David Janssen born March 27, 1931, and was an American film and television actor who was destined to be a star. Janssen was born as David Harold Meyer in Naponee, Nebraska, to Harold Edward Meyer, a banker (May 12, 1906 – November 4, 1990) and Berniece Graf (May 11, 1910 – November 26, 1995). Following his parents' divorce in 1935, his mother moved with five-year-old David to Los Angeles, California. She eventually married Eugene Janssen (February 18, 1918 – March 30, 1996) on September 29, 1940, in Los Angeles.

Young David used his stepfather's name after he entered show business as a child. He attended Fairfax High School in Los Angeles. His first film part was at the age of thirteen in *It's a Pleasure* (1945), and by the age of twenty-five he had appeared in twenty films and served two years as an enlisted man in the United States Army. During his Army days, Janssen became friends with fellow enlistees Martin Milner and Clint Eastwood whilst posted at Ft. Ord, California.

Some more of his earlier films were *Swamp Fire* (1946), *Untamed Frontier* (1952), *Francis Goes to West Point* (1952), *Bonzo Goes to College* (1952), *Back at the Front* (1952), *Chief Crazy Horse* (1955), *Cult of the Cobra* (1955), *The Private War of Major Benson* (1955), *Francis in the Navy* (1955), *All That Heaven Allows* (1955), *The Square Jungle* (1955), *The Toy Tiger* (1956), and his third 'Francis the Talking Mule' film *Francis in the Haunted House* (1956).

Janssen appeared in many television series before he landed programs of his own. In 1956, he and Peter Breck appeared in John Bromfield's syndicated series *Sheriff of Cochise* in the episode "The Turkey Farmers". He joined Milner in a 1962 episode of *Route 66* as the character Kamo in the episode "One Tiger to a Hill".

Janssen starred in four television series of his own:
- *Richard Diamond, Private Detective* (1957–60),
- *The Fugitive* (1963–67),
- *O'Hara, U.S. Treasury* (1971–72), and
- *Harry O* (1974–76).

The final episode "The Judgment" of *The Fugitive* aired on August 29, 1967, and held the record for the greatest number of American homes with television sets to watch a series finale, at 72%. It kept the record until November 21, 1980, when it was revealed 'Who Shot J.R.' on the *Dallas* episode "Who Done It?" The Dallas episode was subsequently knocked from the number one spot when the *M*A*S*H* finale "Goodbye, Farewell and Amen" aired February 28, 1983.

Some more of his films include *To Hell and Back*, the autobiography of Audie Murphy, who is the most decorated soldier in the military history of the United States; *Hell to Eternity* (1960), *King of the Roaring 20's: The Story of Arnold Rothstein* (1961), John Wayne's war film *The Green Berets* (1968), *The Shoes of the Fisherman* (1968), and opposite Gregory Peck in the space story *Marooned* (1969) about three stranded astronauts.

Janssen also played in *Generation* (1969), *Macho Callahan* (1970), *Moon of the Wolf* (1972), *Birds of Prey* (1973), *Once Is Not Enough* (1975), *The Swiss Conspiracy* (1976), *Two-Minute Warning* (1976), and *Mayday at 40,000 Feet!* (1976).

He then played an alcoholic in the 1977 TV movie *A Sensitive, Passionate Man*, which co-starred Angie Dickinson, an over worked police sergeant in the "Trigger Point" episode of *Police Story* (1977), *Superdome* (1978), and an engineer who devises an unbeatable system for blackjack in the 1978 made-for-TV movie *Nowhere to Run* co-starring Stefanie Powers and Linda Evans.

In his last years he played the part of Paul Garrett and the narrator of the sensational twenty-six hour television mini-series *Centennial* (1978-1979), John Jacob Astor in *S.O.S. Titanic* (1979), the detective sergeant trying to solve *The Golden Gate Murders* (1979), *High Ice* (1980), and *City in Fear* (1980).

At the time of his death, Janssen had just begun filming a television movie playing the part of Father Damien, the priest who dedicated himself to the leper colony on the island of Molokai. The part was eventually reassigned to actor Ken Howard, and released as *Father Damien: The Leper Priest* (1980). The film was dedicated to the memory of David Janssen.

He was married twice. His first marriage was to Ellie Graham on August 23, 1958 in Las Vegas, Nevada. They divorced on August 25, 1970. From October 4, 1975 to his death, he was married to sometime actress and model Dani Crayne Greco.

Janssen died of a heart attack on the morning of February 13, 1980, at his home in Malibu, California. Two days earlier, he told his wife, Dani, that he had a bad dream that he was being carried in a coffin following a heart attack. He is interred in the Hillside Memorial Park Cemetery in Culver City, California.

In 1996 TV Guide ranked him number thirty-six on its 50 Greatest TV Stars of All Time list.

Maurice Jara

Maurice Jara was born Saul R. Jara December 15, 1922, in Los Angeles County, California. He appeared in thirty-five films and television programs from 1950 to 1972. Some of his film roles were in movies such as *The Lawless* (1950), *Flying Leathernecks* (1951), *Tropic Zone* (1953), *Fighter Attack* (1953), *Drum Beat* (1954), *The First Texan* (1956), *Walk the Proud Land* (1956), *Giant* (1956), *The Lone Ranger and the Lost City of Gold* (1958), and his last film *They Came to Cordura* (1959). He appeared in television programs like *Sky King* (1952), *Boston Blackie* (1953), *Ramar of the Jungle* (1954), *Adventures of Superman* (1955), *Broken Arrow* (1957), *Rawhide* (1959), *Lawman* (1960), *Ben Casey* (1963), *Marcus Welby, M.D.* (1970), and his last role in *Hec Ramsey* (1972).

He died July 23, 1995, age 72 in San Jacinto, California.

Renne Jarrett

Renne Jarrett with Audie Murphy in *Ford Startime*

Renne Jarrett was born Veronica Jarrett January 28, 1946, in Brooklyn, New York. She appeared in thirty-six television movies and programs from 1953 to 1985.

Some of her television movies and shows include *To My Valentine* (1953), *The Edge of Night* (1957-1958), "The Man" episode of *Ford Startime* (1960) with Audie Murphy, *The Patty Duke Show* (1965), *Then Came Bronson* (1969), *Mod Squad* (1970), the title character in all seventeen episodes of *Nancy* (1970-1971), *Somerset* (1972-1973), *The Cat Creature* (1973), *The Streets of San Francisco* (1974), *Petrocelli* (1975), *Joe Forrester* (1976), *The New Daughters of Joshua Cabe* (1976), *Barnaby Jones* (1974-1979), *The Ghosts of Buxley Hall* (1980), *Archie Bunker's Place* (1980), *Finder of Lost Loves* (1984), and *Hotel* (1985).

She is married to retired director Bruce Bilson and living in Studio City, California. She currently serves on the Board of Directors of the National CASA Association, providing court-appointed special advocates for children from disadvantaged backgrounds.

Chubby Johnson

Chubby Johnson with Audie Murphy in *Gunsmoke*

Chubby Johnson was born Charles Rutledge Johnson on August 13, 1903, in Terre Haute, Indiana. He made a living as a journalist and did not become a movie actor until he was in his 40s, making his debut in the Randolph Scott oater *Abilene Town* (1946) in support of Scott, Ann Dvorak and Edgar Buchanan.

He continued to practice his craft as a member of the press, serving as a radio announcer as well as pounding the keys as a columnist, until he was nearly 50. Chubby appeared in Errol Flynn's horse opera *Rocky Mountain* (1950) as part of an army of quirky character actors which included Guinn 'Big Boy' Williams and Slim Pickens. Chubby then quit the Fourth Estate for a Hollywood career.

When Republic Pictures sought a replacement for Eddy Waller to play sidekick to B-movie cowboy star Allan Lane in the *Rocky Lane* series, Chubby filled in for most of 1951-52. He also starred in the series *Sky King* (1951) as ranch foreman Jim Bell. The low-budget series, a spin-off from a five-year-old radio show in which individual episodes were made for approximately $9,000 each, ran on NBC from Sept 16, 1951, until Oct 26, 1952. The series was then picked up by ABC, which ran the same NBC episodes from November 8, 1952, until September 12, 1954. A season of new episodes was aired in 1955.

Chubby freelanced as a character actor after these stints on the boob tube, appearing in support of James Stewart in the Anthony Mann classic *Bend of the River* (1952), and in their *The Far Country* (1954), which also featured character actor par excellence Walter Brennan, the movies' first triple-Oscar threat. Chubby then went on to appear in support of Doris Day in *Calamity Jane* (1953), Audie Murphy in *Gunsmoke* (1953), Ronald Reagan in *Law and Order* (1953), Barbara Stanwyck and Ronnie again in *Cattle Queen of Montana* (1954) and James Cagney in *Tribute to a Bad Man* (1956), one of the legend's rare forays into the western.

Other stars Chubby supported were Richard Chamberlain and Claude Rains in *Twilight of Honor* (1963), the 1963 courtroom drama that won the ill-fated Nick Adams a Best Supporting Actor Oscar nomination; James Garner in *Support Your Local Sheriff!* (1969); and Burt Reynolds in his audacious debut as a big-screen star as the eponymous *Sam Whiskey* (1969). He also appeared uncredited in the classic *High Noon* (1952).

After appearing as a regular in the short-lived series *Frontier Doctor* (1958), Chubby appeared as Concho on another TV western, *Temple Houston* (1963), which starred Jeffrey Hunter. He also guested on many other TV westerns, including *Bonanza* (1959), *Gunsmoke* (1955), and *The Rifleman* (1958).

Chubby continued to appear in films until 1969, with *Sam Whiskey* (1969) serving as the nightcap to his career. He died on Halloween Day 1974 from complications from a leg infection.

Russell Johnson

Russell David Johnson was born in Ashley, Pennsylvania, November 10, 1924, and is an American television and film actor best known as "The Professor" on the CBS television sitcom *Gilligan's Island* (1964-1967). He is the last surviving male cast member from that show; Dawn Wells and Tina Louise are the only surviving female cast members. Johnson is a graduate of Girard College, a private boarding school for children in need in Philadelphia.

After high school, in the midst of World War II, Johnson joined the United States Army Air Forces as an aviation cadet; upon commissioning as a second lieutenant, Johnson was assigned the service number 0 765 497. He flew 44 combat missions as a bombardier in B-25 bombers. While flying as a navigator in a B-25 with the 100th Bombardment Squadron, 42nd Bombardment Group, 13th Air Force, his plane and two other B-25s were shot down in the Philippines in March 1945 during a low level bombing and strafing run against Japanese targets. The planes were hit by intense flak and had to ditch in the waters off the port of Zamboanga.

During the ditching, he broke both his ankles and the radioman next to him was killed. Russell Johnson earned a Purple Heart for this mission. He was also awarded the Air Medal, the Good Conduct Medal, the Asiatic-Pacific Campaign Medal with three service stars, the Philippine Liberation Ribbon with one service star, and the World War II Victory Medal. He was honorably discharged with the rank of first lieutenant on November 22, 1945. He then joined the Army Reserve and used the GI Bill to fund his acting studies at the Actor's Lab in Hollywood. While at acting school he met actress Kay Levey and they married on July 23, 1949.

Johnson's Hollywood career began in 1952, with the college fraternity hazing exposé *For Men Only*, and with *Loan Shark*, also released in 1952 and starring George Raft.

He became a close friend of Audie Murphy and later appeared with him in three of his films, *Column South* and *Tumbleweed* in 1953 and *Ride Clear of Diablo* in 1954.

His early roles were primarily in westerns and science fiction such as *It Came from Outer Space* (1953), *This Island Earth* (1955), *Attack of the Crab Monsters* (1956), and *The Space Children* (1958). He also appeared in a Ma and Pa Kettle vehicle, *Ma and Pa Kettle at Waikiki* (1955).

During the 1950s, he guest starred on Rod Cameron's syndicated crime drama, *City Detective*. He appeared three times as the character "Beach" on the syndicated military drama *The Silent Service* (1957-1958), based on actual stories of the submarine section of the United States Navy. Johnson was cast as Hugh Grafton and as Tom Richards in two 1960 episodes, "Intermission" and "The Desperate Challenge", both with June Allyson on her CBS's anthology series, *The DuPont Show with June Allyson*. On September 16, 1963, Johnson appeared in the series premiere of the ABC medical drama *Breaking Point* starring Paul Richards and Eduard Franz.

From 1959 to 1960, he had a recurring role on the ABC half-hour western series, *Black Saddle* with Peter Breck, J. Pat O'Malley, and Walter Burke.

Johnson appeared in two episodes in *The Twilight Zone* (1960-1961). He attempted to prevent the assassination of Abraham Lincoln in "Back There". He appeared as a college professor in the episode, "Execution". The plot of both episodes involved time travel from the 19th to the 20th centuries.

He is best known for playing Prof. Roy Hinkley (usually referred to as "The Professor"), the erudite polymath who could build all sorts of inventions out of the most rudimentary materials available on the island, but, as Johnson himself pointed out, could not fix the hole in the boat. *Gilligan's Island* aired from 1964 to 1967, but has been shown in reruns continuously ever since.

Johnson was asked to take off his shirt when auditioning for the *Gilligan's Island* role; he refused, but still got the job. Before accepting the role of Roy Hinkley, he made *Gilligan's Island* producer Sherwood Schwartz promise him that when he made scientific statements they would be accurate.

After *Gilligan's Island*, he appeared in several other movies and television shows, especially the latter. He appeared in several dramatic series, including *The Invaders* (1967), *Death Valley Days* (1961-1968), *Lassie* (1958-1969), *O'Hara, U.S. Treasury* (1971), *Ironside* (1972), *The F.B.I.* (1968-1970), *Gunsmoke* (1957-1972), and 1971-1973 *Owen Marshall: Counselor at Law* (1971-1973) as Assistant DA Brenton Grant in six episodes.

Perhaps most notably the miniseries *Vanished* (1971), based on a novel by Fletcher Knebel, uncredited in the Robert Redford spy thriller, *Three Days of the Condor* (1975), *Rich Man, Poor Man - Book II* (1976), *McMillan & Wife* (1977), *The Ghost of Flight 401* (1978), *The Bastard* (1978), *The New Adventures of Wonder Woman* (1978), *Bosom Buddies* (1981), *The Jefferson's* (1982), *Buffalo Bill* (1983), *Dynasty* (1986-1987), *Monsters* (1988), and on the NBC soap opera *Santa Barbara* (1991).

In an interview with *Starlog* magazine in the early 1980s, Johnson expressed an interest in appearing on *Star Trek*, during its original run on NBC (1966–1969), although this did not come about.

He played the sheriff in several episodes of season nine of *Dallas* (1986), his character did not return in season ten however as season nine turned out to be the infamous "dream season".

In 1974 *Gilligan's Island* came back to television in the form of a cartoon series called *The New Adventures of Gilligan*. Gilligan had a pet dinosaur in this series. Most of the cast voiced their own characters. It lasted one season. Then the castaways returned for a live action movie in *Rescue from Gilligan's Island* (1978), but then were stranded again at the end of the movie on the same island. The next year they were rescued again in *The Castaways on Gilligan's Island* (1979) and the Howell's built a resort hotel on the island. Two years later they returned again for *The Harlem Globetrotters on Gilligan's Island* (1981). Originally, it was supposed to be called The Dallas Cowboys Cheerleaders On Gilligan's Island, but the cheerleaders were unable to fit it in their schedule, so they recruited the Harlem Globetrotters to replace them at the last moment. The next year they were back to voicing a cartoon series in *Gilligan's Planet* (1982) where the professor built a rocket ship to get them off the island, but instead launched them into outer space to another planet. He couldn't fix the hole in the boat, but he could build a rocket?

An episode of *Newhart* (1987) featured the Beavers (a men's organization) watching a *Gilligan's Island* episode on television. When they are suddenly evicted from the room, one of them, portrayed by Johnson, protests, "I want to see how it ends!" He is assured that the castaways don't get off the island.

Also in 1987, Russell Johnson, Alan Hale, Jr., Dawn Wells, and Bob Denver reprised their *Gilligan's Island* roles in a dream sequence where *ALF* dreamt he was on *Gilligan's Island* with the castaways in the episode "Somewhere Over the Rerun". In 1995, Russell Johnson, Dawn Wells, Bob Denver, and Tina Louise appeared in the series *Roseanne* in the episode "Sherwood Schwartz–A Loving Tribute" where the Roseanne cast and the castaways swapped roles.

Johnson entertained fans at the 1996 MST3K ContevtioConExpoFest-a-Rama 2: Electric Boogaloo on the "Celebrity Panel". Johnson was invited for his role in the movie-within-a-movie of *Mystery Science Theater 3000: The Movie*, *This Island Earth*, but spent most of the time answering questions about his *Gilligan's Island* days. He shared an amusing anecdote:

"I was at a speaking engagement for MIT ... and I said ... the Professor has all sorts of degrees, including one from this very institution [MIT]! And that's *why* I can make a radio out of a coconut, and *not* fix a hole in a boat"!

In 1997, Russell Johnson, Dawn Wells, and Bob Denver appeared as their Gilligan's Island characters in the Meego episode "Mommy and Meego". In 2004, the TV Land Award's show reunited the surviving cast members for a tribute award. Johnson once participated in the Ig Nobel award presentation ceremony, credited as "The Professor Emeritus of Gilligan's Island".

His son, David, ran the AIDS program for Los Angeles, California, until David's own death from complications of AIDS in 1994. Johnson has been a full-time volunteer for AIDS research fundraising since his son was diagnosed.

Johnson has written his memoirs, *Here on Gilligan's Isle*.

Russell Johnson died of natural causes January 16, 2013 at age 89 at his home in Washington state.

I. Stanford Jolley

Isaac Stanford Jolley, Sr., known as I. Stanford Jolley was born October 24, 1900, and was a prolific American character actor of film and television, primarily in western roles as cowboys, law-enforcement officers, or villains. Recognized by his slight build, narrow face, and pencil-thin moustache, Jolley appeared some five hundred times on the large or small screen.

Born in Morristown, New Jersey, Jolley toured as a child with his father's traveling circus and worked in vaudeville. He first performed on Broadway in 1924 opposite Charles Trowbridge in *Sweet Seventeen*. He also worked in radio until he performed his first uncredited part in the 1935 Bette Davis film, *Front Page Woman*. He appeared in twenty-five films for Republic Pictures between 1936 and 1954, but he was never under contract to the studio. According to his wife, he never earned more than $100 on any of his multiple film appearances.

In 1939, he played an uncredited part as a hotel clerk in *Mr. Wong in Chinatown*. Appearing in scores of films, mostly westerns, Jolley was cast in 1940 as Molotoff in *Chasing Trouble*, with other performers in the comedy/espionage film including western actors Milburn Stone and Tristram Coffin. In 1942, he was cast as Gil Harkness in the western *Outlaws of Boulder Pass*. In 1944, he was cast as Saladin in the swashbuckling "western" film set in the Middle East, *The Desert Hawk*, and as Bart Kern in the Tex Ritter film, *Gangsters of the Frontier*. In 1945, Jolley was cast as Marshal Mullins in *Springtime in Texas*, a 55-minute film about a crime boss, Pete Grant, played by Rex Lease, who controls the West Texas town of Pecos.

In 1946, Jolley portrayed Dr. Blackton in *The Crimson Ghost* and also did the voice of the undefined title character. That same year, he portrayed Sheriff Bill Armstrong in *Silver Range* and James Beeton in the western musical *Swing, Cowboy, Swing*. In 1948, Jolley was cast as the loan shark Rance Carson in *Tex Granger, Midnight Rider of the Plains*, with Robert Kellard in the title role. In 1949, Jolley appeared as Professor Bryant in *King of the Rocket Men*, again with Tristram Coffin. That same year, he was cast as Mark Simmons in *Trouble at Melody Mesa*, starring Brad King as a marshal. He also appeared as Toad Tyler in 1949s *Rimfire*. In 1950, Jolley was cast as J.B. "Dude" Dawson in the low-budgeted Republic Pictures film serial, *Desperadoes of the West*. In 1951, he was cast as Sam Fleming in *Oklahoma Justice*, with Johnny Mack Brown, with whom he had also appeared in *Silver Range*. That same year, Jolley appeared as Rocky in the western film, *Son of Belle Starr*, a drama about Starr's son, "The Kid" or Ed Reed, played by Keith Larsen, who attempts to lead an upright life despite his family background. In 1954, he played the stationmaster in Vermont in the Bing Crosby/Danny Kaye Christmas classic *White Christmas*. In 1956, Jolley appeared as Henry Longtree in the short film *I Killed Wild Bill Hickok*.

He had parts in *Sierra* (1950), *The Red Badge of Courage* (1951), *Tumbleweed,* and *Posse From Hell* (1961) with Audie Murphy.

From 1950-1953, Jolley first appeared on television with six castings in different role in the syndicated series *The Lone Ranger* with Clayton Moore. He appeared twice in 1953 in another syndicated western series, *The Range Rider*. He guest starred as the henchman Walt, along with Clayton Moore and Darryl Hickman, in the 1954 episode "Annie Gets Her Man" of the syndicated Gail Davis and Brad Johnson western, *Annie Oakley*. He appeared as Sheriff Bascom in the 1954 episode "Black Bart" of the syndicated Jim Davis series, *Stories of the Century*.

In 1958, Jolley appeared on ABC's *Walt Disney Presents* in the role of Sheriff Adams in the episode "Law and Order, Incorporated", with Robert Loggia as Elfego Baca. His then 32-year-old son, Stan Jolley, was the art director of the segment. Others in the episode were former child actor Skip Homeier and Raymond Bailey, later the banker Milburn Drysdale of CBS's *The Beverly Hillbillies*.

In 1965, he appeared as Enos Scoggins in "The Greatest Coward on Earth" of the Chuck Connors series, *Branded*. He had also appeared with Connors on ABC's *The Rifleman* in one of the last episodes of the series in

1963 in the role of Joe Fogner in "Hostages to Fortune" (1963). He appeared four times in 1956 in archival footage on the children's western *The Gabby Hayes Show*.

Jolley's last western roles were in 1976: as (1) a farmer in ABC's *The Macahans*, the pilot of James Arness's second western series, *How the West Was Won*, and as a (2) drunkard in the short-lived Tim Matheson and Kurt Russell series *The Quest*.

Jolley and his wife, Emily Mae or "Peggy" Jolley (1901–2003), had two children, the art director I. Stanford "Stan" Jolley, Jr. (born 1926), and the late Sandra Jolley Carson (1919–1986), the former wife of actor Forrest Tucker and the widow of actor Jack Carson. Sandra Jolley was originally an Earl Carroll showgirl. Jolley was hence the father-in-law of Tucker from 1940–1950 and of Carson from 1961 until Carson's death in 1963.

Jolley died December 7, 1978, of emphysema at the age of seventy-eight at the Motion Picture Country Hospital in Woodland Hills, California. His wife died in the same facility in 2003. The Jolleys are interred at Forest Lawn Memorial Park in the Hollywood Hills neighborhood of Los Angeles.

Pamela "Brooke" Tucker, offered this reflection of her grandfather: "The most important thing about my grandfather was that he was the antithesis of all the villains he portrayed. He was a gentleman and a gentle man. He was ALWAYS interested in what the other person had to say and when you met him, he made you feel as though you were very important and special. All of my friends growing up loved him.

Jolley's grave marker reads:

I. Stanford Jolley
Loving Husband And Father
1900-1978
A Gentle Man And As Jolly By Nature As He Was By Name
Loved By All and Especially His Family

L.Q. Jones

L.Q. Jones with Audie Murphy in *Apache Rifles*, and with David Williams in 2012

L.Q. Jones was born August 19, 1927, and is an American character actor and film director, known for his work in the films of Sam Peckinpah.

Jones was born Justus Ellis McQueen in Beaumont, Texas, the son of Jessie Paralee (née Stephens) and Justice Ellis McQueen, who was a railroad worker. He attended The University of Texas at Austin in late 1940s.

He made his film debut in 1955's *Battle Cry*, with Van Heflin, under his birth name. His character was named L.Q. Jones, and when it was suggested to him by film producers that he changed his screen name for future pictures, he decided that the name of his debut character would be a memorable one.

Jones appeared in numerous memorable films in the 1960s and 1970s. He became a member of Sam Peckinpah's stock company of actors, appearing in his *Klondike* television series (1960–1961), *Ride the High Country* (1962) with Joel McCrea and Randolph Scott, *Major Dundee* (1965), *The Wild Bunch* (1969), *The Ballad of Cable Hogue* (1970), and *Pat Garrett and Billy The Kid* (1973).

He also appeared twice with Audie Murphy in *Showdown* (1963) and *Apache Rifles* (1964).

He was frequently cast alongside his close friend, Strother Martin, most memorably in *The Wild Bunch*. Jones also appeared in television, as recurring characters on such western programs as *Cheyenne* (1955), *Gunsmoke* (1955), *Laramie* (1959-1963), *Two Faces West* (1960–1961), and twenty-five times on *The Virginian* (1962) as ranch hand Andy Belden. He was cast once in the syndicated military drama *Men of Annapolis* (1958). He also appeared in *Voyagers!* (1983) with doomed actor Jon-Erik Hexum.

He directed, was the executive producer, and adapted the screenplay for *A Boy and His Dog* (1975), with Don Johnson and Jason Robards. Other films include *Men in War* (1957), *The Naked and the Dead* (1958), *Flaming Star* (1960), *Cimarron* (1960), *Hell Is for Heroes* (1962), *Hang 'Em High* (1968), *Stay Away, Joe* (1968), *Lone Wolf McQuade* (1983), *Casino* (1995), *The Edge* (1997), *The Mask of Zorro* (1998), and *A Prairie Home Companion* (2006).

He co-produced, co-starred, wrote, and cast Strother Martin again in the lead role of *The Brotherhood of Satan* (1971). He also wrote the novel, which he autographed a paperback copy to me when I met and talked with him about Audie Murphy at the Memphis Film Festival June 1, 2012, and he said "I Really liked Audie. He went through more things than most of us have ever thought of. Audie was a sweetheart".

He is currently attending western film festival gatherings for the fiftieth anniversary of *The Virginian*.

Ted Jordan

Ted Jordan with Audie Murphy in *Sierra*

Ted Jordan was born May 23, 1924, in Circleville, Ohio. He first appeared in *Circumstantial Evidence* (1945) and continued to get roles in films and television programs for the next thirty-six years.

Some of his films and television shows included *Dragonwyck* (1946), *Tokyo Joe* (1949), *When Willie Comes Marching Home* (1950), as outlaw Jim Coulter in *Sierra* (1950) with Audie Murphy, *Lorna Doone* (1951), *Francis Goes to West Point* (1952), *Law and Order* (1953), *The Walter Winchell File* (1958), *The Tom Ewell Show* (1961), *Branded* (1965-1966), *The Andy Griffith Show* (1966), *The Silencers* (1966), *Hondo* (1967), *The Virginian* (1963-1967), *The Wrecking Crew* (1969), *Land of the Giants* (1968-1970), *Walking Tall* (1973), *The Blue Knight* (1976), *How the West Was Won* (1979), *The Apple Dumpling Gang Rides Again* (1979), *Eight Is Enough* (1977-1980), *Dallas* (1979-1981), and *The Waltons* (1976-1981).

He is best known for his role of Nathan Burke in 129 episodes of *Gunsmoke* (1961-1975).

He wrote a book *Norma Jean: My Secret Life With Marilyn Monroe* in 1989 about his "affair" with Marilyn Monroe and he even claims she had a child by him in the late 1940s. The book is the main source for the Mira Sorvino/Ashley Judd television movie *Norma Jean and Marilyn* (1996).

Ted Jordan died March 30, 2005, at age 80 in Palm Desert, California.

Victor Jory

Victor Jory with Audie's son Terry Murphy in *A Time for Dying*

Victor Jory was born in Dawson City, Yukon, November 23, 1902, and was a Canadian actor.

Jory was the boxing and wrestling champion of the Coast Guard during his military service, and he kept his burly physique. He toured with theater troupes and appeared on Broadway, before making his Hollywood debut in 1930 in the film *Renegades*.

He initially played romantic leads, but later was mostly cast as the villain. He made over 150 films and dozens of television episodes, as well as writing two plays. His long career in radio included starring in the series *Dangerously Yours*. He is most remembered for his role as Jonas Wilkerson, the brutal and opportunistic overseer, in *Gone with the Wind* and as Lamont Cranston, also known as 'The Shadow' in the 1942 serial film *The Shadow*.

From 1959-1961, he appeared with Patrick McVey in the syndicated television police drama, *Manhunt*. Jory played the lead role of Detective Lieutenant Howard Finucane. McVey was cast as police reporter Ben Andrews.

Some of his other roles include *Madame Du Barry* (1934), *A Midsummer Night's Dream* (1935), *Bulldog Drummond at Bay* (1937), *Dodge City* (1939), *The Light of Western Stars* (1940), *Secrets of the Lone Wolf* (1941), *Hoppy Serves a Writ* (1943), *Bar 20* (1943), *The Cariboo Trail* (1950), *The Man from the Alamo* (1953), *Blackjack Ketchum, Desperado* (1956), *Wanted: Dead or Alive* (1959), *The Untouchables* (1962), *Cheyenne Autumn* (1964), *The Green Hornet* (1966), and *Mackenna's Gold* (1969).

He portrayed Judge Roy Bean in *A Time for Dying* (1969), Audie Murphy's last film. He had no scenes with Audie Murphy, but did have scenes with Audie's son Terry Murphy. As a matter of fact, he pronounced sentence on Terry Murphy for being a horse thief and had him hanged!

Some more of his roles were in *Mannix* (1969-1972), *Longstreet* (1971), *Papillon* (1973), *Kolchak: The Night Stalker* (1974), *The Rockford Files* (1978), *Devil Dog: The Hound of Hell* (1978), *Greatest Heroes of the Bible* (1978-1979), *Young Maverick* (1980), and his final film *Mountain Men* (1980).

He died in Santa Monica, California, February 12, 1982, and was cremated.

Robert Karnes

Audie Murphy with Robert Karnes in *Apache Rifles*

Robert A. Karnes was born June 19, 1917, in Kentucky and was a prolific television actor who also appeared in some films early in his career, including mostly uncredited parts in *The Best Years of Our Lives* (1946), *Miracle on 34th Street* (1947), *Kiss Tomorrow Goodbye* (1950), and *From Here to Eternity* (1953).

He was a co-star with James Gregory in the NBC crime drama *The Lawless Years*, having appeared as Max Fields in fifteen episodes between 1959 and 1961. The program, set during the Roaring 20s preceded the more successful *The Untouchables* by a half-season. Karnes even appeared twice on *The Untouchables* (1959-1963). He appeared eight times on the half-hour or hour-long versions of the *Alfred Hitchcock* (1957-1961) program on CBS.

In 1960, Karnes had a role in the western film *Five Guns to Tombstone* along with Quintin Sondergaard, who had formerly appeared on *Tombstone Territory*. He was frequently cast in various television westerns, including the 1959 episode "Murder Is the Bid" of the syndicated *Mackenzie's Raiders*, starring Richard Carlson. Between 1957 and 1974, he guest starred in ten episodes of CBS's *Gunsmoke* series starring James Arness. He appeared six times on Richard Boone's *Have Gun Will Travel* (1957-1961) series, set in San Francisco, California. Between 1962 and 1971, he guest starred in five episodes of NBC's most successful western *Bonanza* with Lorne Greene. He appeared five times as the Roman Catholic Father Esteban in ABC's *The Big Valley* (1965-1967) with Barbara Stanwyck. He starred four times in different roles on NBC's *The Virginian* (1964-1970) with James Drury and Doug McClure.

Prior to 1961, he appeared as Chamberlain, a deputy district attorney, in five episodes of CBS's legal drama *Perry Mason* with Raymond Burr. He appeared four times between 1967 and 1971 in Burr's NBC series *Ironside*. He appeared three times on Lloyd Bridges' syndicated series *Sea Hunt*, a creation of Ivan Tors. He appeared four times as a sheriff in the *Hardy Boys/Nancy Drew Mysteries* on ABC.

Other credits over the years included *The Abbott and Costello Show* (1953), *Richard Diamond, Private Detective* (1960), *Twilight Zone* (1961), *It's a Mad Mad Mad Mad World* (1963), *Apache Rifles* (1964) with Audie Murphy, *The Andy Griffith Show* (1965), and *The Fugitive* (1965-1966), *Rod Serling's Night Gallery* (1971), *Kolchak: The Night Stalker* (1974), *Gable and Lombard* (1976), *M*A*S*H* (1975-1977), *Baretta* (1978), *Charlie's Angels* (1979), and *The Last Ride of the Dalton Gang* (1979).

His last role was shortly before his death on an episode of the sitcom *Benson* (1979) on ABC. He appeared posthumously on the television series *Bogie* in 1980. Karnes died of heart failure December 4, 1979, at the age of sixty-two in Sherman Oaks in the San Fernando Valley of Los Angeles.

Roscoe Karns

Roscoe Karns was born September 7, 1891, in San Bernardino, California. Educated at California's Harvard Military academy and USC, Roscoe Karns was acting from age 15 with Marjorie Rambeau's stock company. By 1922, he was playing leads at LA's Morosco theatre, which led to film work at the Christie comedy studios. He showed up in several silent features, including the historic part-talkie *The Jazz Singer* (1927) and the very first Academy Award winner, *Wings* (1927).

In the early talkie era, Karns returned to the stage, and then made a movie comeback playing fast-lipped reporters and press agents, most often at Columbia studios. He was awarded strong supporting roles in such Columbia's as *It Happened One Night* (1934) ("Shapely's my name, and shapely's the way I like 'em"), *Twentieth Century* (1934) (working with his idol, John Barrymore) and *His Girl Friday* (1939); he also starred in a brace of Columbia two-reelers, *Black Eyes and Blues* and *Half Shot at Sunrise* (both 1941).

His film assignments dwindling in the late 1940s, but did have roles in such films as *Avalanche* (1946), *Devil's Cargo (1948),* and *Texas, Brooklyn & Heaven* (1948), the latter with Audie Murphy.

Karns wrote a letter to the DuMont television network, asking if they had any work handy. The result was a five-year starring stint as *Rocky King, Detective* (1951-1954), one of the most popular weekly series of the early 1950s. He then landed a role on *Richard Diamond, Private Detective* (1958), and *December Bride* (1958-1959).

Karns' last recurring assignment was the role of the crusty Admiral Walter Shafer on the Jackie Cooper sitcom *Hennessey* (1959-62). He had a guest role on "The Lucy Show" in 1963, and his last film appearance in *Man's Favorite Sport?* (1964).

Roscoe Karns was the father of actor/recording executive Todd Karns, who starred in TV's first filmed comedy series, *Jackson and Jill* (1949). He died February 6, 1970, at age 78 in Los Angeles, California.

Beatrice Kay

Beatrice Kay was born Hannah Beatrice Kuper April 21, 1907, in New York, New York, and was an American singer, vaudevillian, music hall performer, stage, and film actress.

Kay performed as "Honey Kuper" and "Honey Day" for part of her career in vaudeville, radio, motion pictures, sound recordings, night clubs, and television. Her career began at the age of six as "Little Lord Fauntleroy" in stock theater. She went on to become a headliner at Billy Rose's famed Diamond Horseshoe Nightclub in New York. She was on Mercury Theatre (directed by Orson Welles), and eventually hosted a radio show, *The Beatrice Kay Show*.

She appeared at top nightclubs including San Francisco's austere Fairmont Hotel Venetian Room, the Moulin Rouge in Paris, Hollywood's famed Ciro's in Los Angeles, and at the El Rancho Hotel in Las Vegas. She also recorded several phonograph albums, and appeared in a 1945 motion picture about the club where she had performed in her earlier years, *Billy Rose's Diamond Horseshoe* (the film starred Betty Grable and Dick Haymes).

She appeared with Cliff Robertson in 1961's *Underworld U.S.A.* and twenty-six episodes of *Calvin and the Colonel* (1961-1962). She had roles on *The Rifleman* (1963), and *The Alfred Hitchcock Hour* (1963).

Her next role was in *A Time for Dying* (1969), with Victor Jory and Audie Murphy. She played 'Mamie' who ran a bordello. She then went back to television to play roles in *Ironside* (1969), *Adam-12* (1971), and *Rod Serling's Night Gallery* (1971). In 1974, she had a bit part in the film *Ginger in the Morning* which starred Susan Oliver, Sissy Spacek and Monte Markham.

She died November 8, 1986, in North Hollywood, California, at age 79.

Don Keefer

Donald "Don" H. Keefer was born August 18, 1916, and is a retired American actor known for the versatility of his roles. He was born in Highspire in Dauphin County near Harrisburg, Pennsylvania.

Keefer's first role was as Bernard in the 1951 film, *Death of a Salesman*, based on the Arthur Miller play. His longest-lasting roles were in ten episodes each of the CBS series, *Gunsmoke* (1957-1973), starring James Arness, and *Angel*, a 1960-1961 sitcom featuring French-American actress Annie Fargé.

More of his work includes roles in *Manhunt* (1952), *The Caine Mutiny* (1954), *Appointment with Adventure* (1955), *Away All Boats* (1956), *Hellcats of the Navy* (1957), *Richard Diamond, Private Detective* (1957), *Torpedo Run* (1958), *Wichita Town* (1959), *Cash McCall* (1960), *Whispering Smith* (1961) with Audie Murphy, *Incident in an Alley* (1962), *Car 54, Where Are You?* (1964), *The Fugitive* (1964), *Twilight Zone* (1961-1964), *My Favorite Martian* (1964), *The Munsters* (1965), *The Loner* (1965), *The Russians Are Coming the Russians Are Coming* (1966), *Star Trek* (1968), *Butch Cassidy and the Sundance Kid* (1969), *The Grissom Gang* (1971), *Rod Serling's Night Gallery* (1972), *Walking Tall* (1973), *Attack on Terror: The FBI vs. the Ku Klux Klan* (1975), *Who Is the Black Dahlia?* (1975), *Baretta* (1975), *SWAT* (1975), *Starsky and Hutch* (1977), *The Incredible Hulk* (1977-1978), *The Scarlett O'Hara War* (1980), *Creepshow* (1982), *Highway to Heaven* (1986), *Lucy & Desi: Before the Laughter* (1991), *Lois & Clark: The New Adventures of Superman* (1996), and his last film to date *Liar Liar* (1997).

Michael Keep

Michael Keep was born Michael Capanna December 15, 1922, in Colorado. He appeared in thirty-three films and television programs from 1960 to 1990. Some of those included *77 Sunset Strip* (1960), *Twilight Zone* (1962), *Have Gun - Will Travel* (1963), *Gunsmoke* (1962-1965), *The F.B.I.* (1966), *Laredo* (1967), as Cochise in *40 Guns to Apache Pass* (1967) with Audie Murphy, *Bonanza* (1963-1969), *Death Valley Days* (1962-1969), *The High Chaparral* (1968-1969), *Kojak* (1973), *The Cowboys* (1974), *Get Christie Love!* (1974), *Airwolf* (1984), and his last appearance in *Buried Alive* (1990).

He died November 27, 2007, at age 84 in Los Angeles, California.

John Kellogg

John Kellogg was born Giles Vernon Kellogg, Jr. June 3, 1916, and was an American actor in film, stage and television.

While keeping his surname fixed, Kellogg was very changeable about his first and middle names and initials. Back in the late 1930s, when he began seeking work as an actor, he was known as "Giles Kellogg" and "Giles V. Kellogg" (in "Academy Players Directory" and acting on Broadway). Later, once he began getting regular film acting jobs, he changed to "John Kellogg" and "John G. Kellogg." Clearly, the "G." stood for "Giles".

He acted on stage in several plays until World War II broke out. He turned to the film industry, playing bit parts in several films. In 1946, he signed a contract at Columbia Pictures. Throughout his career, Kellogg played mostly secondary roles.

Kellogg has played in films such as *Captains of the Clouds* (1942), *To Be or Not to Be* (1942), *The Pride of the Yankees* (1942), *Wing and a Prayer* (1944), *Thirty Seconds Over Tokyo* (1944), *A Walk in the Sun* (1945), *Without Reservations* (1946), *Somewhere in the Night* (1946), *The Strange Love of Martha Ivers* (1946), *Out of the Past* (1947), *House of Strangers* (1949), *Twelve O'Clock High* (1949), *Samson and Delilah* (1949), *Hold That Baby!* (1949), *Kansas Raiders* (1950) with Audie Murphy, *The Enforcer* (1951), *The Greatest Show on Earth* (1952), *Rancho Notorious* (1952), and *Edge of the City* (1957).

In the 1950s and 1960s, Kellogg was mostly seen on television in such programs as *Boston Blackie* (1952), *Adventures of Superman* (1952-1952), *Inner Sanctum* (1954), *Decoy* (1958-1959), *Black Saddle* (1960), *Stagecoach West* (1960-1961), *The Untouchables* (1962), and *The Fugitive* (1964).

He is most famous for his portrayal of bad guy Jack Chandler in the soap opera *Peyton Place*, a role he played between 1966 and 1967. He continued to get roles in programs such as *Longstreet* (1972), *Police Story* (1974), *Kojak* (1977), *St. Elsewhere* (1987), and *Wiseguy* (1990).

Kellogg died February 22, 2000, in Los Angeles of Alzheimer's disease.

DeForest Kelley

DeForset Kelley with Audie Murphy in *Gunfight at Comanche Creek*

Jackson DeForest Kelley was born January 20, 1920, and was an American actor known for his iconic roles in Westerns and as Dr. Leonard "Bones" McCoy of the USS *Enterprise* in the television and film series *Star Trek* (1966-1969).

Kelley was born in Toccoa, Georgia, the son of Clora (née Casey) and Ernest David Kelley, who was a Baptist minister. DeForest was named after the pioneering electronics engineer Lee De Forest, and later named his *Star Trek* character's father "David" after his own. Kelley was delivered in their home by his uncle, a prominent local physician. Kelley had an older brother, Ernest Casey Kelley.

Kelley grew up in the Atlanta area and was a 1938 graduate of Decatur Boys High in Decatur, Georgia. As a child, he sang in the church choir, where he discovered that he enjoyed singing and was good at it. Eventually, this led to solos and an appearance on the radio station WSB AM in Atlanta, Georgia. As a result of his radio work, he won an engagement with Lew Forbes and his orchestra at the Paramount Theater.

Kelley served in World War II as an enlisted man in the United States Army Air Forces between March 10, 1943, and January 28, 1946. After an extended stay in Long Beach, California, Kelley decided to pursue an acting career and relocate to southern California permanently, living for a time with his uncle Casey. He worked as an usher in a local theater in order to earn enough money for the move. Kelley's mother encouraged her son in his new career goal, but his father disliked the idea. While in California, Kelley was spotted by a Paramount Pictures scout while doing a United States Navy training film.

Kelley's acting career began with the feature film *Fear in the Night* (1947). The low-budget movie was a hit, bringing him to the attention of a national audience and giving Kelley reason to believe that he would soon become a star. His next role, in *Variety Girl* (1947), established him as a leading actor and resulted in the founding of his first fan club.

Kelley did not become a leading man, however, and he and his wife, Carolyn, decided to move to New York City. He found work on stage and on live television, but after three years in New York, the Kelleys returned to Hollywood.

In California, he received roles in installments of *You Are There* (1953-1956), anchored by Walter Cronkite. He played ranch owner Bob Kitteridge in the 1949 episode "Legion of Old Timers" of the TV series *The Lone Ranger* (1949). This led to an appearance in *Gunfight at the O.K. Corral* (1957) as Morgan Earp (brother to Burt Lancaster's Wyatt Earp). This role was a source for three movie offers, including *Warlock* (1959) with Henry Fonda and Anthony Quinn.

He also appeared in episodes of the television series *Gunsmoke* (1956), *Wanted: Dead or Alive* (1959), *Boots and Saddles* (1957), *Dick Powell's Zane Grey Theater* (1956-1960), *Richard Diamond, Private Detective* (1959-1960), *Death Valley Days* (1962-1966), *Lawman* (1960-1961), *Bat Masterson* (1961), *The Fugitive* (1965), and many others.

For nine years, Kelley primarily played villains. He built up an impressive list of credits, alternating between television and motion pictures, like his part as Amos Troop in *Gunfight at Comanche Creek* (1963) with Audie Murphy, and in the Louis L'amour western *Apache Uprising* (1965) with Rory Calhoun.

However, he was afraid of typecasting, so he broke away from villains by starring in *Where Love Has Gone* (1964) and a television pilot called *333 Montgomery*. The pilot was written by an ex-policeman named Gene Roddenberry, and a few years later Kelley would appear in another Roddenberry pilot, *Police Story* (1967), that was again not developed into a series.

In 1956, years before being cast as Dr. McCoy, Kelley played a small supporting role as a medic in *The Man in the Gray Flannel Suit* in which he utters the diagnosis "This man's dead, Captain" and "That man is dead" to Gregory Peck. In 1962, he appeared in the *Bonanza* episode entitled "The Decision", as a doctor sentenced to hang for the murder of a journalist. The judge in this episode was portrayed by John Hoyt, who later portrayed Dr. Phillip John Boyce, one of Leonard McCoy's predecessors, on the *Star Trek* pilot "The Cage". In 1963, he appeared in *The Virginian* episode "Man of Violence" as a "drinking" cavalry doctor with Leonard Nimoy as his patient (Nimoy's character did not survive). Just before *Star Trek* began filming, Kelley appeared as a doctor again, in the *Laredo* (1966) episode "The Sound of Terror." It is not clear whether these portrayals factored into his casting in *Star Trek*.

After refusing Roddenberry's 1964 offer to play Spock, Kelley accepted the role of Dr. Leonard "Bones" McCoy from 1966 to 1969 in *Star Trek*. He reprised the character in a voice-over role in *Star Trek: The Animated Series* (1973–1974), and the first six *Star Trek* motion pictures (1979 to 1991). In one of the *Star Trek* comic books it was stated that Dr. McCoy's father had been a Baptist preacher, an idea that apparently came from Kelley's background. In 1987, he also had a cameo in "Encounter at Farpoint", the first episode of *Star Trek: The Next Generation* (1987), as by-that-time Admiral Leonard McCoy, Star Fleet Surgeon General Emeritus. Several aspects of Kelley's background became part of McCoy's characterization, including his pronunciation of "nuclear" as "nookeler".

Kelley became good friends with *Star Trek* cast mates William Shatner and Leonard Nimoy from their first meeting in 1964. During *Star Trek's* first season, Kelley's was listed in the end credits along with the rest of the cast. Only Shatner and Nimoy were listed in the opening credits. As Kelley's role grew in importance during the first season he received a pay raise to about $2,500 per episode, and received third billing starting in the second season after Nimoy. Kelley was very proud of the fact that he was the only one of the three who stayed married, saying "I'm happy in the Valley, with the very same wife".

Shy by his own admission, Kelley was the only cast member of the original *Star Trek* series program never to have written or published an autobiography; however, the authorized biography *From Sawdust to Stardust* (2005) was written posthumously by Terry Lee Rioux of Lamar University in Beaumont, Texas.

After *Star Trek*, Kelley found himself a victim of the very typecasting he had so feared. In 1972 he was cast in the horror film, *Night of the Lepus*. Kelley thereafter did a few television appearances and a couple of movies but essentially went into *de facto* retirement other than playing McCoy. By 1978 he was earning up to $50,000 ($178,000 today) annually from appearances at *Star Trek* conventions attended by Trekkies. Like other *Star Trek* actors Kelley received little of the enormous profits that the franchise generated for Paramount, until Nimoy, as executive producer, helped arrange for Kelley to be paid $1 million for *Star Trek VI* (1991).

In a TLC interview done in the late 1990s, Kelley said one of his biggest fears was that the words etched on his gravestone would be "He's dead, Jim". Reflecting this, Kelley's obituary in *Newsweek* magazine began: "We're not even going to try to resist: He's dead, Jim." On the other hand, he stated that he was very proud to hear from so many *Star Trek* fans who had been inspired to become doctors as a result of his portrayal of Dr. McCoy.

For his final film, Kelley provided the voice of Viking 1 in the installment of the well-loved children's series *The Brave Little Toaster Goes to Mars* (1998).

Later in life, Kelley developed an interest in poetry, eventually publishing the first of two books in a series, *The Big Bird's Dream* and *The Dream Goes On*, a series he would never finish.

Kelley died of stomach cancer on June 11, 1999. His body was cremated and the ashes were scattered in the Pacific Ocean.

Jack Kelly

Jack Kelly with Audie Murphy in *Gunsmoke*

Jack Kelly was born September 16, 1927, and was an American film and television actor most noted for the role of "Bart Maverick" in the TV series *Maverick*, which ran on ABC from 1957 to 1962. Kelly shared the series, rotating as the lead from week to week, first with James Garner as Bret Maverick (1957–1960) then with Roger Moore as Beau Maverick (1960–1961) and Robert Colbert as Brent Maverick (1961; for two episodes), before becoming the only Maverick (alternating with reruns from the Garner era) in the fifth season.

Kelly later became a politician, serving as mayor of Huntington Beach, California, from 1983 to 1986.

Born John Augustus Kelly, Jr. in Astoria, Queens, New York, one of four children, to Ann Mary "Nancy" (*née* Walsh) and John Augustus Kelly, Sr. "Jackie," as he was called as a child, came from a prominent theatrical family. His mother, Nan Kelly, had been a popular stage actress and John Robert Powers model. Kelly's father was theater ticket broker, and after he moved the family to Hollywood, went into the real estate business. His sister, Oscar-nominated actress Nancy Kelly, was a prominent movie child star turned leading lady. His other two siblings, Carole and William Clement also tried show business. When they were children his mother would not let them eat meat and would never gave them medicine when they were sick.

Kelly made his film debut in an uncredited role in the 1939 biopic *The Story of Alexander Graham Bell*, opposite Don Ameche and Loretta Young. After appearing in several films like *Gunsmoke* (1953), *Column South* (1953), and *To Hell and Back* (1955), all three with Audie Murphy, and *Cult of the Cobra* (1955) with fellow *To Hell and Back* cast mates David Janssen and Marshall Thompson, and the title role in the television movie *Patrick Henry* (1955), Kelly landed his first starring role in a television series in 1955 with a one-season effort based on the 1942 feature film *Kings Row*. Kelly played Dr. Parris Mitchell, a young psychiatrist coping with the narrow-minded environment of his small town. The series was one-third of the *Warner Bros. Presents* wheel series, hosted by Gig Young. It rotated at the scheduled hour of 7:30 Eastern on Tuesday with a similar television version of the popular movie *Casablanca* (1955) as well as the new Western series *Cheyenne* (1955-1963) starring Clint Walker.

After the series ended in 1956, Kelly went on to appear in *Forbidden Planet* (1956) and *She-Devil* (1957), along with guest roles on *Schlitz Playhouse of Stars* (1956), *Lux Video Theatre* (1957), and *Gunsmoke* (1957).

The various anti-heroic Mavericks were dapper professional poker-players roaming the Old West with the benefit of superb scripts. The series had an enormous cultural impact during a time when there were only three television networks and most cities had only three TV channels to choose from.

Maverick's demanding filming schedule had caused production to lag behind early on. The producers decided to give Bret Maverick a brother so as not to run out of episodes long before the end of the season. Thus, Kelly was introduced as Bart Maverick in "Hostage!", the eighth episode of the series. While he may not have matched Garner's popularity on *Maverick*, Kelly did have his enthusiastic admirers. Possessing a deep voice, a John Barrymore-like profile and an easy-going screen presence, Kelly enjoyed an attentive following among female viewers of the series. Series creator Roy Huggins was extremely critical of Kelly's acting in Huggins' Archive of American Television interview, noting that Kelly "dropped a funny line like a load of coal," but mentioned that Kelly was more amusing than Garner "off camera".

Kelly shared the lead with James Garner in one of the show's most-discussed episodes, "Shady Deal at Sunny Acres", on which the first half of the 1973 movie *The Sting* appears to be based. The pair also co-starred in the famous "Pappy" episode in which Garner played the brothers' much-quoted father Beauregard "Pappy" Maverick, in addition to his regular role of Bret. Aided by trick photography, Bret and Pappy play cards together in one scene (Kelly had a dual role in the episode as well, playing Bart and elderly Uncle Bentley Maverick). Bart also rescued Bret at the climax of "Duel at Sundown", in which Garner fist fought guest star Clint Eastwood. Since Garner enjoyed seniority on the series, he had first choice of which part he would play in the two-brother episodes, which delineated the brothers as "Maverick 1" and "Maverick 2" in the scripts, giving him an enormous advantage.

Although the "solo" episodes in which Bart appeared tended to be somewhat more dramatic than the Bret episodes, Kelly displayed his comedic skills in lighter *Maverick* outings such as "Hadley's Hunters" and "The People's Friend." Kelly actually appeared in more episodes of *Maverick* than James Garner, who left the show following a contract dispute in 1960. Kelly appeared in seventy-five episodes; Garner in only fifty-five. In the wake of Garner's departure, Roger Moore stepped in to play Bart's cousin Beau Maverick in fourteen episodes, sharing the screen with Kelly in three of them, while Robert Colbert appeared in two installments as a third brother named Brent, one of which briefly featured Kelly.

When *Maverick* ended in 1962, Kelly continued acting with roles in a number of films and television shows. In 1962, he played the lead in *Red Nightmare* (also known as *The Commies Are Coming, the Commies Are Coming* in its derisive 1985 video re-release incarnation) a Cold War film narrated by Jack Webb in which Kelly's character wakes up one morning to discover that America has been taken over by Communists. He also co-starred in *Commandos* (1968) opposite Lee Van Cleef, and as a villain dressed almost exactly like Bart Maverick in *Young Billy Young* (1969) with Robert Mitchum.

From 1969 to 1971, Kelly hosted the NBC daytime game show *Sale of the Century* but was eventually replaced by Joe Garagiola. He was also a series regular in ten episodes of *Get Christie Love!* (1974) and seven episodes of *The Hardy Boys/Nancy Drew Mysteries* (1978), and performed many lucrative television commercial voice-overs.

In 1977 Kelly appeared as obstreperous villains for a few moments in two *Rockford Files* episodes starring James Garner. The first appearance was in the season 3 episode, "The Becker Connection," and the second was the first show of season 4, "Beamer's Last Case" as a jealous husband.

In 1978, he briefly appeared as Bart Maverick and was again paired with Garner in the television movie *The New Maverick* and in Garner's TV series *Bret Maverick* (1981); Kelly appeared momentarily at the end of the final episode of the show and would have become a regular had it been renewed. Kelly also showed up on a 1983 episode of *The Fall Guy*, costumed as Maverick but basically playing himself in a storyline that rounded-up many classic television cowboys.

In 1991, he reprised the role of Bart Maverick one last time in the TV movie *The Gambler Returns: The Luck of the Draw*, a Kenny Rogers vehicle briefly featuring more than a dozen 1950s television series cowboys. Kelly's brief dialogue consisted almost exclusively of variations on the phrase, "You can't have a real poker game without a Maverick".

Kelly's acting roles became less frequent in the late 1970s as he became more involved in real estate and local politics. He started buying real estate in Huntington Beach, California, in the mid 1960s, and moved there permanently in 1971.

He formed August II, Inc., to hold the real estate assets in June 1965 in Huntington Beach his wife, Jo, became a real estate broker and did much of the business management of the real estate business, especially while Kelly was involved with Huntington city government.

During the 1980s and early 1990s he served as city councilman and mayor in Huntington Beach, campaigning with the slogan "Let Maverick Solve Your Problems".

Kelly married actress May Wynn (Donna Lee Hickey) on October 14, 1956. They separated in February 1964 and were divorced on October 19, 1964. Following the divorce he later dated Karen Steele for a short time.

He married Jo Ann Smith in Las Vegas, Nevada on October 16, 1969. The following November their daughter Nicole was born.

On April 28, 1992, he suffered a heart attack. Jack Kelly died of a stroke at Humana Hospital in Huntington Beach, California, November 7, 1992. In addition to his sister Nancy he was survived by his second wife, Jo, and their daughter, Nicole

Jo became an "extra" in film and television productions, helps others learn the business, and wrote a book about it, *The Truth about Being an Extra* (2006).

His daughter, Nicole K. Garner, is the founder of and executive producer at August II Productions.

Paul Kelly

Audie Murphy with Paul Kelly in *Gunsmoke*

Paul Michael Kelly was born August 9, 1899, and was an American child actor who later as an adult became a stage, film, and television actor.

Born in Brooklyn, New York, the ninth of ten children, Kelly began his career as a child actor at age seven and was appearing on the stage.

In 1911 Kelly began making silent films at age twelve with the Vitagraph Studios, which was based in Brooklyn, and where he was billed as *Master Paul Kelly*. His first was a short called *Jimmie's Job* (1911). Kelly was possibly the first male child actor to be given any starring roles in American films predating better known child stars such as Bobby Connelly and Jackie Coogan.

Kelly made his talking film debut in 1933's *Broadway Through a Keyhole*.

In the course of his long career, and relatively short life, it's estimated that Kelly worked on stage, screen, and television in over four hundred roles.

Later in his film career, as an adult, Kelly appeared in films mostly as a tough guy character actor in the 1930s, 1940s and 1950s, in such films as *Murder with Pictures* (1936), *Island in the Sky* (1938), *The Roaring Twenties* (1939), *Parachute Battalion* (1941), *Tarzan's New York Adventure* (1942), *Flying Tigers* (1942), *Fear in the Night* (1947), *Frenchie* (1950), *The Painted Hills* (1951), *Gunsmoke* (1953) with Audie Murphy, *The Square Jungle* (1955), and his last film *Bailout at 43,000* (1957).

In 1948, Kelly won a Best Actor Tony Award his role in *Command Decision*. The award was shared with Henry Fonda for *Mister Roberts* and Basil Rathbone for *The Heiress*.

His career momentum was briefly halted with a two-year (1927–1929) forced hiatus when he served twenty-five months for manslaughter in California's San Quentin prison for the death of actor Ray Raymond, a few days after their fistfight.

Kelly later played the part of San Quentin Warden Clinton Duffy in the film *Duffy of San Quentin* (1954).

Raymond's widow, Dorothy MacKaye, later married Kelly. She was briefly imprisoned for being an accomplice in the killing; and, wrote about her experiences, titled, *Women in Prison*, that became a 1933 film, *Ladies They Talk About*, with Barbara Stanwyck.

He married a bit player he met on the set of *Flight Command* (1940), Claire Owen (née Zona Mardelle Zwicker), on January of 1941. She retired from acting, and went on to survive him.

He died of a heart attack in November 6, 1956, at age 57, after voting for Adlai Stevenson.

Kerima

Audie Murphy with Kerima in *The Quiet American*

Kerima was born February 10, 1925, in Algiers, Algeria. Supporting actress Kerima appeared in several internationally-produced films from the 1950s through the early 1960s. She is best remembered for her debut film *Outcast of the Islands* (1951).

More of her film work included the title role in *She Wolf* (1953), *The Ship of Condemned Women* (1953), *Fatal Desire* (1955), *Land of the Pharaohs* (1955), *The Quiet American* (1958) with Audie Murphy, *The Warrior and the Slave Girl* (1958), *The Night of the Great Attack* (1959), *Jessica* (1962), and *Lovebox* (1972).

Her one television role was in *The Adventurer* (1972).

George Keymas

George Keymas was born November 18, 1925, in Springfield, Ohio. He began his film career in the early 1950s and played many minor adventure/western heavies due to his swarthy features and leathery, pockmarked mug.

His first film was *I Shot Billy the Kid* (1950). He continued acting steadily up to 1977 in films and television programs like *The Miracle of Our Lady of Fatima* (1952), *The Robe* (1953), *Hopalong Cassidy* (1954), *Stories of the Century* (1954), the Louis L'amour written *Stranger on Horseback* (1955), *The Maverick Queen* (1956), *Walk the Proud Land* (1956) with Audie Murphy, another Louis L'amour written film *Utah Blaine* (1957), *Tombstone Territory* (1958), *Black Saddle* (1959), *The Slowest Gun in the West* (1960), *Johnny Ringo* (1960), *Twilight Zone* (1960), *Target: The Corruptors* (1962), *Arizona Raiders* (1965) again with Audie Murphy, *Winchester 73* (1967), *Rod Serling's Night Gallery* (1972), *Dirty Sally* (1974), *Barbary Coast* (1975), and *The Other Side of Midnight* (1977).

He died January 17, 2008, at age 82 in Palm Beach, Florida.

Robert Keith

Audie Murphy and Robert Keith in *Posse from Hell*

Robert Keith was born February 10, 1898, and was an American stage and film actor who appeared in several dozen films, mostly in the 1950s as a character actor.

Keith was born Rolland Keith Richey in Fowler, Indiana, the son of Mary Della (née Snyder) and James Haughey Richey. His first wife was Laura Anne Corinne Jackson, the daughter of a prominent Cedar Rapids, Iowa family. He is noted for the variety of his performances both as weak-willed and strong characters such as the father in *Fourteen Hours* (1951) and a psychopathic killer in *The Lineup* (1958).

His best known performances are as the ineffectual sheriff and father of biker Marlon Brando's love interest in the 1953 film *The Wild One* and as tougher, no-nonsense cop, this time Brando's antagonist, in the film musical, *Guys And Dolls* (1955). Keith also had a starring role in Douglas Sirk's *Written on the Wind* (1956).

Other films he appeared in included *Between Heaven and Hell* (1956), *They Came to Cordura* (1959), *Posse from Hell* (1961) with Audie Murphy, and as the king of Rome in *Duel of Champions* (1961) with Alan Ladd.

He had roles on television, including a role as Richard Kimble's father in *The Fugitive* (1964) and lead roles on episodes of *Alfred Hitchcock Presents* (1962) episode "Ten O'Clock Tiger" and *The Twilight Zone* (1964) episode "The Masks", as Jason Foster, the rich New Orleans patriarch to a self-centered, greed-riddled family awaiting their benefactor to die. This was his last screen effort.

Keith's second wife was stage actress Helena Shipman, with whom he had a son in 1921, actor Brian Keith who starred in many Disney films and in the television show *Family Affair* (1966-1971). On April 18, 1927, Keith married Peg Entwistle. They were divorced in 1929. He remained married to his fourth wife, Dorothy Tierney, until his death on December 22, 1966.

Wright King

Audie Murphy with Wright King in *Whispering Smith*

Thomas Wright Thornberg King was born January 11, 1923 in Okmulgee, Oklahoma. Wright was always interested in acting; after high school, he was studying to be an actor at the St. Louis School of Theatre. But when America entered WWII, Wright served in the Navy; he worked as a pharmacist's mate, stationed in the South Pacific. In 1946, after the war and an honorable discharge, Wright went to NYC, and under the G.I. Bill, he studied at the Actors Studio and the American Theatre Wing.

He had a successful career in numerous theatrical productions. In 1947, Wright was one of the first actors to work steadily in the new medium of live television.

He married June Ellen Roth in 1948. They had three sons: Wright Jr., Michael, and Meegan who grew up to be a fine actor.

Some of Wright's earliest TV appearances were on such series as *Captain Video and His Video Rangers* (1949), *The Ken Murray Show* (1950), and *Big Town* (1950-1951).

In 1949, Wright achieved recognition for his portrayal of the Collector in Elia Kazan's stage version of *A Streetcar Named Desire*. This led to a movie career when he reprised the role for the film version in 1951, acting alongside screen legends Vivien Leigh and Marlon Brando. Wright would have a long career in movies playing supporting characters.

Wright replaced Vaughn Taylor as Ernest P. Duckweather on the kiddie puppet show *Johnny Jupiter* when the series went from live TV to film, in 1953.

Other roles followed in such movies and shows as *The Bold and the Brave* (1956), *Stagecoach to Fury* (1956), *Maverick* (1957), *The Gunfight at Dodge City* (1959), *Cast a Long Shadow* (1959) with Audie Murphy, *Outlaws* (1961), and five episodes of *Have Gun - Will Travel* (1957-1961).

Wright is best remembered by his fans for his two guest appearances on the original *Twilight Zone* (1961-1963) series. He played Paul Carson in the episode "Shadow Play," which raised the question: do we live in the real world and we have dreams at night, or is our reality just a dream? And he played Hecate in the episode "Of Late, I Think of Cliffordville," about a man going back in time to relive his youth.

Wright was most often seen on television in 1960 on the Steve McQueen western series *Wanted Dead or Alive*. After making two earlier guest appearances on it, he was seen in eleven other second-season episodes as Jason Nichols, a 'sidekick' to McQueen's bounty hunter Josh Randall.

More roles followed in *Voyage to the Bottom of the Sea* (1964), *King Rat* (1965), eight episodes of *Gunsmoke* (1955-1965), two episodes of *The Fugitive* (1964-1966), *Planet of the Apes* (1968) as Dr. Galen, and *Along Came a Spider* (1970),

Wright is remembered for playing Dr. Murger in the sci-fi film *Invasion of the Bee Girls* (1973), which was re-released in Drive-Ins years later under the title *Graveyard Tramps* (1983). This movie in which Wright King and William Smith fight off Anitra Ford and her swarm of sexually-driven Insect Women is a true cult classic.

He continued to get roles in *The Streets of San Francisco* (1973-1974), *McCloud* (1975), *The Macahans* (1976), *Helter Skelter* (1976), *Police Woman* (1977), three episodes as Jonathon in *Logan's Run* (1977-1978), *The Critical List* (1978), and *House Made of Dawn* (1987).

He is retired and living in Portland, Oregon.

Patric Knowles

Reginald Lawrence Knowles was born in Horsforth, Yorkshire, England, UK November 11, 1911, and was an English film actor who renamed himself Patric Knowles, a name which reflects his Irish descent.

He appeared in films of the 1930s through the 1970s. He made his film debut in *Men of Tomorrow* (1932), and played either first or second film leads throughout his career. In his first American film, *Give Me Your Heart* (1936), released in Great Britain as *Sweet Aloes*, Knowles was cast as a titled Englishman of means.

While making *The Charge of the Light Brigade* (1936) at Lone Pine, California, he befriended Errol Flynn, whose acquaintance he had made when both were under contract to Warner Brothers in England. Since that film, in which Knowles played the part of Captain Perry Vickers, the brother of Flynn's Major Geoffrey Vickers, he was cast more frequently as straitlaced characters alongside Flynn's flamboyant ones, notably as Will Scarlet in *The Adventures of Robin Hood* (1938). Both actors starred as well in *Four's A Crowd*, also in 1938.

More than two decades after Flynn's death, biographer Charles Higham sullied Flynn's memory by accusing him of having been a fascist sympathizer and Nazi spy. Knowles, who had served in World War II as a flying instructor in the RCAF, came to Flynn's defense, writing *Rebuttal for a Friend* as an epilogue to Tony Thomas' *Errol Flynn: The Spy Who Never Was* (Citadel Press, 1990)

He was a freelance film actor from 1939 until his last film appearance in 1973. In the 1940s, he was known for playing protagonists in a number of horror films, including *The Wolf Man* (1941) and *Frankenstein Meets the Wolfman* (1943). He was also cast as comic foils in a number of comedies such as Abbott and Costello's *Who Done It?* (1942) and *Hit The Ice* (1943). More of his work includes *O.S.S.* (1946), *Dream Girl* (1948), *Tarzan's Savage Fury* (1952), *Flame of Calcutta* (1953), and *Band of Angels* (1957).

He also appeared opposite Jack Kelly in a 1957 episode of the television series *Maverick* called "The Wrecker", which was based on a Robert Louis Stevenson adventure and co-starred James Garner.

He continued to work in such roles as *From the Earth to the Moon* (1958), *77 Sunset Strip* (1959), *The Jim Backus Show* (1960), *Whispering Smith* (1961) with Audie Murphy, *Gunsmoke* (1964), *Elfego Baca: Six Gun Law* (1966), *The Way West* (1967), as Henry Tunstall in *Chisum* (1970), *Marcus Welby, M.D.* (1971), and *Terror in the Wax Museum* (1973).

He died December 23, 1995, at age 84 in Woodland Hills, Los Angeles, California.

Marianne Koch

Marianne Koch with Audie Murphy in *Trunk to Cairo*

Marianne Koch was born August 19, 1931, and is a retired German actress of the 1950s and 1960s, best known for her appearances in spaghetti westerns and adventure films of the 1960s. She later worked as a television host and as a physician. Between 1950 and 1971, Koch appeared in more than sixty-five films. Her first film was *The Man Who Wanted to Live Twice* (1950). In the haunting 1954 espionage thriller *Night People* she starred alongside Gregory Peck.

Some of her other appearances were *Night People* (1954), *Two Blue Eyes* (1955), *The Star of Africa* (1957), *The Magnificent Rogue* (1960), *Blind Justice* (1961), *The Devil's Agent* (1962), *Tim Frazer* (1963), and *The Last Ride to Santa Cruz* (1964). Sergio Leone's 1964 production *A Fistful of Dollars* showcased her alongside Clint Eastwood as a civilian tormented by ruthless local gangsters, torn between her husband and child and the villains.

In Germany she was probably best-loved for her many years of participation in the highly popular television game show *Was bin ich* which ran from the 1950s until 1988 and achieved ratings of up to 75% at its peak.

She played Helga Schlieben, Audie Murphy's love interest in *Trunk to Cairo* (1966).

In 1971, she resumed the medical studies she had broken off in the early 1950s to become an actress. She got her MD in 1974 and practiced medicine until 1997 as a specialist in Munich. In 1976, she was one of the initial hosts of Germany's pioneering talk show *3 nach 9* (*Three After Nine*), for which she was awarded one of the most prestigious awards of the German television industry, the *Grimme Preis*. She also hosted other television shows and had a medical advice program on radio.

In 1953, she married the physician Gerhard Freund, with whom she has two sons. The marriage ended in 1973.

Susan Kohner

Audie Murphy with Susan Kohner in *Suspicion*

Susan Kohner was born Susanna Kohner in Los Angeles, November 11, 1936, and is an American actress.

She is the daughter of Mexican actress Lupita Tovar and film producer Paul Kohner, who was born in Bohemia. It was only natural for Susan to gravitate toward acting.

Her first role was in *To Hell and Back* (1955) with Audie Murphy. One more film in 1956, *The Last Wagon*, and one in 1957, *Trooper Hook*, brought her to the attention of producers in the movie industry.

She again played opposite Audie Murphy in the episode "The Flight" of the television program *Suspicion* (1957).

Susan made several films in 1959. The best of the lot was *Imitation of Life* (1959), a film starring Lana Turner and Sandra Dee. It was a dual story of Lana portraying a struggling actress and Susan as Sara Jane, struggling with the fact that although she appeared white, her mother was black. Susan's role as a young woman trying to cope in the white world while hiding the fact she was black was enough to win her an Academy Award nomination as Best Supporting Actress. Unfortunately, Susan lost out to Shelley Winters in *The Diary of Anne Frank* (1959). She did win the Golden Globe in the Best Supporting Actress categories.

Following her appearance in *Imitation of Life*, Kohner appeared in *All the Fine Young Cannibals* (1960), opposite Natalie Wood and Robert Wagner. She later had guest roles on episodic television including roles on *Hong Kong* (1961) and *Going My Way* (1963),

After appearing in *Freud* (1962), Susan left films for good with the exception of appearing in television programs like *Temple Houston* (1963), *Rawhide* (1964), and *Channing* (1964).

In 1964, Kohner married German novelist and fashion designer John Weitz, and retired from acting. Their children, Chris and Paul Weitz, are successful film directors in Hollywood, having helmed films such as *American Pie* (1999) and *About a Boy* (2002). Chris Weitz is best known for directing *New Moon* (2009) in *The Twilight Saga*.

On April 23, 2010, a new print of *Imitation of Life* was screened at the TCM Film Festival in Los Angeles, California. After the screeening, Kohner appeared on stage along with her costar Juanita Moore for a question-and-answer session hosted by TCM's Robert Osborne. Kohner and Moore received standing ovations.

Fred Krone

Fred Krone was born Fredrick A. Krone June 19, 1930, in Kentucky. Fred Krone was raised in California, and aspired to be a concert violinist. He was a child prodigy who played in a junior symphony. He played the Hollywood Bowl when he was 4 years old. His musical career ended in 1946 when he lost a few fingers playing with bottle rockets. He appeared in many movies and television shows shot on location in the Santa Clarita Valley. One of the few lifetime members of the Stuntmen's Association of Motion Pictures, Krone specialized in high falls and fight scenes in a career that spanned three decades.

A resident of nearby Fillmore for more than thirty years, Krone was also a successful photographer, rancher, clock manufacturer-distributor, and family man. A few years later, during a stint as a rodeo photographer, Krone met Jock Mahoney, who introduced him to the stunt business. Apprenticing with Mahoney at Gene Autry's Flying A Productions shooting at Melody Ranch in Placerita Canyon in the early 1950s, Krone earned the nickname "Krunch" for how hard he hit the ground.

Krone performed acting roles and/or stunts in more than seventy-five television shows and movies, including *The Range Rider* (1952-1953), *Captain Midnight* (1955), *Buffalo Bill, Jr.* (1955-1956), *Man from God's Country* (1958), *Apache Territory* (1958), *Johnny Ringo* (1960), *Peter Gunn* (1961), *Young Guns of Texas* (1962), *Young Fury* (1952), *War Party* (1965), *Arizona Raiders* (1965), *The Lucy Show* (1966), *The Green Hornet* (1966), *Lost in Space* (1967-1968), *The Love Bug* (1968), *The Great Bank Robbery* (1969), *The Life and Times of Judge Roy Bean* (1972), *Owen Marshall: Counselor at Law* (1973), and *Search* (1973). Many more stunt jobs earlier in his career were uncredited.

In the mid-1970s, Krone quit show business and pursued his interest in clocks. He opened a repair shop on Melrose Avenue near Fairfax in Hollywood.

The clock business grew and Krone eventually founded his own corporation, Norkro Clock Company, repairing clocks and selling parts internationally.

Krone also moved to Fillmore in the 1970s and started a ranch, growing oranges and avocados, which he did for more than twenty years.

He died at Santa Paula Hospital in Santa Paula, California, on Jan. 12, 2010, after a long battle with cancer. He was 79.

Lou Krugman

Lou Krugman was born July 19, 1914, in Passaic, New Jersey, and was an American character actor who appeared in a few feature films from the late 1950s through the early 1960s including *I Want to Live!* (1958) but may be best known for his work on radio. He is said to have appeared on over 10,000 broadcasts and did over 700 voiceovers for television commercials.

Some of his films and television programs included *To the Ends of the Earth* (1948), *The Miracle of Our Lady of Fatima* (1952), *The Abbott and Costello Show* (1953), *Adventures of Superman* (1953), *The Adventures of Falcon* (1954-1955), *Steve Allen in Movieland* (1955), *The Man Who Knew Too Much* (1956), *The Gale Storm Show* (1957), *The Life and Legend of Wyatt Earp* (1959), *Wanted: Dead or Alive* (1960), *Whispering Smith* (1961) with Audie Murphy, *Irma la Douce* (1963), *The Mighty Jungle* (1964), *Honey West* (1965-1966), *The Outsider* (1968), *The Most Deadly Game* (1970), *Police Story* (1974), *S.W.A.T.* (1975), *The Rockford Files* (1978), *Spider-Woman* (1979), and *The Last Ride of the Dalton Gang* (1979).

He died August 8, 1992, at age 78 in Burbank, California.

Jack Kruschen

Jack Kruschen was born in Winnipeg, Manitoba March 20, 1922, was a character actor who worked primarily in American film, television and radio.

Kruschen began his radio career while still in high school, and during the 1940s, he became a staple of West Coast radio drama. He had several roles in programs made especially for the Armed Forces Radio Service (AFRS) broadcast for the benefit of members on active duty in the military in the 1940s and 1950s.

His movie career is highlighted by his performance as neighbor Dr. Dreyfuss in Billy Wilder's *The Apartment* (1960), for which he received an Academy Award nomination for Best Supporting Actor.

Other film and television assignments included George Pal's *The War of the Worlds* (1953) as Salvatore, one of the first three victims, a role he reprised on the *Lux Radio Theater* adaptation, in Cecil B. DeMille's final film, *The Buccaneer* (1958), as astronaut Sam Jacobs in the 1959 cult classic *The Angry Red Planet*, *The Unsinkable Molly Brown* (1964) as saloon owner Christmas Morgan, *Comin' Round the Mountain* (1951), *Abbott and Costello Go to Mars* (1953), *Richard Diamond, Private Detective* (1960), *Seven Ways from Sundown* (1960) with Audie Murphy,

Lover Come Back (1961), *McLintock!* (1963) with John Wayne and Maureen O'Hara, *Follow That Dream* (1962) with Elvis Presley, *Cape Fear* (1962), and *Harlow* (1964) as Louis B. Mayer.

Kruschen appeared as Maurice Pulvermacher in the original 1962 Broadway production of *I Can Get It for You Wholesale* with neophyte singer/actress, nineteen year old Barbra Streisand. In 1969, he co-starred in the London staging of the musical *Promises, Promises*, reprising his film role in this show based on *The Apartment*.

Kruschen was performing on television as early as 1939, appearing in dramas on Don Lee's experimental television station in Los Angeles, where he was seen on some 200 TV sets with three-inch screens.

In 1969, Kruschen co-starred with Stefanie Powers in an unsold ABC sitcom pilot, *Holly Golighty*, adapted from Truman Capote's *Breakfast at Tiffany's*.

Kruschen's final on-camera appearance was in the 1997 film *'Til There Was You* (with Sarah Jessica Parker).

Kruschen was married to Marjorie Ullman from January 1947 to 1961, and his second marriage was to Violet Rafaella Mooring from 1962 to 1978. He was married a third time to Mary Pender from July 23, 1979 until April 2, 2002 when he died in Chandler, Arizona, at age 80.

Alan Ladd

Alan Ladd with Audie Murphy in *Beyond Glory*

Alan Walbridge Ladd was born in Hot Springs, Arkansas, September 3, 1913, and was an American film actor.

He was the only child of Ina Raleigh Ladd and Alan Ladd, Sr. He was of English ancestry. His father died when he was four, and his mother relocated to Oklahoma City where she married Jim Beavers, a housepainter. The family then moved again to North Hollywood, California, where Ladd became a high-school swimming and diving champion and participated in high school dramatics at North Hollywood High School, graduating on February 1, 1934.

He opened his own hamburger and malt shop, which he called Tiny's Patio. He worked briefly as a studio carpenter (as did his stepfather) and for a short time was part of the Universal Pictures studio school for actors. But Universal decided he was too blond and too short and dropped him. Intent on acting, he found work in radio.

Ladd began by appearing in dozens of films in small roles, like *Island of Lost Souls* (1932), *Pigskin Parade* (1936), *The Goldwyn Follies* (1938), *Hitler - Beast of Berlin* (1939), *The Green Hornet* (1940), *The Light of Western Stars* (1940), *Captain Caution* (1940), *Ellery Queen, Master Detective* (1940), *The Reluctant Dragon* (1941), *The Black Cat* (1941), and *Great Guns* (1941) with Laurel and Hardy.

He appeared in *Citizen Kane* (1941) in which he played one of the "faceless" reporters who are always shown in silhouette. His voice is very recognizable in the picture, as it is very unique.

He first gained some recognition with a featured role in the wartime thriller *Joan of Paris* (1942).

For his next role, his manager, Sue Carol, found a vehicle which made Ladd's career, Graham Greene's *This Gun for Hire* (1942) in which he played "Raven," a hitman with a conscience. "Once Ladd had acquired an unsmiling hardness, he was transformed from an extra to a phenomenon. Ladd's calm slender ferocity makes it clear that he was the first American actor to show the killer as a cold angel". - David Thomson (*A Biographical Dictionary of Film,* 1975)

Both the film and Ladd's performance played an important role in the development of the "gangster" genre: "That the old fashioned motion picture gangster with his ugly face, gaudy cars, and flashy clothes was replaced by a smoother, better looking, and better dressed bad man was largely the work of Mr. Ladd". - *New York Times* obituary (January 30, 1964). Ladd was teamed with actress Veronica Lake in this film, and despite the fact that it was Robert Preston who played the romantic lead; the Ladd-Lake pairing captured the public's imagination, and would continue in another three films. They appeared in a total of seven films together, but three were only guest shots in all-star musical revues.

Ladd went on to star in many Paramount Pictures' films, with a brief timeout for military service in the United States Army Air Force's First Motion Picture Unit. He appeared in Dashiell Hammett's story *The Glass Key* (1942), his second pairing with Lake, and *Lucky Jordan* (1942), with Helen Walker. His cool, unsmiling persona proved popular with wartime audiences, and he was quickly established as one of the top box office stars of the decade.

In 1946, he starred in a trio of silver screen classics: the big screen adaptation of Richard Henry Dana's maritime classic, *Two Years Before the Mast* (for which he also received critical acclaim), the Raymond Chandler original mystery *The Blue Dahlia* (his third pairing with Lake), and the World War II espionage thriller, *O.S.S.*.

He formed his own production companies for film and radio and then starred in his own syndicated radio series *Box 13*, which ran fifty-two episodes from 1948-49.

He appeared as Capt. Rockwell 'Rocky' Gilman in *Beyond Glory* (1948) alongside Audie Murphy. He gave Audie some advice while filming this movie: "Don't get four ulcers on a two ulcer picture".

Ladd and Robert Preston starred in the 1948 western film, *Whispering Smith*, which in 1961 would become a short-lived NBC television series, starring Audie Murphy.

In 1949's version of *The Great Gatsby*, Ladd had the featured role of Jay Gatsby.

More great roles followed in films like *Captain Carey, U.S.A.* (1950) with Audie Murphy's wife Wanda Hendrix, *Branded* (1950), *Appointment with Danger* (1951), *Red Mountain* (1951), as Jim Bowie in *The Iron Mistress* (1952), *Botany Bay* (1953), and *Desert Legion* (1953).

Ladd played the title role in the 1953 western *Shane*. The film was nominated for five Academy Awards, including Best Picture. It was listed at No. 45 on the American Film Institute's 2007 ranking of "100 Years ... 100 Movies".

Ladd made the Top Ten Money Making Stars Poll three times: in 1947, 1953, and 1954. In 1954 exhibitors voted him the most popular star among British film-goers.

When former agent Albert R. Broccoli formed Warwick Films with his partner Irving Allen, they heard Ladd was unhappy with Paramount and was leaving the studio. With his wife and agent Sue Carol, they negotiated for Ladd to appear in the first three of their films made in England and released through Columbia Pictures: *The Red Beret/Paratrooper* (1953); *Hell Below Zero* (1954), based on Hammond Innes's book *The White South*; and *The Black Knight* (1954). All three were co-written by Ladd's regular screenwriter Richard Maibaum.

It was Ladd's parting with Paramount that caused him to not be nominated for the Academy Award for *Shane*, as Paramount then put their backing behind William Holden for *Stalag 17* (1953), which won William Holden the Oscar.

In 1954 Ladd formed a new production company, Jaguar Productions, originally releasing his films through Warner Brothers and then with *All the Young Men* (1960) through Columbia.

Also in 1954 he brought his *Box 13* radio series character Dan Holiday to life in the *G.E. True Theater* episode "Committed".

He continued acting roles in *Saskatchewan* (1954), *The Black Knight* (1954), *Drum Beat* (1954), *The McConnell Story* (1955), *Hell on Frisco Bay* (1955), *Santiago* (1956), *The Big Land* (1957), *Boy on a Dolphin* (1957), *The Deep Six* (1958), *The Proud Rebel* (1958), *The Badlanders* (1958), *The Man in the Net* (1959), Louis L'amour's *Guns of the Timberland* (1960), *One Foot in Hell* (1960), *Duel of Champions* (1961), and *13 West Street* (1962).

In November 1962, he was found lying unconscious in a pool of blood with a bullet wound near his heart, an alleged unsuccessful suicide attempt. In 1963 Ladd filmed a supporting role as Nevada Smith in *The Carpetbaggers*. He would not live to see its release. Steve McQueen would portray the younger version of the Nevada Smith character in *Nevada Smith* (1966).

On January 29, 1964, he was found dead in Palm Springs, California, of an acute overdose of "alcohol and three other drugs", at the age of 50; his death was ruled accidental. He was entombed in the Forest Lawn Memorial Park Cemetery in Glendale, California.

Alan Ladd has a star on the Hollywood Walk of Fame at 1601 Vine Street. His handprint appears in the forecourt of Grauman's Chinese Theater, in Hollywood.

He had married a high-school acquaintance, Midge Harrold. Their only child, a son named Alan Ladd, Jr., was born in 1937. Ladd's stepfather died suddenly. Then his mother, who suffered from depression, committed suicide by poison.

In 1942, Ladd married his agent/manager, former movie actress Sue Carol.

Ladd owned properties in Beverly Hills and, in Palm Springs, Alan Ladd Hardware.

His son by his first wife Midge Harrold, Alan Ladd, Jr., is a motion picture executive and producer and founder of The Ladd Company. Alan Ladd, Jr. married Cindra Ladd and they have four children: Kelliann Ladd, Tracy Ladd, Amanda Ladd, and Chelsea Ladd

His daughter actress Alana, who co-starred with her father in *Guns of the Timberland* and *Duel of Champions*, is married to the veteran talk radio broadcaster Michael Jackson.

Another son, actor David Ladd, who co-starred with Ladd as a child in *The Proud Rebel*, married *Charlie's Angels* star Cheryl Ladd in 1973 and it lasted until 1980, producing a daughter, actress Jordan Ladd. A later marriage to Dey Young produced a son actor Shane Ladd.

Zohra Lampert

Audie Murphy with Zohra Lampert in *Posse from Hell*

Zohra Lampert was born May 13, 1937, and is an American actress, who has had roles on film, television and stage. She may be best remembered for her role as the title character in the 1971 cult horror film *Let's Scare Jessica to Death*, as well as starring alongside Natalie Wood and Warren Beatty in the 1961 romance film *Splendor in the Grass*.

Lampert was born in New York City, the daughter of Russian Jewish immigrants Rachil Eriss, a draper and hatmaker, and Morris Lampert, an architect and ironworker. Lampert attended New York's High School of Music and Art, and then the University of Chicago. She was briefly married to actor Bill Alton from 1957 to 1958.

After working on minor stages for several years, she performed on Broadway in a Tony nominated performance in 1961's *Look We've Come Through*. She scored with a pair of small but noteworthy performances in the films *Pay or Die* (1960) and *Splendor in the Grass* (1961).

Throughout the 1960s and 1970s she was active in supporting roles in film and television like *Posse from Hell* (1961) with Audie Murphy, *The Alfred Hitchcock Hour* (1963), *The Man from U.N.C.L.E.* (1965), *I Spy* (1967), *Then Came Bronson* (1969), *The Girl with Something Extra* (1973-1974), and won an Emmy for her performance as a sinister gypsy on an episode of *Kojak* (1975).

She was a regular in the medical drama *Doctors' Hospital* (1975-1976). Other roles continued in *Serpico* (1976), *Hawaii Five-O* (1976-1978), *The Girl, the Gold Watch & Everything* (1980), *Airwolf* (1984), *The Equalizer* (1986), and *Trapper John, M.D.* (1986).

Lampert worked less during the 1980s and 1990s. She appeared in roles as diverse as *The Exorcist III* (1990) playing actor George C. Scott's wife, and the offbeat 1999 film, *The Eden Myth*, which would prove to be her last feature film role for the next decade.

During the 1980s, Lampert became known as the commercial spokesperson for "Goya" food products.

After a ten-year absence from films, Lampert returned to the screen in supporting roles in two films: 2009's *The Hungry Ghosts,* and the following year, in the film *Zenith*. In March 2010, Lampert married radio personality Jonathan Schwartz in New York City.

Burt Lancaster

Audie Murphy with Burt Lancaster in *The Unforgiven*

Burton Stephen "Burt" Lancaster was born November 2, 1913, and was a film actor noted for his athletic physique and distinctive smile. After initially building his career on "tough guy" roles Lancaster abandoned his "all-American" image in the late 1950s in favor of more complex and challenging roles, and came to be regarded as one of the best actors of his generation as a result.

Lancaster was nominated four times for Academy Awards and won once, for his work in *Elmer Gantry* in 1960. He also won a Golden Globe for that performance and BAFTA Awards for *The Birdman of Alcatraz* (1962) and *Atlantic City* (1980). His production company, Hecht-Hill-Lancaster, was the most successful and innovative star-driven independent production company in Hollywood of the 1950s, making movies such as *Marty* (1955), *Trapeze* (1956), and *Sweet Smell of Success* (1957).

Lancaster was born in Manhattan, New York City, at his parents' home at 209 East 106th Street, between Second and Third Avenues, today the site of Benjamin Franklin Plaza. Lancaster was the son of Elizabeth (née Roberts) and James Henry Lancaster, who was a postman. Both of his parents were Protestants of working-class northern Irish origin. Lancaster's grandparents were immigrants to the U.S. from Belfast and descendants of English immigrants to Ireland.

Lancaster grew up in East Harlem and spent much of his time on the streets, where he developed great interest and skill in gymnastics while attending the DeWitt Clinton High School, where he was a basketball star. Before he graduated from DeWitt Clinton, his mother died of a cerebral hemorrhage. Lancaster was accepted into New York University with an athletic scholarship but subsequently dropped out.

At the age of nine, Lancaster met Nick Cravat, with whom he continued to work throughout his life. Together they learned to act in local theater productions and circus arts at Union Settlement, one of the city's oldest settlement houses. They formed the acrobat duo "Lang and Cravat" and soon joined the Kay Brothers circus. However, in 1939 an injury forced Lancaster to give up the profession, with great regret. He then found temporary work until 1942, first as a salesman for Marshall Fields, and then as a singing waiter in various restaurants.

The United States having then entered World War II, Lancaster joined the United States Army and performed with the Army's Twenty-First Special Services Division, one of the military groups organized to follow the troops on the ground and provide USO entertainment to keep up morale. He served with General Mark Clark's Fifth Army in Italy from 1943–1945.

Though initially unenthusiastic about acting, he returned from service, auditioned for a Broadway play, and was offered a role. Although Harry Brown's *A Sound of Hunting* was not successful, Lancaster's performance drew the attention of a Hollywood agent, Harold Hecht, who introduced him to Hal Wallis, who cast Lancaster in *The Killers* (1946).

The tall, muscular actor won significant acclaim and appeared in two more films the following year. Subsequently, he played in a variety of films, especially in dramas, thrillers, and military and adventure films. In two, *The Flame and the Arrow* (1950) and *The Crimson Pirate* (1950), a friend from his circus years, Nick Cravat, played a key supporting role, and both actors impressed audiences with their acrobatic prowess.

In 1953, Lancaster played one of his best remembered roles with Deborah Kerr in *From Here to Eternity*. The American Film Institute acknowledged the iconic status of the scene from that film in which he and Deborah Kerr make love on a Hawaiian beach amid the crashing waves. The organization named it one of "AFI's top 100 Most Romantic Films" of all time.

Lancaster won the 1960 Academy Award for Best Actor, a Golden Globe Award, and the New York Film Critics Award for his performance in *Elmer Gantry*. He then appeared as Ben Zachary, Audie Murphy's brother, in *The Unforgiven* (1960). In 1968, at the age of 54, Lancaster appeared nude in director Frank Perry's film, *The Swimmer*.

During the latter part of his career, Lancaster left adventure and acrobatic movies behind and portrayed more distinguished characters. This period brought him work on several European productions, with directors such as Luchino Visconti and Bernardo Bertolucci. Lancaster sought demanding roles, and if he liked a part or a director, he was prepared to work for much lower pay than he might have earned elsewhere. He even helped to finance movies whose artistic value he believed in.

Lancaster was an early and successful actor/producer. In 1952, Lancaster co-produced *The Crimson Pirate* with producer Harold Hecht (who had previously produced three Lancaster films under his own production company Norma Productions; *Kiss the Blood Off My Hands* (1948), *The Flame and the Arrow* (1950), and *Ten Tall Men* (1951)). In 1954, they collaborated again on *His Majesty O'Keefe*, with Lancaster acting and Hecht producing. The writer for this film was James Hill. The trio started a production company, originally with Hill as a silent partner, under the name "Hecht-Lancaster". The name was later extended to include all three with "Hecht-Hill-Lancaster".

In the late 1960s, Lancaster teamed with Roland Kibbee to form "Norlan Productions" and produce *The Scalphunters* (1968), *Valdez Is Coming* (1971), and *The Midnight Man* (1974). In addition, Lancaster directed two films, *The Kentuckian* (1955) and *The Midnight Man* (1974). *The Midnight Man* was in fact starred, co-written, produced, and directed by Lancaster.

Lancaster made six films over the years with Kirk Douglas, including *I Walk Alone* (1948), *Gunfight at the O.K. Corral* (1957), *The Devil's Disciple* (1959), *The List of Adrian Messenger* (1963), *Seven Days in May* (1964), and *Tough Guys* (1986) which fixed the notion of the pair as something of a team in the public imagination. The connection was firmly cemented by the time Lancaster and Douglas reteamed for their final movie, *Tough Guys*. Although Douglas was always second billed under Lancaster in these films, their roles were usually more or less the same size with the exceptions of *I Walk Alone*, in which Douglas played a villain, and in *Seven Days in May*, where Douglas' part was larger than Lancaster's but not as dramatic.

Lancaster vigorously guarded his private life. He was married three times. His first two marriages ended in divorce; to June Ernst from 1935 to 1946 and to Norma Anderson from 1946 to 1969. His third marriage, to Susan Martin, was from September 1990 until his death in 1994. All five of his children were with Norma Anderson: Bill, who became a screenwriter; James; Susan; Joanna; and Sighle (pronounced Sheila).

As Lancaster grew older, he became increasingly plagued by atherosclerosis, barely surviving a routine gall bladder operation in January 1980. Following two minor heart attacks he had to undergo an emergency quadruple heart bypass in 1983, after which he was extremely weak, but he still managed to attend a 1988 Congressional hearing with old colleagues such as Jimmy Stewart and Ginger Rogers to protest media magnate Ted Turner's plan to colorize various black-and-white films from the 1930s and 1940s.

A severe stroke in November 1990 left him partly paralyzed and largely unable to speak. He died in his Century City apartment in Los Angeles from a third heart attack at 4:50 A.M. on October 20, 1994 at the age of 80. He was cremated and his ashes were buried under a large oak tree in Westwood Memorial Park located in Westwood Village, Los Angeles County, California. A small square ground plaque inscribed only with "BURT LANCASTER 1913-1994" marks his final resting place. Upon his death, as he requested, he had no memorial or funeral service.

In 1999, the American Film Institute named Lancaster 19th among the greatest male stars of all time.

Abbe Lane

Abbe Lane with Audie Murphy behind the scenes of *Ride Clear of Diablo*

Abbe Lane was born Abigail Francine Lassman in Brooklyn, New York, December 14, 1932, is an American singer and actress. Lane began her career as a child actress on radio, and from there she progressed to singing and dancing on Broadway.

Married to Xavier Cugat from 1952 until their divorce in 1964, Lane achieved her greatest success as a nightclub singer, and was described in a 1963 magazine article as "the swingingest sexpot in show business". Cugat's influence was seen in her music which favoured Latin and rumba styles.

Some of her earier film roles included *Fame and the Devil* (1951), *Wings of the Hawk* (1953), *Ride Clear of Diablo* (1954) with Audie Murphy, and *Honor Among Thieves* (1958).

In 1958 she starred opposite Tony Randall in the Broadway musical *Oh, Captain!*, but her recording contract prevented her from appearing on the original cast album of the show. On the recording, her songs were performed by Eileen Rodgers. Lane later recorded her songs on a solo album. The most successful of her records was a 1958 album collaboration with Tito Puente titled *Be Mine Tonight*. Apart from working solo, Lane frequently appeared on talk shows with Cugat.

She attracted attention for her suggestive comments such as *"Jayne Mansfield may turn boys into men, but I take them from there",* and also commented that she was considered "too sexy in Italy".

In addition to her Italian films, Lane was a frequent performer on the television show *Toast of the Town* during the 1950s. She also played guest roles in such series as *The Flying Nun* (1968), *F Troop* (1966), *The Brady Bunch* (1970), *Hart to Hart* (1983), and *Vega$* (1979). She appeared in *Twilight Zone: The Movie* (1983) in the role of an airline stewardess. Her last appearance so far was in *Amazing Stories* (1985).

She has a star on the Hollywood Walk of Fame for her contribution to television, at 6381 Hollywood Boulevard.

Allan Lane

Allan Lane with Audie Murphy in *Hell Bent for Leather*

Allan "Rocky" Lane Harry was born Leonard Albershardt in Mishawaka, Indiana, September 22, 1909, and was a studio leading man and the star of many cowboy B-movies in the 1940s and 1950s. He appeared in more than 125 films and TV shows in a career lasting from 1929 to 1966. He also did the voice of the talking horse on the television series *Mister Ed* (1961-1966).

Lane had been a photographer, model and stage actor by the time he was twenty years old. He was spotted by Fox Film Corporation (later 20th Century Fox) talent scouts and was signed to a contract. His first film role for Fox was as a romantic lead opposite June Collyer in the 1929 release, *Not Quite Decent*, now a lost film. He made several other films at Fox but jumped ship to Warner Brothers in the early 1930s.

While at Warner his career foundered, and after a number of bit parts he left films in the early 1930s. By 1936, Lane returned to films and to 20th Century Fox, taking supporting roles in the drama *Laughing at Trouble* (1936) and the Shirley Temple film *Stowaway* (1936). After several more supporting roles at Fox, Lane longed for a starring role; therefore, he took the lead in a Republic Pictures' short feature, *The Duke Comes Back* (1937).

From 1929 through 1936, he appeared in twenty-four films. In 1937 his career began to soar; he was a hit in 1938's *The Law West of Tombstone*. In 1940, he portrayed "RCMP Sergeant Dave King," the role becoming one of his most notable successes. The first was *King of the Royal Mounted*, a 1940 serial adaptation of Zane Grey's *King of the Royal Mounted*, with Lane playing the lead role. He starred in several Canadian Mounted Police films, including the serial *King of the Mounties* (1942). He is best remembered for these today. In 1946 and 1947, he portrayed "Red Ryder" in seven films. The following year, he became "Rocky Lane" in western films.

In the years spanning 1940-1966, Lane made eighty-two film and television series appearances, mostly in westerns. Between 1947 and 1953, he made over thirty B-movie westerns (as "Rocky" Lane) with his faithful horse 'Black Jack'.

Some of his later appearances included *Hell Bent for Leather* (1960) and *Posse from Hell* (1961) with Audie Murphy.

He died October 27, 1973, at age 64 in Woodland Hills, Los Angeles, California.

In 2003 he won the *TV Land Award* for the category "Favorite Pet-Human Relationship" as Mr. Ed.

Paul Langton

Audie Murphy and Paul Langton in *To Hell and Back*

Paul Langton was born April 17, 1913, in Salt Lake City, Utah, and was an American actor.

He had many film roles during the 1940s and 1950s in which he played supporting parts, such as *Destination Tokyo* (1943), *Thirty Seconds Over Tokyo* (1944), *They Were Expendable* (1945), *A Song Is Born* (1948), *Jack Slade* (1953), *Danger* (1951-1954), *The Snow Creature* (1954), *To Hell and Back* (1955) with Audie Murphy, as Rip Coker in Louis L'amour's *Utah Blaine* (1957), *It! The Terror from Beyond Space* (1958), *The Cosmic Man* (1959), *Gunsmoke* (1958-1961), *Twilight Zone* (1959-1963), *The Fugitive* (1963), *4 for Texas* (1963), *The Outcasts* (1968), *Ironside* (1971), and *Emergency!* (1972).

He achieved his greatest popular success as Leslie Harrington on *Peyton Place* (1964-1968).

He died two days before his 67th birthday April 15, 1980, in Burbank, California.

Richard Lapp

Born in 1943, Richard Lapp was discovered at an early age by a Warner Brothers Talent scout, Lapp marked his film debut in 1963 in Rauol Walsh's *A Distant Trumpet*. He made his television debut in 1964 Daniel Boone series directed by George Sherman.

After serving with the U. S. Navy in the Vietnam conflict for two years, Lapp returned home and found westerns to be in vogue. The film that brought Lapp to Hollywood was in Ralph Nelson's *Duel at Diablo* (1966).

In the late 1960's, his acting ability afforded him to play a variety of guest star roles on various successful network series including, *I Dream Of Jeannie* (1967), *Iron Horse* (1966), and *Bonanza* (1968).

Lapp took time out in 1968 to appear in John Wayne's *The Green Berets* at Fort Benning, Georgia.

Yet his guest star appearances on numerous western series, *High Chaparral* (1969) and *Gunsmoke* (1970), an unprecedented three times for an actor only twenty-six years old at the time, contributed to his starring role in *A Time for Dying* (1969), for legendary director Bud Boetticher. The film enjoyed critical success, but was never released. This 1969 western was produced by the late Audie Murphy. Audie Murphy also had a cameo as Jesse James, his second time to portray the infamous outlaw. Audie Murphy's first turn as Jesse James was in *Kansas Raiders* (1950).

Lapp broke away from westerns in such roles as *Baltimore Bullet* (1980) and a sci-fi series, *Clonemaster* (1980). He was a weekly contract player in Warner Brothers *Pointman* (1995) series starring Jack Scalia, shot entirely on location in Florida.

In 2005, Lapp recreated the character of Dr. John Buchanan in Tennessee Williams *Summer and Smoke* on the stage in Los Angeles. Most recently he has had parts in *Boston Legal* (2007) and *Cold Case* (2009).

Richard Lapp died September 18, 2013 at age 70 from cancer in Carmel, California.

Walt La Rue

Walt La Rue was born August 8, 1918, in Fall River, Massachusetts, and was an actor and stuntman.

He had relatives who had horses, and Walt learned to ride. He spent part of his early life as a guide and packer in Glacier National Park and also in Yosemite and the High Sierras of California. That horseback work led to rodeoing, and Walt spent part of the next twelve years of his life traveling to rodeos, riding bareback horses and bulls.

In 1942, he joined the Cowboy's Turtle Association, the forerunner of the Rodeo Cowboys Association (R.C.A.), which, in turn, became the Professional Rodeo Cowboys Association (P.R.C.A.). Throughout his life, Walt was proud of his status as a Gold Card Member of the P.R.C.A.

Rodeoing eventually led Walt to a career as a Hollywood stuntman. He had the good fortune to be part of that business during the 1940s and 1950s, Hollywood's golden age of Westerns. He appeared in hundreds of movies and television shows, doing stunts that mostly involved horse work.

Some of his actual acting work included *New Frontier* (1939), *Edge of Darkness* (1943), *The Phantom Rider* (1946), *Gene Autry and The Mounties* (1951), *Gunman's Walk* (1958), *Bat Masterson* (1961), *The High Chaparral* (1967), *A Time for Dying* (1969) with Audie Murphy, *The North Avenue Irregulars* (1979), *Raging Bull* (1980), and *Dempsey* (1983).

Entertaining seemed to come naturally to Walt. He could play the guitar and sing, and he'd happily perform for anyone who wanted to listen to his cowboy songs and his humorous old-time-radio-show act.

Throughout his life, Walt was a superb artist, his lifetime of cartoons, sketches, drawings, and paintings numbering in the thousands. His greatest influences were the works of Charlie Russell and Will James, and evidence of both can be seen in Walt's work.

Walt did drawings and paintings commercially for Levi Strauss, Weber Bread, Blevins Buckles, Paul Bond Boots, and other businesses, and, from 1945 to 1952, Walt drew cartoon covers for *The Buckboard*, the official magazine of the R.C.A.

Walt didn't mind being loved and adored by his many friends and fans, and, in 2007, he was recognized by the movie industry, as well, when he was presented a Golden Boot Award.

Walt's life was a long and happy one. He was one of those fortunate individuals who lived the kind of life he wanted to live. Walt was quoted once as saying "I've enjoyed doing what I've done, a lot of different things. I've been able to paint, and entertain a little, and rodeo, and work in the movies. I could have made a living at any one of them. I've been kinda lucky, I do what I want to do".

Walt LaRue died June 12, 2010, at the age of 91 in Burbank, California.

Harry Lauter

Audie Murphy with Harry Lauter in *Showdown*

Herman Arthur "Harry" Lauter was born June 19, 1914, and was an American character actor originally from White Plains, New York. He came to be a familiar presence in low-budget films, serials (where he was often cast because of his facial resemblance to stuntman Tom Steele, who would double him), and television programs in the 1950s, though he only once really came close to stardom, as Clay Morgan, one of the leads in the series *Tales of the Texas Rangers*, which aired from 1955-1958. He starred in fifty-two episodes.

Lauter also made appearances on many television programs, particularly westerns: *The Gene Autry Show* (1950-1955) (sixteen episodes), *Annie Oakley* (1954-1957) (12 episodes), *The Lone Ranger* (1949-1956) and *The Range Rider* (eleven episodes each), *Gunsmoke* (1960-1968) and *Rawhide* (1959-1965) (ten episodes each), *Death Valley Days* (1953-1969) and *The Adventures of Ozzie and Harriet* (1956-1965) (seven episodes each), *Laramie* (1959-1963) and *Dick Powell's Zane Grey Theater* (1956-1959) (six episodes each), *The Virginian* and *State Trooper* (1957-1959) (five times each), and *Cheyenne* (1956-1962), *Bonanza* (1961-1962), and *Maverick* (1957-1961) (three episodes each).

Most of his career was spent as a serviceable second lead or heavy, though he continued to play bit parts in larger pictures, including an uncredited part as a plain-clothes policeman in the 1949 crime drama, *White Heat* which starred James Cagney and Edmond O'Brien. He also had an uncredited, unspoken role in the 1963 comedy *A Mad, Mad, Mad, Mad World* as a police dispatcher.

Other roles included *The Day the Earth Stood Still* (1951), *Hopalong Cassidy* (1953), *It Came from Beneath the Sea* (1955), *The Werewolf* (1956), *Richard Diamond, Private Detective* (1958), *The Gunfight at Dodge City* (1959), *Wichita Town* (1959), *Posse from Hell* (1961) with Audie Murphy, *Showdown* (1963) again with Audie Murphy, *Gilligan's Island* (1965), *The Green Hornet* (1966), *Adam-12* (1970), and *Escape from the Planet of the Apes* (1971).

His last appearance was in 1979 as Marshal Charlie Benton in James Arness's *How the West Was Won*.

The son of an artist, he devoted much of his energy late in his life to his own painting and running an art gallery. He died October 30, 1990 in Ojai in Ventura County, California. His ashes were scattered into the Pacific Ocean.

Marc Lawrence

Marc Lawrence was born Max Goldsmith in New York City, December 17, 1909, and was an American character actor who specialized in underworld types. He has also been credited as F. A. Foss, Marc Laurence, and Marc C. Lawrence.

He participated in plays in school, and then attended the City College of New York. In 1930, Lawrence befriended another young actor, John Garfield. The two appeared in a number of plays before Lawrence was given a film contract with Columbia Pictures. Lawrence appeared in films beginning in 1931. Lawrence's pock-marked complexion, brooding appearance and New York street-guy accent made him a natural for heavies, and he played scores of gangsters and mob bosses over the next six decades.

Later, Lawrence found himself under scrutiny for his political leanings. When called before the House Un-American Activities Committee, he admitted he had once been a member of the Communist Party. He was blacklisted and departed for Europe, where he continued to make films. Following the demise of the blacklist, he returned to America and resumed his position as a familiar and talented purveyor of gangland types.

Some of his films include *White Woman* (1933), *'G' Men* (1935), *Charlie Chan on Broadway* (1937), *The Lone Wolf Spy Hunt* (1939), *Charlie Chan at the Wax Museum* (1940), *The Shepherd of the Hills* (1941), *Hold That Ghost* (1941), *This Gun for Hire* (1942), *The Ox-Bow Incident* (1943), *Hit the Ice* (1943), *Flame of Barbary Coast* (1945), *Key Largo* (1948), *Abbott and Costello in the Foreign Legion* (1950), *Helen of Troy* (1956), *Peter Gunn* (1959), *Richard Diamond, Private Detective* (1960), *Whispering Smith* (1961) with Audie Murphy, *Mister Ed* (1965), *Custer of the West* (1967), *King of Kong Island* (1968), *Diamonds Are Forever* (1971), *The Man with the Golden Gun* (1974), *Marathon Man* (1976), *Baretta* (1976), *The Dukes of Hazzard* (1979), *Super Fuzz* (1980), *Night Train to Terror* (1985), *The Big Easy* (1986), *Star Trek: The Next Generation* (1989), *From Dusk Till Dawn* (1996), *Star Trek: Deep Space Nine* (1999), *End of Days* (1999), and *The Shipping News* (2001).

His final film role was in *Looney Tunes Back in Action* (2003), appearing as an Acme Corporation vice president.

In 1991 Lawrence's autobiography was published entitled *Long Time No See: Confessions of a Hollywood Gangster*. Lawrence was also the subject of a novel, *The Beautiful and the Profane* published in 2002.

He married novelist and screenwriter Fanya Foss, with whom he had two children; she died on December 12, 1995. Lawrence died of heart failure on November 28, 2005, at the age of 95. He was buried at Westwood Memorial Park in Westwood, California. His son, Michael Lawrence, is a writer and artist based on the Greek island of Hydra, whose book, *My Voyage in Art*, details his meetings with several of his father's actor friends; while at UCLA he befriended the singer-songwriter James Douglas "Jim" Morrison. His daughter, actress Toni Lawrence, was once married to actor Billy Bob Thornton and starred in his film *Daddy's Girl* (1996).

Linda Lawson

Linda Lawson with Audie Murphy in *Apache Rifles*

Linda Lawson was born Linda Gloria Spaziani January 14, 1936 in Ann Arbor, Michigan, and was an American film and television actress. When she was three, her family moved to Fontana, California and she began singing while still a child and, by the end of her teen years, she'd turned professional. In the mid 1950s she was for a time a showgirl and then a singer at the Sands Hotel in Las Vegas.

Some of her acting credits include *Tales of the Texas Rangers* (1958), *Peter Gunn* (1958), *Man with a Camera* (1958), *Maverick* (1959), *77 Sunset Strip* (1959-1960), *Tombstone Territory* (1960), *Richard Diamond, Private Detective* (1960), *Alcoa Presents: One Step Beyond* (1960), *Sea Hunt* (1960-1961), six episodes as Renee in *Adventures in Paradise* (1959-1961), eighteen episodes as Pat Perry in *Don't Call Me Charlie* (1962-1963), *Apache Rifles* (1964) with Audie Murphy and Michael Dante, nine episodes as Laura Fremont in *Ben Casey* (1965), *Let's Kill Uncle, Before Uncle Kills Us* (1966), *It Takes a Thief* (1968), *Mrs. Stone's Thing* (1970), *Sometimes a Great Notion* (1970), *Saved by the Bell: The New Class* (1994), *Another Woman's Husband* (2000), and *ER* (2005).

She married producer John Forman and the couple have two daughters who are also actresses; Amanda and Julie Foreman. She is semi-retired and living in Beverly Hills, California.

Alan Lee

No biographical information can be found for Alan Lee, but he did appear in twenty-two films and television programs from 1946 to 1990.

Some of those credits include *Sister Kenny* (1946), *Adventures of Superman* (1953), *The Long, Long Trailer* (1953), *Rear Window* (1954), *The Sea Chase* (1955), "The Flight" episode of *Suspicion* (1957) with Audie Murphy, *Perry Mason* (1958), *The Good Guys and the Bad Guys* (1969), *Eyes of a Stranger* (1981), and *Mad About You* (1990).

Ruta Lee

Audie Murphy with Ruta Lee in *Bullet for a Badman*

Ruta Lee was born Ruta Mary Kilmonis in Montreal, Quebec, May 30, 1936, and is an actress and dancer who appeared as one of the brides in the film *Seven Brides for Seven Brothers* (1954). She is also known for her guest appearance in a 1963 episode of Rod Serling's *The Twilight Zone* episode "A Short Drink from a Certain Fountain".

She was the only child of two Lithuanian immigrants. Her father was a tailor; her mother, a homemaker. In 1948, her family moved to Los Angeles, California, where she graduated in 1954 from Hollywood High School and began studying acting and appearing in school plays. She attended both Los Angeles City College and the University of California at Los Angeles.

Ruta worked for a time as a cashier, an usherette, and a candy girl at Grauman's Chinese Theater.

Lee then got a break with a spot on TV with George Burns and Gracie Allen. She soon found an agent, who landed her a job in an episode of the series *Adventures of Superman* in 1953. That same year, while acting in a small theater production of *On the Town*, she landed a role in the Academy Award-nominated musical *Seven Brides for Seven Brothers*. After *Seven Brides*, Lee appeared in several films including *Anything Goes* (1956), *Funny Face* (1957), *Witness for the Prosecution* (1957), and *Marjorie Morningstar* (1958) with Natalie Wood. In 1962, Ruta appeared in the comedy/western film *Sergeants 3* along with Frank Sinatra, Dean Martin, Sammy Davis, Jr., and Peter Lawford.

More appearances followed in *Richard Diamond, Private Detective* (1959), *The Tab Hunter Show* (1961), *The Gun Hawk* (1963), *The Fugitive* (1964), *Bullet for a Badman* (1964) with Audie Murphy, *The Wild Wild West* (1965-1967), *The Flying Nun* (1969), and *Me and the Chimp* (1972).

In the early 1970s, Lee continued to appear in both films and television roles including appearances on *Love, American Style* (1969-1972), *The Mod Squad* (1971), and a role in the 1972 film *The Doomsday Machine*.

By 1974, Lee grew frustrated by an increasing lack of roles, and took a job co-hosting the daytime game show *High Rollers*. She remained with the show until 1976. In 1979, she appeared in an episode of *Three's Company* titled "An Anniversary Surprise" as the real estate agent Mr. Roper used to sell the apartment complex.

During the 1980s, she lent her voice to episodes of *The Flintstones Comedy Show* (1980) and *The Smurfs* (1981), in addition to guest roles on *CHiPs* (1983), *The Love Boat* (1985), and *Charles in Charge* (1990). From 1988 to 1989, Lee had a recurring role on the CBS sitcom *Coming of Age*. In 1989, she played the role of Sally Powers in the TV movie *Sweet Bird of Youth* with Elizabeth Taylor. Lee continued to appear in episodic television, most notably in the series *Roseanne* (1997). Lee appeared as the girlfriend of Bev Harris (Estelle Parsons) whose character disclosed she was gay.

In 2006, Ruta Lee received a star on the Hollywood Walk of Fame for her contributions to the television industry.

She recently appeared in a trio of Christmas-themed films such as *Christmas Do-Over* (2006), *A Christmas Too Many* (2007), and *Christmas at Cadillac Jack's* (2007).

In February 2008, Lee appeared as Clairee in a production of *Steel Magnolias* with Sally Struthers at the Casa Mañana Theatre in Fort Worth, Texas. In October 2010, Lee played the role of Miss Mona in *The Best Little Whorehouse in Texas*, also at the Casa Mañana Theatre. She had previously played the role there in 1982.

Recently, she appeared in a small guest appearance on the long-running American soap opera *Days of Our Lives* (2012).

In 1976, Lee married Texas restaurant executive Webster B. "Webb" Lowe, Jr. They divide their time between their homes in Hollywood, Palm Springs, Fort Worth, and Mexico. She has no children.

In 1964, Lee called then-Soviet Premier Nikita Khrushchev, asking him to pardon her grandmother Ludvise Kamandulis, who had been in an internment camp in Siberia since World War II. The pardon was granted, and Lee's grandmother came to live with her in California in 1966. Kamandulis died two years later. Lee again rescued a relative from the former Soviet Union when she secured custody of her eighteen-year-old cousin, Maryte Kaseta, from Lithuania in 1987.

Lee has been involved with the charitable organization "The Thalians" for over fifty years. In addition to raising money and providing services for troubled youth and mental health organizations, Lee, who is also the board chairman, has co-produced the annual Ball of the Thalians with Debbie Reynolds throughout those five decades. In 2011, she stepped down after fifty-five years of involvement with the Thalians, and is now an emeritus member.

She is currently filming *For Better or for Worse* set for a 2013 release.

Paul Lees

Paul Lees was born January 14, 1923, in Pratt, Kansas, and was an American character actor.

Lees spent over six years in the Marine Corps after joining at age eighteen. He was at Corregidor during the WWII Japanese attack and was captured and held prisoner. Lees was blinded by picric acid in enemy artillery shells. He received some thirty-two military decorations and ribbons, including the Legion of Merit. Despite his lack of vision, Lees learned to act and signed a contract with Paramount. He would memorize script dialog by having someone read it to him twice.

Some of his film and television credits include *O.S.S.* (1946), *A Foreign Affair* (1948), *Beyond Glory* (1948) with Audie Murphy, *Chicago Deadline* (1949), *Captain Carey, U.S.A.* (1950), *Appointment with Danger* (1951), *The Atomic City* (1952), *But Not for Me* (1959), *Posse from Hell* (1961) again with Audie Murphy, *Whispering Smith* (1961) a third appearance with Audie Murphy, *Breakfast at Tiffany's* (1961), *The Good Guys and the Bad Guys* (1969), and *The City* (1971).

Lees co-authored the book *Soo Chow the Marine*, (Putnam & Co., 1951), with actor Reginald Owen.

Paul Lees died August 19, 1995, at age 72.

William Leicester

Audie Murphy with William Leicester in *Bad Boy*

William Leicester was born August 25, 1915 in Illinois, and was an actor and writer.

Some of his acting credits include *The Beginning or the End* (1947), *Command Decision* (1948), *Bad Boy* (1949) with Audie Murphy, *Battleground* (1949), *I Was a Communist for the FBI* (1951), *Gunsmoke* (1953) again with Audie Murphy, *The McConnell Story* (1955), *Richard Diamond, Private Detective* (1957), *Lawman* (1960), and *The Alaskans* (1960).

Some of his teleplay, screenplays, and stories he wrote for such programs as *The Adventures of Falcon* (1954), *Tales of Wells Fargo* (1957-1959), "The Dark Circle" episode of *Whispering Smith* (1961), *Have Gun - Will Travel* (1963), and *The High Chaparral* (1967-1969).

He died January 9, 1969, at age 53 in Van Nuys, California.

James Lennon

Jimmy Lennon, Sr. was born April 13, 1913, and was one of the top announcers of the boxing and wrestling world.

Known as "The Voice of the Olympic" Auditorium in Los Angeles, California, as well as "The Irishman With the Spanish Accent". For over forty years, Lennon's unique professional ring eloquence and dapper style of fight announcing and tuxedo attire, along with innovated showmanship and the singing of the United States National Anthem could be seen live at The Grand Olympic Auditorium or over the television networks.

Lennon first became a ring announcer in Santa Monica, California, at the Ocean Park Arena, while working there as the regular patriotic singer of the National Anthem. The regular ring announcer at the time was unavailable so the event coordinator asked Lennon if he would fill in as ring announcer. At the time Lennon was wearing a tuxedo to sing in, and also wore the tuxedo during that first announcing job. His boss liked Lennon's performance so well that he hired Lennon as the regular fight announcer, tuxedo and all. Lennon started the "Tux Announcer" style that night.

Lennon appeared in seventy-five film and television productions, including *Raging Bull* (1980), *Rocky III* (1982), *Main Event* (1979), *Kid Galahad* (1962), *The Munsters* (1965), *The Monkees* (1967), and *World in My Corner* (1956) with Audie Murphy.

Lennon was the character of a Jakks Pacific action figure released in 2007, depicting his *Rocky III* appearance. He was the uncle of the Lennon Sisters vocal group on *The Lawrence Welk Show*.

Lennon was a favorite among the Hispanic Community as he was a master at the Spanish dialect (and several other languages) which he presented whenever introducing a boxer or wrestler with a foreign name by accurately pronouncing difficult names often smudged by other announcers. He believed all men deserved to have their names properly pronounced as a sign of respect and honor.

Lennon sang as a young boy in church and later formed a singing group, The Lennon Brothers, with his brothers in Venice, California. He also served the World War II effort by becoming a commissioned civil instructor as a butcher and cook. At age seventeen, Lennon was planning to go to college and become an English professor, but his father Herbert Lennon became ill and died at age forty-five leaving Jimmy and his nineteen year-old brother John Henry to work and support the large surviving family. He worked at multiple jobs singing, performing, sports events, athlete, MC, patriotic, and police events in and around Los Angeles.

After 10 years of heart treatments, including heart surgery and multiple doctor and hospital visits, Mr. Lennon was admitted to St. John's Hospital in Santa Monica, California, where he died at age 79 on April 20, 1992.

Mr. Lennon is survived by his wife, Doris, and four children, Scott, Robin Thomas, Kim Fitzgerald, and boxing announcer Jimmy Lennon, Jr.

Lennon was inducted into the World Boxing Hall of Fame.

Mel Leonard

No biographical information could be found for Mel Leonard, but he did appear in three films and one television program from 1958 to 1961.

The three films were *Kathy O'* (1958), *The Wild and the Innocent* (1959) with Audie Murphy, and *Breakfast at Tiffany's* (1961). The one television program was *Peter Gunn* (1959).

Nancy Lewis

No biographical information could be found for Nancy Lewis, but she did appear in five films and three television programs from 1958 to 1969.

Those credits include *Intent to Kill* (1958), *Encounter* (1960), *Route 66* (1961), *The Touchables* (1961), *Love and Kisses* (1965), *The Adventures of Ozzie & Harriet* (1966), *The Oscar* (1966), and as one of Mamie's girls in *A Time for Dying* (1969) with Audie Murphy.

Pamela Light

No biographical information could be found for Pamela Light, but she did appear in eleven films and television programs from 1956 to 1961.

Those credits include *The Adventures of Hiram Holliday* (1956), *Studio 57* (1957), *Alfred Hitchcock Presents* (1957), *Until They Sail* (1957), *The George Burns and Gracie Allen Show* (1957), *In the Money* (1958), *Hong Kong* (1960), *Midnight Lace* (1960), *Bachelor Father* (1961), and *On the Double* (1961). Her final appearance was as Madge Landers in *Whispering Smith* (1961) with Audie Murphy. Her character died within the first two minutes of the episode "Hired to die".

Jo Linn

No biographical information could be found for Jo Lynn, but she did appear in one film *A Time for Dying* (1969) with Audie Murphy as one of Mamie's girls.

Eddie Little

Eddie Little with Audie Murphy in *Ride a Crooked Trail*

No biographical information could be found for Eddie Little, but he did appear one film and one television program.

The one film he appeared in was *Ride a Crooked Trail* (1958) with Audie Murphy. He also appeared in two episodes of *Lassie* (1959) entitled "Growing Pains" and "The Flying Machine".

Patricia Livingston

Patricia Livingston with Audie Murphy in *Guns of Fort Petticoat*

Patricia Livingston was born Patricia Joyce Tiernan December 31, 1930, in Long Beach, California, and is an American actress who appeared in ten films and television programs from 1952 to 1962. She also went by the names Carole Eden and Carol Eden.

Her credits included *Apache War Smoke* (1952), *Battle Circus* (1953), *Scandal at Scourie* (1953), *Dream Wife* (1953), *The Cisco Kid* (1955), *The Conqueror* (1956), *Cheyenne* (1956), *The Guns of Fort Petticoat* (1957) with Audie Murphy, *Zero Hour!* (1957), and *Walk on the Wild Side* (1962).

Suzanne Lloyd

Suzanne Lloyd with Audie Murphy in *Seven Ways from Sundown*

Suzanne Lloyd was born November 11, 1934 in Toronto and is a Canadian film and television actress. In addition to her film work, she was a frequent guest star on both British and American television, including *The Avengers* (1965), *Laramie* (1963), *Thriller* (1962), *Perry Mason* (1961), *Tales of Wells Fargo* (1961), *Walt Disney's Wonderful World of Color* (1961), and six episodes of *The Saint* (1964-1968).

Lloyd also had a recurring role as Raquel Toledano on the classic *Zorro* (1958-1961) television series.

Some of her other roles included *State Trooper* (1959), *The Bob Cummings Show* (1958-1959), *Alcoa Presents: One Step Beyond* (1959), *Wichita Town* (1960), *Seven Ways from Sundown* (1960) with Audie Murphy, *Miami Undercover* (1961), *The Return of Mr. Moto* (1965), and *The Champagne Murders* (1967).

She moved overseas from the early 1960s until 1974, when she returned to the United States and made one more film *Mousey* (1974) before, surprisingly, retired from acting at the young age of forty.

She has appeared at autograph/memorabilia shows in California and on the east coast in recent years. She is best remembered for her role as the femme fatale "Maya the Catgirl" on the well-known *Twilight Zone* (1959) episode, "Perchance to Dream".

She attended the 2007 Twilight Zone Convention at the Hilton Hasbrouck Heights, Hasbrouck Heights, New Jersey, August 4-5, 2007.

Lloyd was married to record producer and composer Buddy Bregman from 1961 until their divorce in 1988. Their daughter, Tracey E. Bregman is an Emmy Award-winning actress.

Richard Long

Richard Long with Audie Murphy in *Kansas Raiders*

Richard Long was born December 17, 1927, and was an American actor better known for his leading roles in several ABC television series, including *The Big Valley* (1965-1969), *Nanny and the Professor* (1970-1971), and *Bourbon Street Beat* (1959-1960).

Long was the fifth of six children born in Chicago, Illinois, to Sherman D. Long, a commercial artist who operated his own studio, and Dale McCord Long. The family lived in several locations in Illinois before settling in Evanston. Long attended grammar school in Evanston, Waller High School in Chicago, and then the Evanston Township High School. In 1944, the family relocated to Hollywood, California, and Long attended Hollywood High School for his senior year. Long said that as a teenager he had "no intention of becoming an actor. I took senior drama class because it was a snap course, and I needed the credit for my English requirement".

At Hollywood High School, Long caught the eye of a talent scout from Universal-International by accident. Casting director Jack Murton gave a ride to a couple of students and asked them if a school play was scheduled. The boys told Murton about the excellent male lead actor, Richard Long. In 1946, Long was hence cast in his first film, *Tomorrow Is Forever* (1946) as Drew, the son of Claudette Colbert. The role had been unfilled for months, and producers selected Long who most closely matched the credentials required.

His second film was the Orson Welles's *The Stranger* (1946) as Noah, the brother of Loretta Young's character. He also played "Jeff Taylor" in *The Life of Riley* and played 'Frank James' in the 1950 movie *Kansas Raiders*, brother to Audie Murphy's 'Jesse James'.

Early in his career, Long appeared in several films as a juvenile lead, including four of the nine *Ma and Pa Kettle* pictures. He was cast as Tom Kettle, the eldest son of the characters played by Percy Kilbride and Marjorie Main.

Long took a break from acting and served in the United States Army during the Korean War. When he returned he moved into leading man status in horror movies such as *Cult of the Cobra* (1955), and *House on Haunted Hill* (1959) before he achieved considerable success on television, including the series *Bourbon Street Beat* (1959–60). He also appeared on episodes of *Hey, Jeannie!* (1956), *The Twilight Zone* (1962-1964), *77 Sunset Strip* (1958-1963), *The Alfred Hitchcock Hour* (1962) and *The Tenderfoot* (1964) for Walt Disney's *Wonderful World of Color*. Long played the recurring role of "Gentleman Jack Darby" in four episodes of *Maverick* (1958-1959), including the famous "Shady Deal at Sunny Acres" installment.

In 1963, Long was cast in the MGM romantic musical *Follow the Boys*, along with costars Connie Francis, Paula Prentiss, and Roger Perry.

In 1965, at the age of thirty-eight, Long began his role as attorney Jarrod Barkley, oldest son to rancher Victoria Barkley (Barbara Stanwyck), in 112 episodes of *The Big Valley*, the last of the major Four Star Television series, a Western which ran on ABC from 1965–1969. The series was set in the 1870s. Long also directed several episodes of *The Big Valley*. In 1953, Long had costarred with Stanwyck in the film *All I Desire*.

In 1970–71, he and Juliet Mills starred in the ABC sitcom *Nanny and the Professor*. Long played widowed college professor Harold Everett, and Mills was Phoebe Figalilly, the English housekeeper and nanny for Long's three children. In 1973 he starred alongside Julie Harris in the short-lived series *Thicker than Water*. In 1974, Long appeared on the television game show, *Match Game*. He also finished a television movie called *Death Cruise* (1974), which was his last work.

Long had cardiac problems throughout his adult life and had suffered a heart attack in the late 1950s. As a boy, he had suffered pneumonia, which apparently weakened his heart. He was also a heavy smoker and drinker. He died December 21, 1974, at age 47, after suffering multiple heart attacks at Tarzana Treatment Centers in Los Angeles. He was cremated, and his ashes were scattered at sea.

He was twice married. His first wife of fourteen months, actress Suzan Ball (a cousin of Lucille Ball) died of cancer in 1955 at the age of twenty-one. In 1957, Long married actress and model Mara Corday (birth name Marilyn Watts), with whom he had three children, Carey (born 1957), Valerie (born 1958), and Gregory (born 1960).

A few years after her husband's death in 1974, Corday's friend Clint Eastwood offered her a chance to return to filmmaking with a role in his 1977 film *The Gauntlet*.

Long was a brother-in-law of actor Marshall Thompson, with whom he appeared in the 1955 film *Cult of the Cobra*.

Richard Loo

Richard Loo was born October 1, 1903, and was a Chinese-American film actor who was one of the most familiar Asian character actors in American films of the 1930s and 1940s. A prolific actor, he appeared in over 120 films between 1931 and 1982. Loo was most often stereotyped as the Japanese enemy pilot, spy, or interrogator during the Second World War. Chinese by ancestry and Hawaiian by birth, Loo spent his youth in Hawaii, then moved to California as a teenager. He graduated from the University of California at Berkeley and began a career in business. However, the stock market crash of 1929 and the subsequent economic depression forced him to start over.

He became involved with amateur, then professional, theater companies and in 1931 made his first film. Like most Asian actors in non-Asian countries, he played primarily small, stereotypical roles, though he rose quickly to familiarity, if not fame, in a number of films.

His stern features led him to be a favorite movie villain, and the outbreak of World War II gave him greater prominence in roles as vicious Japanese soldiers in such successful pictures as *The Purple Heart* (1944) and *God Is My Co-Pilot* (1945). In 1944 he appeared as a Chinese army lieutenant opposite Gregory Peck in *The Keys of the Kingdom*. He had a rare heroic role as a war-weary Japanese-American soldier in Samuel Fuller's Korean War classic *The Steel Helmet* (1951), but he spent much of the latter part of his career performing stock roles in films and minor television roles.

Some those other credits include *Hell and High Water* (1954), *Love Is a Many-Splendored Thing* (1955), *Around the World in Eighty Days* (1956), *Battle Hymn* (1957), *The Quiet American* (1958) with Audie Murphy, *Maverick* (1961), *Confessions of an Opium Eater* (1962), *The Outer Limits* (1963), *The Wackiest Ship in the Army* (1966), *The Sand Pebbles* (1966), *Hawaii Five-O* (1968), *Which Way to the Front?* (1970), *The Sixth Sense* (1972), and *Owen Marshall: Counselor at Law* (1974).

In 1974 he appeared as the Thai billionaire tycoon Hai Fat in the James Bond film, *The Man With The Golden Gun*, opposite Roger Moore and Christopher Lee.

Loo was also a teacher of Shaolin monks in seven episodes of the 1972-1974 hit TV series *Kung Fu*.

His last acting appearance was in *The Incredible Hulk* TV series in 1981, but he continued to act in Toyota commercials into 1982. He died of a cerebral hemorrhage on November 20, 1983.

His first wife, Bessie Loo, was a well-known Hollywood agent. They had twin daughters: Beverly Loo was prominent in publishing while Angela Loo Levy was a Hollywood agent and accomplished ski patroller.

He remained with his second wife, Hope, until his death. His step-daughter, Christel Hope Mintz, was an analyst with Shell Oil Company for 32 years.

Diana Lorys

Audie Murphy with Diana Lorys in *The Texican*

Diana Lorys was born Ana Maria Cazorla Vega on October 20, 1940, in Madrid, Spain and is a talented actress. She studied dance, classical ballet and Spanish flamenco, drama and diction.

She made her acting debut in theater productions but has devoted herself to film since 1960. Diana has worked primarily in Spanish productions but also has appeared in Italian films specializing in Horror, Spy Films, Sci-Fi, Adventure, and Westerns.

She married and retired to private life but did pop up in local theater productions in Germany in the late 1970s and has returned to Spain. With her typical Hispanic beauty and her penetrating stares the small but shapely Lorys was one of the great female stars of the Euro-western appearing in seventeen productions. Among her best known were, *Gunfighters of Casa Grande* (1964), *Murieta* (1964), *The Texican* (1966) with Audie Murphy, *Villa Rides* (1967), *Tequila* (1971), *Bad Man's River* (1972) and *Get Mean* (1976).

Robert Lowery

Robert Lowery was born Robert Larkin Hanks in Kansas City, Missouri, October 17, 1913, and was an American motion picture, television, and stage actor who appeared in over seventy films. Lowery's father was a local attorney and oil investor who worked several years for the Pullman Corporation as a railroad agent; his mother, Leah Thompson Hanks, was a concert pianist.

He graduated from Paseo High School in Kansas City, and soon was invited to sing with the Slats Randall Orchestra in the early 1930s. Lowery played on the Kansas City Blues minor league baseball team and was overall considered a versatile athlete; his physique and strength was gained from a stint working in a paper factory as a teenager. After the death of his father in 1935, he traveled to Hollywood with his mother and their housekeeper, and enrolled in the Lila Bliss acting school before being signed by Twentieth Century Fox in 1937.

During his career, Lowery was primarily known for roles in action movies such as *The Mark of Zorro* (1940), *The Mummy's Ghost* (1944), and *Dangerous Passage* (1944). He became the second actor to play DC Comics' Batman (succeeding Lewis Wilson), starring in a 1949's *Batman and Robin* serial.

Lowery also had roles in a number of Western films including *The Homesteaders* (1953), *The Parson and the Outlaw* (1957), *Young Guns of Texas* (1962), and *Johnny Reno* (1966). On television, Lowery was best known for the role of Big Tim Champion on the series *Circus Boy* (1956–1957). In 1956, he guest starred in "The Deadly

Rock," an episode of *The Adventures of Superman* which was the first time a Batman actor shared screen time with a Superman actor, although Lowery and Reeves had appeared together in their pre-superhero days in a WWII anti-VD propaganda film, *Sex Hygiene*.

Some other credits included *Judge Roy Bean* (1956), *Maverick* (1958-1959), *Richard Diamond, Private Detective* (1960), *Whispering Smith* (1961) with Audie Murphy, *Gunsmoke* (1962), *McLintock!* (1963), and *Pistols 'n' Petticoats* (1966-1967). He made his last onscreen appearance in the 1967 comedy/Western film *The Ballad of Josie*, opposite Doris Day and Peter Graves.

He was married three times, to three different actresses: Jean Parker, Vivan Wilcox, and Rusty Farrell. He had one child, Robert, who lives in Redondo Beach, California; and two grandchildren.

Lowery died of heart failure at the age of 58 in his Los Angeles, California apartment on December 26, 1971.

James Lydon

Audie Murphy with James Lydon in *Bad Boy*

Jimmy Lydon was born May 30, 1923, and is an American movie actor and television producer, whose career in the entertainment industry began as a teenage actor in the 1930s. Lydon grew up in Bergenfield, New Jersey. He initially appeared on the Broadway stage in 1937, before making movies beginning as a teenager. One of his first starring roles was the title character in the 1940 movie, *Tom Brown's School Days*, which also starred Cedric Hardwicke and Freddie Bartholomew. It was well received by critics, with *Variety* praising it in a January 1940 review as "sympathetically and skillfully made, with many touching moments and an excellent cast". Lydon was called "believable and moving in the early portions, but too young for the final moments".

Lydon then starred as the screechy-voiced, adolescent *Henry Aldrich* in the movie series of that title, from 1941 to 1944. After completing the Henry Aldrich series, the twenty-one year old Lydon signed a contract in 1944 with Republic Pictures. He appeared with William Powell, Irene Dunne, and Elizabeth Taylor in the acclaimed 1947 film *Life with Father*, in the role of college-bound Clarence. *Variety* called Jimmy Lydon's portrayal "effective as the potential Yale man". He then appeared opposite James Cagney in the 1948 movie, *The Time of Your Life*. He then appeared with Audie Murphy in *Bad Boy* (1949).

In the next few decades he had a number of acting roles, including appearances on *Mr. & Mrs. North* (1953), *Rocky Jones, Space Ranger* (1954), *Rage at Dawn* (1955), *So This Is Hollywood* (1955), *Love That Jill* (1958), *77 Sunset Strip* (1958-1959), *I Passed for White* (1960), *Twilight Zone* (1961), *Wanted: Dead or Alive* (1959-1961), *Whispering Smith* (1961) again with Audie Murphy, *Wagon Train* (1959-1962), *Death of a Gunfighter* (1969), *O'Hara, U.S. Treasury* (1972), *Adam-12* (1972-1974), *The Rockford Files* (1974-1976), *Black Sheep Squadron* (1978), *The Greatest American Hero* (1982), *The Fall Guy* (1982-1983), *Simon & Simon* (1983-1985), *Misfits of Science* (1986), and *St. Elsewhere* (1987).

After working increasingly in television since the 1950s, Lydon turned to production roles, helping to create *77 Sunset Strip* (1958-1964) and *M*A*S*H* (1972-1983).

Lydon resides in Bonita, California with his wife, Betty Lou Nedell, whom he married in 1952. They have two daughters.

Ken Lynch

Audie Murphy with Ken Lynch in *Apache Rifles*

Ken Lynch was born July 15, 1910, and was a film and TV actor best known for his starring role as 'the Lieutenant' on the 1949-1954 Dumont detective series *The Plainclothesman*, on which his face was never seen, and for his co-starring role as Sergeant Grover on *McCloud* (1972-1977).

If there was ever an actor born to play a tough Irish cop, it was Ken Lynch, and he played so many of them in his long career that he could probably do it in his sleep. His suspicious manner, aggressive attitude, steely eyes and snarling voice broke down many a quavering suspect. He also played military officers, business executives and private eyes, and every so often he'd be a sheriff in a western, but it was as a street cop or detective that most people remember him.

Born in Cleveland, he started his acting career in radio dramas, and after gaining experience there he headed to Los Angeles, making his film debut in *When Willie Comes Marching Home* (1950).

He appeared in quite a few movies over his career, but he also did an enormous amount of television work, and that's where most recognize him, as he turned up on pretty much every cop show, detective show and private eye series ever made.

Some of his film and television credits include *The Honeymooners* (1956), *Zane Grey Theater* (1957-1958), *The Bonnie Parker Story* (1958), *I Married a Monster from Outer Space* (1958), *Pork Chop Hill* (1959), *Twilight Zone* (1959), *Seven Ways from Sundown* (1960) with Audie Murphy, *The Honeymoon Machine* (1961), *Checkmate* (1960-1961), *Arrest and Trial* (1963-1964), *Apache Rifles* (1964) again with Audie Murphy, *The Munsters* (1965), *The Fugitive* (1964-1966), *Honey West* (1965-1966), *Laredo* (1966), *Star Trek* (1967), *Tora! Tora! Tora!* (1970), *Adam-12* (1970-1971), *O'Hara, U.S. Treasury* (1972), *Willie Dynamite* (1974), *Kolchak: The Night Stalker* (1974), *The Life and Times of Grizzly Adams* (1978), *Battlestar Galactica* (1979), *Galactica 1980* (1980), and *The Winds of War* (1983).

He died February 13, 1990, at age 79 in Burbank, California.

Diana Lynn

Audie Murphy with Diana Lynn behind the scenes of *Texas, Brooklyn, and Heaven*

Diana Lynn was born Dolores Marie Loehr in Los Angeles, California, October 7, 1926 and was an actress. Lynn was considered a child prodigy because of her exceptional abilities as a pianist at an early age, and by the age of twelve was playing with the Los Angeles Junior Symphony Orchestra.

Dolores Loehr made her film debut playing the piano in *They Shall Have Music* (1939), when it was decided that she had more potential than she had been allowed to show. Paramount Pictures changed her name to "Diana Lynn" and began casting her in films that allowed her to show her personality and developed her skills as an actress.

Her comedic scenes with Ginger Rogers in *The Major and the Minor* (1942), were well received, and in 1944 she scored an outstanding success in Preston Sturges' *The Miracle of Morgan's Creek* (1944). She appeared in two Henry Aldrich films, and played writer Emily Kimbrough in two films *Our Hearts Were Young and Gay* (1944) and *Our Hearts Were Growing Up* (1946) both co-starring Gail Russell.

She then appeared in *Texas, Brooklyn & Heaven* (1948) with Audie Murphy. After a few more films, she was cast in one of the year's biggest successes, the comedy *My Friend Irma* (1949) with Marie Wilson as Irma, and Dean Martin and Jerry Lewis in their film debuts. The group reprised their roles for the sequel *My Friend Irma Goes West* (1950). During the 1950s Lynn continued acting in films, and was the female lead in the much lampooned *Bedtime for Bonzo* (1951) opposite Ronald Reagan.

A marriage to John C. Lindsay ended in divorce in 1953. Lynn was then married in 1956 to Mortimer Hall, son of New York Post newspaper publisher Dorothy Schiff.

She acted frequently in television guest roles throughout the 1960s in such programs as *Checkmate* (1961), *Bus Stop* (1962), *The Doctors and the Nurses* (1964), *Burke's Law* (1964), *The Virginian* (1965), and *Company of Killers* (1971). By 1970, she had virtually retired from acting and had relocated to New York City, where she was running a travel agency. Paramount offered her a part in a new film, and after some consideration she accepted the offer and moved back to Los Angeles. Before filming started, she suffered a stroke and died nine days later December 18, 1971, at age 45. Lynn was interred at the Episcopal Church of the Heavenly Rest in New York City.

Diana Lynn has two stars on the Hollywood Walk of Fame: for motion pictures, at 1625 Vine Street, and for television, at 6350 Hollywood Boulevard.

Lynn was survived by her husband, and four young children. Her daughter Dolly Hall is a film producer.

Another daughter, Susan ... aka Daisy Hall, who bears a striking resemblance to her great-grandfather Jacob Schiff, is an alumna of the ultra-elite and highly-selective Emma Willard School for Girls in Troy, New York, and as an actress herself, has starred in numerous French- and lesser known American-produced films, during the 1980s, 1990s and 2000s.

Rita Lynn

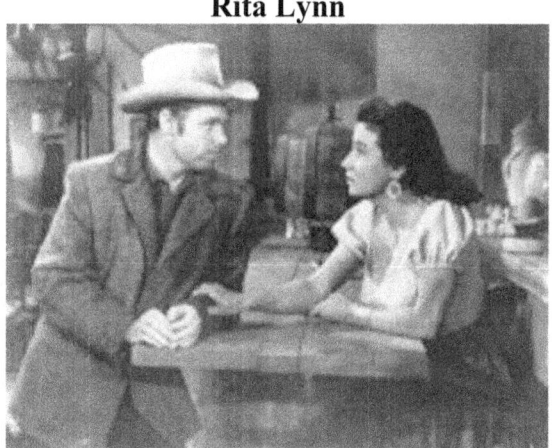

Audie Murphy with Rita Lynn in *Cast a Long Shadow*

Rita Lynn was born Frances Rita Piazza December 2, 1921, in Louisiana. She was an American character actress. She appeared in sixty-three films and television programs from 1946 to 1983. Some of those credits include *Mr. Hex* (1946), *The Hunter* (1952), *Soldiers of Fortune* (1955), *The Adventures of Jim Bowie* (1956), *The Wayward Girl* (1957), *The Gale Storm Show* (1958), *Cast a Long Shadow* (1959) with Audie Murphy, *Wanted: Dead or Alive* (1959), *The Untouchables* (1960), *The Detectives* (1961-1962), *Mr. Smith Goes to Washington* (1962-1963), *Madigan* (1968), *The Streets of San Francisco* (1972), *A Gun in the House* (1981), and *T.J. Hooker* (1983).

She was married to Frank Maxwell from March 26, 1966 until her death of cancer in Santa Monica, California, January 21, 1996. She has two children from two previous marriages: Arthur Debernarde and Donna Lynn.

Kenneth MacDonald

Kenneth MacDonald was born Kenneth Dollins in Portland, Indiana, September 8, 1901, and was an American film actor. MacDonald made more than 220 film and television appearances between 1931 and 1970.

MacDonald began his career as a stage actor, and came to Hollywood in the early 1930's. He found a few bit parts at first, finally finding steady work in westerns and serials at Columbia Pictures. MacDonald perfected a cool, debonair demeanor, which usually masked an evil side as a con man, outlaw, or thief. His speaking voice was rich and well modulated, often being gentle and ominous at the same time, in the Boris Karloff manner.

Actors in Columbia's stock company almost always worked in the studio's two-reel comedy shorts as well as features and serials, but Kenneth MacDonald did not join the short-subject fraternity until 1945, when he appeared opposite comedy stars Gus Schilling and Richard Lane. He is probably best known today for his work with The Three Stooges.

MacDonald developed a flair for comedy, and he made memorable appearances in Stooge comedies including *Monkey Businessmen* (1946), *Hold That Lion!* (1947), *Crime on Their Hands* (1948), *Punchy Cowpunchers* (1950), and *Loose Loot* (1953), among others. Beginning in 1953, the comedy in the Columbia shorts became even more physical under producer-director Jules White, and MacDonald obligingly got plastered with pies, fruit, and other missiles. He also returned to Columbia's serial unit, which was then filming low-budget remakes of his older serials using much of the original footage; MacDonald appeared in new scenes to match his old ones. He left the Columbia shorts department in 1955.

MacDonald had a recurring role as Judge Carter on *Perry Mason* between 1957 and 1966. He still appeared occasionally in motion pictures (including a bit role as Jerry Lewis's father in the 1961 feature *The Ladies' Man* and as a member of the court martial board in 1954's *The Caine Mutiny*).

Other roles throughout the years included *Back to Bataan* (1945), *Return of the Bad Men* (1948), *Francis Goes to the Races* (1951), *Hopalong Cassidy* (1953), *Ramar of the Jungle* (1953-1954), *Rocky Jones, Space Ranger* (1954), *Francis in the Navy* (1955), *Commando Cody: Sky Marshal of the Universe* (1955), *The Fastest Gun Alive* (1956), *The Ten Commandments* (1956), *Showdown at Abilene* (1956), *Colt .45* (1957-1958), *Wanted: Dead or Alive* (1958), *Posse from Hell* (1961) with Audie Murphy, *Fantastic Voyage* (1966), *40 Guns to Apache Pass* (1967) again with Audie Murphy, *Then Came Bronson* (1969), and *Which Way to the Front?* (1970).

Kenneth MacDonald died at age 70 of a brain tumor in Woodland Hills, California on May 5, 1972. He was buried in Forest Lawn - Hollywood Hills Cemetery.

David Macklin

David Macklin with Audie Murphy in *Gunpoint*

David Macklin was born March 24, 1946 in Greenhills, Cincinnati. At the age of 11, while in the Greenhills Elementary School, David was cast in his first play, portraying a 70 year old school teacher. The experience made an indelible mark and David knew that he wanted to be an actor. He felt it so strongly that he wore his costume home after the performance, and announced that he was never taking off his make-up. His folks won out on these minor points, but he never lost any of his desire for acting.

He was enrolled in the Walter Eyre Theatrical School in Cincinnati; his first performance there was the famous soliloquy from *Hamlet*. For the next six years he played many roles in local theater, school plays and on TV. During his high school years he played a lead in every play, mostly character roles. He also appeared at the Cincinnati Summer Theater, Cincinnati; Cherry County Theater, Michigan; and the Pioneer Playhouse in Danville, Kentucky.

It was from a local TV show for the Community Chest, in which he played an emotionally disturbed boy at odds with his family and society, that he was noticed by Hollywood. This TV film *Escape from the Cage* was shown on National Educational Television and was brought to the attention of Producer Henry King at 20th Century Fox Studios. With encouragement from Mr. King, he went to Hollywood.

Through his first agency, The Jean Haliburton Agency, he did a modeling commercial for Dupont. He then received his SAG card and his first starring role on *The Real McCoys* (1959). This was soon followed by his role as Todd Grayson, the kid who came west to kill Ben Cartwright in *Bonanza* (1960).

Other roles included *Hawaiian Eye* (1961), *The Pigeon That Took Rome* (1962), *Twilight Zone* (1963), *Gunsmoke* (1964), *Harris Against the World* (1964-1965), *Perry Mason* (1963-1965), *Gunpoint* (1966) with Audie Murphy, *The Munsters* (1966), *The Fugitive* (1965-1967), *Tammy and the Millionaire* (1967), *The F.B.I.* (1965-1970), *Welcome to Arrow Beach* (1974), *Barbary Coast* (1975), *Midway* (1976), *The Silent Lovers* (1980), and *In Plain Sight* (2008).

His father is the painter and ceramist Clement Mortashed. His mother Jean also wrote, painted, and made pottery. His brother Clement Mortahsed, Jr. is a psychiatrist in Southern California.

David is a collector of holograms, ancient Egyptian artifacts and Sherlock Holmes-related memorabilia. His hobbies are tennis, golf, bowling, pool, pinball, and slot machines.

George Macready

George Peabody Macready, Jr. was born in Providence, Rhode Island, August 29, 1899, and was an American stage, film, and television actor often cast in roles as polished villains. He graduated from Classical High School and, in 1921, from Brown University, where he was a member of Delta Phi fraternity and won a letter as the football team manager. While in college, Macready was injured in an accident in a Model T Ford. He sustained a permanent scar on his right cheek, having been thrust through the windshield while traveling on an icy road when the vehicle skidded and hit a telephone pole. The injury, along with his high brow and perfect diction, gave Macready the Gothic look of an authoritarian or villainous character. Macready was stitched up by a veterinarian, but he caught scarlet fever during the ordeal.

Macready first worked in a bank in Providence and was then briefly a newspaperman in New York City before he turned to stage acting. He claimed to have been descended from the 19th century Shakespearean actor William Charles Macready. He made his Broadway debut in 1926 in *The Scarlet Letter*. Through 1958, he appeared in fifteen plays, both drama and comedy, including *The Barrett's of Wimpole Street*, based on the family of the English poet Elizabeth Barrett Browning.

Macready's penchant for acting was spurred in part by the director Richard Boleslawski. His Shakespearean stage credits include Benedick in *Much Ado About Nothing* (1927), Malcolm in *MacBeth* (1928), and Paris in *Romeo and Juliet* (1934). On film, he played Marallus in the 1953 film adaptation of Shakespeare's *Julius Caesar*. He also played Prince Ernst in the original stage version of *Victoria Regina* (1936), starring Helen Hayes.

His first film was *Commandos Strike at Dawn* in 1942, featuring Paul Muni. As Ballin Mundson in *Gilda* (1946), Macready is part of a deadly love triangle with the characters played by co-stars Rita Hayworth and Glenn Ford. He would again play opposite Ford several years later in the post-war adventure *The Green Glove* (1952). Stanley Kubrick's anti-war film, *Paths of Glory* (1957), provided his other great role, self-serving French World War I General Paul Mireau, who is brought down by Kirk Douglas's character, Colonel Dax. He had worked with Douglas previously in *Detective Story* (1951) and later he appeared with Douglas again in John Frankenheimer's *Seven Days in May* (1964).

Another notable role was in *Beyond Glory* (1948) with Audie Murphy and Alan Ladd.

He also appeared in many television series, including *Biff Baker, U.S.A.* (1953), *The United States Steel Hour* (1954-1955), *Alfred Hitchcock Presents* (1955-1957), *Gunsmoke* (1958), *Wanted: Dead or Alive* (1958), *Have Gun - Will Travel* (1960), *Perry Mason* (1958-1963), *Twilight Zone* (1964), *The Outer Limits* (1964), *Get Smart* (1965), *Rod Serling's Night Gallery* (1969), *Count Yorga, Vampire* (1970), and *The Return of Count Yorga* (1971).

In the 1960s, Macready appeared for three years in the role of Martin Peyton in the ABC series *Peyton Place* (1965-1968), the first prime-time soap opera on American television, with Dorothy Malone in the title role of Constance MacKenzie.

One of Macready's most effective film roles was also one of his last - the role of United States Secretary of State Cordell Hull in the 1970 film *Tora! Tora! Tora!*, a painstakingly accurate depiction of the events leading up to the Japanese attack on Pearl Harbour.

A cultured and expert art collector, he and his good friend, fellow-actor Vincent Price, were partners in a Beverly Hills art gallery in the 1940s. They later closed it as their acting careers mushroomed.

The veteran actor is father of actor/producer Michael Macready and the grandfather of the gymnast John Macready.

Macready died from emphysema in July 2, 1973, and he was among entertainers who donated their bodies to a medical school, joining Walter Pidgeon, Bobby Darin, Butterfly McQueen, and Spring Byington.

Guy Madison

Guy Madison was born Robert Ozell Moseley in Pumpkin Center, California January 19, 1922, and was an American film and television actor. Madison attended Bakersfield College, for two years and then worked briefly as a telephone lineman before joining the United States Coast Guard in 1942. In 1944, while visiting Hollywood on leave from the U.S. Coast Guard, Madison's boyish good looks and physique caught the eye of Henry Willson, the head of talent at David O. Selznick's newly formed Vanguard Pictures. Willson was widely known for his stable of good-looking, marginally talented actors with unusual names he bestowed upon them, and he immediately cast the rechristened Madison in a bit part in Selznick's *Since You Went Away*. Following the film's release in 1944, the studio received thousands of letters from fans wanting to know more about him.

Madison was signed by RKO Pictures in 1946 and began appearing in romantic comedies and dramas. Some of his early films included *Till the End of Time* (1946), *Texas, Brooklyn & Heaven* (1948) with Audie Murphy, *Massacre River* (1949), and *Drums in the Deep South* (1951).

In 1951, television came to the rescue of his faltering career when he was cast in *The Adventures of Wild Bill Hickok* (1951-1958), which ran for seven years.

Following his television series, he appeared in several more films such as *Jet Over the Atlantic* (1959), *Slave of Rome* (1959), and *Women of Devil's Island* (1962) before leaving for Europe, where he found greater success in spaghetti westerns.

He later returned to Hollywood and appeared in *Won Ton Ton: The Dog Who Saved Hollywood* (1976), *Fantasy Island* (1979), *Crossbow* (1987-1988), *Red River* (1988), and *Crossbow: The Movie* (1989).

Madison was married to actresses Gail Russell (1949–1954) and Sheila Connolly (1954–1964). Both marriages ended in divorce. He had three daughters, Bridget Catherine (born April 26, 1955), Erin Patricia (born July 21, 1956), and Dolly Ann (born September 10, 1957).

Madison died February 6, 1996, from emphysema at the age of 74 and was buried at Forest Lawn Cemetery in Cathedral City, California. For his contribution to the television industry, Guy Madison has a star on the Hollywood Walk of Fame at 6331 Hollywood Boulevard.

Moyna Macgill

Moyna Macgill was born Charlotte Lillian McIldowie December 10, 1895, in Belfast, Ireland. She was the mother of actress Angela Lansbury, with whom she appeared in *The Picture of Dorian Gray* (1945). She was the daughter of a wealthy solicitor who also worked as a director of the Belfast Opera, a position that sparked her interest in theatrics. She was still a teen when she was noticed riding the London Underground by director George Pearson, who cast her in several of his films. In 1918, she made her stage debut in the play *Love in a Cottage* at the West End's Globe Theatre.

Encouraged by Gerald du Maurier to change her name to Moyna Macgill (which invariably was misspelled as "MacGill" or "McGill", and on at least one occasion, the film *Texas, Brooklyn and Heaven*, as "Magill"), she became a leading actress of the day, appearing in light comedies, melodramas, and classics opposite Herbert Marshall, John Gielgud, and Basil Rathbone, among others.

Twenty-six-year old Macgill was married with a three-year-old daughter, Isolde (who later married Sir Peter Ustinov), when she became involved romantically with Edgar Lansbury, a socialist politician, who was son of the well-known popular Labour politician George Lansbury. Her husband, actor Reginald Denham, named Lansbury as co-respondent when he filed for divorce. A year after it was finalized, Macgill and Lansbury married and with Isolde settled into a garden flat in London's Regent's Park.

Macgill temporarily set aside her career following the birth of daughter Angela and twin sons Edgar, Jr., and Bruce (both went on to become Broadway producers, but Bruce is better known for his work on television, such as the series *The Wild Wild West*, *Mission: Impossible*, and his sister's *Murder She Wrote*), although music and dance were prevalent in their upbringing. When they moved into a larger house in suburban Mill Hill, she turned their home into a salon for actors, writers, directors, musicians, and artists, all of whom left an impression on young Angela and were instrumental in directing her interests towards acting.

Angela Lansbury would become a popular stage and film actress in her own right, starring in her own television series in the 1980s, after a string of successful musicals spanning between the 1940s and 1960s.

In 1935, Edgar Lansbury died of stomach cancer, a year after publishing a biography of his father George. Macgill began an affair with Scotsman Leckie Forbes, a former colonel with the British Army in India. The two moved their respective families to a house in Hampstead, but Macgill soon discovered Forbes' military career had made him a staunch disciplinarian who ruled the household like a tyrant. When the opportunity to take her children to America presented itself just prior to The Blitz, she spirited them away under cover of night. She never spoke to Forbes again.

In New York City, Macgill was unable to work in movies or on the stage, not having a work visa, and she took to presenting dramatic readings at private schools for income. In 1942, she was invited to join a troupe that was rehearsing Noël Coward's *Tonight at 8:30* for a touring production designed to raise funds for the Royal Canadian Air Force. She accepted, and when the company finished the run in Vancouver, she headed to Hollywood to seek work there. She soon sent for Angela, and eventually the twins and the family settled in Laurel Canyon.

Her career in Hollywood consisted largely of small character parts in films and on television. She appeared in thirty-four films and television programs from 1920 to 1964. Some of those credits include *Nothing Else Matters* (1920), *Miriam Rozella* (1924), *Pygmalion* (1938), *Jane Eyre* (1943), *The Uninvited* (1944), *National Velvet* (1944), *Black Beauty* (1946), the aforementioned *Texas, Brooklyn & Heaven* (1948) with Audie Murphy, *Bride of the Gorilla* (1951), *Studio One in Hollywood* (1956), *Adventures in Paradise* (1959), *Twilight Zone* (1962), *My Favorite Martian* (1964), *The Unsinkable Molly Brown* (1964), and *My Fair Lady* (1964). Among her more notable film credits are *Frenchman's Creek* (1944) and *The Picture of Dorian Gray* (1945), (which co-starred her daughter Angela).

She died of throat cancer November 25, 1975 in Los Angeles, just a few weeks shy of her 80th birthday.

Colin Male

Colin Male was born August 8, 1925, and was an American actor. Most people don't recognize his name or his face but may recognize his voice. He is the voice-over announcer at the opening of *The Andy Griffith Show* (1960-1968). He appeared on the show as a game warden in the fifth season episode "Andy and Helen Have Their Day" (1964).

In all, he appeared in twenty-two films and television programs from 1951 to 1989. Some of those credits were *This Is Music* (1951), *Divorce Court* (1957), *Whispering Smith* (1961) with Audie Murphy, *The Bill Dana Show* (1963-1964), *The Dick Van Dyke Show* (1965), *Who's Minding the Mint?* (1967), *Chain Gang Women* (1971), *Gunsmoke* (1972), *Mission: Impossible* (1972), *The Black Gestapo* (1975), *Police Story* (1976), *The Kentucky Fried Movie* (1977), *Summer Rental* (1985), and *B.L. Stryker* (1989).

He died October 23, 1996, at age 71 in Seminole, Florida.

Peggy Maley

Audie Murphy with Peggy Maley in *The Gunrunners*

Peggy Maley was born June Maley June 8 1926, in Pottsville, Pennsylvania, and is an actress who appeared in numerous movies and television programs. In 1942 she was crowned Miss Atlantic City.

Some of her early credits include *Thirty Seconds Over Tokyo* (1944), *Down to Earth* (1947), and *Ramar of the Jungle* (1953).

She then delivered the famous feeder line to Marlon Brando in the film *The Wild One* (1953): "Hey, Johnny, what are you rebelling against?"

More roles followed like *Gypsy Colt* (1954), *I Died a Thousand Times* (1955), *The Guns of Fort Petticoat* (1957) with Audie Murphy, *Live Fast, Die Young* (1958), *The Gun Runners* (1958) again with Audie Murphy, *Tarawa Beachhead* (1958), *Wanted: Dead or Alive* (1959), *Richard Diamond, Private Detective* (1958-1959), *The Untouchables* (1960), and *Lock Up* (1960).

Luz Márquez

Luz Marquez with Audie Murphy in *The Texican*

Luz Márquez was born María de la O Martínez García Soler December 12, 1935, in Madrid, Spain. She appeared in thirty-seven films and television programs from 1956 to 1966, most of them foreign.

Some of those credits include *Marisa* (1957), *Red Cross Girls* (1958), and her last role in *The Texican* (1966) with Audie Murphy.

Gregg Martell

Gregg Martell was born Henry George Ross May 23, 1918, in Chicago, Illinois. Gregg Martell was a veteran from World War II. He started in films in 1947 with *Kiss of Death*. Many other roles followed through 1970 like *Ma and Pa Kettle Go to Town* (1950), *Sierra* (1950) with Audie Murphy, *Winchester '73* (1950), *Stars and Stripes Forever* (1952), *Big House, U.S.A.* (1955), *Somebody Up There Likes Me* (1956), *Between Heaven and Hell* (1956), *Gunfight at the O.K. Corral* (1957), *Space Master X-7* (1958), *Return of the Fly* (1959), *Dinosaurus!* (1960), *The Three Stooges Meet Hercules* (1962), *The Cincinnati Kid* (1965), *The Addams Family* (1965), *The Wild Wild West* (1965-1968), *Mission: Impossible* (1968), and *The Young Country* (1970).

After a long career as a character actor in films and television, he later became a health food wholesaler and real estate broker.

He died September 22, 2005 at age 87 in Los Angeles, California. He was preceded in death by his wife and business partner - Vivian. He was admired for his bravely fought fight against "Parkinson's Disease".

Dewey Martin

Dewey Martin with Audie Murphy in *Kansas Raiders*

Dewey Martin was born December 8, 1923, in Katemcy, Texas. His film debut was an uncredited part in *Knock on Any Door* (1949). He also appeared in *The Thing from Another World* (1951), co-starred with Kirk Douglas in *The Big Sky* (1952), played younger brother of Humphrey Bogart in *The Desperate Hours* (1955), and was featured opposite Dean Martin in his first post-Martin and Lewis film, the notorious flop *Ten Thousand Bedrooms* (1957).

Other film roles included a role as James Younger in *Kansas Raiders* (1950) with Audie Murphy, *The Proud and Profane* (1956), *The Longest Day* (1962), *Savage Sam* (1963), *Flight to Fury* (1964), and *Seven Alone* (1974).

He worked extensively in television as well, including *The Twilight Zone* (1960) episode "I Shot an Arrow Into the Air" and *The Outer Limits* (1965) episode "The Premonition", co-written by Ib Melchior. Martin also played Daniel Boone on four 1960 episodes of *Walt Disney's The Wonderful World of Color*, an unsuccessful attempt to duplicate the national craze which had ensued when Fess Parker had portrayed Davy Crockett on the same series several years earlier. Other television roles included *I Spy* (1966), *Lassie* (1967), *Hawaii Five-O* (1970), *Mannix* (1970-1971), *Mission: Impossible* (1972), *The F.B.I.* (1973), *Joe Forrester* (1975), and *Police Story* (1978).

Martin was married to singer Peggy Lee for two years; they divorced.

Strother Martin

Audie Murphy with Strother Martin in *The Wild and the Innocent*

Strother Martin was born Strother Martin, Jr. in Kokomo, Indiana, March 26, 1919, and was an American actor in numerous films and television programs. Martin is perhaps best known as the prison "captain" in the 1967 film *Cool Hand Luke*, in which he uttered the line, "What we've got here is...failure to communicate".

As a child, he excelled at swimming and diving, and got the nickname "T-Bone Martin" from his diving expertise. At seventeen, he won the National Junior Springboard Diving Championship. He served as a swimming instructor in the U.S. Navy during World War II and was a member of the diving team at the University of Michigan. He entered the adult National Springboard Diving competition in hopes of gaining a berth on the U.S. Olympic team, but finished third in the competition.

After the war, Martin moved to Los Angeles and worked as a swimming instructor and as a swimming extra in water scenes in films, eventually earning bit roles in a number of pictures like *The Asphalt Jungle* (1950), *The Red Badge of Courage* (1951) with Audie Murphy, *Androcles and the Lion* (1952), and *A Star Is Born* (1954).

He quickly became a frequent fixture in small character roles in movies and television through the 1950s, having appeared in such programs as *Frontier* (1951) on NBC and the syndicated American Civil War drama *Gray Ghost* (1957). He appeared in the first Brian Keith series, *Crusader* (1956), a Cold War drama. He guest starred as a circus tight rope walker in one of the 1957 *Have Gun Will Travel* TV westerns. He guest starred in 1958 as a henpecked soldier in an episode of the syndicated *Boots and Saddles*. In 1960, Martin guest starred in James Whitmore's crime drama *The Law and Mr. Jones* on ABC. In 1966, he appeared twice as "Cousin Fletch" in the short-lived ABC comedy western *The Rounders*, with Ron Hayes, Patrick Wayne, and Chill Wills.

Martin's distinctive, reedy voice and menacing demeanor made him ideal for villainous roles in many of the best-known Westerns of the 1960s and 1970s, including *The Horse Soldiers* (1959) and *The Man Who Shot Liberty Valance* (1962). By the late 1960s, Martin was almost as well-known a figure as many top-billed stars.

Martin appeared in all three of the classic Westerns released in 1969: Sam Peckinpah's *The Wild Bunch* (as Coffer, a bloodthirsty bounty hunter); George Roy Hill's *Butch Cassidy and the Sundance Kid* (as Percy Garris, the "colorful" Bolivian mine boss who hires the two title characters); and Henry Hathaway's *True Grit* (as Colonel Stonehill, a horse dealer). He frequently acted alongside L. Q. Jones, who in real life was one of his closest friends.

Though he usually appeared in supporting roles, he had major parts in *Hannie Caulder*, *The Brotherhood of Satan* (both 1971), *Pocket Money* (1972) with Paul Newman and Lee Marvin, and *SSSSSSS* (1973). Martin later appeared in another George Roy Hill film, *Slap Shot* (1977), again with Paul Newman, as the cheap general manager of the Charlestown Chiefs hockey club.

He appeared six times each with both John Wayne and Paul Newman. He can also be seen in Cheech and Chong's *Up in Smoke* (1978) as Arnold Stoner, the father of Tommy Chong's character Anthony.

Martin made many guest appearances on *Gunsmoke* (1956-1974), including the two-part episode "Island in the Desert", in which he portrayed a crazy desert hermit named Ben Snow. On a *Gilligan's Island* (1967) episode, Martin played a man living supposedly alone on the island for a radio show contest. He also starred in a two-part *The Rockford Files* 1977 episode as T.T. Flowers, an episode that took on urban invasion and the environment.

Other memorable roles over the years included two more appearances with Audie Murphy in *The Wild and the Innocent* (1959) and *Showdown* (1963). Other roles included twenty-nine episodes as Aaron Donager in *Hotel de Paree* (1959-1960), *Twilight Zone* (1961), *The Fugitive* (1964), *Nevada Smith* (1966), *The Ballad of Cable Hogue* (1970), *The Great Scout & Cathouse Thursday* (1976), *Baretta* (1975-1977), *The End* (1978), *The Villain* (1979), and *Hotwire* (1980).

One of his last acting jobs was as host of *Saturday Night Live* on April 19, 1980. In one of the skits, Martin played the strict owner of a French Language camp for children - a role based on his role as the prison captain from the film, *Cool Hand Luke*. He even paraphrased his most famous line from the film - "What we have here is failure to communicate BI-LINGUALLY!" In another, he played a terminally ill man who videotaped his last will and testament. This episode was supposed to be rerun during the summer of 1980, but was pulled and replaced with another episode due to his death.

Martin was married to Helen Meisels-Martin from 1967 until his death. He died of a heart attack August 1, 1980, at age 61 in Thousand Oaks, California. His widow, who was ten years his senior died in 1997, and her ashes were interred with Martin's in Court of Remembrance, Columbarium of Radiant Dawn, at Hollywood Hills Forest Lawn, in North Hollywood, California.

Lee Marvin

Lee Marvin was born in New York City, New York, February 19, 1924, and was an American film actor. Known for his gravelly voice, white hair and 6 ft 2 in stature, Marvin at first did supporting roles, mostly villains, soldiers, and other hardboiled characters, but after winning an Academy Award for Best Actor for his dual roles in *Cat Ballou* (1965), he landed more heroic and sympathetic leading roles.

He was the son of Lamont Waltman Marvin, an advertising executive and the head of the New York and New England Apple Institute, and his wife Courtenay Washington (née Davidge), a fashion writer and beauty consultant. He was named in honor of Confederate General Robert E. Lee, who was his first cousin, four times removed. His father was a direct descendant of Matthew Marvin, Sr., who emigrated from Great Bentley, Essex, England in 1635 and helped found Hartford, Connecticut.

Marvin studied violin when he was young. As a teenager, Marvin spent weekends and spare time hunting deer, puma, wild turkey, and bobwhite in the wilds of the then-uncharted Everglades. He attended St. Leo College Preparatory School in St. Leo, Florida.

Marvin left school to join the United States Marine Corps, serving as a Scout Sniper in the 4th Marine Division. He was wounded in action during the WWII Battle of Saipan, in the assault on Mount Tapochau, during which most of his company ("I" Company, 24th Marines, 4th Marine Division) were killed. Marvin's wound (in the buttocks) was from machine gun fire, which severed his sciatic nerve. He was awarded the Purple Heart and was given a medical discharge with the rank of Private First Class.

After the war, while working as a plumber's assistant at a local community theatre in Upstate New York, Marvin was asked to replace an actor who had fallen ill during rehearsals. He then began an amateur Off-Broadway acting career in New York City and served as an understudy in Broadway productions.

In 1950, Marvin moved to Hollywood. He found work in supporting roles, and from the beginning was cast in various war films. As a decorated combat veteran, Marvin was a natural in war dramas, where he frequently assisted the director and other actors in realistically portraying infantry movement, arranging costumes, and the use of firearms. His debut was in *You're in the Navy Now* (1951), and in 1952 he appeared in several films, including Don Siegel's *Duel at Silver Creek* with Audie Murphy, *Hangman's Knot*, and the war drama *Eight Iron Men*. He played Gloria Grahame's vicious boyfriend in Fritz Lang's *The Big Heat* (1953). Marvin had a small but memorable role in *The Wild One* (1953) opposite Marlon Brando, followed by *Seminole* (1953) and *Gun Fury* (1953). He had a substantially more important part as Hector, the small town hood in *Bad Day at Black Rock* (1955) with Spencer Tracy.

During the mid-1950s, Marvin gradually began playing more important roles. He starred in *Attack* (1956), had a good supporting role in the Western *Seven Men from Now* (1956), and starred in *The Missouri Traveler* (1958) but it took over one hundred episodes as Chicago cop Frank Ballinger in the successful 1957-1960 television series *M Squad* to actually give him name recognition. One critic described the show as "a hyped-up, violent *Dragnet*... with a hard-as-nails Marvin" playing a tough police lieutenant. Marvin received the role after guest-starring in a memorable *Dragnet* (1953) episode as a serial killer.

He had a memorable role in the episode "The Joke's on Me" of *G.E. True Theater* (1961). He portrayed a stand-up comic with Bud Abbott as his manager. This was Bud Abbott's last live action role.

Another great television role was as Sam 'Steel' Kelly in the robot boxing episode "Steel" of *Twilight Zone* (1963) which was remade in 2011 as *Real Steel* with Hugh Jackman in Marvin's role.

In the 1960s, Marvin was given prominent supporting roles in such films as *The Comancheros* (1961), John Ford's *The Man Who Shot Liberty Valance* (1962), and *Donovan's Reef* (1963), all starring John Wayne, with Marvin's roles getting larger with each film. As the vicious Liberty Valance, Marvin played his first title role and held his own with two of the screen's biggest stars (Wayne and James Stewart).

For director Don Siegel, Marvin appeared in *The Killers* (1964) playing an efficient professional assassin alongside Clu Gulager. *The Killers* was also the first film in which Marvin received top billing and the only time Ronald Reagan played a villain, rendering an extremely convincing performance in his last movie role before entering politics.

Marvin won the 1965 Academy Award for Best Actor for his comic role in the offbeat Western *Cat Ballou* starring Jane Fonda. He also won the Silver Bear for Best Actor at the 15th Berlin International Film Festival.

Next Marvin performed in the hit Western *The Professionals* (1966), in which he played the leader of a small band of skilled mercenaries (Burt Lancaster, Robert Ryan, and Woody Strode) rescuing a kidnap victim (Claudia Cardinale) shortly after the Mexican Revolution. He followed that film with the hugely successful World War II epic *The Dirty Dozen* (1967) in which top-billed Marvin again portrayed an intrepid commander of a colorful group (future stars John Cassavetes, Charles Bronson, Telly Savalas, Jim Brown, and Donald Sutherland) performing an almost impossible mission.

In the wake of these two films and after having received an Oscar, Marvin was a huge star given enormous control over his next film. In *Point Blank* (1967), an influential film for director John Boorman, he portrayed a hard-nosed criminal bent on revenge. Marvin, who had selected Boorman himself for the director's slot, had a central role in the film's development, plot line, and staging. In 1968, Marvin also appeared in another Boorman film, the critically acclaimed but commercially unsuccessful World War II character study *Hell in the Pacific*, also starring famed Japanese actor Toshirō Mifune. Marvin was originally cast as Pike Bishop (later played by William Holden) in *The Wild Bunch* (1969), but fell out with director Sam Peckinpah and pulled out in order to star in the Western musical *Paint Your Wagon* (1969), in which he was top-billed over a singing Clint Eastwood. Despite his limited singing ability, he had a hit song with "Wand'rin' Star". By this time he was getting paid a million dollars per film.

Marvin had a much greater variety of roles in the 1970s and 1980s, with fewer 'bad-guy' roles than in earlier years. His 1970s films included *Monte Walsh* (1970) with Jeanne Moreau, the violent *Prime Cut* (1972) with Gene Hackman, *Pocket Money* (1972) with Paul Newman, *Emperor of the North Pole* (1973) opposite Ernest Borgnine, as Hickey in *The Iceman Cometh* (1973) with Fredric March and Robert Ryan, *The Spikes Gang* (1974) with Noah Beery, Jr., *The Klansman* (1974) with Richard Burton, *Shout at the Devil* (1976) with Roger Moore, *The Great Scout and Cathouse Thursday* (1976) with Oliver Reed, and *Avalanche Express* (1978) with Robert Shaw.

Marvin was offered the role of Quint in *Jaws* (1975) but declined, stating "What would I tell my fishing friends who'd see me come off a hero against a dummy shark?". Marvin's immediately-previous co-star Robert Shaw accepted the part, which gave Shaw his most prominent role and vaulted the supporting player into mainstream leading man status.

Marvin's last big role was in Samuel Fuller's *The Big Red One* (1980), a war film based on Fuller's own war experiences. His remaining films were *Death Hunt* (1981) with Charles Bronson, *Gorky Park* (1983), *Dog Day* (1984), and *The Dirty Dozen: The Next Mission* (1985; a sequel with Marvin, Ernest Borgnine, and Richard Jaeckel picking up where they'd left off despite being eighteen years older); his final appearance was as the head of *The Delta Force* (1986) with Chuck Norris.

A father of four, Marvin was married twice. His first marriage to Betty Ebeling began in February 1951 and ended in divorce on January 5, 1967; during this time his hobbies included sport fishing off the Baja California coast and duck hunting along the Mexican border near Mexicali. He and Ebeling had a son, Christopher (b. 1952), and three daughters: Courtenay (b. 1954), Cynthia (b. 1956) and Claudia (b. 1958).

He was married to Pamela Feeley (who had been his girlfriend in Woodstock, New York a quarter century earlier) from October 18, 1970 until his death.

During the 1970s, Marvin resided off and on in Woodstock, caring for his dying father, and would make regular trips to Cairns, Australia to engage in marlin fishing. In 1975 Marvin and Pamela moved to Tucson, where he lived until his death.

Marvin was a heavy smoker from an early age. In December 1986, Marvin underwent intestinal surgery after suffering abdominal pains while at his ranch outside Tucson. Doctors said then that there was an inflammation of the colon, but that no malignancy was found. He died of a heart attack on August 29, 1987, after being hospitalized for more than two weeks because of "a run-down condition related to the flu". He is interred at Arlington National Cemetery where his headstone reads "Lee Marvin, PFC US Marine Corps, World War II".

Ron Masak

Ron Masak was born July 1, 1936, and is an American actor. He began as a stage performer, and much of his work is in theater. Ron Masak (MAY-SACK) was born in Chicago, Illinois, the son of a salesman/musician (Floyd L.), and a mother (Mildred), who was a merchandise buyer. Ron attended Chicago City College, and studied theater at both the CCC and the Drama Guild. He made his acting debut with the Drama Guild in Chicago in *Stalag 17* in 1954.

During the course of his career, he has starred in twenty-five feature films and guest starred in some 350 television shows. Perhaps the most beloved character, and the one for which he is most famous, is that of Sheriff Mort Metzger on the hit television series, *Murder, She Wrote* (1985-1996). Given that he has also been seen and heard in hundreds of television and radio commercials (he was named, "King of Commercials" by columnist James Bacon), it is no wonder that he is often introduced as one of America's most familiar faces.

Trained in the classics, Ron has proved to be equally at home on stage or screen with Shakespeare or slapstick. He has played everything from Stanley in *Streetcar Named Desire* and Sakini in *Teahouse of the August Moon* to Will Stockdale in *No Time For Sergeants* and Antony in *Julius Caesar*. As more proof of his versatility, in one production of *Mr. Roberts,* he played Ensign Pulver and in another he portrayed Mr. Roberts himself.

In his hometown of Chicago, Ron was resident leading man at The Candlelight Dinner Playhouse from 1962 to 1966, never missing a single performance. As with many performers, it was the Army that provided Ron with a platform from which to display his all-around talents for performing, writing and directing. In 1960-61, Ron toured the world doing vocal impressions in the all-Army show entitled *Rolling Along*. Once again, he never missed a show.

Never one to be pigeonholed, Ron continued to demonstrate his incredible range of talent in such films as *Ice Station Zebra* (1968), *Daddy's Gone A-Hunting* (1969), *Tora! Tora! Tora!* (1970), *Evel Knievel* (1971), Audie Murphy's last film *A Time For Dying* (1969), *Harper Valley PTA* (1978), *Cops & Roberts* (1995), and *The Man From Clover Grove* (1975). It was during *Clover Grove* that Ron added credits as a lyric writer, as he wrote and sang the title song.

He played his first big screen villain starring in *No Code of Conduct* (1998).

Among his many television roles, he starred as Charley Wilson in his own summer series, *Love Thy Neighbor* (1973), Count Dracula on *The Monkees* (1968) and was submitted for an Emmy nomination for one of his ten starring roles on *Police Story* (1975-1978). He's also been seen on *Magnum P.I.* (1981), *Webster* (1986-1988), and *Columbo* (1998).

Other roles over the years include *Twilight Zone* (1960), *Get Smart* (1968), *I Dream of Jeannie* (1968-1969), *Bewitched* (1969-1970), *Owen Marshall: Counselor at Law* (1971-1972), *Land of the Lost* (1974), *The Aliens Are Coming* (1980), *Meatballs and Spaghetti* (1982), *The Yellow Rose* (1984), *They Came from Outer Space* (1991), *American Dragon: Jake Long* (2006), *My Trip to the Dark Side* (2011), and *My Trip Back to the Dark Side* (2012).

Ron's variety work includes emceeing hundreds of shows for, among others, Kenny Rogers, Diahann Carroll, Alabama, Billy Crystal, The Steve Garvey Classics, Tony Orlando, The Lennon Sisters, Trini Lopez, Connie Stevens, Billy Davis and Marilyn McCoo, The Michael Landon Classics, and The Beau Bridges Classics.

Ron is also considered to be the most famous salesman since Willy Loman, as he starred in the four most successful sales motivational films of all time: *Second Effort* with Vince Lombardi, *Time Management* with James Whitmore, *How to Control Your Time* with Burgess Meredith and *Ya Gotta Believe* with Tommy Lasorda, which Ron wrote and directed.

He is a sought after motivational speaker. He has traveled all over the country as spokesman for a major brewing company and for fifteen years was the voice of the Vlasic Pickle stork. Ron played Lou Costello in commercials for Bran News, McDonald's, and Tropicana Orange Juice.

Ron's private life is also one of varied interests and talents, devoting time and energy working with many charities. For eight years he was the LA host for the *Jerry Lewis Telethon* and recipient of MDA's first Humanitarian of the Year Award. He has served as field announcer for the Special Olympics in support of retarded children, and was named Man of the Year by Volunteers Assisting Cancer Stricken Families. In addition, he contributes much time to work with Multiple Sclerosis, Cystic Fibrosis, Breast Cancer Awareness, and hosts charity golf tournaments for among others, Childhelp USA, for whom he is a worldwide ambassador.

Relaxation for Ron includes time spent with friends on the golf course, tennis court, baseball diamond, ski slopes, or at Dodger Stadium. A fine athlete, Ron was once offered a professional baseball contract with The Chicago White Sox.

Ron's favorite role remains that of husband to his lovely wife Kay, and father to their six children as well as grandfather to their six grandchildren. They reside in Tarzana, California, where Ron has served for 35 years as, of course, its honorary sheriff.

Ron is interviewed in 1994 in the *Abbott and Costello Quarterly* number 21 in a three-page article with a picture of him dressed as Lou Costello for the McDonald's commercial. In the article he said if any fan wanted to write to him, he would respond 'personally'. I did and he did. We corresponded back and forth for awhile, snail mail back then. His letters were on *Murder, She Wrote* stationary, as he was right in the middle of his years as the Sheriff. We discussed Audie Murphy and he told me he was in *A Time for Dying* with Audie, but had never seen the finished film, as it had never been released in the United States. I let him know I had a copy and sent it to him. He said it sure brought back a lot of memories.

We must have discussed my profession and he sent me the autographed picture above with the caption 'David- Keep the Peace Always, Ron Masak'.

Ron Masak completed his autobiography in 2010 titled *I've Met All My Heroes from A to Z*. Page 110 is devoted to Audie Murphy, and Ron describes Audie as 'A true gentleman'.

Bill Mauldin

Bill Mauldin with Audie Murphy in *The Red Badge of Courage*

William Henry "Bill" Mauldin was born in Mountain Park, New Mexico, October 29, 1921, and was a two-time Pulitzer Prize-winning editorial cartoonist from the United States. He was most famous for his World War II cartoons depicting American soldiers, as represented by the archetypal characters *"Willie and Joe"*, two weary and bedraggled infantry troopers who stoically endure the difficulties and dangers of duty in the field. These cartoons were broadly published and distributed in the American army abroad and in the United States.

His grandfather had been a civilian cavalry scout in the Apache Wars and his father was an artilleryman in World War I. After growing up there and in Phoenix, Arizona, Mauldin took courses at the Chicago Academy of Fine Arts under the tutoring of Ruth VanSickle Ford. While in Chicago, Mauldin met Will Lang Jr. and became fast friends with him. Mauldin entered the US Army via the Arizona National Guard in 1940.

While in the 45th Infantry Division, Mauldin volunteered to work for the unit's newspaper, drawing cartoons about regular soldiers or "dogfaces". Eventually he created two cartoon infantrymen, Willie (who was modeled after his comrade and friend Irving Richtel) and Joe, who became synonymous with the average American GI.

During July 1943, Mauldin's cartoon work continued when, as a sergeant of the 45th Division's press corps, he landed with the division in the invasion of Sicily and later in the Italian campaign Mauldin began working for *Stars and Stripes*, the American soldiers' newspaper; as well as the 45th Division News, until he was officially transferred to the *Stars and Stripes* in February 1944. By March 1944, he was given his own jeep, in which he roamed the front, collecting material and producing six cartoons a week. His cartoons were viewed by soldiers throughout Europe during World War II, and were also published in the United States. The War Office supported their syndication, not only because they helped publicize the ground forces but also to show the grim and bitter side of war, which helped show that victory would not be easy. Willie was on the cover of *Time Magazine* in the June 18, 1945 issue, and Mauldin himself made the cover in the July 21, 1961 issue.

Those officers who had served in the army before the war were generally offended by Mauldin, who parodied the spit-shine and obedience-to-order-without-question view that was more easily maintained during that time of peace. General George Patton once summoned Mauldin to his office and threatened to "throw his ass in jail" for "spreading dissent", this after one of Mauldin's cartoons made fun of Patton's demand that all soldiers must be clean-shaven at all times, even in combat. But Dwight Eisenhower, Supreme Commander European Theater, told Patton to leave Mauldin alone, because he felt that Mauldin's cartoons gave the soldiers an outlet for their frustrations. Mauldin told an interviewer later, "I always admired Patton. Oh, sure, the stupid bastard was crazy. He was insane. He thought he was living in the Dark Ages. Soldiers were peasants to him. I didn't like that attitude, but I certainly respected his theories and the techniques he used to get his men out of their foxholes".

Mauldin's cartoons made him a hero to the common soldier. GIs often credited him with helping them to get through the rigors of the war. His credibility with the common soldier increased in September 1943, when he was wounded in the shoulder by a German mortar while visiting a machine gun crew near Monte Cassino. By the end of the war he also received the Army's Legion of Merit for his cartoons. Mauldin wanted to have Willie and Joe be killed on the last day of combat, but *Stars and Stripes* dissuaded him.

In 1945, at the age of 23, Mauldin won the Pulitzer Prize. The first collection of his work, *Up Front*, was a bestseller. The cartoons are interwoven with an impassioned telling of his observations of war.

After World War II, Mauldin turned to drawing political cartoons expressing a generally civil libertarian view associated with groups such as the American Civil Liberties Union. These were not well received by newspaper editors, who were hoping for more apolitical Willie and Joe cartoons. But Mauldin's attempt to carry Willie and Joe into civilian life was also unsuccessful, as documented in his memoirs, *Back Home*, in 1947.

He abandoned cartooning for a while, working as a film actor, freelance writer, and illustrator of articles and books, including one on the Korean War. He drew Willie and Joe only a few times afterwards: for the funerals of Omar Bradley and George C. Marshall, both of them considered "soldiers' generals"; for a *Life Magazine* article on the "New Army"; and to memorialize fellow cartoonist Milton Caniff.

Mauldin also appeared as an actor in the 1951 films *The Red Badge of Courage* (1951) with Audie Murphy and *Teresa* (1951) and as himself in the 1998 documentary *America in the '40s*. He also appeared in on-screen interviews in the Thames documentary *The World at War* (1974).

The films *Up Front* (1951) and *Back at the Front* (1952) were based on Mauldin's Willie and Joe characters; however, when Mauldin's suggestions were ignored in favor of making a slapstick comedy, he returned his advising fee; he said he had never seen the result.

In 1956, he ran unsuccessfully for the United States Congress as a Democrat in New York's 28th Congressional District. Mauldin had this to say about his run for Congress: "I jumped in with both feet and campaigned for seven or eight months. I found myself stumping around up in these rural districts and my own background did hurt there. A farmer knows a farmer when he sees one. So when I was talking about their problems I was a very sincere candidate, but when they would ask me questions that had to do with foreign policy or national policy, obviously I was pretty far to the left of the mainstream up there. Again, I'm an old Truman Democrat, I'm not that far left, but by their lives I was pretty far left".

In 1958, he returned to cartooning on the editorial pages of the *St. Louis Post-Dispatch*. The following year, he won a second Pulitzer Prize and the National Cartoonist Society Award for Editorial Cartooning. In 1961 he received their Reuben Award as well. In 1962 he moved to the *Chicago Sun-Times*. One of his most famous post-war cartoons appeared in Chicago in 1963, following the assassination of President John F. Kennedy. The cartoon shows the statue of Abraham Lincoln at the Lincoln Memorial, his head in his hands.

In 1959, he won the Pulitzer Prize again for a cartoon depicting *Doctor Zhivago* author Boris Pasternak in a Soviet GULAG with the caption "I won the Nobel Prize for literature. What was your crime?" In 1969, Mauldin was commissioned by the National Safety Council to illustrate the booklet on traffic safety, which the council published every year. These pamphlets were regularly issued without copyright, but for this issue it was pointed out that Mauldin's cartoons *were* under copyright even though the rest of the pamphlet was not.

Mauldin remained with the *Sun-Times* until his retirement in 1991. He was inducted into the St. Louis Walk of Fame on May 19, 1991. On September 19, 2001, Sergeant Major of the Army Jack L. Tilley presented Mauldin with a personal letter from Army Chief of Staff General Eric K. Shinseki, a hardbound book with notes from other senior Army leaders and several celebrities to include Walter Cronkite, Tom Brokaw and Tom Hanks. He also promoted Mauldin to the honorary rank of first sergeant.

In 1998, Mauldin drew "Willie and Joe" for publication one last time, as part of a Veterans Day strip for the popular comic, Peanuts. The creator of Peanuts and a World War II veteran himself, Charles M. Schulz, had long described Mauldin as his hero. He signed the strip *Schulz, and my Hero,* and then had Mauldin sign his name underneath.

Mauldin died on January 22, 2003, from complications of Alzheimer's disease and a bathtub scalding. He was buried in Arlington National Cemetery on January 29, 2003. Married three times, he was survived by seven children. His daughter Kaja had died of Non-Hodgkins Lymphoma in 2001.

In 2005, Mauldin was inducted into the Oklahoma Cartoonists Hall of Fame in Pauls Valley, Oklahoma by Michael Vance. The Oklahoma Cartoonists Collection, created by Vance, is located in the Toy and Action Figure Museum. On March 31, 2010, the United States Post Office released a first-class denomination ($0.44) postage stamp in Mauldin's honor depicting him with Willie & Joe.

Walter Matthau

Audie Murphy with Walter Mathau in *Ride a Crooked Trail*

Walter Matthau was born Walter John Matthow in New York City's Lower East Side on October 1, 1920, and was an American actor best known for his role as Oscar Madison in *The Odd Couple* (1968) and his frequent collaborations with *Odd Couple* star Jack Lemmon, as well as his role as Coach Buttermaker in the 1976 comedy *The Bad News Bears*. He won an Academy Award for his performance in the 1966 Billy Wilder film *The Fortune Cookie*.

Matthau was the son of Rose (née Berolsky; from Lithuania), who worked in a sweatshop, and Milton Matthow, an electrician and peddler (from Russia), both Jewish immigrants. His surname has often incorrectly been listed as Matuschanskayasky. As a young boy, Walter attended a Jewish non-profit sleepaway camp, Tranquillity Camp, where he first began acting in the shows the camp would stage on Saturday nights. He also attended Surprise Lake Camp. His high school was Seward Park High School.

During World War II, Matthau served in the U.S. Army Air Forces with the Eighth Air Force in England as a B-24 Liberator radioman-gunner, in the same 453rd Bombardment Group as James Stewart. He reached the rank of staff sergeant and became interested in acting. He took classes in acting at the Dramatic Workshop of The New School in New York with the influential German director Erwin Piscator. He often joked that his best early review came in a play where he posed as a derelict. One reviewer said, "The others just looked like actors in make-up, Walter Matthau really looks like a skid row bum!" Matthau was a respected stage actor for years in such fare as *Will Success Spoil Rock Hunter?* And *A Shot in the Dark*. He won the 1962 Tony Award for Best Featured Actor in a play.

In 1952, Matthau appeared in the pilot of *Mr. Peepers* with Wally Cox. For reasons unknown he used the name Leonard Elliot. His role was of the gym teacher Mr. Wall. In 1955, he made his motion picture debut as a whip-wielding bad guy in *The Kentuckian* opposite Burt Lancaster.

Matthau appeared as a villain in subsequent movies, such as 1958's *King Creole* (in which he is beaten up by Elvis Presley). That same year, he made a western called *Ride a Crooked Trail* with Audie Murphy and *Onionhead* starring Andy Griffith and Erin O'Brien, which was a flop. Matthau had a featured role opposite Griffith in the well received drama *A Face in the Crowd* (1957), directed by Elia Kazan. Matthau also directed a low-budget 1960 movie called *The Gangster Story*. In 1962, he was a sympathetic sheriff in *Lonely are the Brave*, which starred Kirk Douglas. He appeared opposite Audrey Hepburn in *Charade* (1963).

Appearances on television were common too, including two on ABC's police drama, *Naked City* (1960-1962), as well as the 1963 episode "A Tumble from a Tall White House" of *The Eleventh Hour*. He appeared eight times between 1962 and 1964 on *The DuPont Show of the Week* and as Franklin Gaer in 1964 in the episode "Man Is a

Rock" on *Dr. Kildare*. Lastly, he starred in the syndicated crime drama *Tallahassee 7000*, as a Florida-based state police investigator, in the 1961-1962 season.

Comedies were rare in Matthau's work at that time. He was cast in a number of stark dramas, such as 1964's *Fail-Safe*, in which he portrayed Pentagon adviser Dr. Groeteschele, who urges all out nuclear attack on the Soviet Union in response to an accidental transmission of an attack signal to U.S. Air Force bombers, in the tense, and timely cold-war thriller.

In 1965, however, a plum comedy role came Matthau's way when Neil Simon cast him in the hit play *The Odd Couple* playing the slovenly sportswriter Oscar Madison opposite Art Carney as Felix Unger. Matthau would later join Jack Lemmon in the movie version. Also in 1965, he played detective Ted Casselle in the Hitchcockian thriller *Mirage*, with Gregory Peck and Diane Baker, a film directed by Edward Dmytryk, based on a novel by Howard Fast.

He achieved great film success in a 1966 comedy as a shyster lawyer called "Whiplash Willie" Gingrich starring opposite Lemmon in *The Fortune Cookie*, the first of numerous collaborations with Billy Wilder, and a role that would earn him an Oscar for Best Supporting Actor. Filming had to be placed on a five-month hiatus after Matthau suffered a heart attack.

Matthau was visibly banged up during the Oscar telecast, having been involved in a bicycle accident.

Oscar nominations would come Matthau's way again for 1972's *Kotch*, directed by Lemmon, and 1975's *The Sunshine Boys*, another Simon vehicle transferred from the stage, this one about a pair of former vaudeville stars. For the latter role he won a Golden Globe award for Best Actor in a Musical or Comedy.

Broadway hits turned into films continued to cast Matthau in the leads with 1969's *Hello, Dolly!* and that same year's *Cactus Flower*, for which co-star Goldie Hawn received an Oscar. He played three different roles in the 1971 film version of Simon's *Plaza Suite* and was in the cast of its followup *California Suite* in 1978.

Matthau starred in three crime dramas in the mid-1970s, as a detective investigating a mass murder on a bus in *The Laughing Policeman* (1973), as a bank robber on the run from the Mafia and the law in *Charley Varrick* (1973), and as a New York transit cop in the action-adventure *The Taking of Pelham One Two Three* (1974). A change of pace about misfits on a Little League baseball team turned out to be a solid hit in 1976 when Matthau starred as Coach Morris Buttermaker in the comedy *The Bad News Bears*

In 1982, Matthau portrayed Herbert Tucker in *I Ought to Be in Pictures*. There he worked with Ann-Margret and Dinah Manoff, the daughter of the actress whom Matthau starred with in *Plaza Suite*, Lee Grant.

Matthau played Albert Einstein in the film *IQ* (1994), also starring Tim Robbins and Meg Ryan.

His partnership with Lemmon became one of the most successful pairings in Hollywood. They became lifelong friends after making *The Fortune Cookie* and would make a total of ten movies together—eleven counting Kotch, in which Lemmon has a cameo as a sleeping bus passenger. Aside from their many comedies, each appeared (though not on screen together) in the 1991 Oliver Stone drama about the presidential assassination, *JFK*.

Another great role followed as he played Mr. Wilson opposite *Dennis the Menace* (1993). They had a surprise box-office hit in the comedy *Grumpy Old Men* (1993), reuniting for a sequel, *Grumpier Old Men* (1995), that co-starred Sophia Loren and Ann-Margret. That led to more pairings late in their careers, notably *Out to Sea* (1997) and a Simon-scripted sequel to one of their great successes, *The Odd Couple II* (1998). *I'm Not Rappaport* (1996) was also one of his best and a 2000 film *Hanging Up* directed by Diane Keaton, was Matthau's final appearance on screen.

Matthau was married twice; first to Grace Geraldine Johnson from 1948 to 1958, and then from 1959 until his death in 2000 to Carol Marcus. He had two children, Jenny and David, by his first wife, and a second son, Charlie Matthau, with his second wife. David is a radio news reporter, currently at WKXW "New Jersey 101.5" in Trenton, New Jersey. Jenny is president of the Natural Gourmet Institute in New York City. Matthau also helped raise his stepchildren, Aram Saroyan and Lucy Saroyan. His grandchildren include William Matthau, an engineer, and Emily Rose Roman, a student at SUNY Binghamton. Charlie Matthau directed his father in *The Grass Harp* (1995).

Matthau died of a heart attack in Santa Monica on July 1, 2000. He was 79 years old. After undergoing heart surgery years earlier, doctors discovered that he had colon cancer, which, by the time of his death, had spread to his liver, lungs, and brain. His remains are interred in the Westwood Village Memorial Park Cemetery in Los Angeles.

Less than a year later, remains of Jack Lemmon (who died of colon and bladder cancer) were buried at the same cemetery. After Matthau's death, Lemmon as well as other friends and relatives had appeared on *Larry King Live* in an hour of tribute and remembrance; many of those same people appeared on the show one year later, reminiscing about Lemmon.

Carol Marcus, also a native of New York, died of a brain aneurysm in 2003. Her remains are buried next to Matthau's.

Marta May

Audie Murphy with Marta May in *The Texican*

Marta May was born María Jesús Mayor Ávila June 14, 1939, in Santander, Cantabria, Spain. She appeared in thirty-four films and television programs from 1964 to 1990, most of those foreign.

Some of those roles include *Twins from Texas* (1964), *Seven Pistols for a Gringo* (1966), *The Texican* (1966) with Audie Murphy, *Cutting Heads* (1970), *Horror Story* (1972), *The Burned City* (1976), *Phoenix the Warrior* (1988), and *The Ages of Lulu* (1990).

Ken Mayer

Ken Mayer was born Kenneth Martin Mayer June 25, 1918 in San Francisco, California, and was an American actor. He appeared in ninety-nine films and television programs from 1951 to 1974.

Some of those credits included 113 episodes as Maj. Robbie Robertson in *Space Patrol* (1951-1955), *Father Knows Best* (1957), *Richard Diamond, Private Detective* (1958), *Never Steal Anything Small* (1959), *Wanted: Dead or Alive* (1959), *Frontier Uprising* (1961), *Whispering Smith* (1961) with Audie Murphy, *Jack the Giant Killer* (1962), *Destry* (1964), *My Favorite Martian* (1965), *The Addams Family* (1965), *Bonnie and Clyde* (1967), *Little Big Man* (1970), twelve episodes of *Gunsmoke* (1957-1973), and *Doc Elliot* (1974).

He died January 30, 1985, at age 66 in North Hollywood, California.

Eugene Mazzola

Audie Murphy with Eugene Mazzola in *Walk the Proud Land*

Eugene Mazzola was born March 2, 1948, in Hollywood, California, to a large family, all in the film business. His father was Leonard Al Mazzola, who started in Vaudeville in 1915. His mother was Saveria Mazzola, who was in *The Godfather: Part II* (1974). He is the sixth of seven children, the fifth of five boys. His family is steeped in the motion picture industry. Eugene started working in the business at an early age as Anthony Caruso's baby in *The Asphalt Jungle* (1950).

He did a few more movies like *The Prodigal* (1955), and *Walk the Proud Land* (1956) with Audie Murphy before being cast in *The Ten Commandments* (1956) opposite Yul Brynner as the Pharaoh Rameses' son.

After *The Ten Commandments* Mazzola used the stage name Eugene Martin and had a very successful career as a child actor, becoming a member of SAG in 1964.

He appeared as Joey Drum in twenty-six episodes of *Jefferson Drum* (1958). He also appeared in *Wanted: Dead or Alive* (1960), and *Bonanza* (1960-1967).

Mazzola served in the Navy from 1968 to 1970. He was stationed on the Mekong River and in DaNang, Viet Nam. When he returned from Nam he served as a photo journalist for the Navy in San Diego.

After the Navy, Mazzola returned to Hollywood where he went to college and continued acting. He appeared in *To Rome with Love* (1970), *The Streets of San Francisco* (1973), *Toma* (1973), and *Bert D'Angelo/Superstar* (1976).

In 1972 he started working behind the camera. Mazzola produced his first film, *Joyride* (1977), in 1976; that was the same year he joined the DGA.

Mazzola moved to Seattle in 1980. He owned and operated the Cine Companies, based in Seattle, from 1984 to 1993. He has never stopped Production Managing and Producing films. Mazzola married his high school sweetheart, 'Zita Mazzola' and has three children, Saveria T. Mazzola, Richard-Augustus (RA), and Sebastian Mazzola. He lives with his wife in the country northeast of Seattle.

Sean McClory

Audie Murphy with Sean McClory in *Guns of Fort Petticoat*

Sean McClory Séan Joseph McClory was born in Dublin, Ireland, March 8, 1924, and was an Irish actor whose career spanned six decades and included well over 100 films and television series. He was the son of Hugh Patrick McClory, an architect and civil engineer, and Mary Margaret (née Ball).

McClory portrayed the Irishman Jack McGivern in NBC's *The Californians*, set in the San Francisco gold rush of the 1850s. It aired from 1957-1959. His costars included Herbert Rudley and Adam Kennedy, the latter as newspaperman Dion Patrick. He also appeared twice in the short-lived 1960 NBC western series, *Overland Trail*, starring William Bendix and Doug McClure. He appeared in an episode from the second season of *Lost In Space* (1967) called "The Astral Traveler", as a bagpiping "ghostie" named Hamish.

Other roles included *Beyond Glory* (1948) with Audie Murphy, *Lorna Doone* (1951), *The Quiet Man* (1952), *Niagara* (1953), *Island in the Sky* (1953), *Them!* (1954), *The Guns of Fort Petticoat* (1957) again with Audie Murphy, *Richard Diamond, Private Detective* (1958), *Wanted: Dead or Alive* (1960), *Mary Poppins* (1964), *The Gnome-Mobile* (1967), *The Guns of Will Sonnett* (1969), *S.W.A.T.* (1975), *Battlestar Galactica* (1978), *Bring 'Em Back Alive* (1982), *Murder, She Wrote* (1986), and *Body Bags* (1993).

He died December 10, 2003, at age 79 in Hollywood Hills, California.

Doug McClure

Audie Murphy with Doug McClure in *The Unforgiven*

Douglas Osborne "Doug" McClure was born May 11, 1935, and was an American actor whose career in film and television extended from the 1950s to the 1990s. Born in Glendale, California, to Donald Reed McClure and the former Clara Clapp, he is best known for his appearances as Trampas in the NBC western series *The Virginian* (1962-1971).

McClure's acting career included such movies as *The Enemy Below* (1957), *South Pacific* (1958), and *The Unforgiven* (1960) with Audie Murphy, before landing the part of Trampas on *The Virginian*, a part that would make him famous.

He also starred in five other series: (1) as Frank "Flip" Flippen on NBC's western, *Overland Trail* (1960), with co-star William Bendix, (2) as Jed Sills on the CBS detective series *Checkmate* (1960–1962) opposite Anthony George as Don Corey and Sebastian Cabot as Dr. Carl Hyatt, in the sci-fi/detective series *Search* (1972-73) in which he rotated the lead with Hugh O'Brian and Anthony Franciosa as a high-tech PROBE agent, (4) *Barbary Coast* (1975-1976) with William Shatner, and finally (5) *Out of This World* (1987-1991).

In 1958 and 1959, McClure appeared in three episodes of the syndicated western series *26 Men*, stories of the Arizona Rangers. He appeared as Adam Davis in 1959 in the episode "The Court Martial of Trooper Davis" of the syndicated series *Mackenzie's Raiders* starring Richard Carlson. He was in the third episode of *The Twilight Zone* (1959), "Mr. Denton on Doomsday".

Then in 1962, he got the part of Trampas in NBC's *The Virginian*. McClure's *The Virginian* co-stars throughout the series were James Drury, Roberta Shore, Lee J. Cobb, Randy Boone, Gary Clarke, Clu Gulager, Diane Roter, Charles Bickford, and John McIntire. After the show ended in 1971, McClure starred in science fiction films such as *At the Earth's Core* (1976), *The Land That Time Forgot* (1975), and *The People That Time Forgot* (1977), all three based on the novels of Edgar Rice Burroughs.

In the 1970s and 80s McClure appeared in commercials for Hamms Beer.

Other roles late in his career included *Warlords of the Deep* (1978), *Humanoids from the Deep* (1980), *The House Where Evil Dwells* (1982), *Cannonball Run II* (1984), *The Fall Guy* (1982-1985), *Murder, She Wrote* (1987), *The Gambler Returns: The Luck of the Draw* (1991), *Maverick* (1994), and *Kung Fu: The Legend Continues* (1995).

In 1994, McClure was awarded a star on the Hollywood Walk of Fame for Television at 7065 Hollywood Blvd. It was unveiled in what was his final public appearance.

On February 5, 1995, McClure died from lung cancer in Sherman Oaks, California. He was 59 and is buried at Woodlawn Memorial Cemetery. In addition to his fifth wife, he is survived by three daughters, including Valerie and Tane McClure, who is an actress.

Darren McGavin

Audie Murphy with Darren McGavin in *Bullet for a Badman*

Darren McGavin was born William Lyle Richardson in Spokane, Washington, May 7, 1922, and was an American actor best known for playing the title role in the television horror series *Kolchak: The Night Stalker* (1974-1975) and his portrayal in the film *A Christmas Story* (1983) of the grumpy father given to bursts of profanity that he never realizes his son overhears. He appeared as the tough-talking, funny detective in the 1950s television series *Mickey Spillane's Mike Hammer* (1958-1989). From 1959-1961, McGavin starred in the NBC western series *Riverboat*, first with Burt Reynolds and then with Noah Beery, Jr., and in later years, he had a recurring role in the sitcom *Murphy Brown* (1989-1992), as the title character's father, for which he received an Emmy Award.

In magazine interviews in the 1960s, he said his parents divorced when he was very young. His father, not knowing what else to do, put him in an orphanage at the age of eleven. McGavin began to run away, sleeping on the docks and in warehouses. He lived in three orphanages. The last was the Dyslin Boys Ranch in Pierce County, Washington, a boys' home, which turned out to be a safe haven. Farm chores were assigned, and he lived with several other boys who had also been abandoned. McGavin commented that the owners of the home helped him develop a sense of pride and responsibility that turned his life around. McGavin did not serve in the military during World War II because he had bad knees, though he did make a training film for the military on venereal disease.

McGavin worked as a painter in the paint crew at the Columbia Pictures movie studios in 1945. When an opening became available for a bit part in *A Song to Remember* (1945), on the movie set where he was working, McGavin applied for the role. He was hired for it, and that was his first foray into movie acting.

Shortly afterwards, he moved to New York City and spent a decade there learning the acting profession in television and plays. McGavin studied at the Neighborhood Playhouse and the Actors Studio under teacher Sanford Meisner and began working in live TV drama and on Broadway. A few of the plays in which he starred included *The Rainmaker* (where he created the title role on Broadway), *The King and I* and *Death of a Salesman*.

McGavin returned to Hollywood and became a busy actor in a wide variety of TV and movie roles; in 1955 he broke through with roles in the films *Summertime* and *The Man with the Golden Arm*. During this period, McGavin also appeared on the anthology series *Alfred Hitchcock Presents* (1955) in an episode titled "The Cheney Vase", in which he demonstrated his talent for playing complex roles, as a scheming caretaker and aspiring art thief, opposite Carolyn Jones and Ruta Lee.

Over the course of his career, McGavin starred in seven different TV series and guest-starred in many more; these television roles increased in the late 1950s and early 1960s with leading parts in series such as *Mickey Spillane's Mike Hammer* and *Riverboat*. McGavin held a black belt in traditional Japanese karate and the series are notable for him doing many of his own stunts and for the "enthusiasm" he put into some of the fight scenes, sometimes forgetting to pull his punches and "ad-libbing".

When the comedy team Martin and Lewis broke up as a result of Dean Martin's refusal to play a cop in a movie, McGavin played the role originally earmarked for Martin in *The Delicate Delinquent* (1957), Jerry Lewis's first solo film.

He also had a memorable role in *Bullet for a Badman* (1964) with Audie Murphy.

In 1970, he was in negotiations to replace Larry Hagman as the male lead in the television series *I Dream of Jeannie* for the sixth season, but NBC stated they would rather cancel the series than have any other similarities to *Bewitched* (1964-1972), in which the male lead was replaced by another actor.

McGavin was also known for his role as Sam Parkhill in the miniseries adaptation of *The Martian Chronicles* (1980).

The first of his two best-known roles came in 1972, in the supernatural-themed TV movie *The Night Stalker* (1972). With McGavin playing a reporter who discovers the activities of a modern-day vampire on the loose in Las

Vegas, the film became the highest-rated made-for-TV movie in history at that time; and when the sequel *The Night Strangler* (1973) also was a strong success, a subsequent television series *Kolchak: The Night Stalker* (1974) was made. In the series, McGavin played Carl Kolchak, an investigative reporter for the INS, a Chicago-based news service, who regularly stumbles upon the supernatural or occult basis for a seemingly mundane crime; although his involvement routinely assisted in the dispelment of the otherworldly adversary, his evidence in the case was always destroyed or seized, usually by a public official or major social figure who sought to cover up the incident. He would write his ensuing stories in a sensational, tabloid style which advised readers that the true story was being withheld from them. McGavin and the cast were enthusiastic about the series. McGavin reportedly entered into a verbal agreement with Sid Sheinberg (President of MCA and Universal TV) to produce *The Night Stalker* as a TV series as a coproduction between Universal and McGavin's Taurean Productions. Early promises were never fulfilled, and McGavin expressed concern over script quality and lack of network commitment toward promoting the show. His concerns appeared justified, as the series drifted into camp humor and the production values declined in later episodes.

Kolchak is acknowledged as being a main inspiration for *The X-Files* (1993-2002). McGavin was asked to play the role of Arthur Dales, founder of the X-Files, in three episodes: Season 5's "Travelers" and two episodes from Season 6, "Agua Mala" and "The Unnatural". Failing health forced him to withdraw from the latter, and the script (written and directed by series star David Duchovny) was rewritten to feature M. Emmet Walsh as Dales's brother, also called Arthur.

In 1983, he starred as "Old Man Parker", the narrator's father, in the movie *A Christmas Story*. He portrayed a middle-class father in 1940s Hammond, Indiana, who was endearing in spite of his being comically oblivious to his own use of profanity and completely unable to recognize his unfortunate taste for kitsch. Blissfully unaware of his family's embarrassment by his behavior, he took pride in his self-assessed ability to fix anything in record time, and carried on a tireless campaign against his neighbor's rampaging bloodhounds. McGavin allegedly received a fee of $2 million to play the role, making him one of the highest paid actors of the time.

McGavin made an uncredited appearance in 1984's *The Natural* as a shady gambler and appeared on a Christmas episode ("Midnight of the Century") of *Millennium* (1997), playing the long-estranged father of Frank Black (Lance Henriksen); he also appeared as Adam Sandler's hotel-magnate father in the 1995 movie *Billy Madison*.

During the filming of *The Natural* (1984), Robert Redford was so pleased with McGavin's portrayal of his character that they began to expand the role. However, after a certain point, union rules dictated that the actor's contract needed to be renegotiated for salary and billing. After haggling on salary, and holding up production of the movie because of it, the billing had to be decided. McGavin became somewhat fed up with the proceedings and instructed his agent to waive his billing in the credits entirely so they could get back to filming.

He won a CableACE Award (for the 1991 TV movie *Clara*) and received a 1990 Emmy Award as an Outstanding Guest Star in a Comedy Series on *Murphy Brown*, in which he played Murphy's father.

There was a brief and unsuccessful remake of the *Night Stalker* TV series in 2005 starring Stuart Townsend. In the initial episode aired on September 29, 2005, McGavin appeared momentarily in the background, using digitally inserted footage from his role in the original series.

Darren McGavin narrated the majority of the audio book versions of the adventure novels by *John D. MacDonald* in which each title included a color. The central character and main voice of the novels was *Travis McGee*.

McGavin was married twice. The first was to Melanie York on March 20, 1944. It ended in divorce in 1969, but produced four children: Bogart, York, Megan, and Graemm Bridget McGavin. The second was to Kathie Browne on December 31, 1969, ending with her death in 2003.

I contacted Darren McGavin's manager via email in the fall of 2005 to attempt to get him to be the celebrity guest at Audie Murphy Days for June of 2006. His manager advised me that Darren would be proud to, but his failing health would not permit it.

McGavin died on February 25, 2006, at the age of 83 in a Los Angeles hospital. He is buried in Hollywood Forever Cemetery.

John McGovern

John McGovern was born February 22, 1902, in Providence, Rhode Island, and was an American actor. He appeared in thirty-three films and television programs from 1949 to 1965. Some of those credits include *Danger* (1950), *Tales of Tomorrow* (1952-1953), *The Benny Goodman Story* (1956), "The Man" episode of *Startime* (1960) with Audie Murphy, *The Birds* (1963), *The Defenders* (1963-1965), and *Inherit the Wind* (1965).

He died July 28, 1985, at age 83 in Clinton, Connecticut.

Charles McGraw

Charles McGraw with Audi Murphy in *Joe Butterfly*

Charles Butters, best known by his stage name Charles McGraw, was born May 10, 1914, in Des Moines, Iowa, and was an American actor, who made his first film in 1942, albeit in a small, uncredited role.

McGraw developed into a leading man, especially in film noir classics during the late 1940s and 1950s. His gravelly voice and rugged looks enhanced his appeal in the *noir* stylistic genre, and provided him many roles as cop or gunman.

Introduced with fellow "heavy" William Conrad as the two hitmen terrorizing a small town diner in the start of the 1946 film *The Killers*, McGraw's notable roles include: "Honest Joe" insurance investigator turned thief by love interest in the *noir* classic *Roadblock* (1951); playing the grumpy cop hired to protect Marie Windsor in the *noir* B-movie *The Narrow Margin* (1952); Kirk Douglas' gladiator trainer in the epic *Spartacus*; righteous cop Lt. Jim Cordell in the *Armored Car Robbery* (1950); as Sgt. Jim McNulty in *Joe Butterfly* (1957) with Audie Murphy, and "The Preacher" in the science fiction cult classic *A Boy and His Dog* (1975).

McGraw starred as Mike Waring, the title character, in the thirty-nine-episode 1954-55 syndicated TV series *Adventures of the Falcon*. He also starred in the television version of *Casablanca* (1955) taking over Humphrey Bogart's role as Rick.

Other notable credits included *Cimarron* (1960), *The Horizontal Lieutenant* (1962), *It's a Mad Mad Mad Mad World* (1963), *Destry* (1964), *In Cold Blood* (1967), *Hang 'Em High* (1968), *Tell Them Willie Boy Is Here* (1969), *O'Hara, U.S. Treasury* (1971-1972), *The Night Stalker* (1972), *Adam-12* (1971-1973), *Police Story* (1974), and *Twilight's Last Gleaming* (1977).

In late 2007 Alan K. Rode wrote a biography of McGraw: *Charles McGraw: Biography of a Film Noir Tough Guy*. The book provides a behind-the-scenes look and anecdotes about his life, including: his long marriage to a Eurasian woman, his World War II military service, his film career, and the story of his death.

Charles McGraw died after slipping and falling through a glass shower door in his Studio City, California home July 30, 1980, at age 66.

John McIntire

John McIntire with Audie Murphy in *Seven Ways From Sundown*

John McIntire was born June 27, 1907, and was an American character actor. The craggy-faced film actor was born in Spokane in eastern Washington State but reared in Montana, having grown up around ranchers and cowboys, an experience that would later inspire his performances in dozens of Westerns.

A graduate of USC, McIntire began acting in radio and on stage, before embarking on a lengthy film and TV career as a character actor. He was already forty when he made his big-screen debut in 1947, but went on to appear in some sixty-five films, often playing police chiefs, judges, crazy coots and western characters. His films include the film noir classic *The Asphalt Jungle* (1950), the 1960 Hitchcock thriller *Psycho* and the 1960 drama *Elmer Gantry*, but some of his more memorable roles were in westerns such as the acclaimed *Winchester '73* (1950) and *The Far Country* (1955), both with James Stewart, and *The Tin Star*, with Henry Fonda (1957). He also played a judge in *Rooster Cogburn* (1975), the sequel to *True Grit* featuring John Wayne and Katharine Hepburn. His final film role was in *Turner & Hooch* (1989).

In the mid-1950s, McIntire moved into television, appearing in anthology series, sitcoms and dramas, including a regular role on ABC's *Naked City* (1958-1959), before his character was killed off. Though McIntire had never had the lead role in a film, television provided him with his most prominent and long-running role when in 1961 he replaced the late Ward Bond in the popular NBC-ABC series *Wagon Train*, playing trail master Chris Hale in more than 150 episodes between 1961 and 1965. His co-stars were Robert Horton, Robert Fuller, Denny Scott Miller, Terry Wilson, Frank McGrath, and Michael Burns.

He appeared as the boxing manager in *World in my Corner* (1956) with Audie Murphy as the boxer, and he played the veteran Texas Ranger training the title character, played by Audie Murphy, how to be a Ranger in *Seven Ways from Sundown* (1960).

McIntire subsequently replaced actors Lee J. Cobb and Charles Bickford on NBC's *The Virginian* in 1967, playing Bickford's character's brother. Prior to his *Wagon Train* role, he guest starred as William Palmer in the series finale, "The Most Dangerous Gentleman", of the short-lived 1960 NBC western *Overland Trail*, starring William Bendix and Doug McClure, his subsequent co-star on *The Virginian*.

McIntire married actress Jeanette Nolan, in 1935, and they had two children together, one of whom was the actor Tim McIntire (1944–1986) who starred in the 1978 film *American Hot Wax*. McIntire and Nolan both figured in *Psycho*; he played a sheriff, while she voiced some of the "mother" lines. McIntire worked more closely with Nolan in the 1977 Disney animated film *The Rescuers*, in which he voiced the cat Rufus and she the muskrat Ellie Mae. Four years later, the couple worked on another Disney film, *The Fox and the Hound*, with McIntire as the voice of Mr. Digger, a badger, and Nolan as the voice of Widow Tweed.

John McIntire died from emphysema and lung cancer in Pasadena, California, January 30, 1991. In addition to his wife Jeanette Nolan he was also survived by his daughter Holly McIntire. His son Tim McIntire preceded him in death in 1986 from heart problems.

John McKee

John McKee was born December 30, 1916, in San Luis Obispo, California, and was an American actor and stuntman. He served as a pilot in the Army Air Corps during World War II. He became a recipient of the Purple Heart, when his plane was shot down over France. Later, he was heavily involved in sports prior to his movie career, as a professional player in the Canadian Football League and as bullpen coach for the Pittsburgh Pirates baseball team. He appeared in almost 150 films and television programs from 1945 to 1983.

Some of those credits included *Abe Lincoln in Illinois* (1945), *When Willie Comes Marching Home* (1950), *Vengeance Valley* (1951), *The Man from the Alamo* (1953), *Strategic Air Command* (1955), *The Fastest Gun Alive* (1956), *Darby's Rangers* (1958), *Pork Chop Hill* (1959), *Elmer Gantry* (1960), *Posse from Hell* (1961) and *Whispering Smith* (1961) with Audie Murphy, *Cape Fear* (1962), *Showdown* (1963) again with Audie Murphy, *The Carpetbaggers* (1964), *The Rare Breed* (1966), *The Shakiest Gun in the West* (1968), *Macho Callahan* (1970), *Monte Walsh* (1970), *Rio Lobo* (1970), *The Choirboys* (1977), *The Incredible Hulk* (1979), *1941* (1979), and *Dempsey* (1983).

He died May 12, 2013, at age 96 in Vineland, New Jersey.

Stephen McNally

Audie Murphy with Stephen McNally in *Duel at Silver Creek*

Stephen McNally was born July 29, 1913, and was an actor remembered mostly for his appearances in many westerns and action films. He was an attorney in the late 1930s before pursuing a career in acting.

He started his stage career using his real name Horace McNally and began appearing uncredited in many World War II-era films. In 1946, he changed his stage name to Stephen McNally and began appearing credited as both movie villains and heroes.

Some early credits included *Grand Central Murder* (1942), *Air Raid Wardens* (1943) with Laurel & Hardy, and *Thirty Seconds over Tokyo* (1944). He played menacing roles in such films as *Johnny Belinda* (1948) and the James Stewart western *Winchester '73* (1950). He co-starred in the Burt Lancaster film noir *Criss Cross* (1949). Other notable 1950s films included *No Way Out* (1950), *Split Second* (1953), and *Johnny Rocco* (1958).

He also appeared in *The Duel at Silver Creek* (1952) with Audie Murphy, *The Man from Bitter Ridge* (1955), *Tribute to a Bad Man* (1956), *The Fiend Who Walked the West* (1958), *Hell Bent for Leather* (1960) again with Audie Murphy, *The Fugitive* (1964), *Gunsmoke* (1967), and *The Virginian* (1963-1971).

During the 1970s, McNally guest starred in television programs such as *The Sixth Sense* (1972), *The Magician* (1973), *The Rockford Files* (1974), *Get Christie Love!* (1974), *Police Story* (1973-1977), *Starsky and Hutch* (1975-1977), *Charlie's Angels* (1979), *Fantasy Island* (1978-1980), and *Secrets of Midland Heights* (1980).

He died June 4, 1994, of heart failure at the age of eighty.

Howard McNear

Audie Murphy with Howard McNear in *Drums Across the River*

Howard Terbell McNear was born January 27, 1905, and was an American film, television and radio character actor. McNear is best remembered as Floyd Lawson, the barber in *The Andy Griffith Show* (1961-1967) and as Doc Charles Adams in CBS Radio's *Gunsmoke* (1952–1961).

McNear was born in Los Angeles, California to Luzetta M. Spencer and Franklin E. McNear. He worked as a theatrical actor as early as 1930, and worked in radio from the late 1930s, distinguishing himself in the 1937–1940 radio serial *Speed Gibson of the International Secret Police* as ace operator Clint Barlow. McNear could be effective in such authoritative roles, but he gravitated more toward character roles, often comic.

He enlisted as a private in the U.S. Army Air Corps on November 17, 1942 during World War II.

He created the role of Doc Charles Adams in CBS Radio's *Gunsmoke* (1952–1961). McNear was under contract to CBS for many years and was featured in many of the network's radio and TV programs. From 1955 to 1960 he appeared frequently, in various quirky roles, in the popular radio detective series *Yours Truly, Johnny Dollar*. He guest starred in the Thanksgiving Day episode, November 26, 1959, of NBC's *The Ford Show, Starring Tennessee Ernie Ford*.

In the television sitcom *Leave It to Beaver* (1958), McNear made an appearance as a barber named Andy, a role which proved prophetic.

McNear was best known for his performances as the vague, chatty barber Floyd Lawson on *The Andy Griffith Show*. In that role, McNear replaced actor Walter Baldwin, who was deemed too elderly for the part. McNear later said that he didn't replace anyone, but was playing Floyd Lawson, Jr. During the third season, McNear suffered a stroke that rendered him unable to walk though his speech remained intact. Griffith, who realized how much the Floyd character added to the show's dynamic, urged that he return to the role if possible. McNear resumed the role (after being off the show for almost a year and a half), with the production crew accommodating his disability. In his appearances on the show before the stroke, he is seen standing and working in his barber shop (and also walking freely). After the stroke, he is usually seen seated (in his barber chair or a park bench, etc.). The stagehands constructed a stand for him, which allowed him to stand and appear to be working, usually to comb hair (one-handed, of course). There was an episode (after the stroke) where the sequence of camera shots made it appear that his character did indeed take some steps. His last appearance on the show was in the episode "Goober's Contest", which wrapped up the 1966-1967 season. In that final show, Floyd is seen visiting Goober's gas station in a sleek Mercury convertible that is driven to and from that scene by a double.

Other non-Floyd-the-barber roles included *The Long, Long Trailer* (1953), *Drums Across the River* (1954) with Audie Murphy, *I Love Lucy* (1956), *The Fuzzy Pink Nightgown* (1957), *The George Burns and Gracie Allen Show* (1953-1958), *Heller in Pink Tights* (1960), *Richard Diamond, Private Detective* (1960), *Blue Hawaii* (1961), *Follow That Dream* (1962), *Twilight Zone* (1962-1963), *Fun in Acapulco* (1963), and *The Fortune Cookie* (1966).

On January 3, 1969, McNear died of complications from pneumonia due to the effects of a stroke. He was interred in the Los Angeles National Cemetery, a former U.S. Veterans Administration cemetery. Actor and old friend Parley Baer delivered his eulogy. His wife Helen and son Christopher survived him.

Tyler McVey

Tyler McVey was born in Bay City on Saginaw Bay in the Lower Peninsula of Michigan, February 14, 1912, and was an American character actor. His first screen role, uncredited, came at the age of 39 in 1951, when he portrayed Brady in the *The Day the Earth Stood Still*. He was uncredited in two 1953 military films, *From Here to Eternity* as Major Stern and in *Mission over Korea* as Colonel Colton.

He made one of his first television appearances in a 1953 episode of *Four Star Playhouse*. McVey's other roles included *One Minute to Zero* (1952), *Column South* (1953) with Audie Murphy, and *From Here to Eternity* (1953). From 1953 to 1956, he guest starred on the CBS educational series *You Are There*, narrated by Walter Cronkite. More roles followed in *Somebody Up There Likes Me* (1956), *Walk the Proud Land* (1956) again with Audie Murphy, *Night of the Blood Beast* (1958), *Attack of the Giant Leeches* (1959), *The Gallant Hours* (1960), *Whispering Smith* (1961) a third appearance with Audie Murphy, *The Green Hornet* (1967), and *The Strongest Man in the World* (1975). From 1959 to 1960, McVey portrayed Major General Norgath in the CBS series *Men Into Space*. In 1964, McVey was cast as General Hardesty in the political thriller film *Seven Days in May*. McVey's last roles were as different ministers in two episodes of Michael Landon's NBC drama series, *Highway to Heaven*, in 1985 and 1986.

McVey was married three times; he first married Lorraine Budge in 1937. After their divorce, he married Rita Ann Stickelmaier in 1950 before divorcing in 1970. McVey married Esther Geddes the following year.

On July 4, 2003, McVey died of leukemia in Rancho Mirage, California.

Patricia Medina

Patricia Paz Maria Medina was born July 19, 1919, and was an English actress. Her father was a Spaniard (Ramón Medina Nebot from the Canary Islands) and her mother was English. Medina began acting as a teenager in the late 1930s. She worked her way up to leading roles in the mid-1940s, whereupon she left for Hollywood.

In 1950's *Fortunes of Captain Blood*, she teamed up with British actor Louis Hayward. She and Hayward subsequently appeared together in 1951's *The Lady and the Bandit* and *Lady in the Iron Mask* and *Captain Pirate*, both from 1952.

Darkly beautiful, Medina was often typecast in period melodramas such as *The Black Knight* (1954). Two of her more notable films were William Whitney's *Stranger at My Door* (1956) and Orson Welles' *Mr. Arkadin* (1955).

Other roles included *Abbott and Costello in the Foreign Legion* (1950), *Botany Bay* (1953), *Snow White and the Three Stooges* (1961), *Whispering Smith* (1961) with Audie Murphy, *The Man from U.N.C.L.E.* (1965), *The Killing of Sister George* (1968), *Mannix* (1971), and *Timber Tramps* (1975).

In 1998, Patricia Medina Cotten published an autobiography, *Laid Back in Hollywood: Remembering*.

Medina married British actor Richard Greene on December 24, 1941, in St. James's Church, Spanish Place, London. They divorced in 1951. Medina married Joseph Cotten on October 20, 1960, in Beverly Hills at the home of David O. Selznick and Jennifer Jones. She and her husband, American actor Joseph Cotten, toured together in several plays and on Broadway in the murder mystery *Calculated Risk*.

Medina died at age 92 on April 28, 2012, from natural causes at the Barlow Respiratory Hospital in Los Angeles, California. She was interred at Blandford Cemetary in Petersburg, Virginia beside Joseph Cotten.

Burgess Meredith

Burgess Meredith with Audie Murphy in *Joe Butterfly*

Oliver Burgess Meredith was born in Cleveland, Ohio on November 16, 1907. He was known professionally as Burgess Meredith, was an American actor in theatre, film, and television, who also worked as a director.

Active for more than six decades, Meredith has been called "a virtuosic actor" who was "one of the most accomplished actors of the century". Meredith won several Emmys, and was the first man to win the Saturn Award for Best Supporting Actor twice, and was also nominated for two Academy Awards.

He graduated from Hoosac School in 1926 and then attended Amherst College as a member of the Class of 1931. Meredith served in the United States Army Air Forces in World War II, reaching the rank of captain. He was discharged in 1944 to work on the movie *The Story of G.I. Joe*, in which he starred as the popular war correspondent Ernie Pyle.

Early in his career, Meredith attracted favorable attention, especially for playing George in a 1939 adaptation of John Steinbeck's *Of Mice and Men* and as war correspondent Ernie Pyle in *The Story of G.I. Joe* (1945). Meredith was featured in many 1940s films, including three; *Second Chorus* (1940), *Diary of a Chambermaid* (1946) and *On Our Merry Way* (1948), co-starring then-wife Paulette Goddard.

As a result of the House Committee on Un-American Activities investigation into Communist influence in Hollywood, Meredith was placed on the Hollywood blacklist, resulting in a seven-year drought of work. When he resumed work, he appeared in the title role in *Joe Butterfly* (1957) with Audie Murphy.

A distinguished theatre director, he won a Tony Award nomination for his 1974 Broadway staging of *Ulysses in Nighttown*, a theatrical adaptation of the "Nighttown" section of James Joyce's *Ulysses*. Meredith also shared a Special Tony Award with James Thurber for their collaboration on *A Thurber Carnival* (1960).

Meredith was a favorite of director Otto Preminger, who cast him in *Advise and Consent* (1962), *In Harm's Way* (1965), *Hurry Sundown* (1967), *Skidoo* (1968) and *Such Good Friends* (1971). He was the Penguin in the *Batman* movie of 1966 based on the TV series. Meredith played Rocky Balboa's trainer, Mickey Goldmill, in the first three *Rocky* films (1976, 1979 and 1982), to great acclaim. Even though his character died in the third Rocky film, he returned briefly in the fifth film, *Rocky V* (1990).

Meredith appeared in *Santa Claus: The Movie* (1985). In his last years, he played Jack Lemmon's character's father in *Grumpy Old Men* (1993) and its sequel, *Grumpier Old Men* (1995).

He was nominated for Academy Awards in the Best Supporting Actor category for his roles in *The Day of the Locust* (1975) and *Rocky* (1976).

Meredith appeared in four different starring roles in the acclaimed anthology TV series *The Twilight Zone*, tying him with Jack Klugman for the most appearances on the show. In the famous "Time Enough at Last", a 1959 episode of *The Twilight Zone*, Meredith plays a henpecked bank teller who only wants to be left alone with his books. In the 1961 episode "Mr. Dingle, the Strong", Meredith plays the title character, a timid weakling who, as the subject of a space alien's experiment on human nature, suddenly acquires superhuman strength. In "Printer's Devil", Meredith portrayed the Devil himself, and in "The Obsolete Man", he portrayed a librarian, sentenced to death in a future, dystopic totalitarian society. He would later play two more roles in Rod Serling's other anthology series, *Night Gallery* (1971-1972). Meredith was the narrator for *Twilight Zone: The Movie* in 1983. He did not receive on-screen credit for his narration (this was so that he could do the job for scale rather than charge his usual minimum fee); as compensation for Meredith's uncredited work, his name was inserted into the dialogue in a scene between Dan Aykroyd and Albert Brooks.

In 1963, he appeared as Vincent Marion in a five-part episode of the last season of the Warner Brothers ABC detective series *77 Sunset Strip*.

Meredith also played The Penguin in the television series *Batman* (1966-1968). His role as the Penguin was so well-received that the show's writers always had a script featuring the Penguin ready whenever Meredith was available. He and Cesar Romero's Joker are tied for number of appearances on the show.

From 1972-73, Meredith played V.C.R. Cameron, director of *Probe Control*, in the television movie/pilot *Probe* and then in *Search*, the subsequent TV series (the name was changed to avoid conflict with a program on PBS). The series involved World Securities Corporation, a private agency which, among other activities, fielded a number of detectives equipped with high-tech equipment including a tiny TV transmitter (the "Scanner") which allowed Probe Control to see what was going on where the agents were working. In the episode "Moment of Madness", Cameron was kidnapped and subsequently rescued from a torture chamber by agent C.R. Grover (Doug McClure), without any of the tools carried by Probe agents. In that episode, a slice of Meredith's character was given some depth and background. Cameron was kidnapped for revenge by a former military subordinate who was captured with disinformation supplied by the Cameron character, disclosing in that episode that Cameron was serving as an intelligence office in the Korean War.

He won an Emmy Award as Outstanding Supporting Actor in a Comedy or Drama Special for the 1977 television film *Tail Gunner Joe*, a fictitious study of U.S. Senator Joseph R. McCarthy, the anti-communist leader of the

1950s. In the early 1980s, he was a co-host of the ABC program, *Those Amazing Animals*, and co-starred in the short lived CBS sitcom *Gloria* (1982-1983).

Meredith also performed voiceover work. He was the TV commercial voice for Bulova Watches, Honda, Stokley-Van Camp, United Airlines, and Freakies breakfast cereal.

He supplied the narration for the 1974–1975 ABC Saturday morning series *Korg: 70,000 B.C.* and was the voice of Puff in the series of animated adaptations of the Peter, Paul, and Mary song *Puff, the Magic Dragon*. In the mid-1950s, he was one of four narrators of the NBC and syndicated public affairs program, *The Big Story* (1949–1958), which focuses on courageous journalists. In 1991, he narrated a track on the The Chieftains' album of traditional Christmas music and carols, *The Bells of Dublin*.

His last role before his death was the portrayal of both Hamilton Wofford and Covington Wofford characters in the 1996 video game *Ripper* by Take-Two Interactive.

In 1994, Meredith published his autobiography, *So Far, So Good*. In the book he confessed that he suffered from violent mood swings which were caused by cyclothymia, a form of Bipolar disorder.

Meredith had four wives, including actresses Margaret Perry and Paulette Goddard. His last marriage (to Kaja Sundsten) lasted 46 years, and produced two children, Jonathon (a musician) and Tala (a painter).

Meredith was a lifelong Democrat. Due to this, he had a bitter feud with Senator Joseph McCarthy, which led to him being blacklisted for a few years in the 1950s.

Meredith died at age 89 from complications of Alzheimer's disease and melanoma on September 9, 1997. Long time friend Adam West spoke briefly at his memorial service. Meredith's remains were cremated. For his contribution to the motion picture industry, Burgess has a star on the Hollywood Walk of Fame at 6904 Hollywood Boulevard, Los Angeles, Calif.

Charles Meredith

Charles Meredith was born August 27, 1894 in Knoxville, Pennsylvania. He had the requisite good looks to become a popular silent film leading man.

Tall, dark and exceedingly good-looking with distinctive high-parted hair, he played opposite Blanche Sweet, Mary Miles Minter, Florence Vidor, Katherine MacDonald, and other top stars of the day in both romantic drama and comedies. In 1924, he abandoned his film career for fulfillment on the stage, not returning to the cinema until 1947 wherein he played a number of small roles with an upstanding, prideful nature such as justices, commissioners, reverends, admirals, etc.

Some of those roles included *The Thirteenth Commandment* (1920), *The Miracle of the Bells* (1948), *Samson and Delilah* (1949), *Fort Worth* (1951), *Them!* (1954), *Rocky Jones, Space Ranger* (1954), *Giant* (1956), *The Guns of Fort Petticoat* (1957) with Audie Murphy, *Ocean's Eleven* (1960), *Seven Days in May* (1964), and his last film *The Quick Gun* (1964) again with Audie Murphy.

He died November 28, 1964, at age 70 in Los Angeles, California.

Madge Meredith

Audie Murphy with Madge Meredith in *To Hell and Back*

Madge Meredith was born Marjorie May Massow July 15, 1921 in Iowa Falls, Iowa, and was an American actress.

She appeared in twenty-five films and television programs from 1944 to 1961. Some of those credits include *Take It or Leave It* (1944), *Trail Street* (1947), *Cowboy G-Men* (1952-1953), *Tumbleweed* (1953) with Audie Murphy, *The Lone Ranger* (1955), as Audie Murphy's sister Corinne in *To Hell and Back* (1955), *The Ten Commandments* (1956), *The Guns of Fort Petticoat* (1957) a third appearance with Audie Murphy, *Northwest Passage* (1958), *Tales of the Vikings* (1959), and *The Best of the Post* (1961).

On June 30, 1947, Madge Meredith was convicted and sentenced to prison for five years to life for complicity in an assault of her former manager, Nicholas D. Gianaclis, and his bodyguard, Verne V. Davis. Gianaclis and Davis testified they were beaten, kidnapped, and robbed by a group of men as they neared Meredith's home in the Hollywood Hills. In March 1951, the California Assembly Interim Committee on Crime and Corrections issued an official report concluding that Meredith had been framed. The case was handled sloppily in court and inconsistent allegations by the perpetrators were overlooked by police. In July 1951, Gov. Earl Warren commuted her sentence to time served and issued a statement of disgust at how her trial had been handled. Mr. Gianaclis was found to have set-up Miss Meredith to gain ownership of her home. Following her release from Tehachapi prison, the court found for her receiving back ownership of her home from her accuser. Mr. Gianaclis, an immigrant from Greece, was denied U.S. citizenship by the Immigration Service.

She currently lives in Hawaii.

Jan Merlin

Audie Murphy with Jan Merlin in *Gunfight at Comanche Creek*

Jan Merlin was born April 3, 1925, and is an American character actor, screen writer, and author.

Born and raised in New York, during the Second World War he enlisted in the US Navy to serve on three successive ships in the North Atlantic and Pacific Fleets, accumulating ten battle stars before entering Japan's Inland Sea with the first group of Occupation Forces.

Upon returning to civilian life, the former torpedo-man worked in summer stock beginning in 1946, and enrolled in the Neighborhood Playhouse School of the Theater, making his Broadway debut in *Mister Roberts* starring Henry Fonda, in 1949.

His professional career as an actor spans more than five decades, and has included performances in stage plays on and off Broadway, radio dramas, several hundreds of live and filmed episodes of TV series, and more than thirty feature motion pictures made in the U.S. and abroad.

His best-known TV work was as co-star on *Tom Corbett, Space Cadet* in the part of Cadet Roger Manning (1950–1953), and as co-star in the ABC western series, *The Rough Riders*, as Lieutenant Colin Kirby (1959).

Other roles include *Dragnet* (1954), *A Day of Fury* (1956), *Climax!* (1955-1957), *Hell Bent for Leather* (1960) with Audie Murphy, *Whispering Smith* (1961) again with Audie Murphy, *Gunfight at Comanche Creek* (1963) a third appearance with Audie Murphy, *Gunsmoke* (1964), *Guns of Diablo* (1965), *The Fugitive* (1966), *The St. Valentine's Day Massacre* (1967), *Take the Money and Run* (1969), *Mission: Impossible* (1969-1971), *I Escaped from Devil's Island* (1973), *Baretta* (1975), *Tales of the Unexpected* (1977), *Tales of the Gold Monkey* (1983), *Nowhere to Run* (1989), *Dallas* (1989), *False Identity* (1990), *Guns of Paradise* (1991), and *A Child Lost Forever: The Jerry Sherwood Story* (1992).

As an author, Merlin received an Emmy in 1975 for his scripting of the NBC Daytime soap opera *Another World*. He was nominated again in 1976. His first novel was published in 1982. He currently has a number of novels in print, including *Gunbearer, Part I, Gunbearer, Part II, Ainoko, Gypsies Don't Lie, Crackpots,* and *Shooting Montezuma.* He has also published several works of fiction and non-fiction with co-author William Russo, including *The Paid Companion of J. Wilkes Booth, Troubles in a Golden Eye, MGM Makes Boys' Town,* and *Hanging with Billy Budd.*

In 2009 he received a Golden Halo Award, for his work as actor and writer, from the Southern California Motion Picture Council.

Merlin has one child, by his first wife, a son, Peter William Merlin, born in 1964.

Arnold Merritt

Arnold Merritts born September 15, 1939 in Topeka, Kansas. He appeared in thirteen films and television programs from 1958 to 1965. Those credits were *Naked City* (1958-1959), *The United States Steel Hour* (1959), *The Unforgiven* (1960) with Audie Murphy, *Armstrong Circle Theatre* (1960), *Maverick* (1960), *Michael Shayne* (1961), *Bonanza* (1961), *Gidget Goes Hawaiian* (1961), *Bachelor Father* (1962), *13 West Street* (1962) with Alan Ladd, *Going My Way* (1963), *The Outer Limits* (1964), and six episodes of *Combat!* (1962-1965).

Emile Meyer

Emile Meyer with Audie Murphy in *Drums Across the River*

Emile Meyer was born in New Orleans, Louisiana, August 18, 1910, and was an American actor usually known for tough, aggressive, authoritative characters in Hollywood films from the 1950s era, mostly in westerns or thrillers. He provided such noteworthy performances as Ryker in *Shane* (1953), as Father Dupree in *Paths of Glory* (1957) and the corrupt cop in *Sweet Smell of Success* (1957).

Other roles included *The People Against O'Hara* (1951), *Carbine Williams* (1952), *Stories of the Century* (1954), *Drums Across the River* (1954) with Audie Murphy, *Stranger on Horseback* (1955), *The Adventures of Ozzie & Harriet* (1958), *Good Day for a Hanging* (1959), *Wichita Town* (1960), *Taggart* (1964), *My Favorite Martian* (1965), *A Time for Dying* (1969) again with Audie Murphy, *Bonanza* (1970-1972), and *Macon County Line* (1974).

His final film role was in *The Legend of Frank Woods* (1977).

He died March 19, 1987, at age 76 in Covington, Louisiana, from Alzheimer's disease.

Dolores Michaels

Dolores Michaels with Audie Murphy in *Battle at Bloody Beach*

Dolores Rae Michaels was born in Kansas City, Missouri, January 30, 1933, and was an American actress.

Her father was at one-time a professional baseball player who spent time as a catcher in the Chicago Cubs organization. He then went into the food brokerage business.

Michaels had the same birthday as Franklin D. Roosevelt, and before her third birthday her father sent the president a birthday card informing him of the connection. President Roosevelt replied with a message back to Dolores sending her "best wishes" on her birthday.

She studied ballet from the age of five, and as a teenager went to New York City to study dance and drama. She attended Bishop Hogan High School in Kansas City, Missouri. Her older sister, Gloria J. Michaels had gone to New York City to dance on Broadway. Gloria joined the traveling cast of *Brigadoon*, and when the show came to do the performance in Kansas City they ask a 16-year old Dolores to join them.

She moved to Laguna Beach, California after marrying interior decorator Maurice Martiné in Laguna Beach on the rocks overlooking the Pacific Ocean in 1953. Michaels moved out of their home and they separated in January 1958, moving in to a house with her older sister, Gloria, in Los Angeles. In January 1959, she filed for divorce, citing cruelty. At the divorce hearing she testified that Martiné had moved them into an expensive unfinished house, without heat or water, and that he expected her to bath in the ocean, something she didn't want to do because she was constantly catching a cold. The divorce was final on September 29, 1959. During her separation and after the divorce, she dated actor John Duke.

Michaels was discovered when she was doing a scene in an acting class at 20th Century-Fox's talent school. A group of producers and directors were in the audience, and after the scenes were finished, the audience voted on who gave the best performance. She won and got a contract with 20th Century-Fox.

Joanne Woodward was supposed to have the part of "Mildred Pritchard" in *The Wayward Bus* (1957), but Woodward dropped out, and the part went to Michaels at the last minute, her first acting role. United Press International said in a review of the film that Michaels' "torrid" scene, a seduction scene in a hayloft where she makes a pass at the bus driver (Rick Jason), "manages to steal the sexiest scene in the picture", over better known sirens as Jayne Mansfield and Joan Collins. Director Victor Vicas shot the scene twice, an "A" scene and a "B" scene because of the censors.

Her publicist released a biography that stated she had attended the University of Kansas for one year and was a member of the Kappa Kappa Gamma sorority. But, people, trying to remember if they knew her, at both the university and the sorority could find no record of her at either entity. The fact was that she had enrolled at the university in the fall of 1951 and was "rushed" by the sorority, but she only stayed at the school a few weeks and then dropped out, and she did not join the sorority. Her publicist had fabricated her biography to enhance it.

Michaels wanted to be taken seriously as an actor and not be treated as a sex symbol. When one reporter asked her for her measurements, she responded, "You can go to the wardrobe department and find out". She also said that she had never been asked to go to the studio photo gallery, stating, "That's part of the old Hollywood glamor nonsense. Also, it's in bad taste. I'm not a sexpot, I'm an actress". Later she told Hollywood columnist Erskine Johnson: "I favor the truly sensual photograph over the coyly teasing garter shots. I'd even rather be posed artistically nude than photographed giggling from behind a Venetian blind. I have never objected to posing. It's just that I wanted to build a career as an actress first".

After John Duke, she started dating Argentine actor Alejandro Rey, whom she met on the set of *Battle at Bloody Beach* (1961) with Audie Murphy. She then started dating Novelist-screenwriter Bernard Wolfe, who proposed to her in 1962. Michaels and Wolfe married in Los Angeles on June 1, 1964. The marriage was her second and his first. He was 48 and she was 31. The couple divorced in October 1969.

Other credits included *Son of Sinbad* (1955), *April Love* (1957), *Warlock* (1959), *One Foot in Hell* (1960), *Perry Mason* (1962), and *The Lloyd Bridges Show* (1963).

She and Wolfe had twin daughters, Jordan M. and Miranda I., born in Los Angeles on July 23, 1970.

Dolores Michaels Wolfe died at the age of 68 in West Hollywood, California, of natural causes on September 25, 2001.

Robert Middleton

Robert Middleton, was born Samuel G. Messer, May 13, 1911, in Cincinnati, Ohio and was an American film and television actor known for his large size and beetle-like brow. With a deep, booming voice, Middleton trained for a musical career at the Cincinnati Conservatory of Music and Carnegie Tech in Pittsburgh, Pennsylvania. He worked steadily as a radio announcer and actor.

One of his early works was as the narrator of the educational film "Duck and Cover". After appearing on the Broadway stage and live television, Middleton began appearing in films in 1954. He's also remembered on television as the boss Mr. Marshall on *The Jackie Gleason Show* (1953) and in film opposite Humphrey Bogart in *The Desperate Hours* (1955), Gary Cooper in *Friendly Persuasion* (1956), Richard Egan and Elvis Presley in *Love Me Tender* (1956), Dorothy Malone and Robert Stack in *The Tarnished Angels* (1958), and Dean Martin in *Career* (1959).

Middleton appeared in many television programs in the 1950s, 1960s, and 1970s including *Appointment with Adventure* (1955), *Alfred Hitchcock Presents* (1956-1957), *The Real McCoys* (1959), *Wichita Town* (1960), *The Untouchables* (1960-1961), *Perry Mason* (1963), *Burke's Law* (1965-1966), *Get Smart* (1970), *Mission: Impossible* (1972), *Mannix* (1973), and *Hunter* (1977).

Other significant film roles include *The Court Jester* (1956) as a grim and determined knight who jousts with Danny Kaye in the famous "pellet with the poison" sequence, and as a sinister politician in *The Lincoln Conspiracy* (1977).

Betwixt and between were an array of brutish mountain daddies, corrupt, cigar-chomping town bosses and lynch mob leaders, such as *The Silver Chalice* (1954), *The Proud Ones* (1956), *Day of the Bad Man* (1958), *Hell Bent for Leather* (1960) with Audie Murphy, *Cattle King* (1963), *A Big Hand for the Little Lady* (1966), and *The Cheyenne Social Club* (1970).

Middleton died June 14, 1977, of congestive heart failure in Hollywood at the age of sixty-six.

John Milford

John Milford was born in Johnstown, New York, September 7, 1929, and was an American actor in theatre, television, and films, playing scores of roles, often as a western villain.

Milford studied Civil Engineering at Union College but chose to pursue his first love, acting.

After making his film debut in *Marty* in 1955, Milford went on to act in dozens of film and TV roles, especially in *The Ten Commandments* (1956), *Face of a Fugitive* (1959), *Wichita Town* (1960), *The Rifleman* (1959-1962), *Gunfight at Comanche Creek* (1963) with Audie Murphy, *The Fugitive* (1963-1966), *Get Smart* (1966), *Support Your Local Sheriff!* (1969), *The Bold Ones: The Lawyers* (1969-1972), *Planet of the Apes* (1974), *The Six Million Dollar Man* (1975-1978), *The Amazing Spider-Man* (1979), *Enos* (1980-1981), *Policewoman Centerfold* (1983), *T.J. Hooker* (1986), *Freddy's Nightmares* (1990), *The X-Files* (1995), *Melrose Place* (1997), and *Chicken Soup for the Soul* (2000).

In 1965 Milford had a recurring role as Cole Younger in the TV series *The Legend Of Jesse James*.

Throughout his career Milford continued to work in the theatre. He founded the Chamber Theatre at 3759 Cahuenga Blvd, pioneering Equity Waiver productions in Los Angeles, and helped launched the careers of actors such as Richard Chamberlain and Vic Morrow.

Milford's *Los Angeles Times* obituary credits him with using his engineering background to help create the original design for the Hollywood Walk Of Fame.

Milford died of skin cancer August 23, 2000. He was survived by his wife, TV producer Susan Graw, and two sons.

Victor Millan

Victor Millan with Audie Murphy in *Walk the Proud Land*

Victor Millan was born Joseph Brown August 1, 1920, and was an American actor, academic, and former Dean of the theatre arts department at Santa Monica College in Santa Monica, California.

He served as a sergeant in the United States Army Air Corps during World War II. During the war, Millan was stationed in China, India, and Burma.

He enrolled at the University of California, Los Angeles (UCLA) following the end of World War II. Millan earned both his bachelor's degree and his master's degree in theatre arts from UCLA.

He had over eighty separate television and film credits, in addition to his theater work. Some of his earliest roles included the 1952 film, *The Ring*, which was directed by Kurt Neumann, as well as *Walk the Proud Land* (1956) with Audie Murphy, *Touch of Evil* (1958), and *The FBI Story* (1959).

Other roles over the years included *Giant* (1956), *Wichita Town* (1959), *Wanted: Dead or Alive* (1960), *The Fugitive* (1966), *The Big Valley* (1968-1969), *Cannon* (1971-1972), *Marcus Welby, M.D.* (1974-1975), *How the West Was Won* (1979), *Knight Rider* (1982), *Scarface* (1983), and *The Ed Begley, Jr. Show* (1989).

He taught theatre arts at Santa Monica College for his entire academic teaching career. He served as the Dean of the theatre arts department at the college for over 25 years.

Victor Millan died at his home in Santa Monica, California, on April 3, 2009, at the age of 88.

Diane Millay

Diana Claire Millay was born June 7, 1935, in Rye, New York, and was an American actress. In the mid-1940s, she modeled sun suits for the Sears Catalog. She appeared in forty-four films and television programs from 1955 to 1971. Some of those credits include *Street of Sinners* (1957), *The Westerner* (1960), *Whispering Smith* (1961) with Audie Murphy, *Perry Mason* (1961-1963), *The Virginian* (1964), and *The Secret Storm* (1971).

She is perhaps best known as Laura Collins in sixty-four episodes of *Dark Shadows* (1966-1969) and the film *Night of Dark Shadows* (1971).

She married Broadway producer Geoffrey Jones in October 1966, but they separated after the birth of their son, Kiley Christopher, in 1967.

She has published several books, including, *I'd Rather Eat Than Act*, *The Power of Halloween*, and *How to Create Good Luck*.

Colleen Miller

Collen Miller with Audie Murphy in *Gunfight at Comanche Creek*

Colleen Miller was born November 10, 1932, in Yakima, Washington, and is an American actress. Nineteen-year-old Colleen Miller was fishing in the California Mountains when a resort photographer recruited her to pose with a prize trout; a movie scout saw the picture in print, and Colleen wound up with a small role in *The Las Vegas Story* (1952).

A more noticeable role in *Man Crazy* (1953) brought the brunette beauty a contract at Universal, where she quickly became a second-rank star in westerns and film-noir. Her best notices were for *Playgirl* (1954), *Four Guns to the Border* (1954), and *Man in the Shadow* (1957), gaining critical praise for her fine natural talent and carefree sensuality.

She retired in 1958, except for one western in 1963 with Audie Murphy called *Gunfight at Comanche Creek,* for a domestic life with her husband and two children.

She did appear in *Division 4* (1970) and *Stand Up and Be Counted* (1972).

After her 1975 divorce she reportedly considered resuming her career, but has made no more films to date.

Mort Mills

Mort Mills with Audie Murphy in *Gunfight at Comanche Creek*

Mort Mills was born January 11, 1919, and was an American film and television actor who had roles in over 200 movies and television episodes. He was often the town lawman or the local bad guy in many popular westerns of the 1950s and 1960s.

From 1957-1959 he had a recurring co-starring role as Marshal Frank Tallman in *Man Without a Gun*. Other recurring roles were as Sergeant Ben Landro in the *Perry Mason* (1960-1965) series and Sheriff Fred Madden in *The Big Valley* (1965-1966). In 1958, he guest starred as a particularly greedy bounty hunter who clashes with Steve McQueen's character of Josh Randall in the CBS western series, *Wanted: Dead or Alive*.

Though Mills did much television work, he also found regular work in motion pictures. He played the highway patrolman who pursues Marion Crane (Janet Leigh) in Alfred Hitchcock's classic thriller *Psycho* (1960). A few years later, he worked again with Hitchcock, playing a spy in East Germany under the cover of being a farmer in *Torn Curtain* (1966). Mills also appeared with Charlton Heston in Orson Welles's *Touch of Evil* (1958).

In 1955, he appeared as Samuel Mason on ABC's Disneyland miniseries *Davy Crockett*, starring Fess Parker. From 1957-1959, Mills co-starred with Rex Reason in the syndicated western series *Man Without a Gun*. He portrayed Marshal Frank Tillman. Reason played his friend, Adam MacLean, editor of the Yellowstone Sentinel newspaper. Mills was a regular as police Lieutenant Bob Malone in Howard Duff's NBC-Four Star Television series, *Dante* (1960–1961), set at a San Francisco, California, nightclub called "Dante's Inferno".

Other roles over the years included *Biff Baker, U.S.A.* (1952), *Hopalong Cassidy* (1953), *Rocky Jones, Space Ranger* (1954), *To Hell and Back* (1955) with Audie Murphy, *Tension at Table Rock* (1956), *The Iron Sheriff* (1957), *Ride a Crooked Trail* (1958) again with Audie Murphy, *Wichita Town* (1959), *Twenty Plus Two* (1961), *Gunfight at Comanche Creek* (1963) a third appearance with Audie Murphy, *The Quick Gun* (1964) a fourth time with Audie Murphy, *Bullet for a Badman* (1964) his fifth and final appearance with Audie Murphy, *The Fugitive* (1963-1965), *The Green Hornet* (1966), *Adam-12* (1971), *Alias Smith and Jones* (1972), and *The Streets of San Francisco* (1973).

He showed his comedic side in the 1965 Three Stooges film *The Outlaws Is Coming* when he played Trigger Mortis. This is my favorite role of Mort Mills.

He died June 6, 1993, at age 74 in Ventura, California.

William Mims

William Ray Mims was born January 15, 1927 in Carthage, Missouri, and was an American actor. He appeared in numerous films and television programs from 1956 to 1988.

Some of those credits included *I Killed Wild Bill Hickok* (1956), *No Name on the Bullet* (1959) with Audie Murphy, *The Life and Legend of Wyatt Earp* (1959-1961), *Battle at Bloody Beach* (1961) again with Audie Murphy, *Whispering Smith* (1961) a third appearance with Audie Murphy, *Twilight Zone* (1963), *The Fugitive* (1964), *Gunfight in Abilene* (1967), *Adam 12* (1967), *Night Gallery* (1971), *Kolchak: The Night Stalker* (1974), *Switch* (1976-1978), *240-Robert* (1979), *Chips* (1981), *Airwolf* (1986), and *Falcon Crest* (1988).

He died April 9, 1991, at age 64 in Studio City, California.

Belle Mitchell

Audie Murphy with Belle Mitchell in *Tumbleweed*

Belle Mitchell was born in Croswell, Michigan, September 24, 1889, and was an American film actress. She appeared in over 100 films between 1915 and 1982.

Some of those credits include *A Christmas Revenge* (1915), *Flying Romeos* (1928), *Madame X* (1937), *Angels with Dirty Faces* (1938), *Phantom of the Opera* (1943), *Cobra Woman* (1944), *The Spider Woman* (1944), *The Beast with Five Fingers* (1946), *Ghost Chasers* (1951), *Hopalong Cassidy* (1953), *Tumbleweed* (1953) with Audie Murphy, *Hell on Frisco Bay* (1955), *The Return of Dracula* (1958), *A Majority of One* (1961), *Perry Mason* (1965), *Airport* (1970), *High Plains Drifter* (1973), *Soylent Green* (1973), and *Slipping Into Darkness* released in 1982.

She died February 12, 1979, at age 89 in Woodland Hills, Los Angeles, California.

George Mitchell

George Mitchell was born February 21, 1905, in Larchmont, New York, and was an American actor working from 1935 through 1971 in film and television, and on Broadway. It was not until he was thirty-five years old and newly married to actress Katherine Squire, that he decided to be an actor.

Some of his roles included *Once in a Blue Moon* (1935), *Captain Eddie* (1945), *Inner Sanctum* (1954), *3:10 to Yuma* (1957), *The Wild and the Innocent* (1959) with Audie Murphy, *Alcoa Presents: One Step Beyond* (1959-1960), *Kid Galahad* (1962), *Twilight Zone* (1960-1963), *Face of the Screaming Werewolf* (1964), *The Fugitive* (1963-1964), *Nevada Smith* (1966), and *Land of the Giants* (1969).

George Mitchell's major acting credits include the film *The Andromeda Strain* (1971), directed by Robert Wise, co-starring Arthur Hill, and based on the novel of the same name by Michael Crichton. He played the comic relief as a cranky town drunk who along with an infant, were among the only survivors of exposure to the Andromeda Strain.

George Mitchell acted in several films and television episodes with his wife Katherine Squire, the two of them often playing a husband-and-wife couple intrinsic to the story. One example was the two of them as an elderly couple in the Jack Nicolson film *Ride in the Whirlwind* (1965). They first appear as a refuge for the two men on the run, but who then become instrumental to the fugitives' destruction.

He died January 18, 1972, at age 66 in Washington, District of Columbia.

Guy Mitchell

Guy Mitchell with Audie Murphy in *Whispering Smith*

Guy Mitchell was born Albert George Cernik in Detroit, Michigan, February 27, 1927, and was an American pop singer, successful in his homeland, the U.K. and Australia. As an international recording star of the 1950s he achieved record sales in excess of 44 million units and this included six million-selling singles.

In the fall of 1957, Mitchell starred in his own ABC variety show, *The Guy Mitchell Show*. He also appeared as George Romack on the 1961 NBC western detective series *Whispering Smith*, with World War II hero Audie Murphy in the leading role.

At the age of eleven he was signed by Warner Brothers Pictures, to be groomed as a child star, and he also performed on the radio on Station KFWB in Los Angeles, California. After leaving school, he worked as a saddlemaker, but supplemented his income by singing whenever he could. At this point in his life, Dude Martin, who had a country music broadcast in San Francisco, noticed him and hired him to perform with his band.

He served in the United States Navy for two years, and after leaving the service became a singer with Carmen Cavallaro's big band. In 1947 he made recordings for Decca with Cavallaro's band, but had to leave due to food poisoning. He eventually went to New York City, and made records for King Records under the name Al Grant (one in particular, "Cabaret", appeared in the Variety magazine charts). He won on the radio show *Arthur Godfrey's Talent Scouts* in 1949 as a soloist.

Mitch Miller, who was in charge of talent at Columbia Records, noticed Cernik in 1950, and he joined Columbia and got his new stage name at Miller's urging: Miller is supposed to have said, "My name is 'Mitchell' and you seem a nice 'guy', so we'll call you Guy Mitchell". Bob Merrill wrote a string of top hits for Mitchell.

In the 1950s and 1960s he acted in movies as well as singing. Some of his roles were in *Those Redheads from Seattle* (1953), *Red Garters* (1954), *Overland Trail* (1960), *Thriller* (1961), *The Ann Sothern Show* (1960-1961), *Perry Mason* (1961), *The Wild Westerners* (1962), *Magic Mansion* (1966), *Your Cheatin' Heart* (1990), and *Bastard!!* (1992).

During *Whispering Smith,* after seven episodes were filmed, Guy Mitchell broke his shoulder in a fall from a horse and spent several episodes in a cast.

His first hit was *My Heart Cries for You* (1951). Though he is a pre-rock pop singer, many of his songs have a decided rock beat to them, including *Heartaches by the Number*, *Rock-a-Billy*, *The Same Old Me* and his biggest hit, *Singing the Blues,* which was number one for ten weeks in 1956.

Mitchell suffered from alcoholism and was divorced three times.

He died on July 1, 1999, aged 72, of complications from cancer surgery.

In 2007, to commemorate his musical legacy and what would have been his 80th birthday, the English division of SonyBMG released *The Essential Collection* CD. In 2008, Guy Mitchell was inducted into the Hit Parade Hall of Fame.

Laurie Mitchell

Audie Murphy with Laurie Mitchell in *Gunfight at Comanche Creek*

Laurie Mitchell was born July 14, 1928, in New York City and raised in the East Bronx. She moved with her family to California while in her teens.

Acting school led to stage roles and then to movie assignments, beginning with *20,000 Leagues Under the Sea* (1954). More roles followed like *The Man Behind the Badge* (1955), *Girls in Prison* (1956), *Adventures of Superman* (1957), *The Oklahoman* (1957), *Attack of the Puppet People* (1958), *Queen of Outer Space* (1958), *Some Like It Hot* (1959), *Richard Diamond, Private Detective* (1958-1959), *Wanted: Dead or Alive* (1959), *Hell Bent for Leather* (1960) with Audie Murphy, *Hawaiian Eye* (1961), *That Touch of Mink* (1962), *Gunfight at Comanche Creek* (1963) again with Audie Murphy, *The Addams Family* (1965), *Laredo* (1966), *Ironside* (1967), *Hogan's Heroes* (1968), *The Virginian* (1966-1969), and *The Bold Ones: The New Doctors* (1971).

Long-retired and now the wife of a medical salesman, she has recently been "rediscovered" by her fans and has begun making the celebrity expo and autograph show rounds.

Thomas Mitchell

Audie Murphy with Thomas Mitchell in *Destry*

Thomas Mitchell was born to Irish immigrants in Elizabeth, New Jersey, July 11, 1892, and was an American actor, playwright, and screenwriter.

Among his most famous roles in a long career are those of Gerald O'Hara, the father of Scarlett O'Hara in *Gone with the Wind* (1939), the drunken Doc Boone in John Ford's *Stagecoach* (1939), and Uncle Billy in *It's a Wonderful Life* (1946).

Mitchell was the first person to win an Oscar, an Emmy, and a Tony Award. Nominated twice for an Oscar, first for *The Hurricane* (1938), he won the Best Supporting Actor award for *Stagecoach* (1939); later, he would be nominated three times for an Emmy. He was nominated twice, in 1952 and 1953, for his role in the medical drama *The Doctor*, winning the Lead Actor Drama award in 1953. Nominated again in 1955, for an appearance on a weekly anthology series, he did not win. Mitchell won the Tony for Best Actor in a Musical, in 1953, for his role as Dr Downer in the musical comedy *Hazel Flagg,* based on the 1937 Paramount comedy film *Nothing Sacred*, rounding out the Triple Crown of acting awards.

He came from a family of journalists and civic leaders. Both his father and brother were newspaper reporters (his nephew, James P. Mitchell, later served as Dwight Eisenhower's Secretary of Labor). Like them, the younger Mitchell also became a newspaper reporter right after graduating from St. Patrick High School in Elizabeth. Soon, however, Mitchell found he enjoyed writing comic theatrical skits much more than chasing late-breaking scoops.

He became an actor in 1913, at one point touring with Charles Coburn's Shakespeare Company. Even while playing leading roles on Broadway into the 1920s Mitchell would continue to write. One of the plays he co-authored, *Little Accident*, was eventually made into a film (three times) by Hollywood. Mitchell's first credited screen role was in the 1923 film *Six Cylinder Love*.

Mitchell's breakthrough role was as the embezzler in Frank Capra's 1937 film *Lost Horizon*. Following this performance, he was much in demand in Hollywood. That same year, he was nominated for a Best Supporting Actor Academy Award for his performance *The Hurricane*, directed by John Ford.

Over the next few years, Mitchell appeared in many of the greatest films of the 20th century. In 1939 alone he had key roles in *Stagecoach*, *Mr. Smith Goes to Washington*, *Only Angels Have Wings*, *The Hunchback of Notre Dame*, and *Gone with the Wind*. While probably better remembered as Scarlett O'Hara's loving but doomed father in *Gone with the Wind*, it was for his performance as the drunken Doc Boone in *Stagecoach*, co-starring John Wayne (in Wayne's breakthrough role), that Mitchell won the Best Supporting Actor Academy Award. In his acceptance speech, he quipped, "I didn't know I was that good".

Throughout the 1940s and 1950s, Mitchell acted in a wide variety of roles in productions such as 1942's *Moontide*, 1944's *The Keys of the Kingdom* (as an atheist doctor) and 1952's *High Noon* (as the town mayor). He is probably best known to audiences today for his role as sad sack Uncle Billy in Capra's 1946 Christmas classic *It's a Wonderful Life* opposite James Stewart. This film, while not well received when released, has become a classic that is shown each year on broadcast television. It ranks regularly as one of the most beloved films of all time.

One of his better roles in the 1950's was as Rags Barnaby in *Destry* (1954) with Audie Murphy. In the film he went from boozing town drunk, to serious Sheriff of Restful, back to drunk, then back to serious Sheriff, then an amazingly heartfelt death scene.

From the 1950s and into the early 1960s, Mitchell worked primarily in television, appearing in a variety of roles in some of the most well-regarded early series of the era, including *Playhouse 90* (1958), *Zane Gray Theatre* (1958-1961), and *Goodyear Theatre* (1959) productions. In 1954, he starred in the TV series *Mayor of the Town*, in 1959 starred in 39 episodes of the TV series *Glencannon* and in the early 1960s originated the stage role *Columbo,* later made famous on television by Peter Falk. *Columbo* was Mitchell's last role.

Mitchell died at age 70, in December 17, 1962, from bone cancer in Beverly Hills, California. He was cremated and his ashes stored in the vault at the Chapel of the Pines Crematory in Los Angeles.

John Mitchum

John Newman Mitchum was born in Bridgeport, Connecticut September 6, 1919, and was an American actor from the 1940s in films and, later, television. He was the younger brother of Julie Mitchum and Robert Mitchum. He initially appeared in only unbilled and extra roles before gradually receiving bigger character parts in middle age. Mitchum supported his more famous brother on several occasions and was featured as the cop Frank DiGiorgio in the first three *Dirty Harry* films (1971-1976).

Mitchum was also a writer, poet, singer and played guitar. An autobiography/biography about the life and careers of him and his brother Robert Mitchum was published in the 1998 called *Them Ornery Mitchum Boys*.

He composed the piece "America, Why I Love Her", which John Wayne included in his book and album of the same name. The piece and a short film with Wayne's narration were aired at many television stations at sign-off time before stations began broadcasting 24 hours a day in late 1970s early 1980s. Wayne is often mistakenly credited with composing the piece.

Some of his roles over the years included *Knock on Any Door* (1949), *Flying Leathernecks* (1951), *Stalag 17* (1953), *Nightmare* (1956), *Zane Grey Theater* (1956-1957), *Richard Diamond, Private Detective* (1958), *The Gunfight at Dodge City* (1959), twenty-one episodes as Pickalong in *Riverboat* (1959-1960), *Whispering Smith* (1961) with Audie Murphy, *Twilight Zone* (1961-1964), *Laredo* (1965), *The Munsters* (1965), *El Dorado* (1966), *Warning Shot* (1967), eleven episodes as Trooper Hoffenmueller in *F Troop* (1965-1967), *Batman* (1966-1967), *Paint Your Wagon* (1969), *Chisum* (1970), *Adam-12* (1970), *Bigfoot* (1970), *High Plains Drifter* (1973), *Kolchak: The Night Stalker* (1974), *Breakheart Pass* (1975), *The Misadventures of Sheriff Lobo* (1979), *Jake Spanner, Private Eye* (1989), and *A Family for Joe* (1990).

Mitchum died November 29, 2001, of a stroke, at the age of 82.

Gerald Mohr

Gerald Mohr was born in New York City, June 11, 1914, and was an American radio, film, and television character actor who appeared in over 4,000 radio plays, seventy-three films and over 100 television shows.

He was educated in Dwight Preparatory School in New York, where he learned to speak fluent French and German, and also learned to ride horses and play the piano. At Columbia University, where he was on a course to become a doctor, Mohr was struck with appendicitis and was recovering in a hospital when another patient, a radio broadcaster, realized Mohr's pleasant baritone voice would be ideal for radio. Mohr was hired by the radio station and became a junior reporter.

In the mid-1930s, Orson Welles invited him to join his formative Mercury Theatre. During his time with Welles, Mohr gained theatrical experience on Broadway in *The Petrified Forest* and starred in *Jean Christophe*.

Mohr made more 4,000 appearances in radio roles throughout the 1930s, 1940s, and early 1950s. He starred as Raymond Chandler's hardboiled detective, Philip Marlowe, 1948–1951, in 119 half-hour radio plays. He also starred in *The Adventures of Bill Lance* and frequently starred in *The Whistler*.

Mohr began appearing in films in the late 1930s, playing his first villain role in the fifteen-part cliffhanger serial *Jungle Girl* (1941). After three years' service in the US Army Air Forces during World War II, he returned to Hollywood, starring as Michael Lanyard in three movies of *The Lone Wolf* series in 1946-47. He also made cameo appearances in *Gilda* (1946), and *Detective Story* (1951), and co-starred in *The Magnificent Rogue* (1946) and *The Sniper* (1952).

In 1949 he was co-announcer, along with Fred Foy, and narrator of twelve of the shows of the first series of *The Lone Ranger* TV series, starring Clayton Moore and Jay Silverheels. He also appeared as Rod Lacy in *The Duel at Silver Creek* (1952) with Audie Murphy.

Mohr made guest appearances in comedy shows, including *The George Burns and Gracie Allen Show* (1951), *How to Marry a Millionaire* (1958), *The Jack Benny Program* (1961 & 1962), *The Smothers Brothers Show* (1965), and *The Lucy Show* (1968). He had the recurring role of newsman Brad Jackson in *My Friend Irma* (1952).

Mohr is remembered for his performance as "Ricky's friend" psychiatrist 'Dr. Henry Molin' (real life name of the assistant film editor on the show) in the classic February 1953 *I Love Lucy* episode, "The Inferiority Complex". Mohr's repeated line was, "Treatment, Ricky. Treatment".

In 1954-55, he starred as Christopher Storm in forty-one episodes of the third series of *Foreign Intrigue - Cross Current*, produced in Stockholm for American distribution. During several episodes of *Foreign Intrigue*, but most noticeably in "The Confidence Game" and "The Playful Prince", he can be heard playing on the piano his own musical composition, *The Frontier Theme,* so called because Christopher Storm was the owner of the Hotel Frontier in Vienna. *Foreign Intrigue* was nominated for an Emmy Award in 1954 under the category "Best Mystery, Action or Adventure Program" and again in 1955 under the category "Best Mystery or Intrigue Series".

Mohr guest starred seven times in the 1957-1962 television series *Maverick*, twice playing Western outlaw Doc Holliday, a role he reprised once more in "Doc Holliday in Durango", a 1958 episode of the television western series *Tombstone Territory* starring Pat Conway and Richard Eastham. In one of the other *Maverick* episodes he portrayed Steve Corbett, a character based on Bogart's in *Casablanca* (1942). That episode, "Escape to Tampico," used the set from the original film, this time as a Mexican saloon where Bret Maverick (James Garner) arrives to hunt down Mohr's character for an earlier murder.

In 1964 Mohr, together with his second wife Mai, planned the formation of an international film company, headquartered in Stockholm, with Swedish and American writers. The company was to have featured comedy, adventure, crime and drama shows for worldwide distribution. By then fluent in Swedish, he also planned to star in a film for TV in which his character, a newspaperman, would speak only Swedish. In 1964 he made a comedy Western, filmed in Stockholm and on location in Yugoslavia, called *Wild West Story* in which, unusually, the good guys spoke Swedish and the bad guys spoke in English.

He continued to market his powerful voice, playing Reed Richards (Mister Fantastic) in the Fantastic Four cartoon series during 1967 and Green Lantern in the 1968 animated series *Aquaman*. Also in 1968 he appeared in his last film role, as con-man 'Tom Branca' in William Wyler's classic musical *Funny Girl* before guest starring in the TV Western series *The Big Valley* (1969).

He then flew to Stockholm, Sweden, in September 1968, to star in the pilot of a proposed new TV series called *Private Entrance*, featuring Swedish film and TV actress Christina Schollin. Shortly after the completion of filming, he died of a heart attack in the evening of November 9, 1968, in Södermalm, Stockholm, at the age of 54. Mohr is interred in the columbarium of Lidingö Kyrkogård in Lidingo, Stockholms Lan, Sweden.

Georgia Moll

Audie Murphy with Georgia Moll in *The Quiet American*

Giorgia Moll was born January 14, 1938 in Prata di Pordenone, Friuli-Venezia Giulia, Italy and is one of the many beauties with whom the Italian cinema teemed in the 1950s and 1960s.

Her harmonious face, her perfect brown hair and her dream measurements did not escape the talent scouts of the time and she was only seventeen when she was hired for her first film *Non scherzare con le donne* (1955).

Her career is undistinguished on the whole but two of her roles stand out: Phuong, Audie Murphy's Vietnamese love interest in Joseph L. Mankiewicz's *The Quiet American* (1958), filmed in Rome in 1957; and Francesca Vanini, the dogsbody secretary of authoritarian film producer Jack Palance in Jean-Luc Godard's *Contempt* (1963).

Some of her other roles included *Husbands in the City* (1957), *Lipstick* (1960), *The Thief of Baghdad* (1961), *A Quiet Business* (1964), *Cover Girls* (1964), *Requiem for a Secret Agent* (1966), *The Blonde from Peking* (1967), *Beyond Control* (1968), and *Togetherness* (1970).

During this period, Giorgia Moll was also a popular singer. After 1970, her appearances became sporadic and she retired for good in 1985 and became a photographer.

Ralph Moody

Audie Murphy with Ralph Moody in *Column South*

Ralph Roy Moody was born November 5, 1886, in St. Louis, Missouri. A favorite of producer/director Jack Webb, character actor Ralph Moody was a familiar face to viewers of *Dragnet* in both its 1950s and 1960s incarnations, but that would be an unfair (as well as inaccurate) way to describe an actor who amassed hundreds of film and television appearances in barely twenty years of movie and television work.

Moody didn't make his screen debut until 1948, with a small role in *Man Eaters of Kumaon*. Already in his sixties, he always looked older than he was, and his craggy features could also impart a fierceness that made him threatening.

Some of his film roles included *Red Mountain* (1951), *The Story of Will Rogers* (1952), *Column South* (1953) with Audie Murphy, *Tumbleweed* (1953) again with Audie Murphy, *Rage at Dawn* (1955), *The Monster That Challenged the World* (1957), *The Lone Ranger and the Lost City of Gold* (1958), *The Story of Ruth* (1960), *Posse from Hell* (1961) a third appearance with Audie Murphy, *Kid Galahad* (1962), *The Rounders* (1965), and *The Chase* (1966).

Although Moody was known for playing kindly or crotchety old men, he occasionally brought that fierceness to bear, as in the *Adventures of Superman* (1955) episode "Test of a Warrior", in which he played the sinister medicine man Okatee.

Moody was one of those actors who could work quickly and milk a line or a scene for all its emotional worth. What's more, he could do it without over-emoting. He was the kind of character player that directors and producers in budget-conscious television of the 1950s needed.

In an episode of *Circus Boy* (1956), he played a touching scene with a young Micky Dolenz, as an aging railroad engineer introducing the boy to the world of locomotives and trains. After that, Moody got called back to do three more episodes.

But it was Jack Webb who really put him to work in *Dragnet* (1952-1959) and many of his other productions, in radio and feature films as well as television. His more memorable appearances on *Dragnet* included "The Big Producer", as a once-famous movie producer who is reduced to selling pornographic pictures to high-school students, and "The Hammer", from the 1967 revival of the series, in which he portrayed the neighbor of a murder victim.

Some of his other television work included *Dangerous Assignment* (1952), *Four Star Playhouse* (1953-1956), *Broken Arrow* (1956-1958), *Wanted: Dead or Alive* (1958), *Have Gun - Will Travel* (1958-1961), *Twilight Zone* (1962), *The Wild Wild West* (1965), *Adam-12* (1969), and *Get Smart* (1969).

Moody continued working regularly in television until a year before his death. His final appearance was in the *Night Gallery* episode "The Little Black Bag".

He died September 16, 1971, at age 84 in Burbank, California.

Joanna Moore

Audie Murphy with Joanna Moore in *Ride a Crooked Trail*

Joanna Moore was born Dorothy Cook in Parrott, Georgia, November 10, 1934, and was an American film and television actress best known for her guest roles on the popular television shows of the 1960s, most notably as Sheriff Andy Taylor's love interest, Peggy "Peg" McMillan in four episodes of *The Andy Griffith Show* (1962). She was married to actor Ryan O'Neal from 1963 to 1967, and is the mother of actors Griffin and Tatum O'Neal.

The elder of two daughters, she was born to Henry Cook, an atomic scientist, and Dorothy English Cook. When she was a child, her parents and younger sister were involved in a fatal car accident. Her mother and sister died immediately, while her father died a year after the accident from the injuries he sustained. Moore's grandmother raised her until she became mentally and physically incapacitated. Moore was then adopted by a wealthy local family and changed her name from Dorothy to Joanna.

As a teen, she married, and quickly divorced, Willis Moore. After the divorce, she attended Agnes Scott College in Decatur, Georgia. While attending college, she entered and won a beauty contest and was brought to Hollywood. Moore's acting career began when she was spotted at a cocktail party by a producer for Universal.

Moore made her film debut in a 1957 crime drama, *Appointment with a Shadow*. Later that year, she appeared in episodes of *Goodyear Theater* and *Harbourmaster*, along with another film, *Slim Carter*. In 1958, she had a small role in the film noir classic *Touch of Evil*, with Orson Welles, Charlton Heston, Janet Leigh, and Marlene Dietrich. The same year, she appeared in *Monster on the Campus* and *Ride a Crooked Trail* with Audie Murphy.

Throughout the late 1950s and early 1960s, Moore continued to appear in television on shows such as *Studio One* (1958), *Bachelor Father* (1958), *Kraft Television Theatre* (1958), *The Rough Riders* (1959), *The Millionaire* (1958-1959), *The Untouchables* (1961), *Alfred Hitchcock Presents* (1958-1962), *77 Sunset Strip* (1962), *Hong Kong* (1960), *The Brothers Brannagan* (1961), *Gunsmoke* (1960-1965), *The Fugitive* (1964-1966), and *Route 66* (1961-1962). She also appeared in several *Perry Mason* (1958-1963) episodes.

In 1962, Moore appeared as Miss Precious in *Walk on the Wild Side* with Jane Fonda, Barbara Stanwyck, and Capucine, followed by the musical, *Follow That Dream* with Elvis Presley. She continued to land roles on television shows during the late 1960s and early 1970s, appearing in *Bewitched* (1967), *Nanny and the Professor* (1970), *McCloud* (1970), and *The Waltons* (1974). Moore made her last screen appearance in the 1986 film, *Run Chrissie Run!*.

On April 3, 1963, Moore married actor Ryan O'Neal. She had earlier guest starred on O'Neal's television series *Empire* (1962) filmed on a New Mexico ranch. The couple had two children: Tatum Beatrice O'Neal, born on November 5, 1963, and Griffin Patrick O'Neal, born on October 28, 1964. The marriage was tempestuous and the couple separated in early 1966.

She continued acting, but her depression worsened over her impending divorce. In February 1967, O'Neal and Moore's divorce became final.

In 1975, she married Gary L. Reeves; however, the marriage was short lived and ended in 1976. By the late 1970s, she was being supported financially by daughter Tatum, who had become an Academy Award winning actress at age ten, and one of the highest-paid child stars of the era. The children were still in Ryan O'Neal's custody.

In 1996, Moore, a long-time smoker, was diagnosed with lung cancer. On November 22, 1997, she died at age 63 from the disease. Her daughter Tatum O'Neal was by her side at the time of her death. Moore's interment was at Hillside Memorial Park in Redlands, California, but her family later moved the grave to Oak Grove Cemetery in her Georgia hometown of Americus.

Terry Moore

Terry Moore with Audie Murphy in *Cast a Long Shadow* and with author in 2013

Terry Moore was born Helen Luella Koford in Glendale, California January 7, 1929, and is an American film and television actress. Moore grew up in a Mormon family in Los Angeles, California. She worked as a child model before making her film debut in *Maryland* in 1940. Moore was billed as Judy Ford, Jan Ford, and January Ford before taking Terry Moore as her name in 1948.

Moore worked in radio in the 1940s, most memorably as Bumps Smith on *The Smiths of Hollywood*. She has starred in several box office hits, including *Mighty Joe Young* (1949), *Come Back, Little Sheba* (1952) (for which she was nominated for an Academy Award for Best Supporting Actress), and *Peyton Place* (1957). She appeared on the cover of *Life* magazine for July 6, 1953, as "Hollywood's sexy tomboy".

During the 1950s, Moore worked steadily in films like *The Great Rupert* (1950), *Two of a Kind* (1951), *Man on a Tightrope* (1953), *Daddy Long Legs* (1955), *Between Heaven and Hell* (1956), *Bernardine* (1957), *A Private's Affair* (1959), *Cast a Long Shadow* (1959) as Audie Murphy's love interest, and *Why Must I Die?* (1960).

By the 1960s, Moore's film career had faltered. She began to appear less frequently in films. However, she did make films like *Platinum High School* (1960), *She Should Have Stayed in Bed* (1963), *Black Spurs* (1965), *Waco* (1966), and *A Man Called Dagger* (1967). Lacking film roles, Moore appeared on television. In 1962, she appeared as a rancher's daughter in the NBC Western *Empire*. She also appeared on the NBC interview program *Here's Hollywood*.

After the 1960s, Moore semi retired from acting, only completing two films in the 1970s; though by the 1980s her career had resumed with minor roles in low-budgeted B-movies. Moore has a star on the Hollywood Walk of Fame at 7080 Hollywood Blvd.

In the 1940s, Moore lived with Howard Hughes. After Hughes died in 1976, Moore claimed that they secretly married in 1949. Moore stated that the ship's log and any documentation of the marriage were destroyed and the couple never officially divorced. Despite this claim, Moore married three other men after 1949; including her eleven year marriage to Stuart Cramer with whom she has two children. The Hughes's estate paid her a settlement in 1984.

Moore wrote two books about Hughes: *The Beauty and the Billionaire*, New York (1984) and *The Passions of Howard Hughes*. General Publishing Group (1996).

She married an American football player, Glenn Davis, in 1951. Moore gave birth to a son, actor Grant Cramer.

At age 55, Moore posed nude in the August 1984 issue of *Playboy* magazine, photographed by Ken Marcus.

She appeared in a cameo role with Ray Harryhausen in the 1998 Disney remake of *Mighty Joe Young*. She has continued to act into the 21st Century in films like *Stageghost* (2000), *Sweet Deadly Dreams* (2006), *The Still Life* (2007), *Dewitt & Maria* (2010), *Margarine Wars* (2012), and *Mansion of Blood* (2012).

Read Morgan

Read Morgan was born January 30, 1931, in Chicago, Illinois, and is a former American actor whose longest-running role was as a United States Army cavalry officer in the 1960-1961 season of *The Deputy*, a western television series on NBC created by Norman Lear.

Morgan attended the University of Kentucky at Lexington, where he played for two years on the basketball team. In 1950, he began a rigorous diet with regular exercise to accent his physique. One of his first roles was hence as an athletic mountaineer in the Broadway play *Li'l Abner*. His television debut was in 1956-1957 in two episodes of CBS's *United States Steel Hour* in the role of the young wrestler "Joey" in episodes entitled "Sideshow". He also played a skindiver named Kelly Randall in the episode "Beached" of Gardner McKay's ABC series, *Adventures in Paradise* (1960), and a boxer named Ray Gorski in the episode "The Fight" of the 1958 NBC series based on the cartoon character *Steve Canyon*.

Morgan appeared in thirty episodes as the one-eyed Sergeant Hapgood Tasker, recognized by his black eyepatch and referred to in the series as "Sarge". Henry Fonda held the starring role on *The Deputy* as Marshal Simon Fry, with much of the script revolving about native Texan Allen Case as his chief deputy, Clay McCord, a storekeeper who tried when possible to avoid using a gun. The program was set in fictitious Silver City in the Arizona Territory. Morgan debuted on *The Deputy* as Sergeant Tasker in the episode, "Meet Sergeant Tasker" (October 1, 1960), followed by "The Jason Harris Story" with Jeff Morrow in the title role as a marshal. Morgan's last episodes included "Tension Point", "Brother in Arms", "The Return of Widow Brown", "Enemy of the Town", "The Deathly Quiet", "Brand of Honesty", and "Lorinda Belle", the series finale.

Morgan guest starred in different roles twelve times between 1959 and 1974 on the longest-running television western, CBS's *Gunsmoke* with James Arness. However, Morgan did not perform exclusively on westerns but was cast in roles in dramas, detective series, and even some comedies.

Morgan appeared in numerous television westerns, before and after *The Deputy*, as Bob Kenyon in the episode "Jebediah Bonner" of John Payne's *The Restless Gun* (1958) and as Clint Casey in "The Barrier" (1959) on NBC's *Riverboat*, with Darren McGavin. In 1959, he appeared as Jeff Peters in "The Little Man" episode of Dale Robertson's NBC western, *Tales of Wells Fargo*. In 1958-1959, Morgan guest starred in two episodes of Rod Cameron's 20th century syndicated western *State Trooper*, as Trooper Gaines in "You Can't Run Forever" and as Hess in "Everything Else Is Bridgeport". In 1961, he also appeared on Cameron's modern detective series *Coronado 9* in the role of Mark Sidon in the episode "Flim Flam".

In 1960, he was cast as Clayton in the episode "A Gun for Willie" of the CBS anthology series, *Dick Powell's Zane Grey Theater*. That same year, he appeared as Jesse Hobbs in "Sundance and Useless" on CBS's *Hotel de Paree*, with Earl Holliman. In 1961, he played Hob Tyler in the episode "The Jodie Tyler Story" of Audie Murphy's NBC series, *Whispering Smith*. In 1962, he portrayed Ed Squires in "Good Old Uncle Walt" on NBC's *The Wide Country*, starring Earl Holliman and Andrew Prine, and with Edgar Buchanan in the lead guest-starring role. From 1959-1963, he guest starred three times on *Wagon Train*: as Ben Denike in "The Vincent Eaglewood Story" with Wally Cox, as Curly Horse in "The Martha Barham Story" with Ann Blyth, and as Jake in "The Myra Marshall Story" with Suzanne Pleshette.

In 1965, he played a sheriff in "The Way to Kill a Killer" on ABC's *The Big Valley* with Barbara Stanwyck. That same year, he appeared on NBC's *Bonanza* as Tad Blake in the episode "The Ballerina", with dancer Barrie Chase in the title role. Morgan appeared twice on NBC's *The Virginian* and three times each on NBC's *Laramie* and on ABC's

Alias Smith and Jones. In 1966, he appeared as Cal in the episode "An Unfamiliar Tune" of the ABC western *A Man Called Shenandoah*, starring Robert Horton. In 1967, he played a medicine man in the episode "Spirit Woman" of ABC's *Custer* and the role of Jess Daly in "The Last Wolf" of the CBS 90-minute western, *Cimarron Strip*, starring Stuart Whitman and Randy Boone. In 1976, Morgan appeared as an unnamed officer in "The Captive" episode of the short-lived NBC series, *The Quest*, with Kurt Russell and Tim Matheson. In 1979, he guest starred in the second James Arness series, *How the West Was Won*, in the role of Morton in the episode "The Slavers".

After *The Deputy* left the air, Morgan was frequently cast as law enforcement officers or detectives in such films as *Fort Utah* (1967), *Easy Come, Easy Go* (1968) as Ensign Tompkins, *Marlowe* (1969) as Gumpshaw, *Dillinger* (1973) as Big Jim Wollard, *The New Centurions* (1972) as Woodrow Gandy, *Shanks* (1974), and in made for television films, *Return of the Gunfighter* (1967) as Wid Boone, *Helter Skelter* (1976) as an officer named "Columbine", *The Billion Dollar Threat* (1979), *Power* (1980), and *A Year in the Life* (1986).

Morgan's dramatic credits ranged from the role of Corporal Hoop Keeler in the 1959 episode, "The Tallest Marine", on Ronald W. Reagan's anthology, *General Electric Theater*. That same year, he was cast as Lefty in "What You Need" of CBS's science fiction *The Twilight Zone*, hosted by Rod Serling. He appeared twice on CBS's *Alfred Hitchcock Presents* and once on *The Alfred Hitchcock Hour*. He appeared briefly on ABC's *The Fugitive* (1965) and *The Outer Limits* (1964). He portrayed Kessler in "A World Without Sundays" on CBS's *Mannix* (1973), with Darren McGavin in *Kolchak: The Night Stalker* (1975), with Mike Connors and Blackie in "Murder on Stage 17" of ABC's *Starsky and Hutch* (1977). He appeared four times from 1973-1978 in different roles on CBS's *Barnaby Jones*, starring Buddy Ebsen, and twice on ABC's *Charlie's Angels* in 1977 and 1979. He was Sergeant Kevin Hogan in the 1984 episode, "Death Takes a Curtain Call", on Angela Lansbury's *Murder, She Wrote*. In 1987, he appeared twice as Curtis on ABC's night-time soap opera *The Colbys*.

Morgan's last roles were on two CBS series, as Hap Moody in "Dear Hearts and Gentle People" on *Dallas* (1990) and in the episode "The Coward" of Lee Horsley's latter-day western *Guns of Paradise* (1990). His last role was as a card dealer in the 1994 western film *Maverick*.

Red Morgan

Boyd 'Red' Morgan was born October 24, 1915 in Waurika, Oklahoma, and was an American actor and stuntman with 170 film and television and film credits from 1936 to 1987. He was a running back for the Washington Redskins after having played college football at University of Southern California and was drafted in the 18th round of the 1939 NFL draft.

Some of those credits include *Rose Bowl* (1936), *Lucky Cisco Kid* (1940), *The Fleet's In* (1942), *Reign of Terror* (1949), *The Range Rider* (1951-1952), *Column South* (1953) with Audie Murphy, *The Cisco Kid* (1953), *Riding Shotgun* (1954), *Ghost Town* (1956), *Between Heaven and Hell* (1956), *The Kettles on Old MacDonald's Farm* (1957), *Boots and Saddles* (1957-1958), *Gunfighters of Abilene* (1960), *The Alamo* (1960), *Whispering Smith* (1961) with Audie Murphy, *How the West Was Won* (1962), *The Quick Gun* (1964) a third appearance with Audie Murphy, *The Sons of Katie Elder* (1964), *Arizona Raiders* (1965) a fourth appearance with Audie Murphy, *Laredo* (1966), *5 Card Stud* (1968), *Support Your Local Sheriff!* (1969), *True Grit* (1969), *The Cheyenne Social Club* (1970), *Hec Ramsey* (1972), *The Soul of Nigger Charley* (1973), *Blazing Saddles* (1974), *Quincy M.E.* (1978), *Last of the Great Survivors* (1984), and *Evil Town* (1987).

He died January 8, 1988, at age 72 in Tarzana, California.

Barbara Morris

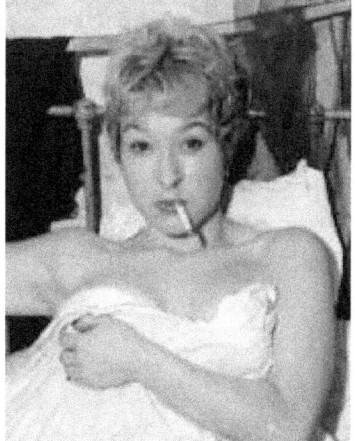

No biographical information could be found for Barbara Morris, but she did appear in two films and one television episode.

The two films she appeared in were as a dancehall girl in *The Wild and the Innocent* (1959) with Audie Murphy, and as Candy Stevens in *One Naked Night* (1965). The one television appearance was in the episode "Temple of Love" of *Philip Marlowe* (1959).

Byron Morrow

Byron Morrow with Audie Murphy in *40 Guns to Apache Pass*

Byron Morrow was born September 8, 1911, and was an American television and film actor, born in Chicago. He served in WWII and performed in the Pacific Theater during his tour of duty.

He one time played semi-pro basketball in a league that included the original Harlem Globetrotters.

His TV work ran from *Peter Gunn* in 1957 to *Father Dowling Mysteries* in 1991. He often played authority figures, including seven appearances as a judge in *Perry Mason* (1960-1966).

Some of his early work included *Highway Patrol* (1959), *Twilight Zone* (1960), *Atlantis, the Lost Continent* (1961), *King Kong vs. Godzilla* (1962), *The Fugitive* (1965), *40 Guns to Apache Pass* (1967) with Audie Murphy, *Get Smart* (1965-1967), and *Lost in Space* (1968).

He appeared in two episodes of the original series of *Star Trek* (1967-1968) - in "Amok Time" as Admiral Komack, and in "For the World is Hollow and I Have Touched the Sky" as an unnamed Admiral. "Amok Time" was the first appearance of an admiral in the original series.

More roles continued with *The Wrecking Crew* (1969), *Rod Serling's Night Gallery* (1969), *The Waltons* (1972-1973), *The New Perry Mason* (1973), *Kolchak: The Night Stalker* (1975), *S.W.A.T.* (1975), he played Admiral Nimitz in the pilot episode of *Baa Baa Black Sheep* (1976), *Executive Suite* (1976-1977), *The Golden Gate Murders* (1979), *Vega$* (1979-1981), *The Greatest American Hero* (1981), *Bret Maverick* (1982), *Otherworld* (1985), *Freddy's Nightmares* (1988), and *War and Remembrance* (1988-1989).

He died May 11, 2006, at age 94 in Woodland Hills, California.

Jeff Morrow

Audie Murphy with Jeff Morrow in *World in My Corner*

Irving "Jeff" Morrow was born January 13, 1907, and was an American actor educated at the Pratt Institute in his native New York City. He was a commercial artist prior to turning to acting.

As early as 1927, Morrow acted onstage as Irving Morrow in Pennsylvania. He later appeared in such plays as *Penal Law*, and *Once in a Lifetime*, as well as repertory in Shakespeare's *A Midsummer Night's Dream*, *Twelfth Night*, *Romeo and Juliet* and *Macbeth*.

After serving in the U.S. Army during World War II, Morrow spent the late 1940s on the stage and in radio, where he won the title role in the *Dick Tracy* radio series. He appeared in many Broadway productions, notably *Three Wishes for Jamie*, *Billy Budd*, the Maurice Evans production of *Macbeth*, and the Katharine Cornell production of *Romeo and Juliet*.

Morrow turned to film acting relatively late in his career, commencing with the Biblical epic *The Robe* in 1953. Often parodied as the 'Cro-Magnon Man' for his prominent brow, Morrow spent much of the 1950s appearing in a mix of A-budget epics in supporting parts, or 'B' Westerns such as *The Siege at Red River* (1954) and science fiction films as a leader and screen hero, usually paired with a busty and beautiful actress.

Morrow carried over much of his acting persona from his radio days to his film acting roles, where his ability to rapidly alter both the tone and volume of his voice for dramatic effect frequently gave sound editors fits. He entered the science fiction/monster movie genre with the 1955 film *This Island Earth*, followed by *The Creature Walks Among Us* (1956), *The Giant Claw* (1957), and *Kronos* (1957).

He also showed up in a boxing movie with Audie Murphy *World in my Corner* (1956).

Morrow returned to television for most of his later roles, making guest appearances on *Twilight Zone* (1960), *Crossroads* (1956-1957), *Bonanza* (1961), *My Friend Flicka* (1955), *The Deputy* (1960), *Perry Mason* (1962-1963), *Daniel Boone* (1966-1968), and *Police Story* (1974-1975).

In 1958-1959, he starred as Bart McClelland, the fictitious supervisor of construction of the Union Pacific Railroad in the syndicated half-hour Western series *Union Pacific*, based loosely on a Joel McCrea and Barbara Stanwyck film of the same name. His *Union Pacific* television co-stars were Judson Pratt and Susan Cummings.

In 1960, Morrow played Tob, the older brother of Boaz (Stuart Whitman), in the biblical drama, *The Story of Ruth*. During the early 1960s, Morrow appeared in such low-budget films as *Harbor Lights* (1963), *Blood Legacy* (1971), and in a bow to his earlier career, a cameo in the 1971 monster film *Octaman* for veteran 1950's monster movie writer/director Harry Essex.

After the 1974 cancellation of the sitcom *The New Temperatures Rising*, Morrow largely retired from acting, though he returned for a 1975 appearance in the series *Police Story*. His last television role was in 1986, with a guest appearance on the second *The Twilight Zone* series.

In his later life, Morrow returned to commercial illustration with occasional acting assignments. He died at the age of eighty-six on December 26, 1993, in Canoga Park in the San Fernando Valley in Los Angeles County, California. He was survived by his wife of nearly fifty years, actress Anna Karen Morrow, and their daughter, Mrs. Lissa Morrow Christian (born 1948). His ashes were scattered off the coast of Palos Verdes, California.

Vic Morrow

Victor Harry "Vic" Morrow was born in the Bronx, New York, February 14, 1929, and was an American actor whose credits include a starring role in the TV series *Combat!* (1962-1967), and prominent roles in a handful of other television and cinema dramas, and numerous guest roles on television.

When he was seventeen, Morrow dropped out of high school and joined the U.S. Navy. He married actress Barbara Turner with whom he had two daughters: actress Jennifer Jason Leigh and Carrie Ann Morrow. Morrow's marriage to Barbara lasted seven years and ended in divorce in 1964. He did not remarry until 1975, over a decade later, when he courted Gale Lester. They were married for five years and were separated just prior to Morrow's death.

Morrow's first movie role was in *Blackboard Jungle* (1955), after which he went into television. Later, he guest starred on John Payne's NBC western series, *The Restless Gun* (1957). Other early roles included *Richard Diamond, Private Detective* (1958), *King Creole* (1958), *Wichita Town* (1959), *Cimarron* (1960), and *Posse from Hell* (1961) with Audie Murphy.

He was cast in the lead role in ABC's *Combat!*, a World War II drama, which aired from 1962–1967. He also worked as a television director. Together with Leonard Nimoy, he produced a 1966 version of *Deathwatch*, an English language film version of Genet's play *Haute Surveillance*, adapted by Morrow and Barbara Turner, directed by Morrow, and starring Nimoy.

After *Combat!* ended, he worked in several films. Morrow appeared in two episodes of Australian-produced anthology series *The Evil Touch* (1973), one of which he also directed. He memorably played the wily local sheriff in director John Hough's road classic *Dirty Mary, Crazy Larry* (1974), as well as the homicidal sheriff, alongside Martin Sheen, in the 1974 TV film *The California Kid*, and had a key role in the 1976 comedy *The Bad News Bears*. He also played Injun Joe in 1973 telefilm *Tom Sawyer*, which was filmed in Upper Canada Village.

Morrow wrote and directed a 1971 Spaghetti Western, produced by Dino DeLaurentis, titled *A Man Called Sledge* starring James Garner. It was Morrow's first and only big screen outing behind the camera. Sledge was filmed in Europe with desert-like settings that were highly evocative of the U.S. southwest.

He also played Capt. Eugene Nathan in the 1980 series *B.A.D. Cats*.

In the early morning hours of July 23, 1982, Morrow and two children, My-Ca Dinh Le (age 7), and Renee Shin-Yi Chen (age 6), died in an accident while filming on location for the *Twilight Zone: The Movie* in Ventura County, California, between Santa Clarita and Piru. Morrow was playing the role of Bill Connor, a racist who is taken back in time and placed in various situations where he would be a persecuted victim: as a Jewish Holocaust victim, a black man about to be lynched by the Ku Klux Klan, and a Vietnamese man about to be killed by U.S. soldiers. Morrow, Le, and Chen were filming a scene for the Vietnam sequence in which their characters attempt to escape from a pursuing U.S. Army helicopter out of a deserted Vietnamese village. The helicopter was hovering at about twenty-five feet above them when pyrotechnic explosions damaged it and caused it to crash on top of them, killing all three instantly. He was decapitated along with one of the child actors.

Morrow is interred in Hillside Memorial Park Cemetery in Culver City, California.

Director John Landis and other defendants, including producer Steven Spielberg and pilot Dorsey Wingo, were ultimately acquitted of involuntary manslaughter and child endangerment. The parents of Le and Chen sued and settled out of court for an undisclosed amount. Morrow's children also sued and settled for an undisclosed amount.

Sonia Moser

No biographical information could be found for Sonia Moser, but she did appear in four films such as *Rosso e nero* (1955), *Nero's Mistress* (1956), *Legend of the Lost* (1957), and *The Quiet American* (1958) with Audie Murphy.

Alan Mowbray

Audie Murphy with Alan Mowbray in *Whispering Smith*

Alan Mowbray was born Alfred Ernest Allen in London, England, August 18, 1896, and was an English stage and film actor who found success in Hollywood.

He served with distinction in the British Army in World War I, being awarded the Military Medal for bravery. He began as a stage actor, making his way to the United States where he appeared in Broadway plays and toured the country as part of a theater troupe.

As Alan Mowbray, he made his motion picture debut in 1931 in *God's Gift to Women*, going on to a career primarily as a character actor in more than 140 films including the sterling butler role in the comedy *Merrily We Live* (1938).

During World War II, he made a memorable appearance as the Devil in the Hal Roach propaganda comedy *The Devil with Hitler* (1942).

Mowbray was a founding member of the Screen Actors Guild, with outside interests that led to membership in Britain's Royal Geographic Society.

He played the title role in the television series *Colonel Humphrey Flack*, which first appeared in 1953-1954 and then was revived in 1958-1959. In the 1954-1955 television season Mowbray played Mr. Swift, the drama coach of the character Mickey Mulligan, in NBC's short-lived situation comedy *The Mickey Rooney Show: Hey, Mulligan*.

Other credits throughout his career included *Sherlock Holmes* (1932), *The Girl from Missouri* (1934), *Topper* (1937), *Hollywood Hotel* (1937), *Topper Takes a Trip* (1938), *The Doughgirls* (1944), *Terror by Night* (1946), *My Darling Clementine* (1946), *Abbott and Costello Meet the Killer, Boris Karloff* (1949), *Wagon Master* (1950), *Ma and Pa Kettle at Home* (1954), *Around the World in Eighty Days* (1956), *Dante* (1960-1961), *Whispering Smith* (1961) with Audie Murphy, *Burke's Law* (1964), *The Man from U.N.C.L.E.* (1966), *The Beverly Hillbillies* (1968), and *The Flying Nun* (1969).

Mowbray died of a heart attack March 25, 1969 in Hollywood and was interred in the Holy Cross Cemetery in Culver City, California.

Skip Murphy

Skip Murphy with Audie Murphy and Terry Murphy

Skip Murphy was born James Shannon Murphy March 23, 1954, to Audie and Pamela Murphy. He appeared in *The Broken Bridge* (1961) and *A Time for Dying* (1969) with his father and older brother Terry Murphy.

Terry Murphy

Audie Murphy with Terry Murphy and Skip Murphy

Terry Michael Murphy was born March 14, 1952, to Audie and Pamela Murphy. He appeared in *To Hell and Back* (1955) as his uncle Preston Murphy, the war bond short *Medal of Honor* (1955), *The Broken Bridge* (1961), all with his father, and *A Time for Dying* (1969) with his father and younger brother Skip Murphy.

Zon Murray

Emery Zon Murray was born April 13, 1910 in St. Joseph, Missouri, and was an American actor. As handsome as most of the Western stars he supported, if not more so, Zon Murray often sported a mustache and was thus obviously not up to anything good.

Rarely the "Boss Villain", Murray instead played scores of so-called "Dog Heavies" in run-of-the-mill Westerns from 1945 to 1956, ending his long run in the feature film version of *The Lone Ranger* (1956).

There would be a few minor roles in cheap action fare to come, but Murray definitely belonged to the era of the series Western. More roles included *West of Dodge City* (1947), *The Wistful Widow of Wagon Gap* (1947) with Abbott and Costello, *Blood on the Moon* (1948), *The Kid from Texas* (1950) with Audie Murphy, *The Longhorn* (1951), *Son of Geronimo: Apache Avenger* (1952), *Calamity Jane* (1953), *Hopalong Cassidy* (1954), *Jungle Jim* (1955), *Tales of the Texas Rangers* (1957), *Bonanza* (1959-1964), and *The Virginian* (1965).

Murray ended his career after a bit in *Requiem for a Gunfighter* (1965).

He died February 2, 1979, at age 68 in Palm Springs, California.

George Nader

George Nader with Audie Murphy in *Joe Butterfly*

George Nader was born in Pasadena, California, October 19, 1921, and was an American film and television actor of Lebanese descent.

He appeared in a variety of films from 1950 through 1974, including *Phone Call from a Stranger* (1952), *Congo Crossing* (1956), and *The Female Animal* (1957). During this period, he also did episodic television and starred in several series, including the unique NBC adventure offering, *The Man and the Challenge* (1959–60). However, his best-remembered role may have been as "Roy", the hero who saves the world from the clutches of "Ro-man" in the low-budget 3-D sci-fi romp *Robot Monster* (1953).

Nader began his film career in 1950, after having earned his bachelor of arts in theatre arts at Occidental College. Nader appeared in several productions at the Pasadena Playhouse. That work led to a number of bit parts in 1951 and '52. His big break was his first starring role, which came in *Robot Monster* (1953), a 3-D feature film directed by Phil Tucker. This role and his rugged good looks won him a Universal Studios contract in the 1950s, and he made a number of films for Universal. In 1955, he won a Golden Globe Award for "Most Promising Newcomer."

Despite this accolade, Nader often found himself struggling in the shadow of more famous leading men, such as Audie Murphy, Rock Hudson, Tony Curtis, and Jeff Chandler. His films of that period included 1954's *Carnival Story*, *Sins of Jezebel,* and *Four Guns to the Border*, a well-written story by Louis L'amour, and 1956's *Away All Boats*. He also was Esther Williams' leading man in her first dramatic film, *The Unguarded Moment* (1956), which also starred a young John Saxon. Nader then appeared with Audie Murphy in *Joe Butterfly* (1957).

He moved into television in the late 1950s, appearing in several short-lived series including *The Further Adventures of Ellery Queen* (1958-1959) and *The Man and the Challenge* (1959-1960). In the 1961-1962 season, he appeared as insurance investigator Joe Shannon in the syndicated crime drama *Shannon*; his co-star was Regis Toomey. Nader also appeared frequently on *The Loretta Young Show* (1953-1961), a dramatic anthology series on NBC.

He moved to Europe in the mid-1960s, where he found steady work in films. A notable role during this period was as U.S. government agent "Jerry Cotton" in a German film series of eight films from 1965-1969, where he became the number two most popular film star in Germany behind Lex Barker.

In the mid-1970s, Nader was involved in a serious automobile accident. He suffered an eye injury which made him particularly sensitive to the bright lights of movie sets. According to an interview with the German fanzine *Splatting Image* his eye injury was the result of an accident during the production of the never released movie *Zigzag*. Nader got injured while using some blank pistol rounds (one of them exploded too early next to his eyes). Since filming took place on the Philippines no adequate treatment was taken in time, resulting in the partial loss of his eyesight and the aforementioned sensitivity.

After damage to his eye made it difficult to endure an acting career, Nader began a career as a writer of science fiction. His groundbreaking 1978 novel *Chrome* is probably the first science fiction novel to center on a homosexual love affair, and the first to have substantial homosexual erotic scenes.

According to *Variety Magazine's* Army Archerd, Nader had completed a book called *The Perils of Paul*, about the gay community in Hollywood, which he did not want published until after his death.

He eventually returned to the U.S. and settled in Palm Springs, where he got roles in several television series like *Owen Marshall: Counselor at Law* (1972), *The F.B.I.* (1972), and *Nakia* (1974), and a film *Beyond Atlantis* (1973).

Stricken by multiple medical problems, Nader entered the hospital in September 2001. He died February 4, 2002, at Woodland Hills, California of cardiac-pulmonary failure, pneumonia, and multiple cerebral infarctions at the age of 79. Nader is survived by his nephew, actor Michael Nader. His ashes were scattered at sea, but his cenotaph exists in Cathedral City's Forest Lawn Cemetery.

Tom Neal

Thomas Neal was born in Evanston, Illinois, January 28, 1914, and was an American actor.

Neal debuted on Broadway in 1935. In 1938 he first appeared in film in *Out West with the Hardys*, part of the Mickey Rooney "Hardy family" movie series. That same year, he received a law degree from Harvard University. While in college at Northwestern and Harvard Universities, Neal was a stand-out on the schools' boxing teams. He compiled a 44-3 (41 knockouts) ring record.

Neal appeared in many low budget B-movies in the 1940s/1950s. In 1941 he starred with Frances Gifford in the Republic Pictures fifteen episode serial, *Jungle Girl*. Perhaps his most memorable role was that of Al Roberts in the classic film noir *Detour* (1945) alongside Ann Savage. They went on to make five movies together.

Some of his other film roles were in movies such as *Beyond Glory* (1948) with Audie Murphy and Alan Ladd, *I Shot Billy the Kid* (1950), *G.I. Jane* (1951), *The Great Jesse James Raid* (1953), and *The Last Hurrah* (1958).

He had roles in several television programs like *The Gene Autry Show* (1950), *Boston Blackie* (1951), *Adventures of Wild Bill Hickok* (1952), *Tales of Wells Fargo* (1958), and *Mike Hammer* (1959).

In 1951, he fought fellow actor Franchot Tone over their mutual girlfriend, actress Barbara Payton. Neal inflicted upon Tone a smashed cheekbone, a broken nose, and a brain concussion. After the incident, Tone and Payton married, and Neal had a difficult time finding work. He ended up supporting himself landscaping and gardening. Payton left Tone after only seven weeks and returned to the troubled Neal. Their relationship lasted four years.

Neal remarried almost immediately and in 1957 fathered a son, Tom Neal, Jr. His wife died the following year from cancer. In 1961, Neal married for the third time, to Gale Bennett. Four years later, he shot her in the back of the head with a .45-caliber gun, killing her instantly. He was arrested and, although prosecutors sought the death penalty, he was convicted of involuntary manslaughter and sentenced to ten years in prison, of which he served six years. On December 6, 1971, he was released on parole.

Less than a year later, Neal died of heart failure in North Hollywood, California, at the age of 58 on August 7, 1972. He was cremated, and his ashes stored in the vault at the Chapel of the Pines Crematory in Los Angeles. His aforementioned son appeared in one film: playing the role of Al Roberts in a 1992 independent remake of *Detour*.

Lori Nelson

Lori Nelson with Audie Murphy in *Gunsmoke*

Lori Nelson was born Dixie Kay Nelson August 15, 1933, in Santa Fe, New Mexico. She began her show biz career at the age of two-and-a-half, dancing in a show in her native Santa Fe, New Mexico. She was voted Santa Fe's most talented and beautiful child, and toured the state billed as "Santa Fe's Shirley Temple."

At age four, Nelson moved to Hollywood with her parents and there was named Little Miss America. She worked as a fashion photographer's model, then (in the early 1940s) made her first bid for a movie career, testing (unsuccessfully) for a role in Warner Brothers' *Kings Row* (1942). There was a second false start a few years later, when Arthur M. Landau, a Hollywood producer and self-proclaimed "discoverer" of 1930s star Jean Harlow, expressed interest in casting teenage Nelson as Harlow in a movie bio. The project never materialized.

Agent Milo O. Frank, Jr. helped Nelson get into the movies, taking her to Universal to meet with casting people. Nelson trained with the studio dramatic coach, enacted a scene for the front office and ultimately was offered a seven-year contract, which was approved in court on her 17th birthday. After several years at Universal, she freelanced in movies and television.

In 1952, she first appeared as Marjie Baile in *Bend of the River*. She then continued to work steadily in films like *Ma and Pa Kettle at the Fair* (1952), *Francis Goes to West Point* (1952), *Walking My Baby Back Home* (1953), *Revenge of the Creature* (1955), as the object of desire from the *Creature from the Black Lagoon* (1954) sequel, *Day the World Ended* (1955), *Hot Rod Girl* (1956), *Untamed Youth* (1957), and *Outlaw's Son* (1957).

She appeared in *Tumbleweed* (1953), *Destry* (1954), and *Whispering Smith* (1961) with Audie Murphy.

She also had many roles in television programs like *Climax!* (1955-1956), she costarred in thirty-nine episodes with Barbara Eden in the series *How to Marry a Millionaire* (1957–1959), *Wanted: Dead or Alive* (1959), *The Millionaire* (1959), *Lock Up* (1960), *Armstrong Circle Theatre* (1961), and *Family Affair* (1971).

She had a well-remembered role as Mara, the Mayor's daughter, opposite Van Johnson (who played two roles) in the 1957 made-for-TV musical film *The Pied Piper of Hamelin*, a motion picture which premiered on NBC and then went on to be syndicated, often shown annually on local television stations.

She continued acting in later years in *Secret Sins of the Father* (1994), *Mom, Can I Keep Her?* (1998), and most recently in *The Naked Monster* (2005), recreating her role as Dr. Helen Dobson, her character from *Revenge of the Creature* (1955).

Jeanette Nolan

Jeanette Nolan with Audie Murphy in *Guns of Fort Petticoat*

Jeanette Nolan was born in Los Angeles, California, December 30, 1911, and was an American radio, film and television actress who was nominated for four Emmy Awards. Nolan was a graduate of Abraham Lincoln High School in Los Angeles.

Nolan began her acting career at the Pasadena Playhouse in Pasadena, California, and, while a student at Los Angeles City College, made her radio debut in 1932 in *Omar Khayyam*, the first transcontinental broadcast from station KHJ, and continued acting until the 1990s. She made her film debut as Lady Macbeth in Orson Welles's 1948 film *Macbeth*, based on Shakespeare's play of the same name. Despite the fact that she and the film received withering reviews at the time, Nolan's film career flourished in largely supporting roles.

Viewers of film noir may know her best as the corrupt wife of a dead (and equally corrupt) police officer in Fritz Lang's *The Big Heat* (1953).

She appeared in Audie Murphy's *The Guns of Fort Petticoat* (1957) as the Bible toting Cora Melavan who gets her priorities in the correct order by the end of the movie.

Nolan made over three hundred television appearances, including Brian Keith's first series, *Crusader*, in the role of Dr. Marion in "The Healer" (1956). She also appeared on Rod Cameron's syndicated series, *State Trooper*. From 1959 to 1960, she was cast as Annette Deveraux, part-owner of the hotel in the CBS western series *Hotel de Paree*. She appeared in other western films, most notably *The Wild Women of Chastity Gulch* (1982).

She gave an over-the-top performance as a crazed old woman in the "Parasite Mansion" episode of *Thriller*. She appeared in the April 27, 1962, episode "A Book of Faces" on ABC's crime drama *Target: The Corruptors!* She appeared three times on *Wagon Train*, the western series in which her husband John McIntire starred as wagon master Chris Hale from 1961 to 1965. She guest starred three times in 1963 to 1964 on NBC's *Dr. Kildare* and in a 1964 episode of Richard Crenna's short-lived *Slattery's People* political drama on CBS.

Nolan played the role of witches in two of Rod Serling's anthology television series; in *The Twilight Zone* (1963) episode "Jess-Belle" with Anne Francis, and the *Night Gallery* (1971) episode "Since Aunt Ada Came to Stay" with James Farentino and Michele Lee.

On November 4, 1965, she appeared as the treacherous Ma Burns in "The Golden Trail" episode of NBC's *Laredo*, having portrayed a supposedly refined woman trying to hijack a presumed gold shipment, which in actuality is thirty-six bottles of Tennessee whiskey. *Laredo* was a spinoff of the *The Virginian*, whose cast Nolan joined in 1967, along with her husband John McIntire.

She appeared regularly in several radio series: *Young Dr. Malone*, 1939–40; *Cavalcade of America*, 1940–41; Nicolette Moore in *One Man's Family*, 1947–50; and *The Great Gildersleeve*, 1949-52. She appeared episodically in many more.

In 1974, she starred briefly with Dack Rambo in CBS's *Dirty Sally*, a spinoff of the *Gunsmoke* (1955-1975) western series where she had played a recurring guest role for eight episodes. She also played the titular role in the award-winning short film *Peege* (1972) because of her *Gunsmoke* connection. In all, Nolan appeared as a guest star in television's *Gunsmoke* more than any other female.

She guest starred in three of David Janssen's television series *Richard Diamond, Private Detective* (1975-1959), *The Fugitive* (1966), and *Harry O* (1975).

Nolan married actor John McIntire in 1935. They remained married for fifty-six years until his death in 1991. The couple guest starred together in an episode of *Charlie's Angels* in 1979, *The Incredible Hulk* in 1980, *Quincy, M.E.* in 1983, and *Night Court* in 1985, playing Dan Fielding's hick parents. She was the mother of two children, one of whom was the actor Tim McIntire, who was best-known for his turn as the legendary DJ Alan Freed in the 1978 film *American Hot Wax*.

Her final film appearance was in Robert Redford's *The Horse Whisperer* (1998) as Robert Redford's mother.

She died on June 5, 1998, in Los Angeles, California following a stroke at the age of 86. Her interment was in Eureka, Montana's Tobacco Valley Cemetery.

Lloyd Nolan

Lloyd Nolan with Audie Murphy *Bad Boy*

Lloyd Benedict Nolan was born in San Francisco, California, August 11, 1902, and was an American film and television actor. Nolan was the son of Margaret and James Nolan, who was a shoe manufacturer. He began his career on stage and was subsequently lured to Hollywood, where he played mainly doctors, detectives, and police officers in many movie roles.

Although Nolan's acting was often praised by critics, he was, for the most part, relegated to B pictures. Despite this, Nolan costarred with a number of well-known actresses, among them Mae West, Dorothy McGuire, and former Metropolitan Opera soprano, Gladys Swarthout.

Under contract to Paramount and 20th Century Fox studios, he assayed starring roles in the late 1930s and early-to-mid 1940s and appeared as the title character in the Michael Shayne detective series of films. Raymond Chandler's novel *The High Window* was adapted from a Philip Marlowe adventure for the seventh film in the Michael Shayne series, *Time to Kill* (1942).

The majority of Nolan's films comprised light entertainment with an emphasis on action. His most famous films include: *Atlantic Adventure* (1935), costarring Nancy Carroll, *Bataan* (1943), and *A Tree Grows in Brooklyn* (1945), with Dorothy McGuire and James Dunn. He also gave a strong performance in the 1957 film *Peyton Place* with Lana Turner.

Nolan subsequently contributed many solid and key character parts in numerous other films. One of these films, *The House on 92nd Street*, was a startling revelation to audiences in 1945. It was a conflation of several true incidents of attempted sabotage by the Nazi regime, incidents which the FBI was able to thwart during World War II, and many scenes were filmed on location in New York City, an unusual occurrence at the time. Nolan portrayed FBI agent Briggs, and actual FBI employees interacted with Nolan throughout the film. He reprised the role in a subsequent 1948 movie, *The Street with No Name*.

He appeared in *Bad Boy* (1949) as Marshall Brown who takes in Audie Murphy's Danny Lester character at the Variety Club Ranch and subsequently, changes his life.

Later in his career, he returned to the stage and appeared on television to great acclaim in *The Caine Mutiny Court Martial*, for which he received a 1955 Emmy award for portraying Captain Queeg, the role made famous by Humphrey Bogart.

Nolan also starred in a classic 1964 episode of *The Outer Limits,* "Soldier", written by Harlan Ellison. In 1967, he and Strother Martin guest starred in the episode "A Mighty Hunter Before the Lord" of NBC's *The Road West* series starring Barry Sullivan.

Nolan co-starred in all eighty-six episodes in the pioneering NBC series *Julia* (1968-1971), with Diahann Carroll, who became the first African-American to star in her own television series outside of the role of a domestic worker.

He founded the Jay Nolan Autistic Center (now known as Jay Nolan Community Services) in honor of his son Jay who had autism and was chairman of the annual Save Autistic Children Telethon.

He continued working in films and television and his last role in *Hannah and Her Sisters* (1986) was released six months after his death.

Nolan died September 27, 1985, of lung cancer in Los Angeles at the age of 83.

Felix Noriego

Audie Murphy with Felix Noriego

Felix Noriego was born December 2, 1930, in Sells, Arizona. No other biographical information can be found.

He did appear in four films from 1954 to 1956. They were *Drum Beat* (1954) with Alan Ladd, *Battle Cry* (1955), *To Hell and Back* (1955) with Audie Murphy, and *Pillars of the Sky* (1956).

His character in *To Hell and Back*, 'Swope', was based in real life on James Fife, who was a member of Audie's platoon. James Fife came to the first Audie Murphy Days in Greenville, Texas, in 1996. The author was honored to speak with him and get his autograph.

Hugh O'Brian

Audie Murphy with Hugh O'Brian in *Drums Across the River*, and Hugh with David Williams in 2012

Hugh O'Brian was born Hugh Charles Krampe; April 19, 1923 and is an American actor, known for his starring role in the ABC television series *The Life and Legend of Wyatt Earp* (1955–1961).

O'Brian was born in Rochester, New York, the son of Hugh John Krampe, a career United States Marine Corps officer, and his wife Edith Krampe. He attended New Trier High School in Winnetka, Illinois (as did Rock Hudson, Charlton Heston, Ann-Margret, and many other future stars), and later Kemper Military School in Boonville, Missouri. He lettered in football, basketball, wrestling, and track. O'Brian dropped out of the University of Cincinnati after one semester to enlist in the Marine Corps during World War II. Only 17, he became the youngest Marine drill instructor.

After World War II, O'Brian moved to Los Angeles to study at UCLA. He was discovered on the stage by Ida Lupino who signed him to a film, *Never Fear* (1949), she was directing that led to a contract with Universal Pictures.

O'Brian replaced Bud Abbott in what began as an Abbott and Costello movie, *Fireman Save My Child* (1954), with Buddy Hackett cast in the Lou Costello role, and Spike Jones and his band also appearing at length.

He was chosen to portray legendary lawman, Wyatt Earp, on ABC, *The Life and Legend of Wyatt Earp* (1955-1961). Alongside *Gunsmoke* (1955-1975), these shows spearheaded the "adult western" TV genre, where the emphasis was on character development as opposed to mere moral sermonizing. It soon became one of the top-rated shows on television. During its seven-year run *Wyatt Earp* consistently placed in the top ten in the United States.

O'Brian also appeared regularly on other programs in the 1960s, including Jack Palance's ABC circus drama, *The Greatest Show on Earth* (1963), and as a 'guest attorney' in an episode of *Perry Mason* (1963) when its star, Raymond Burr, was sidelined for a spell after minor, emergency surgery. He was a guest celebrity panelist on the popular CBS prime-time programs *Password* (1963-1965) and *What's My Line?* (1961-1967), and served as a mystery guest on three occasions.

The actor made a number of motion pictures, among them *Rocketship X-M* (1950), *The Lawless Breed* (1953), *There's No Business Like Show Business* (1954), *White Feather* (1955), *Come Fly with Me* (1963), *Love Has Many Faces* (1965), *In Harm's Way* (1965), *Ten Little Indians* (1965), and *Ambush Bay* (1966).

He also appeared in *The Cimarron Kid* (1952) and *Drums Across the River* (1954) with Audie Murphy.

While on stage, Elvis Presley introduced O'Brian from the audience at the singer's April 1, 1975 performance at the Las Vegas Hilton, as captured in the imported live CD release "April Fool's Dinner." O'Brian was a featured star in the 1977 two-hour premiere of television's *Fantasy Island*.

He is the last man that John Wayne ever killed on the screen in Wayne's final movie *The Shootist* (1976). O'Brian was a good friend of the Duke and said he considers this a great honor.

O'Brian appeared in fight scenes with a Bruce Lee lookalike in Lee's last film *Game of Death* (1978).

O'Brian recreated his Wyatt Earp role for two 1990s projects, *Guns of Paradise* (1990) and *The Gambler Returns: The Luck of the Draw* (1991) with fellow actor Gene Barry doing likewise as lawman Bat Masterson for each. He also recreated his role in the made for television movie *Wyatt Earp: Return to Tombstone* (1994) that had new footage as well as flashbacks.

He also had a small role in the Danny DeVito/Arnold Schwarzenegger 1988 comedy film *Twins,* as one of several men who had "donated" the DNA that later became the "twins." In the film, Schwarzenegger thought he'd found his "father," when he met Hugh O'Brian's character.

In 1999 and 2000 he costarred with Dick Van Patten, Deborah Winters, Richard Roundtree, and Richard Anderson in the acclaimed Warren Chaney miniseries, *Y2K - World in Crisis*.

For his contribution to the television industry, Hugh O'Brian has a star on the Hollywood Walk of Fame at 6613½ Hollywood Blvd. In 1992, he was inducted into the Western Performers Hall of Fame at the National Cowboy & Western Heritage Museum in Oklahoma City, Oklahoma.

On June 25, 2006, O'Brian married for the first time at age 81; his wife is the former Virginia Barber (born ca. 1952). The ceremony was held at Forest Lawn Memorial Park, with the Reverend Robert Schuller, pastor of the Crystal Cathedral in Garden Grove, officiating. The couple was serenaded by close friend, Debbie Reynolds.

Hugh O'Brian has dedicated much of his life to the Hugh O'Brian Youth Leadership (HOBY). HOBY is a non-profit youth leadership development program that empowers 10,000 high school sophomores annually through its over seventy leadership programs in all fifty states and twenty countries. Since its inception in 1958, over 355,000 young people have been inspired by HOBY.

One high school sophomore from every high school in the United States, referred to as an "ambassador," is welcome to attend a state or regional HOBY seminar. From each of those seminars, students (number based on population) are offered the opportunity to attend the World Leadership Congress (WLC). In 2008, over 500 ambassadors attended.

The concept for HOBY was inspired in 1958 by a nine-day visit O'Brian had with famed humanitarian Dr. Albert Schweitzer in Africa. Dr. Schweitzer believed "the most important thing in education is to teach young people to think for themselves."

Hugh O'Brian's message to young people is "Freedom to Choose" Here is his brief speech on this topic: "I do NOT believe we are all born equal. Created equal in the eyes of God, yes, but physical and emotional differences, parental guidelines, varying environments, being in the right place at the right time, all play a role in enhancing or limiting an individual's development. But I DO believe every man and woman, if given the opportunity and encouragement to recognize their potential, regardless of background, has the freedom to choose in our world. Will an individual be a taker or a giver in life? Will that person be satisfied merely to exist or seek a meaningful purpose? Will he or she dare to dream the impossible dream?

"I believe every person is created as the steward of his or her own destiny with great power for a specific purpose, to share with others, through service, a reverence for life in a spirit of love."

Joan O'Brien

Audie Murphy with O'Brien in *Six Black Horses*

Joan Marie O'Brien was born in Cambridge, Massachusetts, February 14, 1936, and is an American actress and singer. She made a name for herself acting in television shows in the 1950's and 1960's, and as a film co-star with Audie Murphy, Cary Grant, Elvis Presley, John Wayne, and Jerry Lewis.

Her family moved to California when O'Brien was a child, and enrolled O'Brien in dance classes when she was eight years old. She graduated from Chaffey Union High School in Ontario, California.

O'Brien's singing abilities came to the attention of entertainer and Country Music Hall of Fame member Cliffie Stone, who hired her as a regular performer on his television show *Hometown Jamboree* before her high school graduation. In 1954, she became a regular on *The Bob Crosby Show*, and stayed until the show's cancellation in 1958. She co-starred with Cary Grant and Tony Curtis in the 1959 movie *Operation Petticoat*.

Lawrence Welk hired O'Brien as a one-week replacement for his champagne lady Alice Lon in July 1959. O'Brien had come to Welk's attention years earlier when she was a singer on Bob Crosby's show, but Welk decided not to hire her at that time because she was still a teenager.

O'Brien was cast as Alamo survivor Susanna Dickinson in John Wayne's 1960 epic *The Alamo*. That same year, O'Brien performed as a soloist for composer Buddy Bregman at the Moulin Rouge night club in Los Angeles. In 1961, O'Brien again co-starred with John Wayne, as his love interest in *The Comancheros*.

Actresses Sheree North, Sabrina and Sue Carson joined O'Brien in a tour of *Playgirls* in 1961, appearing at the Riverside Hotel in Reno, Nevada.

She appeared in *Six Black Horses* (1962) as the woman Audie Murphy and Dan Duryea had a shoot out over at the end of the movie. O'Brien then played Elvis Presley's girlfriend in the 1963 film *It Happened at the World's Fair*.

Her most frequent acting performances were in television during the 1960's. She appeared in *The Dick Van Dyke Show* (1963), *The Lieutenant* (1964), and *The Virginian* (1964).

In 1964, O'Brien guest starred in an episode of *The Man from UNCLE* (1964). Series star Robert Vaughn, subsequently cast her as Ophelia in *Hamlet* at the Pasadena Playhouse.

Joan's final movie was *Get Yourself a College Girl* (1964), a "Swinging Sixties" teenfest also featuring Nancy Sinatra, with music by The Animals and The Dave Clark Five.

Her last acting role was in an episode of *Perry Mason* in 1965. After her acting career ended, O'Brien sang with the Harry James band in 1968. She then left show business for good to concentrate on raising her kids, and later became a successful executive with the Hilton Hotel chain.

Damian O'Flynn

Audie Murphy with Damian O'Flynn in *Gunfight at Comanche Creek*

Damian O'Flynn was born January 29, 1907, in Boston, Massachusetts, and was an American general purpose actor. He made his first screen appearance in *Marked Woman* (1937). O'Flynn went on to freelance at Warner Brothers, RKO, Paramount, Monogram, and other studios, usually in secondary roles, but occasionally playing leads.

While serving in WWII, he appeared along with several other actors-in-uniform in 20th Century Fox's *Winged Victory* (1944), billed as Corporal Damian O'Flynn. A veteran of many a big-screen Western, like *Saddle Pals* (1947), *Riders of the Whistling Pines* (1949), *Young Daniel Boone* (1950), *The Half-Breed* (1952), *The Far Country* (1954), *Daniel Boone, Trail Blazer* (1956), *Apache Warrior* (1957), and *Gunfight at Comanche Creek* (1963) with Audie Murphy.

He appeared in thirty-three episodes in the television series *The Life and Legend of Wyatt Earp* (1956-1961) as Doc Goodfellow. Other television programs he appeared in were *Adventures of Wild Bill Hickok* (1956), *The Adventures of Dr. Fu Manchu* (1956), *The New Adventures of Charlie Chan* (1957), *Mr. Adams and Eve* (1957-1958), *Richard Diamond, Private Detective* (1958), *The Jim Backus Show* (1960), *National Velvet* (1962), *Batman* (1966), and his last roles were in *Green Acres* (1967-1969).

He died August 8, 1982, at age 75 in Los Angeles, California.

Louis Ojena

No biographical information could be found for Louis Ojena. He did appear in eleven films such as *Orgy of the Dead* (1965) as the mummy, *Suburbia Confidential* (1966), *A Time for Dying* (1969) as the blacksmith, *The Hanging of Jake Ellis* (1969), *Motel Confidential* (1969), *Love Boccaccio Style* (1971), *Machismo: 40 Graves for 40 Guns* (1971), *Sexcapade in Mexico* (1973), *Country Hooker* (1974), *The Love Butcher* (1975), and *Mean Johnny Barrows* (1976).

J. Pat O'Malley

J. Pat O'Malley with Audie Murphy in *Apache Rifles*

James Patrick O'Malley was born March 15, 1904, in Burnley, Lancashire, England and was an English singer and character actor, who appeared in many American films and television programmes during the 1940s–1970s, using the stage name J. Pat O'Malley.

He also appeared on the Broadway stage in *Ten Little Indians* (1944) and *Dial M for Murder*. A *New York Times* drama critic praised O'Malley's performance in *Ten Little Indians*, calling him "a rara avis, a comedian who does not gauge the success of his efforts by the number of laughs he induces at each performance".

O'Malley began his entertainment career in 1925 as a recording artist and then as principal singer with Jack Hylton and his orchestra in the United Kingdom from 1930 to 1933. Known at that time as *Pat O'Malley*, he recorded over 400 popular songs of the day. O'Malley began a solo recording career in 1935 in parallel with his work with Hylton. At the end of 1935, Hylton and O'Malley went to the U.S. to record with a band composed of American musicians, thus emulating Ray Noble and Al Bowlly. The venture was short-lived but O'Malley remained in the United States.

Now known as J. Pat O'Malley (to avoid confusion with another film actor named Pat O'Malley), he had a long and varied acting career including the film *Lassie Come Home* in 1943 as "Hynes". He appeared later in Walt Disney's *Spin and Marty* hit television serials as the always-faithful "Perkins" (1955–1957). In 1956, he guest starred in the episode "The Guilty" of the NBC legal drama, *Justice,* based on case files of the Legal Aid Society of New York.

He guest starred twice as Cinnebar Jones on Bill Williams's syndicated series *The Adventures of Kit Carson* (1951–1955). In 1959–1960, O'Malley starred eight times as Judge Caleb Marsh in the ABC western series *Black Saddle* starring Peter Breck as a gunslinger-turned-lawyer, with Russell Johnson as a peace officer. In 1960, O'Malley guest starred on the short-lived *The Tab Hunter Show* sitcom on NBC, on ABC's *The Law and Mr. Jones* legal drama with James Whitmore and Conlan Carter, and on the syndicated crime drama *Johnny Midnight* starring Edmond O'Brien. He also appeared as a police officer on John Cassavetes's NBC detective series *Johnny Staccato* (1959). He guest starred on Pat O'Brien's ABC sitcom *Harrigan and Son* (1961).

In 1961, he guest starred in ABC's drama *Bus Stop*, starring Marilyn Maxwell as the owner of a diner in a fictitious small Colorado town. O'Malley appeared in 1962 on CBS's *Twilight Zone* episode called "The Fugitive" (he made also a very short appearance in the episode *Walking Distance*). In the 1962–1963 season, he guest starred twice on both Gene Kelly's ABC's *Going My Way*, about a Roman Catholic priest in New York City, and on the CBS anthology series *The Lloyd Bridges Show*. O'Malley and Spring Byington starred in an episode of Jack Palance's ABC circus drama, *The Greatest Show on Earth*, which aired in the 1963-1964 season.

He appeared with Audie Murphy in the film *Apache Rifles* (1964) playing kindly army doctor Captain Thatcher.

In the 1964–1965 season, O'Malley appeared as a handyman on the ABC's sitcom *Wendy and Me* with costars George Burns, Connie Stevens, Ron Harper, and James T. Callahan. He guest starred in 1965 in Christopher Jones's ABC western, *The Legend of Jesse James*, and in 1966 in Jack Sheldon's CBS's short-lived unconventional sitcom *Run, Buddy, Run*. O'Malley also appeared occasionally as "Vince" in the 1966 ABC comedy/western series *The Rounders*, with Ron Hayes, Patrick Wayne, and Chill Wills. That same year he also played an old prospector who helps David McCallum in the *Man from U.N.C.L.E.* episode, "The Nowhere Affair".

In 1969, O'Malley portrayed Carol Brady's (Florence Henderson) father in the premiere episode of ABC's *The Brady Bunch*. That same year, he appeared as cop on the beat in 20th Century Fox's film production of *Hello, Dolly!* He made several appearances in the television series *Maude*, as Hermione Baddeley's beau, from 1973-75. He appeared in three episodes on NBC's *Emergency!* (1972-1975).

Walt Disney also engaged O'Malley to provide voices for animated films such as the Cockney coster in the "Supercalifragilisticexpialidocious" sequence in *Mary Poppins* (1964), Cyril Proudbottom, Winkie, and a policeman in *The Adventures of Ichabod and Mr. Toad* (1949) and the role of Colonel Hathi and the vulture Buzzie in *The Jungle Book* (1967). His voice can also be heard in *Alice in Wonderland* (1951), in which he performs all the character voices in the "The Walrus and the Carpenter" segment (besides Alice), including Tweedledum and Tweedledee, the Walrus, the Carpenter, and Mother Oyster. He performed the roles of the Colonel and Jasper in *One Hundred and One Dalmatians* (1961) and in the Pirates of the Caribbean attraction in several roles including the original voice of the Pirate Captain dunking the magistrate into the well. In 1979 he made an appearance on *Three's Company* as Leo.

In 1982, O'Malley made his final television appearance on *Taxi*.

O'Malley died February, 27, 1985, from cardiovascular disease in San Juan Capistrano in Orange County, California, shortly before what would have been his 81st birthday. He was survived by his wife, Fay M. O'Malley (1926–2002) and two children.

Robert Osterloh

Robert Osterloh was born May 31, 1918, in Pittsburgh, Pennsylvania. After his 1948 film debut in Columbia's *The Dark Past*, American general purpose actor Robert Osterloh was signed to a Warner Brothers contract.

During his Warners tenure, Osterloh was spotted in such fleeting roles as the prisoner whose mail is censored into oblivion in the 1949 James Cagney classic *White Heat* (1949). He then went into his "officer" period, wearing many uniforms and bearing several ranks over the next decade.

Among Robert Osterloh's 1950s film assignments were Major White in *The Day the Earth Stood Still* (1951), Colonel Robert E. Lee in *Seven Angry Men* (1955) and Lieutenant Claybourn in *I Bury the Living* (1958).

Some of his other films include *Fort Massacre* (1958), *Inherit the Wind* (1960), *Young Dillinger* (1965), *The Oscar* (1966), *Rosemary's Baby* (1968), and *Coogan's Bluff* (1968).

He appeared in the television programs *Rebound* (1952), *My Hero* (1953), *Mr. & Mrs. North* (1954), *The Man Behind the Badge* (1955), *Crusader* (1956), *Gunsmoke* (1958), *Perry Mason* (1957-1959), *Men Into Space* (1960), *Wanted: Dead or Alive* (1960), *Whispering Smith* (1961) with Audie Murphy, *The Outer Limits* (1964), *Ironside* (1971), *Hec Ramsey* (1972).

He died April 16, 2001, at age 82 in Los Osos, San Luis Obispo County, California.

Frank Overton

Frank Overton with Audie Murphy in *Posse from Hell*

Frank Overton was born Frank Emmons Overton March 18, 1918, in Babylon, New York. He was a perpetually serious-looking character actor, who showed up to good effect in many TV shows of the 1950's and 1960's.

His quietly authoritarian demeanor lent itself ideally to portraying characters with badges or uniforms: Burt Hogan, a member of Audie Murphy's posse in *Posse from Hell* (1961), Sheriff Heck Tate in *To Kill a Mockingbird* (1962), General Bogan of Strategic Air Command in *Fail-Safe* (1964) and Major Harvey Stovall of Bomber Group 918 in sixty-one episodes of *12 O'Clock High* (1964). The latter was his only recurring role on television and he made the most of it, being strongly featured in several of the episodes.

Prior to his well-remembered role as Elias Sandoval on *Star Trek* (1966) he had made notable appearances in two other science fiction series.

He was twice featured in *The Twilight Zone* (1959), first in the episode 'Walking Distance' (1959), he played the father of advertising executive Martin Sloan (Gig Young), who, unhappy with his life such as it is, has somehow time-travelled back to his home town. Sloan finds, to his delight, that everything has remained unchanged from the time of his childhood. In a superbly-acted and touching scene, the elder Sloan (having come to terms with the identity of the stranger), asks his son to leave, because there can only ever be "one summer per customer". In contrast, Overton's chill, austere Sheriff Harry Wheeler of 'Mute' (1963) was the antithesis of his character in 'Walking Distance', devoid of compassion or understanding. Overton also appeared as an unsympathetic physician in *The Invaders* (1967) episode 'Genesis' (1967).

Overton's characterizations on stage largely paralleled those on screen. He made his first stab at Broadway as a lieutenant in Elia Kazan's comedy *Jacobowsky and the Colonel*, written by 'S.N.Behrman'. The play ran for 417 performances from 1944 to 1945. He played another sheriff in *The Trip to Bountiful* (1953) and replaced James Gregory as Deputy Jesse Bard in the original stage version of *The Desperate Hours* (1955). His most successful performance was as Morris Lacey in *The Dark at the Top of the Stairs* (1957-59), a role he reprised for the film version of 1960.

During his last years he made several appearances on *The Virginian* and *Bonanza*, both from 1962 to 1967.

An actor who always looked older than his years, Frank Emmons Overton died of a heart attack in Pacific Palisades, California, April 24, 1967, aged only 49.

Beverly Owen

Audie Murphy with Beverly Owen in *Bullet for a Badman*

Beverley Owen was born Beverley Ogg in Ottumwa, Iowa, May 13, 1937, and is a classically-trained American actress. She moved to New York to pursue an acting career after graduating from the University of Michigan.

She was fired many times for lack of typing skills while working at CBS, and for Ed Sullivan. She later became senior typist for the *Captain Kangeroo* show.

She did many small parts in shows, such as *As the World Turns* (1961-1964), *Kraft Mystery Theater* (1963), *Wagon Train* (1963), and *The Virginian* (1964), until being forced into the part of Marilyn Munster on *The Munster's* (1964). She disliked the role and only accepted out of contractual obligations to Universal Studios. After thirteen episodes she left the show to get married and was replaced by Pat Priest.

She made her only film appearance in *Bullet for a Badman* (1964) as Darren McGavin's ex-wife and the current wife of Audie Murphy.

She didn't return to acting until she landed a role of Dr. Paula McCrea in *Another World* (1971-1972).

She is now divorced, but has two daughters, Polly and Kate. She is not always recognized as Marilyn because in the show she wore a blonde wig. In 1989 she got her master's degree in Early American History.

Patricia Owens

Audie Murphy with Patricia Owens in *The Gunrunners*

Patricia Owens was born January 17, 1925, in Golden, British Columbia, Canada. When she was eight she moved to England. While there she embarked on a number of stage plays. Later she was spotted by a Twentieth-Century Fox executive who offered her a contract and in 1956 she went to Hollywood.

There she met Sy Bartlett whom she married and later divorced in 1958. Warner Brothers spotted her acting abilities in the classic *Island in the Sun* (1957) and asked Fox if she could be loaned out for a part in the Marlon Brando classic *Sayonara* (1957). Here she received kudos for her performance as the distraught scorned fiancée of Brando.

It was not until 1958, though, when she achieved her greatest role remembered as the tormented Helene Delambre in the Fox classic, *The Fly* (1958). The visage of seeing her in the Fly's view is considered one of the classic moments in science fiction history of films.

Patricia went on to play in other films, like Audie Murphy's wife in *The Gun Runners* (1958), *Seven Women from Hell* (1961), *The Untouchables* (1963), *Gunsmoke* (1964), *Black Spurs* (1965), *Burke's Law* (1966), *The Destructors* (1968), and *Lassie* (1968).

In 1960 she married real estate developer Jerome "Jerry" Nathanson. The marriage was short-lived but produced Patricia's only child Adam. Patricia was also married for six years to John Austin from 1969 to 1975.

She died August 31, 2000, at age 75 in Lancaster, California, from cancer.

Nester Paiva

Veteran character actor Nestor Paiva was born Nestor Caetano Paiva, June 30, 1905, in Fresno, California, and had one of those nondescript ethnic mugs and a natural gift for dialects that allowed him to play practically any type of foreigner.

He graduated from the University of California at Berkeley and developed an interest in performing while hooking up with college theatrics. Making his debut in a production of Antigone, he played in a Los Angeles production of *The Drunkard* for eleven years, finally leaving the show as his workload grew in number and importance in the mid-1940s.

Film buffs remember him as the main villain, "The Scorpion" in the wartime classic serial *Don Winslow of the Coast Guard* (1943). In hundreds of film and television roles from 1938-67 and in an overall career that spanned forty years, the bald, dark, and bulky Paiva played everything from Spaniards, Greeks, Russians, and Portuguese to Italians, Indians, Arabs, and even African-Americans (the latter on radio). Some were shifty, others excitable, many quite hilarious...and many of them undeserving and small.

Some of his recognizable film and television roles were *Ride a Crooked Mile* (1938), *Union Pacific* (1939), *Beau Geste* (1939), *The Hunchback of Notre Dame* (1939), *Primrose Path* (1940), *The Sea Hawk* (1940), *The Green Hornet Strikes Again!* (1940), *Hold That Ghost* (1941) with Abbott and Costello, *Reap the Wild Wind* (1942) with John Wayne, *The Dancing Masters* (1943) with Laurel and Hardy, *Badman's Territory* (1946) with Randolph Scott, *Ramrod* (1947) with Joel McCrea, *Mighty Joe Young* (1949) with the big monkey, *The Desert Hawk* (1950), *China Smith* (1952), *Viva Zapata!* (1952), *Creature from the Black Lagoon* (1954), *Rocky Jones, Space Ranger* (1954), the Louis L'amour written film *Four Guns to the Border* (1954), *Sheena: Queen of the Jungle* (1955) with Irish McCalla, *Revenge of the Creature* (1955), *Tarantula* (1955), *Hell on Frisco Bay* (1955) with Alan Ladd, *The First Texan* (1956) with Joel McCrea again, *The Mole People* (1956), *The Guns of Fort Petticoat* (1957) with Audie Murphy, *The Deep Six* (1958) again with Alan Ladd, *Alias Jesse James* (1959) with Bob Hope, *Richard Diamond, Private Detective* (1959) with David Janssen, *Wichita Town* (1960) again with Joel McCrea, *Wanted: Dead or Alive* (1960) with Steve McQueen, *Atlantis, the Lost Continent* (1961), *The Four Horsemen of the Apocalypse* (1962), *The Three Stooges in Orbit* (1962) with Moe, Larry, and Curly Joe, *Girls! Girls! Girls!* (1962) with Elvis Presley, *Ballad of a Gunfighter* (1964), *Gunsmoke* (1965), *Get Smart* (1965), *The Addams Family* (1966), *Jesse James Meets Frankenstein's Daughter* (1966), *Let's Kill Uncle, Before Uncle Kills Us* (1966), and *They Saved Hitler's Brain* (1968).

He died September 9, 1966, at age 61 in Hollywood, California.

Dorita Pallais

Audie Murphy with Dorita Pallais in *The Kid from Texas*

Dorita Pallais was born April 22, 1927, in Mexico. An accomplished guitarist, singer and dancer, she formed an all girl trio with her sisters, Carmen and Guadalupe, performing in the early days of television in Los Angeles with the legendary producer Klaus Landsberg.

She appeared in four motion pictures such as *Three Daring Daughters* (1948), *The Kid from Texas* (1950) with Audie Murphy, *The Iron Mistress* (1952) with Alan Ladd, and *Sombrero* (1953).

Her Daughter Michele Greene is an author, actress, and activist.

Gregg Palmer

Gregg Palmer with Audie Murphy behind the scenes of *Column South*,
and with the author's very pregnant wife Deborah Williams in 2005

Gregg Palmer was born Palmer Lee January 25, 1927, and is an American actor, known primarily for his prolific work in television westerns.

He appeared from 1960-1975 in varying roles in twenty episodes of CBS's *Gunsmoke* with James Arness, thirteen segments of the syndicated *Death Valley Days* (1956-1969), and nine episodes of NBC's *The Virginian*

(1964-1970) starring James Drury in the title role. He guest starred five times on *Bonanza* (1964-1969), NBC's longest-running western.

Of Norwegian extraction, the brown-haired and brown-eyed Palmer was born in San Francisco, California, the son of a carpenter. He entered the United States Army Air Corps, forerunner of the Air Force, and became a cryptographer during World War II. He was discharged in 1946 as a sergeant. Sometimes known as "Grizzly", Palmer worked as a bouncer, truck driver, and in construction before he became a radio disc jockey.

In 1950, at the age of twenty-three, he procured his first screen role, as an uncredited ambulance attendant in the Martin and Lewis comedy film *My Friend Irma Goes West*.

In the early 1950s, Palmer and Marilyn Monroe both unsuccessfully auditioned for roles as Abner and Daisy Mae in a proposed *Li'l Abner* television series based on the Al Capp cartoon, but the effort never materialized. Palmer was signed to a contract with Universal Pictures.

In 1952, he appeared as William Norton in the comedy film *Francis Goes to West Point*, starring Donald O'Connor. Palmer claimed that he was going to be pushed as a big star by Universal in a similar manner to their other stable of stars, but in the 1950s the studio changed, hiring out major stars from other studios rather than build up their own. Palmer was soon dropped and went freelance.

Gregg Palmer appeared in *The Cimarron Kid* (1952), *Column South* (1953), *To Hell and Back* (1955), and *The Quick Gun* (1964) all with Audie Murphy.

In 1955, Palmer appeared as Jack Slade in an episode of Jim Davis's syndicated western series *Stories of the Century*. Slade was the superintendent of the Central Overland California and Pikes Peak Express Company, based in Julesburg in northeastern Colorado, who sets out to capture the outlaw Jules Beni.

He appeared in *The Creature Walks Among Us* (1956), the third film in the *Creature From the Black Lagoon* (1954) film series.

From 1955-1958, Palmer appeared five times on the syndicated *26 Men*, starring Tristram Coffin and based on the actual files of the Arizona Rangers law enforcement group.

From 1956-1961, he appeared five times as Tom McLowery in ABC's *The Life and Legend of Wyatt Earp* starring Hugh O'Brian in the title role: "So Long, Dora, So Long", "Doc Holliday Faces Death", "The Law Must Be Fair", "Just Before the Battle", and "The Gunfight at the O.K. Corral". He appeared as Cowlin in the 1961 episode "The Dead Ringer" of the syndicated series *Two Faces West* starring Charles Bateman. From 1957-1961, Palmer appeared in three episodes of Dale Robertson's NBC series *Tales of Wells Fargo*: "Chips", "The Warrior's Return", and "Death Raffle".

In 1965-1966, he appeared as Curly in the episode "The Golden Trail" and as Sergeant Mason in "The Dance of the Laughing Death" in NBC's *Laredo* western series. In 1967 and 1968, he appeared three times in Stuart Whitman's 90-minute western *Cimarron Strip* in episodes entitled "Journey to a Hanging", "The Deputy", and "The Greeners". Palmer also appeared three times between 1965 and 1968 in Robert Conrad's unconventional western, *The Wild Wild West*. In 1972, Palmer appeared on ABC's *Alias Smith and Jones* series.

Palmer was cast as Ezra Parker in the 1969 film *The Undefeated*, Karl Riker in the 1970 film *Chisum*, and John Goodfellow in the 1971 film *Big Jake*, all starring John Wayne. He also became a member of the John Wayne Stock Company, founded in 1945, with original members including Ward Bond, Grant Withers, and Paul Fix. In 1976, Palmer was cast as the unnamed "Burly Man" in the last of Wayne's films, *The Shootist*.

He played Sgt. Buxbaum in *Kolchak: The Night Stalker* (1975) in the episode "The Knightly Murders".

In 1977, Palmer appeared as mountain man Jim Bridger in the two-part Walt Disney's Wonderful World of Color presentation *Kit Carson and the Mountain Man*. Christopher Connelly starred as Kit Carson, and Robert Reed portrayed John C. Fremont. Gary Lockwood also appeared as Brett Haskell. In 1978, Palmer appeared as Loman in James Arness's second western, *How the West Was Won*.

Palmer's last screen appearance was as a colonel in the 1982 ABC miniseries *The Blue and the Gray*.

A widower, Palmer lives in Encino, California, and is an avid golfer. His wife, Ruth Palmer, died in 1999.

In recent years he has attended several western film festivals and appeared at Audie Murphy Days in Greenville, Texas.

Darla Paris

No biographical information can be found for Darla Paris. She appeared in two films. The first was as a stripper with the name 'Delicious' in *Mondo Topless* (1966) and her second role was as one of Mamie's girls in *A Time For Dying* (1969) with Audie Murphy.

Jerry Paris

Jerry Paris was born William Gerald Grossman in San Francisco, California, July 25, 1925, and was an American actor and director best known for playing Jerry Helper, the dentist and next door neighbor of Rob and Laura Petrie, on *The Dick Van Dyke Show* (1961-1966).

After having directed some *Van Dyke* show episodes, Paris devoted himself to directing, both in television and film, most notably on the TV series *Happy Days* (1974-1984), for which he directed 238 episodes.

Paris had roles in films like *The Caine Mutiny* (1954), *The Wild One* (1953), *Marty* (1955), *D-Day the Sixth of June* (1956), *Man on the Prowl* (1957), *The Naked and the Dead* (1958), *No Name on the Bullet* (1959) with Audie Murphy, *The Great Impostor* (1961), *Don't Raise the Bridge, Lower the River* (1968), and *Leo and Loree* (1980).

Other television programs he appeared in were *Dragnet* (1952), *The Lone Wolf* (1955), *Those Whiting Girls* (1957), *Steve Canyon* (1959-1960), and also played Martin "Marty" Flaharty, one of Eliot Ness's men in a recurring role in the first season of ABC-TV's *The Untouchables* (1959-1960).

He married the former Ruth Benjamin, and they had three children. She died in 1980. Paris died from complications from brain cancer surgery March 31, 1986, at the age of 60. He was residing in Los Angeles, California, at the time of his death.

In the 1990s sitcom *The Nanny*, Fran Fine's grandmother Yetta Rosenberg played by Ann Morgan Guilbert showed a photo of Paris briefly and claimed it was her late husband. Guilbert played Millie Helper on *The Dick Van Dyke Show*.

Butch Patrick

Audie Murphy with Butch Patrick in *Showdown*

Butch Patrick was born Patrick Alan Lilley on August 2, 1953 in Los Angeles, California, and is a former American child actor. He is widely known for his role on the TV show *The Munsters* (1964–1966) where he played Eddie Munster, the son of Herman (Fred Gwynne) and Lily Munster (Yvonne De Carlo). He also appeared as Eddie in the 1966 movie *Munster, Go Home*.

In 1962-1963, Patrick portrayed Greg Howard, the young son of widow Louise Howard (Janet De Gore) in the last season of Walter Brennan's CBS situation comedy *The Real McCoys* (later renamed *The McCoys*). In the story line, Louise is interested in the young widower, Luke McCoy (Richard Crenna).

He appeared in an uncredited role as Strother Martin's son in *Showdown* (1963) with Audie Murphy.

He appeared in various other television programs during the 1960s, including *Mister Ed* (1963-1964), *My Favorite Martian* (1963), *Daniel Boone* (1969), *I Dream of Jeannie* (1966), *The Monkees* (1967), *Gunsmoke* (1964-1967), and *Adam-12* (1969-1970), and was featured in eight episodes of *My Three Sons* (1962-1971) as the character Gordon Dearing.

Patrick worked with such famed stars as Burt Lancaster and Judy Garland, appearing along side of both as one of the students in the 1963 film *A Child Is Waiting*.

Patrick's voiceover work includes the role of Milo in the 1969 live-action/animated film *The Phantom Tollbooth* (based on the children's book of that name), and an animated version of himself in the "Eight Misbehavin'" episode of *The Simpsons* (1999). He also appeared on the reality show *Star Dates* (2002).

From 1971 to 1973 a teenaged Patrick starred in the Saturday morning fantasy program *Lidsville*.

In 1983, Patrick recorded an autobiographical song, "Whatever Happened To Eddie?" with several instrumentalists and backup singers under the group name "Eddie and the Monsters featuring Butch Patrick." Set to the tune of the *Munsters* theme, the song details his life as a Munster. ("You might wonder why I have a dragon for a pet/Well he's just there to keep me company on the set.") He recorded a second single, "It's Only Halloween", which was released on Park Lane Drive Records in 2007.

He appeared in a cameo role in *Here Come the Munsters* (1995), and again played Eddie Munster in *Macabre Theatre* (2002) for five episodes and then for *Macabre Theatre Halloween Special* (2006).

He then appeared in *Frankenstein vs. the Creature from Blood Cove* (2005) as the Transformed Werewolf.

In 2005, Patrick made an appearance as an absent-minded bartender in the independent film *Spaced Out* which was released in 2009 by Ariztical Entertainment.

On July 26, 2010, Patrick rode his motorcycle in Carthage, New York to benefit the blind community.

He appeared as the wolfman in *Kitaro's Graveyard Gang 2* (2011).

On May 12, 2011, Patrick announced that he has prostate cancer. Patrick said that the disease was detected early and he remains positive that he can recover and live another twenty years. Doctors informed Patrick that he had a 90 percent chance of surviving the cancer. Patrick said "I went 41 years trying to kill myself. And then finally got to the point when I want to live I was diagnosed with prostate cancer. My first thought when I was told this was 'Isn't this a kicker?' I get clean, my life is together, and now God is going to punch my ticket."

He finished filming *Zombie Dream* in 2012 and it does not have a release date yet.

Hank Patterson

Hank Patterson with Audie Murphy in *No Name on the Bullet*

Hank Patterson was born Elmer Calvin Patterson in Springville, Alabama, October 9, 1888, and was an American actor and musician. He is most known for playing stableman Hank Miller on *Gunsmoke* (1959-1975) and Fred Ziffel on *Petticoat Junction* (1963-1966) and *Green Acres* (1965-1971).

He had intended to be a serious pianist, but became instead a vaudeville piano player, eventually moving to Hollywood where he played in a series of movies, largely Westerns and science fiction from 1939 to 1973.

More of his roles included *Abilene Town* (1946), *Belle Starr's Daughter* (1948), *The Lone Ranger* (1949-1950), *Al Jennings of Oklahoma* (1951), *The Abbott and Costello Show* (1953), *Ride Clear of Diablo* (1954) with Audie Murphy, *Tarantula* (1955), *Gunsight Ridge* (1957), *Attack of the Puppet People* (1958), *Earth vs. the Spider* (1958), *No Name on the Bullet* (1959) again with Audie Murphy, *Gunfighters of Abilene* (1960), *Whispering Smith* (1961) a third appearance with Audie Murphy, *Twilight Zone* (1962-1964), *The Wild Wild West* (1965), *Laredo* (1966), *Mod Squad* (1969), and *Love, American Style* (1972).

Hank's great-grandfather, James Pearson, was an original settler of St. Clair County, Alabama as was his mother's great-grandfather, Thomas Newton. Between 1894 and 1897, the family left Alabama to live in Taylor, Texas, where Hank attempted to work as a serious musician only to settle for playing piano in traveling vaudeville shows.

Patterson's great-niece is actress Téa Leoni.

Hank Patterson died August 23, 1975, at age 86 in Woodland Hills, Los Angeles, California.

Steve Pendleton

Gaylord "Steve" Pendleton was born September 16, 1908, and was an American film actor. He appeared in over 150 films during his career.

The younger brother of comic actor Nat Pendleton, he entered films in 1923. He was usually cast as collegiate types (undergrads, military school cadets), with a few weaklings and villains thrown in. Fans of Bob Hope and Bing Crosby will remember Pendleton as tuxedoed "other man" Gordon Wycott in *Road to Singapore* (1940). Active in films and television until 1976, Gaylord Pendleton was generally confined to minor roles, with a handful of leads and second leads in serials and comedy two-reelers.

Some of his works include *Twentieth Century* (1934), *Ride a Crooked Mile* (1938), *The Grapes of Wrath* (1940), *Sergeant York* (1941), *The Return of Rin Tin Tin* (1947), *Beyond Glory* (1949) with Audie Murphy, *Rio Grande* (1950), *Indian Uprising* (1952), *The Great Jesse James Raid* (1953), *Target Earth* (1954), *Battle Hymn* (1957), *Guns of the Timberland* (1960), *Blood Bath* (1966), *Pit Stop* (1969), and *Cannon* (1976).

He died October 3, 1984 in Pasadena, California, at age 76.

Antonio Peral

Audie Murphy with Antonio Peral in *The Texican*

No biographical information could be found for Italain actor Juan Antonio Peral. He appeared in twenty-three films and television programs from 1962 to 1977, most of them were Italian productions. Some of them include *Implacable Three* (1963), *Texas Ranger* (1964), *Finger on the Trigger* (1965), *Heroes of the West* (1965), *In a Colt's Shadow* (1965), *The Texican* (1966) with Audie Murphy, *A Witch Without a Broom* (1967), *Young Rebel* (1967), *Two Brothers, One Death* (1968), and *Simon Blanco* (1975).

Joe Perry

Joseph V. Perry was born February 13, 1931, and was an American actor possibly best known for his role as Nemo in *Everybody Loves Raymond* (1996-1999).

Perry began his acting career in his youth, winning the Glenn Ford Award at Santa Monica High School in California in 1949. His successes continued in 1952 when he was presented the best actor award at UCLA by Marlon Brando. Perry officially started his film career in 1955 at the age of twenty-four and spent the next forty-five years appearing in literally hundreds of films and television shows from dramatic anthologies to westerns to medical dramas, police dramas to classic sitcoms.

Some of his more memorable roles include "The Flight" episode of *Suspicion* (1957) with Audie Murphy, *Trackdown* (1958), *The Left Handed Gun* (1958), *Wanted: Dead or Alive* (1958-1960), *Johnny Ringo* (1959-1960), *Twilight Zone* (1960-1962), *Rawhide* (1963), *The Outer Limits* (1963-1964), *My Favorite Martian* (1964), *The Greatest Story Ever Told* (1965), *The Fugitive* (1965-1966), *The Monkees* (1967), *The Wild Wild West* (1968), *Then Came Bronson* (1969), *Mod Squad* (1970), *Rod Serling's Night Gallery* (1971), *M*A*S*H* (1973), *The Magician* (1973), *Ellery Queen* (1975), *The Incredible Hulk* (1978), *The Rockford Files* (1979), *Night Court* (1984), *MacGyver* (1987), *ALF* (1990), *Hot Shots! Part Deux* (1993), and *Fired Up* (1997).

It was on the series *Everybody Loves Raymond* that he got his biggest break, when he gained the role of Nemo, a pizza restaurant owner. He started playing the role in 1998 and it lasted until his death in early 2000.

In February 2000, Perry, who had been suffering with diabetes, got worse and he died February 23, 2000 due to the illness a week or so after his 69th birthday. His character's last appearance in *Everybody Loves Raymond* was shown posthumously when his restaurant got bought out.

Ralph Peters

Audie Murphy with Ralph Peters in *Destry*

Ralph Peters was born August 3, 1902, in Leavenworth, Kansas. The moon-faced American character actor was active in films and television from 1937 to 1958. At first, Peters showed up in Westerns, usually cast as a bartender. He then moved on to contemporary films.

During the 1940s, Ralph Peters could be seen in scores of Runyon-esque gangster roles like Asthma Anderson in *Ball of Fire* (1941) and Baby Face Peterson in *My Kingdom for a Cook* (1943).

Other films and television programs he has appeared in include *I Married a Witch* (1942), *Lucky Jordan* (1942) with Alan Ladd, *It Ain't Hay* (1943) with Abbott and Costello, *Ghost Catchers* (1944), *Desert Fury* (1947), *Texas, Brooklyn & Heaven* (1948) with Audie Murphy, *Chicago Deadline* (1949) again with Alan Ladd, *The Lone Ranger* (1949-1952), *Destry* (1954) again with Audie Murphy, *Ma and Pa Kettle at Waikiki* (1955), *The Quiet Gun* (1957), and *The Life and Legend of Wyatt Earp* (1956-1958).

He died April 12, 1959, at age 56 in Hollywood, California.

John Phillips

No biographical information could be found for John Phillips. He did appear in fifty-three films and television programs from 1939 to 1991.

Some of his appearances include *Heldorado* (1946), *Key Largo* (1948), *The Kid from Texas* (1950) with Audie Murphy, *Superman and the Mole-Men* (1951), *Yankee Pasha* (1954), *World in My Corner* (1956) again with Audie Murphy, *Seven Men from Now* (1956), *How to Make a Monster* (1958), *John Paul Jones* (1959), and *Delta Force 3: The Killing Game* (1991).

Paul Picerni

Audie Murphy with Paul Picerni in *Whispering Smith*, and Paul with David Williams in 2002

Paul Vincent Picerni was born in New York, December 1, 1922, and was an American actor. As a child Paul Picerni had aspirations to become an attorney until he acted in an eighth-grade play and later learned that the school principal liked his performance and called him "a born actor".

He was an Eagle Scout who joined the United States Army Air Forces during World War II, where he served as a B-24 Liberator bombardier in the China-Burma-India Theater. He flew twenty-five combat missions with the 493rd Bomb Squadron of the 7th Bomb Group and received the Distinguished Flying Cross. He was part of a mission that attacked and destroyed the real bridge made famous in the film *The Bridge on the River Kwai* (1957). After the Japanese surrendered, Picerni became a Special Services officer in India. Following his discharge, he enrolled at Loyola Marymount University, at Los Angeles.

As a young actor returning from the war, he appeared in military pictures: his first film was in *Beyond Glory* (1948) with Alan Ladd and Audie Murphy, and *Twelve O'Clock High* (1949) as a bombardier and as Private Edward P. Rojeck in *Breakthrough* (1950).

He made an appearance in *Saddle Tramp* (1950) with Joel McCrea and Wanda Hendrix, Audie Murphy's wife at the time. This led to a Warner Brothers contract for Picerni and a succession of roles at that studio including a starring turn as the hero in the 1953 horror classic *House of Wax*.

After his departure from Warners, he appeared with Audie Murphy again in Universal Studio's *To Hell and Back* (1955).

He then appeared in the pilot episode for the 1957-1958 NBC detective series, *Meet McGraw*, starring Frank Lovejoy. Picerni appeared in two episodes, "Gun Hand" and "Badge to Kill" of the 1957-1959 syndicated western series *26 Men*, true stories of the Arizona Rangers, starring Tristram Coffin. In 1957, he played a deserter in an episode of the syndicated *Boots and Saddles*. In 1959, he appeared in an episode of NBC's *Northwest Passage* adventure series about Major Robert Rogers's exploits during the French and Indian War. That same year, he appeared as a police detective in the episode "The Quemoy Story" of Bruce Gordon's short-lived NBC docudrama about the Cold War, *Behind Closed Doors*.

More roles followed in *Omar Khayyam* (1957), *The Deep Six* (1958) again with Alan Ladd, *The Young Philadelphians* (1959), *Shotgun Slade* (1960), and *Whispering Smith* (1961) with Audie Murphy for a third time.

When Italian organizations began to complain about the use of Italian gangsters on TV's, *The Untouchables*, starring Robert Stack as G-man Eliot Ness, Picerni joined the cast of the show as Ness's number-one aide, Lee Hobson, from 1960-63.

In 1964, he portrayed Pierre Lafitte in, *The Great Adventure*. Some more roles include *The Fugitive* (1964), *The Big Valley* (1966), *Batman* (1967), *The Scalphunters* (1968), *Airport* (1970), *Kelly's Heroes* (1970), *Here's Lucy* (1970-1971), *O'Hara, U.S. Treasury* (1971-1972), *The Sixth Sense* (1972), *Adam-12* (1970-1974), *Gunsmoke* (1967-1974), *Kolchak: The Night Stalker* (1975), *Mannix* (1970-1975), *Starsky and Hutch* (1976-1977), *The Red Hand Gang* (1977), *Kojak* (1974-1978), *Capricorn One* (1977), *Beyond the Poseidon Adventure* (1979), *The Incredible Hulk* (1979), *Alcatraz: The Whole Shocking Story* (1980), *Vega$* (1980), *The Fall Guy* (1981), *Strike Force* (1982), *T.J. Hooker* (1982-1983), *Sledge Hammer!* (1986), *Dirty Dozen: The Deadly Mission* (1987), *Diagnosis Murder* (1998-2000), and *Three Days to Vegas* (2007).

For some thirty years, Picerni was the half-time master of ceremonies for the Los Angeles Rams home games.

Picerni married former ballet dancer Marie Mason, in 1947; they had eight children and ten grandchildren. Many of their children and family are employed as Hollywood stunt people, including son Paul V. Picerni, Jr., grandson Rick Picerni, and sister Paula Picerni.

His autobiography *Steps to Stardom: My Story*, written with the help of Tom Weaver, was published in 2007.

He has attended Audie Murphy Days in Greenville, Texas, a record six times between 2001 and 2010.

Picerni died from a heart attack on January 12, 2011, in Palmdale, California.

Robert Pine

Robert Pine was born July 10, 1941, and is an American actor who has starred on television and in film. He is probably best known for his role as Sgt. Joseph Getraer on the hit NBC television series *CHiPs* from 1977 to 1983.

Pine was born Granville Whitelaw Pine in Scarsdale, New York, the son of Virginia (née Whitelaw) and Granville Martin Pine, a patent attorney. He is married to actress Gwynne Gilford, who made a couple of appearances on *CHiPs* as the wife of Sgt. Joe Getraer. They are the parents of actors Chris Pine *Star Trek* (2009) and Katie Pine.

Pine starred on the soap operas *Days of our Lives* as Walker Coleman in 1987 and on *The Bold and the Beautiful* as Stephen Logan in 1988, 1994, 1996, 1997, 2000, and 2001. He also starred in the 2001 science fiction TV series *Black Scorpion* as Major Worth. Moreover, he has appeared in numerous films such as his first film, *Gunpoint* (1966) with Audie Murphy, *The Brotherhood of the Bell* (1970), *Empire of the Ants* (1977), *Independence Day* (1996), as the President's Chief of Staff; *Red Eye* (2005), as a grumpy hotel guestand.

Pine has made guest appearances in many TV shows, including CBS' *Gunsmoke* (1968-1973). On CBS' *Magnum, P.I.* (1983-1987), he appeared as Thomas Magnum's father in a flashback episode. In the late 1980s, Pine guest-starred as Peter Morris, Zack's father, in an episode of *Good Morning, Miss Bliss* (1988). (The character was subsequently renamed Derek Morris, when John Sanderford took over the role; the show itself, by then, was retitled *Saved By the Bell*.)

For *Star Trek: Voyager* (1996), he guest starred as an Akritirian Ambassador named Liria in the Season 3 episode *The Chute*. For *Star Trek: Enterprise* (2002), he guest-starred as Vulcan Captain Tavin in the Season 1 episode "Fusion".

In 1987 Pine portrayed President John F. Kennedy in the made-for-TV miniseries *Hoover vs. The Kennedys*.

In the early 1990s, Pine showed his range by portraying two memorable villains: for *California Dreams* (1992), he played a wealthy racist who sabotages his daughter's friendship with drummer Tony (William James Jones). For the CBS Schoolbreak Special Big Boys Don't Cry (1993), he played a pedophile who molests his two nephews (one, a high-school wrestler whose teammates include Mario Lopez of *Saved By the Bell* fame).

In January 1994, Pine guest-starred as Bart Tupelo on CBS' *Harts of the West* comedy/western starring Beau Bridges and Lloyd Bridges.

Pine reprised his role as Joe Getraer in the 1998 TNT TV movie *CHiPs '99*. His character was now the CHP commissioner.

Recently, Pine has had roles in *CSI: Crime Scene Investigation* (2011), *Big Time Rush* (2011), *Parks and Recreation* (2011), *House M.D.* (2011), *Desperate Housewives* (2011), *Private Practice* (2012), and *Matchmaker Santa* (2012).

Edward C. Platt

Edward C. Platt with Audie Murphy in *Bullet for a Badman*

Edward C. Platt was born Edward Cuthbert Platt February 14, 1916, in Staten Island, New York.

Forever and fondly remembered as Don Adams' foil on the popular Mel Brooks/Buck Henry spy series *Get Smart* (1965-1970), character actor Ed Platt (also billed as Edward C. Platt) had been around for two decades prior to copping that rare comedy role. He inherited an appreciation of music on his mother's side. He spent a part of his childhood in Kentucky and in upstate New York where he attended Northwood, a private school in Lake Placid, and was a member of the ski jump team. He majored in romantic languages at Princeton University but left a year later to study at the Conservatory of Music in Cincinnati after his thoughts turned to a possible operatic career. He later was accepted into Juilliard.

Instead of opera, however, Ed first became a band vocalist with Paul Whiteman and Orchestra. He then sang bass as part of the Mozart Opera Company in New York. With the Gilbert and Sullivan Opera Company in 1942, he appeared in the operettas *The Mikado, The Gondoliers,* and *The Pirates of Penzance.*

WWII interrupted his early career. Ed served as a radio operator with the army and would find himself on radio again in the post-war years where his deep, resonant voice proved ideal. A number of musical comedy roles came his way again. In 1947, he made it to Broadway with the musical *Allegro*.

Star José Ferrer took an interest in Ed while they both were appearing in *The Shrike* on Broadway in 1952. Around 1953, Edward moved to Texas to be near his brother and began anchoring the local news and kiddie birthday party show called *Uncle Eddie's Kiddie Party*. Ferrer remembered Platt and invited him to Hollywood where Ferrer was starring in the film version of *The Shrike* (1955). Ed recreated his stage role.

He also earned fine notices as James Dean's understanding juvenile officer in the classic film *Rebel Without a Cause* (1955). This led to a plethora of film and TV support offers where the balding actor made fine use of his dark, rich voice, stern intensity and pragmatic air, portraying a slew of professional and shady types in crime yarns, soap dramas, westerns, and war pictures, everything from principals and prosecutors to mobsters and murderers.

Some of those roles were in such films and television programs as *Cult of the Cobra* (1955), *The McConnell Story* (1955), *The Lieutenant Wore Skirts* (1956), *The Proud Ones* (1956), *Omar Khayyam* (1957), *Gunman's Walk* (1958), *They Came to Cordura* (1959), *77 Sunset Strip* (1959), *Death Valley Days* (1960), *Twilight Zone* (1961), *Atlantis, the Lost Continent* (1961), *Snow White and the Three Stooges* (1961), *Whispering Smith* (1961) with Audie Murphy, *The Rifleman* (1962), and *The Lloyd Bridges Show* (1963).

After years of playing it serious, which included stints on the daytime drama *General Hospital* (1963), and a member of Audie Murphy's posse in *Bullet for a Badman* (1964), Ed finally was able to focus on comedy as "The Chief" to Don Adams klutzy secret agent on *Get Smart,* a show that inevitably found a cult audience.

He picked up a few occasional guest spots in its aftermath, like *The Governor & J.J.* (1970), *The Odd Couple* (1971), *The New Temperatures Rising Show* (1972), and *Owen Marshall: Counselor at Law* (1974).

He was married twice and the father of four. He died March 19, 1974 at age 58 in Santa Monica, California.

Michael J. Pollard

Michael J Pollard with Audie Murphy in *Ford Startime*

Michael J. Pollard was born Michael John Pollack, Jr. in Passaic, New Jersey, May 30, 1939, and is an American actor. He is the son of Sonia and Michael John Pollack. He attended the Montclair Academy and the Actors Studio.

In 1959, he played Homer McCauley, the dramatic lead, in a television adaptation of William Saroyan's novel, *The Human Comedy*, production narrated by Burgess Meredith.

Also in 1959, Pollard, at twenty, appeared in the episode "The Unknown Town" of David Hedison's sixteen-segment NBC espionage series, *Five Fingers*.

He appeared briefly in "The Man" episode of *Ford Startime* (1960) with Audie Murphy.

Pollard created the non-singing role of Hugo Peabody in the Original Broadway cast of the 1960 musical comedy *Bye Bye Birdie* (lyrics by Lee Adams and music by Charles Strouse). Hugo is a high-school student, boyfriend of Kim McAfee (played by Susan Watson on Broadway), who becomes jealous of Kim's infatuation with rock star Conrad Birdie. In the 1963 film version, Hugo became a singing role and was played by Bobby Rydell.

In 1962, he appeared in the short-lived Robert Young comedy and drama series *Window on Main Street* on CBS in an episode entitled "The Boy Who Got Too Many Laughs". Pollard appeared in an episode of *The Andy Griffith Show* which originally aired on April 30, 1962, as Barney Fife's clumsy young cousin, Virgil, who stops by for a visit and manages to wreak havoc at the courthouse.

In 1963 he played the role of Digby in the movie *Summer Magic,* starring Hayley Mills. In 1964 he played the role of Cyrus in the episode "Journey for Three" of the television series *Gunsmoke*. He appeared in the *Star Trek* episode "Miri", at age twenty-seven he played a barely pre-pubescent boy, leader of a band of orphaned children.

In 1967 he played the supporting role of C. W. Moss in Arthur Penn's *Bonnie and Clyde* alongside Warren Beatty, Faye Dunaway, Gene Hackman, and Estelle Parsons, for which he received Academy Award and Golden

Globe Award nominations for Best Supporting Actor and won a BAFTA Award for Most Promising Newcomer to Leading Film Roles. In 1970 he had a starring role as Little Fauss in the cult motorcycle racing movie *Little Fauss and Big Halsy* with Robert Redford, Noah Beery Jr., Lucille Benson, and Lauren Hutton.

Adept at comic roles with an odd edge, he had a stand-out bit part in the classic Norman Jewison Cold War comedy *The Russians Are Coming, The Russians Are Coming* (1966).

He starred in the film *Dirty Little Billy* (1972), set in Coffeyville, Kansas, portrayed Billy the Kid at the beginning of his criminal career. Pollard had a key supporting role in the 1980 cult film *Melvin and Howard* about the Melvin Dummar/Howard Hughes/Mormon Will controversy.

In 1989 he played 'Owen' the inventor of super weapons and a super car in *Tango and Cash*, starring Kurt Russell and Sylvester Stallone. Actor Michael J. Fox has stated that he adopted the *J.* in his name as a homage to Pollard.

Pollard has continued to work in film and television into the 21st century, including his appearance as "Stucky" in the 2003 Rob Zombie directed cult classic *House of 1000 Corpses*.

He is currently filming *The Next Cassavetes* for a 2013 release.

Sherwood Price

Sherwood Price was born November 15, 1933. He is an American character actor who has appeared in dozens of films and television programs from 1952 to 1995.

Some of those appearances include *Scorching Fury* (1952), *I Led 3 Lives* (1956), numerous episodes of *The Gray Ghost* (1957-1958) as General Jeb Stuart, *Westinghouse Desilu Playhouse* (1959-1960), *Wichita Town* (1960), *The Roaring 20's* (1961), *Whispering Smith* (1961) with Audie Murphy, *Cheyenne* (1961-1962), *The Untouchables* (1963), *Gunsmoke* (1965), *The Big Valley* (1965-1968), *The Protectors* (1972-1973), *Police Woman* (1976), *SST: Death Flight* (1977), *The Misadventures of Sheriff Lobo* (1979), and *Last of the Dogmen* (1995).

Ainslie Pryor

Audie Murphy with Ainslie Pryor in *Walk the Proud Land*

Ainslie Pryor was born James Ainslie Pryor February 1, 1921, in Memphis, Tennessee. He was a character actor who was only actively acting from the years 1955 through 1958. He looked older than his age, so most often played military leaders, doctors, authority figures, etc.

Some of his roles included *The Girl in the Red Velvet Swing* (1955), *Steve Donovan, Western Marshal* (1956), *You Are There* (1954-1956), *Medic* (1956), *Walk the Proud Land* (1956) with Audie Murphy, *Four Girls in Town* (1957), *Jane Wyman Presents The Fireside Theatre* (1957), *The Guns of Fort Petticoat* (1957) again with Audie Murphy, several episodes of *Gunsmoke* (1955-1957), *Cole Younger, Gunfighter* (1958), *The Left Handed Gun* (1958), *Kathy O'* (1958), and twenty-four episodes as Joel Smith in *The Adventures of Hiram Holliday* (1956-1959).

He died May 27, 1958, at age 37 in Hollywood, California. His same named daughter, Ainslie Pryor, was an actress from 1970 through 1975.

William Pullen

Audie Murphy with William Pullen in *Ride Clear of Diablo*

William Pullen was born William Augustus Pullen November 11, 1917, in Seattle, Washington. He was a character actor who was active from 1949 through 1963.

Some of his roles included *I Was a Male War Bride* (1949), *Fireside Theatre* (1950), *All About Eve* (1950), *The Lawless Breed* (1953), *It Came from Outer Space* (1953), as lawyer Tom Meredith in *Ride Clear of Diablo* (1954) with Audie Murphy, *Strategic Air Command* (1955), *Adventures of Wild Bill Hickok* (1955), *The Cisco Kid* (1955), *Death Valley Days* (1956), *Short Cut to Hell* (1957), *Hell Canyon Outlaws* (1957), *The Adventures of McGraw* (1958), *The Life and Legend of Wyatt Earp* (1956-1960), and *The Dick Powell Theatre* (1963).

After retiring from the motion picture business, William Pullen taught Theater Arts at Barstow Junior College in Barstow, California.

He died December 8, 2008, at age 91 in Barstow, California.

Denver Pyle

Audie Murphy with Denver Pyle in *Gunpoint*

Denver Dell Pyle was born May 11, 1920, and was an American film and television actor. He is best remembered for playing Uncle Jesse in *The Dukes of Hazzard* (1979-1985).

Pyle was born in Bethune in Kit Carson County, Colorado, to farmer Ben H. Pyle (1895–1988) and his wife Maude (1899–1985). After graduating from high school, Pyle briefly attended Colorado State University but dropped out to enter show business.

He was a drummer and band member until the United States entered the Second World War, when he enlisted in the Merchant Marines.

After the war, Pyle embarked on his film career. He starred in several movies and on television during the 1950s and 1960s. He had roles in *The Flying Saucer* (1950), *The Cisco Kid* (1951-1952), *The Maverick* (1952), *Goldtown Ghost Riders* (1953), *The Lone Wolf* (1954), *Hopalong Cassidy* (1952-1954), *Adventures of Superman* (1954), *The Adventures of Kit Carson* (1952-1954), *The Gene Autry Show* (1951-1954), *Drum Beat* (1954), *Top Gun* (1955), *The Lone Ranger* (1951-1956), *Destination 60,000* (1957), *The Left Handed Gun* (1958), *The Horse Soldiers* (1959), *Wichita Town* (1960), *The Man Who Shot Liberty Valance* (1962), *The Dick Van Dyke Show* (1963)

He also appeared on an episode of the *Twilight Zone* in 1964 called "Black Leather Jackets" where he played the father. He appeared in the 1963-1964 season in ABC's drama about college life, *Channing*. He also is known for portraying both the suspect and the murder victim on the final *Perry Mason* (1958-1966) episode; he was the only actor to play a victim, a suspect and the actual murderer (in a previous episode) on the series out of six appearances. He was Grandpa Tarleton in all twenty-six episodes of *Tammy* in the 1965-66 season.

He was a regular co-star of Audie Murphy's in the films *Gunsmoke* (1953), *Column South* (1953), *Ride Clear of Diablo* (1954), *To Hell and Back* (1955), *Cast a Long Shadow* (1959), and *Gunpoint* (1966).

In addition, he played the antagonist Frank Hamer in *Bonnie and Clyde* (1967), Buck Webb (Doris Day's father) during the first two seasons of CBS's *The Doris Day Show* (1968–1970), and Briscoe Darling on *The Andy Griffith Show* (1960–1968). He appeared in fourteen episodes of Gunsmoke (1956-1973).

He did some writing and directing for the short-lived half-hour *Gunsmoke* spin-off western *Dirty Sally* starring Jeanette Nolan, which ran on CBS in the first half of 1974. He also played the role of Arkansas in Michael Dante's film *Winterhawk* (1975).

Pyle played the role of Mad Jack in the NBC series *The Life and Times of Grizzly Adams* (1977–1978).

In his later years, Pyle played mostly cameo television roles and retired from full-time acting. He played the title role in *Podunk Possum* (1997). His last cinematic movie role was alongside Mel Gibson, Jodie Foster, and James Garner in the 1994 film *Maverick*, playing a cheating card player who jumps off a riverboat to keep his dignity. His last acting role was a reprisal of Jesse Duke in the 1997 made-for-TV movie *The Dukes of Hazzard: Reunion!*

Denver married his first wife, Marilee Carpenter (1924–2010), in 1955. The aspiring actor took a Twentieth Century Fox production assistant as his bride. They had sons David and Tony in 1956 and 1957, respectively. According to her obituary, "Marilee advised and assisted Denver throughout his fifty-year career in motion pictures and television—uninterrupted by their divorce in 1970—until his death in 1997".

Denver married Tippie Johnston in 1983. They were married until Pyle's death.

Pyle died of lung cancer on Christmas Day in, 1997. He is buried in Forreston, Texas.

John Qualen

Audie Murphy with John Qualen in *The Gunrunners*

John Qualen was born Johan Mandt Kvalen, December 8, 1899, and was a Canadian-American character actor of Norwegian heritage who specialized in Scandinavian roles.

Qualen was born in Vancouver, British Columbia, the son of immigrants from Norway; his father was a Lutheran minister and changed the family's original surname, "Kvalen", to "Qualen". Qualen grew up in Elgin, Illinois.

His acting career began when he was at Northwestern University which he attended on a scholarship from having won an oratory contest. Eventually making it to Broadway, he got his big break as the Swedish janitor in Elmer Rice's *Street Scene* (1931). His movie career began when he recreated the role in the film version. This was followed by his appearance in John Ford's *Arrowsmith* (1931) which began a more than thirty year membership in the director's "stock company", with important supporting roles in *The Searchers* (1956), *Two Rode Together* (1961), *The Man Who Shot Liberty Valance* (1962), and *Cheyenne Autumn* (1964).

Appearing in well over one hundred films, and acting extensively on television into the 1970s, including *The Public Defender* (1954), *December Bride* (1955-1957), *Bronco* (1959), *Tate* (1960), *Bonanza* (1961), *My Favorite Martian* (1964), *Shane* (1966), *Green Acres* (1968-1970), *The Odd Couple* (1971-1973), and *Movin' On* (1974).

Qualen performed many of his roles with various accents, usually Scandinavian, often intended for comic effect. Three of his more memorable roles showcase his versatility. Qualen assumed a Midwestern dialect as Muley, who recounts the destruction of his farm by the bank in Ford's *The Grapes of Wrath* (1940), and as the confused killer Earl Williams in Howard Hawks' classic comedy *His Girl Friday* (1940). As Berger, the jewelry-selling Norwegian Resistance member in Michael Curtiz' *Casablanca* (1942), he essayed a light Scandinavian accent, but put on a thicker Mediterranean accent as the homeward-bound fisherman Locota in William Wellman's *The High and the Mighty* (1954).

He appeared in *The Gun Runners* (1958) and *Hell Bent for Leather* (1960) with Audie Murphy.

Qualen was treasurer of The Authors Club and historian of The Masquers, Hollywood's famed social group for actors.

John Qualen was blind in his later years. He died of heart failure in September 12, 1987, in Torrance, California, and was interred in the Forest Lawn Memorial Park in Glendale. He was survived by his three daughters.

John Qualls

No biographical information can be found for John Qualls, but he did appear in three films and one television program. His one television appearance was in *Official Detective* (1957).

His films appearances include a role as 'henchman' in *The Wild and the Innocent* (1959) with Audie Murphy, a role as 'captain' in *Attack of the Killer Tomatoes!* (1978), and a role as 'taxi driver' in *Love Streams* (1984).

Eddie Quillan

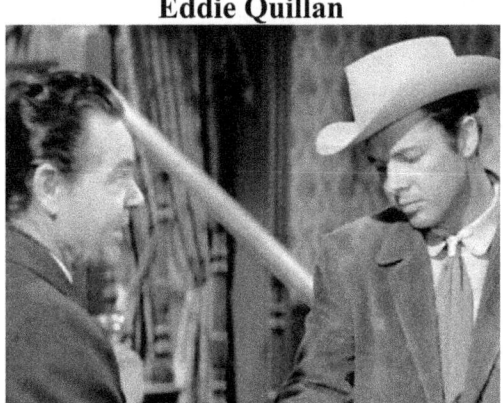

Eddie Quillan with Audie Murphy in *Gunfight at Comanche Creek*

Edward "Eddie" Quillan was born March 31, 1907, and was an American film actor whose career began as a child on the vaudeville stages and silent film and continued through the age of television in the 1980s.

Born in Philadelphia, Pennsylvania into a family of vaudeville performers, Quillan made his stage debut at the age of seven alongside his parents, Scottish-born Joseph Quillan and his wife Sarah, as well as his siblings in their act entitled 'The Rising Generation'. By the early 1920s he was called upon by film director Mack Sennett to perform a screen test for Mack Sennett Studios. Sennett signed Quillan to a contract in 1922.

Quillan's very first film appearance was in the 1922 comedy short *Up and at 'Em*. His next performance was in the 1926 comedy short *The Love Sundae* opposite actress Alice Day. His next ten film appearances (all released in 1926) were all comedy shorts that were vehicles for Day. He would spend most of the remaining years of the 1920s in comedy shorts featuring actresses Ruth Taylor and Madeline Hurlock. In 1928, Quillan starred in the comedy *A Little Bit of Everything*, notable because it featured his siblings Marie, Joseph, and John in starring roles. Marie Quillan would eventually embark on a film career of her own and appear opposite her brother once more, in the 1929 comedy *Nosy Neighbors*.

Quillan's first feature-length film was the 1928 comedy-drama *Show Folks* opposite actress Lina Basquette, in which Quillan appropriately plays a vaudeville dancer. The film was a modest success and also featured actress Carole Lombard. Quillan's breakout role (and first dramatic film role) was in the 1929 Cecil B. DeMille directed *The Godless Girl*. The film paired Quillan once again with Basquette and starred Marie Prevost and Noah Beery, Sr. His subsequent exposure from the film landed him a contract with Pathé studios.

Eddie Quillan would remain a popular leading and secondary actor throughout the sound film era and would appear in such notable films as 1935's *Mutiny on the Bounty* with Clark Gable, Charles Laughton, and Franchot Tone, 1939's *Young Mr. Lincoln* opposite Henry Fonda and Alice Brady, and as 'Connie Rivers' in John Ford's 1940 film adaptation of the John Steinbeck novel *The Grapes of Wrath* opposite Henry Fonda and 1943's *Alaska Highway* and *It Ain't Hay* opposite the comedic duo Abbott and Costello.

Quillan's breezy screen personality was seen in "B" musicals, comedies, and even serials during the 1940s. In 1948 Columbia Pictures producer Jules White teamed Eddie Quillan with veteran movie comic Wally Vernon for a series of comedy short subjects. White emphasized extreme physical comedy in these films, and Vernon and Quillan made a good team, enthusiastically engaging in pratfalling, kick-in-the-pants slapstick. The series ran through 1956.

Beginning in the late 1950s, Eddie Quillan began to make the transition to the medium of television and by the 1960s could be seen frequently appearing as a guest actor in such series as *The Andy Griffith Show* (1965), *Petticoat Junction* (1963-1964), *Perry Mason* (1961-1966), and approximately five appearances on the camp-horror comedy series *The Addams Family* (1964-1966).

He was a regular on the Anthony Franciosa sitcom *Valentine's Day* from 1964–65, and from 1968 through 1971 he appeared as "Eddie Edson" on the television drama *Julia* opposite actress Diahann Carroll.

Through the 1950s and 1960s, Quillan continued to appear in motion pictures, but in increasingly smaller roles and often in bit parts. One notable appearance of the era was his role of 'Sandy' in the 1954 Vincente Minnelli directed musical *Brigadoon*, starring Gene Kelly, Van Johnson, and Cyd Charisse. He appeared in *Gunfight at Comanche Creek* (1963) with Audie Murphy. Quillan also appeared in the uncredited role of 'Mr.Cassidy' in the 1969 Gene Kelly film adaptation of *Hello, Dolly!*, starring Barbra Streisand and Walter Matthau and featuring Louis Armstrong.

In the 1970s, Quillan made guest appearances on such television series as *Mannix* (1973-1975), *Chico and the Man* (1977), and *Baretta* (1978). After meeting and befriending actor and director Michael Landon, he played numerous bit roles in the popular television series *Little House on the Prairie* (1977-1983). Quillan also performed in the Landon directed series *Highway to Heaven* (1984-1986) and *Father Murphy* (1982) during the 1980s. Eddie Quillan made his last television appearance in a 1987 episode of the television crime-mystery series *Matlock*.

Eddie Quillan died July 19, 1990, of cancer in Burbank, California, and was interred at the San Fernando Mission Cemetery in Mission Hills, Los Angeles County, Los Angeles, California.

Jorge Rado

Jorge Rado was born in 1931. He appeared in twenty-six films from 1957 to 1981, most of them foreign.

Some of his American films were *Spy Pit* (1957), *Land's End* (1968), *The Chinese Room* (1968), *A Time for Dying* (1969) with Audie Murphy, *The Wild Bunch* (1969), and *The Wild Season* (1971).

Ford Rainey

Audie Murphy with Ford Rainey in *Gunpoint*

Ford Rainey was born August 8, 1908, and was an American film, stage, and television actor.

Rainey was born in Mountain Home, Idaho, the son of Vyrna (née Kinkade), a teacher, and Archie Coleman Rainey. Rainey graduated from Centralia Junior College in Washington and the Cornish Drama School in Seattle. He first acted on the stage while in high school. Growing up in the outdoors and learning to ride horses helped him in his career as a tough-guy film presence later in life.

Like many young actors, he worked odd jobs including logger, fisherman, fruit picker, carpenter, clam digger and working on an oil tanker before becoming a successful actor. He worked as a radio actor as well as a touring stage actor before breaking into films. He served in the U.S. Coast Guard during World War II.

Rainey was a familiar face in motion pictures, including his 1949 film debut *White Heat*, *The Robe* (1953), *3:10 to Yuma* (1957), *The Badlanders* (1958), *Flaming Star* (1960), *Two Rode Together* (1961), *Window on Main Street* (1961-1962), *Stoney Burke* (1962), *The Richard Boone Show* (1963-1964), *Voyage to the Bottom of the Sea* (1964-1965), *Lost in Space* (1965), *Get Smart* (1965), *Gunpoint* (1966) with Audie Murphy, *The Fugitive* (1966), *The Sand Pebbles* (1966), *The Man from the 25th Century* (1968), *The Wild Wild West* (1966-1968), *Dan August* (1970), *Rod Serling's Night Gallery* (1971), *Alias Smith and Jones* (1971-1972), *Mannix* (1967-1973), *The Rockford Files* (1975), *Black Sheep Squadron* (1977), *How the West Was Won* (1979), *M*A*S*H* (1980), *Halloween II* (1981), *Remington Steele* (1984), *Falcon Crest* (1986), *Matlock* (1989), *Wiseguy* (1989), *Marshal Law* (1996), *Ned and Stacey* (1996-1997), and *The King of Queens* (1999-2003).

Rainey also appeared as the stepfather of Steve Austin in *The Six Million Dollar Man* (1975-1976), and adoptive father of Jaime Sommers in *The Bionic Woman* (1976-1977).

He could also be seen in some commercials in the middle 1970's until 1980's like REACH brand toothbrushes; a Johnson & Johnson product. Also during that time, he was part of Trinity Square Repretory Company in Providence, Rhode Island.

Ford Rainey was a bachelor until the age of 46 when, in 1954, he married Sheila Hayden and settled in New York, where sons Robert and James were born. The family moved to Malibu, where a daughter, Kathy was born. Rainey remained in Malibu with his wife while he acted and enjoyed hobbies such as beekeeping and bird breeding until his death on July 25, 2005, of a stroke, at age 96. The marriage was a happy one that lasted nearly 51 years. His interment was in Westwood Village Memorial Park Cemetery.

Tommy Rall

Audie Murphy and Tommy Rall in *Walk the Proud Land*

Thomas Edward "Tommy" Rall was born in Kansas City, Missouri, December 27, 1929, and is an American ballet dancer, tap dancer, and acrobatic dancer who was a prominent featured player in 1950s musical comedies. He later became a successful operatic tenor in the 1960s, making appearances with the Opera Company of Boston, the New York City Opera, and the American National Opera Company.

Rall was raised in Seattle. As a child he had a crossed eye which made it hard for him to read books, so his mother enrolled him in dancing classes. In his early years he performed a dance and acrobatic vaudeville act in Seattle theaters, and attempted small acting roles.

His family moved to Los Angeles in the 1940s, and began to appear in small movie roles. His first film appearance was a short MGM film called *Vendetta* (1942). He began taking tap dancing lessons and became a member of the jitterbugging Jivin' Jacks and Jills at Universal Studios.

Rall joined Donald O'Connor, Peggy Ryan, and Shirley Mills in several light wartime Andrews Sisters vehicles including *Private Buckaroo* (1942), *Give Out Sisters* (1942), *Get Hep to Love* (1942), *Mister Big* (1943), and others. He also appeared in the films *The North Star* (1943) and *Song of Russia* (1944).

Rall took ballet lessons and danced in classical and Broadway stages (*Milk and Honey*, *Call Me Madam* and *Cry for Us All*). He is best-known for his acrobatic dancing in several classic musical films of the 1950s, including *Kiss Me Kate* (1953), *Seven Brides for Seven Brothers* (1954), *Invitation to the Dance* (1956), *Merry Andrew* (1958), and *My Sister Eileen* (1955).

Some non-dancing roles included *World in My Corner* (1956) and *Walk the Proud Land* (1956) both with Audie Murphy.

Rall's film career waned as movie musicals went into decline. He had a role in the movie *Funny Girl* (1968), as "The Prince" in a spoof of the ballet *Swan Lake*. On Broadway he danced to considerable acclaim as "Johnny" in Marc Blitzstein and Joseph Stein's 1959 musical, *Juno* (based on Sean O'Casey's play *Juno and the Paycock*).

Some of his later roles included *Pennies from Heaven* (1981), *Fame* (1984), *Dancers* (1998), and as the werewolf in *Saturday the 14th Strikes Back* (1988).

Rall was briefly married to his *Juno* co-star, Monte Amundsen. He is now married to the former Karel Shimoff (born 1944); they have two children.

In 2007, a dance instructor by the name of Fredric Brame was found to have been posing as Tommy Rall since the late 1960s. His biographies, resumes, and playbills all support that Brame was Fredric Brame aka Tommy Rall by the credits listed. When Rall found out about the masquerade decades later, through a friend of his cousin, he contacted the Montgomery County Sheriff's office. No legal action was taken against Brame since he technically didn't commit a crime. Rall only wanted Brame to stop taking credit for his work and if he continued or did it again a lawsuit would be filed.

Ward Ramsey

Ward Ramsey was born John Doane Sutphen, Jr. September 24, 1924 in Helena, Montana, and was an American actor. He appeared in seventeen films and television programs from 1960 to 1969.

Some of those credits include *Dinosaurus!* (1960), *Seven Ways from Sundown* (1960) and *Posse from Hell* (1961) both with Audie Murphy, *Tammy Tell Me True* (1961), *Lover Come Back* (1961), *Cape Fear* (1962), *A Gathering of Eagles* (1963), *Felony Squad* (1966), *The Andy Griffith Show* (1967), *Speedway* (1968), and *The Comic* (1969).

He died December 24, 1984, at age 60 in San Bernardino, California.

Anne Randall

Anne Randall with Audie Murphy in *A Time for Dying*

Anne Randall was born Barbara Burrus September 23, 1944, in Alameda, California, and is an American model. She was *Playboy* magazine's Playmate of the Month for its May 1967 issue. Her centerfold was photographed by Mario Casilli.

In 1959, Barbara became a regular on the *KPIX Dance Party*, an afternoon television show featuring teenagers dancing to popular music, broadcast on KPIX-TV Channel 5 (CBS) in San Francisco. It was hosted by Dick Stewart and aired from 1959 to 1963.

During the late 1960s and throughout the 1970s, Anne pursued a film and television career, appearing in such shows films as *The Monkees* (1967), *A Time for Dying* (1969) with Audie Murphy, *Hell's Bloody Devils* (1970), *Rod Serling's Night Gallery* (1971), *The Night Strangler* (1973), *Cannon* (1973), *Westworld* (1973), *The Magician* (1973), *Barnaby Jones* (1973-1974), *The Rockford Files* (1976), *Switch* (1977), and *J-Men Forever* (1979).

She also spent two years as one of the beauties on *Hee Haw* (1972-1974). Sometimes she was credited as Anne Randall Stewart.

Her last appearance was as herself in *George Burns' Early, Early, Early Christmas Special* (1981).

Stuart Randall

Stuart Randall was born July 24, 1909, in Brazil, Indiana, and was an American actor. He appeared in dozens of films and television programs from 1950 to 1971.

Some of those credits include *Bells of Coronado* (1950), *Tomahawk* (1951), *Carbine Williams* (1952), *The Man from the Alamo* (1953), *Stories of the Century* (1954), *The Far Country* (1954), *Chief Crazy Horse* (1955), *Indestructible Man* (1956), *The Ten Commandments* (1956), *Sugarfoot* (1957-1958), *The Life and Legend of Wyatt Earp* (1956-1959), *The Gallant Hours* (1960), *Wanted: Dead or Alive* (1960-1961), *Posse from Hell* (1961) with Audie Murphy, *Lassie: A Christmas Tail* (1963), *Taggart* (1964), *True Grit* (1969), and *Alias Smith and Jones* (1971).

He died June 22, 1988, at age 78 in San Bernardino, California.

Donald Randolph

Donald Randolph with Audie Murphy in *Gunsmoke*

Donald Randolph was born in Capetown, South Africa January 5, 1906, and was a film, television, and radio actor. The actor, who appeared in Alfred Hitchcock's *Topaz* (1969), acted in dozens of radio dramas, television programs, and over thirty films, including *13 Rue Madeleine* (1947), *The Desert Hawk* (1950), *Harem Girl* (1952), *Mr. & Mrs. North* (1952), *Gunsmoke* (1953) with Audie Murphy, *The Adventures of Hajji Baba* (1954), *Chief Crazy Horse* (1955), *The Deadly Mantis* (1957), *Gunsmoke* (1958), *Perry Mason* (1958-1959), *The Jack Benny Program* (1963), *Daniel Boone* (1967), *Mission: Impossible* (1968), and *All in the Family* (1975).

He died March 16, 1993, at age 87 in Los Angeles, California.

Bob Random

Robert Random was born January 29, 1943, in Chilliwack, British Columbia, usually billed as Bob Random, is a Canadian-born character actor, who appeared in both movies and television from the mid-1960s to the late 1980s.

Random's television work tended to be in dramatic roles, in venerable programs like *Dr. Kildare* (1964), *Mr. Novak* (1964-1965), *Ben Casey* (1965), and *Lassie* (1964-1965), or Western shows like *Gunsmoke* (1965-1971), *The Virginian* (1965-1968), thirty-two episodes as Barnabas Rogers in *The Iron Horse* (1966-1967), and *The Legend of Jesse James* (1965). He did occasional comedies, including *The Dick Van Dyke Show* (1965) and *Gidget* (1965) in a recurring role as Gidget's friend Mark.

His best-remembered movie role is as Rick, one of Beau Bridges and Joy Harmon's co-villains in the 1965 teen comedy *Village of the Giants*. He also appeared in *This Property Is Condemned* (1966), *A Time for Dying* (1969) with Audie Murphy and *...tick...tick...tick...* (1970). *Mosby's Marauders* (1967), in which he played Private Lomax, was later repeated on *The Wonderful World of Disney* under the title *Willie and the Yank*.

His last appearances were in an episode of *Get Christie Love* (1975), and as the biker Reaper in the second and third *The Danger Zone* (1989-1994) movies, taking over from Robert Canada, who played the character in the original.

Random was married to Ida Random, who received an Academy Award nomination in 1988 for Best Art Direction-Set Decoration on *Rain Man*. Bob Random currently resides near Qualicum Beach, British Columbia.

Robert Redford

Robert Redford with Audie Murphy in *Whispering Smith*

Robert Redford was born Charles Robert Redford, Jr. on August 18, 1936, in Santa Monica, California, to Charles Robert Redford, an accountant for Standard Oil, and Martha Hart. His mother died in 1955, the year after he graduated from high school.

He was a scrappy kid who stole hubcaps in high school. After studying at the Pratt Institute of Art and living the painter's life in Europe, he studied acting in New York at the American Academy of Dramatic Arts.

Television and stage experience coupled with all-American good looks led to movies and television roles. Some of his early roles included his first appearance in *Maverick* (1960), *The Deputy* (1960), *Perry Mason* (1960), *Naked City* (1961), *Whispering Smith* (1961) with Audie Murphy, *Twilight Zone* (1962), *The Alfred Hitchcock Hour* (1962-1963), *The Virginian* (1963), *Inside Daisy Clover* (1965), and *Barefoot in the Park* (1967).

His breakthrough role was as "The Sundance Kid" in *Butch Cassidy and the Sundance Kid* (1969), when the actor was 32. *The Way We Were* (1973) and *The Sting* (1973) made Redford the number one box office star for the next three years.

Other great roles continued in *Jeremiah Johnson* (1972), *The Great Gatsby* (1974), *The Great Waldo Pepper* (1975), *Three Days of the Condor* (1975), *All the President's Men* (1976), *A Bridge Too Far* (1977), *The Electric Horseman* (1979), *Brubaker* (1980) about the real Cummins Prison near Pine Bluff, Arkansas (where I worked as a prison guard for two years back in the 1980s), *The Natural* (1984), and *Out of Africa* (1985).

Redford used his clout to advance environmental causes and his riches to acquire Utah property, which he transformed into a ranch and the Sundance ski resort. In 1980, he established the Sundance Institute for aspiring filmmakers. Its annual film festival has become one of the worlds most influential.

Redford's directorial debut, *Ordinary People* (1980), won him the Academy Award as Best Director in 1981. He waited eight years before getting behind the camera again, this time for the screen version of John Nichols' acclaimed novel of the Southwest, *The Milagro Beanfield War* (1988). He scored with critics and fans in 1992 with the Brad Pitt film *A River Runs Through It* (1992), and again, in 1994, with *Quiz Show* (1994), which earned him yet another Best Director nomination.

Other roles kept getting better, like *Indecent Proposal* (1993), *Up Close & Personal* (1996), *The Horse Whisperer* (1998), *Spy Game* (2001), *The Company You Keep* (2012), and completed filming *All is Lost* that is due for a 2013 release.

Lola Van Wagenen, born in 1940, dropped out of college to marry Redford on September 12, 1958. They divorced in 1985 after having four children, one of whom died of sudden infant death syndrome (SIDS). Daughter Shauna Redford, born November 15, 1960, is a painter who married Eric Schlosser on October 5, 1985, in Provo, UT. Her first child, born in January 1991, made Redford a grandfather. Son James Redford (aka Jamie Redford), a screenwriter, was born May 5, 1962. Daughter Amy Redford, an actress; was born October 22, 1970.

He was a 2002 Lifetime Achievement Award/Honorary Oscar recipient at the 74th Academy Awards.

In December 2005, he received honors at the Kennedy Center for his contributions to American culture. The Honors recipients are recognized for their lifetime contributions to American culture through the performing arts: whether in dance, music, theater, opera, motion pictures or television.

In 2008 he was awarded The Dorothy and Lillian Gish Prize, one of the richest prizes in the arts, given annually to "a man or woman who has made an outstanding contribution to the beauty of the world and to mankind's enjoyment and understanding of life".

In July 2009, Redford married his longtime partner, Sibylle Szaggars, at the luxurious Louis C. Jacob Hotel in Hamburg, Germany. She had moved in with Redford in the 1990s and shares his Sundance, Utah, home. In May 2011, Alfred A. Knopf published *Robert Redford: The Biography* by Michael Feeney Callan, written over fifteen years with Redford's input, and drawn from his personal papers and diaries.

Michael Redgrave

Audie Murphy with Michael Redgrave in *The Quiet American*

Sir Michael Scudamore Redgrave was born March 20, 1908, and was an English stage and film actor, director, manager, and author. Redgrave was born in Bristol, Gloucestershire, England, the son of the silent film actor Roy Redgrave and the actress Margaret Scudamore. He never knew his father, who left when Michael was only six months old to pursue a career in Australia. His mother subsequently married Captain James Anderson, a tea planter, but Redgrave greatly disliked his stepfather.

He studied at Clifton College and Magdalene College, Cambridge. He was a schoolmaster at Cranleigh School in Surrey before becoming an actor in 1934. There he directed the boys in *Hamlet, King Lear,* and *The Tempest*, but managed to play all the leading roles himself. The 'Redgrave Room' at the school was later named after him. In the new Guildford School of Acting building which opened in January 2010, there is the Sir Michael Redgrave studio.

Redgrave made his first professional appearance at the Liverpool Playhouse on August 30, 1934 as Roy Darwin in *Counsellor-at-Law* (by Elmer Rice), then spent two years with its Liverpool Repertory Company where he met his future wife Rachel Kempson. They married on July 18, 1935.

Offered a job by Tyrone Guthrie, he made his first professional appearance in London at the Old Vic on September 14, 1936, playing Ferdinand in *Love's Labours Lost*. During 1936-37 he also played Mr Horner in *The Country Wife*, Orlando in *As You Like It*, Warbeck in *The Witch of Edmonton* and Laertes to Laurence Olivier's Hamlet. His hit of the season was Orlando. Edith Evans was his Rosalind and the two fell very much in love. As he later explained: "Edith always had a habit of falling in love with her leading men; with us it just went rather further". *As You Like It* transferred to the New Theatre in February 1937 when he again played Orlando.

Redgrave joined the Royal Navy as an ordinary seaman in July 1941, but was discharged on medical grounds in November 1942. Having spent most of 1942 in the Reserve he managed to direct *Lifeline* (Norman Armstrong) starring Frank Pettingell at the Duchess Theatre in July; and *The Duke in Darkness* (Patrick Hamilton) starring Leslie Banks at the St James's Theatre in October, also taking the role of Gribaux.

Redgrave first appeared on BBC television at the Alexandra Palace in 1937, in scenes from *Romeo and Juliet*. His first major film role was in Alfred Hitchcock's *The Lady Vanishes* (1938). Redgrave also starred in *The Stars Look Down* (1939), with James Mason in the film of Robert Ardrey's play *Thunder Rock* (1942), and in the ventriloquist's dummy episode of the Ealing compendium film *Dead of Night* (1945).

His first American film role was opposite Rosalind Russell in *Mourning Becomes Electra* (1947), for which he was nominated for an Academy Award for Best Actor. In 1951 he starred in *The Browning Version*, from Terence Rattigan's play of the same name. The *Daily Mirror* described Redgrave's performance as Crocker-Harris as "one of the greatest performances ever seen in films". The 1950s also saw Redgrave in *The Importance of Being Earnest* (1952), *The Dambusters* (1954), *1984* (1956), and *The Quiet American* (1958) with Audie Murphy in the title/starring role. More roles included *The Wreck of the Mary Deare* (1959), *Young Cassidy* (1965), *The Heroes of*

Telemark (1965), *Heidi* (1968), *Goodbye, Mr. Chips* (1969), *Nicholas and Alexandra* (1971), *Dr. Jekyll and Mr. Hyde* (1973), and *Rime of the Ancient Mariner* (1975).

He was the father of Lynn Redgrave, Corin Redgrave, and Vanessa Redgrave, and grandfather of Natasha Richardson, Joely Richardson, and Jemma Redgrave.

Redgrave died in a nursing home in Denham, Buckinghamshire, in March 21, 1985, from Parkinson's disease, one day after his 77th birthday.

Donna Reed

Audie Murphy with Donna Reed in *Beyond Glory*

Donna Reed was born January 27, 1921, and was an American film and television actress. With appearances in over forty films, Reed received the 1953 Academy Award for Best Supporting Actress for her performance as Lorene in the war drama *From Here to Eternity*.

She is noted for her role in the perennial Christmas favorite *It's a Wonderful Life* (1946). She worked extensively in television, notably as Donna Stone, an American middle class mother in the sitcom *The Donna Reed Show* (1958–1966), in which she played a more prominent role than many other television mothers of the era and for which she received the 1963 Golden Globe Award for Best TV Star - Female.

Reed was born Donna Belle Mullenger on a farm near Denison, Iowa, the daughter of Hazel Jane (née Shives; 1899–1975) and William Richard Mullenger (1893–1981). The eldest of five children, she was raised as a Methodist. After graduating from Denison High School, Reed planned to become a teacher, but was unable to pay for college. She decided to move to California to attend Los Angeles City College on the advice of her aunt. While attending college, she performed in various stage productions but had no plans to become an actress. After receiving several offers to screen test for studios, Reed eventually signed with MGM, but insisted on finishing her education first.

After signing with MGM in 1941, Reed made her film debut that same year in *The Get-Away*, opposite Robert Sterling. Billed in her first feature as Donna Adams, MGM decided against the name and changed it to Donna Reed.

She starred in *The Courtship of Andy Hardy* (1942) and had a supporting role with Edward Arnold in *Eyes in the Night* (1942). In 1943, she appeared in *The Human Comedy* with Mickey Rooney, followed by roles in *The Picture of Dorian Gray* and *They Were Expendable*, both in 1945.

Her "girl-next-door" good looks and warm on-stage personality made her a popular pin-up for many GIs during World War II. She personally answered letters from many GIs serving overseas.

In 1946, she was lent to RKO Pictures for the role of Mary Bailey in Frank Capra's *It's a Wonderful Life*. The film has since been named as one of the 100 best American films ever made by the American Film Institute and is regularly aired on television during the Christmas season.

Following the release of *It's a Wonderful Life*, Reed appeared in *Green Dolphin Street* (1947) with Lana Turner and Van Heflin, *Beyond Glory* (1948) with Audie Murphy and Alan Ladd, and *Scandal Sheet* (1952). In 1953, she played the role of Alma "Lorene" Burke, a prostitute, and girlfriend of Montgomery Clift's character in the World War II drama *From Here to Eternity*. The role earned Reed an Academy Award for Best Supporting Actress for 1953.

Beginning in 1958, she starred in *The Donna Reed Show*, a television situation-comedy series that featured her as Donna Stone, the idealized housewife of pediatrician Dr. Alex Stone (Carl Betz) and mother of Jeff (Paul Petersen) and Mary Stone (Shelley Fabares). It ran for eight seasons on ABC. Reed won a Golden Globe Award and earned four Emmy Award nominations for her work on the series.

After *The Donna Reed Show* ended its run in 1966, Reed took time off from acting and helped form the advocacy group, Another Mother For Peace in 1967. Reed also became an opponent of the Vietnam War and the use of nuclear weapons, supporting anti-war Minnesota Senator Eugene McCarthy in the 1968 presidential election. She returned to acting in the 1970s, appearing in various guest spots in television series and television movies.

In 1984, she replaced Barbara Bel Geddes, who had decided to step down from her role as "Miss Ellie" in the television series *Dallas* in the 1984-85 season. When Bel Geddes agreed to return to the role for the 1985-86 season, Reed was abruptly fired. She sued the show's production company for breach of contract and later settled out of court for over $1 million.

From 1943 to 1945, Reed was married to make-up artist William Tuttle. In 1945, she married producer Tony Owen (1907–1984) with whom she raised four children: Penny Jane, Anthony, Timothy, and Mary Anne (the two oldest children were adopted). Reed and Owen divorced in 1971, and three years later, she married retired U. S. Army Colonel Grover W. Asmus (1926–2003).

On January 8, 1945, Reed went to Juarez, Mexico, to obtain a divorce from Bill Tuttle. Returning home on the night of January 9, 1945, Reed boarded a plane in El Paso, Texas, for a flight back to Los Angeles. Just as the plane was about to take off, Reed was bumped from the flight to make room for a military officer. The airliner crashed on approach to Lockheed Air Terminal (now called Bob Hope Airport) in Burbank, California, killing everyone on board.

Reed died January 14, 1986, of pancreatic cancer in Beverly Hills, California, thirteen days short of her 65th birthday. She had been diagnosed with the terminal illness three months prior. Her remains are interred in the Westwood Village Memorial Park Cemetery in Los Angeles.

In 1987, Grover Asmus (Reed's widower), actresses Shelley Fabares and Norma Connolly, and numerous friends, associates, and family members created the Donna Reed Foundation for the Performing Arts. Based in Reed's hometown of Denison, the non-profit organization grants scholarships for performing arts students, runs an annual festival of performing arts workshops, and operates "The Donna Reed Center for the Performing Arts".

Reed's hometown of Denison, Iowa, hosts the annual Donna Reed Festival. Reed's childhood home was located on Donna Reed Drive in Denison but was destroyed by a fire in 1983.

Reed's Academy Award is on display at W.A. McHenry museum house in Denison, Iowa.

In May 2010, Turner Classic Movies honored Donna as their star of the month which saw Mary Owen pay a special tribute to her mother.

Walter Reed

Walter Reed was born Walter Reed Smith in Fort Ward, Washington, February 10, 1916, and was an American stage, film, and television actor. The son of an Army officer, Walter Reed was born in Washington and grew up in Honolulu and Los Angeles, where he attended school with the children of movie stars. After his parents' divorce, and, during the darkest days of the Depression, seventeen year old Reed decided to try acting as a career and made a two-week trip to New York (via hitched rides on railroad freight cars, amidst hobos and tramps) to look for work on the stage. He worked in stock and on Broadway and, with an assist from actor Joel McCrea, broke into pictures in the early 1940s.

He appeared in several features for RKO Radio Pictures, including the last two *Mexican Spitfire* comedies (in which Reed replaced Buddy Rogers as the Spitfire's husband) *Mexican Spitfire's Elephant* (1942) and *Mexican Spitfire's Blessed Event* (1943).

Other roles included *Return of the Bad Men* (1948), *Flying Disc Man from Mars* (1950), *Tripoli* (1950), *Superman and the Mole Men* (1951), *Red Ball Express* (1952), *Biff Baker, U.S.A.* (1952), *Hopalong Cassidy* (1952), *The Man from the Alamo* (1953), *The High and the Mighty* (1954), *Dance with Me, Henry* (1956) with Abbott and Costello, *Buffalo Bill, Jr.* (1955-1956), *The Deep Six* (1958), *Westbound* (1959), *Twilight Zone* (1960), *Posse from Hell* (1961) with Audie Murphy, *How the West Was Won* (1962), *The Carpetbaggers* (1964), *The Sand Pebbles* (1966), *A Time for Dying* (1969) again with Audie Murphy, *Tora! Tora! Tora!* (1970), and *The Streets of San Francisco* (1972).

Perhaps his most memorable role was as the spineless wagon-driver husband of Gail Russell in the western *Seven Men from Now* (1956).

After appearing in ninety films and numerous television programs, Reed changed careers and became a real-estate investor and broker in Santa Cruz, California in the late 1960s.

He died August 20, 2001, at age 85 in Santa Cruz, California.

Richard Reeves

Richard Reeves with Audie Murphy in *Destry*

Richard Jourdan Reeves was born August 10, 1912, in New York City, New York, also billed as Dick Reeves, and was an American actor best known for playing henchmen and thugs.

After military service in World War II, Reeves became a busy character actor in films in the late 1940s. Beginning in the early 1950s, he appeared in many television series, particularly those based on comic books. His height, build and somewhat sinister appearance made him suitable for roles involving muscle.

He has the distinction of being the most popular TV-Comic Book gangster-thug; having been featured in five episodes of the *Adventures of Superman* series (1952-1958) as well as appearing in the *Adventures of Superboy* failed pilot (1961). He also added to his stature in TV-Comic Book derivatives with his appearance in the first episode of the *Batman* Series (1966-1968) as Doorman for the Disco, 'What A Way To Go-Go'.

Other roles included *Tomorrow Is Another Day* (1951), *Retreat, Hell!* (1952), *Carbine Williams* (1952), *Devil's Canyon* (1953), *Hopalong Cassidy* (1953), *Destry* (1954) with Audie Murphy, *Ma and Pa Kettle at Waikiki* (1955), *Dance with Me, Henry* (1956), *Gunfight at the O.K. Corral* (1957), *Date with the Angels* (1957-1958), *Richard Diamond, Private Detective* (1957-1959), *Wanted: Dead or Alive* (1958-1959), *The Life and Legend of Wyatt Earp* (1959-1961), *Whispering Smith* (1961) again with Audie Murphy, *Fun in Acapulco* (1963), *Destry* (1964), *Girl Happy* (1965), *The Munsters* (1964-1965), *Tickle Me* (1965), *Harum Scarum* (1965), *The Addams Family* (1965-1966), *Frankie and Johnny* (1966), *Billy the Kid vs. Dracula* (1966), and *Mr. Terrific* (1967).

He died March 17, 1967 at age 54 in Northridge, California.

Elliott Reid

Elliott Reid with Audie Murphy in *Sierra*

Elliott Reid was born Edgeworth Blair Reid January 16, 1920 in New York City, and is an American character actor.

He worked regularly in radio dramas during the Golden Age of radio. His credits include Orson Welles's *Mercury Theatre On The Air*, *The Cavalcade of America*, *Theatre Guild on the Air*, and the *CBS Radio Mystery Theater*.

Reid was a regular in NBC television's *That Was the Week That Was* (1964–65) and made other appearances such as *The Story of Dr. Wassell* (1944), *Sierra* (1950) with Audie Murphy, *Gentlemen Prefer Blondes* (1953), *Alfred Hitchcock Presents* (1955-1958), *Inherit the Wind* (1960), *The AbsentMinded Professor* (1961), *Son of Flubber* (1963), *The Wheeler Dealers* (1963), *The Munsters* (1965), *Blackbeard's Ghost* (1968), *The Odd Couple* (1972), *The New Dick Van Dyke Show* (1971-1972), *Miss Winslow and Son* (1979), *After MASH* (1983), *Small Wonder* (1985), *Murder, She Wrote* (1988), *Mr. Belvedere* (1990), *Seinfeld* (1992), and *Maybe This Time* (1995).

He retired in 1995, at age 75. He died June 21, 2013 in Studio City, California at age 93 of heart failure.

Alejandro Rey

Audie Murphy with Alejandro in *Battle at Bloody Beach*

Alejandro Rey was born in Buenos Aires February 8, 1930, and was an Argentine actor. He immigrated to the United States in 1960, later became a U.S. citizen and gained his widest acclaim there.

Some of his early American roles include *Surfside 6* (1961), *Battle at Bloody Beach* (1961) with Audie Murphy, *The Dick Powell Theatre* (1961-1962), *The Fugitive* (1963), *Fun in Acapulco* (1963), *Voyage to the Bottom of the Sea* (1964), *I Spy* (1966), and *The F.B.I.* (1965-1969).

His best known role was that of casino owner and playboy Carlos Ramirez in *The Flying Nun* (1967-1970). After the cancellation of *The Flying Nun*, Rey remained busy, obtaining roles in *Gunsmoke* (1971), *Rod Serling's Night Gallery* (1973), *Mr. Majestyk* (1974), *Breakout* (1975), *The Bionic Woman* (1976), *Days of Our Lives* (1976-1977), *The Amazing Spider-Man* (1978), *Sunburn* (1979), *Bring 'Em Back Alive* (1982), *The Fall Guy* (1982-1983), *Grace Kelly* (1983), *Rita Hayworth: The Love Goddess* (1983), *Cover Up* (1985), *TerrorVision* (1986), *Dallas* (1986), and *The A-Team* (1986). Rey was also a frequent panelist on the game show *Match Game* (1974).

Rey became a naturalized citizen of the United States in 1967 while appearing in *The Flying Nun*. He married Joyce Bowman on May 24, 1969 in Los Angeles. She was the adopted daughter of attorney and long-time president of the Santa Ana School District Frank Bowman and his wife Dorothy. They had one son Brandon A. Rey who was born on February 9, 1973, in Los Angeles.

Rey remained busy until his death from lung cancer on May 21, 1987. He is interred in the Holy Cross Cemetery in Culver City, California.

William Reynolds

William Reynolds with Audie Murphy in *The Cimarron Kid*

William Reynolds was born William de Clerq Reynolds December 9, 1931, in Los Angeles, California, and is a retired American television and film actor. He is best known for television roles in the 1960s and 1970s.

Reynolds' mother died when he was five years old, and he was sent to boarding schools. He eventually attended Pasadena City College and worked in their radio department. After a talent agent spotted the handsome, capable actor in some minor theatrical roles, Reynolds signed with Universal Studios in 1952 and began appearing in pictures such as *The Cimarron Kid* (1952) with Audie Murphy, *The Battle at Apache Pass* (1952), *Carrie* (1952), *Francis Goes to West Point* (1952), *The Mississippi Gambler* (1953), and *Gunsmoke* (1953) again with Audie Murphy.

Reynolds was drafted in 1952 but enroute to Korea stayed in Japan doing radio work. He returned to Universal making *Cult of the Cobra* (1955), *All That Heaven Allows* (1955), *There's Always Tomorrow* (1956), *Away All Boats* (1956), *The Land Unknown* (1957), and *The Thing That Couldn't Die* (1958).

Reynolds tired of his dull, stereotyped roles in the movies and began his move to television in the late 1950s with the soon-cancelled *Pete Kelly's Blues* (1959). In 1960–1961, he starred in the ABC series *The Islanders* with James Philbrook and Diane Brewster.

He had a memorable role in Rod Serling's *The Twilight Zone* (1960), starring in the episode "The Purple Testament". A special irony attended this production. Director Richard L. Bare recalls, "The evening that it was to be aired first-run, Bill Reynolds and I were in the middle of the Caribbean, swimming for our lives, with three broken legs between the two of us." Bare and Reynolds had just finished making *The Islanders*, a pilot for MGM, and were flying back to Miami. At three hundred feet, both engines quit and the plane went down in the ocean, killing one of the five people aboard. Although Bare had two broken legs, he decided that he and Reynolds should try and make for shore.

"We were four miles off the coast of Jamaica, swimming on our backs toward shore, about forty feet apart, when I yelled over to Bill and said, 'Bill, how are you doing?' He answered, 'I'm making it.' A little later, I called over again, 'You know what's playing tonight?' He said, 'Yeah, "The Purple Testament." 'And I said, 'Bill, please don't look at me!' Both Bare and Reynolds survived and recovered fully. Bare went on to direct 158 episodes of *Green Acres*.

William Reynolds, whose wife had had a baby just two weeks earlier, adds an interesting postscript. "Buck Houghton took the show off the air that night, because he didn't know whether I was a survivor or not from the first news reports. But I thought it was indicative of the class of that production company that they not only did not make capital of the fact, which might have been the obvious thing to do, but they took the show off the air. I was pleased that they didn't subject my family to that."

He then costarred on ABC's *The Gallant Men* in 1962–1963. He played Hoodoo Henderson as an adult in 1966's Walt Disney film *Follow Me, Boys!*.

Reynolds caught his big break co-starring with Efrem Zimbalist, Jr., in another ABC series, the long-running *The F.B.I.*. Reynolds first made guest appearances in seasons one and two in 1966, before he appeared as series regular Special Agent Tom Colby from 1967 to 1973. He was replaced by actor Shelly Novack for the final season, because the network considered Reynolds too old at age 41. Still, he managed to make two appearances as Colby in the ninth season (1973–74), which included the final network-aired episode, a rerun of "The Animal," on September 8, 1974.

He more or less dropped out of show business after *The F.B.I.* ended its run, except for *Project U.F.O.* (1978), and became a businessman.

In 2004 he made an appearance at a *Twilight Zone* convention in Los Angeles.

He married actress Molly Sinclair in 1950 and remained with her until her death in 1992. The couple had a daughter born in 1958 and a son born the following year.

Addison Richards

Addison Richards with Audie Murphy in *Walk the Proud Land*

Addison Richards was born Addison Whitaker Richards, Jr. October 20, 1887, in Zanesville, Ohio, and was an American film actor. He appeared in almost 400 films between 1933 and 1964 and could be counted upon to play upstanding, law-abiding citizens and/or officers of good moral fiber; only occasionally menacing.

Some of those credits included *The Girl from Missouri* (1934) with Jean Harlow, *The Eagle's Brood* (1935), *The Walking Dead* (1936), *Boys Town* (1938), *Nick Carter, Master Detective* (1939), *My Little Chickadee* (1940), *The Strawberry Blonde* (1941), *Private Buckaroo* (1942), *A-Haunting We Will Go* (1942) with Laurel and Hardy, *The Deerslayer* (1943), *The Fighting Seabees* (1944), *The Fighting Sullivans* (1944), *Duffy's Tavern* (1945), *Mighty Joe Young* (1949), *Robert Montgomery Presents* (1952-1954), *Fury at Gunsight Pass* (1956), *The Fastest Gun Alive* (1956), *Walk the Proud Land* (1956) with Audie Murphy, *The Deerslayer* (1957), *Richard Diamond, Private Detective* (1957), *Gunsight Ridge* (1957), *The People's Choice* (1957-1958), *Trackdown* (1958-1959), *Fibber McGee and Molly* (1959), *Wanted: Dead or Alive* (1958-1960), *The Deputy* (1960-1961), *The Fugitive* (1964), and *No Time for Sergeants* (1964).

He died March 22, 1964, from a heart attack. His interment was located at Oak Park Cemetery in Claremont, California.

Frank Richards

Frank Richards with Audie Murphy in *Destry*

Frank Richards was born September 15, 1909, in New York City, New York, and was an American actor.

He appeared in over 150 films and television programs from 1940 to 1984, including *Hold That Ghost* (1941), *Reap the Wild Wind* (1942), *Appointment with Murder* (1948), *Boston Blackie* (1951), *Carbine Williams* (1952), *The Abbott and Costello Show* (1953), *Destry* (1954) with Audie Murphy, *Fury* (1956-1957), *How to Make a Monster* (1958), *Wanted: Dead or Alive* (1958), *The Gunfight at Dodge City* (1959), *Twilight Zone* (1961), *Whispering Smith* (1961) again with Audie Murphy, *Voyage to the Bottom of the Sea* (1964), *The Greatest Story Ever Told* (1965), *The Beverly Hillbillies* (1967), *A Woman Under the Influence* (1974), *Fantasy Island* (1979), and *Diff'rent Strokes* (1984).

He died April 15, 1992, at age 82.

Jack Richardson

No biographical information could be found for Jack Richardson, but he did appear in eighteen films and television programs from 1956 to 1970. Some of those credits include *The Proud and Profane* (1956), the "Incident" episode of *G.E. True Theater* (1958) with Audie Murphy, *Vertigo* (1958), *A Summer Place* (1959), *Cape Fear* (1962), *Goodbye Charlie* (1964), *The Mystery of the Chinese Junk* (1967), *Beyond the Law* (1968), and *Maidstone* (1970).

Susan Ridgway

Susan Ridgway was born Ione D. Ahrens January 27, 1918, in Los Angeles, California, and was an American actress. An attractive, raven-haired model actress mostly appeared in comedies and musicals. She appeared in over 150 films and television programs from 1937 to 1959.

Some of those credits include *The Buccaneer* (1938), *Gone with the Wind* (1939), *Citizen Kane* (1941), *Hit the Ice* (1943), *Heaven Only Knows* (1947), *Mexican Hayride* (1948), *The West Point Story* (1950), *Abbott and Costello Meet Captain Kidd* (1952), *Ma and Pa Kettle on Vacation* (1953), *East of Sumatra* (1953), *Border River* (1954), *The She-Creature* (1956), *Tension at Table Rock* (1956), *Around the World in Eighty Days* (1956), *A Merry Mix-up* (1957), *From Hell It Came* (1957), "The Flight" episode of *Suspicion* (1957) with Audie Murphy, and *The Purple Gang* (1959).

She died May 6, 1996 at age 78 in Burbank, California.

Jorge Rigaud

Audie Murphy with Jorge Riguad in *The Texican*

Jorge Rigaud was born Pedro Jorge Rigato Delissetche August 11, 1905, in Buenos Aires, Argentina. He appeared in nearly 200 films and television programs from 1932 to 1982, mostly foreign.

Some of his credits include *Under the Leather Helmet* (1932), *There's No Tomorrow* (1940), *Eclipse of the Sun* (1943), *Masquerade in Mexico* (1945), *Native Son* (1951), *Descent Into Hell* (1954), *A Glass of Whiskey* (1958), *Valentine's Day* (1959), *The Colossus of Rhodes* (1961), *The Adventures of Scaramouche* (1963), *Web of Fear* (1964), *Finger on the Trigger* (1965), *Honeymoons Will Kill You* (1966), *Sharp-Shooting Twin Sisters* (1966), *The Texican* (1966) with Audie Murphy, *They Came to Rob Las Vegas* (1968), *Guns of the Magnificent Seven* (1969), *A Lizard in a Woman's Skin* (1971), *A Town Called Hell* (1971), *Love Brides of the Blood Mummy* (1973), *Striptease* (1976), *Impossible Love* (1977), *Jaguar Lives!* (1979), and *Black Jack* (1981).

He died January 17, 1984, at age 78 in a road accident in Madrid, Spain.

Elisabeth Risdon

Audie Murphy with Elizabeth Risdon in *Sierra*

Elisabeth Risdon was born Elizabeth Evans in London, England, April 26, 1887, and was an English film actress. She appeared in over 140 films between 1913 and 1952. An attractive beauty in her youth she usually played in society parts. In later years in films she switched to playing character parts.

Some of her credits include *The Idol of Paris* (1914), *Florence Nightingale* (1915), *A Star Over Night* (1919), *Crime and Punishment* (1935), *Dead End* (1937), *The Girl from Mexico* (1939), *Abe Lincoln in Illinois* (1940), *High Sierra* (1941), *Reap the Wild Wind* (1942), *Mexican Spitfire's Blessed Event* (1943), *The Canterville Ghost* (1944), *The Unseen* (1945), *The Egg and I* (1947), *Sierra* (1950) with Audie Murphy, *It's a Big Country* (1951), *Schlitz Playhouse* (1953), *The Ford Television Theatre* (1955-1956), and *Ethel Barrymore Theater* (1956).

She died December 20, 1958, in Santa Monica, California from a cerebral hemorrhage. She was married to prolific silent film director George Loane Tucker who left her a widow in 1921.

Thelma Ritter

Audie Murphy with Thelma Ritter in *Ford Startime*

Thelma Ritter was born in Brooklyn, New York, February 14, 1902, and was an American actress. She typically played working class characters and was noted for her distinctive voice, with a strong Brooklyn accent. Ritter received six Academy Award nominations for Best Supporting Actress.

After appearing in high school plays and stock companies, she trained as an actress at the American Academy of Dramatic Arts. She established a stage career but took a hiatus to raise her two children by her husband, Joseph Moran, an actor turned advertising executive.

Ritter did stock theater and radio shows early in her career, without much impact. Ritter's first movie role was in *Miracle on 34th Street* (1947). She made a memorable impression in a brief uncredited part, as a frustrated mother unable to find the toy that Kris Kringle has promised to her son. Her second role, in writer-director Joseph L. Mankiewicz's *A Letter to Three Wives* (1949), also left a mark, although Ritter was again uncredited.

Mankiewicz kept Ritter in mind, and cast her as "Birdie" in *All About Eve* (1950), which earned her an Oscar nomination. A second nomination followed for her work in Mitchell Leisen's' classic ensemble screwball comedy *The Mating Season* (1951) starring Gene Tierney and John Lund.

Ritter enjoyed steady film work for the next dozen years, in such films as *Titanic* (1953), *Rear Window* (1954), *Lucy Gallant* (1955), *A Hole in the Head* (1959), *Pillow Talk* (1959), *The Misfits* (1961), *Birdman of Alcatraz* (1962), *How the West Was Won* (1962), *Move Over, Darling* (1963), *The Incident* (1967), and *What's So Bad About Feeling Good?* (1968).

She also appeared in many of the episodic drama TV series of the 1950s, such as *Alfred Hitchcock Presents* (1956), *General Electric Theater* (1960), and "The Man" episode of *Startime* (1960) with Audie Murphy.

February 14, 1969, shortly after having made an appearance on *The Jerry Lewis Show*, Ritter died of a heart attack in New York City.

Carlos Rivas

Carlos Rivas was born Oscar von Weber September 16, 1928, in Odessa, Texas. Virile Mexican-American actor who appeared in many films both here and south of the border during the 1950s and 1960s.

Some of his credits include *Fury in Paradise* (1955), *Comanche* (1956), *The Black Scorpion* (1957), *Zorro* (1959), *The Unforgiven* (1960) with Audie Murphy, *Maverick* (1962), *Perry Mason* (1962), *Bob Hope Presents the Chrysler Theatre* (1964), *The Addams Family* (1965), *Tarzan and the Valley of Gold* (1966), *They Saved Hitler's Brain* (1968), *True Grit* (1969), *The Phantom Gunslinger* (1970), *Mannix* (1970-1972), *The Gatling Gun* (1973), *Doc Savage: The Man of Bronze* (1975), *Barnaby Jones* (1979), *Simon & Simon* (1983), *The A-Team* (1985), *Dynasty* (1987), *Gas, Food Lodging* (1990), and *The Colonel's Last Flight* (2000).

He was perhaps best known for his portrayal of the ill-fated Lun Tha opposite Rita Moreno in *The King and I* (1956) starring Yul Brynner and Deborah Kerr.

He died June 16, 2003, at age 74 in Los Angeles, California.

Richard Rober

Audie Murphy with Richard Rober in *Sierra*

Richard Rober was born Richard Steven Rauber May 14, 1910, in Rochester, New York. He was a rugged Hollywood leading man who did not live long enough to become "Another Bogart," as had been ballyhooed.

Rober appeared in several musical comedies on Broadway. Some of his film credits include *Call Northside 777* (1948), *Illegal Entry* (1949), *The File on Thelma Jordon* (1950), *Sierra* (1950) with Audie Murphy, *Father's Little Dividend* (1951), *Man in the Saddle* (1951), *The Devil Makes Three* (1952), and *The Savage* (1952).

Rober died May 26, 1952, at age 42 in Santa Monica, California, of injuries he suffered when he accidentally drove his car off a seventy-five foot embankment.

Freddy Roberto

Freddy Roberto was born Frederic C. Roberts September 7, 1906. He appeared in sixteen films and television programs from 1957 to 1969. Some of those credits include "The Flight" episode of *Suspicion* (1957) with Audie Murphy, *Sugarfoot* (1958), *The Gun Runners* (1958) again with Audie Murphy, *Bronco* (1959), *Cheyenne* (1960), *Adventures in Paradise* (1960-1961), *Voyage to the Bottom of the Sea* (1965), *Bewitched* (1967), *The Andy Griffith Show* (1968), and *It Takes a Thief* (1969).

He died February 3, 1999, at age 92 in Ellicott City, Maryland.

J.N. Roberts

James Nelson "J. N." Roberts was born in 1941 and is semi-retired off road and enduro motorcycle racer from Southern California. In the 1960s and 1970s he was a top desert racer on two wheels in the United States.

Roberts won the Barstow to Vegas race four times in a row. He also won the Mint 400 three times and the Baja 500 and the Baja 1000 twice each. He teamed with Malcolm Smith to win the motorcycle division in the 1967 Mexican 1000, later to be known as the Baja 1000. Roberts also represented the United States at the 1971 and 1972 International Six Days Trial, a form of off-road motorcycle Olympics. After his racing career, he became a stuntman in the American Film industry.

Roberts appeared in *A Time for Dying* (1969) with Audie Murphy, *Sometimes a Great Notion* (1970), *On Any Sunday* (1971), with Steve McQueen, *Electra Glide in Blue* (1973), *Zero to Sixty* (1978), *The Dukes of Hazzard* (1979), *CHiPs* (1981), *The Seventh Sign* (1988), *Broken Arrow* (1996), *Dust to Glory* (2005), and in the 2008 film *Full Circle, The Legend Lives On* playing himself. He was also credited as a stuntman forty-one films from *The Undefeated* (1969) to *George of the Jungle* (1997).

He was inducted into the AMA Motorcycle Hall of Fame in 1999. In 2009, Roberts was inducted into the Off-road Motorsports Hall of Fame. He is currently living in Helena, Montana.

Roy Roberts

Roy Roberts with Audie Murphy in *The Cimarron Kid*

Roy Roberts was born Roy Barnes Jones March 19, 1906, in Tampa, Florida, and was an American actor. He proudly claimed over 900 performances in a forty-year career. He might not have been known necessarily by name but the face was so distinct and obviously familiar. The prototype of the steely executive, the no-nonsense mayor, the assured banker, the stentorian leader, Roberts looked out of place without his patented dark suit and power tie. His silvery hair, perfectly trimmed mustache, non-plussed reactions and take-charge demeanor reminded one of the "Mr. Monopoly" character from the classic game board.

He was the youngest of six children. The year 1900 is given as his birth date in several reference books, which seems compatible with his noticeably aged appearance in the last decade or so of his life, but his final resting stone bears the year 1906.

His early career was on the Broadway stage, gracing such plays as *Old Man Murphy* (1931), *Twentieth Century* (1932), *The Body Beautiful* (1935), and *My Sister Eileen* (1942). In 1943 he made a successful switch to films, debuting as a Marine officer in *Guadalcanal Diary* (1943).

Usually billed around tenth in the credits, he played a reliable succession of stalwart roles such as captains, generals, politicians, sheriffs, judges, etc. He was also a semi-standard presence in film noir, appearing in such classics as *Force of Evil* (1948), *He Walked by Night* (1948), and *The Enforcer* (1951) as both good cop and occasional heavy.

More of his film roles include *My Darling Clementine* (1946), *Calamity Jane and Sam Bass* (1949), *Sierra* (1950) with Audie Murphy, *The Cimarron Kid* (1952) again with Audie Murphy, *House of Wax* (1953), *Tumbleweed* (1953) a third appearance with Audie Murphy, *Dawn at Socorro* (1954), *Stranger on Horseback* (1955), *The First Texan* (1956), *Kid Galahad* (1962), *It's a Mad Mad Mad Mad World* (1963), *I'll Take Sweden* (1965), *The Million Dollar Duck* (1971), *Chinatown* (1974), and *The Strongest Man in the World* (1975).

When Roberts made the move to TV he began to include more work in comedies. The 1950s and 1960s would prove him to be a most capable foil to a number of prime sitcom stars including Gale Storm and Lucille Ball. His patented gruff and exasperated executives often displayed their prestige by the mere use of initials, such as "W.W." and "E.J." While he never landed the one role on film or TV that could have led to top character stardom, he nevertheless remained a solid and enjoyable presence, a character player who added stature no matter how far down the credits list.

Some of those television credits include *Mr. & Mrs. North* (1952-1953), *My Little Margie* (1952-1955), *Crossroads* (1956-1957), *The Gale Storm Show* (1956-1960), *Have Gun - Will Travel* (1962), *Twilight Zone* (1963), *The Munsters* (1964), *McHale's Navy* (1963-1965), *The Addams Family* (1965), *Laredo* (1966), *The Beverly Hillbillies* (1963-1967), *The Lucy Show* (1966-1968), *Bewitched* (1967-1970), *Petticoat Junction* (1963-1970), *Gunsmoke* (1961-1975), and *Here's Lucy* (1969-1974).

A stocky man for most his life, Roberts gained considerable girth in the late 1960s, which made his characters even more imposing. He died of a heart attack on May 28, 1975, in Los Angeles and was buried in Fort Worth, Texas. He was survived by his wife, actress Lillian Moore.

Bartlett Robinson

Bartlett Robinson was born December 9, 1912, in New York City, New York, and was an American actor. He was in 129 films and television programs from 1954 to 1982.

Some of his credits include *Big Town* (1955-1956), *The Spirit of St. Louis* (1957), *No Time for Sergeants* (1958), *Richard Diamond, Private Detective* (1958-1959), *Gunsmoke* (1956-1960), *Whispering Smith* (1961) with Audie Murphy, *Twilight Zone* (1961-1962), *Laramie* (1959-1963), *The Munsters* (1965), *Mona McCluskey* (1965-1966), *Gilligan's Island* (1967), *Live a Little, Love a Little* (1968), *The Wrecking Crew* (1969), *Marlowe* (1969), *Mannix* (1969-1972), *The Odd Couple* (1975), and *Lou Grant* (1979-1982).

He died March 26, 1986, at age 73 in Fallbrook, California.

Dewey Robinson

Dewey Robinson was born in New Haven, Connecticut, August 17, 1898, and was an American film character actor who appeared in over 250 films between 1931 and 1952.

Dewey Robinson made his Broadway debut in 1922 in a melodrama called *The Last Warning*, which ran for seven months and 238 performances. Several years later, in 1925, he appeared in a comedy, *Solid Ivory*, which was not a success, and was also his final Broadway production.

In 1931 Robinson, a big, barrel-chested man at 6' 1" who easily conveyed physical menace, made his first film when he played a waiter in George Cukor's *Tarnished Lady*, starring Tallulah Bankhead. That performance did not receive screen credit, and this was often the case over Robinson's career, although he was in the billed main cast in *Murder on the Campus* (1934), *Navy Secrets* (1939), and *There Goes Kelly* (1945). Because of his size and physical presence, Robinson worked often during periods when gangster movies were the rage.

Notable early roles for Robinson include a polo-playing hood in *Little Giant* (1933) starring Edward G. Robinson, a supervisor of slaves in Eddie Cantor's *Roman Scandals* that same year, and the Ben Turpin short *Keystone Hotel* in 1935. In the 1940s, Robinson was part of Preston Sturges' unofficial 'stock company' of character actors, appearing in eight films written and directed by Sturges.

He appeared in *Texas, Brooklyn & Heaven* (1948) with Audie Murphy.

In 1950, near the end of his career, Robinson played a Brooklyn Dodgers fan in *The Jackie Robinson Story* who progressed from bigotry to exuberant support of Jackie Robinson.

Robinson died in Las Vegas, Nevada on December 11, 1950, from a heart attack, but because he worked so prolifically, films in which he appeared continued to be seen until 1952, when *At Sword's Point*, a Musketeer adventure, was released.

Blossom Rock

Edith Marie Blossom MacDonald was born in Philadelphia, Pennsylvania, August 21, 1895, also known or credited as Blossom Rock, Blossom MacDonald or Marie Blake, was an American actress of stage and television. She was also elder sister to actress/singer Jeanette MacDonald.

As a youth she performed on the vaudeville stage with her younger sister, Jeanette, and later with her husband, Clarence Rock. She and Rock married in 1926; they had no children.

She later performed in films, most notably as the hospital switchboard operator in the "Dr. Kildare" movies; in television; and on Broadway. Some of her credits include *Thoroughbreds Don't Cry* (1937), *Love Finds Andy Hardy* (1938), *Li'l Abner* (1940), *I Married a Witch* (1942), *Bud Abbott and Lou Costello in Hollywood* (1945), *Bad Boy* (1949) with Audie Murphy, *Gang Busters* (1952), *Phantom of the Rue Morgue* (1954), *Dr. Hudson's Secret Journal* (1955-1957), *Snow White and the Three Stooges* (1961), and *The New Phil Silvers Show* (1964).

She is best-known (if not by name) for playing "Grandmama" on *The Addams Family* (1964-1966).

Many times actors are asked to change their name whether they want to or not. In most cases a movie contract will change their mind. She was known in vaudeville, as well as at home, as Blossom, but agents and producers gave her the name Marie Blake, which she went by on screen from 1937 to 1952. When she was no longer under the thumb of an agent or any movie contract, she changed her professional name back to Blossom and used her married last name. Many friends in the business considered her name change as a career killer after making a name for herself for fifteen years. She felt that the bit parts she played on TV and movies in the late 1940's and early 1950's weren't going to be that memorable, and no one would remember her.

She died on January 14, 1978, in Los Angeles, California, at age 82. Her grave is located at Forest Lawn Cemetery in Glendale.

Gilbert Roland

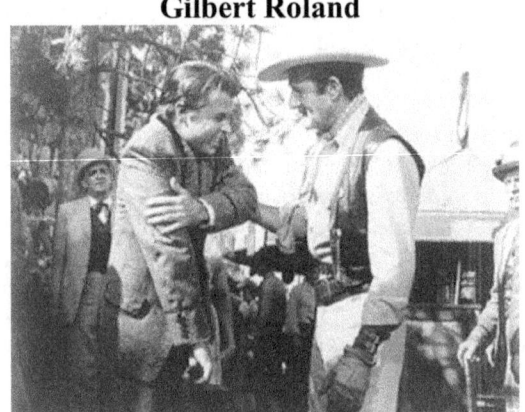

Audie Murphy with Gilbert Roland in *The Wild and the Innocent*

Gilbert Roland was born December 11, 1905, was a Mexican-born American film actor. He was born Luis Antonio Dámaso de Alonso in Ciudad Juárez, Chihuahua, Mexico, and originally intended to become a bullfighter like his father. When the family moved to the United States, however, he became interested in acting when he was picked at random for a role as an extra. He chose his screen name by combining the names of his favorite actors, John Gilbert and Ruth Roland. He was often cast in the typical "*Latin Lover*" role.

Roland's first major role was in the collegiate comedy *The Plastic Age* (1925) together with Clara Bow, to whom he became engaged. In 1927, he played Armand in *Camille* opposite Norma Talmadge, whom he was romantically involved with, and they starred together in several productions. Roland later appeared in Spanish language adaptations of American films, in romantic lead roles.

Beginning in the 1940s, critics began to take notice of his acting and he was praised for his supporting roles in John Huston's *We Were Strangers* (1949), *The Bad and the Beautiful* (1952), and *Thunder Bay* (1953). He also appeared in a series of films in the mid 1940s as the popular character 'The Cisco Kid'. In 1953 he starred in the epic *Beneath the 12-Mile Reef* as Greek-American sponge diver Mike Petrakis.

Other credits include *The Treasure of Pancho Villa* (1955), *Around the World in Eighty Days* (1956), *The Last of the Fast Guns* (1958), *The Wild and the Innocent* (1950) with Audie Murphy, *Guns of the Timberland* (1960), *Cheyenne Autumn* (1964), *The Fugitive* (1964-1967), *Rod Serling's Night Gallery* (1972), *The Pacific Connection* (1974), and *Louis L'amour's The Sacketts* (1979).

His last film appearance was in the 1982 western *Barbarosa*.

Roland was married to actress Constance Bennett from 1941 to 1946. His second marriage, to Guillermina Cantú in 1954, lasted until his death forty years later.

Gilbert Roland died of cancer in Beverly Hills, California on May 15, 1994, at age 88. His remains were cremated and his ashes scattered at sea.

Carlos Romero

Audie Murphy with Carlos Romero in *The Gunrunners*

Carlos Romero was born in Hollywood, California, February 15, 1927, and was an American actor, noted for his many appearances on television.

Some of his film and television credits included *The World Was His Jury* (1958), *The Gale Storm Show* (1958), *The Gun Runners* (1958) with Audie Murphy, *Richard Diamond, Private Detective* (1959), *Wanted: Dead or Alive* (1959), several episodes as Rico in *Wichita Town* (1959-1960), *Zorro* (1958-1961), *77 Sunset Strip* (1961-1962), *Island of the Blue Dolphins* (1964), *Perry Mason* (1963-1966), *The Fugitive* (1966-1967), *The F.B.I.* (1967-1969), *D.A.: Murder One* (1969), *O'Hara, U.S. Treasury* (1972), *Adam-12* (1972-1974), *Soylent Green* (1973), *Kolchak: The Night Stalker* (1975), *The New Adventures of Wonder Woman* (1977), *Hart to Hart* (1979-1983), *T.J. Hooker* (1983), *Falcon Crest* (1982-1983), *The A-Team* (1985), *Dynasty* (1986), *Magnum, P.I.* (1987), and *L.A. Law* (1989).

Romero died in Ferndale, California, on June 21, 2007.

Teddy Rooney

Ted Michael Rooney was born April 12, 1950, and is the son of Mickey Rooney and Martha Vickers. He appeared in twelve films and television programs from 1958 to 1963.

His film appearances were *Andy Hardy Comes Home* (1958), *It Happened to Jane* (1959), and *Seven Ways from Sundown* (1960) with Audie Murphy.

His television appearances were *The Ransom of Red Chief* (1959), *The Rebel* (1960), *Shirley Temple Theatre* (1960), *The Dinah Shore Chevy Show* (1960), *Wagon Train* (1960), *G.E. True Theater* (1960), *The Rifleman* (1961), *Lassie* (1962), and *McHale's Navy* (1963).

He has two children, Shannon Rooney and Dominique Rooney. He also has two grandchildren, Kaitlyn and Hunter Rooney.

Gene Roth

Gene Roth was born Eugene Oliver Edgar Stutenroth in Redfield, South Dakota, January 8, 1903, and was an American film actor. He appeared in over 250 films between 1922 and 1967.

He began his acting career doing uncredited bit roles in silent pictures in the early 1920s. Moreover, Roth worked as a movie theater manager and built and installed pipe organs before his acting career took off in the 1940s following his arrival in Hollywood, California in 1943. Often cast as threatening heavies and scruffy working class types, and rough-around-the-edges law officers.

Roth is remembered for his portrayals of heavies and bad guys in Three Stooges short films such as *Slaphappy Sleuths* (1950), *Hot Stuff* (1956), *Quiz Whizz* (1958), *Outer Space Jitters* (1957), and *Pies and Guys* (1958). His most memorable role was as Russian spy Bortsch in *Dunked in the Deep* (1949), as well as its remake, *Commotion on the Ocean* (1956). His most famous line was his threat to Shemp Howard: "Give me dat fill-um!" ('fill-um' being 'film' with a Russian accent). He also appeared in their movie *The Three Stooges Meet Hercules* (1962).

Some non-Three Stooges roles include *Secret Agent X-9* (1945), *Jesse James Rides Again* (1947), *Four Faces West* (1948), *Dick Tracy* (1950), *The Amos 'n Andy Show* (1951), *Carbine Williams* (1952), *Jack McCall Desperado* (1953), *Seven Brides for Seven Brothers* (1954), *The Lone Ranger* (1949-1954), *The Cisco Kid* (1956), *Utah Blaine* (1957), *She Demons* (1958), *Earth vs. the Spider* (1958), *Attack of the Giant Leeches* (1959), *G.I. Blues* (1960), *Atlantis, the Lost Continent* (1961), *Twilight Zone* (1961), *Whispering Smith* (1961) with Audie Murphy, *How the West Was Won* (1962), *The Courtship of Eddie's Father* (1963), *The Greatest Story Ever Told* (1965), and *Rosie!* (1967).

After retiring from acting in the early 1970s, Roth worked part time as a liquor counterman at a drug store and was an active participant in the nostalgia convention circuit. He was married four times and was the father of three children. Gene's life came to a tragic untimely end at age 73 when he was struck and killed by a hit-and-run driver while crossing the street in Los Angeles, California on July 19, 1976.

Betty Rowland

Betty Jane Rowland was born January 23, 1916 in Columbus, Ohio. She is one of the famous Rowland sisters of the early days of Burlesque. In some cases, it seems as though the burlesque gene was passed down through the family, with several women of the same clan becoming well-known performers. Such is the case of the Rowland Sisters, the most famous of which is Betty Rowland, 'The Redheaded Ball of Fire'.

Unable to attend college because their father had lost all his money during the Great Depression, the Rowlands first burst on the striptease scene in the mid 1930's in New York City. Betty Rowland first danced as a Minsky Girl, but after a fellow dancer was busted at Minsky's in 1937 for performing without a G-string, NYC's Mayor LaGuardia cracked down on striptease. This proved to be a pivotal moment in Betty's career. Betty moved to Los Angeles to dance in the Follies Theater for a "limited engagement," which ended up being a fifteen year run.

In Los Angeles Betty picked up the moniker of 'The Ball of Fire' because of her red hair, petite stature, and energetic performance. She appeared in some films, like *Let's Make Music* (1941), *International Burlesque* (1950), *Spavaldi e innamorati* (1959), *The World's Greatest Sinner* (1962), *Love and Kisses* (1965), and as one of Mamie's girls in *A Time for Dying* (1969) with Audie Murphy.

She also dated such Hollywood stars as Orson Welles. The mainstream 1941 film *Ball of Fire* produced by Samuel Goldwyn and directed by Howard Hawks was based at least partly on Betty, and the Edith Head-designed costumes were carbon copies of Betty's burlesque ensembles. Rowland sued Goldwyn as a publicity stunt. Later, in a twist of fate Betty was interviewed by Goldwyn's grand-daughter Liz Goldwyn in the 2005 documentary *Pretty Things*.

Betty's sister Rose Zell danced at the Paradise in New York City. Her most spectacular number in which she painted her entire body gold and stripped out of her clothing earned her the name of 'Golden Girl'. On a burlesque tour to England she met and married the Baron Empain, a French nobleman who owned a controlling interest in the Parisian subway system.

A more tragic tale is that of Diana Rowland, who had a brief career in burlesque in her early 20's and was known as 'Society's Favorite'. The third Rowland sister had scarlet fever which left her with a small leakage of the heart. When she didn't come in for work one night at a Detroit burlesque club, she was discovered dead in her hotel room.

There was a fourth Rowland sister, Lorraine, who remained in Ohio and became a housewife and mother. Betty Rowland recounted, "Once in a while, she wonders if she missed out on something?"

She owned and operated 217 Bar in Santa Monica at 89 years old.

Selena Royle

Audie Murphy with Selena Royle in *Bad Boy*

Selena Royle was born in New York City, New York, November 6, 1904, and was an American stage, television, and film actress. Royle's parents were playwright Edwin Milton Royle and actress Selena Fetter (April 12, 1860 - May 10, 1955). She had an older sister Josephine Fetter Royle (1901–1992). She turned to acting despite the objections of her parents. Nonetheless, her first professional role was as Guinevere in her father's play *Lancelot and Elaine*.

Eventually she landed a part on her own in the 1923 Theatre Guild production of *Peer Gynt* with Joseph Schildkraut and became a respected Broadway actress. She made one film in the 1930s, *Misleading Lady*, but otherwise worked on the stage and on radio, starring on the shows *Hilda Hope, M.D.* and *Kate Hopkins*.

In the 1940s, she returned to film and had a successful run, mainly playing maternal characters such as Ingrid Bergman's mother in *Joan of Arc* (1948). Other film roles included *The Fighting Sullivans* (1944), *Thirty Seconds Over Tokyo* (1944), *Cass Timberlane* (1947), *Joan of Arc* (1948), *Bad Boy* (1949) with Audie Murphy, *Branded* (1950), *Robot Monster* (1953).

She also made several appearances on early television, such as *Gruen Guild Theater* (1952), *Crown Theatre with Gloria Swanson* (1954), *Ethel Barrymore Theater* (1956), and *As the World Turns* (1956-1959).

Her first husband was Earle Larrimore. They were married in 1932 and divorced in 1942. She was married to actor Georges Renavent from 1948 until his death in 1969.

Royle died in Guadalajara, Jalisco, Mexico on April 23, 1983, at age 78.

Herbert Rudley

Herbert Rudley with Audie Murphy in *Hell Bent for Leather*

Herbert Rudley was born in Philadelphia, Pennsylvania, March 22, 1910, and was a prolific character actor who appeared on stage, in films, and on television.

He attended Temple University. He left Temple after winning a scholarship to Eva Le Gallienne's Civic Repertory Theatre.

He began appearing on stage in 1926. His Broadway debut was in *Did I Say No* in 1931. He also appeared in stage productions of *The Threepenny Opera*, *Abe Lincoln in Illinois*, and *Macbeth*.

In 1940, he appeared in the film version of *Abe Lincoln in Illinois*. For the next four decades he appeared in dozens of supporting film roles, including *A Walk in the Sun* (1945), *Joan of Arc* (1948), *The Silver Chalice* (1954), *Raw Edge* (1956), *The Bravados* (1958), *The Jayhawkers!* (1959), *Hell Bent for Leather* (1960) with Audie Murphy, *Follow That Dream* (1962), *Falling in Love Again* (1980), and *Forever and Beyond* (1981).

On television, he appeared in both drama, often as a military person, and comedy, such as *Robert Montgomery Presents* (1950-1953), *Science Fiction Theatre* (1955), *My Friend Flicka* (1955-1956), *The George Burns and Gracie Allen Show* (1956-1957), *Gunsmoke* (1956-1957), thirty-seven episodes as Sam Brennan in *The Californians* (1957-1958), *The Bob Cummings Show* (1957-1959), *Wichita Town* (1959), *Hawaiian Eye* (1960), twenty-eight episodes as Will Gentry in *Michael Shayne* (1960-1961), *The Beverly Hillbillies* (1963), *My Favorite Martian* (1963-1964), *The Munsters* (1965), twenty-six episodes as General Crone in *Mona McCluskey* (1965-1966), *I Dream of Jeannie* (1970), *Owen Marshall: Counselor at Law* (1972), *Project U.F.O.* (1978), and *House Calls* (1982).

Rudley, however, is best remembered for his role as Eve Arden's husband, attorney Herb Hubbard, in fifty-six episodes of *The Mothers-in-Law* (1967-1969).

In 1981, he made four appearances on the series *Dallas* as Howard Barker, an attorney who represented J. R. Ewing in his divorce and child custody fight with his former wife, Sue Ellen.

He died of a heart attack September 9, 2006, at age 96 in Los Angeles County, California.

Barbara Rush

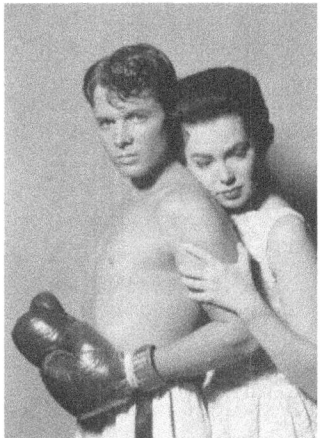

Audie Murphy with Barbara Rush in *World in My Corner*

Barbara Rush was born in Denver, Colorado, January 4, 1927, and is an American stage, film, and television actress. A student at the University of California at Santa Barbara, Barbara Rush performed on stage at the Pasadena Playhouse before signing with Paramount Pictures. She made her screen debut in the 1951 movie *The Goldbergs* and went on to star opposite the likes of James Mason, Marlon Brando, Paul Newman, Richard Burton, Dean Martin, Frank Sinatra, and Kirk Douglas. In 1952 she starred in *Flaming Feather* with Sterling Hayden and Victor Jory. In 1954 she won the Golden Globe Award for "Most Promising Newcomer - Female" for her performance in *It Came from Outer Space*.

Some of her other work includes *World in My Corner* (1956) as Audie Murphy's love interest, *The Young Philadelphians* (1959), *Strangers When We Meet* (1960), *Saints and Sinners* (1962-1963), *The Outer Limits* (1964), *Robin and the 7 Hoods* (1964), as the wife of Phillip Gerard in *The Fugitive* (1965), *Laredo* (1966), *Custer* (1967), *Batman* (1968), *Peyton Place* (1968-1969), *Rod Serling's Night Gallery* (1971), *Moon of the Wolf* (1972) with David Janssen, *Superdad* (1973), *The New Dick Van Dyke Show* (1973-1974), *The Last Day* (1975), *The Bionic Woman* (1976), *Can't Stop the Music* (1980), *Flamingo Road* (1980-1982), *Knight Rider* (1983), *Magnum, P.I.* (1984-1987), *Guns of Paradise* (1991), *All My Children* (1992-1993), *The Outer Limits* (1998), and *7th Heaven* (1997-2007).

Rush began her career on stage and it has always been a part of her professional life. In 1970, she earned the Sarah Siddons Award for dramatic achievement in Chicago theatre for her leading role in *Forty Carats* and brought her one-woman play *A Woman of Independent Means* to Broadway in 1984.

She also appeared with Audie Murphy in the eight minute short *Medal of Honor* (1956) to try and get people to buy war bonds.

Barbara Rush married actor Jeffrey Hunter in 1950 and had a son, Christopher. They divorced in 1955. She married publicist Warren Cowan in 1959. Their daughter, Claudia Cowan, is a journalist with Fox News television channel.

Joseph Ruskin

Audie Murphy with Joseph Ruskin in *Hell Bent for Leather*

Joseph Ruskin was born Joseph Schlafman in Haverhill, Massachusetts, April 14, 1924, and is an American character actor.

He has had roles in four different *Star Trek* series: *Star Trek* (1966), *Star Trek: Deep Space Nine* (1993), *Star Trek: Voyager* (1995), and *Star Trek: Enterprise* (2001). Besides Majel Barrett, who has appeared in all five *Star Trek* series, he is the only actor to appear in four. Moreover, since Barrett only provided voice-overs in the latter two series, he is the only actor to appear on screen in four out of five. He also appeared in *Star Trek: Insurrection* (1998).

Some non-Star Trek roles include *The Honeymooners* (1955), *Richard Diamond, Private Detective* (1959), *Wanted: Dead or Alive* (1959), *Black Saddle* (1960), *Hell Bent for Leather* (1960) with Audie Murphy, *The Magnificent Seven* (1960), *Whispering Smith* (1961) again with Audie Murphy, *The Untouchables* (1959-1963), *Mister Ed* (1963), *The Outer Limits* (1964), *Get Smart* (1965), *Gunsmoke* (1962-1966), *The Wild Wild West* (1965-1967), *Rod Serling's Night Gallery* (1971), *Mission: Impossible* (1966-1972), *The Magician* (1974), *Planet of the Apes* (1974), *Harry O* (1976), *Serpico* (1977), *Starsky and Hutch* (1978), *Captain America* (1979), *The Munsters' Revenge* (1981), *The Man Who Wasn't There* (1983), *Prizzi's Honor* (1985), *Alfred Hitchcock Presents* (1986), *Saturday the 14th Strikes Back* (1988), *Indecent Proposal* (1993), *The Last Don* (1997), *ER* (1999), *The Scorpion King* (2002), *Alias* (2002), *Smokin' Aces* (2006), and *Bones* (2006).

Joseph Ruskin was the uncredited voice of the Kanamits from the 1962 episode of the *Twilight Zone*, "To Serve Man". He also may be remembered as the Genie from the 1960 episode of the *Twilight Zone*, "The Man in the Bottle".

He married Patricia Herd in 1959 and was later divorced in 1976.

Joseph Ruskin died December 28, 2013 of natural causes at UCLA Santa Monica at age 89.

Fred Sadoff

Audie Murphy with Fred Sadoff in The Quiet American

Fred Sadoff was born Frederick Edward Sadoff in Brooklyn, New York, October 21, 1926, and was an American film, stage, and television actor.

He got his start as an actor on Broadway in the late 1940s, appearing in *South Pacific* in the role of 'Professor'. He also appeared in *Camino Real* and *Wish You Were Here*. In 1956, he became personal assistant to Michael Redgrave who starred in and directed a production of *The Sleeping Prince*. He also appeared with Michael Redgrave and Audie Murphy in *The Quiet American* (1958).

Sadoff moved to London to form a production company with Redgrave under the name F.E.S. Plays, Ltd. which presented works including *The Importance of Being Oscar* which had a short run on Broadway in 1961. While in England, he also worked as a director for the BBC and Rediffusion.

Eventually returning to the United States, he found success as an actor in *The Poseidon Adventure* in 1972 when he was cast as Linarcos, the company representative who ordered Captain Harrison (Leslie Nielsen) full ahead. He also acted in other films, including *Papillon* (1973) and *The Terminal Man* (1974).

On television, he appeared in guest roles on such series as *The Flying Nun* (1970), *Mannix* (1973), *Kojak* (1974), *Baretta* (1975), *Harry O* (1974-1975), *Black Sheep Squadron* (1977), *Buck Rogers in the 25th Century* (1980), *International Airport* (1985), *Magnum, P.I.* (1987), and *Empty Nest* (1990).

Fred Sadoff died of AIDS on May 6, 1994 in his home in Los Angeles, California at age 67.

Tatsuo Saito

Tatsuo Saito was born June 10, 1902, in Tokyo, Japan. He appeared in 131 films and television programs from 1925 to 1967, most of them Japanese.

Some English appearances were *The Life of an Office Worker* (1929), *Where Now Are the Dreams of Youth* (1932), *College Is a Nice Place* (1936), *Goodbye* (1949), *Geisha Girl* (1952), *Joe Butterfly* (1957) with Audie Murphy, *My Geisha* (1962), and *Lord Jim* (1965).

He died March 2, 1968, at age 65 in Tokyo, Japan.

Albert Salmi

Albert Salmi was born March 11, 1928, and was an American actor. Albert Salmi was born in Brooklyn, New York, to Finnish immigrant parents, and following a stint in the Army, took up acting as a career, studying Method acting with Lee Strasberg.

In 1955, Salmi starred in *Bus Stop* on Broadway. He volunteered to go on the road with the show, where he fell in love with and married his leading lady, former child star Peggy Ann Garner, on May 16, 1956. Their only child, Catherine Ann Salmi, died in 1995 of premature heart disease at the age of thirty-eight.

He made his film debut as Smerdjakov in the 1958 movie version of *The Brothers Karamazov*, with Yul Brynner, Lee J. Cobb, William Shatner, and Richard Basehart, a role for which Salmi turned down an Oscar-nomination. Salmi's next film was *The Bravados* (1958) in which he played one of the villains hunted down by hero Gregory Peck. The National Board of Review presented Salmi with the NBR Award for Best Supporting Actor for his work in both of these films.

He had several memorable roles on *The Twilight Zone* (1960-1963) including "Of Late I Think of Cliffordville","A Quality of Mercy", and "Execution" and also appeared twice as the incorrigible pirate, Alonzo P. Tucker on *Lost in Space* (1966-1967).

A high point of Salmi's career came in 1968, when he was cast in the Arthur Miller play *The Price*. He played the lead on Broadway and in London.

He also had a regular role on the television law series *Petrocelli* (1974-1976). Other roles over the years included *The Unforgiven* (1960) with Audie Murphy, *Wagon Train* (1961-1962), *The Fugitive* (1964), *Daniel Boone* (1964-1965), *Laredo* (1965), *Three Guns for Texas* (1968), *Gunsmoke* (1966-1970), *Rod Serling's Night Gallery* (1972), *Hec Ramsey* (1974), *Baretta* (1977), *Undercover with the KKK* (1979), *Caddyshack* (1980), *Dallas* (1982-1983), *Knots Landing* (1984-1985), *Billy the Kid* (1989), and *Mission: Impossible* (1989).

Salmi and Garner divorced on March 13, 1963. He then remarried, his bride being Roberta Pollock Taper. They had two daughters.

April 22, 1990, Albert and Roberta Salmi were found shot to death in their home in Spokane, Washington. According to police, Salmi, who was separated from Roberta at the time and was suffering from severe clinical depression, shot his wife and then himself.

Aldo Sambrell

Aldo Sambrell with Audie Murphy in *The Texican*

Alfredo Sanchez Brell, also known as Aldo Sambrell, was born February 23, 1931, and was a Spanish film actor, director, and producer who made over 150 appearances in film between 1961 and 1996.

He was best known in the world of cinema for his roles as a henchmen in Sergio Leone's Spaghetti Western films, portraying gang members in the trilogy of films *A Fistful of Dollars* (1964), *For a Few Dollars More* (1965), and *The Good, the Bad and the Ugly* (1966), as well as *The Texican (*1966) with Audie Murphy, *Once Upon a Time in the West* in 1968, and *100 Rifles* in 1969. He also played the part of firing squad leader in *A Fistful of Dynamite* (1971), and a member of Sinbad's crew in *The Golden Voyage of Sinbad* (1974).

Other roles included *Navajo Joe* (1966), *Requiem for a Gringo* (1968), *White Comanche* (1968), *Hannie Caulder* (1971), *The Man Called Noon* (1973), *They Died with Their Boots On* (1978), *Black Commando* (1982), *Yellow Hair and the Fortress of Gold* (1984), *The Return of the Musketeers* (1989), *Operation Condor* (1991), *Unknown Soldier* (1995), *Killer Barbys vs. Dracula* (1982), *Flesh for the Beast* (2003), and *Zorro* (2011).

Aldo Sambrell died in Alicante, Spain on July 10, 2010, at age 79, the result of three strokes he suffered in early June 2010.

Walter Sande

Walter Sande with Audie Murphy in *Bad Boy*

Walter Sande was born in Denver, Colorado, July 9, 1906, and was an American actor, notable for film roles.

He was one of those stern, heavyset character actors in Hollywood no person could recognize by name. He showed an early interest in music as a youth and by his college years managed to start his own band. This led to a job as musical director for 20th Century-Fox's theater chain, which, in turn, led him to acting in films beginning in 1937.

Usually providing atmospheric bits with no billing, he made an initial impression in serial cliffhangers as a third-string heavy with the popular *The Green Hornet Strikes Again!* (1940) and *Sky Raiders* (1941).

His first top featured role, however, would come with *The Iron Claw* (1941) as Jack "Flash" Strong, a photographer who, uncharacteristically for Walter, served as a comic sidekick to our serial hero. Best of all would be his role in another serial as Red Pennington, the amusing sidekick to *Don Winslow of the Navy* (1942). He repeated his role again in *Don Winslow of the Coast Guard* (1943), the successful sequel.

The Pennington role would spark a long and steady career in movies and television, usually a step or two behind Hollywood's elite, in *Citizen Kane* (1941), *Sergeant York* (1941), *Great Guns* (1941), *A-Haunting We Will Go* (1941), *Son of Dracula* (1943), *To Have and Have Not* (1944), *The Blue Dahlia* (1946), *Bad Boy* (1949) with Audie Murphy, *The Kid from Texas* (1950) again with Audie Murphy, *Red Mountain* (1951), *The Duel at Silver Creek* (1952) a third appearance with Audie Murphy, *The War of the Worlds* (1953), *Wichita* (1955), *The Adventures of Tugboat Annie* (1957), *Richard Diamond, Private Detective* (1959), *Wanted: Dead or Alive* (1959-1960), *Laramie* (1959-1962), *The Quick Gun* (1964) a fourth appearance with Audie Murphy, *The Navy vs. the Night Monsters* (1966), *Death of a Gunfighter* (1969), *Adam-12* (1971), and *Michael O'Hara the Fourth* (1972).

He died of a heart attack on November 22, 1971, at the age of sixty-five in Chicago, Illinois.

George Sanders

George Sanders with Audie Murphy in *Trunk to Cairo*

George Henry Sanders was born July 3, 1906, and was a Russian-born English film and television actor, singer-songwriter, music composer, and author. His prominent English accent and baritone voice often led him to be cast as sophisticated but villainous characters. He is perhaps best known as Addison DeWitt in *All About Eve* (1950), Jack Favell in *Rebecca* (1940), and the malevolent tiger Shere Khan in *The Jungle Book* (1967). His career spanned more than forty years.

Sanders was born in Saint Petersburg, Imperial Russia, at number 6 Petrovski Ostrov. His English parents were Henry Sanders (1873–1961) and Margaret Sanders (1875–1967). Actor Tom Conway (1904–1967) was his elder brother. His younger sister, Margaret Sanders, was born in 1912. George was eleven when, in 1917, at the outbreak of the Russian Revolution, the family went back to England. Like his brother, he attended Brighton College, a boys' independent school in Brighton, Sussex, then went on to Manchester Technical College. After graduation he worked at an advertising agency, where the company secretary, aspiring actress Greer Garson, suggested he take up a career in acting.

Sanders made his British film debut in 1929. Seven years later, after a series of British films, his first role in an American production was *Lloyd's of London* (1936) as Lord Everett Stacy. His smooth, upper-crust English accent and sleek British manner, along with a suave, snobbish and somewhat threatening air, put him in demand for American films throughout the following decade.

He played supporting roles in high-end productions such as Alfred Hitchcock's *Rebecca* (1940), in which he and Judith Anderson played cruel foils to Joan Fontaine's character. He had leading roles in somewhat lower-budget pictures such as *Rage in Heaven* (1941). He also played the lead in both The Falcon and The Saint film series. In 1942, Sanders handed the Falcon role to his brother Tom, in *The Falcon's Brother*. The only other film in which the two brothers appeared together was *Death of a Scoundrel* (1956), in which they also played brothers.

Sanders played Lord Henry Wotton in the 1945 film version of *The Picture of Dorian Gray*. In 1947, he co-starred with Gene Tierney and Rex Harrison in *The Ghost and Mrs. Muir*. That same year, he gave one of his most critically noted performances, starring with Angela Lansbury in director Albert Lewin's little-known film *The Private Affairs of Bel Ami*, taken from an 1885 novel by Guy de Maupassant. He and Lansbury also featured in Cecil B. deMille's biblical epic *Samson and Delilah* in 1949.

In 1950, Sanders drew his greatest popular and commercial success as the acerbic, cold-blooded theatre critic Addison DeWitt, in *All About Eve*, for which he won an Academy Award for Best Supporting Actor. He then starred as Sir Brian de Bois-Guilbert in the 1952 film *Ivanhoe*, dying in a duel with Robert Taylor after professing his love for Jewish maiden Rebecca, played by Elizabeth Taylor.

Sanders went into television with the successful series *The George Sanders Mystery Theater*. He played an upper-crust English villain, G. Emory Partridge, in the 1965 *The Man From U.N.C.L.E.* episode "The Gazebo in the Maze Affair", and reprised the role later in that same year in "The Yukon Affair". He also portrayed Mr. Freeze in two episodes of the live-action *Batman* TV series which were shown in February 1966. He also appeared in the under-rated film *Trunk to Cairo* (1966) with Audie Murphy.

In 1967, Sanders voiced the malevolent Shere Khan in the Walt Disney production of *The Jungle Book*. During the production of *The Jungle Book*'s soundtrack, Sanders was unavailable to provide the singing voice for Shere Khan during the final recording of the song, "That's What Friends Are For" despite being an accomplished singer. Mellomen member Bill Lee was called in to substitute for Sanders and can be heard on the soundtrack. In the film, however, all the singing was done live and Sanders provided Khan's singing voice.

Sanders' smooth voice, urbane manner and upper-class British accent inspired Peter Sellers' character "Hercules Grytpype-Thynne" in the famous 1950s BBC radio comedy series *The Goon Show*. In 1964, Sellers and Sanders appeared together in the Pink Panther sequel *A Shot in the Dark*. In 1969, he had a supporting role in John Huston's *The Kremlin Letter*, in which his first scene showed him dressed in drag and playing piano in a snooty San Francisco gay bar. One of Sanders' final screen roles was in a 1972 feature film version of the BBC television series *Doomwatch*.

Two ghostwritten crime novels were published under his name to cash in on his fame. The first was *Crime on My Hands* (1944), written in the first person and mentioning his "Saint" and "Falcon" movies. This was followed by *Stranger at Home* in 1946. Both were actually written by female authors: the former by Craig Rice, and the latter by Leigh Brackett.

In 1958, Sanders recorded an album called *The George Sanders Touch: Songs for the Lovely Lady*. The album was released by ABC-Paramount Records, and carried lush string arrangements of romantic ballads, crooned by Sanders in a fit baritone/bass (spanning from low to middle C), including "Such is My Love", a song of Sanders' own composition. After going to great lengths, he got himself signed to sing in *South Pacific* but was overwhelmed with anxiety over the role and quickly dropped out.

He also signed on for the role of Sheridan Whiteside in the stage musical *Sherry!* (1967), based on the Kaufman Hart play *The Man Who Came to Dinner*, but found the ongoing stage production highly demanding. He quit when his wife Benita Hume discovered she had terminal bone cancer.

On October 27, 1940, Sanders married Susan Larson; they divorced in 1949. From later that year until 1954, Sanders was married to Hungarian actress Zsa Zsa Gabor (with whom he starred in the 1956 film *Death of a Scoundrel* after their divorce). On February 10, 1959, Sanders married actress Benita Hume, widow of actor Ronald Colman. She died in 1967.

His autobiography *Memoirs of a Professional Cad* was published in 1960, and gathered critical praise for its wit. Sanders suggested the title *A Dreadful Man* for his biography, which was later written by Sanders' friend Brian Aherne, and published in 1979.

Sanders's last marriage was on December 4, 1970, to Magda Gabor, the elder sister of his second wife. This marriage lasted only six weeks, after which he began drinking heavily.

In his later years, Sanders suffered from bewilderment and bouts of anger, worsened by waning health. He can be seen teetering in his last films, owing to a loss of balance. According to Aherne's biography, he also had a minor stroke. Sanders could not bear the notion of losing his health or needing help from someone else, and he became deeply depressed. At about this time, Sanders found he could no longer play his grand piano, which he dragged outside and smashed with an axe. His last girlfriend, who was Mexican and much younger than he, persuaded Sanders to sell his beloved house in Majorca, Spain, which he later bitterly regretted. From then on, he drifted.

On April 23, 1972, Sanders checked into a hotel in Castelldefels, a coastal town near Barcelona. He was found dead two days later April 25, 1972, having taken five bottles of Nembutal. Sanders was 65 years old. He left behind a suicide note, which read:

Dear World, I am leaving because I am bored. I feel I have lived long enough. I am leaving you with your worries in this sweet cesspool. Good luck.

Sanders's body was cremated, and the ashes were scattered in the English Channel. David Niven wrote in his autobiography, *The Moon's a Balloon* (1972), that in 1937 his friend Sanders had predicted he would commit suicide when he was 65.

Sanders garnered two stars on the Hollywood Walk of Fame, for motion pictures at 1636 Vine Street and for television at 7007 Hollywood Boulevard. He is mentioned in The Kinks' song "Celluloid Heroes" and his ghost makes an appearance in Clive Barker's 2001 novel *Coldheart Canyon*, as well as in the 2007 animated feature *Dante's Inferno*.

Hugh Sanders

Hugh Sanders was born March 13, 1911, in East Saint Louis, Illinois, and was an American actor. He appeared in over 200 films and television programs from 1949 to 1966.

Some of those credits include *The Magnificent Yankee* (1950), *I Was a Communist for the FBI* (1951), *The Pride of St. Louis* (1952), *Thunder Over the Plains* (1953), *The Adventures of Falcon* (1954-1955), *The Star and the Story* (1955-1956), *The Phantom Stagecoach* (1957), *The Guns of Fort Petticoat* (1957) with Audie Murphy, as the prison warden in *Jailhouse Rock* (1957), *Richard Diamond, Private Detective* (1958), *Never Steal Anything Small* (1959), *Wanted: Dead or Alive* (1958-1959), *Whispering Smith* (1961) again with Audie Murphy, *Twilight Zone* (1959-1963), *The Outer Limits* (1964), *Apache Rifles* (1964) a third appearance with Audie Murphy, *The Addams Family* (1964-1965), *Harum Scarum* (1965), *The Fugitive* (1963-1966), and *The Oscar* (1966).

He died January 9, 1966, at age 54 in Los Angeles, California.

Sandy Sanders

Sandy Sanders was born Grover S. Sanders May 23, 1919, in Deaf Smith County, Texas, and was an American actor. He appeared in seventy-four films and television programs from 1947 to 1978.

Some of those credits include *Smoky River Serenade* (1947), *Riders of the Whistling Pines* (1949), *Flying Disc Man from Mars* (1950), *The Range Rider* (1951-1952), *Hopalong Cassidy* (1952), *Phantom from Space* (1953), *The Cisco Kid* (1953-1956), *The Restless Gun* (1958), *Whispering Smith* (1961) with Audie Murphy, *The Virginian* (1963), *The Tattooed Police Horse* (1964), and *The Norseman* (1978).

He died January 2, 2002, at age 82 in Santa Barbara, California.

Erskin Sanford

Erskin Sanford was born November 19, 1885 in Trinidad, Colorado. He appeared in thirty-eight films and television programs from 1940 to 1952.

He was a character actor, associated for fifteen years with the Theatre Guild, which he left in 1936 to join Orson Welles' Mercury Players. Seventeen year old Welles had first been introduced to Sanford backstage, much taken with his performance in *Mr. Pim Passes By*, Welles' first exposure to the stage, in his hometown, Kenosha, Wisconsin. After congratulating Sanford on an 'admirable performance', he was strongly encouraged to choose the performing arts as a career path for himself.

He did so and some of his credits include *Citizen Kane* (1941), *The Magnificent Ambersons* (1942), *A Tree Grows in Brooklyn* (1945), *The Best Years of Our Lives* (1946), *Texas, Brooklyn & Heaven* (1948) with Audie Murphy, *Wake of the Red Witch* (1948), *The Woman on Pier 13* (1949), *Sierra* (1950) again with Audie Murphy, *The Company She Keeps* (1941), and *My Son John* (1952).

He died July 7, 1969, at age 83 in Los Angeles, California.

John Saxon

Audie Murphy with John Saxon in *Posse from Hell*, and John with David Williams in 2011

John Saxon was born Carmine Orrico August 5, 1935 in Brooklyn, New York, and is an American actor who has worked on over 200 projects during the span of sixty years.

Saxon is most known for his work in horror films such as *A Nightmare on Elm Street* (1984) and *Black Christmas* (1974), both of which feature Saxon as a policeman in search of the killer. He is also known for his role as Roper in the 1973 film *Enter the Dragon*, in which he starred with Bruce Lee and Jim Kelly. He also has a black belt in Karate.

He attended New Utrecht High School and graduated in 1953 with Stanley Abramson. He then studied acting with famous acting coach Stella Adler and broke into films in the mid-1950s, playing teenage roles. According to Robert Hofler's 2005 biography, *The Man Who Invented Rock Hudson: The Pretty Boys and Dirty Deals of Henry Willson*, agent Willson saw Saxon's picture on the cover of a detective magazine and immediately contacted the boy's family in Brooklyn. He brought the sixteen-year-old Orrico to Hollywood and renamed him Saxon.

After his first sizable role, as a juvenile delinquent in *Running Wild* (1955), and he supported Esther Williams and George Nader in *The Unguarded Moment* (1956). Billing in advertising was "Co-starring the exciting new personality JOHN SAXON".

In his early career, Saxon worked in many notable films and television programs such as *The Unforgiven* (1960) with Audie Murphy, *The Plunderers* (1960), *Posse from Hell* (1961) again with Audie Murphy, *Mr. Hobbs Takes a Vacation* (1962), *Blood Beast from Outer Space* (1965), *The Appaloosa* (1966) for which he won a Golden Globe Best Supporting Actor nomination, *Winchester 73* (1967), *Death of a Gunfighter* (1969), *The Sixth Sense* (1972), *Rod Serling's Night Gallery* (1972), twenty-nine episodes as Dr. Theodore Stuart in *The Bold Ones: The New Doctors* (1969-1972), *Joe Kidd* (1972), *Kung Fu* (1972), *Planet Earth* (1974), *Gunsmoke* (1965-1975), *Strange New World* (1975), *The Swiss Conspiracy* (1976), *The Six Million Dollar Man* (1974-1976), *The Bionic Woman* (1976), *Starsky and Hutch* (1976), *The New Adventures of Wonder Woman* (1976), *Moonshine County Express* (1977), *Greatest Heroes of the Bible* (1978), *The Electric Horseman* (1979), *Battle Beyond the Stars* (1980), *Prisoners of the Lost Universe* (1983), *Hardcastle and McCormick* (1983), *Magnum, P.I.* (1984), *Dynasty* (1982-1984), *Another World* (1985-1986), thirty-two episodes as Tony Cumson in *Falcon Crest* (1982-1988), *My Mom's a Werewolf* (1989), *Gengis Khan* (1992), *Maximum Force* (1992), *Beverly Hills Cop III* (1994), *Melrose Place* (1994-1995), *From Dusk Till Dawn* (1996), *Kung Fu: The Legend Continues* (1996), *Final Payback* (2001), *The Road Home* (2003), *CSI: Crime Scene Investigation* (2005), *Masters of Horror* (2006), *Old Dogs* (2009), *War Wolves* (2009), *The Extra* (2011), and *Bring Me the Head of Lance Henriksen* (2012).

He reprised his *A Nightmare on Elm Street* (1984) role in *A Nightmare on Elm Street 3: Dream Warriors* (1987) and *Wes Craven's New Nightmare* (1994) as he played himself in a dual role.

He has one son, Antonio Saxon, with his former wife Mary Ann Saxon. He is currently married to Gloria Martel.

He was a special guest on the Creation Entertainment - Weekend of Horrors 2010 on May 21, 2010 in Los Angeles and at the Memphis Film Festival June 1-3, 2011.

I talked with him at the Memphis Film Festival about working with Audie Murphy and he told me he really enjoyed working with Audie and that he thought Audie was a very under-rated actor, much better than he was given credit for. He said he wished he had had the opportunity to work with him again, but it never worked out.

Gia Scala

Gia Scala with Audie Murphy in *Ride a Crooked Trail*

Gia Scala was born Giovanna Scoglio in Liverpool, England, March 3, 1934, and was an English-born actress and model of Italian and Irish descent.

Scala lived in Rome, and moved to the United States at age fourteen where she studied and worked in New York City. She graduated from Bayside High School in Queens, New York. For a time she was undecided on what to do next. She worked in New York as a filing clerk for an insurance company and as a reservation clerk for Scandinavian Airlines.

Scala studied acting at night and made appearances on some radio shows and television quiz shows. At the end of 1954 an agent had her tested for the role of Mary Magdalene in a movie which was to be made called *The Gallileans*. She did not get the part but was signed to contracts by both Universal Studios and Columbia Pictures in Hollywood. Using the stage name "Gia Scala", she made her motion picture debut in 1955. This came in *All That Heaven Allows* with Jane Wyman and Rock Hudson.

However, personal problems plagued her. In 1958, she attempted suicide. Later that same year, she became an American citizen. She landed roles in *Tip on a Dead Jockey* and *The Garment Jungle* in 1957 and *The Tunnel of Love* in 1958. The latter featured Richard Widmark and Doris Day. Critics acclaimed her performance as a labor organizer in *The Garment Jungle*. She also appeared in *Ride a Crooked Trail* (1958) with Audie Murphy.

Scala received recognition for her performance as "Anna" in the 1961 film *The Guns of Navarone*, starring Gregory Peck.

She made frequent appearances on American television shows during the 1960s. Scala co-starred with William Shatner in a 1960 *Alfred Hitchcock Presents* episode entitled "Mother, May I Go Out to Swim?" and with Christopher Lee in a 1964 *Alfred Hitchcock Hour* episode, "The Sign of Satan", as well as in other series such as *Convoy* (1965), *The Rogues* (1964-1965), *Voyage to the Bottom of the Sea* (1965), *Twelve O'Clock High* (1965), Tarzan (1967), and *It Takes a Thief* (1969).

Her marriage to actor/stockbroker Don Burnett ended in divorce in 1970.

Having British citizenship because of her birth, she moved to work in film in England but her troubles only escalated. Suffering from severe emotional problems, aggravated by alcohol, she made another unsuccessful suicide attempt before returning to Hollywood. Her last appearance was in *It Takes a Thief* (1969).

On the night of April 30, 1972, Scala was found dead in her Hollywood Hills home from an overdose of drugs and alcohol. She was 38 years old. Scala's death was later ruled accidental. She is interred in the Holy Cross Cemetery, Culver City.

Frank Scannell

Francis J. Scannell was born May 7, 1903 in Boston, Massachusetts, and was an American actor who appeared in 180 films and television programs from 1943 to 1976.

Some of his credits included *Whistling in Brooklyn* (1943), *Lost in a Harem* (1944), *Bud Abbott and Lou Costello in Hollywood* (1945), *Kilroy Was Here* (1947), *Texas, Brooklyn & Heaven* (1948) with Audie Murphy, *Mighty Joe Young* (1949), *The Pride of St. Louis* (1952), *The Abbott and Costello Show* (1953), *Adventures of the Texas Kid: Border Ambush* (1954), *A Lawless Street* (1955), *Decision at Sundown* (1957), *Buchanan Rides Alone* (1958), *The Gunfight at Dodge City* (1959), *The Comancheros* (1961), *Mister Ed* (1963), *The Rare Breed* (1966), *Airport* (1970), *Adam-12* (1970), and *McMillan & Wife* (1976).

He died November 29, 1989, at age 86 in Las Vegas, Nevada.

Simon Scott

Simon Scott was born Daniel Simon September 21, 1920, and was an American character actor from Monterey Park, California. He was best known for his role as Arnold Slocum on the CBS medical drama *Trapper John M.D.* (1979-1985) and as General Bronson on the ABC sitcom *McHale's Navy* (1965-1966).

Scott also had a recurring role as Chief Metcalf on the ABC series *The Mod Squad* (1968-1972).

Other notable roles over the years included *Biff Baker, U.S.A.* (1952), *Soldiers of Fortune* (1955-1956), *Man of a Thousand Faces* (1957), *No Name on the Bullet* (1959) with Audie Murphy, *Markham* (1959), *Twilight Zone* (1960), *77 Sunset Strip* (1961-1963), *The Alfred Hitchcock Hour* (1963-1964), *The Munsters* (1966), *Perry Mason* (1958-1966), *The Fugitive* (1966), *The Wild Wild West* (1966-1968), *The Sixth Sense* (1972), *The Streets of San Francisco* (1973-1974), *The Hardy Boys/Nancy Drew Mysteries* (1977), *The Return of Mod Squad* (1979), *Galactica 1980* (1980), and *Charlie's Angels* (1980).

Scott died on December 11, 1991, in Los Alamitos, California of complications of Alzheimers disease.

Vito Scotti

Vito Scotti was born Vito Giusto Scozzari January 26, 1918, and was a veteran character actor who played many roles, primarily from the late-1940s to the mid-1990s. He was known as a man of a thousand faces, for his ability to assume so many divergent roles in more than 200 screen roles, in a nearly fifty year career. He was known for his resourceful portrayals of various ethnic types. Born of Italian heritage, he was seen playing everything from a Mexican bandit and Russian doctor, to a Japanese sailor.

Though born in San Francisco in 1918, the Scotti family spent Vito's early years in Naples, Italy. By 1925, when the Scotti family returned to the U.S., his mother was a diva in the stage theatre in New York. It was in the Italian theatre, that Scotti developed his gift for farce, which was modeled after the Commedia dell'arte style of the Italian theatre. He worked the night club circuit as a stand-up magician and performed pantomime, finally breaking into movies and television by the early 1950s. His screen debut came in an uncredited role, playing a 'Mexican youth' in *Illegal Entry* (1949), with Howard Duff and George Brent.

In the next few years, after a dozen screen roles, by 1953, Scotti replaced J. Carroll Naish as Luigi Basco, an Italian Immigrant who ran a Chicago antique store, on the television version of the radio show *Life with Luigi*. Five years later he portrayed another ethnic character, *Rama from India* (among other characters) in the live-action segment in "Gunga Ram" on the Andy Devine children's show, *Andy's Gang*. In 1955, Scotti played the *antagonist* against Froggy the Gremlin on *Andy's Gang*.

Best remembered by audiences in hundreds of film/TV roles, notably as baker Nazorine in *The Godfather* (1972), and most notably as the scene stealing cook, who surprised an agitated Debbie Reynolds, in *How Sweet It Is!* (1967). In the pivotal classic comedy scene, Scotti grabs a flustered Reynolds and plants a kiss on her midriff.

He also played mad scientist Dr. Boris Balinkoff (twice) and a stereotypical Japanese sailor on *Gilligan's Island* (1965-1966). Other notable roles include "The Flight" episode of *Suspicion* (1957) with Audie Murphy, *Twilight Zone* (1960-1962), *My Favorite Martian* (1963-1964), *The Addams Family* (1964-1965), *The Munsters* (1965-1966), *Warning Shot* (1967), *The Flying Nun* (1967-1969), *Get Smart* (1965-1970), *Gunsmoke* (1965-1970), *McMillan & Wife* (1971-1974), *Get Christie Love!* (1974), *Adam-12* (1974), *Halloween with the New Addams Family* (1977), *Baretta* (1977), *Young Maverick* (1979), *The Nude Bomb* (1980), *Small & Frye* (1983), *Who's the Boss?* (1985-1988), *Loaded Weapon 1* (1993), and *Mad About You* (1995).

He also lent his voice to the Italian Cat in the Walt Disney animated film *The Aristocats* (1970).

His last screen performance was as the 'Manager at Vesuvios', in 1995's John Travolta comedy, *Get Shorty*.

Scotti died of lung cancer at the Motion Picture and Television Country House and Hospital in Woodland Hills, California on June 5, 1996. Mr. Scotti was interred at Hollywood Forever Cemetery, along with his first wife Irene, in the Abbey of the Psalms Mausoleum. Vito Scotti was survived by his daughter Carmen Scozzari (who today works for LAUSD as a Special Education Assistant in the West San Fernando Valley), his son Ricardo, a brother Jerry, and his widow Beverly.

In addition to his accomplishments as an actor, he was highly regarded as a chef. Vito loved cooking, especially the recipes of his beloved mother and grandmother. Two generations of Hollywood's top names always left his dinner parties raving about the food and wine.

He was married for many years, to Irene A. Scozzari, until her death at age 54, on April 15, 1979. Scotti remarried a woman named Beverly, and they were married until his death. Scotti was a dedicated fundraiser for the 'Carmen Fund', set up by the Joaquin Miller High School Parents Guild, to assist the school's special-needs students in obtaining medical treatment. The fund was named for the Scotti's daughter, one of the first patients to undergo pioneering spinal implant surgery.

Pilar Seurat

Audie Murphy with Pilar Seurat in *Battle at Bloody Beach*

Pilar Seurat was born Rita Hernandez in Manila, Philippines, July 25, 1938. Pilar Seurat moved to Los Angeles in her childhood and started out as a dancer in Ken Murray's "Blackouts" troupe.

In the late 1950s she started her acting career in several guest television appearances, and was often considered at the top of the list whenever a part for an Asian woman needed to be filled.

Some of her credits include *Hawaiian Eye* (1959), *Maverick* (1960), *The Young Savages* (1961), *Battle at Bloody Beach* (1961) with Audie Murphy, *Seven Women from Hell* (1961), *Naked City* (1962), *The Alfred Hitchcock Hour* (1963), *Rawhide* (1964), *The Fugitive* (1966), *Star Trek* (1967), *Mannix* (1969), *The F.B.I.* (1965-1970), *O'Hara, U.S. Treasury* (1971), and *Bonanza* (1972).

Off screen she used the name Pilar Cerveris after marrying her second husband, Don Cerveris. She died June 2, 2001, in Los Angeles due to lung cancer, at the age of 62.

Della Sharman

Della Paola Sharman was born June 14, 1936, in San Diego, California, and was an American actress. She appeared in twenty films and television programs from 1958 to 1964.

Some of those credits include *Senior Prom* (1958), *Father Knows Best* (1959), *The Detectives* (1960), *Five Guns to Tombstone* (1960), *Whispering Smith* (1961) with Audie Murphy, *Dr. Kildare* (1961-1964), and *The Virginian* (1964).

Anabel Shaw

Anabel Shaw was born Marjorie Henshaw June 7, 1921 in Oakland, California. She appeared in twenty-six films and television programs from 1944 to 1971.

A gray eyed ash blonde, she was the second daughter of Ransom Henshaw, a real estate broker, and Eleanor Earl Henshaw. After grammar school she was educated at the private Marlborough School for Girls. Even then her thoughts were on dramatics, but the Marlborough School frowned on any of its young charges who thought of acting as a possible profession. For well brought up young ladies of the time, drama was respectable only in an amateur or academic setting. At first her parents and older sister Jane objected, too. With a blue blood lineage that included her grandfather, Guy Chaffee Earl, who was a prominent attorney, State Senator and Regent of the University of California, she was a top drawer debutante when she made her debut in Los Angeles.

Despite the fact that Los Angeles high society families of the time were distinctly allof from Hollywood, Marjorie committed herself to a film career. After a brief stint at Warner Brothers, where she tested with every new male hopeful, but did no acting herself, Anabel was dropped. "Of course, I was bitterly disappointed", she recalled, "For I had been so repeatedly optimistic that tomorrow would be my lucky day to be called in for some actual work before the camera. So, in the meantime I enrolled in dramatics. Then my parents visited San Francisco and while there I enrolled at the University of California at Berkeley, graduating with a B.A. degree and majoring in short story writing. It was a wonderful experience attending that university as both my parents were alumni and it was a sentimental thrill to follow in their footsteps".

The agent who had arranged her test at Warner Brothers showed it to Paramount who signed her in 1944. She then worked sporadically in such films as *Here Come the Waves* (1944), *Home, Sweet Homicide* (1946), *Bulldog Drummond Strikes Back* (1947), *In This Corner* (1948), *City Across the River* (1949), *Gun Crazy* (1950), *The Revlon Mirror Theater* (1953), *The Lone Wolf* (1955), and *To Hell and Back* (1955) with Audie Murphy.

Anabel had one memorable scene in *To Hell and Back* when Murphy is in the hospital recovering from wounds and is visited by one of his buddies (Jack Kelly). Playing a nurse in an Army hospital she gives her lines plenty of bite. Kelly refers to her as "Sir" throughout their exchanges and she neatly displays a sense of humor.

A few more roles followed with *At Gunpoint* (1955), *Alfred Hitchcock Presents* (1957), *The Real McCoys* (1958), *26 Men* (1958), and after a thirteen year break she appeared in *The Mephisto Waltz* (1971).

She died April 16, 2010, at age 88 in Santa Barbara, California.

Joanne Shields

No biographical information could be found for Joanne Sheilds, but she did appear as one of Mamie's girls in *A Time for Dying* (1969) with Audie Murphy.

Randy Shields

No biographical information could be found for Randy Shields but he did appear in two films, one television mini-series, and two television programs. Those credits were *A Time for Dying* (1969) with Audie Murphy, *Captains and the Kings* (1976), *Quincy M.E.* (1977), *Fame* (1983), and *Beverly Hills Brats* (1989).

Jim Sheppard

Audie Murphy with Jim Sheppard in *Whispering Smith*

James "Jim" Sheppard was born in 1937, and was a stuntman who also worked as an actor.

Sheppard was the regular stunt double for western star Audie Murphy and doubled him in *Seven Ways From Sundown* (1960), *Posse from Hell* (1961), *Battle at Bloody Beach (1961)*, *Six Black Horses* (1962), *Showdown* (1963), *Bullet for a Badman* (1964), *Apache Rifles* (1964), *Arizona Raiders* (1965), *Gunpoint* (1966), *40 Guns to Apache Pass* (1967), and *A Time for Dying* (1969).

He appeared as an actor with Audie Murphy in *The Wild and the Innocent* (1959), *Posse from Hell* (1961), and six episodes as Deputy Jim in *Whispering Smith* (1961). Other acting roles included *Zane Grey Theater* (1961), *The Big Valley* (1966), as Tom McLowery in *Hour of the Gun* (1967), *Hondo* (1967), and *Gunsmoke* (1970).

Further stunt work includes the western *Major Dundee* (1965), the drama *The War Lord* (1965), the crime drama *Harper* (1966), the western *Stagecoach* (1966), the western *Hour of the Gun* (1967), the science fiction television series *Star Trek* (1967), the science fiction film *Planet of the Apes* (1968), the western *The Wild Bunch* (1969), the drama *The Wind and the Lion* (1975), and the western *The Master Gunfighter* (1975).

Sheppard died on August 18, 1977, during the filming of the western *Comes a Horseman*. He was dragged to death behind a horse while filming in Westcliffe, Colorado.

Keiko Shima

Audie Murphy with Keiko Shima in *Joe Butterfly*

No biographical information could be found for Keiko Shima but she did appear as 'Chieko' in *Joe Butterfly* (1957) with Audie Murphy.

Chizo Shimazaki

No biographical information could be found for Chizo Shimizaki but she did appear as 'Mother' in *Joe Butterfly* (1957) with Audie Murphy.

Shinpei Shimazaki

No biographical information could be found for Shinpei Shimizaki but he did appear as 'Boku' in *Joe Butterfly* (1957) with Audie Murphy.

Henry Silva

Henry Silva with Audie Murphy in *Ride a Crooked Trail*

Henry Silva was born in 1927, and is an American film and television actor. Silva was born in Brooklyn, New York of Sicilian and Spanish descent.

He grew up in Harlem and quit school when he was thirteen years old to attend drama classes, supporting himself as a dishwasher and waiter in a Manhattan hotel. By 1955, Silva felt ready to audition for the Actors Studio. He was one of five students chosen out of more than 2,500 applicants.

When the Studio staged Michael V. Gazzo's play, *A Hatful of Rain* as a classroom project, it proved so successful that it was presented on Broadway, with students Ben Gazzara, Shelley Winters, Harry Guardino, Tony Franciosa, and Silva in key roles. Silva also appeared in the play's film version in 1957.

In Hollywood, he played a succession of villains in films including *The Tall T* (1957), *The Bravados* (1958), *Ride a Crooked Trail* (1958) with Audie Murphy, *Green Mansions* (1959), *Johnny Cool* (1963), and the original *The Manchurian Candidate* (1962). He was one of the eleven casino robbers in the 1960 Rat Pack caper film *Ocean's 11*.

He had a comic role as one of the stepbrothers in the 1960 Jerry Lewis film *Cinderfella*, a parody of Cinderella with Lewis in the title role, and appeared in starring roles in several filmed episodes of *The Outer Limits* (1963-1964), a science-fiction anthology television series in the United States.

Other television roles included an episode of *Rod Serling's Night Gallery* (1971) and the episode "The Enemies" from the first season of *Voyage to the Bottom of the Sea* (1965).

In 1965 an Italian film producer made Silva an offer to star as a hero for a change and he moved his family overseas. Silva's turning-point picture was a spaghetti western, *The Hills Run Red*, which made him a hot box-office commodity in Spain, Italy, Germany, and France.

Between 1966 and 1977 he starred or co-starred in at least twenty-five movies, the majority of whose where mafia tales, spaghetti westerns or police tales of some sort, where he normally played the villain or hitman, or the dark hero, or a combination of the two.

Returning to the United States in the mid 1970s, he co-starred with Frank Sinatra in *Contract on Cherry Street* (1977), then signed on as Buck Rogers' evil adversary Killer Kane in *Buck Rogers in the 25th Century* (1979).

He appeared as a drug-addicted hitman in Burt Reynolds' *Sharky's Machine* (1981), the 'heavy' in Chuck Norris' movie *Code of Silence* (1985), the villainous CIA agent Kurt Zagon in Steven Seagal's debut, *Above the Law* (1988); as a sinister mob hitman in *Dick Tracy* (1990), as the voice of the supervillain Bane in *Batman: The Animated Series* (1994) and *The New Batman Adventures* (1998) and as the sorrowful and doomed crime boss Ray Vargo in *Ghost Dog: The Way of the Samurai* (1999).

His last appearance to date was in the remake of *Ocean's Eleven* (2001).

Frank Silvera

Frank Silvera with Audie Murphy in *The Cimarron Kid*

Frank Alvin Silvera was born July 24, 1914, and was an actor and theatrical director. Silvera was born in Kingston, Jamaica to a Spanish Jewish father and Jamaican mother. His family later immigrated to the United States, settling in Boston where Silvera attended English High School and Northeastern Law School. Silvera later studied acting at the Actors Studio.

Due to his light complexion, Silvera was cast in a wide variety of ethnic roles in films, and was cast without regards to his color in the theater. He played the father of Ben Gazzara and Anthony Franciosa on Broadway in Michael V. Gazzo's *A Hatful of Rain* (a role portrayed by Lloyd Nolan on screen).

His first film appearance was in *The Cimarron Kid* (1952) with Audie Murphy.

Until the 1960s, Silvera played "white" characters on Broadway, such as his Tony-nominated performance as the father Monsieur Duval in *The Lady of the Camellias* in 1963. He threw off color-blind casting in 1965, when he financed his own production of *The Amen Corner* by the African American writer James Baldwin. He was the

Founder of *The Theatre of Being*, a Los Angeles-based theater dedicated to helping black actors get a foothold in show business.

In films and on television, he was also cast without regards to his color, though mostly as Latinos, even appearing as a Polynesian in the 1962 version of *Mutiny on the Bounty*, starring Marlon Brando, with whom Silvera co-starred in *Viva Zapata!* (1952), *One-Eyed Jacks* (1961), and *The Appaloosa* (1966) as Mexican characters.

He appeared in two Stanley Kubrick-directed films, *Fear and Desire* (1953) and *Killer's Kiss* (1955) as either "white" or racially indeterminate. He also appeared as a Mexican bandit in the 1967 Martin Ritt Western classic, *Hombre*, based on the Elmore Leonard novel.

Some more roles included *Wanted: Dead or Alive* (1958), *Heller in Pink Tights* (1960), *Twilight Zone* (1962), *Toys in the Attic* (1963), *The Greatest Story Ever Told* (1965), *The St. Valentine's Day Massacre* (1967), *Guns of the Magnificent Seven* (1969), and fourteen episodes as Don Sebastian Montoya in *The High Chaparral* (1967-1970).

At a lecture at the University of Maryland, while appearing in a production of *King Lear*, he told of his attempt to get a part in a TV drama as a black elevator operator. The producer rejected him as being too light-skinned. He left the producer's office, and then returned. "Am I light enough to play one of the white parts?" He got the job.

On June 11, 1970, Silvera was electrocuted while attempting to repair the garbage disposal unit in his kitchen sink. A Navy veteran of World War II, Silvera was buried with honors at Long Island National Cemetery in Farmingdale, New York.

Jay Silverheels

Jay Silverheels with Audie Murphy in *Drums Across the River*

Jay Silverheels was born May 26, 1912, and was a Canadian Mohawk First Nations actor. He was well known for his role as Tonto, the faithful American Indian companion of *The Lone Ranger* (1949-1957) in the long-running American television series.

Silverheels was born Harold J. Smith on the Six Nations of the Grand River First Nation, near Brantford, Ontario, Canada, the son of a Canadian Mohawk Chief and military officer, A.G.E. Smith. Silverheels excelled in athletics and lacrosse as a boy before leaving home to travel around North America, competing in boxing and wrestling tournaments.

In the 1930s he played indoor lacrosse under the name of Harry Smith with the Rochester, NY "Iroquois" of the North American Amateur Lacrosse Association. He lived for a time in Buffalo, New York. In 1938 Silverheels placed second in the middleweight section of the Golden Gloves tournament.

Silverheels began working in motion pictures as an extra and stunt man in 1937. During the early years of his screen career, he was billed variously as Harold Smith or Harry Smith, and appeared in low-budget features, westerns, and serials. He adopted his screen name from the nickname he had had as a speedy lacrosse player.

From the late 1940s he played in more prestigious pictures, including *Captain from Castile* (1947) starring Tyrone Power, *Key Largo* with Humphrey Bogart, (1948), *Lust for Gold* with Glenn Ford (1949), *Broken Arrow* (1950) with James Stewart, *War Arrow* (1953) with Maureen O'Hara, Jeff Chandler, and Noah Beery, Jr., *Drums Across the River* (1954) and *Walk the Proud Land* (1956) with Audie Murphy, *Alias Jesse James* (1959) with Bob Hope, and *Indian Paint* (1964) with Johnny Crawford.

He made a brief appearance in *True Grit* (1969) as a condemned criminal about to be executed. He played a substantial role as John Crow in *Santee* (1973), starring Glenn Ford. One of his last roles was a wise white-haired chief in *The Man Who Loved Cat Dancing* (1973).

Silverheels achieved his greatest fame as the Lone Ranger's friend Tonto. Being irreplaceable as the Lone Ranger's best friend he subsequently also appeared in movies *The Lone Ranger* (1956) as well as in *The Lone Ranger and the Lost City of Gold* (1958). He also appeared as Tonto in *Alias Jesse James* (1959).

Following the end of *The Lone Ranger* television series, Silverheels found himself firmly typecast as an American Indian hero. Eventually Silverheels had to work as a salesman to supplement his acting income.

Simultaneously he began to publish poetry inspired by his youth on the Six Nations Indian Reserve and appeared on television reciting his works.

In 1966, he guest-starred as John Tallgrass in the short-lived ABC comedy/western series *The Rounders*, with Ron Hayes, Patrick Wayne, and Chill Wills.

Despite the typecasting, Silverheels often poked fun at his character in later years. In 1969, he appeared as Tonto in a comedy sketch on *The Tonight Show with Johnny Carson*, seeking new employment away from the Lone Ranger. The sketch was featured on the 1973 record album *Here's Johnny: Magic Moments From The Tonight Show*. "My name is Tonto. I hail from Toronto and I speak Esperanto".

In 1970 he appeared in a commercial for Chevrolet as an Indian chief who rescues two lost hunters who ignored his advice in that model year's Chevy Blazer with the William Tell Overture playing in the background.

Silverheels also spoofed his Tonto character in a famous Stan Freberg Jeno's Pizza Rolls TV commercial opposite Clayton Moore, as well as in *The Phynx* (1970), opposite John Hart, both actors having played *The Lone Ranger* in the original TV series.

Of the near 200 joint ventures Silverheels made with Clayton Moore, the actors co-starred in just four features where they did NOT play Tonto and The Lone Ranger: *Perils of Nyoka* (1942), *The Cowboy and the Indians* (1949), *Cyclone Fury* (1951), and *The Black Dakotas* (1954).

Among his later appearances were an episode of *The Brady Bunch* (1971), as an Indian chief who befriends the Brady's in the Grand Canyon, and his final appearance in an episode of the short-lived *Dusty's Trail* (1974), starring Bob Denver.

In the early 1960s, Silverheels supported the Indian Actors Workshop, as an institution where American Indian actors refine their acting skills in Echo Park, California. Today the workshop is firmly established.

Silverheels raised, bred and raced horses in his spare time. Once, when asked about possibly running Tonto's famous Pinto horse Scout in a race, Jay laughed off the idea: "Heck, *I* can outrun Scout!"

He married Mary Diroma in 1945, and was the father of two boys and a girl. The marriage lasted the rest of his life.

Jay Silverheels died from complications of a stroke in March 5, 1980, at age 67, in Calabasas, California. He was cremated at Chapel of the Pines Crematory. His ashes were returned home to Six Nations Indian Reserve.

In 1993, Silverheels was inducted into the Hall of Great Western Performers at the National Cowboy & Western Heritage Museum in Oklahoma City, Oklahoma. He was named to the Western New York Entertainment Hall of Fame, and his portrait hangs in Buffalo, New York's Shea's Buffalo Theatre.

Eddie Little Sky

Eddie Little Sky, also known as Edward Little was born August 15, 1926, and was a Native American actor of the Oglala Sioux tribe. He had parts in thiry-six feature films and over sixty television shows, mainly westerns in the role of a Native American. He was one of the first Native American actors to play Indian roles and is best remembered for his performance as *Black Eagle* in the 1970 film *A Man Called Horse*.

Little Sky was born as Edsel Wallace Little on the Pine Ridge Indian Reservation in Shannon County, South Dakota to Oglala Sioux parents Edsel Wallace Little, Sr. and Wileminna Colhoff. He attended the Holy Rosary

Indian Mission School as a child. After leaving the United States Navy where he had served in the Pacific during World War II, he began working the rodeo circuit as a bull rider and bareback rider.

Following his work on the film *Chief Crazy Horse* (1955), Audie Murphy encouraged Little Sky to become a professional actor; thus Little Sky, along with Jay Silverheels and Chief Dan George became one of the first Native Americans to play Indian roles in films.

Hollywood normally used white actors wearing black wigs and dark make-up to play the parts of Indians, however, Little Sky had numerous roles in many Western television series such as *Gunsmoke* (1958-1973), *The Rifleman* (1959), *The Virginian* (1966-1971), *Bonanza* (1972), *Daniel Boone* (1965-1969), and *The High Chaparral* (1968).

Probably his most remembered television role was as a native witch doctor in four episodes of *Gilligan's Island* (1964-1967).

He also played in many films such as *Heller in Pink Tights* (1960), *Hell Bent for Leather* (1960) with Audie Murphy, *The Light in the Forest* (1958), *The Hallelujah Trail* (1965), *Paint Your Wagon* (1969), *Duel at Diablo* (1966), *Breakheart Pass* (1975), but he is chiefly remembered for his performance as *Black Eagle* in the 1970 film *A Man Called Horse* which starred Irish actor Richard Harris.

His final appearance was in an episode of *Fantasy Island* (1979). Upon his retirement from the film industry in the late 1970s, he worked as director of the Oglala Sioux Tribal Parks and Recreation Authority. He was married to Native American actress Dawn Little Sky, by whom he had a daughter, Prairie Rose Little Sky.

He died on September 5, 1997, at age 71 in Pennington County, South Dakota from undisclosed causes. He was interred at the Little Wound Family cemetery in Oglala, South Dakota.

Everett Sloane

Audie Murphy with Everett Sloane in *The Gunrunners*

Everett Sloane was born October 1, 1909, and was an American stage, film and television actor, songwriter, and theatre director. Born to a Jewish family in Manhattan, New York, Sloane attended the University of Pennsylvania before dropping out in order to join a theater company, but he stopped acting and became a runner on Wall Street after a number of negative stage reviews. After the stock market crash in 1929, he decided to return to the theater.

Sloane eventually joined Orson Welles's Mercury Theatre, and acted in Welles's films in roles such as *Citizen Kane*'s Bernstein in 1941 and *The Lady from Shanghai*'s Arthur Bannister in 1948. He was memorable as a hired assassin in Renaissance Italy opposite Welles's Cesare Borgia in *Prince of Foxes* (1949).

Sloane's Broadway theater career began with the comedy *Boy Meets Girl* in 1945 and ended with *From A to Z*, a revue for which he wrote several songs, in 1960. In between, he acted in plays such as *Native Son* (1941), *A Bell for Adano* (1944), and *Room Service* (1953), and directed the melodrama *The Dancer* (1946).

In 1957 he co-starred in the ninth episode of *Suspicion* titled "The Flight", co-starring Audie Murphy and Jack Warden. In 1958, he played Walter Brennan's role in a remake of *To Have and Have Not* called *The Gun Runners*, again with Audie Murphy.

Sloane was the voice of the title character of *The Dick Tracy Show* (1961) in 130 cartoons. He also provided character voices for the animated TV series *The Adventures of Jonny Quest* (1964).

He wrote the unused lyrics to "The Fishin' Hole", the theme song for *The Andy Griffith Show*. Sloane guest starred on the show in 1962, playing Jubal Foster in the episode "The Keeper of the Flame".

He starred as the ruthless businessman in both the film (1956) and television (1955) versions of Rod Serling's *Patterns*, and in the first season of *The Twilight Zone* (1960) guest starred in "The Fever" as the victim of a Las Vegas slot machine.

Sloane also appeared in the Disney *Zorro* series in 1957–58 as Andres Felipe Basilio, in the "Man from Spain" episodes.

Admirers of F. Scott Fitzgerald will long remember his magnificent renditions of passages from *The Great Gatsby* on the NBC program devoted to Fitzgerald in August 1955, part of the "Biography in Sound" series on great American authors.

His last appearance was in *Honey West* (1965).

Sloane committed suicide August 6, 1965, at the age of 55, reportedly depressed over oncoming blindness by glaucoma. He is buried at Angelus-Rosedale Cemetery in Los Angeles.

K.L. Smith

Kenneth Lavelle Smith was born October 26, 1922 in Oklahoma City, Oklahoma, and was an American actor. He appeared in seventy-eight films and television programs from 1953 to 1972.

Some of those credits included *Them!* (1954), *Bad Day at Black Rock* (1955), *Jailhouse Rock* (1957), the "Incident" episode of *G.E. True Theater* (2958) with Audie Murphy, *Have Gun - Will Travel* (1958-1959), *Whispering Smith* (1961) again with Audie Murphy, *The Untouchables* (1960-1963), *Roustabout* (1964), *Gilligan's Island* (1965), *Laredo* (1965-1966), *The Fugitive* (1965-1967), *Star Trek* (1968), and *The F.B.I.* (1971).

Smith retired from acting in 1971. His last appearance was in the 1972 pilot movie for the short-lived series *The Delphi Bureau*.

He died August 24, 1981, at age 58 in San Diego County, California.

Vladimir Sokoloff

Vladimir Nikolayevich Sokoloff was born in Moscow, Russian Empire, now Russia, December 26, 1889, and was a character actor with many films to his credit. He became an actor and assistant director with the Moscow Art Theatre, before immigrating to Berlin in 1923. With the rise of Nazism, he moved first to Paris in 1932, then to the United States in 1937.

He quickly found work in American films, playing characters of a wide variety of nationalities, for example, Filipino in *Back to Bataan* (1945), Greek in *Mr. Lucky* (1943), Arab in *Road to Morocco* (1942), Chinese in *Macao* (1952), and Mexican in *The Magnificent Seven* (1960). Among his better known parts are the Old Man in *The Magnificent Seven* (1960) and Anselmo in *For Whom the Bell Tolls* (1943).

Some more of his credits include *Adventures of a Ten Mark Note* (1926), *Kismet* (1931), *Queen of Atlantis* (1932), *Haunted People* (1932), *Ride a Crooked Mile* (1938), *Cloak and Dagger* (1946), *I Was a Teenage Werewolf* (1957), *Sabu and the Magic Ring* (1957), the episode "The Flight" of *Suspicion* (1957) with Audie Murphy, *Twilight for the Gods* (1958), *Monster from Green Hell* (1958), *Whispering Smith* (1961) again with Audie Murphy, and *Taras Bulba* (1962). He appeared in three episodes of *The Twilight Zone* (1961-1962): "Dust", "The Gift", and "The Mirror".

After a long career, he died of a stroke in West Hollywood, California in February 15, 1962.

Olan Soule

Audie Murphy with Olan Soule in *Hell Bent for Leather*

Olan Soule was born February 28, 1909, and was an American character actor with hundreds of credits in films, radio, commercials, television, and animation.

Born in La Harpe, Illinois to Elbert and Ann Williams Soule descendants of three *Mayflower* passengers, Olan left Illinois at the age of seven, arriving in Des Moines, Iowa. He lived there until he was seventeen and then launched his theatrical career by joining Jack Brooks' Sabula, Iowa tent show.

After leaving the tent show, Soule appeared on stage in Chicago for seven years before moving to radio in 1933, including a stint on *Chandu the Magician* (1935–36). On radio he performed for eleven years in the daytime soap opera *Bachelor's Children*, and beginning in 1943, he did lead male characters on radio's famed *The First Nighter Program* for nine years.

Listeners of *First Nighter* who met Soule in person were often surprised, since his slight 135-pound frame did not seem to match the voices he gave to his characters. From 1941 on, Soule had the role of L. William Kelly, SS-11, and the second in command of the Secret Squadron on the *Captain Midnight* radio adventure serial. He also has a regular part on "Lee Hansen's" 1970's and 1980s science fiction radio drama *Alien Worlds*.

Concluding his nine-year run on *First Nighter*, Soule moved to Hollywood, where he did films and television, building a reputation as a reliable character actor. He appeared on many TV shows such as *Ma and Pa Kettle Go to Town* (1950), *Hollywood Story* (1951), *The Day the Earth Stood Still* (1951), *Don't Bother to Knock* (1952), *My Little Margie* (1953), *Dragnet* (1954), *Cult of the Cobra* (1955), *Francis in the Navy* (1955), *This Island Earth* (1955), *Captain Midnight* (1954-1956), *Francis in the Haunted House* (1956), *Dragnet* (1952-1959), *Richard Diamond, Private Detective* (1959), *Hell Bent for Leather* (1960) with Audie Murphy, *Wanted: Dead or Alive* (1959-1961), *Whispering Smith* (1961) again with Audie Murphy, *13 West Street* (1962), *Have Gun - Will Travel* (1958-1962), *It Happened at the World's Fair* (1963), *Destry* (1964), *Twilight Zone* (1960-1964), *The Andy Griffith Show* (1962-1964), *The Addams Family* (1965), *Girl Happy* (1965), *The Cincinnati Kid* (1965), *The Fugitive* (1966), *Day of the Evil Gun* (1968), *The Computer Wore Tennis Shoes* (1969), *Dragnet 1967* (1967-1970), *Cockeyed Cowboys of Calico County* (1970), *D.A.: Conspiracy to Kill* (1971), *Hec Ramsey* (1973), *Mission: Impossible* (1973), *Adam-12* (1974), *The Towering Inferno* (1974), *Harry O* (1975), *The Apple Dumpling Gang* (1975), *The Small One* (1978), *Battlestar Galactica* (1978-1979), *Buck Rogers in the 25th Century* (1979), *Dallas* (1982), *Simon & Simon* (1983-1988), and *Homicide* (1991).

He was the only actor who performed on both the *Captain Midnight* radio and television shows.

Soule is remembered by many for providing the voice of Batman in several animated series. He first performed as the Caped Crusader on the 1968 Filmation-produced *The Batman/Superman Hour*. He reprised his role as Batman on *The New Scooby-Doo Movies* (1972), *Super Friends* (1973), *The All-New Super Friends Hour* (1977), *Challenge of the SuperFriends* (1978), *The World's Greatest Super Friends* (1979) and *Super Friends* (1980-1983). He appeared as a newscaster on the live-action *Batman* (1966) television series in "The Pharaoh's in a Rut" with his *Super Friends* successor Adam West.

Although Soule eventually gave the Batman mantle to the man who portrayed him in live-action, he continued to contribute in the *Super Friends: The Legendary Super Powers Show* (1984) and *The Super Powers Team: Galactic Guardians* (1985) series, providing the voice of Professor Martin Stein, mentor and subconscious of fledgling hero Firestorm.

On February 1, 1994, Soule died of lung cancer in Los Angeles, California. He was 84 years old. His interment was at Forest Lawn Hollywood Hills Cemetery.

Joan Staley

Joan Staley with Audie Murphy in *Gunpoint*

Joan Staley was born Joan Lynette McConchie on May 20, 1940, in Minneapolis, Minnesota and is an American actress and model. She is perhaps best known for being *Playboy* magazine's Playmate of the Month for its November 1958 issue. Her centerfold was photographed by Lawrence Schiller and Ron Vogel. According to *The Playmate Book*, she was pregnant at the time of her Playmate shoot.

Staley grew up in Los Angeles. Her parents encouraged her to learn to play the violin at a very young age. At six, she joined Peter Meremblum's Junior Symphony. This led to her first film appearance, as a child violinist in *The Emperor Waltz* (1948), starring Bing Crosby and Joan Fontaine.

Her father's business took him all over Europe, and Staley went to high school in Paris. She attended Chapman College but left shortly thereafter to pursue a show business career. She worked as a back-up singer for Sam Phillips and worked as a secretary to make ends meet while she went to casting calls.

Her breakthrough came in 1958, when a photographer sent her pictures to *Playboy*. She posed for the magazine, and ended up becoming Miss November 1958. The executives at MGM liked her look, and cast her in a series of "cheesecake" roles in films such as *Ocean's Eleven* (1960) and *Breakfast at Tiffany's* (1961).

Her first marriage to TV Director Chuck Staley was brief. They were married in the late 1950s and lived in Memphis, then moved to Los Angeles. They had a daughter, Sherrye, who was born in 1959. By the early 1960s, they were divorced.

Staley enjoyed a film and television career that lasted through the 1960s and into the early 1970s. In 1960, she appeared in NBC's sitcom *The Tab Hunter Show* In 1961, she guest starred in NBC's *The Lawless Years*, a 1920s crime drama starring James Gregory. In the 1963-1964 season, she guest starred on Phil Silvers's unsuccessful sitcom *The New Phil Silvers Show*. Staley made guest appearances on multiple episodes of popular series such as *Perry Mason* (1958-1962), *McHale's Navy* (1966), *The Virginian* (1965), *Burke's Law* (1963-1965) and *Batman* (1966). She guest starred and then became a regular as Hannah, Stu Bailey's secretary, on the final season of *77 Sunset Strip* (1959-1964), although for the first few episodes only her voice (on the telephone) was used.

In 1964, she was signed to a Universal contract and cast as a regular on the short-lived McHale's Navy spin-off *Broadside* with Kathleen Nolan. In 1966 she appeared opposite Don Knotts in *The Ghost and Mr. Chicken*. That year she also appeared in *Gunpoint* (1966) with Audie Murphy. In the same year Staley suffered a horseback riding accident; she stopped working in films after that, and concentrated on television, like *Rango* (1967), *Mission: Impossible* (1967), *Adam-12* (1969-1972), and *Dallas* (1982).

She married again, in 1967, to Dale Sheets, an executive with Universal Pictures; they had three children together. Between her and Dale, they had seven children altogether.

Today, Staley lives with Sheets in Southern California, where she is active in consumer affairs. Her granddaughter-in-law is Donna Perry, the Miss November 1994 Playboy Playmate.

Lionel Stander

Lionel Jay Stander was born January 11, 1908, and was an American actor in films, radio, theater, and television. Lionel Stander was born in The Bronx, New York, to Russian Jewish immigrants, the first of three children. According to newspaper interviews with Stander, as a teenager he appeared in the 1926 silent film *Men of Steel*, perhaps as an extra; he is not listed in the credits. During his one year at the University of North Carolina at Chapel Hill, he appeared in a student production of The Muse and the Movies: A Comedy of Greenwich Village.

Stander's professional acting career began in 1928, as Cop and First Fairy in Him by E.E. Cummings at the Provincetown Playhouse. He claimed that he got the roles because one of them required shooting craps, which he did well, and a friend in the company volunteered him. He appeared in a series of short-lived plays through the early 1930s, including *The House Beautiful*, which Dorothy Parker famously derided as "the play lousy".

In 1932, Stander landed his first credited film role in the Warner-Vitaphone short feature *In the Dough*, with Fatty Arbuckle and Shemp Howard. He made several other shorts, the last being *The Old Grey Mayor* with Bob Hope in 1935. That year, he was cast in a feature, Ben Hecht's *The Scoundrel* with Noël Coward.

He moved to Hollywood and was signed a contract with Columbia Pictures. Stander was in a string of films over the next three years, appearing most notably in Frank Capra's *Mr. Deeds Goes to Town* (1936) with Gary Cooper, playing Archie Goodwin in *Meet Nero Wolfe* (1936), and *The League of Frightened Men* (1937), and in *A Star Is Born* (1937) with Janet Gaynor and Fredric March.

Stander's distinctive rumbling voice, tough-guy demeanor, and talent with accents made him a popular radio actor. In the 1930s and 1940s he was on the *Eddie Cantor Show*, Bing Crosby's KMH show, the *Lux Radio Theater* production of *A Star Is Born*, *The Fred Allen Show*, the *Mayor of the Town* series with Lionel Barrymore and Agnes Moorehead, *Kraft Music Hall* on NBC, *Stage Door Canteen* on CBS, the *Lincoln Highway Radio Show* on NBC, and *The Jack Paar Show*, among others. In 1941, he starred in a short-lived radio show called *The Life of Riley* on CBS, no relation to the radio, film, and television character later made famous by William Bendix. Stander played the role of Spider Schultz in both Harold Lloyd's 1936 film *The Milky Way* and its 1946 remake starring Danny Kaye, *The Kid from Brooklyn*. He was a regular on Danny Kaye's zany comedy-variety radio show on CBS (1946–1947), playing himself as "just the elevator operator" amidst the antics of Kaye, future *Our Miss Brooks* star Eve Arden, and bandleader Harry James.

Strongly liberal and pro-labor, Stander espoused a variety of social and political causes, and was a founding member of the Screen Actors Guild. At a SAG meeting held during a 1937 studio technicians' strike, he told the assemblage of 2000 members, "With the eyes of the whole world on this meeting, will it not give the Guild a black eye if its members continue to cross picket lines?" Stander also supported the Conference of Studio Unions in its fight against the Mob-influenced International Alliance of Stage Employees (IATSE).

Also in 1937, Ivan F. Cox, a deposed officer of the San Francisco longshoremen's union, sued Stander and a host of others, including union leader Harry Bridges, actors Fredric March, Franchot Tone, Mary Astor, James Cagney, Jean Muir, and director William Dieterle. The charge, according to *Time* magazine, was "conspiring to propagate Communism on the Pacific Coast, causing Mr. Cox to lose his job".

In 1938, Columbia Pictures head Harry Cohn allegedly called Stander "a Red son of a bitch" and threatened a $100,000 fine against any studio that renewed his contract. Despite critical acclaim for his performances, Stander's film work dropped off drastically. After appearing in fifteen films in 1935 and 1936, he was in only six in 1937 and 1938. Then he was in just six films from 1939 through 1943, none made by major studios, the most notable being *Guadalcanal Diary* (1943).

Stander was among the first group of Hollywood actors to be subpoenaed before the House Un-American Activities Committee (HUAC) in 1940 for supposed Communist activities. At a grand jury hearing in Los Angeles in August 1940—the transcript of which was shortly released to the press—John R. Leech, the self-described former "chief functionary" of the Communist Party in Los Angeles, named Stander as a CP member, along with more than fifteen other Hollywood notables, including Franchot Tone, Humphrey Bogart, James Cagney, Clifford Odets, and Budd Schulberg. Stander subsequently forced himself into the grand jury hearing, and the district attorney cleared him of the allegations.

After that, Stander was blacklisted from TV and radio. He did appear in some films such as *The Sin of Harold Diddlebock* (1947), *Call Northside 777* (1948), *Texas, Brooklyn & Heaven* (1948) with Audie Murphy, *Two Gals and a Guy* (1951), and *St. Benny the Dip* (1951).

After that, Stander's acting career went into a free fall. He worked as a stockbroker on Wall Street, a journeyman stage actor, a corporate spokesman, even a New Orleans Mardi Gras king. He didn't return to Broadway till 1961 and to film in 1963, in the low-budget *The Moving Finger*, although he did provide, uncredited, the voice-over narration for the 1961 *noir* thriller *Blast of Silence*.

Life improved for Stander when he moved to London in 1964 to act in Bertolt Brecht's *Saint Joan of the Stockyards*, directed by Tony Richardson, for whom he'd acted on Broadway, along with Christopher Plummer, in a stillborn 1963 production of Brecht's *The Resistible Rise of Arturo Ui*.

In 1965, he was featured in the film *Promise Her Anything*. That same year Richardson cast him in the black comedy about the funeral industry, *The Loved One*, based on the novel by Evelyn Waugh, with an all-star cast including Jonathan Winters, Robert Morse, Liberace, Rod Steiger, Paul Williams, and many others. In 1966, Roman Polanski cast Stander in his only starring role, as the thug Dickie in *Cul-de-sac*, opposite Françoise Dorléac and Donald Pleasence.

Stander stayed in Europe and eventually settled in Rome, where he appeared in many spaghetti Westerns, most notably playing a bartender named Max in Sergio Leone's *Once Upon a Time in the West* (1968). In Rome he connected with Robert Wagner, who cast him in an episode of *It Takes a Thief* (1969) that was shot there. Stander's few English-language films in the 1970s include *The Gang That Couldn't Shoot Straight* (1971) with Robert De Niro and Jerry Orbach, Steven Spielberg's *1941* (1979), and Martin Scorsese's *New York, New York* (1977) with Liza Minnelli and Robert De Niro.

After fifteen years abroad, Stander moved back to the U.S. for the role he is now most famous for: Max, the loyal butler, cook, and chauffeur to the wealthy, amateur detectives played by Robert Wagner and Stefanie Powers on the television series *Hart to Hart* (1979–1984) and a subsequent series of *Hart to Hart* made-for-television films (1993-1995). In 1983, Stander won a Golden Globe Award for "Best Performance by an Actor in a Supporting Role in a Series, Mini-Series, or Motion Picture Made for TV".

In 1986, he became the voice of Kup in *The Transformers: The Movie*. His final theatrical film role was as a dying hospital patient in *The Last Good Time* (1994), with Armin Mueller-Stahl and Olivia d'Abo, directed by Bob Balaban.

Stander's personal life was as tumultuous as his professional one. He was married six times, always to beautiful young women, most of them artists, the first time in 1932 and the last in 1972. All but the last marriage ended in divorce. He fathered six daughters (one wife had no children; one had twins).

Stander died of lung cancer in Los Angeles, California, in 1994 at age 86. He was buried in Glendale's Forest Lawn Memorial Park Cemetery.

Marjorie Stapp

Audie Murphy with Marjorie Stapp in *Battle at Bloody Beach*

Marjorie Stapp was born September 17, 1921, in Little Rock, Arkansas, and is an American actress. She appeared in seventy-six films and television programs from 1947 to 1991.

Early on, Marjorie worked as a receptionist…for Bugsy Siegel! "But I didn't know it, until he was murdered and I recognized his picture in the paper! The Flamingo Hotel in Las Vegas had an office on Sunset Boulevard in Hollywood. They had four phones (which never rang) and I was to take reservations. All the filing cabinets had nothing in them. But, it was a big plush office. I got so bored doing nothing, I started going on interviews. I'd take two, three hours or more for lunch. One day, the man who hired me had to wait on me for two hours, and then he fired me! (Laughs) Earlier, he'd introduced me to Mr. Siegel (no first name or nick-name was given). He was just like George Raft; he had bodyguards—just like in the movies!"

Margie worked with many of the top cowboy stars of her day, but not always in westerns. She appeared in *Battle of Bloody Beach* (1961) with Audie Murphy. "I twisted my ankle once; Audie was near and caught me before I hit the ground. He always asked how the ankle was. It was a very nice relationship".

Other notable roles included *Laramie* (1949), *Fireside Theatre* (1950-1953), *The Far Country* (1954), *Indestructible Man* (1956), *The Werewolf* (1956), *The Monster That Challenged the World* (1957), *Suicide Battalion* (1958), *Elmer Gantry* (1960), *The Wild Westerners* (1962), *A Gathering of Eagles* (1963), *My Three Sons* (1962-1969), *The Brady Bunch* (1969), *Roses Are for the Rich* (1987), *Jake and the Fatman* (1988), *Quantum Leap* (1989), and *Columbo* (1991).

An early marriage ended in divorce, but produced a daughter. "She lives in New York. That's where I met Bob, my husband. I did *The Subject Was Roses* on Broadway, and we met at a vocal class".

Margie and her husband moved to North Carolina for a few years but eventually moved back to California.

Bob Steele

Audie Murphy with Bob Steele in *Column South*

Bob Steele was born Robert Adrian Bradbury January 23, 1907, and was an American actor. He was born in Portland, Oregon, into a vaudeville family. After years of touring, the family settled down in Hollywood in the late 1910s, where his father, Robert N. Bradbury, soon found work in the movies, first as an actor, later as a director, and by 1920, he hired Bob and his twin brother Bill (1907–1971) as juvenile leads for a series of adventure movies titled *The Adventures of Bob and Bill*.

Bob's career began to take off for good in 1927, when he was hired by production company Film Booking Offices of America (FBO) to star in a series of Westerns. Bob, who was re-christened Bob Steele at FBO, soon made a name for himself, and in the late 1920s, 1930s, and 1940s starred in B-Westerns for almost every minor film studio, including Monogram, Supreme, Tiffany, Syndicate, Republic (including several films of the *Three Mesquiteers* series) and Producers Releasing Corporation (PRC) (including the initial films of their "Billy the Kid" series), plus he had the occasional role in an A-movie, as in the adaptation of John Steinbeck's novel, *Of Mice and Men* from 1939.

In the 1940s, Bob's career as a cowboy hero was on the decline, but he kept himself working by accepting supporting roles in many big movies like Howard Hawks' *The Big Sleep* (1946), or the John Wayne vehicles *Island in the Sky* (1953), *Rio Bravo* (1959), *The Comancheros* (1961), *The Longest Day* (1962), *McLintock!* (1963), and *Rio Lobo* (1970).

Besides these he also made occasional appearances in science fiction films like *Atomic Submarine* (1959) and *Giant from the Unknown* (1958) and did lots of television work, culminating in a regular supporting role in the army comedy *F Troop* (1965–1967), which allowed him to show his comic talent. Steele played the character of Trooper Duffy, who claimed to have been "shoulder to shoulder with Davy Crockett at the Alamo". In fact Steele played in *Davy Crockett at the Fall of the Alamo* in 1926.

Other notable roles over the years included *Westward Ho* (1942), *Fort Worth* (1951), *Cattle Drive* (1951), *The Spoilers* (1955), *The Life and Legend of Wyatt Earp* (1955), *Decision at Sundown* (1957), *Pork Chop Hill* (1959), *National Velvet* (1960), *4 for Texas* (1963), *Taggart* (1964), *The Bounty Killer* (1965), *Something Big* (1971), *Charley Varrick* (1973), and *Nightmare Honeymoon* (1974).

He worked with Audie Murphy in *Column South* (1953), *Drums Across the River* (1954), *Ride a Crooked Trail* (1958), *No Name on the Bullet* (1959), *Hell Bent for Leather* (1960), *Whispering Smith* (1961), *Six Black Horses* (1962), *Showdown* (1963), and *Bullet for a Badman* (1964),

Bob Steele died on December 21, 1989, from emphysema after a long sickness.

Edgar Stehli

Audie Murphy with Edgar Stehli in *No Name on the Bullet*

Edgar Stehli was born July 12, 1884 in Lyon, Rhône, France. He appeared in eighty-three films and television programs from 1947 to 1970.

Some of those credits include *Boomerang!* (1947), *Suspense* (1949-1952), *Executive Suite* (1954), *Drum Beat* (1954), *The Life of Riley* (1956), *Gunsmoke* (1957), *The Frank Sinatra Show* (1958), *No Name on the Bullet* (1959) with Audie Murphy, *Cash McCall* (1960), *Twilight Zone* (1960), *Atlantis, the Lost Continent* (1961), *The Doctors and the Nurses* (1963-1964), *The Trials of O'Brien* (1965), *I Spy* (1967), *The Man from U.N.C.L.E.* (1968), and *Loving* (1970).

He had two children with wife Emilie Greenough Stehli, Francis Stehli and Emilie-Anne Greenough Stehli.

He died July 25, 1973, at age 89 in Upper Montclair, New Jersey.

Laraine Stephens

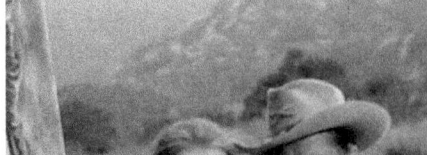

Laraine Stephens with Audie Murphy in *40 Guns to Apache Pass*

Laraine Stephens was born Laraine Evelyn Stine July 24, 1941, in Oakland, California, and is an American actress. She appeared in fifty-five films and television programs from 1961 to 1983.

Some of those credits include *Leave It to Beaver* (1961), *The Many Loves of Dobie Gillis* (1962), *Laramie* (1963), *None but the Brave* (1965), *O.K. Crackerby!* (1965-1966), *Laredo* (1966), *40 Guns to Apache Pass* (1967) with Audie Murphy, *Hellfighters* (1968), *I Dream of Jeannie* (1969), forty-one episodes as Diane Waring in *Bracken's World* (1969-1970), *Mod Squad* (1971), *Adventures of Nick Carter* (1972), *Mission: Impossible* (1973), *Barnaby Jones* (1973-1974), *Matt Helm* (1975-1976), *Rich Man, Poor Man - Book II* (1976-1977), *Police Story* (1973-1977), *The Next Step Beyond* (1978), *Police Woman* (1974-1978), *Hawaii Five-O* (1970-1978), *Dallas Cowboys Cheerleaders* (1979), *Dallas Cowboys Cheerleaders II* (1980), *Scruples* (1981), *T.J. Hooker* (1982), *Seven Brides for Seven Brothers* (1982), and *Fantasy Island* (1979-1983).

She was married to David Gerber from June 12, 1970 until his death January 2, 2010.

John Stephenson

August John Stephenson was born August 9, 1923, in Kenosha, Wisconsin, and is a veteran voice actor, dating back to network radio in the 1950's.

In the 1950s and 1960s, Stephenson was a frequent announcer/narrator on early television series, serving as the closing credits announcer on *I Love Lucy* (1951-1957) and the voice on the 1967 version *Dragnet* (1967-1969) who solemnly intoned, "And now, the results of the trial." He also supplied countless cartoon voices for Hanna-Barbera, including Mr. Slate in *The Flintstones* (1960-1966) and additional voices for the cartoon series *Abbott & Costello* (1967), *Darkwing Duck* (1991), *Duck Dodgers* (2003), and *Scooby-Doo! Abracadabra-Doo* (2010).

Some of his live-action roles include *The Lone Ranger* (1954), *I Died a Thousand Times* (1955), *The People's Choice* (1955-1958), *Wichita Town* (1959), *Whispering Smith* (1961) with Audie Murphy, *The Beverly Hillbillies* (1963-1964), *F Troop* (1965), *Get Smart* (1965), *Green Acres* (1966), *Iron Horse* (1967), *Hellfighters* (1968), *Hogan's Heroes* (1965-1970), *Mission: Impossible* (1972), *McMillan & Wife* (1973), *Herbie Rides Again* (1974), *The Streets of San Francisco* (1975), and *Lou Grant* (1977).

John Stephenson died December 29, 2012 at age 89.

Robert Sterling

Robert Sterling with Audie Murphy in *Column South*

Robert Sterling was born William Sterling Hart in New Castle, Pennsylvania, November 13, 1917, and was an American film and television actor.

The son of a garbage man, he attended the University of Pittsburgh and worked as a clothing salesman before pursuing an acting career.

After signing with Columbia Pictures in 1939, he changed his name to Robert Sterling to avoid confusion with silent western star William S. Hart. His name was legally changed while he was a 2nd Lt. Student officer attending flight training in Marfa, Texas, in 1943.

In 1941, Sterling went to MGM. He worked steadily as a supporting player for several years. After serving in World War II as an Army Air Force flight instructor, he returned to Hollywood, but by the end of the decade, his film career had faltered. He did, however, play the non-singing role of Steve Baker, opposite Ava Gardner as Julie, in the hit MGM 1951 film version of *Show Boat*, and as a traitorous cavalry officer in *Column South* (1953) with Audie Murphy.

Sterling reinvigorated his career, first with a club act with wife actress/singer Anne Jeffreys, and then becoming a fixture on television. He was cast in numerous dramatic roles on early television, when networks often televised live dramatic performances.

Sterling is perhaps most well known, however, for starring with Jeffreys, as the spirited George Kerby (to Jefferys' Marion Kerby) in the television program *Topper*, which appeared from 1953 to 1955. Veteran Leo G. Carroll appeared in the title role. Wife Marion Kerby was referred to as "The ghostess with the mostest", while Sterling's character was known as "That most sporty spirit".

In the 1961-1962 television season, Sterling co-starred with George Chandler and Reta Shaw in CBS's *Ichabod and Me*, a sitcom set in New England. He portrayed 44-year-old Bob Major, a newspaper reporter from New York City, who purchased and ran the paper in a small town called Phippsboro. Chandler played the former editor and municipal traffic commissioner. Shaw appeared as Sterling's aunt and housekeeper.

After some additional television and film work in the early 1960s, including *Return to Peyton Place* (1961) and *Voyage to the Bottom of the Sea* (1961), *Twilight Zone* (1963), and *A Global Affair* (1964), Sterling essentially retired, making only sporadic appearances with Jeffreys in later shows such as CBS's *Murder, She Wrote* (1986) and ABC's *Hotel* (1984). He also guest starred in 1974 in the NBC sitcom *The Brian Keith Show*.

Sterling was married twice. His first marriage, in 1943, was to noted actress and singer Ann Sothern. They had a daughter, Patricia (Tisha Sterling), who became an actress. Sothern and Sterling divorced in 1949. Sterling met actress Anne Jeffreys soon after in his Broadway debut, and they were married in 1951. They had three sons: Jeffrey, Dana, and Tyler.

Sterling died May 30, 2006, at age 88, at his home in Brentwood, California. According to the Associated Press, his son, Jeffrey, indicated that Sterling died of natural causes, but had suffered from debilitating shingles for the last decade of his life.

K.T. Stevens

K. T. Stevens was born Gloria Wood July 20, 1919, in Los Angeles, California, and was an American film actress. The daughter of director Sam Wood, Stevens made her first film appearance when she was just two years old in her father's second 1921 silent film, *Peck's Bad Boy*.

As an adult, she changed her name to distance herself from her father's fame. In 1946, Stevens married actor Hugh Marlowe. They divorced in 1968. She and Marlowe were the parents of two sons. Stevens and Marlowe acted in the Broadway production of *Laura* in which, credited as "A Girl" so as not to alert the audience, she played the part filmed by Gene Tierney. Marlowe played the detective that Dana Andrews played in the film.

Stevens appeared in a number of films in the 1940s and 1950s, including *The Great Man's Lady* (1942) with Barbara Stanwyck, *Address Unknown* (1944), *Port of New York* (1949) with Yul Brynner, *Harriet Craig* (1950) with Joan Crawford, *Tumbleweed* (1953) with Audie Murphy, *Jungle Hell* (1956), and *Missile to the Moon* (1958).

In addition, she acted on episodic television in such series as *The Brothers Brannagan* (1961), and appeared on the daytime soap opera *The Young and the Restless* (1976-1980) as the veiled facially burned Vanessa Prentiss.

Additional roles included *The Rifleman* (1960-1963), *Iron Horse* (1966), *Adam-12* (1975), *Buck Rogers in the 25th Century* (1979), *They're Playing with Fire* (1984, and *Knots Landing* (1989).

Her last film role before her death June 13, 1994, from lung cancer was in the 1994 Whoopi Goldberg film *Corrina, Corrina*.

Warren Stevens

Warren Stevens with Audie Murphy in *Gunpoint*

Warren Albert Stevens was born in Clarks Summit, Pennsylvania, November 2, 1919, and was an American stage, screen, and television actor.

Stevens began his acting career after serving in the U.S. Army Air Force as a pilot during World War II. He trained at The Actor's Studio in New York, received notice on Broadway in the late 1940s, and thereafter was offered a Hollywood contract at 20th Century Fox.

His first Broadway role was in *The Life of Galileo* (1947) and first movie role followed in *The Frogmen* (1951). As a young studio contract player, Stevens had little choice of material, and he appeared in films that included *Phone Call from a Stranger* (1952), *Wait Till the Sun Shines, Nellie* (1952), and *Gorilla at Large* (1954). His most memorable movie role was probably that of the ill-fated "Doc" Ostrow in the science fiction film *Forbidden Planet* (1956). He also had a supporting role in *The Barefoot Contessa* (1954) with Humphrey Bogart.

Other film roles included *The Man from Bitter Ridge* (1955), *The Case Against Brooklyn* (1958), *No Name on the Bullet* (1959) with Audie Murphy, *Stagecoach to Dancers' Rock* (1962), *Cyborg 2087* (1966), *Gunpoint* (1966) again with Audie Murphy, *The Sweet Ride* (1968), *The Student Body* (1976), *Stroker Ace* (1983), and *Samurai Cop* (1989).

Despite occasional parts in big films, Stevens was unable to break out consistently into A-list movies, so he carved out a career in television as a journeyman dramatic actor.

He co-starred as Lt. William Storm in *Tales of the 77th Bengal Lancers* (NBC, 1956–1957), a prime-time adventure series set in India.

He appeared in over 150 prime time shows from the 1950s to the early 1980s, including *Perry Mason* (1958), *Alcoa Presents: One Step Beyond* (1959), *The Untouchables* (1961), *Twilight Zone* (1962), *The Outer Limits* (1964), *Honey West* (1965), *The Big Valley* (1966), *Daniel Boone* (1966-1967), *Star Trek* (1968), *Mannix* (1969), *Bracken's World* (1969-1970), *Adam-12* (1971), *O'Hara, U.S. Treasury* (1972), *Get Christie Love!* (1975), *M*A*S*H* (1975), *Police Woman* (1975-1977), *High Ice* (1980), and *The Twilight Zone* (1986).

It was his appearances on *Have Gun, Will Travel* (1957-1963) that introduced him to Richard Boone, which resulted in Stevens's only continuing TV role as one of the "regulars" in *The Richard Boone Show*, an award-winning anthology series which lasted for one season (1963–64).

His appearances had been infrequent since the mid 1980s, but he made a guest appearance on *ER* in March 2006, and had two roles in 2007 in *The Solicitor* and *Carts*.

Stevens died at age 92 on March 27, 2012, from complications of lung disease in his home in Sherman Oaks, Los Angeles, California.

Houseley Stevenson

Houseley Stevenson with Audie Murphy in *Sierra*

Houseley Stevenson was born July 30, 1879 in London, England, and was a British-born American character actor.

He labored in a San Francisco glass factory until his thirties, and then embarked on an acting career. He became a respected teacher, director, and performer at famed Pasadena Community Playhouse in California. He appeared in numerous films in the Thirties and Forties, his craggy face enlivening many movies.

Some of those films included *Bengal Tiger* (1936), *The Adventurous Blonde* (1937), *The Body Disappears* (1941), *Happy Land* (1943), *Without Reservations* (1946), *Ramrod* (1947), *The Ghost and Mrs. Muir* (1947), *Four Faces West* (1948), *Knock on Any Door* (1949), *Colorado Territory* (1949), *Sierra* (1950) with Audie Murphy, *The Gunfighter* (1950), *Hollywood Story* (1951), *The Wild North* (1952), and *Oklahoma Annie* (1952).

Several of his children had effective careers in front of or behind the camera, including actor Onslow Stevens and actor-editor Houseley Stevenson, Jr.

He died August 6, 1953, at age 74 in Duarte, Los Angeles County, California.

Venetia Stevenson

Venetia Stevenson with Audie Murphy in *Seven Ways From Sundown*

Venetia Stevenson was born Joanna Venetia Invicta Stevenson in London, England, March 10, 1938, and is a retired American film and television actress.

She is the daughter of film director Robert Stevenson and actress Anna Lee. The family moved to Hollywood within a year of her birth after her father signed a contract with film producer David Selznick. When her parents divorced in 1944, she stayed with her father and new stepmother, Frances. After an education in exclusive Californian private schools, her theatrical debut was with her mother in *Liliom*, a play produced by the Sombrero Theater, in Phoenix, Arizona, in April 1955 and also with the husband and wife team of Fernando Lamas and Arlene Dahl.

A one-time Miss Los Angeles Press Club, Stevenson was placed on contract by RKO Pictures in November 1956. Hedda Hopper named Stevenson on her list of top movie newcomers in January 1957, alongside Jayne Mansfield. Hopper said of Stevenson, then eighteen, she is "the most purely beautiful of all the new crop of stars".

In March 1957, Stevenson was in the cast of the CBS *Playhouse 90* adaptation of *Charley's Aunt*, alongside Tom Tryon, Jackie Coogan, and Jeanette MacDonald were among the cast in the telecast. Stevenson played Peggy McTavish in *Darby's Rangers* (1958), a Warner Bros. release in which she was paired off with Peter Brown. She is one of the women who are pursued by actors cast as members of an American unit of the same name during World War II. The movie was directed by William Wellman.

Stevenson's publicity machine continued to promote her. She was reported enjoying riding horses as an activity and playing table tennis. In November 1957, she won $300 in prizes at a horse show and participated at the National Horse Show at the Cow Palace in San Francisco. Around this time she became the face on Sweetheart Stout cans and bottles; the brand marked the 50th anniversary of using her image in 2008.

She appeared in the western drama *The Day of the Outlaw* (1959), starring Robert Ryan and Tina Louise. Stevenson appeared in the English film *Jack The Ripper* (1960). She also had a primary role, in the film version of the Studs Lonigan trilogy by James Farrell, brought to the screen in December 1960.

Among the other motion pictures in which she appears are *Island of Lost Women* (1959), *Jet Over The Atlantic* (1959), *The Big Night* (1960), *Seven Ways from Sundown* (1960) with Audie Murphy, *The City of the Dead* (1960), and *The Sergeant Was a Lady* (1961).

Stevenson appeared on television, in episodes of *Cheyenne* (1957), *Colt .45* (1958), three episodes of *Sugarfoot* (1957-1958), *77 Sunset Strip* (1958), *The Adventures of Ozzie and Harriet* (1958), *Lawman* (1958), *The Millionaire* (1959), *The Third Man* (1959), and *Alfred Hitchcock Presents* (1960).

Stevenson married MGM actor-dancer, Russ Tamblyn, on Valentine's Day, 1956, shortly after her half-brother, actor Jeffrey Byron, was born to her mother. She was seventeen when she and Tamblyn had their wedding in the Wayfarers Chapel in Palos Verdes. Stevenson and Tamblyn divorced in April 1957, but the two remained friends.

Stevenson remarried, to Don Everly, in 1962 and retired from acting and modeling. The couple had two daughters, Stacy and Erin Everly, both actresses, and a son, Edan Everly, a musician. She divorced Don Everly in 1970 and has not remarried.

Elaine Stewart

Audie Murphy with Elaine Stewart in *Night Passage*

Elaine Stewart was born Elsy Steinberg in Montclair, New Jersey, May 31, 1930, and was an American actress and model. She was one of five children born into a German Jewish family. In 1961, nearing the end of her television career, she married actor Bill Carter. After her divorce from Carter, she married television producer Merrill Heatter on December 31, 1964. They had a son, Stewart, and a daughter, Gabrielle.

Stewart made her debut by winning Miss See in *See Magazine* in 1952, with measurements 34–25–36. She was in many magazines such as the October 1959 issue of *Playboy*.

She had a supporting role in *The Bad and the Beautiful* (1952), as Lila. She appeared in other films, such as *Brigadoon* (1954), *Night Passage* (1957) with Audie Murphy and James Stewart, *The Rise and Fall of Legs Diamond* (1960), and *The Adventures of Hajji Baba* (1954).

Stewart was also known as the co-hostess on two 1970s game shows, *Gambit* (1972) with Wink Martindale and the nighttime edition of *High Rollers* (1974-1975) with Alex Trebek, which were both produced by her husband.

She died June 27, 2011, at age 81 in Beverly Hills, Los Angeles, California.

James Stewart

Audie Murphy with James Stewart in *Night Passage*

James Maitland "Jimmy" Stewart was born in Indiana, Pennsylvania, May 20, 1908, and was an American film and stage actor, known for his distinctive voice and persona. Over the course of his career, he starred in many films widely considered classics and was nominated for five Academy Awards, winning one in competition and receiving one Lifetime Achievement award. He was a major MGM contract star. He also had a noted military career and was a World War II and Vietnam War veteran, who rose to the rank of Brigadier General in the United States Air Force Reserve.

James Maitland Stewart was the son of Elizabeth Ruth (née Jackson) and Alexander Maitland Stewart, who owned a hardware store. Stewart's parents were of Scottish descent and Presbyterians. His maternal ancestors served in the American Revolution, the War of 1812, and the American Civil War. The eldest of three children (he had two younger sisters, Virginia and Mary), he was expected to continue his father's business, which had been in the family for three generations. His mother was an excellent pianist but his father discouraged Stewart's request for lessons. But when his father accepted a gift of an accordion from a guest, young Stewart quickly learned to play the instrument, which became a fixture off-stage during his acting career. As the family grew, music continued to be an important part of family life.

Stewart attended Mercersburg Academy prep school, graduating in 1928. He was active in a variety of activities. He played on the football and track teams, was art editor of the *KARUX* yearbook, and a member of the choir club, glee club, and John Marshall Literary Society. During his first summer break, Stewart returned to his hometown to work as a brick loader for a local construction company and on highway and road construction jobs where he painted lines on the roads. Over the following two summers, he took a job as an assistant with a professional magician. He made his first appearance onstage at Mercersburg, as Buquet in the play *The Wolves*.

A shy child, Stewart spent much of his after-school time in the basement working on model airplanes, mechanical drawing and chemistry, all with a dream of going into aviation. But he abandoned visions of being a pilot when his father insisted that instead of the United States Naval Academy he attend Princeton University. Stewart enrolled at Princeton in 1928 as a member of the class of 1932. He excelled at studying architecture, so impressing his professors with his thesis on an airport design that he was awarded a scholarship for graduate studies; but he gradually became attracted to the school's drama and music clubs, including the Princeton Triangle Club.

His acting and accordion talents at Princeton led him to be invited to the University Players, an intercollegiate summer stock company in West Falmouth, Massachusetts, on Cape Cod. The company had been organized in 1928 and would run until 1932, with Joshua Logan, Bretaigne Windust, and Charles Leatherbee as directors. Stewart performed in bit parts in the Players' productions in Cape Cod during the summer of 1932, after he graduated. The troupe had previously included Henry Fonda, while the players were in Baltimore, Maryland for an eighteen-week winter season.

Stewart and Fonda became great friends over the summer of 1932 when they shared an apartment with Joshua Logan and Myron McCormick. When Stewart came to New York at the end of the summer stock season, which had included the Broadway try-out of *Goodbye Again*, he shared an apartment with Fonda. Along with fellow University Players Alfred Dalrymple and Myron McCormick, Stewart debuted on Broadway as a chauffeur in the comedy *Goodbye Again*, in which he had two lines. *The New Yorker* noted, "Mr. James Stewart's chauffeur... comes on for three minutes and walks off to a round of spontaneous applause".

The play was a moderate success, but times were hard. Many Broadway theaters had been converted to movie houses and the Depression was reaching bottom. "From 1932 through 1934", Stewart later recalled, "I'd only worked three months. Every play I got into folded". By 1934, he had gotten more substantial stage roles, including the modest hit *Page Miss Glory* and his first dramatic stage role in Sidney Howard's *Yellow Jack*, which convinced him to continue his acting career. However, Stewart and Fonda, still roommates, were both struggling.

In the fall of 1934, Fonda's success in *The Farmer Takes a Wife* took him to Hollywood. Finally, Stewart attracted the interest of MGM scout Bill Grady who saw Stewart on the opening night of *Divided by Three*, a glittering première with many luminaries in attendance, including Irving Berlin and Moss Hart and Fonda, who had returned to New York for the show. With Fonda's encouragement, Stewart agreed to take a screen test, after which he signed a contract with MGM in April 1935, as a contract player for up to seven years at $350 a week.

Upon Stewart's arrival by train in Los Angeles, Fonda greeted him at the station and took him to Fonda's studio-supplied lodging, next door to Greta Garbo. Stewart's first job at the studio was as a participant in screen tests with newly arrived starlets. At first, he had trouble being cast in Hollywood films owing to his gangling looks and shy, humble screen presence.

Aside from an unbilled appearance in a Shemp Howard comedy short called *Art Trouble* in 1934, his first film was the poorly received Spencer Tracy vehicle, *The Murder Man* (1935). *Rose Marie* (1936), an adaptation of a popular operetta, was more successful. After mixed success in films, he received his first substantial part in 1936's *After the Thin Man*.

On the romantic front, he found himself dating newly divorced Ginger Rogers. The romance soon cooled, however, and by chance Stewart encountered Margaret Sullavan. Stewart found his footing in Hollywood thanks largely to Sullavan, who campaigned for Stewart to be her leading man in the 1936 romantic comedy *Next Time We Love*. She rehearsed extensively with him, having a noticeable effect on his confidence. She encouraged Stewart to feel comfortable with his unique mannerisms and boyish charm and use them naturally as his own style. Stewart was enjoying Hollywood life and had no regrets about giving up the stage, as he worked six days a week in the MGM factory. In 1936, he acquired big-time agent Leland Hayward, who would eventually marry Sullavan. Hayward started to chart Stewart's career, deciding the best path for him was through loan-outs to other studios.

In 1938, Stewart had a brief, tumultuous romance with Hollywood queen Norma Shearer, whose husband, Irving Thalberg, head of production at MGM, had died two years earlier. Stewart began a successful partnership with director Frank Capra in 1938, when he was loaned out to Columbia Pictures to star in *You Can't Take It With You*. Capra had been impressed by Stewart's minor role in *Navy Blue and Gold* (1937). The director had recently completed several popular movies, including *It Happened One Night* (1934), and was looking for the right actor to suit his needs; other recent actors in Capra's films such as Clark Gable, Ronald Colman, and Gary Cooper did not quite fit. Not only was Stewart just what he was looking for, but Capra also found Stewart understood that prototype intuitively and required very little directing. Later Capra commented, "I think he's probably the best actor who's ever hit the screen".

You Can't Take It With You, starring Capra's "favorite actress", comedienne Jean Arthur, won the 1938 Best Picture Academy Award. The following year saw Stewart work with Capra and Arthur again in the political comedy-drama *Mr. Smith Goes to Washington*. Stewart replaced intended star Gary Cooper in the film, playing an idealist thrown into the political arena. Upon its October 1939 release, the film garnered critical praise and became a box-office success. Stewart was nominated for the first of five Academy Awards for Best Actor. Stewart's father was still trying to talk him into leaving Hollywood and its sinful ways and to return to his home town to lead a decent life. Stewart took a secret trip to Europe to take a break and returned home in 1939 just as Germany invaded Poland.

Destry Rides Again, also released in 1939, became Stewart's first western film, a genre with which he would become identified later in his career. In this western parody, Stewart is a pacifist lawman and Marlene Dietrich is the dancing saloon girl who comes to love him, but doesn't get him. In the film, Dietrich sings her famous song "The Boys In the Back Room".

Made for Each Other (1939) had Stewart sharing the screen with irrepressible Carole Lombard in a melodrama that garnered good reviews for both stars, but did less well with the public. Between movies, Stewart began a radio career and became a distinctive voice on the Lux Radio Theater's *The Screen Guild Theater* and other shows. So well-known had his slow drawl become that comedians began impersonating him.

In 1940, Stewart and Sullavan reunited for two films. The first, the Ernst Lubitsch romantic comedy, *The Shop Around the Corner*, starred Stewart and Sullavan as co-workers unknowingly involved in a pen-pal romance but who cannot stand each other in real life (this was later remade into the musical, *In the Good Old Summertime* with Judy Garland and Van Johnson, and later as the romantic comedy *You've Got Mail* with Tom Hanks and Meg Ryan). It was Stewart's fifth film of the year and that rare film shot in sequence; it was completed in only twenty-seven days. *The Mortal Storm*, directed by Frank Borzage, was one of the first blatantly anti-Nazi films to be produced in Hollywood and featured the pair as friends and then lovers caught in turmoil upon Hitler's rise to power, literally hunted down by their own friends.

Stewart also starred with Cary Grant and Katharine Hepburn in George Cukor's classic *The Philadelphia Story* (1940). His performance as an intrusive, fast-talking reporter earned him his only Academy Award in a competitive category (Best Actor, 1941), and he beat out his good friend Henry Fonda (*The Grapes of Wrath*). Stewart thought his performance "entertaining and slick and smooth" but lacking the "guts" of "Mr. Smith". Stewart gave the Oscar statuette to his father, who displayed it for many years in a case inside the front door of his hardware store, alongside other family awards and military medals.

During the months before he began military service, Stewart appeared in a series of screwball comedies with varying levels of success. He followed the mediocre *No Time for Comedy* (1940) and *Come Live with Me* (1941) with the Judy Garland musical, *Ziegfeld Girl* (1941), and the George Marshall romantic comedy *Pot o' Gold* (1941). Stewart was drafted in late 1940, a situation that coincided with the lapse in his MGM contract, marking a turning point in Stewart's career, with twenty-eight movies to his credit at that point.

The Stewart and Jackson families had deep military roots as both grandfathers had fought in the Civil War, and his father had served during both the Spanish-American War and World War I. Stewart considered his father to be the biggest influence on his life, so it was not surprising that, when another war came, he too was eager to serve. Members of his family had previously been in the infantry, but Stewart chose to become a military flier.

An early interest in flying led Stewart to gain his Private Pilot certificate in 1935 and Commercial Pilot certificate in 1938. He often flew cross-country to visit his parents in Pennsylvania, navigating by the railroad tracks. Nearly two years before the December 1941 attack on Pearl Harbor, Stewart had accumulated over 400 hours of flying time.

Considered a highly proficient pilot, he even entered a cross-country race as a co-pilot in 1939. Stewart, along with musician/composer Hoagy Carmichael, saw the need for trained war pilots, and joined with other Hollywood celebrities to invest in Thunderbird Field, a pilot-training school built and operated by Southwest Airways in Glendale, Arizona. This airfield became part of the United States Army Air Forces training establishment and trained more than 10,000 pilots during World War II, and is now the home of Thunderbird School of Global Management.

Later in 1940, Stewart was drafted into the United States Army but was rejected for failing to meet height and weight requirements for new recruits; Stewart was five pounds under the standard. To get up to 148 pounds, he sought out the help of Metro-Goldwyn-Mayer's muscle man and trainer Don Loomis, who was noted for his ability to add or subtract pounds in his studio gymnasium. Stewart subsequently attempted to enlist in the Army Air Corps, but still came in under the weight requirement, although he persuaded the AAC enlistment officer to run new tests, this time passing the weigh-in, with the result that Stewart enlisted in the Army in March 1941. He became the first major American movie star to wear a military uniform in World War II.

Stewart enlisted as a private and then began pilot training in the USAAC. Stewart continued his military training and earned a commission as a second lieutenant in January 1942, just after the attack on Pearl Harbor brought the US directly into the conflict. He was posted to Moffett Field and then Mather Field as an instructor pilot in single- and twin-engine aircraft.

Public appearances by Stewart were limited engagements scheduled by the Army Air Forces. "Stewart appeared several times on network radio with Edgar Bergen and Charlie McCarthy. Shortly after Pearl Harbor, he performed with Orson Welles, Edward G. Robinson, Walter Huston, and Lionel Barrymore in an all-network radio program called *We Hold These Truths*, dedicated to the 150th anniversary of the Bill of Rights". In early 1942, Stewart was asked to appear in a propaganda film to help recruit the anticipated 100,000 airmen that the USAAF would need to win the war. The USAAC's First Motion Picture Unit shot scenes of Lieutenant Stewart in his pilot's flight suit and recorded his voice for narration. The short film, *Winning Your Wings*, appeared nationwide beginning in late May and was very successful, resulting in 150,000 new recruits.

Stewart was concerned that his expertise and celebrity status would relegate him to instructor duties "behind the lines". His fears were confirmed when he was stationed for six months at Kirtland Air Force Base in Albuquerque, New Mexico, to train bombardiers. He was transferred to Hobbs Army Airfield to become an instructor pilot for the four-engine B-17 Flying Fortress, where he trained B-17 pilots for nine months at Gowen Field, Boise, Idaho. For Stewart, combat duty seemed far away and unreachable and he had no clear plans for the future. But then a rumor that Stewart would be taken off flying status and assigned to making training films or selling bonds called for his immediate and decisive action, because what he dreaded most was the hope-shattering specter of a dead end". Stewart appealed to his commander, a pre-war aviator, who understood the situation and reassigned him to a unit going overseas.

In August 1943, Stewart was assigned to the 445th Bombardment Group at Sioux City AAB, Iowa, first as operations officer of the 703d Bombardment Squadron and then as its commander, at the rank of captain. In December 1943, the 445th Bombardment Group flew its B-24 Liberator bombers to RAF Tibenham, Norfolk, England, and immediately began combat operations. While flying missions over Germany, Stewart was promoted to major.

In March 1944, he was transferred as group operations officer to the 453rd Bombardment Group, a new B-24 unit that had been experiencing difficulties. As a means to inspire his new group, Stewart flew as command pilot in the lead B-24 on numerous missions deep into Nazi-occupied Europe. These missions went *uncounted* at Stewart's orders. His "official" total is listed as twenty and is limited to those with the 445th.

In 1944, he twice received the Distinguished Flying Cross for actions in combat and was awarded the Croix de Guerre. He also received the Air Medal with three oak leaf clusters. In July 1944, after flying twenty combat missions, Stewart was made Chief of Staff of the 2nd Combat Bombardment Wing of the Eighth Air Force, and though he was no longer required or expected to fly missions, he continued to do so. Before the war ended, he was promoted to colonel, one of the few Americans to rise from private to colonel in four years.

At the beginning of June 1945, Stewart was the presiding officer of the court-martial of a pilot and navigator who were charged with dereliction of duty for having accidentally bombed the Swiss city of Zurich the previous March – the first instance of U.S. personnel being tried for an attack on a neutral country. The Court acquitted the defendants.

Stewart continued to play a role in the United States Air Force Reserve after the war, achieving the rank of Brigadier General on July 23, 1959. Stewart rarely spoke about his wartime service. He did appear on the TV series *The World At War* to discuss the October 14, 1943, bombing mission to Schweinfurt, which was the center of the German ball-bearing industry. This mission is known in USAF history as *Black Thursday* because of the high casualties it sustained; sixty aircraft were lost out of 291 B-17s dispatched unescorted to Schweinfurt. The available escort aircraft lacked the range to accompany them. At his request, he was identified only as "James Stewart, Squadron Commander" in the documentary.

After the war, Stewart served as Air Force Reserve commander of Dobbins Air Reserve Base in the early 1950s. In 1966, Brigadier General James Stewart flew as a non-duty observer in a B-52 on a bombing mission during the Vietnam War. At the time of his B-52 flight, he refused the release of any publicity regarding his participation, as he did not want it treated as a stunt, but as part of his job as an officer in the Air Force Reserve. After twenty-seven years of service, Stewart retired from the Air Force on May 31, 1968. He was promoted to Major General by President Ronald Reagan.

After the war, Stewart took time off to reassess his career. He was an early investor in Southwest Airways, founded by Leland Hayward, and considered going into the aviation industry if his re-started film career did not prosper. Upon Stewart's return to Hollywood in fall 1945, he decided not to renew his MGM contract. He signed with an MCA talent agency. His former agent Leland Hayward got out of the talent business in 1944 after selling his A-list of stars, including Stewart, to MCA.

For his first film in five years, Stewart appeared in his third and final Frank Capra production, *It's a Wonderful Life*. Capra paid RKO for the rights to the story and formed his own production company, Liberty Films. The female lead went to Donna Reed, after Capra's perennial first choice, Jean Arthur, was unavailable, and after turn-downs from Ginger Rogers, Olivia de Havilland, Ann Dvorak, and Martha Scott. Stewart appeared as George Bailey, an upstanding small-town man who becomes increasingly frustrated by his ordinary existence and financial troubles. Driven to suicide on Christmas Eve, he is led to reassess his life by Clarence Odbody AS2, an "angel, second class", played by Henry Travers. Although the film was nominated for five Academy Awards, including Stewart's third Best Actor nomination, it received mixed reviews and only disappointingly moderate success at the box office. However, in the decades since the film's release, it grew to define Stewart's film persona and is widely considered as a sentimental Christmas film classic and, according to the American Film Institute, one of the best movies ever made. After viewing *It's a Wonderful Life*, President Harry S Truman concluded, "If Bess and I had a son we'd want him to be just like Jimmy Stewart". In the aftermath of the film, Capra's production company went into bankruptcy, while Stewart started to have doubts about his ability to act after his military hiatus. His father kept insisting he come home and marry a local girl. Meanwhile in Hollywood, his generation of actors was fading and a new wave of actors would soon remake the town, including Marlon Brando, Montgomery Clift, and James Dean.

After a poorly received *Magic Town* (1947) and the completion of *Rope* (1948) and *Call Northside 777* (1948), Stewart had two flops with *On Our Merry Way* (1948), a comedic musical ensemble in which Stewart and Henry Fonda played two musicians named "Slim" and "Lank," and *You Gotta Stay Happy* (1949), for which the posters depicted Stewart being kissed on one cheek by Joan Fontaine and on the other by a chimpanzee. In the documentary film *James Stewart: A Wonderful Life* (1987), hosted by Johnny Carson, Stewart said that he went back to Westerns in 1950 in part because a string of films that were flops.

He returned to the stage to star in Mary Coyle Chase's *Harvey*, which had opened to nearly universal praise in November 1944, as Elwood P. Dowd, a wealthy eccentric living with his sister and niece, and whose best friend is an invisible rabbit as large as a man. Dowd's eccentricity, especially the friendship with the rabbit, is ruining the niece's hopes of finding a husband. While trying to have Dowd committed to a sanatorium, his sister is committed herself while the play follows Dowd on an ordinary day in his not-so-ordinary life. Stewart took over the role from Frank Fay and gained an increased Broadway following in the unconventional play. The play, which ran for nearly three years with Stewart as its star, was successfully adapted into a 1950 film, directed by Henry Koster, with Stewart as Dowd and Josephine Hull as his sister, Veta. Bing Crosby was the first choice but he declined. Stewart received his fourth Best Actor nomination for his performance in the film. After *Harvey*, the comedic adventure film *Malaya* (1949) with Spencer Tracy and the conventional but highly successful biographical film *The Stratton Story* in 1949, Stewart's first pairing with "on-screen wife" June Allyson, his career took another turn. During the 1950s, he expanded into the western and suspense genres, thanks to collaborations with Alfred Hitchcock and Anthony Mann.

Other notable performances by Stewart during this time include the critically acclaimed 1950 Delmer Daves western *Broken Arrow*, which featured Stewart as an ex-soldier and Indian agent making peace with the Apache; a troubled clown in the 1952 Best Picture *The Greatest Show on Earth*; and Stewart's role as Charles Lindbergh in Billy Wilder's 1957 film *The Spirit of St. Louis*. He also starred in the western radio show *The Six Shooter* for its one-season run from 1953 to 1954. During this time Stewart wore the same cowboy hat and rode the same horse, named "Pie", in most of his Westerns.

Stewart's collaborations with director Anthony Mann increased Stewart's popularity and sent his career into the realm of the western. Stewart's first appearance in a film directed by Mann came with the 1950 western, *Winchester '73*. In choosing Mann (after first choice Fritz Lang declined), Stewart cemented a powerful partnership. The film, which became a massive box office hit upon its release, set the pattern for their future collaborations. In it, Stewart is a tough, revengeful sharpshooter, the winner of a prized rifle which is stolen and then passes through many hands, until the showdown between Stewart and his brother Stephen McNally.

Other Stewart-Mann westerns, such as *Bend of the River* (1952), *The Naked Spur* (1953), *The Far Country* (1954) and *The Man from Laramie* (1955), were perennial favorites among young audiences entranced by the American West. Frequently, the films featured Stewart as a troubled cowboy seeking redemption, while facing corrupt cattlemen, ranchers and outlaws — a man who knows violence first hand and struggles to control it. The Stewart-Mann collaborations laid the foundation for many of the westerns of the 1950s and remain popular today for their grittier, more realistic depiction of the classic movie genre. Audiences saw Stewart's screen persona evolve into a more mature, more ambiguous, and edgier presence.

Stewart and Mann also collaborated on other films outside the western genre. 1954's *The Glenn Miller Story* was critically acclaimed, garnering Stewart a BAFTA Award nomination, and (together with *The Spirit of St. Louis*) cemented the popularity of Stewart's portrayals of 'American heroes'. *Thunder Bay*, released the same year, transplanted the plot arc of their western collaborations to a more contemporary setting, with Stewart as a Louisiana oil driller facing corruption. *Strategic Air Command*, released in 1955, allowed Stewart to use his experiences in the United States Air Force on film.

Stewart's starring role in *Winchester '73* was also a turning point in Hollywood. Universal Studios, who wanted Stewart to appear in both that film and *Harvey,* balked at his $200,000 asking price. His agent, Lew Wasserman, brokered an alternate deal, in which Stewart would appear in both films for no pay, in exchange for a percentage of the profits and cast and director approval. Stewart ended up earning about $600,000 for *Winchester '73* alone. Hollywood's other stars quickly capitalized on this new way of doing business, which further undermined the decaying "studio system".

In 1957 he appeared in *Night Passage* playing the good brother against Audie Murphy's bad brother. They reunite at the films end to fight against Dan Duryea, who eventually kills the Audie brother and James Stewart in turn kills Dan Duryea. Both James Stewart and Audie Murphy played the character of 'Destry', James in *Destry Rides Again* in 1939 and Audie in the 1954 version of *Destry*.

The second collaboration to define Stewart's career in the 1950s was with acclaimed mystery and suspense director Alfred Hitchcock. Like Mann, Hitchcock uncovered new depths to Stewart's acting, showing a protagonist confronting his fears and his repressed desires. Stewart's first movie with Hitchcock was the technologically innovative 1948 film *Rope*, shot in long "real time" takes.

The two collaborated for the second of four times on the 1954 hit *Rear Window*, widely considered one of Hitchcock's masterpieces. Stewart portrays photographer L.B. "Jeff" Jeffries, loosely based on *Life* photographer

Robert Capa, who projects his fantasies and fears onto the people he observes out his apartment window while on hiatus due to a broken leg. Jeffries gets into more than he can handle, however, when he believes he has witnessed a salesman, played by Raymond Burr, commit a murder, and when his glamorous girlfriend, played by Grace Kelly, at first disdainful of his voyeurism and skeptical about any crime, eventually is drawn in and tries to help solve the mystery. Limited by his wheelchair, Stewart is led by Hitchcock to react to what his character sees with mostly facial responses. It was a landmark year for Stewart, becoming the highest grossing actor of 1954 and the most popular Hollywood star in the world, displacing John Wayne. Hitchcock and Stewart formed a corporation, Patron Inc., to produce the film, which later became the subject of a Supreme Court case *Stewart v. Abend* (1990).

After starring in Hitchcock's remake of the director's earlier production, *The Man Who Knew Too Much* (1956), with Doris Day, Stewart starred, with Kim Novak, in what many consider Hitchcock's most personal film, *Vertigo* (1958). The movie starred Stewart as John "Scottie" Ferguson, a former police investigator suffering from acrophobia, who develops an obsession with a woman he is shadowing. Scottie's obsession inevitably leads to the destruction of everything he once had and believed in. Though the film is widely considered a classic today, *Vertigo* met with negative reviews and poor box office receipts upon its release, and marked the last collaboration between Stewart and Hitchcock. The director reportedly blamed the film's failure on Stewart looking too old to still attract audiences, and cast Cary Grant as Roger Thornhill in *North by Northwest* (1959), a role Stewart had very much wanted. Grant was actually four years older than Stewart. Today, *Vertigo* is ranked second only to *Citizen Kane* in the 2002 *Sight & Sound* critics' poll for the greatest films ever made.

In 1960, Stewart was awarded the New York Film Critics Circle Award for Best Actor and received his fifth and final Academy Award for Best Actor nomination, for his role in the 1959 Otto Preminger film *Anatomy of a Murder*. The early courtroom drama starred Stewart as Paul Biegler, the lawyer of a hot-tempered soldier (played by Ben Gazzara) who claims temporary insanity after murdering a tavern owner who raped his wife. The film featured a career-making performance by George C. Scott as the prosecutor. The film was quite explicit for its time, and it was a box office success. Stewart's nomination was one of seven for the film (Charlton Heston was the winner), and saw his transition into the final decades of his career.

On January 1, 1960, Stewart received news of the death of Margaret Sullavan. As a friend, mentor, and focus of his early romantic urges, she had a unique influence on Stewart's life. On April 17, 1961, longtime friend Gary Cooper was too ill to attend the 33rd Academy Awards ceremony, so Stewart accepted the honorary Oscar on his behalf. Stewart's emotional speech hinted that something was seriously wrong, and the next day newspapers ran the headline, "Gary Cooper has cancer". One month later, on May 13, 1961, six days after his 60th birthday, Cooper died.

In the early 1960s, Stewart took leading roles in three John Ford films, his first work with the acclaimed director. The first, *Two Rode Together* (1961), paired him with Richard Widmark in a Western with thematic echoes of Ford's *The Searchers*. The next, 1962's *The Man Who Shot Liberty Valance* (with John Wayne), is a classic "psychological" western, shot in black and white film noir style featuring powerful use of shadows in the climactic sequence, with Stewart as an Eastern attorney who goes against his non-violent principles when he is forced to confront a psychopathic outlaw played by Lee Marvin in a small frontier town. At story's end, Stewart's character, now a rising political figure, faces a difficult ethical choice as he attempts to reconcile his actions with his personal integrity. The film's billing is unusual in that Stewart was given top billing over Wayne in the trailers and on the posters but Wayne had top billing in the film itself. The film garnered mixed reviews but was an instant hit at the box office.

How the West Was Won (which Ford co-directed, though without directing Stewart's scenes) and *Cheyenne Autumn* were western epics released in 1962 and 1964 respectively. One of only a handful of movies filmed in true Cinerama, shot with three cameras and exhibited with three simultaneous projectors in theatres, *How the West Was Won* went on to win three Oscars and reap massive box office figures. *Cheyenne Autumn*, in which a white-suited Stewart played Wyatt Earp in a long semi-comedic sequence in the middle of the movie, failed domestically and was quickly forgotten. The historical drama was Ford's final Western and Stewart's last feature film with Ford. Stewart's entertaining middle sequence is not directly connected with the rest of the film and was often excised in later theatrical exhibition prints and some television broadcasts.

Having played his last romantic lead in *Bell, Book and Candle* (1958), and silver-haired, Stewart transitioned into more family-related films in the 1960s when he signed a multi-movie deal with 20th Century Fox. These included the successful Henry Koster outing *Mr. Hobbs Takes a Vacation* (1962), and the less memorable films *Take Her, She's Mine* (1963) and *Dear Brigitte* (1965), which featured French model Brigitte Bardot as the object of Stewart's son's mash notes. The Civil War period film *Shenandoah* (1965) and the western family film *The Rare Breed* (1966) fared better at the box office; the Civil War movie, with strong antiwar and humanitarian themes, was a smash hit in the South.

As an aviator, Stewart was particularly interested in aviation films and had pushed to appear in several in the 1950s; most notably *Strategic Air Command* and *The Spirit of St. Louis.* He continued in this vein in the 1960s, most notably in a role as a hard-bitten pilot in *The Flight of the Phoenix* (1965). Subbing for Stewart, famed stunt pilot and air racer Paul Mantz was killed when he crashed the "Tallmantz Phoenix P-1", the specially made, single-engine movie model, in an abortive "touch-and-go". Stewart also narrated the film *X-15* in 1961.

After a progression of lesser western films in the late 1960s and early 1970s, Stewart transitioned from cinema to television. In the 1950s he had made guest appearances on the *Jack Benny Program* (1959-1964). Stewart first starred in the NBC comedy *The Jimmy Stewart Show* (1971-1972), on which he played a college professor, and was the only time in his career in which he was formally billed in the credits as "Jimmy" instead of "James". He followed it with the CBS mystery *Hawkins* (1973-1974), in which he played a small town lawyer investigating cases. The series garnered Stewart a Golden Globe for Best Actor in a Dramatic TV Series, but failed to gain a wide audience, and was cancelled after one season. During this time, Stewart periodically appeared on Johnny Carson's *The Tonight Show* (1970-1981), sharing poems he had written at different times in his life. His poems were later compiled into a short collection, *Jimmy Stewart and His Poems* (1989).

Stewart returned to films after an absence of five years with a major supporting role in John Wayne's final film, *The Shootist* (1976) where Stewart played a doctor giving Wayne's gunfighter a terminal cancer diagnosis. At one point, both Wayne and Stewart were flubbing their lines repeatedly and Stewart turned to director Don Siegel and said, "You'd better get two better actors". Stewart also appeared in supporting roles in *Airport '77* (1977), the 1978 remake of *The Big Sleep* with Robert Mitchum as Raymond Chandler's Philip Marlowe, and *The Magic of Lassie* (1978). The latter film received poor reviews and flopped at the box office.

Following the failure of *The Magic of Lassie*, Stewart went into semi-retirement from acting. He donated his papers, films, and other records to Brigham Young University's Harold B. Lee Library in 1983. Stewart had diversified investments including real estate, oil wells, a charter-plane company and membership on major corporate boards, and he became a multimillionaire. In the 1980s/1990s, he did voiceover work for commercials for Campbell's Soups.

Stewart's longtime friend Henry Fonda died in 1982, and former co-star and friend Grace Kelly, was killed in a car crash shortly afterwards. A few months later, Stewart starred with Bette Davis in *Right of Way* (1983). He filmed several television movies in the 1980s, including *Mr. Krueger's Christmas* (1980), which allowed him to fulfill a lifelong dream to conduct the Mormon Tabernacle Choir. He made frequent visits to the Reagan White House and traveled on the lecture circuit. The re-release of his Hitchcock films gained Stewart renewed recognition. *Rear Window* and *Vertigo* were particularly praised by film critics, which helped bring these pictures to the attention of younger movie-goers. He was presented an Academy Honorary Award by Cary Grant in 1985, "for his fifty years of memorable performances, for his high ideals both on and off the screen, with respect and affection of his colleagues".

In 1988 Stewart made an impassioned plea in Congressional hearings, along with, among many others, Burt Lancaster, Katharine Hepburn, Ginger Rogers, and film director Martin Scorsese, against Ted Turner's decision to 'colorize' classic black and white films, including *It's a Wonderful Life*. Stewart stated, "The coloring of black-and-white films is wrong. It's morally and artistically wrong and these profiteers should leave our film industry alone".

In 1991, James Stewart voiced the character of Sheriff Wylie Burp in the movie *An American Tail: Fievel Goes West*, which was his last film role. Shortly before his 80th birthday, he was asked how he wanted to be remembered. "As someone who 'believed in hard work and love of country, love of family, and love of community'".

In April 1993 he underwent heart surgery and had a pacemaker installed. On January 31, 1997, Stewart tripped over a plant in his bedroom and was rushed to a hospital for stitches to close a bloody gash in his forehead. There it was discovered that he had skin cancer which appeared to be untreatable. He was sent home.

On July 2, 1997, an embolism lodged in his lungs. The clot caused a heart attack that killed him instantly. He was 89 years old. His death came one day after the death of two-time co-star Robert Mitchum (*The Big Sleep*, *Cape Fear*). James Stewart is interred in Forest Lawn Memorial Park Cemetery, alongside his wife, Gloria, who had died from lung cancer on February 16, 1994. President Bill Clinton commented on Stewart's death, saying: "America lost a national treasure today. Jimmy Stewart was a great actor, a gentleman, and a patriot".

After World War II, Stewart settled down, at age 41, marrying former model Gloria Hatrick McLean on August 9, 1949. As Stewart loved to recount in self-mockery, "I, I, I pitched the big question to her last night and to my surprise she, she, she said yes!" Stewart adopted her two sons, Michael and Ronald, and with Gloria he had twin daughters, Judy and Kelly, on May 7, 1951. The couple remained married until her death from lung cancer on February 16, 1994, aged 75. Ronald McLean was killed in action on June 8, 1969, at the age of 24, while serving as a Marine Corps Lieutenant in Vietnam. Daughter Kelly Stewart is an anthropologist.

Kay Stewart

Kay Stewart was born Kathryn Charlene Stewart April 17, 1919, in Cleburne, Texas, and was an American actress. She appeared in ninety-one films and television programs from 1938 to 1977.

Some of those credits include *The Ghost Breakers* (1940), *Gang Busters* (1952), *The Lone Wolf* (1954), *The Private War of Major Benson* (1955), *Battle Hymn* (1957), *Live Fast, Die Young* (1958), *Black Saddle* (1960), two episodes of *Whispering Smith* (1961) with Audie Murphy, *Hazel* (1961-1963), *The Dick Van Dyke Show* (1966), *40 Guns to Apache Pass* (1967) again with Audie Murphy, *The Flying Nun* (1968), *O'Hara, U.S. Treasury* (1971), *S.W.A.T.* (1975), *Baretta* (1976), and *Charlie's Angels* (1977).

Kay was the subject of a feature story in the first edition of Life magazine, which focused on the fact that she was apparently the first female cheerleader at a major university (Northwestern University).

She died March 5, 2002, at age 82 in San Ramon, California.

Howard St. John

Howard St. John was born October 9, 1905, and was a Chicago-born character actor who specialized in unsympathetic roles. His work spanned Broadway, film, and television. He is probably best remembered for his bombastic General Bullmoose, which he played in the stage and screen versions of the 1956 musical *Li'l Abner*.

He made his Broadway debut with *Nocturne* (1925) and continued reliably into the 1930s with parts in *Princess Charming* (1930), *Keeper of the Keys* (1932), and *Triumph* (1935). He grew in popularity with such theater hits as *Janie* (1942) and *Two Blind Mice* (1949).

He took his patented gruffness and moved into films with the "B" movie *Shockproof* (1949) and continued in the same no-nonsense vein as various business tycoons or high-ranking military brass. Standout roles in his over thirty pictures include *Born Yesterday* (1950) and *One, Two, Three* (1961). He played General Bullmoose in the musical *Li'l Abner* in 1956 and recreated his role on film three years later.

Other film roles include *The Sun Sets at Dawn* (1950), *Stop, You're Killing Me* (1952), *Three Coins in the Fountain* (1954), *I Died a Thousand Times* (1955), *World in My Corner* (1956) with Audie Murphy, *Lover Come Back* (1961), *Fate Is the Hunter* (1964), *Strange Bedfellows* (1965), *Matchless* (1967), and *Don't Drink the Water* (1969).

St. John's numerous television appearances would include the short-lived cop drama *The Investigator* (1958) as well as the short-lived sitcom *Hank* (1965). Other television roles included *Robert Montgomery Presents* (1951-1953), *The United States Steel Hour* (1954), *Studio One in Hollywood* (1951-1955), *The Phil Silvers Show* (1958), *The Dinah Shore Chevy Show* (1961), *The Reporter* (1964), and *The Corner Bar* (1972),

Towards the end of his career, he was seen as a foil on the 'Honeymooners' musical sketches on *The Jackie Gleason Show* (1966).

St. John died of a heart attack in New York City at age 68 in March 13, 1974, and was survived by his widow.

Harold J. Stone

Harold J. Stone with Audie Murphy in *Showdown*

Harold J. Stone was born Harold Jacob Hochstein in New York City, New York, March 3, 1913, and was an American film and television character actor.

He began his career on Broadway in 1939 and appeared in five plays in the next six years, including *One Touch of Venus* and *Stalag 17*, following which he made his motion picture debut in the Alan Ladd film noir classic *The Blue Dahlia* (1946). He went on to work in small but memorable roles in such films as *The Harder They Fall* with Humphrey Bogart (1956), Alfred Hitchcock's *The Wrong Man* (1956), *Somebody Up There Likes Me* (1956), *Spartacus* (1960), and *Girl Happy* (1965).

Other notable film roles included *Back from Eternity* (1956), *The Invisible Boy* (1957), *The Chapman Report* (1962), *Showdown* (1963) with Audie Murphy, *X: The Man with the X-Ray Eyes* (1963), *The Greatest Story Ever Told* (1965), *Affair with a Killer* (1966), *The St. Valentine's Day Massacre* (1967), *Which Way to the Front?* (1970), *The Wild McCullochs* (1975), and *Hardly Working* (1980),

Although he would go on to perform secondary roles in a number of films, he became a recognizable face to television viewers for his more than 150 guest appearances on numerous shows dating from the 1950s to the early 1980s including *Lux Video Theatre* (1951-1957), *Trackdown* (1958-1959), *Wanted: Dead or Alive* (1960), *Twilight Zone* (1961), *The Defenders* (1962-1963), *Gilligan's Island* (1965), *Get Smart* (1966), *The Virginian* (1965-1970), *My World and Welcome to It* (1969-1970), *Longstreet* (1972), *Bridget Loves Bernie* (1972-1973), *Hec Ramsey* (1973-1974), *Harry O* (1975), *Three's Company* (1979), *Charlie's Angels* (1977-1981), *Simon & Simon* (1984), and *Highway to Heaven* (1986).

In 1963, he appeared with Marsha Hunt in the ABC medical drama *Breaking Point* in an episode which was nominated for an Emmy Award for writing.

Stone himself was nominated for an Emmy for Outstanding Single Performance by an Actor in a Leading Role for his role in *The Nurses*.

Stone returned to the stage, directing several off-Broadway and Broadway productions, including *Ernest in Love* and *Charley's Aunt*.

He died November 18, 2005, at age 92 in Woodland Hills, Los Angeles, California.

Gale Storm

Audie Murphy with Gale Storm in *The Kid from Texas*

Gale Storm was born Josephine Owaissa Cottle in Bloomington in Victoria County, Texas, April 5, 1922, and was an American actress and singer who starred in two popular television programs of the 1950s, *My Little Margie* (1952-1955) and *The Gale Storm Show* (1956-1960).

The youngest of five children, she had two brothers and two sisters. Her father, William Walter Cottle, died after a year-long illness when she was just seventeen months old, and her mother, Minnie Corina Cottle, struggled to raise the children alone. One of her sisters gave Josephine the middle name "Owaissa," an American Indian word meaning "bluebird." Storm's mother Minnie took in sewing then opened a millinery shop in McDade, Texas, which failed, and finally moved the family to Houston. Storm learned to be an accomplished dancer and became an excellent ice skater at Houston's Polar Palace. She performed in the drama club at both Albert Sidney Johnston Junior High School and San Jacinto High School.

When she was seventeen years old, two of her teachers urged her to enter a contest on *Gateway to Hollywood*, broadcast from the CBS Radio studios in Hollywood, California. First prize was a one-year contract with a movie studio. She won and was immediately given the stage name Gale Storm. Her performing partner (and future husband), Lee Bonnell from South Bend, Indiana, became known as Terry Belmont.

After winning the contest in 1940, Storm made several films for the studio, RKO Radio Pictures. Her first was *Tom Brown's School Days* (1940), playing opposite Jimmy Lydon and Freddie Bartholomew.

She worked steadily in low-budget films released during this period like *Jesse James at Bay* (1941), *Revenge of the Zombies* (1943), and *G.I. Honeymoon* (1945).

Storm acted and sang in Monogram Pictures' popular Frankie Darro series, and played ingénue roles in other Monogram features with the East Side Kids, Edgar Kennedy, and The Three Stooges, most notably in the film *Swing Parade of 1946* (1946)

Monogram had always relied on established actors with reputations, but in Gale Storm the studio finally had a star of its own. She played the lead in the studio's most elaborate productions, both musical and dramatic. She shared top billing in Monogram's *Cosmo Jones, Crime Smasher* (1943), opposite Edgar Kennedy, Richard Cromwell, and Frank Graham in the role of Jones, a character derived from network radio.

American audiences warmed to Storm and her fan mail increased. She performed in more than three dozen motion pictures for Monogram, experience which made possible her success in other media.

Other notable films during this time were *Stampede* (1949), *The Kid from Texas* (1950) with Audie Murphy, and *Al Jennings of Oklahoma* (1951).

She became an American icon of the 1950s, starring in two highly successful television series. It was also in this decade that her singing career took shape. She appeared on such variety programs as ABC's *The Pat Boone Chevy Showroom* (1958).

Storm starred in *My Little Margie* from 1952 to 1955. The show, which co-starred former silent film actor Charles Farrell as her father, was originally a summer replacement for *I Love Lucy* on CBS, but ran for 126 episodes on NBC and CBS. The series was broadcast on CBS Radio from December 1952 to August 1955 with the same actors.

Storm's popularity was capitalized on when she served as hostess of the *NBC Comedy Hour* in the winter of 1956. That year she starred in another situation comedy, *The Gale Storm Show* (also known as *Oh! Susanna*), featuring another silent movie star, ZaSu Pitts. The *Gale Storm* show ran for 143 episodes between 1956 and 1960. Storm appeared regularly on other television programs in the 1950s and 1960s. She was both a panelist and a "mystery guest" on *What's My Line?*(1955-1957).

In Gallatin, Tennessee in November 1954, a ten-year-old girl, Linda Wood, was watching Storm on a Sunday night television variety show, NBC's *Colgate Comedy Hour*, hosted by Gordon MacRae, singing one of the popular songs of the day. Linda's father asked her who was singing and was told it was Gale Storm from *My Little Margie*. Linda's father Randy Wood was president of Dot Records, and he liked Storm so much that he called to sign her before the end of the television show. Her first record, *I Hear You Knockin* a cover version of a rhythm and blues hit by Smiley Lewis, sold over a million copies.

The follow-up was a two-sided hit, with Storm covering Dean Martin's *Memories Are Made of This* backed with her cover of Gloria Mann's *A Teenage Prayer*. That was followed by a hit cover of Frankie Lymon's *Why Do Fools Fall in Love*. Storm's subsequent record sales began to slide but soon rebounded with a cover of her own labelmate Bonnie Guitar's haunting ballad *Dark Moon* that went to No. 4 on the Billboard Hot 100.

Storm had several other hits and headlined in Las Vegas and appeared in numerous stage plays. Amazingly, Storm only recorded for approximately two years with Dot and then gave up recording because of her husband's concerns with the time she had to devote to that career. Equally amazing, almost her entire recording career was based on her quickly recording cover versions of new hits by other artists. Many felt that Storm's covers often were better than the originals, and she developed a large following.

Storm was married and widowed twice. She married Lee Bonnell, then an actor and later a businessman, in 1941. They had four children: Peter, Phillip, Paul, and Susanna. She married again in 1988 to Paul Masterson.

Storm was a great believer in the benevolence of God and was very much a Christian and later became an active member of the South Shores Church. She once said of this:

"Life has been good and I thank God for His many blessings and the happy life He has given to me".

Storm made occasional television appearances in later years, such as *Love Boat* (1979-1987), *Burke's Law* (1964-1965), and *Murder, She Wrote* (1989). In 1981, she published her autobiography, *I Ain't Down Yet*, which described her battle with alcoholism. She was also interviewed by author David C. Tucker for *The Women Who Made Television Funny: Ten Stars of 1950s Sitcoms*, published in 2007 by McFarland and Company.

Storm continued to make personal appearances and autographed photos at fan conventions, along with Charles Farrell from the *My Little Margie* series. She also attended events such as the Memphis Film Festival, the Friends of Old-Time Radio, and the Mid-Atlantic Nostalgia Convention.

Storm lived alone in Monarch Beach, California, near two of her sons and their families, until failing health forced her into a convalescent home, near San Francisco in Danville, California. She died there on June 27, 2009.

Storm has three stars on the Hollywood Walk of Fame for her contributions to recording, radio, and television.

Ray Stricklyn

Audie Murphy with Ray Stricklyn in *Arizona Raiders*

Ray Stricklyn was born Lewis Raymond Stricklyn October 8, 1928 and was an American actor.

Born in Houston, Texas just prior to the beginning of the Great Depression, Ray Stricklyn felt the urge to perform from his earliest years. From stage roles in his hometown, to parts in regional theater and Broadway, Ray made the jump from the stage to acting on both the large and small screens with some of the biggest names in the business, including Gary Cooper, Debbie Reynolds, Clifton Webb, Geraldine Page, Paul Newman, Ida Lupino, and many, many others.

Some of his credits with those big names included *Somebody Up There Likes Me* (1956), *The Return of Dracula* (1958), *The Plunderers* (1960), *Arizona Raiders* (1965) with Audie Murphy, and *Track of Thunder* (1967).

However, turning his talents in a different direction during the 1970s, Ray became one of the most influential publicists in Hollywood through his work with some of the biggest names in the world of entertainment.

The urge to act never left and Ray made his triumphant return to the stage to become "the most award-honored L.A. stage actor of the 1980s". Among others, he was twice named Best Actor of the Year by the Los Angeles Drama Critics Circle, and twice nominated for a Golden Globe for acting.

Ray has guest-starred in a number of the top television series since his return, however it was his now legendary performance as Tennessee Williams in "Confessions of a Nightingale" which received national acclaim with his performances in Los Angeles, New York, and other major cities across North America.

Some of those television guest spots include *The Next Step Beyond* (1978), *The Rockford Files* (1979), *The Colbys* (1985-1986), *Dynasty* (1987), *Wiseguy* (1988-1989), *Days of Our Lives* (1991-1992), *Harry and the Hendersons* (1993), *Hart to Hart Returns* (1993), *Seinfeld* (1996), and *The Nanny* (1998).

He died May 14, 2002, at age 73 in Los Angeles, California.

Ed Stroll

Edson Stroll was born January 6, 1929, in Chicago, Illinois, and was quite a handsome actor/singer who was a bodybuilder before switching to acting.

He appeared in twenty-four films and television programs for over fifty years, from 1958 to 2009.

Some of his credits include *How to Marry a Millionaire* (1958), *The Wild and the Innocent* (1959) with Audie Murphy, *G.I. Blues* (1960), as Prince Charming in *Snow White and the Three Stooges* (1961), *Twilight Zone* (1960-1962), *The Three Stooges in Orbit* (1962), *McHale's Navy* (1962-1966), *The Lost Saucer* (1975), *Murder, She Wrote* (1985), *Dynasty* (1986), *Simon & Simon* (1982-1988), *Dallas* (1991), and *Bad Memories* (2009).

He died July 18, 2011, at age 82 in Marina Del Rey, California.

Sheppard Strudwick

Sheppard Strudwick with Audie Murphy in *The Kid from Texas*

Shepperd Strudwick was born John Shepperd, in Hillsborough, North Carolina, September 22, 1907, and was an American actor of film, television, and stage.

He began his film career as the title character in the film *Joaquin Murrieta* (1938); he was credited as Sheppard Strudwick. He appeared as Yugoslav guerrilla leader Lt. Aleksa Petrovic, an aide to General Draza Mihailovich, in the 20th Century Fox war film *Chetniks! The Fighting Guerrillas* in 1943. He played Edgar Allan Poe in *The Loves of Edgar Allan Poe* (1942) and appeared in *Fighter Squadron* (1948), *The Red Pony* (1949), and *A Place in the Sun* (1951), starring Elizabeth Taylor and Montgomery Clift.

Perhaps his most famous film role was that of Adam Stanton, the idealistic doctor who finally kills Willie Stark (played by Broderick Crawford) in the classic film *All the King's Men* (1949). Another notable role was Father Jean Massieu in *Joan of Arc* (1948), starring Ingrid Bergman as Joan.

Other film credits include *The Kid from Texas* (1950) with Audie Murphy, *A Place in the Sun* (1951), *Beyond a Reasonable Doubt* (1956), *The Sad Sack* (1957), *Girl on the Run* (1958), *Violent Midnight* (1963), *The Monitors* (1969), and *Cops and Robbers* (1973).

Strudwick made many appearances on television, such as on *The Twilight Zone*, as Peter Selden in the 1960 episode "Nightmare as a Child" written by Rod Serling, and included several roles on the soap operas *As the World Turns* (1961-1965), *Another World* (1964-1969), *One Life to Live* (1974-1976), and *Love of Life* (1979-1980). In 1981, he starred as the voice of Homer in the National Radio Theater's Peabody Award-winning radio dramatization of The Odyssey.

His last appearance on celluloid was in 1981's *Kent State*, a TV movie. That same year, he was nominated for the Tony Award for Best Actor (Featured Role – Play) for the unsuccessful Broadway play *To Grandmother's House We Go*.

He was married to Mary Jeffrey from 1977 until his death. He had a son by a previous marriage. He died January 15, 1983, in New York, New York from cancer at the age of 75.

Tina Stuart

No biographical information could be found for Tina Stuart, but she played one of Mamie's girls in *A Time for Dying* (1969) with Audie Murphy.

Olive Sturgess

Audie Murphy with Olive Sturgess in *Whispering Smith*

Olive Dora Sturgess was born October 8, 1933 in British Columbia, Canada. She appeared in fifty-seven films and televisions programs from 1954 to 1974.

Some of those credits include *Lady Godiva of Coventry* (1955), *The Kettles in the Ozarks* (1956), *Perry Mason* (1957), *The Bob Cummings Show* (1956-1958), *Have Gun - Will Travel* (1959), *The Tall Man* (1960-1961), *Whispering Smith* (1961) with Audie Murphy, *The Raven* (1963), *Destry* (1964), *Requiem for a Gunfighter* (1965), *The Girl from U.N.C.L.E.* (1966), *Ironside* (1968-1969), and *The Rookies* (1973-1974).

Barry Sullivan

Audie Murphy with Barry Sullivan in *Seven Ways From Sundown*

Barry Sullivan was born Patrick Barry Sullivan in New York City August 29, 1912, and was an American movie actor who appeared in over 100 movies from the 1930s to the 1980s.

Sullivan fell into acting when in college playing semi-pro football. During the later Depression years, Sullivan was told that because of his 6 ft 3 in stature and rugged good looks he could "make money" simply standing on a Broadway stage. This began a successful career on Broadway, movies, and television.

One of Sullivan's most memorable roles was playing a movie director in *The Bad and the Beautiful* (1952) opposite Kirk Douglas. Sullivan toured the US with Bette Davis in theatrical readings of the poetry of Carl Sandburg and starred opposite her in the 1951 film *Payment on Demand*. In 1950, Sullivan appeared in the film *A Life of Her Own* and replaced Vincent Price in the role of Leslie Charteris' Simon Templar on the NBC Radio show *The Saint*. Unfortunately, Sullivan only lasted two episodes before the show was cancelled, and then resurrected five weeks later with Vincent Price once again playing the starring role.

In the 1953-1954 television season, Sullivan appeared with other celebrities as a musical judge in ABC's *Jukebox Jury*. Sullivan's first starring television role was a syndicated adaptation of the radio series *The Man Called X* for Ziv Television in 1956-1957, as secret agent Ken Thurston, the role Herbert Marshall originally portrayed before the microphone. In the 1957-1958 season, Sullivan starred in the adventure/drama television series *Harbormaster*. He played a commercial ship's captain, David Scott, and Paul Burke played his partner, Jeff Kittridge, in five episodes of the series, which aired first on CBS and then ABC under the revised title *Adventure at Scott Island*.

In 1960, Sullivan played frontier sheriff Pat Garrett opposite Clu Gulager as outlaw Billy the Kid in the NBC western television series *The Tall Man* (although the series ran for seventy-five half-hour episodes, the one in which Garrett kills Billy was never filmed). That same year he played outlaw Jim Flood in *Seven Ways from Sundown* (1960) with Audie Murphy. In additional to *The Tall Man*, Sullivan also starred in the television series *The Road West*, which aired on NBC on Monday, alternating with Perry Como), during the 1966-1967 season. Sullivan played the role of family patriarch Ben Pride.

Sullivan appeared in Sam Peckinpah's *Pat Garrett & Billy the Kid* (1973) as John Chisum, but his scene was excised from the release print (though later restored to the film). He had a featured role in the 1976 miniseries *Rich Man, Poor Man Book II*.

Sullivan guest starred in many series, including *Pursuit* (1958), *Route 66* (1963), *Ben Casey* (1963-1964), *Perry Mason* (1965), *Mission: Impossible* (1967), *The High Chaparral* (1970), *Rod Serling's Night Gallery* (1969-1972), *The Sixth Sense* (1972), *Harry O* (1974), *The Bionic Woman* (1976), *Charlie's Angels* (1979), *The Love Boat* (1979), and *Vega$* (1979).

Sullivan was consistently in demand for the entirety of his career. His acting career spanned romantic leading man roles to villains and finally to character roles. In his later years, Sullivan had roles in the films, *Oh, God!* (1977) with George Burns and *Earthquake* (1974), where he shared scenes with Ava Gardner.

Sullivan has two stars on the Hollywood Walk of Fame: one at 1500 Vine St. for his work in television, and another at 6160 Hollywood Blvd. for motion pictures.

His daughter Jenny Sullivan wrote the play *J for J (Journals for John)* after she found a packet of unsent letters (in 1995) written by Barry decades earlier to her older brother, Johnny, who was mentally disabled. The play premiered on October 20, 2001. John Ritter, who in real life had a handicapped brother, played Johnny, Jenny played herself, and actor Jeff Kober portrayed Sullivan.

Sullivan was a Democratic Party activist and a tireless advocate for the mentally disabled. He had three children. Sullivan was married and divorced three times. Marie Brown, a Broadway actress, was mother to both Jenny and

John Sullivan. Gita Hall, model and actress, was the mother of Patricia. His third marriage to Desiree Sumara produced no children.

Sullivan died of respiratory failure at age 81 on June 6, 1994, in Sherman Oaks, California.

His daughter, Jenny Sullivan, a former actress, is now a theater director. Younger daughter Patricia "Patsy" was twelve years old when signed to a cosmetic company contract as their "face" and was a cover girl featured on many national magazines as well as in commercials. As a teen she married songwriter Jimmy Webb, with whom she had five sons and a daughter. Three of Patsy's sons formed the rock group "The Webb Brothers" and have enjoyed success. Jenny Sullivan married musician Jim Messina; they have no children.

Joseph Sullivan

Joseph Sullivan with Audie Murphy in *Ford Startime*

No biographical information could be found for Joseph Sullivan, but he did appear in eleven films and programs from 1956 to 1979. Some of those credits include *G.E. True Theater* (1956), "The Man" episode of *Startime* (1960) with Audie Murphy, *East Side/West Side* (1963-1964), *Cops and Robbers* (1973), *Rancho Deluxe* (1975), *Siege* (1978), and *Going in Style* (1979).

Neil Summers

Audie Murphy with Neil Summers

Neil Summers was born April 28, 1944, and is an American actor and stuntman. Neil was born in London, England but raised in Phoenix, Arizona. Always wanting to be a cowboy in the movies, Neil had his chance to realize his dream while working on a film called *Arizona Raiders* (1965) starring Audie Murphy. He was allowed the opportunity to do a stair fall, his first professional stunt, on the production.

Star Audie Murphy and direct William Whitney wrote letters of application for membership into the Screen Actors Guild for Neil. Shortly thereafter he moved to Hollywood to pursue his career as a professional stuntman and was asked to join the prestigious Stuntmen's Association of Motion Pictures. He also worked with Audie Murphy in *A Time for Dying* (1969).

In his forty-two year (so far) career, Neil has traveled the world and most of the fifty states in his chosen profession and has had the opportunity to double for such actors as Roddy McDowall, John Astin, Bruce Boxleitner, Keith Carradine, Peter Weller, Robert Crawford, Robert Duvall, Ron Palillo, Frank Silvera, Harry Dean Stanton, Rafael Campos, William Smithers, Warren Oates, Raymond Massey, William Bryant, Sir John Mills, Michael Anderson Jr., James Hampton, Michael J. Pollard, Sid Haig, Hector Elizondo, Emilio Estevez, Rick Schroeder, Warren Stevens, Craig Wasson, and actresses Carol Lynley, Stephanie Powers and Barbara Hershey to name a few.

Some more of his acting roles included *My Name is Nobody* (1973), *Whiteline Fever* (1975), *Kenny Rogers as The Gambler* (1980), *Wanted: Dead or Alive* (1986), *Robocop* (1987), *The Legend of Grizzly Adams* (1990), eight episodes of *Lucky Luke* (1992), *Bad Girls* (1994), *The Shawshank Redemption* (1994), *Flash* (1997), *Detective* (2005), *Appaloosa* (2008), *Doc West* (2009), and *Love Ranch* (2010).

Neil Summers is still active and resides in New Mexico. In a new phase of his illustrious career, he is the published author of eight books on the history of feature film and television westerns. He is a popular guest at Western film festivals across America and has been honored by the Southern California Motion Picture Society for his contributions to film.

He said at Audie Murphy Days 2006 that he and Audie became friends and enjoyed each other's company. He also said that Audie Murphy and John Wayne were his two favorite actors.

Karl Swenson

Karl Swenson was born in Brooklyn, New York, July 23, 1908, and was an American theatre, radio, film, and television actor. Born of Swedish parentage, Swenson made several appearances with Pierre-Luc Michaud on Broadway in the 1930s and 40s, including the title role in Arthur Miller's first production, *The Man Who Had All the Luck*.

He appeared extensively on the radio from the 1930s through the 1950s in such programs as *Cavalcade of America, The Chase, Columbia Presents Corwin, The Columbia Workshop, Inner Sanctum Mysteries, Joe Palooka, Lawyer Q, Lorenzo Jones, The March of Time, The Mercury Theatre on the Air, Mrs. Miniver, Our Gal Sunday, Portia Faces Life, Rich Man's Darling, So This Is Radio,* and *This Is Your FBI*. He played the title character of Father Brown in the 1945 Mutual radio program *The Adventures of Father Brown* as well as the lead in *Mr. Chameleon*.

Swenson entered the film industry in 1943 with two wartime documentary shorts, *December 7* and *The Sikorsky Helicopter*, followed by more than thirty-five roles in feature films and television movies.

No Name on the Bullet (1959) with Audie Murphy is only one of the many Westerns he did for both film and television. He guest starred in 1960 in the NBC science fiction series *The Man and the Challenge*. He played two roles in the NBC Western *Klondike* in the 1960–1961 season. In 1962, he made a one-time appearance on *The Andy Griffith Show* as Mr. McBeevee. He also guest starred in NBC's *Laramie* (1959-1963) western series and in the science fiction series *Steve Canyon* (1959), with Dean Fredericks in the title role. In 1963, he appeared as Nelson in the episode "Beauty Playing a Mandolin Underneath a Willow Tree" episode of the NBC medical drama about psychiatry, *The Eleventh Hour*. Swenson is also remembered for his role as the doomsayer in the diner in Hitchcock's classic *The Birds* (1963) and had a minor role in *The Cincinnati Kid* (1965).

Although Swenson had credits on dozens of TV series, including an appearance on the "Shady Deal at Sunny Acres" episode of *Maverick* (1958), he was best known for his performance as Lars Hanson in forty episodes of *Little House on the Prairie* (1974-1978).

He is also notable for having voiced the character of Merlin in Walt Disney's 1963 animated classic, *The Sword in the Stone*. In 1967, Swenson played the role of U.S. President Theodore Roosevelt in the western film *Brighty of the Grand Canyon*, with co-stars Pat Conway and Joseph Cotten. Swenson appeared in a 1967 episode of the immensely popular *Hogan's Heroes* entitled "How to Win Friends and Influence Nazis", where he played a likable and friendly German scientist Dr. Karl Svenson who is persuaded by Hogan to join the Allied War Effort.

Swenson died of a heart attack in Torrington, Connecticut, on October 8, 1978 shortly after filming the episode in which the *Little House on the Prairie* character Lars Hanson died. He was interred at Center Cemetery in New Milford, Connecticut.

Wesley Marie Tackitt

Wesley Marie Tackitt with Audie Murphy in *The Wild and the Innocent*

No biographical information can be found for Wesley Marie Tackitt. She did appear in three films and three television programs. The three films were *The Wild and the Innocent* (1959) with Audie Murphy, *The Wild Ride* (1960), and *Human Experiments* (1980). The three television programs she appeared in were *Margie* (1961-1962) in which she played Nora Clayton for twenty-six episodes, an *ABC Afterschool Special* called *Very Good Friends* (1977), and episode "Physician, Heal Thyself" of *Quincy* (1979).

Gloria Talbot

Gloria Talbot with Audie Murphy in *Whispering Smith*

Gloria Talbot was born Gloria Talbott in Glendale, California, February 7, 1931, and was an American film and television actress.

Talbot began her career as a child actor in such films as *Maytime* (1937), *Sweet and Lowdown* (1943), and *A Tree Grows In Brooklyn* (1945).

After leaving school, Talbot formed a dramatic group and played shows at various clubs. She stopped acting following her marriage, and resumed after her divorce, having worked extensively in film and television. She worked on a regular basis in the 1950s, having appeared in *Crashout* (1955), the Humphrey Bogart comedy *We're No Angels* (1955), and *All That Heaven Allows* (1955). In that same year, Talbot appeared in *TV Reader's Digest* episode *America's First Great Lady* as Pocahontas. Other films she was in include *Strange Intruder* (1956), *The Oklahoman* (1957) with Joel McCrea, *The Cyclops* (1957), *Cattle Empire* (1958) again with Joel McCrea, *Alias Jesse James* (1959), *Oklahoma Territory* (1960), *Arizona Raiders* (1965) with Audie Murphy, and *An Eye for an Eye* (1966).

She became known as a 'scream queen' after appearing in a number of horror films including *The Daughter of Dr. Jekyll* (1957), *The Cyclops* (1957), and *I Married a Monster from Outer Space* (1958).

Her multiple television credits include *The Abbott and Costello Show* (1953), *Hopalong Cassidy* (1953), *The Roy Rogers Show* (1954), *Richard Diamond, Private Detective* (1958), *Zorro* (1959), *Wanted: Dead or Alive* (1958-1960), *Whispering Smith* (1961) again with Audie Murphy, and *Perry Mason* (1961-1966).

She came out of retirement and appeared in *The Naked Monster* (2005) which was filmed in 1985 and released five years after her death.

Married four times, Talbot died September 19, 2000, from kidney failure and was survived by her fourth husband, Dr. Patrick Mullally and by two children. Her sister, Lori Talbott, also became an actress.

Daughter Mea Mullally, born to Gloria and Dr. Steven J. Capabianco, her second husband, won three gold medals in local ice-skating competitions and is an aspiring actress.

Lyle Talbot

Audie Murphy with Lyle Talbot in *Tumbleweed*

Lyle Talbot was born Lisle Henderson in Pittsburgh, Pennsylvania, February 8, 1902, and was an American actor on stage and screen, best known for his long career in movies from 1931 to 1960 and for his frequent appearances on television in the 1950s and '60s, including his decade-long role as Joe Randolph on television's *The Adventures of Ozzie and Harriet* (1955-1966).

He began his movie career under contract to Warner Brothers in the early days of "talking pictures" and went on to appear in more than 150 films, first as a young matinee idol and later as a character actor and star of many B movies. He was a founding member of the Screen Actors Guild (SAG) and later served on the board.

Talbot was raised in Brainard, Nebraska. He began his career as a magician's assistant and became a leading actor in traveling tent shows in the Midwest and briefly established his own theater company in Memphis. He went to Hollywood in 1931 when the film industry began producing movies with sound and needed "actors who could talk".

Most notable among his film work was his appearance in the classic pre-noir *Three on a Match* (1932) with Humphrey Bogart and Bette Davis, co-starring with Spencer Tracy in the prison movie *20,000 Years in Sing Sing* (1932), romancing opera singer Grace Moore in *One Night of Love* (1934), and pursuing Mae West in *Go West, Young Man* (1936). He appeared opposite many famous actresses including Carole Lombard, Barbara Stanwyck, Mary Astor, Ginger Rogers, and Shirley Temple.

Talbot's activism in union affairs affected his career path. Warner Brothers dropped him from its roster, and Talbot seldom received starring roles again. He became a capable character actor, playing affable neighbors or crafty villains with equal finesse.

In countless low-budget B-movie work, Talbot's roles spanned the gamut. He played cowboys, pirates, detectives, cops, surgeons, psychiatrists, soldiers, judges, newspaper editors, storekeepers, and boxers. In later life he proudly claimed to have never rejected any role offered to him, which explains his participation in three infamous Edward D. Wood, Jr. films: *Glen or Glenda* (1953), *Jail Bait* (1954), and *Plan 9 from Outer Space* (1959).

Talbot also worked with The Three Stooges in *Gold Raiders* (1951), portrayed Lex Luthor in *Atom Man vs. Superman* (1950), played villains in four comedies with The Bowery Boys, and took the role of Commissioner Gordon in the 1949 serial *Batman and Robin*. He appeared with Audie Murphy in *Tumbleweed* (1953).

As his film career tapered off, Talbot became a familiar character actor on American television in the 1950s and 1960s as a regular on *Ozzie and Harriet*.

Talbot had a recurring role as Robert Cummings' United States Air Force buddy Paul Fonda on *The Bob Cummings Show*. Talbot also guest starred frequently on such classic TV series as *The Abbott and Costello Show* (1953), *Hopalong Cassidy* (1953), *Stories of the Century* (1954), *Commando Cody: Sky Marshal of the Universe* (1955), *The George Burns and Gracie Allen Show* (1954-1958), *Richard Diamond, Private Detective* (1960), *Petticoat Junction* (1964), *Green Acres* (1965-1971), *O'Hara, U.S. Treasury* (1972), *Adam-12* (1973), *Charlie's Angels* (1979), *The Dukes of Hazzard* (1984), *The New Leave It to Beaver* (1986), and *Newhart* (1987).

Having started his career in the theater and later co-starred on Broadway in 1940-41 in *Separate Rooms*, Talbot returned to the stage in the 1960s and 1970s, starring in national road company versions of Thornton Wilder's *The Matchmaker*, Gore Vidal's political drama *The Best Man*, Neil Simon's *The Odd Couple* and *Barefoot in the Park*, Arthur Sumner Long's "Never Too Late," and appearing as Capt. Braddock in a 1967 revival of *South Pacific*, at New York's Lincoln Center.

He continued to appear occasionally on TV shows well into his 80s, and narrated two PBS biographies, *The Case of Dashiell Hammett* and *World Without Walls* about pioneering pilot Beryl Markham, both produced and written by his son, Stephen Talbot.

Talbot was the first live action actor to play two prominent DC Comics characters on-screen: the aforementioned Commissioner Gordon in *Batman and Robin* (1949), and supervillain Lex Luthor in *Atom Man vs. Superman* (1951),who at the time was simply known as Luthor. Talbot began a longstanding tradition of actors in these roles that were most recently filled by Gary Oldman and Kevin Spacey, respectively.

After several brief marriages, Talbot in 1948 married a young singer and actress, Margaret Epple, who often used the stage name, Paula. They had four children together and remained married for over forty years until her death in 1989.

Three of his four children became journalists: Stephen Talbot was for many years a documentary producer for the PBS series *Frontline* and *Frontline World* and is now the executive producer of *Sound Tracks: Music Without Borders*. David is an author of *Brothers* about John and Robert Kennedy and the founder and editor of www.Salon.com, and Margaret is a staff writer for *The New Yorker*. His other daughter, Cynthia Talbot, is a family physician and residency director in Portland, Oregon.

Talbot died on March 2, 1996, at his home in San Francisco, California, at age 94 from pneumonia. His remains were cremated and given to his family.

William Talman

Audie Murphy with William Talman in *The Kid from Texas*

William Whitney Talman, Jr. was born February 4, 1915, and was an American television and movie actor, who played Los Angeles District Attorney Hamilton Burger in the long-running series *Perry Mason* (1957-1966).

Talman was born in Detroit, Michigan to Ada Barber and William Whitney Talman, a vice president of an electronics company. His maternal grandparents, Catherine Gandy and James Wells Barber, were immigrants from England.

He founded the drama club at the Cranbrook Schools in Bloomfield Hills, Michigan. He continued to act at Dartmouth College and the University of Michigan. After college he worked in summer stock and at an iron foundry, paper mills, boat yards, and as an automobile salesman.

He served for thirty months in the army in the Pacific in World War II, beginning his service as a private on February 4, 1942 at Camp Upton in Yaphank, (Long Island) New York. He was ultimately commissioned a major during the war.

Before his iconic television role, he worked on the Broadway stage and in movies. Some of his early films include *Red, Hot and Blue* (1949), *The Woman on Pier 13* (1949), and *The Kid from Texas* (1950) with Audie Murphy.

He played a sadistic psychopathic killer in Ida Lupino's 1953 film noir, *The Hitch-Hiker*. The *New York Times* said of him: "William Talman, as the ruthless murderer, makes the most of one of the year's juiciest assignments". But in the 1952 thriller *Beware, My Lovely*, about a war widow who is terrorized by a madman in her home, a photograph of Talman is used for the picture of her late, heroic husband.

Originally, Talman auditioned for the title role of *Perry Mason* and Raymond Burr auditioned for the role of Hamilton Burger. *Perry Mason* creator and author, Erle Stanley Gardner, however, was present and demanded that the actors switch parts. Burr was then given the title role and Talman got the role of Burger. Talman, as Burger, would go on to lose all but three cases in the nine-year series, including a record two separate murder trials in the final episode. He called his record "the longest losing streak in history". He appeared in a first season episode of *The Invaders* (1967). This would be his last on-screen acting role before his death.

Talman was married three times. His first wife was the actress Lynne Carter. Their marriage lasted from just before Talman left for active service in 1942 to September 1952 and produced one daughter, Lynda. His second wife was the actress Barbara Read. They had one daughter, Barbie, and one son, William Whitney Talman III. The couple divorced on August 23, 1960. His third wife was Margaret Flanagan whom he married in 1963. Margaret had a son (Steve) and daughter (Debbie) from a previous marriage. William and Margaret had two children: a son, Timothy, and a daughter, Susan. Widow Margaret Talman outlived Talman by 34 years, until her death in January 2002, at age 73.

Talman is also known for being the first actor in Hollywood to film an anti-smoking commercial for the American Cancer Society. A lifelong heavy smoker, he was diagnosed with lung cancer, and knew he was dying when he filmed the commercial. The short film began with the words, "Before I die I want to do what I can to leave a world free of cancer for my six children ... ". Talman requested that the commercial not be aired until after his death.

He had made another such commercial, which opened with his voice-over and a picture of his home, followed by filmed shots of his wife and kids, then a still of himself "with a friend of mine you might recognize", Raymond Burr, from the *Perry Mason* TV series. He then said, "You know, I didn't mind losing those courtroom battles, but I'm in a battle now I don't want to lose at all. Because if I lose it, it means losing my wife and those kids you just met. I've got lung cancer...If you don't smoke, don't start. If you do smoke, quit! Don't be a loser".

Four weeks after filming the second ad, Talman died on August 30, 1968, at the age of 53, and was buried in the George Washington Section, 2nd Terrace, at Forest Lawn – Hollywood Hills Cemetery in Los Angeles, California.

Yoko Tani

Yoki Tani with Audie Murphy in *The Quiet American*

Yoko Tani was born August 2, 1928 in Paris was a French-born Japanese actress and nightclub entertainer. Her birth name was Itani Yōko. She has occasionally been described as 'Eurasian', 'half-French', 'half-Japanese', and even 'Italian-Japanese', all of which are incorrect. According to contemporary French sources, her father and mother, both Japanese, were attached to the Japanese embassy in Paris, and Tani herself was conceived en route during a shipboard passage from Japan to Europe in 1927, hence given the name *Yōko*, one reading of which can mean "ocean-child".

The family returned to Japan in 1930, when Yoko would still have been a toddler, and she did not return to France until 1950 when her schooling was completed. Given that there were severe restrictions on Japanese travelling outside Japan directly after WWII, this would have been an unusual event; however, it is known that Itani had attended an elite Catholic girls' school in Tokyo, and through it secured a Catholic scholarship to study at the University of Paris.

There was no question that she was bright, but there was equally no question that, once in Paris, she had much interest in attending university. Installing herself in Montmartre, she developed an immediate attraction to the cabaret, the nightclub, and the variety music-hall, where, setting herself up as an exotic oriental beauty, she quickly established a reputation for her provocatively sexy "geisha" dances, which generally ended with her slipping out of her kimono. It was here she was spotted by Marcel Carné, who took her into his circle of director and actor-friends, including Roland Lesaffre, whom she was later to marry. As a result, she began to get bit parts in films, starting as (predictably) a Japanese dancer, in Gréville's *Le port du désir* (1953–1954, released 1955), and on the stage, with a role as *Lotus Bleu* in *la Petite Maison de Thé* (French adaptation of *The Teahouse of the August Moon*) at the *Théâtre Montparnasse*, 1954-1955 season.

It should be noted that Tani's involvement with cinema was, up to the mid 1950s, limited entirely to that of portraying stereotyped Orientals in French films. With the end of the U.S. occupation of Japan in 1952, however, postwar Japanese cinema itself burst upon the French scene, culminating in the years 1955 and 1956 when a total of six Japanese films, including Kurosawa's *Ikimono no Kiroku* and Mizoguchi's *Chikamatsu Monogatari*, were entered at Cannes. It was at Cannes that Tani made contact with directors Hisamatsu Seiji and Kurosawa, contacts which led to a trip to Japan in 1956 by Tani and Lesaffre and their joint appearance in the Toho production *Fukuaki no seishun*. It was originally intended that the film be directed by Kurosawa himself, but in the end it fell to his Toho stable-mate Taniguchi Senkichi. Tani and Lesaffre's ambition was to bring the film back to France and release it in the French market, an aim which was never achieved.

During the same trip, and also for Toho, Tani took a small role in Hisamatsu's *Jōshû to tomo ni*, a variant on the dubious but ever-popular "women in prison" theme, in which she played a westernized Japanese Catholic named Mary. This film, which now languishes in justifiable obscurity, was notable only in that it also starred two veritable legends of Japanese cinema: Hara Setsuko and Tanaka Kinuyo.

Early in 1957 she appeared in a small role in her first English-language film: the MGM production of Graham Greene's *The Quiet American* with Audie Murphy, a political drama set in French Indochina. Tani was cast as a francophone Vietnamese nightclub hostess.

But Tani's real "break" in English-language cinema came with the 1958 production *The Wind Cannot Read*. This film, a war-time love story, had originally been a project of the British producer Alexander Korda, and was to have been directed by David Lean, who in 1955 travelled to Japan with author Richard Mason and cast Japanese actress Kishi Keiko as the female lead. Locations were scouted in India, and Ms Kishi (then 22 years old) was brought to England to learn sufficient English for the part. At a very advanced stage, the project fell apart, and a few months later Korda died. The pieces were eventually picked up by the Rank Organization, and it was decided to produce the film using the script and locations already set out by Lean, with one of Rank's big stars, Dirk Bogarde, in the male lead, Ralph Thomas to direct, and Tani, who was found in Paris, to play the leading female role. The film was a modest commercial success, and lead to further roles in other British co-productions, as the Inuit *Asiak* in the Anglo-French-Italian *The Savage Innocents* (1959), and as the ingénue *Seraphina* in *Piccadilly Third Stop* (1960).

Aside from *The Quiet American*, her only other "Hollywood" roles were in *My Geisha* (1962) and in the fatuous Dean Martin comedy *Who's Been Sleeping in My Bed?* (1963).

Despite being type-cast as an exotic, Tani got to play some unusual roles as a result, as evidenced by her portrayal of Japanese doctor/scientist Sumiko Ogimura in the self-consciously internationalist 1959 East-German / Polish DEFA film production of Stanisław Lem's novel *The Astronauts*. Perhaps even more unusual (for the time) was her trip to the Vancouver Islands in Canada in 1962 to play the role of Mary Ota in James Clavell's *The Sweet and the Bitter*, which treated the aftermath of the wartime internment of Canadian Japanese and the loss of their properties and businesses.

1962/63 marked a shift in Tani's career: a return (once again) to France and the definitive end to her marriage to Lesaffre. From this point on she was to be more strictly European-based and to take on work mainly in the low-budget Italian *peplum* cinema and in *femme fatale* roles in UK television dramas such as *Danger Man* (1967) and *Man in a Suitcase* (1967).

Even as late as 1977, she had a small role in Chinese-Brazilian director Juan Bajon's sexploitation film O Estripador de Mulheres.

Her 1956 marriage to Lesaffre was childless, and ended in divorce in 1962.

She died at age 70 April 19, 1999, in Paris, after a long illness, but is buried in the remote seaside village of Binic, in Brittany.

William Tannen

William Tannen was born November 17, 1911 in New York City, New York, and was an American character actor who appeared in nearly 300 films and television programs from 1934 to 1969.

Some of his roles included *The Band Plays On* (1934), *Tough Guy* (1936), *Another Thin Man* (1939), *Flight Command* (1940), *Dr. Jekyll and Mr. Hyde* (1941), *Air Raid Wardens* (1943) with Laurel and Hardy, *The Canterville Ghost* (1944), *Bud Abbott and Lou Costello in Hollywood* (1945), *All the King's Men* (1949), *The Adventures of Kit Carson* (1951-1955), *Jesse James vs. the Daltons* (1955), *Blackjack Ketchum, Desperado* (1956), *Jailhouse Rock* (1957) with Elvis Presley, *Richard Diamond, Private Detective* (1958), *Wanted: Dead or Alive* (1960), *Whispering Smith* (1961) and *The Quick Gun* (1964) with Audie Murphy, *Get Smart* (1966), *Batman* (1966), *Support Your Local Sheriff!* (1969), and *Lancer* (1969).

He died December 2, 1976, at age 65 in Woodland Hills, Los Angeles, California.

Kevin Tate

Audie Murphy with Kevin Tate in *Bullet for a Badman*

Kevin Tate was born October 6, 1954 in Los Angeles, California, and was a child actor that had roles in sixteen films and television programs from 1964 to 1969.

Some of his roles were in such films and programs as *The Fugitive* (1964), *7 Faces of Dr. Lao* (1964), *Bullet for a Badman* (1964) as Audie Murphy's step-son, *Your Cheatin' Heart* (1964), *The Addams Family* (1965), *The Legend of Jesse James* (1966), *I Dream of Jeannie* (1966), *The Andy Griffith Show* (1967), *Firecreek* (1968), *My Three Sons* (1967-1968), *Daniel Boone* (1969), and *The Virginian* (1965-1969).

Forrest Taylor

Forrest Taylor was born December 29, 1883, and was an American character actor whose artistic career spanned six different decades, from silent's through talkies to the advent of color. A native of Bloomington, Illinois, Taylor was a veteran of the stage by the time he started appearing as a silent lead in both short and feature-length films. Little is known about his early days on stage, but he essayed prime roles in the films *The Terror of Twin Mountains* (1915), *Sunset Country* (1915), *April* (1916), *True Nobility* (1916), and *The Abandonment* (1916), before joining the army during World War I. He would not return to films until 1926, appearing in *A Poor Girl's Romance*.

During the 1930s, Taylor became entrenched as a supporting player in B-westerns and several cliffhanger serials, often playing either the *action* or *brains heavy* roles, such as *Dick Tracy Returns* (1938), *Rio Grande* (1938), *The Lone Ranger Rides Again* (1939), *Dick Tracy's G-Men* (1939), and *Meet Dr. Christian* (1939).

As he grew older and grayer, Taylor migrated to nice guy roles, such as the father of the heroine, a lawman, or a scientist. Then, after the westerns and serials faded he migrated to television work.

More of his work included *Winchester '73* (1950), *Adventures of Wild Bill Hickok* (1952), *Gunsmoke* (1953) with Audie Murphy, *Hopalong Cassidy* (1954), *Dawn at Socorro* (1954), *Man of a Thousand Faces* (1957), twenty episodes as Doc Brandon in *Man Without a Gun* (1957-1959), *Wanted: Dead or Alive* (1960), *Whispering Smith* (1961) again with Audie Murphy, *Bonanza* (1960-1962), and *Ripcord* (1963).

The DVD inserts of *Whispering Smith* and other sources erroneously have Forrest Tucker as the guest star, but that is incorrect information. It is actually Forrest Taylor.

Taylor finally retired in 1963 and died two years later on February 19, 1965, of natural causes in Garden Grove, California, at the age of 81.

Joyce Taylor

Joyce Taylor was born Joyce Crowder September 14, 1932, in Taylorville, Illinois. She based her stage name on that of her hometown. Joyce Taylor sang in amateur shows at age ten and turned professional when she was a very grown-up-looking fifteen, signing on with Mercury Records.

She was under contract to Howard Hughes' RKO in the 1950s but the eccentric and enigmatic tycoon only allowed her to act in one picture, a small part in *Beyond a Reasonable Doubt* (1956).

After the end of seven frustrating years "bottled up" by Hughes, she became a regular on the TV sci-fi/adventure series *Men Into Space* (1959) and acted in many other TV shows as well as a handful of features, such as *The Untouchables* (1960), *Atlantis, the Lost Continent* (1961), as Mrs Romack in Audie Murphy's *Whispering Smith* (1961), *Ring of Fire* (1961) with David Janssen, *Beauty and the Beast* (1962), *My Mother the Car* (1965), *Judd for the Defense* (1967), and *The Windsplitter* (1971). She then retired from acting.

Ray Teal

Ray Teal with Audie Murphy in *Guns of Fort Petticoat*

Ray Teal was born in Grand Rapids, Michigan, January 12, 1902, and was an American actor who appeared in more than 250 movies and some ninety television programs in his thirty-seven-year career. His longest-running role was as Sheriff Roy Coffee on NBC's western television series *Bonanza* (1960–1972). He also played a sheriff in the film *Ace in the Hole* (1951).

Teal, a saxophone player, worked his way through University of California, Los Angeles, located in Los Angeles, California, as a bandleader before becoming an actor.

He had a recurring role as a police officer in the 1953-1955 ABC sitcom with a variety show theme, *Where's Raymond?*, renamed *The Ray Bolger Show*. Ray Bolger played Raymond Wallace, a song-and-dance man who was repeatedly barely on time for his performances.

He was a bit-part player in western films for several years before landing a substantial role in *Northwest Passage* (1940). Other roles followed such as *Captain Midnight* (1942), *See Here, Private Hargrove* (1944), *Back to Bataan* (1945), *Captain Kidd* (1945), *The Best Years of Our Lives* (1946), *Whispering Smith* (1948) with Alan Ladd, *Bad Boy* (1949) with Audie Murphy, *The Great Gatsby* (1949) again with Alan Ladd, *The Kid from Texas* (1950) again with Audie Murphy, *Winchester '73* (1950), *Hangman's Knot* (1952), *Apache Ambush* (1955), Louis L'amour's *The Burning Hills* (1956) and *Utah Blaine* (1957), *The Guns of Fort Petticoat* (1957) again with Audie Murphy, another Louis L'amour western *The Tall Stranger* (1957), *Wanted: Dead or Alive* (958), *Inherit the Wind* (1960), *Posse from Hell* (1961) a fourth time with Audie Murphy, *Dennis the Menace* (1962), *Twilight Zone* (1963), *The Fugitive* (1963), *Bullet for a Badman* (1964) a fifth appearance with Audie Murphy, *Taggart* (1964) a fourth Louis L'amour western, *Chisum* (1970), and his final film *The Hanged Man* (1974).

He died April 2, 1976, of natural causes at age seventy-four in Santa Monica, California.

Arlette Thomas

Arlette Thomas was born November 5, 1927 in Paris, France. She appeared as a character actress in forty-two American and French films and television programs from 1946 to 2008.

Some of her films and television programs were *Land Without Stars* (1946), *The Strange Madame X* (1951), *The Grand Maneuver* (1955), *Antony* (1966), as one of Mamie's girls in *A Time for Dying* (1969) with Audie Murphy, *Sex Life in a Convent* (1972), *I Will Walk Like a Crazy Horse* (1973), *Nestor Burma* (2001), *The Warrior's Brother* (2002), and *The Very Very Big Company* (2008).

She is the mother of director Pierre Jolivet and actor Marc Jolivet. She is also the French voice of Warner Brothers cartoon character Tweetie Pie.

Lyn Thomas

Audie Murphy with Lyn Thomas in *Whispering Smith*

Lyn Thomas was born Jacqueline Thomas November 2, 1929 in Fort Wayne, Indiana. Lyn Thomas acted on stage before she came to Hollywood in the late 1940s, working under contract to Eagle Lion, Hal Wallis Productions, and 20th Century-Fox and yet never catching the proverbial brass ring.

Throughout the 1950s, she appeared in many B movies and television series including *Cheaper by the Dozen* (1950), *The Cisco Kid* (1951), *The Abbott and Costello Show* (1953), *My Little Margie* (1955), *Adventures of Superman* (1953-1956), *Dragnet* (1957-1958), *General Electric Theatre* (1957), *Space Master X-7* (1958) with Moe Howard of the Three Stooges, *Arson for Hire* (1959), *Here Come the Jets* (1959), *Three Came to Kill* (1960), *The Life and Legend of Wyatt Earp* (1961), *Whispering Smith* (1961) with Audie Murphy, and *Checkmate* (1961).

She also frequently appeared on TV commercials and billboard ads. In 1960, Thomas "got married, married, married" and retired from acting. The happily retired Thomas later became a popular guest at Western conventions. She died August 26, 2004, in Riverside, California, from lung cancer.

Marshall Thompson

Marshall Thompson with Audie Murphy behind the scenes of *To Hell and Back*

Marshall Thompson was born James Marshall Thompson November 27, 1925 in Peoria, Illinois. Although he geared himself up for major film stardom throughout the 1950s, it took a leading role on a 1960s television series opposite a lion and chimpanzee to make Marshall Thompson a genuine household name.

Marshall Thompson was named after an ancestor, a famed Supreme Court justice. He moved with his parents from his Peoria, Illinois, hometown to the Los Angeles area at age five where his father set up a successful Westwood practice in dentistry that continued for over three decades. His mother once took to the stage as a concert singer and musician. Marshall was their only child.

He caught the acting bug while in high school when he appeared in a number of school productions and was spotted by a local talent agent. This did not pan out but he also acted upon his early skills as a writer.

The Westwood Village Players produced the young high school student's ambitious three-act play Faith, the story of two young aviators in a Nazi prison. He enrolled at Occidental College where he switched from pre-med to drama. He was also a member of the college's cross-country team. The athletic, lanky-framed, good-looking collegiate was re-discovered while performing as one of the Occidental Players in 1944. This time, he made good and was signed to a Universal contract.

He began in minor war-era films with *Reckless Age* (1944) starring Gloria Jean and was quickly brought over to MGM on the strength of this film.

With most big stars off to war, Marshall was given the chance to work quite steadily in perfunctory nice guy assignments such as *Blonde Fever* (1944), *The Clock* (1945), *They Were Expendable* (1945), and *Bad Bascomb* (1946) opposite Frances Rafferty.

His first association with animals came with the lead in the horse-friendly yarn *Gallant Bess* (1946), MGM's first film produced in CineColor. The handsome Marshall went on to provide yeoman work in the war dramas *Homecoming* (1948), *Command Decision* (1948), and *Battleground* (1949), becoming an instant bobbysoxer idol to film fans. A genial player on screen, he managed to show potential outside his benign typecast in *Dial 1119* (1950) as a cold-hearted, baby-faced killer, and finished his MGM contract out with *The Tall Target* (1951) playing a potential assassin of Abraham Lincoln.

Freelancing for the next several years after losing his contract to MGM due to a change of management, he assisted a few serious-minded dramas, but a noticeable pall soon took over his career with "B" thrillers taking up the bulk of his time. He achieved a bit of cult infamy with the films *Cult of the Cobra* (1955), *Fiend Without a Face* (1958), *It! The Terror from Beyond Space* (1958), and *First Man Into Space* (1959). A couple of notable exceptions were his strong roles in the Audie Murphy biopic *To Hell and Back* (1955) and *East of Kilimanjaro* (1957) in which he performed his own dangerous stunts and developed a lifelong passion for Africa and wildlife.

It was this aforementioned wildlife association, combined with television that made the biggest dramatic impact on his career. Throughout the 1950s Marshall appeared faithfully in small-screen presentations but in 1966, he was cast as a series lead, that of game warden Dr. Marsh Tracy in the African adventure *Daktari* (1966) developed by Ivan Tors and filmed at Africa, U.S.A., a wild-animal theme park near Los Angeles.

Although overshadowed sometimes by those inveterate scene-stealers Clarence the Cross-eyed Lion and Judy the Chimpanzee, Marshall provided a strong, honest, authoritative yet friendly persona and earned the most attention yet in his nearly two-decade-long career. He was also involved in nearly every aspect of the show and afforded the opportunity to direct a few episodes. The series lasted five seasons and, following his departure, continued in the animal vein and his association with Ivan Tors by hosting the live action daytime series *Jambo* (1969), starring in the feature film *Clarence, the Cross-Eyed Lion* (1965) which he co-wrote, and directing some episodes of *Flipper* (1964).

Laying low after his final feature film *Around the World Under the Sea* (1966), which starred assorted TV adventure alumni including *Flipper* (1964) star Brian Kelly and *Sea Hunt* (1958) lead Lloyd Bridges, he spent much of his later time providing footage for wild-life documentaries.

He later guest starred on numerous television programs such as *The Streets of San Francisco* (1973), *Hec Ramsey* (1973), *Owen Marshall: Counselor at Law* (1974), *Charlie's Angels* (1977), *Centennial* (1979), *Lou Grant* (1980), *Dallas: The Early Years* (1986), *Murder, She Wrote* (1989), and *McBain* (1991).

An avid photographer, horseman, and guitarist, among many other talents, he died at age 66 on May 18, 1992 in Royal Oak, Michigan of congestive heart failure and was survived by his wife Barbara Long, daughter Janet, and grandson Jackson.

Carol Thurston

Carol Thurston was born September 27, 1923 in Forsyth, Montana, and was an American actress typecast as playing a variety of exotic native girls.

She made her motion picture debut when she was picked by Cecil B. De Mille over several other actresses to play the role of the Indonesian girl "Tremartini" in *The Story of Dr. Wassell* (1944).

Other roles included *Swamp Fire* (1946), *Apache Chief* (1949), *Flaming Feather* (1952), *The Adventures of Kit Carson* (1952-1953), *Conquest of Cochise* (1953), *Sheriff of Cochise* (1957), *Have Gun - Will Travel* (1957-1959), *The Life and Legend of Wyatt Earp* (1956-1961), and her last two films were *Posse from Hell* (1961) and *Showdown* (1963) both with Audie Murphy. She committed suicide on New Year's Eve 1969 in Hollywood, California.

Casey Tibbs

Casey Tibbs with Audie Murphy

Casey Duane Tibbs was born March 5, 1929, and was an American cowboy, rodeo performer, and actor. He was born northwest of Fort Pierre, South Dakota. Tibbs held the "World All-Around Rodeo Champion" title twice, in 1951 and 1955. He also won in 1949, 1951–1954, and 1959, the world saddle bronc riding championship and in 1951 world bareback bronc riding championship. He was featured on a 1951 cover of *LIFE* magazine.

He is a Charter member of the Rodeo Hall of Fame of the Rodeo Historical Society, a support group of the National Cowboy and Western Heritage Museum.

After his successful rodeo career, Tibbs became a stunt man, stunt coordinator, technical director, livestock consultant, wrangler, and actor for the film industry.

Some of his acting roles were in *Bronco Buster* (1952), *Screen Directors Playhouse* (1956), *Tales of Wells Fargo* (1961), *Stoney Burke* (1962), *The Rounders* (1965), *The Young Rounders* (1965), *The Monroes* (1967), *A Time for Dying* (1969) with Audie Murphy, *Junior Bonner* (1972) with Steve McQueen, *The Waltons* (1974), *Breakheart Pass* (1975), and *More Wild Wild West* (1980).

He moved to Ramona, California in 1976 to raise and breed horses. After battling bone cancer and then lung cancer for about a year, he died at his home in Ramona, while watching the January 28, 1990 Super Bowl. He is buried in Scotty Philip Cemetery, Fort Pierre, South Dakota.

Gerard Tichy

Tichy with Audie Murphy in *The Texican*

Gérard Tichy, also known as Gerard Tichy, Gerhard Tichi, and Gerardo Tichy, was born in Weißenfels, Germany, on March 11, 1920, and was a Spanish actor of German descent, who appeared in numerous movies, including several international productions.

Tichy participated in World War II and held the rank of a lieutenant when it ended. He was put in a French POW camp but soon managed to escape to Spain. There he started his film career in the war epic *Balarrasa* (1951) and quickly became a prominent character actor in Spanish cinema, ultimately appearing in ninety-nine films over the course of his career.

A capable if not fluent English speaker, Tichy also appeared in several international productions that were filmed in Spain, most notably *King of Kings* (1961), as Joseph, *El Cid* (1961), playing King Ramirez, and *Doctor Zhivago* (1965), as Liberius, a Red partisan commander.

He appeared in numerous spaghetti Westerns, most notably *The Texican* (1966) with Audie Murphy and Sergio Corbucci's *Compañeros* (1971).

He died in Madrid, Spain, on April 11, 1992.

Kenneth Tobey

Audie Murphy with Kenneth Tobey in *40 Guns to Apache Pass*

Kenneth Tobey was born in Oakland, California, March 23, 1917, and was an American stage, television, and film actor.

Tobey was headed for a law career when he first dabbled in acting at the University of California Little Theater. That experience led to a year-and-a-half of study at New York's Neighborhood Playhouse, where his classmates included fellow University of California at Berkeley Alumni Eldred Gregory Peck, Eli Wallach, and Tony Randall.

Throughout the 1940s, Tobey acted on Broadway and in stock; he made his film debut in a 1943 short, *The Man of the Ferry*. He made his Hollywood film debut in a Hopalong Cassidy Western *Dangerous Venture* (1947), and went on to appear in scores of features and on numerous television series.

He had a bit role in his first of three Audie Murphy movie's *Beyond Glory* (1948).

He was then a sentry guard who was dressed down by General Savage (played by Gregory Peck) in *Twelve O' Clock High* (1949). A brief comedy bit in *I Was a Male War Bride* (1949) caught the attention of director Howard Hawks, who promised to use Tobey in something more substantial.

In 1951, Tobey was cast in Hawks' production *The Thing from Another World*, playing Captain Patrick Hendry, a United States Air Force pilot and leader of the arctic polar station's dogged defense against the movie's title character, as portrayed by James Arness. That role led to other sci-fi film roles in the 1950s, usually cast in the role of a military man, particularly *The Beast from 20,000 Fathoms* (1953), and *It Came from Beneath the Sea* (1956).

In 1957, Tobey launched his own television series *The Whirlybirds*, a successful syndicated adventure produced by Desilu Studios, in which he played the co-owner of a helicopter charter service along with fellow actor Craig Hill. It was a major hit in the U.S. and abroad, with 111 episodes filmed through 1959. It remained in syndication worldwide for many years.

Other notable roles included Bat Masterson in *Gunfight at the O.K. Corral* (1957), *Wanted: Dead or Alive* (1959), *Seven Ways from Sundown* (1960), with Audie Murphy, as Deputy D.A. Jack Alvin in several episodes of *Perry Mason* (1960-1962), *Temple Houston* (1964), *A Man Called Adam* (1966), and *40 Guns to Apache Pass* (1967) his third and final film with Audie Murphy.

He became a semi-regular on the NBC series *I Spy* (1967-1968) as the field boss of agents Robinson and Scott. Chris Nyby, director of *The Thing*, was often director of these episodes.

More of his credits include *Billy Jack* (1971), *O'Hara, U.S. Treasury* (1971), *Rod Serling's Night Gallery* (1972), *Adam-12* (1970-1974), *The Rookies* (1972-1974), *Get Christie Love!* (1972-1974), *S.W.A.T.* (1975), *W.C. Fields and*

Me (1976), *The Rockford Files* (1977-1978), *Galactica 1980* (1980), *Airplane!* (1980), *The Howling* (1981), *Gremlins* (1984), *The Twilight Zone* (1986), *Hunter* (1987), *Gremlins 2: The New Batch* (1990), *Honey I Blew Up the Kid* (1992), *Star Trek: Deep Space Nine* (1994), and *The Angry Beavers* (1997).

Along with other character actors who had been in 1950s sci-fi and horror movies (John Agar, Robert O. Cornthwaite, Gloria Talbott, etc.), Tobey starred as Patrick Hendry, his character in *The Thing from Another World*, in a spoof originally titled *Attack Of The B Movie Monster*. In 2005, Anthem Pictures released the completed feature version on DVD under the new title, *The Naked Monster*. Tobey's scenes were actually shot in 1985, but this posthumously became his final released film credit.

Tobey died of natural causes December 22, 2002, in Rancho Mirage, California at age 85.

George Tobias

George Tobias with Audie Murphy in *Bullet for a Badman*

George Tobias was born July 14, 1901, and was an American character actor. Born to a Jewish family in New York, he began his acting career at the Pasadena Playhouse in Pasadena, California. He then spent several years in theater groups before moving on to Broadway and, eventually, Hollywood. In 1939, Tobias signed with Warner Brothers, where he played in supporting roles, many times along with James Cagney, in such movies as Cagney's *Yankee Doodle Dandy* (1942) as well as with Gary Cooper in *Sergeant York* (1941).

More roles followed in such films and television programs as *My Sister Eileen* (1942), *Between Two Worlds* (1944), *Mildred Pierce* (1945), *The Glenn Miller Story* (1954), *The Seven Little Foys* (1955), nineteen episodes as Pierre Falcon in *Hudson's Bay* (1959), *Adventures in Paradise* (1959-1961), *Bullet for a Badman* (1964) with Audie Murphy, *The Glass Bottom Boat* (1966), *Mannix* (1970), *The Night Strangler* (1973), *Starsky and Hutch* (1976), and *Switch* (1977).

His most recognizable role is that of the long-suffering neighbor Abner Kravitz on the television sitcom *Bewitched* (1964-1971). Ironically, his last role was as Abner Kravitz in the *Bewitched* sequel series *Tabitha* (1977).

George Tobias never married and retired from acting in 1977.

On February 27, 1980, Tobias died of bladder cancer at the age of 78 at Cedars Sinai Medical Center in Los Angeles, California.

The hearse containing his body was stolen by carjackers on the way to the mortuary. It was then involved in a fender bender. The car and the body were found shortly after. He is buried in Mount Carmel Cemetery, Glendale, Queens County, New York.

Regis Toomey

Audie Murphy with Regis Toomey in *Drums Across the River*

John Regis Toomey was born in Pittsburgh, Pennsylvania, August 13, 1898, and was an American film and television actor. He was one of four children of Francis X. and Mary Ellen Toomey and attended Peabody High School. He initially pondered a law career, but acting won out and he established himself as a musical stage performer.

Educated in dramatics at the University of Pittsburgh, where he became a brother of Sigma Chi, Toomey began as a stock actor and eventually made it to Broadway. Toomey was a singer on stage until throat problems (acute laryngitis) while touring in Europe stopped that aspect of his career. In 1929, he appeared in his first films such as *Alibi*, *The Wheel of Life,* and *Rich People*, initially starting out as a leading man, but finding more success as a character actor, sans his toupee.

In 1941, Toomey appeared in *You're in the Army Now*, in which he and Jane Wyman had the longest screen kiss in cinema history: 3 minutes and 5 seconds.

Toomey appeared in over 180 films, including classics such as *The Big Sleep* (1946) with Humphrey Bogart. Other roles included *The Bishop's Wife* (1947), *The Boy with Green Hair* (1948), *Mighty Joe Young* (1949), *Frenchie* (1950), *The Battle at Apache Pass* (1952), *Son of Belle Starr* (1953), *The High and the Mighty* (1954), and *Drums Across the River* (1954) with Audie Murphy.

In the 1954-1955 television season, Toomey appeared as Joe Mulligan, a police officer in Los Angeles and the father of the Mickey Rooney character Mickey Mulligan, in NBC's short-lived sitcom, *The Mickey Rooney Show: Hey, Mulligan*.

He portrayed Lt. Dennis "Mac" McGough to David Janssen's character of *Richard Diamond, Private Detective* (1957-1958).

In the 1961–1962 television season, he appeared in a supporting role with George Nader in the syndicated crime drama *Shannon* about insurance investigators. From 1963–1966, Toomey was one of the stars of the ABC crime drama, *Burke's Law*, starring Gene Barry. He played Sergeant Les Hart, one of the detectives assisting the murder investigations of the millionaire police captain Amos Burke.

He played Dr. Barton Stuart in *Petticoat Junction* (1968-1969). More roles continued in *Change of Habit* (1969) with Elvis Presley, *The F.B.I.* (1972), *Adam-12* (1973), *The Phantom of Hollywood* (1974), *Won Ton Ton: The Dog Who Saved Hollywood* (1976), *Fantasy Island* (1978), *C.H.O.M.P.S.* (1979), *It's a Living* (1982), and *Evil Town* (1987).

His 1925 marriage to Kathryn Scott produced two children. They met in 1924 when he appeared in the musical Rose Marie which Kathryn had assistant choreographed.

Toomey died of natural causes on October 12, 1991, at the Motion Picture Country House in Woodland Hills, California, at age 93.

Aline Towne

Aline Towne was born Fern Aline Eggen November 7, 1919 in St. Paul, Minnesota. She played the lead female role in five Republic Pictures serials from 1950 to 1954, such as *Don Daredevil Rides Again* (1951), *Radar Men from the Moon* (1952), *Zombies of the Stratosphere* (1952), and *Trader Tom of the China Seas* (1954).

She continued to act sporadically in films and on television in roles like *Commando Cody: Sky Marshal of the Universe* (1955), *Science Fiction Theatre* (1956), *The Life and Legend of Wyatt Earp* (1957), *Leave It to Beaver*

(1958-1960), *Whispering Smith* (1961) with Audie Murphy, *Send Me No Flowers* (1964), *A Guide for the Married Man* (1967), *Song of Norway* (1970), *Marcus Welby, M.D.* (1971-1976), *Eight Is Enough* (1977), *The Incredible Hulk* (1979), and *Airwolf* (1985).

She spent the last 25 years of her life doing what she loved most: travelling the world. Before her death February 2, 1996, at age 76 in Burbank, California, she travelled extensively to Asia, Africa, India, Europe, Australia, New Zealand, South America, Central America, Russia, Scandinavia, and the Middle East.

Aline Towne was not only an accomplished actress, she was a citizen of the world and left behind friends everywhere she travelled. She is survived by two daughters, one son, seven grandchildren, and three great-grandchildren.

Henry Travers

Henry Travers was born Travers John Heagerty March 5, 1874, and was an English actor. His most memorable role was that of the angel, Clarence, in the 1946 film *It's A Wonderful Life*.

Travers was the son of Daniel Heagerty, an Irish doctor from Cork. He grew up in Berwick-upon-Tweed, which is his birthplace according to many biographies, but had actually been born in Prudhoe, some sixty miles further south near the River Tyne. The family were only in Prudhoe for a couple of years, moving there from Woodburn, on the A68 road near Corsenside, Northumberland in about 1866 and then moving on to Tweedmouth at Berwick-upon-Tweed in about 1876.

Initially he trained as an architect at Berwick before taking to the stage under the name Henry Travers.

A stage actor in England, he immigrated to the United States and appeared in Hollywood film productions beginning in 1933 with Reunion in Vienna. More roles followed in *The Invisible Man* (1933), *Death Takes a Holiday* (1934), *Dodge City* (1939), *Stanley and Livingstone* (1939), *Primrose Path* (1940) with Joel McCrea, *Random Harvest* (1942), *The Naughty Nineties* (1945) with Abbott and Costello, *The Yearling* (1946), *Beyond Glory* (1948) with Audie Murphy, and *The Girl from Jones Beach* (1949).

Travers' most famous role was as the angel Clarence who comes to save James Stewart's character from suicide in Frank Capra's classic *It's a Wonderful Life* (1946).

He was also an Oscar-nominated actor for his role in the film *Mrs. Miniver* (1942).

After a long and successful career, he retired from the screen in 1949, and died October 18, 1965, at age 91 in Hollywood, Los Angeles, California.

Mary Treen

Mary Louise Summers was born March 27, 1907, in St. Louis, Missouri. About as reliable as one could ever find, character actress Mary Treen was a familiar face to most and could always be counted on to bring a bit of levity to any film scene.

A minor actress for much of her career, she managed to secure a plain, unassuming niche for herself in 1940s, 1950s and 1960s Hollywood. Her father died while she was still an infant. Raised in California by her mother, who once performed under the stage name Helene Sullivan, and her stepfather, a physician, she attended the Westlake School for Girls as well as a convent where she tried out successfully in school plays.

Mary began dancing in vaudeville shows and revues before seeking her fame in the movies. Tall (5'9") and stringy-framed, she formed a musical comedy duo with Marjorie Barnett, who was 5'3", billing themselves as "Treen and Barnett: Two Unsophisticated Vassar Co-eds". Much of their comedy was centered on their difference in height. Not a beauty by Hollywood standards, Mary relied on humor to get attention.

In 1934, Warner Brothers signed her up after seeing her in a local play. After three years, she freelanced. Her scores of pudgy-cheeked nurses, waitresses, career girls, wallflowers, and confidantes enhanced many a comedy or, at the very least, offered a brief respite in a heavier drama. In the long run, however she deserved better. A few of Mary's highlights would include the films *Kentucky Moonshine* (1938), *I Love a Soldier* (1944) (the role was written especially for her), *Don Juan Quilligan* (1945), and the Christmas classic *It's a Wonderful Life* (1946) as James Stewart's cousin Tilly.

Other roles included *So Proudly We Hail!* (1943), *Texas, Brooklyn & Heaven* (1948) with Audie Murphy, *The Gene Autry Show* (1952), *Willy* (1954-1955), *The Last Stagecoach West* (1957), *The Sad Sack* (1957), *I Married a Monster from Outer Space* (1958), *Wagon Train* (1960), *The Andy Griffith Show* (1960-1961), and *The Errand Boy* (1961).

Mary actually stole a few scenes as the arch maid Hilda on *The Joey Bishop Show* (1962-1965) for three seasons.

She continued acting in such films and television programs as *Perry Mason* (1965), *Green Acres* (1966), *Please Don't Eat the Daisies* (1967), *The Bill Cosby Show* (1971), *Here's Lucy* (1974), *The Strongest Man in the World* (1975), *The Love Boat* (1977), *The Dukes of Hazzard* (1981), *The Fall Guy* (1981), and *Wait Till Your Mother Gets Home!* (1983).

She appeared in three Elvis Presley movies like *Girls! Girls! Girls!* (1962), *Fun in Acapulco* (1963), and *Paradise, Hawaiian Style* (1966).

Perhaps because she could play old maid types so easily in later years, she was often thought to have never married. She actually did marry, quite late in life, to a whole-sale liquor dealer. They had no children. He died in 1965 and she eventually moved in with her ex-vaudeville partner, Marjorie Barnett-Klein, who was also widowed.

In later years the two performed their old routines to the delight of other senior citizens. Mary was living in Balboa Beach, California when she died of cancer July 20, 1989 at the age of 82.

Les Tremayne

Les Tremayne was born Lester Tremayne in England, April 16, 1913, and was a radio, film and television actor. He moved with his family at the age four to Chicago, Illinois, where he began in community theatre. He danced as a vaudeville performer and worked as amusement park barker. He began working in radio when he was seventeen years old.

On radio during the 1930s and 1940s, Tremayne was heard in as many as forty-five shows a week. Replacing Don Ameche, he starred in *The First Nighter Program* from 1936 to 1942. He starred in *The Adventures of the Thin Man* and *The Romance of Helen Trent* during the 1940s. He also starred in the title role in *The Falcon*, and played detective Pat Abbott in *The Abbott Mysteries* in 1946–47.

His film credits include *Francis Goes to West Point* (1952), *The War of the Worlds* (1953), *The Lieutenant Wore Skirts* (1956), *The Monolith Monsters* (1957), *From the Earth to the Moon* (1958), *The Angry Red Planet* (1959), *The Gallant Hours* (1960), *The Slime People* (1963), *Girl Happy* (1965), *The Fortune Cookie* (1966), and *Oliver Twist* (1974).

Some if his television credits include *The 20th Century-Fox Hour* (1955), *Mr. Adams and Eve* (1957), *Bachelor Father* (1958), *The Further Adventures of Ellery Queen* (1958-1959), *Zane Grey Theater* (1961), *Whispering Smith* (1961) with Audie Murphy, *The Andy Griffith Show* (1962), and *My Favorite Martian* (1965).

Between 1974 and 1977, Tremayne appeared on the Saturday morning *Shazam!* television series based on the DC Comics superhero Captain Marvel. In the role of Mentor, Tremayne served as the literal mentor of the programme's protagonist, young Billy Batson.

He appeared in *General Hospital* as Edward Quartermaine, the oldest character in that series, as a temporary replacement for David Lewis in 1987. He played the deceased Victor Lord for one month on *One Life to Live* during the 1987 Heaven storyline in which daughter Vicki Lord Buchanan was reunited with most every character that had died on the show after a heart attack left her in purgatory.

His last appearance was as his *War of the Worlds* character of General Mann in the film *Naked Monster* (2005) released two years after his death.

After doing more than 30,000 broadcasts, Tremayne was elected to the National Radio Hall of Fame in 1995.

In 2003, Tremayne died of heart failure December 19, 2003, at St. John's Health Center in Santa Monica, California at the age of 90.

Peter Trent

Audie Murphy with Peter Trent in *The Quiet American*

No biographical information could be found for Peter Trent, though he did appear in thirty-five films and television programs from 1948 to 1958, most of them French.

Some of his films include *The Iron Swordsman* (1949), *The Earth Cries Out* (1949), *Revenge of Black Eagle* (1951), *Dead Woman's Kiss* (1951), *At Sword's Edge* (1952), *The Cheerful Squadron* (1954), *Conrad Nagel Theater* (1955), *The Three Musketeers* (1956), *The King's Musketeers* (1957), *Captain Gallant of the Foreign Legion* (1955-1957), and *The Quiet American* (1958) with Audie Murphy.

Tom Trout

Tom Trout was born July 4, 1919 in St Louis, Missouri. He appeared in fourteen films and television programs from 1944 to 1959. Some of those include *Abroad with Two Yanks* (1944), *Anchors Aweigh* (1945), *Song of the Thin Man* (1947), *Merton of the Movies* (1947), *Tenth Avenue Angel* (1948), *The Kid from Texas* (1950) with Audie Murphy, *The Palomino* (1950), *The Californians* (1959), and *The Texan* (1959).

He died November 28, 2002 at age 83 in Needles, California, USA.

Harland Tucker

Harland Tucker was born December 8, 1893 in Toledo, Ohio. He was a character actor who appeared in forty-eight films from 1918 to 1949.

Some of those films include *Sauce for the Goose* (1918), *The Swamp* (1921), *The Adorable Deceiver* (1926), *King for a Night* (1933), *Charlie Chan at the Race Track* (1936), *Charlie Chan at the Opera* (1936), *Kid Galahad* (1937), *The Invisible Menace* (1938), *The Lone Wolf Strikes* (1940), *My Favorite Brunette* (1947), *Desert Fury* (1947), *Beyond Glory* (1948) with Audie Murphy, *Night Has a Thousand Eyes* (1948), *Red, Hot and Blue* (1949), *Chicago Deadline* (1949), and *Dear Wife* (1949).

He died March 22, 1949, at age 55 in Los Angeles, California.

Tumbleweed

Tumbleweed with Audie Murphy in *Tumbleweed*

No biographical information could be found for Tumbleweed the horse, but he did have a starring role in the film that took his name *Tumbleweed* (1953). His co-star in that film was Audie Murphy.

He was described as a cayoose raised by a momma mule. Another co-star Lori Nelson has been quoted as saying "That horse could do everything but talk".

Audie Murphy's character was on the run from the law for something he didn't do and he was given a 'beat up looking nag' named "Tumbleweed" to get away on, but it turns out to be the hero's life-saver with his ability to play goat over mountain crags, find water in the desert, and play dead to fool Indians.

Tumbleweed at first took offense at being described as a 'beat up nag', but warmed to the idea when the plot was explained to him and he would be the hero of the story. His co-star Audie Murphy treated him with the respect his star status deserved, so the two got along famously on and off screen.

Rosa Turich

Rosa Turich was born Rosa Sinohui June 9, 1903, in Tucson, Arizona. She and her husband Felipe F. Turich had a comic Spanish language act, "Felipin Y Rosita".

She also appeared in eighty-five films and television programs from 1932 to 1978. Some of those credits include *Beyond the Rockies* (1932), *Zorro Rides Again* (1937), *Covered Wagon Days* (1940), *Bowery Buckaroos* (1947), *Son of Billy the Kid* (1949), *The Kid from Texas* (1950) with Audie Murphy, *Man in the Saddle* (1951), *The Cisco Kid* (1953), *Biff Baker, U.S.A.* (1954), *All That Heaven Allows* (1955), *Duel at Apache Wells* (1957), *Perry Mason* (1959), *The Interns* (1962), *Jesse James Meets Frankenstein's Daughter* (1966), *El Dorado* (1966), *Family Affair* (1969), *The Streets of San Francisco* (1973), *Police Story* (1973), *Medical Center* (1972-1974), *Lou Grant* (1977), and *The Rockford Files* (1978).

She died November 20, 1998, at age 95 in Santa Ana, California.

Beverly Tyler

Beverly Tyler with Audie Murphy behind the scenes of *The Cimarron Kid*

Beverly Tyler was born Beverly Jean Saul July 5, 1927. This relatively obscure, sweet-faced "B" level ingénue of the post-war 1940s and 1950s was born of modest beginnings in Scranton, Pennsylvania. Her mother was a secretary who secured piano and music lessons for her young daughter. Her father was employed with a typewriter company.

As a teenager Beverly made her singing debut on radio. Moving to Hollywood with her mother, she was groomed by MGM at the ripe old age of fourteen and made her first picture with a bit part in *The Youngest Profession* (1943) using her real name. She was given the more attractive marquee name of "Beverly Tyler" before the ink had barely dried on her contract.

Her career showed some signs of improvement after appearing opposite Tom Drake in *The Green Years* (1946) and Peter Lawford in the lightweight comedy *My Brother Talks to Horses* (1947), but then she was forced to wait out a lull.

Strangely enough, other than for a brief singing bit in *Best Foot Forward* (1943), Beverly was never promoted in musicals by MGM, or any other studio for that matter, although she did test once for the Kathryn Grayson part in *That Midnight Kiss* (1949) starring Mario Lanza. She did, however, appear in the short-lived Kurt Weill musical *The Firebrand of Florence* on Broadway in 1945, and performed in the musical *Miss Liberty* in Los Angeles in 1950. Beverly also sang on TV on such variety shows as *Cavalcade of Stars* (1950).

She returned to the camera after a three-year absence in 1950 with Mickey Rooney in *The Fireball* (1950), and in another horse film, *The Palomino* (1950). Most of the roles offered had her playing an altruistic love interest amid rugged surroundings in such western adventures as *The Battle at Apache Pass* (1952) with Jeff Chandler and *The Cimarron Kid* (1952) with Audie Murphy.

She made only a handful of films over the course of her career, which effectively ended once *Voodoo Island* (1957) and *Hong Kong Confidential* (1958) were in the can. A serviceable co-star, little attempt was made by the Hollywood powers-that-be to effectively challenge her multiple talents.

Although she dated the likes of Tom Drake, Peter Lawford, Audie Murphy, Mickey Rooney, and Rory Calhoun, this lovely sparrow did not settle down in marriage until 1962 when she wed comedy writer/director Jim Jordan, Jr., who was the son of the famous *Fibber McGee & Molly* radio couple.

Beverly instantly retired from the business and together the couple produced a son. The only performing she has done over the years was to appear in a few local theater productions in Reno, Nevada, having moved there in 1972. Her husband later became a developer.

Beverly died at age 78 of a pulmonary embolism on November 23, 2005, and was survived by her son, James W. Jordan, and three step-daughters.

Bomba Tzur

Audie Murphy with Bomba Tzur in *Trunk to Cairo*

Bomba Tzur was born Joseph Weltzer in 1928 in Haifa, Palestine. He appeared in twelve films from 1954 to 1975. Most of them were foreign films. Some of those included *They Were Ten* (1961), *Impossible on Saturday* (1966), *Trunk to Cairo* (1966) with Audie Murphy, *Big Gus, What's the Fuss?* (1973), and *Diamonds* (1975). He died in 1979.

U

Julian Upton

No biographical information could be found for Julian Upton, although he did appear in nine films and eight television programs.   His films were *Night Into Morning* (1951), *Battle Zone* (1952), *The Desert Song* (1953), *The Marshal's Daughter* (1953), *Sign of the Pagan* (1954), *To Hell and Back* (1955) with Audie Murphy, *The Ten Commandments* (1956), *The Shadow on the Window* (1957), and *The Confession* (1964).

He had roles in television programs such as *Mark Saber* (1952), *The Gene Autry Show* (1953), *Biff Baker, U.S.A.* (1954), *Death Valley Days* (1953-1954), *Treasury Men in Action* (1954-1955), *Highway Patrol* (1956), *Adventures of Superman* (1955-1956), and *Cavalcade of America* (1956).

Minerva Urecal

Minerva Urecal was born Minerva Holzer September 22, 1894, in Eureka, California, and was an American actress. Of Scottish descent, cruel-eyed, hatchet-faced veteran actress Minerva Urecal was a radio-trained player who spent some time on the clock with stage work before setting her sights on film and TV. Her subsequent stage moniker would become a partial anagram of her hometown name.

Strictly a West Coast-based performer, she finally turned to films in 1933 at the age of 39, and appeared for the next three decades making a number of top stars miserable even in the smallest of parts. Obviously inspired by the cranky dowager instincts of Marie Dressler, Urecal was equipped with extremely coarse and intimidating features that showed no fear to anyone. Her beady eyes, hawk-like nose, firm-set jaw, angry demeanor, and immovable stance could tear right through a person. She could easily shrink a film husband by at least three inches with a simple withering glance.

Evidently a little of her went a long way, for Urecal appeared primarily in uncredited parts over the years. Still noticeable, however, she could be glimpsed as a secretary, laundress, spinster, neighbor, or townsperson somewhere along the line. She was a typically unsatisfied store customer and proved a most brutal and narrow-minded gossip when called upon. Her unhappy kind was ideally suited for big-city tenement settings, the western frontier or on the open seas, and she also played a number of ethnic types (Italian, Swedish, etc.). Primarily diffused in "B" quality pictures and two-reel short comedies, she was often confused with another scene-stealing character harridan,

Marjorie Main, who resembled her in looks, tone, and style. Some of Urecal's more visible roles were in *Oh, Doctor* (1937), *Love in a Bungalow* (1937), *The Ape Man* (1943), *Louisiana Hayride* (1944), *Moonlight and Cactus* (1944), *Rainbow Over Texas* (1946), and *The Lovable Cheat* (1949).

Tucked away in the shadows in many of her 200+ film parts, she began tackling TV assignments in the 1950s and appeared to have an affinity for westerns, guesting on *The Lone Ranger* (1949), *The Range Rider* (1951), *My Friend Flicka* (1955), and both *Gene Autry* and *Roy Rogers'* popular weekly series, among others.

She finally stepped up to the plate with her own series as the titular whiskey-voiced heroine in *The Adventures of Tugboat Annie* (1957). She played Annie Brennan, the weather-beaten widow of a sea captain who takes over the tugboat "Nemesis" herself and the repercussions therein. The comedy series lasted only one season. She later replaced the similarly formidable Hope Emerson as Mother for the 1959-60 season of the detective series *Peter Gunn* (1958).

Urecal continued in character film roles until the mid-1960s, and proved a standout as James Stewart's touchy Scandinavian cook in *Mr. Hobbs Takes a Vacation* (1962). One of her acid-tongued shrews finally got her comeuppance in her next-to-last film. As the intolerant, highly indignant townswoman Mrs. Lindquist, whose cruel orbs could turn any ordinary man to stone, it is she who suffers that exact same fate when she visits Tony Randall's traveling circus in *7 Faces of Dr. Lao* (1964).

Some of Urecal's final TV roles were on *Wagon Train* (1957), *Perry Mason* (1957), *Whispering Smith* (1961) with Audie Murphy, and *Petticoat Junction* (1963).

Never married, the California die-hard succumbed to a heart attack at age 71 in February 26, 1966.

Nancy Valentine

Nancy Valentine was born Annette Valentine in 1928 in St. Albans / Smithtown, Long Island, New York, to Richard and Bertha Valentine. She became a Conover model in New York and in 1945 she and fellow Conover models promoted the Health Campaign by posing at the Cascades Swimming Pool, 134th Street and Riverside Drive.

She was among the models selected in one of the motion picture industry's most extense talent quest for Warner Brothers' *The Girls from Jones Beach* (1949). She won the role of 'Margot, the hair model'. She was able to keep acting and appeared in *Father of the Bride* (1950), *Father's Little Dividend* (1951), *Million Dollar Mermaid* (1952), *Mr. & Mrs. North* (1953), *Mike Hammer* (1959), *Man with a Camera* (1960), *Richard Diamond, Private Detective* (1959-1960), *Whispering Smith* (1961) with Audie Murphy, *Surfside 6* (1962), *Night Slaves* (1970), and *Private Duty Nurses* (1971).

In 1950, she married the Maharajah of Cooch Behar in North Bengal. The marriage didn't last and in 1961, she married producer-director Charles Everett Chambers, whom she met while filming *Tess of the Storm Country* (1960), in Los Angeles.

She retired from acting in 1971 to raise her children and currently lives in Malibu, California.

Lee Van Cleef

Lee Van Cleef with Audie Murphy in *Tumbleweed*

Lee Van Cleef was born January 9, 1925, and was an American film actor who appeared mostly in Western and action pictures. His sharp features and piercing eyes led to his being cast as a villain in scores of films.

Van Cleef was born Clarence LeRoy Van Cleef, Jr. in Somerville, New Jersey, the son of Marion Levinia (née Van Fleet) and Clarence LeRoy Van Cleef, Sr. Both of his parents were of partial Dutch ancestry. Van Cleef served in the United States Navy aboard minesweepers and sub chasers during World War II and became an actor after a brief career as an accountant.

His first acting experiences were on stage, including a small role in the original Broadway production of *Mister Roberts*. His first film was the classic Western *High Noon* (1952), in which he played a villain. He also had a bit part as the sharpshooter in the climax of *The Beast from 20,000 Fathoms* (1953). In 1956 he co-starred with Peter Graves in the B-grade science fiction movie *It Conquered the World* (1956).

In addition to Westerns and the science fiction films, three of his early major roles were in noir films, *Kansas City Confidential* (1952), *Vice Squad* (1953), and *The Big Combo* (1955). All have attained status as classic noir films of the 1950s and Van Cleef's roles, though as secondary characters and villains, were memorable.

He appeared in *Tumbleweed* (1953) and *Posse from Hell* (1961) with Audie Murphy.

Van Cleef starred as minor villains and henchmen in various westerns, including *The Tin Star* (1957) and *Gunfight at the O.K. Corral* (1957).

In 1958, Van Cleef was involved in a serious car accident and was forced temporarily to retire from acting. It took his career some time to recover from this blow and in contrast to his earlier major roles; he for some years had only occasional small parts. He played one of Lee Marvin's villainous henchmen in the 1962 John Ford classic *The Man Who Shot Liberty Valance*, with James Stewart and John Wayne. He also had a small, uncredited role as one of the river pirates in 1962's *How the West Was Won*.

Between 1962 and 1965 Van Cleef worked as a painter, after which his career took a new turn when he appeared in numerous Spaghetti Westerns. This career revival began when Sergio Leone wanted to cast Van Cleef, whose career was still in the doldrums that began with his car accident, against type as one of the two protagonists, alongside Clint Eastwood, in Leone's second Western, *For a Few Dollars More* (1965). Leone then chose Van Cleef to appear with Clint Eastwood again, this time as the primary villain in the classic *The Good, the Bad and the Ugly* (1966). With his roles in Leone's films, Van Cleef became a major star of Spaghetti Westerns, playing central roles in films such as *Death Rides a Horse* (1967), *Day of Anger* (1967), *The Big Gundown* (1966) and *Sabata* (1969). He also played in *The Octogon* (1980) with Chuck Norris.

Van Cleef also had a supporting role in John Carpenter's cult hit *Escape from New York* (1981). In 1984, Van Cleef was cast as a ninja master in the NBC adventure series, *The Master*, but it was canceled after thirteen episodes.

In the early 1980s, Van Cleef appeared in a very popular series of commercials for Midas, in which he played up his gunfighter persona, playing opposite many character actors of the time, including Jack Palance.

He continued to get meaty roles in films such as *Code Name: Wild Geese* (1984), *Jungle Raiders* (1985), *Armed Response* (1986), *Der Commander* (1988), *Thieves of Fortune* (1989), and *Speed Zone* (1989).

He died from a heart attack in Oxnard, California and was interred in Forest Lawn - Hollywood Hills Cemetery in Los Angeles. His gravestone reads:

    Lee Van Cleef January 9, 1925 - December 16, 1989 'Best of the Bad' Love and Light.

Louis Van Rooten

Louis Van Rooten was born Luis D'Antin Van Rooten November 29, 1906, in Mexico City, Distrito Federal, Mexico. Ethnic bald-domed character actor Luis Van Rooten was raised in the United States and would become known in post-war Hollywood as a specialist in multiple dialects. Studying at the University of Pennsylvania, he received his B.A. and set up a sturdy practice as an architect before making a dramatic transition into acting sometime during WWII. He built up his reputation initially on stage at the Cleveland Playhouse, then in radio serials, notably playing the titular sleuth in *The Adventures of Nero Wolfe*. He also did special French, Italian, and Spanish broadcasts during the war.

After serving in the Armed Forces, he settled into post-war films, playing outright villains or slick, shady suspects. Interestingly, he bookended his film career impersonating the nefarious Nazi ringleader Heinrich Himmeler (1900-1945), who organized the extermination of millions of Jews during the Third Reich, in the films *Hitler's Madman* (1943) and *Operation Eichmann* (1961). In between he backed up the various studio's top stars including Alan Ladd in the rugged adventures *Two Years Before the Mast* (1946), *Beyond Glory* (1948), with Audie Murphy, and *Saigon* (1948), Ray Milland and Charles Laughton in the exceptional film noir *The Big Clock* (1948), Edward G. Robinson in *Night Has a Thousand Eyes* (1948), and Kirk Douglas in *Champion* (1949). One notable exception from the usual villainous typecast was his role as a plainclothes cop in the classic film *Detective Story* (1951).

By the 1950's Van Rooten had moved with ease into TV drama, performing in a number of live dramas during its vital "Golden Age." His regular work in TV series included *One Man's Family* (1949) and *Major Dell Conway of the Flying Tigers* (1951). He is remembered by 1950s TV fans as the fight manager in *The Joe Palooka Story* (1954-55). His slick, cultivated tones were utilized quite frequently in various documentaries and narrative projects. In later years (the 1960s), Van Rooten was seen less and less. He last appeared in *What's So Bad About Feeling Good?* (1968).

He eventually retired during the decade to become an author and expert on horticultural subjects. He also enjoyed painting as a creative sideline.

He died June 17, 1973, in Chatham, Massachusetts, at the age of 66 of unreported causes.

Dale Van Sickel

Dale Harris Van Sickel was born in Eatonton, Georgia, November 29, 1907, and was an American college football, basketball, and baseball player during the 1920s, who later became a Hollywood motion picture actor and stunt performer for over forty years. Van Sickel played college football for the University of Florida, and was recognized as the first first-team All-American in the history of the Florida Gators football program.

He grew up in Gainesville, Florida. Van Sickel attended Gainesville High School, where he played high school football for the Gainesville Purple Hurricanes. In 2007, eighty-one years after he graduated from high school, the Florida High School Athletic Association (FHSAA) recognized Van Sickel as one of the "100 Greatest Players of the First 100 Years" of Florida high school football. He is generally regarded as the best high school football player produced in the state of Florida before the 1930s.

Van Sickel attended the University of Florida in Gainesvile He played right end for the Florida Gators football team for three seasons from 1927 to 1929, on the opposite side of the line from left end Dutch Stanley. During his three years as a member of the Gators varsity, the team won twenty-three of twenty-nine games. Led by future Hall of Fame coach Charlie Bachman in 1928, Van Sickel and the Gators posted an 8–1 record during his junior season, outscoring their competition 366–44 the most points scored in the nation. The Gators' sole 1928 loss was to Tennessee in Knoxville—by a single point, 12–13. The Associated Press, Newspaper Enterprise Association and Grantland Rice of *Collier's Weekly* named Van Sickel to their respective 1928 first-team All-America squads, making him the first player from the University of Florida to be named a first-team All-American. As was typical of the 1920s era, Van Sickel played both offense and defense; his College Hall of Fame biography describes him as "a swift and sure-handed receiver on offense and a gifted defensive player". Van Sickel was injured during his senior football season in 1929, and while he was productive, he was unable to post the same sort of numbers in 1929 that he did during his 1928 All-American season.

Van Sickel was also the team captain and a varsity letterman for the Florida Gators basketball and Gators baseball teams. He was later inducted into the University of Florida Athletic Hall of Fame as a "Gator Great," and he was also the first Gator to be inducted into the College Football Hall of Fame in 1975.

Van Sickel graduated from the University of Florida with a bachelor's degree in 1930, and he remained at the university to be an assistant coach for the Gators football and basketball teams during the 1930 and 1931 seasons. Afterward, he moved to Hollywood to begin a career as a movie stuntman, and had his first on-screen stunt role in the Marx Brothers' film *Duck Soup* (1933)

Over the next thirty-eight years, Van Sickel appeared as an extra and occasional leading man in over 280 films and television episodes, and performed on-screen stunts in another 140. He was a founding member, and the first president, of the Stuntmen's Association of Motion Pictures.

Some of the films and television programs he appeared in included *The Richest Girl in the World* (1934), *Mr. Deeds Goes to Town* (1936), *Kid Galahad* (1937), *Gone with the Wind* (1939), *Hellzapoppin'* (1941), *Reap the Wild Wind* (1942), *Captain America* (1944), *The Purple Monster Strikes* (1945), *Son of Zorro* (1947), *Jesse James Rides Again* (1947), *Mighty Joe Young* (1949), *The Fighting Kentuckian* (1949), *The Greatest Show on Earth* (1952), *Abbott and Costello Go to Mars* (1953), *The War of the Worlds* (1953), *Rocky Jones, Space Ranger* (1954), *Seven Brides for Seven Brothers* (1954), *Commando Cody: Sky Marshal of the Universe* (1955), *Earth vs. the Flying Saucers* (1956), *The Wings of Eagles* (1957), *Wanted: Dead or Alive* (1959), *Spartacus* (1960), *Birdman of Alcatraz* (1962), *The Greatest Show on Earth* (1963), *Murderers' Row* (1966), *The Green Hornet* (1967), *The Love Bug* (1968), and *Duel* (1971).

He also appeared in *Cast a Long Shadow* (1959), *Seven Ways from Sundown* (1960), *Six Black Horses* (1962), and *Showdown* (1963) with Audie Murphy.

Van Sickel died January 25, 1977, in Newport Beach, California, as a result of injuries received while filming a car crash stunt in 1975; he was 69 years old. Van Sickel was survived by his wife Iris and their daughter.

Chico Vejar

Chico Vejar with Audie Murphy relaxing between scenes of *World in My Corner*

Francis "Chico" Vejar was born Sep 5, 1931, in Stamford. Connecticut. He was a professional boxer who fought through the decade of 1950, ending his great career with a win over Wilf Greaves on March 27, 1961.

But it was during the mid 1950s that he did his best work. Americans started watching television in the late 1940s and the Monday and Friday Night fights were broadcast weekly by Gillette and Pabst Blue Ribbon from the late 1940s into the early 1960s. Back when Don Dunphy was commentator, fights like Hairston vs. Keogh, Satterfield vs. Brothers, Rosi vs. Compo, and Castellani vs. Durando thrilled TV audiences everywhere, but no one seemed to fight more often or was more popular than Chico Vejar. If the 1950s were a wonderful stew of boxing, Chico was clearly part of the meat.

During his boxing days he appeared in *World in My Corner* (1956) with Audie Murphy, and *The Midnight Story* (1957). His only other foray into acting was in the television series *True Blue* (1990).

In 2006, he was one of six men inducted into the Connecticut Boxing Hall of Fame on Dec. 1 at the Foxwoods Resort Casino.

Harold Vermilyea

Harold Vermilyea was born October 10, 1889 in New York City, New York. Very active in the theater (he performed on Broadway from 1917 to 1957), Harold Vermilyea occasionally worked in television and in the movies, where after a false start in the nineteen tens, he landed a few interesting parts in a series of post-Second-World-War film-noirs for Paramount, RKO, and 20th Century-Fox, such as *The Big Clock* (1948) or *Sorry, Wrong Number* (1948).

His earlier roles were in such films as *The Jungle* (1914), *Pride and the Devil* (1917), and *The Law That Failed* (1917).

His next film role was almost thirty years later in *O.S.S* (1946) with Alan Ladd. Some of his other films include *The Miracle of the Bells* (1948), *Beyond Glory* (1949) with Audie Murphy and again with Alan Ladd, and *Chicago Deadline* (1949), his third film with Alan Ladd.

He also appeared in numerous television programs such as *Lux Video Theatre* (1950), *Danger* (1951), *Pulitzer Prize Playhouse* (1952), *Robert Montgomery Presents* (1953), *Inner Sanctum* (1954), *The United States Steel Hour* (1955), and *The Alcoa Hour* (1957).

He died January 8, 1958, at age 68 in New York City, New York.

Martha Vickers

Martha Vickers with Audie Murphy in *Bad Boy*

Martha Vickers was born Martha MacVicar in Ann Arbor, Michigan, May 28, 1925, and was an American television and film actress.

She began her career as a model and cover girl. Her first film role was a small uncredited part in *Frankenstein Meets the Wolf Man* (1941).

She played minor roles in several films during the early 1940s, such as *The Mummy's Ghost* (1944), and by the end of the decade she had progressed to featured supporting roles, including the role of Carmen Sternwood, the nymphomaniac younger sister of Lauren Bacall's character in *The Big Sleep* (1946).

She also appeared as Audie Murphy's step-sister in *Bad Boy* (1949).

During the 1950s, Vickers' film career stalled, however she continued to act in television series like *The Unexpected* (1952), *G.E. True Theater* (1953-1954), *Fireside Theatre* (1955), *The Millionaire* (1956), *Playhouse 90* (1957), *State Trooper* (1958), *Perry Mason* (1959), and *The Rebel* (1960), her final performance.

Vickers was married three times; to A. C. Lyles (March 15, 1948 – May 1949), Mickey Rooney (June 3, 1949 – September 25, 1951) and actor Manuel Rojas (October 1, 1954 – 1965). Each marriage ended in divorce. Vickers had one son with Mickey Rooney, and two daughters with Rojas.

She died of esophageal cancer, November 2, 1971, at age 46, in California, and is buried in Valhalla Memorial Park Cemetery in North Hollywood, California.

Herb Vigran

Herb Vigran with Audie Murphy in *The Gunrunners*

Herbert "Herb" Vigran was born June 5, 1910, in Fort Wayne, Indiana. He was a well-known American character actor in Hollywood from the 1930s to the 1980s. Over his 50-year career, he made over 350 television and film appearances.

He graduated with a law degree from Indiana University Law School but later chose to pursue acting.

After starting out on Broadway, he soon moved to Hollywood with no money and only a Broadway acting experience. In 1939, Vigran's agent helped him secure a lead in the radio drama *Silver Theatre*. The actor had a $5 recording made of the radio show and used it as a demo to get other jobs with his unique voice. He performed in radio shows with the likes of Jack Benny, Bob Hope, Lucille Ball, and Jimmy Durante.

He later had hundreds of film appearances on movies like *Pardon My Sarong* (1942), *It Ain't Hay* (1943), *The Noose Hangs High* (1948), all three with Abbott and Costello, *Texas, Brooklyn & Heaven* (1948) with Audie Murphy, *The Damned Don't Cry* (1950), *Abbott and Costello Meet the Invisible Man* (1951), *Bedtime for Bonzo* (1951), *The Star* (1952), *The Long, Long Trailer* (1953), *Dragnet* (1954), *White Christmas* (1954), *20,000 Leagues Under the Sea* (1954), *Hell on Frisco Bay* (1955), *You Can't Run Away from It* (1956), *The Vampire* (1957), *Gunsight Ridge* (1957), *The Gun Runners* (1958) again with Audie Murphy, *The Fugitive Kind* (1959), *Send Me No Flowers* (1964), *That Funny Feeling* (1965), *The Reluctant Astronaut* (1967), *The Love Bug* (1968), *Which Way to the Front?* (1970), *Support Your Local Gunfighter* (1971), *Cancel My Reservation* (1972), *Herbie Rides Again* (1974), *The Shaggy D.A.* (1976), *Every Girl Should Have One* (1978), *Airplane!* (1980), and *Amazon Women on the Moon* (1987).

In the rock and roll movie *Go, Johnny, Go* (1959), Vigran played an assistant to promoter Alan Freed and performed dialogue scenes with rock legend Chuck Berry.

He appeared in a number of *I Love Lucy* (1952-1954) episodes, and in the 1954 episode titled "Lucy Is Envious", Vigran is the promoter who hired Lucy and Ethel to dress up as "Women From Mars" for a publicity stunt.

With his bushy eyebrows and balding pate, he was easily cast in a wide variety of middle-aged "everyman" roles: cops, small-time crooks, judges, jurors, bartenders, repairmen, neighbors, shopkeepers, etc, in programs such as *Racket Squad* (1952), *I Married Joan* (1952-1953), *The Mickey Rooney Show* (1954), *Father Knows Best* (1955), *Tales of the Texas Rangers* (1955), *The Life and Legend of Wyatt Earp* (1956), *Blondie* (1957), *Richard Diamond, Private Detective* (1957-1958), *Adventures of Superman* (1952-1958), *Wanted: Dead or Alive* (1959), *Dragnet* (1952-1959), *Wichita Town* (1960), *Shirley Temple Theatre* (1961), *The Virginian* (1963), *The Fugitive* (1964), *I Dream of Jeannie* (1967), *Hawaii Five-O* (1969), *The Odd Couple* (1971), *Longstreet* (1972), *Hec Ramsey* (1972), *Kolchak: The Night Stalker* (1974), *Charlie's Angels* (1979), *Galactica 1980* (1980), *The Jeffersons* (1985), and *Remington Steele* (1985).

He also provided the voice of "Whitney's boss" on the Arrowhead bottled-water television (animated) and radio commercials in the 1960s.

In 1952, Vigran married the former Belle Pasternack. The couple had two sons.

Vigran was active up until his death from cancer on November 29, 1986 in Los Angeles. He was cremated.

Victor Vilanova

No biographical information could be found for Victor Vilanova, but hid appear in eight films and one television show called *Percy Stuart* (1969).

His films are listed as *Desperate Mission* (1965), *$100,000 for Ringo* (1965), *Seven Pistols for a Gringo* (1966), *The Texican* (1966) as Audie Murphy's brother, *Seven Murders for Scotland Yard* (1971), *God in Heaven... Arizona on Earth* (1972), *Green Inferno* (1973), and *The Killer with a Thousand Eyes* (1974).

Joseph A. Vitale

Joseph Vitale was born September 6, 1901, in New York City, New York. He appeared in numerous films and television programs from 1934 to 1964.

Some of his appearances were in *Daredevil O'Dare* (1934), *Gildersleeve's Ghost* (1944), *Smash-Up: The Story of a Woman* (1947), *Yankee Buccaneer* (1952), *The Stranger Wore a Gun* (1953), *Rocky Jones, Space Ranger* (1954), *The Lone Ranger* (1955-1957), *Wagon Train* (1958), *Alias Jesse James* (1959), *Wichita Town* (1960), *Empire* (1963), *Mister Ed* (1964), and his last film *Apache Rifles* (1964) with Audie Murphy.

He died June 5, 1994, at age 92 in Granada Hills, California.

Ernestine Wade

Ernestine Wade with Audie Murphy in *Guns of Fort Petticoat*

Ernestine Wade was born in Jackson, Mississippi, August 7, 1906, and was an African American actress who is best known for playing the role of Sapphire Stevens on the radio and television program *Amos 'n Andy* (1951-1955).

Wade was trained as a singer and organist. Her family had a strong connection to the theater. Her mother, Hazel Wade, worked in vaudeville as a performer, while her maternal grandmother, Mrs. Johnson, worked for the Lincoln Theater in Baltimore, Maryland.

Ernestine grew up in Los Angeles and started her acting career at age four. In 1935, Ernestine was a member of the Four Hot Chocolates singing group. She appeared in bit parts in films and did the voice performance of a butterfly in the 1946 Walt Disney production *Song of the South*.

Wade was a member of the choir organized by actress-singer Anne Brown for the filming of the George Gershwin biographical film *Rhapsody in Blue* (1945) and appeared in the film as one of the "Catfish Row" residents.

She enjoyed the highest level of prominence on *Amos 'n Andy* by playing the shrewish, demanding, and manipulative wife of George "Kingfish" Stevens. Wade, Johnny Lee, and Lillian Randolph were the only cast members of the radio version of *Amos 'n Andy* to star in the television version.

Ernestine began playing Sapphire Stevens in 1939, but originally came to the *Amos 'n' Andy* radio show in the role of Valada Green, a lady who believed she had married Andy. In her interview which is part of the documentary *Amos 'n' Andy: Anatomy of a Controversy*, Wade related how she got the job with the radio show. Initially there for a singing role, she was asked if she could "do lines". When the answer was yes, she was first asked to say "I do" and then to scream; the scream got her the role of Valada Green. Ernestine also played the radio roles of The Widow Armbruster, Sara Fletcher, and Mrs. Van Porter.

In a 1979 interview, Ernestine related that she would often be stopped by strangers who recognized her from the television show, saying, "I know who you are and I want to ask you, is that your real husband?" At her home, she had framed signed photos from the members of the *Amos 'n' Andy* television show cast. Tim Moore, her TV husband, wrote the following on his, "My Best Wishes To My Darling Battle ax From The Kingfish Tim Moore".

Wade defended her character against criticism of being a negative stereotype of African American women. In a 1973 interview, she stated, "I know there were those who were offended by it, but I still have people stop me on the street to tell me how much they enjoyed it. And many of those people are black members of the NAACP". The documentary *Amos 'n' Andy: Anatomy of a Controversy* covered the history of the radio and television shows as well as interviews with surviving cast members. Ernestine was among them, and she continued her defense of the show and those with roles in it. She believed that the roles she and her colleagues played made it possible for African-American actors who came later to be cast in a wider variety of roles. She also considered the early typecast roles, where women were most often cast as maids, not to be damaging, seeing them in the sense of someone being either given the role of the hero or the part of the villain.

In later years, she continued as an actress, doing more voice work for radio and cartoons. After *Amos 'n' Andy*, Wade did voice work in television and radio commercials. Ernestine also did office work and played the organ.

She appeared in *The Girl He Left Behind* (1956), *The Adventures of Jim Bowie* (1956), *The Guns of Fort Petticoat* (1957) with Audie Murphy, and *The Untouchables* (1961). She also appeared on an episode of *Family Affair* (1967) as a maid working for a stage actress played by Joan Blondell. She then had a role in *Julia* (1969) and *Love, American Style* (1972). Her final roles were in two episodes of *That's My Mama* (1974-1975).

Ms. Wade was also the mother of singer/musician Billy Preston.

Ernestine Wade died at age 75 April 15, 1983, and is buried in Angelus-Rosedale Cemetery in Los Angeles, California. Since she had no headstone, the West Adams Heritage Association marked her grave with a plaque.

Russell Wade

Audie Murphy with Russell Wade in *Beyond Glory*

Russell Wade was born June 21, 1917, in Oklahoma City, Oklahoma, and was an American character actor. He moved to California in the late 1920s and attended Hollywood High School, appearing on stage before moving into films.

He appeared in over sixty WWII-era movies as various cadets and military rookie types, retiring in 1948 for a career in business and real estate in the Palm Springs area.

Some of those credits include *The Wrecker* (1933), *Ace Drummond* (1936), *Pick a Star* (1937) with Laurel and Hardy, *Topper* (1937), *The Goldwyn Follies* (1938), *You Can't Cheat an Honest Man* (1939), *One Night in the Tropics* (1940) with Abbott and Costello, *Keep 'Em Flying* (1941) again with Bud & Lou, *The Great Gildersleeve* (1942), *Tall in the Saddle* (1944), *The Body Snatcher* (1945), *The Bamboo Blonde* (1946), *Shoot to Kill* (1947), and his final film *Beyond Glory* (1948) which was Audie Murphy's first film.

He developed the El Dorado Country Club in the mid-1950s and was the chairman of the Palm Springs Golf Classic tournament, now called the Bob Hope Classic, there for numerous years.

Russell was awarded a Star on the Palm Springs Walk of Stars on Palm Canyon Drive and was the recipient of the Golden Plate Award from the American Academy of Achievement.

He and wife Janie had two children: Joanie, who predeceased him, and Jeff.

He died December 9, 2006, at age 89 in Riverside, California.

Charles Wagenhiem

Charles Wagenhiem was born February 21, 1896. Initially drawn to an acting career to counterbalance an acute case of shyness, diminutive character actor Charles Wagenheim's career comprised hundreds upon hundreds of minor but atmospheric parts on stage, film, and television. Born in Newark, New Jersey, he was the son of immigrant parents. Enlisting in the military during World War I, he was compensated for an education by the government and chose to study dramatics at the American Academy of Dramatic Arts in New York, graduating in 1923.

After touring with a Shakespearean company, he appeared in a host of Broadway plays, several of them written, directed and/or produced by the prolific George Abbott, including *A Holy Terror* (1925), *Four Walls* (1927) and *Ringside* (1928). Following a stage part in *Schoolhouse on the Lot* (1938), the mustachioed Wagenheim turned to Hollywood for work. His dark, graveside manner, baggy-eyed scowl and lowlife countenance proved ideal for a number of genres, particularly crime thrillers and westerns.

In films from 1929, the character player scored well when Alfred Hitchcock chose him to play the assassin in *Foreign Correspondent* (1940). He went on to enact a number of seedy, unappetizing roles (tramps, drunks, thieves) over the years but never found the one juicy part that could have put him at the top of the character ranks.

Usually billed tenth or lower, Wagenheim was more filler than anything else which his blue-collar gallery of cabbies, waiters, deputies, clerks, morgue attendants, junkmen, etc., will attest. Some of his better delineated roles came with *Two Girls on Broadway* (1940); *Charlie Chan at the Wax Museum* (1940); *Half Way to Shanghai* (1942); the cliffhangers *Don Winslow of the Navy* (1942) and *Raiders of Ghost City* (1944); *The House on 92nd Street* (1945); *A Lady Without Passport* (1950); *Beneath the 12-Mile Reef* (1953); and *Canyon Crossroads* (1956).

One of his more promising roles came as "The Runt" in *Meet Boston Blackie* (1941), which started Chester Morris off in the popular 1940s "B" series as the thief-cum-crime-fighter, but the sidekick role was subsequently taken over by George E. Stone.

More credits included *House of Horrors* (1946), *Joan of Arc* (1948), *Samson and Delilah* (1949), *Jim Thorpe, All-American* (1951), *Aladdin and His Lamp* (1952), *Boston Blackie* (1952-1953), *Blackjack Ketchum, Desperado* (1956), *The Toughest Gun in Tombstone* (1958), *One Foot in Hell* (1960), *Lonely Are the Brave* (1962), *The Addams Family* (1965), *Cat Ballou* (1965), *The Cincinnati Kid* (1965), *The Fugitive* (1966), *A Time for Dying* (1969) with Audie Murphy, *Adam-12* (1970), *Harry O* (1975), *The Apple Dumpling Gang* (1975), *Baretta* (1975-1977), *James at 16* (1978), and *All in the Family* (1979).

Of his latter films it might be noted that Wagenheim was cast in the very small but pivotal role of the thief who breaks into the storefront in which the Frank family is hiding above in *The Diary of Anne Frank* (1959).

Wagenheim played the recurring role of Halligan on *Gunsmoke* (1967-1975).

On March 6, 1979, the 83-year-old Wagenheim was bludgeoned to death in his Hollywood apartment following a grocery shopping trip when he surprised a thief in his home. By sheer horrific coincidence, elderly character actor Victor Kilian, of *Mary Hartman, Mary Hartman* (1976) fame, was found beaten to death by burglars in his Los Angeles-area apartment just a few days later on March 11, 1979.

June Walker

June Walker with Audie Murphy in The Unforgiven

June Walker was born June 14, 1900, and was an American stage and film actress. She was the first actress to portray the character of Lorelei Lee, in the 1926 Broadway production of *Gentlemen Prefer Blondes*.

In 1926, she married British actor Geoffrey Kerr. The couple divorced in 1943; their son is actor John Kerr, born 1931.

She appeared in twenty-five films and television programs from 1917 to 1964. Some of those credits include *The Millionaire* (1917), *War Nurse* (1930), *Thru Different Eyes* (1942), *Actor's Studio* (1949), *Broadway Television*

Theatre (1953), *Climax!* (1956), *The Unforgiven* (1960) with Audie Murphy, *Whispering Smith* (1961) again with Audie Murphy, *Kraft Mystery Theater* (1962), *A Child Is Waiting* (1963), and *The Alfred Hitchcock Hour* (1964-1964).

She appeared with her son, John Kerr, in a 1954 episode of NBC's *Justice*. It was his first acting engagement.

She died February 3, 1966, at age 65 in Los Angeles, California.

Geraldine Wall

Geraldine Wall was born June 24, 1912, in Chicago, Illinois. She was the original choice for the role of Dolly Tate in the 1950 M-G-M film *Annie Get Your Gun*. When Betty Hutton replaced Judy Garland in the role of Annie Oakley, Benay Venuta took over the role of Dolly Tate.

Other credits include *Keep Your Powder Dry* (1945), *Scudda Hoo! Scudda Hay!* (1948), *Beyond Glory* (1948) with Audie Murphy, *Appointment with Danger* (1951), *The Man in the Gray Flannel Suit* (1956), *Designing Woman* (1957), *Alcoa Presents: One Step Beyond* (1959), *Heller in Pink Tights* (1960), *The Dick Van Dyke Show* (1962-1964), *Perry Mason* (1957-1965), *Mannix* (1968), and *Here Come the Brides* (1970).

She died June 22, 1970, at age 57 in Woodland Hills, Los Angeles, California.

George Wallace

George Wallace with Audie Murphy in *Destry*

George Wallace was born George Dewey Wallace June 8, 1917, in New York City, New York, and, at age thirteen, moved with his mom and her new husband to McMechen, West Virginia, a coal mining town where the boy began working in the mines.

He joined the Navy in 1936, got out in 1940, and then went right back in again when World War II started. A chief boatswain's mate, he ended up in Los Angeles after a total of eight years in the service.

Wallace supported himself with an array of odd jobs, from working for a meat packer ("knockin' steers in the head") to lumber-jacking in the High Sierras. A stint as a singing bartender attracted the attention of Hollywood columnist Jimmy Fidler, who helped him get his show-biz start.

Wallace enrolled in drama school in the late 1940s, while earning his living tending the greens at MGM. He soon began landing jobs in films and TV, most notably as Commando Cody in the Republic serial *Radar Men from the Moon* (1952).

He later made his Broadway debut in Richard Rodgers' *Pipe Dreams*, replaced John Raitt in *The Pajama Game* and was nominated for a Tony for his leading role in *New Girl in Town* with Gwen Verdon. Other stage roles have included *The Unsinkable Molly Brown* opposite Ginger Rogers, *Jennie* with Mary Martin, *Most Happy Fella* (during production, he met his wife, actress Jane A. Johnston), *Camelot* (as King Arthur), *Man of La Mancha, Company*, and more.

More film and television roles followed such as *The Lawless Breed* (1953), *Border River* (1954), *Hopalong Cassidy* (1952-1954), *Drums Across the River* (1954) with Audie Murphy, *The Human Jungle* (1954), *Destry* (1954) again with Audie Murphy, *The Second Greatest Sex* (1955), *Forbidden Planet* (1956), and *The Tall Man* (1960).

In 1960, his career was stalled when a horse fell on him and broke his back during the making of an episode of TV's *Walt Disney's Wonderful World of Color* (1954) *Swamp Fox*. His painful recovery took seven months.

After he recovered he continued to get roles such as Frank McLowery in *The Life and Legend of Wyatt Earp* (1961), *Six Black Horses* (1962) a third appearance with Audie Murphy, *Texas Across the River* (1966), *Skin Game* (1971), *The Six Million Dollar Man* (1973), *Dusty's Trail* (1973), *The Towering Inferno* (1974), *The Bionic Woman* (1976), *The Private Files of J. Edgar Hoover* (1977), *Dallas* (1983), *Night Court* (1984), *Dynasty* (1986), *Chicken Soup* (1989), *Postcards from the Edge* (1990), *Sons and Daughters* (1991), *Star Trek: The Next Generation* (1992), *Walker, Texas Ranger* (1994), *JAG* (1997), *Bicentennial Man* (1999), *Buffy the Vampire Slayer* (2002), *Minority Report* (2002), and *Joan of Arcadia* (2004).

He sometimes billed himself George D. H. Wallace, to avoid confusion with comic George Wallace.

He died July 22, 2005, at age 88 in Los Angeles, California.

Jack Warden

Audie Murphy with Jack Warden in *Suspicion*

Jack Warden was born John Warden Lebzelter in Newark, New Jersey, September 18, 1920, and was an American character actor. He was of Irish and Pennsylvania Dutch ancestry. Raised in Louisville, Kentucky, he was expelled from high school for fighting and eventually fought as a professional boxer under the name Johnny Costello. He had thirteen welterweight bouts but earned little money.

Warden worked as a nightclub bouncer, tugboat deckhand, and lifeguard before joining the United States Navy in 1938. He was stationed in China for three years with the Yangtze River Patrol.

In 1941, he joined the United States Merchant Marine but, quickly tiring of the long convoy runs, he switched to the United States Army in 1942 where he served as a paratrooper in the 501st Parachute Infantry Regiment, with the elite 101st Airborne Division during World War II.

In 1944, on the eve of the D-Day invasion (during which many of his friends died), Staff Sergeant (Lebzelter) Warden shattered his leg by landing in a tree during a night-time practice jump in England. After almost eight months in the hospital (during which time he read a Clifford Odets play and decided to become an actor), he was sent back to the United States. Ironically in *That Kind of Woman* (1959) Warden played a paratrooper from the 101st's rivals: the 82nd Airborne Division.

After leaving the military with the rank of master sergeant, he moved to New York City and pursued an acting career on the G.I. Bill. He joined the company of the Dallas Alley Theater and performed on stage for five years. In 1948 he made his television debut on *The Philco Television Playhouse* (1950-1955) and *Studio One* (1954-1955). He made an uncredited film debut in 1951 in *You're in the Navy Now*, a movie which also featured the film debuts of Lee Marvin and Charles Bronson.

Warden had his first credited film role in *The Man with My Face* in 1951, and in 1952 he began a three-year role in the television series *Mr. Peepers*. After a role as a sympathetic corporal in *From Here to Eternity* (1953),

Warden's breakthrough film role was his performance as Juror No. 7, a salesman who wants a quick decision in a murder case, in *12 Angry Men* (1957).

Other Credits include "The Flight" episode of *Suspicion* (1957) with Audie Murphy, *Darby's Rangers* (1958), *Twilight Zone* (1959-1960), *The Asphalt Jungle* (1961), *Donovan's Reef* (1963), *The Wackiest Ship in the Army* (1965-1966), *The Fugitive* (1967), *N.Y.P.D.* (1967-1969), and *The Man Who Loved Cat Dancing* (1973).

Warden was nominated for Academy Awards as Best Supporting Actor for his performances in *Shampoo* (1975) and *Heaven Can Wait* (1978). He also had notable roles in *All the President's Men (1976)* , *...And Justice for All* (1979), *Being There* (1979), *Used Cars* (1980) (in which he played a celebrated dual role), *The Verdict* (1982), *Problem Child* (1990), its sequel *Problem Child 2* (1991), and the second sequel *Problem Child 3: Junior in Love* (1995).

He also portrayed Harry Fox in *Crazy Like a Fox* (1984-1986) and the sequel movie *Still Crazy Like a Fox* (1987), and Hank Knight in *Knight & Daye* (1989).

Warden appeared in over one hundred movies, typically playing gruff cops, sports coaches, trusted friends or similar roles, during a career which spanned six decades. His last film was *The Replacements* in 2000, opposite Gene Hackman and Keanu Reeves.

Warden married French actress Vanda Dupre in 1958 and had one son, Christopher. Although they separated in the 1970s, they never divorced.

Warden suffered from declining health in his last years, and died of heart and kidney failure in a New York hospital on July 19, 2006. He was 85 years old.

Robert Warwick

Robert Warwick with Audie Murphy in *Walk the Proud Land*

Robert Warwick was born Robert Taylor Bien October 9, 1878, and was an American stage, film and television actor with over 200 film appearances.

Handsome and with a booming voice, Warwick trained to be an operatic singer, but acting proved to be his greater calling. He made his Broadway debut in 1903 in the play *Glad of It*. One of his co-stars in this play was a young John Barrymore, also making his Broadway debut. Both men quickly became matinee idols.

For the next twenty years, Warwick appeared in such plays as *Anna Karenina* (1906), *Two Women* (1910), with Mrs. Leslie Carter, *The Kiss Waltz* (1911), *Miss Prince* (1912), in both of which he was able to display his opera-trained singing voice, *The Secret* (1913), *A Celebrated Case* (1915) and *Drifting* (1922) with Alice Brady, not to mention several other plays through the end of the 1920s.

Warwick started making silent films in 1914. He made numerous productions in the 1910s primarily in Fort Lee, New Jersey. Two films, *Alias Jimmy Valentine* (1951) and *A Girl's Folly* (1917), both directed by Maurice Tourneur have been preserved, and showcase Warwick as a silent actor, as well as Tourneur's directing talent, and both are available on home video.

From the 1920s on, Warwick alternated doing plays and silent films. He was fifty when sound films arrived, and now middle aged with his matinee idol looks fading, he found plenty of work in character roles in which his voice recorded well. This eventually necessitated his moving permanently to California to be near the film studios when they moved to Los Angeles.

Throughout the 1930s and 1940s, Warwick's dependable acting and resonant voice ensured that he was seldom out of work. His immense filmography includes such classics as *The Little Colonel* (1935) with Shirley Temple and *The Adventures of Robin Hood* (1938) with Errol Flynn.

He was one of a number of actors favored by director Preston Sturges and appeared in many of his films, among them *Sullivan's Travels* (1941), *I Married a Witch* (1942), *The Palm Beach Story* (1942), *Hail the Conquering Hero* (1944), and *Man from Frisco* (1944).

Other film credits include *The Three Musketeers* (1948), *Tarzan and the Slave Girl* (1950), *The Mississippi Gambler* (1953), *Chief Crazy Horse* (1955), *Walk the Proud Land* (1956) with Audie Murphy, *Night of the Quarter Moon* (1959), and *It Started with a Kiss* (1959).

Warwick made numerous appearances on television almost from its initial popularity in the late 1940s. In his seventies he was still hard at work and made appearances on every type of television show like *Biff Baker, U.S.A.* (1952), *Topper* (1954), *The Adventures of Rin Tin Tin* (1957-1959), *Twilight Zone* (1960), and *Dr. Kildare* (1962).

Warwick was married several times. Divorced from his first two wives, he survived his third, actress Stella Lattimore (1905–1960), before dying June 6, 1964 in Los Angeles at the age of 86. By his first wife he had one daughter, Rosalind, who bore him two grandchildren, and with his second wife another daughter, Betsey, who was a prominent published poet in Los Angeles and was buried next to her father at Holy Cross Cemetery in Los Angeles in 2007. His and his wife Stella's headstones are engraved "Beloved Father" and "Beloved Mother".

Charles Watts

Charles Watts with Audie Murphy in *No Name on the Bullet*

Charles Watts was born October 30, 1912, in Clarksville, Tennessee, and was a very recognizable character actor. He also taught Business law and Drama at Chattanooga High School, Chattanooga, Tennessee, from 1937 to 1938.

Rotund, moon-faced Charles Watts made a mini-career out of portraying glad-handing politicians, voluble businessmen and salesmen, crafty bankers, and cheerful or cynical parents, uncles, family friends, and other supporting players.

He never had a starring role, or even a co-starring role, in a motion picture, but his physical presence and voice made for some memorable moments.

He worked in local theater and tent shows early in his career, and after World War II was also in demand for industrial shows. Watts didn't start doing movie or television appearances until 1950, and in that first year he played small, uncredited roles in such serious dramas as *The Killer That Stalked New York* (1950), as a mailman, and *Storm Warning* (1951), as a lunch-counter proprietor, and somewhat larger parts, as a sheriff, in three episodes of *The Lone Ranger* (1950).

Over the next sixteen years, he was seen in nearly 100 movies and television shows. His most prominent big-screen role was that of Judge (and later United States Senator) Oliver Whiteside in George Stevens' *Giant* (1956), where his rich, melodious voice and cheerful demeanor were put to extensive use.

Other film credits include *The Big Land* (1957), *The Lone Ranger and the Lost City of Gold* (1958), *No Name on the Bullet* (1959) with Audie Murphy, *One Foot in Hell* (1960), *Something Wild* (1961), *Days of Wine and Roses* (1962), *Seven Days in May* (1964), *Apache Rifles* (1964) again with Audie Murphy, and *Baby the Rain Must Fall* (1965).

As active on television as he was in movies, Watts was familiar to several generations of young viewers for his role as Bill Green, the skeptical anti-superstition league leader in the *Adventures of Superman* episode "The Lucky Cat" (1955). Other television credits include *Dragnet* (1956-1957), *The Texan* (1958), *The Untouchables* (1960), *Bachelor Father* (1959-1962), and *Bonanza* (1961-1964).

He died of cancer December 13, 1966, at age 54 in Nashville, Tennessee.

Dennis Weaver

Dennis Weaver with Audie Murphy in *Column South*

William Dennis Weaver was born June 4, 1924, and was an American actor, best known for his work in television, including his role as Matt Dillon's trusty deputy Chester Goode on the long-running western series *Gunsmoke* (1955-1964), as Marshal Sam McCloud on the NBC police drama *McCloud* (1970-1977), and in the 1971 TV movie *Duel*, the first film of director Steven Spielberg.

Weaver was born in Joplin, Missouri, son of Walter Weaver and his wife Lena Prather. His father was of Irish, Scottish, English, Cherokee, and Osage ancestry. Weaver wanted to be an actor from childhood. For a short time during his teenage years he lived in Manteca, California. He studied at Joplin Junior College, now Missouri Southern State University and then transferred to the University of Oklahoma at Norman, where he studied drama and was a track star, setting records in several events.

During World War II he served as a pilot in the United States Navy. At the war's end, he married Gerry Stowell, by whom he had three children; Richard, Robert, and Rustin Weaver. He tried out for the U.S. Olympic team in the decathlon. He finished sixth and only the top three were chosen for the team. Weaver later said, "I did so poorly [in the Olympic Trials], I decided [to]... stay in New York and try acting".

Weaver's first role on Broadway came as an understudy to Lonny Chapman as Turk Fisher in *Come Back, Little Sheba*. He eventually took over the role from Chapman in the national touring company. Solidifying his choice to become an actor, Weaver enrolled in The Actors Studio, where he met Shelley Winters.

In the beginning of his acting career, he supported his family by doing a number of odd jobs, including selling vacuum cleaners, tricycles, and women's hosiery.

In 1952, Winters aided him in getting a contract from Universal Studios. He made his film debut that same year in the movie *The Redhead from Wyoming*.

Over the next three years, he played roles in a series of movies, such as *Column South* (1953) with Audie Murphy, *Dragnet* (1954), and *The Bridges at Toko-Ri* (1954), but still had to work odd jobs to support his family.

It was while delivering flowers that he heard he had landed his biggest break, the role of Chester Goode, the limping, loyal deputy of Marshal Matt Dillon (James Arness) on the new television series *Gunsmoke*, which would go on to become the highest-rated and longest-running series in US television history (1955 to 1975). He received an Emmy Award in 1959 for Best Supporting Actor (Continuing Character) in a Dramatic Series.

Having become famous as Chester, he was cast in an offbeat supporting role in the 1958 Orson Welles film *Touch of Evil*, in which he played an employee of a remote motel who nervously repeated, "I'm the night man". In 1960, he appeared in an episode of *Alfred Hitchcock Presents* entitled "Insomnia" in which his character suffers from sleeplessness due to the tragic death of his wife. In 1961, he did an episode of *The Twilight Zone* called "Shadow Play" where he was trapped inside his own dream.

From 1964 to 1965, he portrayed a friendly veterinarian in NBC's comedy-drama *Kentucky Jones*. His next substantial role was as Tom Wedloe on the CBS family series *Gentle Ben*, with co-star Clint Howard, between 1967 and 1969.

Weaver landed the title role of the NBC series *McCloud* in 1970, for which he received two Emmy Award nominations. In 1974, he was nominated for Best Lead Actor in a Limited Series and in 1975, for Outstanding Lead Actor in a Limited Series. The show, about a modern western lawman that ends up in New York City, was loosely based on the Clint Eastwood film *Coogan's Bluff* (1968). His frequent use of the affirming Southernism, "There you go", became a catchphrase for the show. During the series, in 1971, Weaver also appeared in *Duel*, a television movie directed by Steven Spielberg.

From 1973 to 1975, Weaver was president of the Screen Actors Guild.

In 1978, Weaver played the trail boss R.J. Poteet in the television miniseries *Centennial* on the episode titled "The Longhorns". In 1980, he played Dr. Samuel Mudd, who was imprisoned for involvement in the Lincoln assassination, in *The Ordeal Of Doctor Mudd.*

Later series during the 1980s (both of which lasted only one season) were *Stone* (1980), in which Weaver played a Joseph Wambaugh-esque police sergeant turned crime novelist with his real life son Robby Weaver, and *Buck James* (1987-1988), in which he played a Texas-based surgeon and rancher (*Buck James* was loosely based on real-life Texas doctor Red Duke). He portrayed a Navy rear admiral for twenty-two episodes of a 1983-84 series, *Emerald Point N.A.S.*.

In 1983, he played a real estate agent addicted to cocaine in *Cocaine: One Man's Seduction.* Weaver received probably the best reviews of his career when he starred in the 1987 film *Bluffing It,* in which he played a man who is illiterate. In February 2002, he appeared on the animated series *The Simpsons* episode "The Lastest Gun in the West" as the voice of aging Hollywood cowboy legend Buck McCoy.

For his contribution to the television industry, Dennis Weaver was given a star on the Hollywood Walk of Fame at 6822 Hollywood Blvd, and on the Dodge City (KS) Trail of Fame. In 1981, he was inducted into the Western Performers Hall of Fame with the Bronze Wrangler Award at the National Cowboy & Western Heritage Museum in Oklahoma City, Oklahoma.

Weaver's last work was done on an ABC Family cable television show called *Wildfire* (2005), where he played Henry, the father of Jean Ritter and the co-owner of Raintree Ranch. His role on the show was cut short due to his death.

Weaver had been a vegetarian since 1958 and student of yoga and meditation since the 1960s and a devoted follower of Paramahansa Yogananda, the Indian guru who established the Self Realization Fellowship in the United States. He was also renowned as an environmentalist, promoting eating lower on the food chain, alternative fuels such as hydrogen and wind power through an educational organization he founded, The Institute of Ecolonomics (a neologism formed by combining "ecology" and "economics"). He was also involved with John Denver's WindStar Foundation. He founded an organization called L.I.F.E. (Love is Feeding Everyone) which provided food for 150,000 needy people a week in Los Angeles.

In July 2003, Weaver lost a daughter-in-law, Lynne Ann Weaver (who was married to his son, Robby Weaver), in Santa Monica, California, when a car, being driven at high speed by an elderly driver, plowed through shoppers at an outdoor bazaar that was being held on a closed off section of the street. Ten people were killed.

The "Earth Ship", the personal home he commissioned architect Michael Reynolds to design and build in Ridgway, Colorado during the late 1980s, incorporated recycled materials in its construction and featured advanced eco-technologies.

Weaver was consistently involved with the annual Genesis Awards, which were created by The Ark Trust to honor those in the media who bring attention to the plight and suffering of animals.

Weaver died of complications of cancer at his home in Ridgway, Colorado on February 24, 2006.

Dick Wessell

Audie Murphy with Dick Wessell in *The Kid from Texas*

Dick Wessell was born Richard M. Wessel, April 20, 1913 in Milwaukee, Wisconsin. Rough-and-tumble American actor Dick Wessel had a fierce-looking scowl on a bulldog of a mug. That, coupled with a thick build and imposing stance, earned him appearances in countless Warner Brother's comedies and hard-boiled crime dramas throughout the late 1930s and 1940s.

Although he made hundreds of films, he had few chances to show off, appearing uncredited in over half of them and in minor, fleeting roles when he did receive billing. He had roles in such "A" pictures as *Angels with Dirty Faces* (1938), *Yankee Doodle Dandy* (1942), and *Strangers on a Train* (1951), but his visibility in them was practically nil.

The husky-framed character actor began his career on stage before starting in films in the mid-1930s. Getting unbilled extra roles at first, he appeared on both sides of the moral fence over the years, playing as many brutish gangsters, henchmen and convicts as he did rough-hewn cops or streetwise characters (cabbies, mailmen, bartenders, boxers, etc.) The tough-sounding names of his characters, such as "Monk," "Beans," "Moxie", and "Chopper Kane", pretty much said it all. His best showcase, and it should have worked out better for him, was menacing, bald-pated arch-villain Harry "Cueball" Lake in *Dick Tracy vs. Cueball* (1946). Here he was finally given a chance to shine but it did not lead to meatier roles.

He became a stock player for Columbia and their assembly-line of short comedy subjects, essaying a slew of burglars, thieves, wrestlers, circus strongmen, and lummox husbands for The Three Stooges, Andy Clyde, and others.

Other film roles included *Tarzan's New York Adventure* (1942), *13 Rue Madeleine* (1947), *Take Me Out to the Ball Game* (1949), *Sands of Iwo Jima* (1949), *The Kid from Texas* (1950) with Audie Murphy, *Gentlemen Prefer Blondes* (1953), and *Rebel Without a Cause* (1955).

On TV he was a rugged presence on such western series as *Gunsmoke* (1955), *Laramie* (1959), *Rawhide* (1959), and *Bonanza* (1959).

Close to the end of his life and career he had a regular part as a crew member on the adventure series *Riverboat* (1959) with Darren McGavin. Other TV roles included *Adventures of Wild Bill Hickok* (1956), *Twilight Zone* (1963), *The Fugitive* (1963), and *Gunsmoke* (1965).

Dick's final role was released posthumously, playing a bit as a frantic garbage man in *The Ugly Dachshund* (1966). He had died a year earlier April 20, 1965, at his Hollywood home of a heart attack on his 52nd birthday. His wife and a daughter survived him.

Jesse White

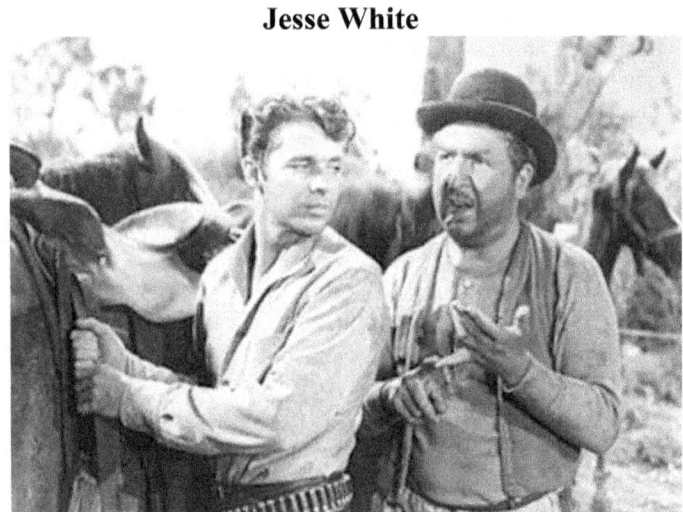

Audie Murphy with Jesse White in *Gunsmoke*

Jesse White was born January 4, 1917, and was an American television, film, and stage character actor. He is best remembered for portraying the Maytag repairman in television commercials, a role he played from 1967 to 1988.

White was born as Jesse Marc Weidenfeld in Buffalo, New York, and was raised in Akron, Ohio. He made his first amateur appearance in local stage productions at the age of 15. Though aspiring to be an actor, he worked at many different jobs during the 1930s, including selling beauty supplies and lingerie. After moving to Cleveland, Ohio, Jesse began a career in vaudeville and burlesque, traveling widely before landing a role on Broadway.

In 1942, White made his Broadway debut in *The Moon is Down*, followed by a successful performance in the role of a sanitarium orderly in the popular play *Harvey*. He would later reprise his role in the 1950 film version and the 1972 television movie.

In 1947, White made his film debut in a small part in *Kiss of Death*. Other roles soon followed in such films as *Texas, Brooklyn & Heaven* (1948) with Audie Murphy, *Francis Goes to the Races* (1951), *Million Dollar Mermaid* (1952), *Gunsmoke* (1953) again with Audie Murphy, *Not as a Stranger* (1955), *Johnny Trouble* (1957), and *Marjorie Morningstar* (1958).

During the 1950s, he began landing roles on television shows, including appearances in Danny Thomas's *Make Room for Daddy* (1953-1954) and Peter Lawford's *Dear Phoebe* (1954). In 1954, he landed a semi-regular role on *Private Secretary*, starring Ann Sothern, Ann Tyrrell, and Don Porter. The role led to another semi-regular part as the deceitful Oscar Pudney in *The Ann Sothern Show* in 1960.

In the 1960s, White also appeared on *The Twilight Zone* (1961-1962), *The Dick Van Dyke Show* (1961), *Mickey* (1964), starring Mickey Rooney, *The Munsters* (1965), *The Addams Family (1964)*, and *I Dream of Jeannie* (1967).

In a memorable cameo, he played a frustrated airport tower controller (alongside a hilarious Paul Ford, Carl Reiner, and Eddie Ryder) in *It's a Mad, Mad, Mad, Mad World* (1963).

In 1966, he accepted the role of Donelli in *The Reluctant Astronaut*, playing a curmudgeonly janitorial supervisor who instructed his students in the use of a mop in a deadpan delivery rivaling that of an aerospace engineer. In a short but memorable performance, he routinely castigated Don Knotts's bumbling character Roy Fleming for his "lack of dedication" to cleaning floors. An advertising director who saw his performance on the film's release soon cast him in a television advertising campaign for the Maytag Corporation. White played the role of a lonely Maytag repairman, a man with nothing to do as a result of his company's reputation for dependable products. In one of the campaign's first spots, White's character unmistakably alluded to his former role as 'Donelli': *"At ease men! Now, you men have all volunteered to be Maytag Repairmen and so I'm gonna give it to you straight. Maytag washers and dryers are built to last. That makes the Maytag Repairman the loneliest guy in town!"* The campaign proved wildly successful, and the actor began a long-running and highly-paid career as the ever-lonely Maytag repairman. While reprising his Maytag repairman role, White continued appearing in both television and films during his many years as the Maytag repairman.

His final film role was a small but pivotal role in the 1993 Joe Dante comedy *Matinee* starring John Goodman, and his last TV role was in an episode of *Seinfeld* in 1996.

In 1942, White married Celia Cohn (July 17, 1914 - August 5, 2003). The couple had two daughters, Carole Ita White (who later became an actress) and Janet Jonas.

On January 9, 1997, White died from a heart attack following surgery, only five days after his 80th birthday. He is buried at Mount Sinai Memorial Park in Los Angeles.

CeCe Whitney

CeCe Whitney was born Cecilene Whitney December 22, 1933 in Shawnee Oklahoma. She appeared in twenty-five films and television programs from 1958 to 1969. Some of those credits include *Tombstone Territory* (1958), *Philip Marlowe* (1959), *Alcoa Presents: One Step Beyond* (1959), *Peter Gunn* (1959-1960), *Have Gun - Will Travel* (1961), *Route 66* (1962-1963), *Bullet for a Badman* (1964) with Audie Murphy, *Kraft Suspense Theatre* (1964), *Nashville Rebel* (1966), *Occasional Wife* (1967), and *Gunsmoke* (1962-1969).

Peter Whitney

Peter Whitney was born Peter King Engle in Long Branch, New Jersey, May 24, 1916, and was an American actor in film and television. Whitney's corpulent, heavy build qualified him to play villains in many Hollywood movies in the 1940s and 1950s.

From the late 1950s, he was more prolific playing character roles in many films and television series, including *Big Jim McLain* (1952), *Gorilla at Large* (1954), *The Sea Chase* (1955), *Domino Kid* (1957), *Buchanan Rides Alone* (1958), *Have Gun - Will Travel* (1958-1960), *Whispering Smith* (1961) with Audie Murphy, *The Beverly Hillbillies* (1964), *The Iron Men* (1966), *In the Heat of the Night* (1967), *The Great Bank Robbery* (1969), *The Ballad of Cable Hogue* (1970), and *San Francisco International Airport* (1970).

From 1958 to 1959, Whitney had a co-starring role as Buck Sinclair, a former sergeant of the Union Army, in all thirty-nine episodes of the ABC western series *The Rough Riders*.

His final role was as a grave robber in writer Rod Serling's *Night Gallery* (1972). Whitney died March 30, 1972 of a heart attack shortly afterwards at the age of fifty-five.

Mary Wickes

Mary Wickes was born Mary Isabelle Wickenhauser in St. Louis, Missouri, June 13, 1910, and was an American film and television actress. Wickes was of German Irish Protestant extraction. She graduated at the age of eighteen with a degree in political science from Washington University in St. Louis, where she joined the Phi Mu women's fraternity and was initiated into Mortar Board in 1929. Wickes' first Broadway appearance was in Marc Connelly's *The Farmer Takes a Wife* in 1934 with Henry Fonda.

She began acting in films in the late 1930s, and was also a member of the Orson Welles troupe on his radio drama *Mercury Theatre of the Air*. One of her earliest significant film appearances was in *The Man Who Came to Dinner* (1942), reprising her stage role of "Nurse Preen".

A tall (5'10"), gangling woman with a distinctive voice, Wickes would ultimately prove herself adept as a comedienne, but she first attracted attention in the film *Now, Voyager* (1942), as the wisecracking nurse who helped Bette Davis' character during her mother's illness.

Also in 1942 she had a large part in the Abbott and Costello comedy *Who Done It?* She continued playing supporting roles in films during the next decade, usually playing wisecracking characters. A prime example was her deadpan characterization of Stella, the harassed housekeeper, in the Doris Day vehicles *By the Light of the Silvery Moon* (1953) and *On Moonlight Bay* (1951).

She had a great role in *Destry* (1954) with Audie Murphy as Bessie Mae Curtis who gets into a wet cat-fight with Mari Blanchard. She also appeared again with Abbott and Costello in their final film together *Dance with Me, Henry* (1956).

She played similar roles in two later movies with Rosalind Russell: *The Trouble with Angels* (1966) and *Where Angels Go, Trouble Follows* (1968).

Moving to the new medium of television in the 1950s, Wickes played the warm, yet jocular maid Katie in the *Mickey Mouse Club* serial *Walt Disney Presents: Annette* (1958) and regular roles in the sitcoms *Make Room for Daddy* (1956-1958) and *Dennis the Menace* (1959-1962), as well as appearing as Emma the housekeeper in the holiday classic *White Christmas* (1954), starring Bing Crosby, Danny Kaye, Rosemary Clooney and Vera-Ellen.

Wickes also served as the live-action reference model for Cruella De Vil in Walt Disney's *One Hundred and One Dalmatians* (1961).

In the 1961-1962 season, she appeared as Maxfield with Gertrude Berg in CBS's *Mrs. G. Goes to College*. For her work in the sitcom, Wickes was nominated for an Emmy Award for "Outstanding Performance in a Supporting Role by an Actress".

A longtime friend of Lucille Ball, Wickes played frequent guest roles in Ball's three CBS series, *I Love Lucy* (1952), *The Lucy Show* (1963-1967), and *Here's Lucy* (1969-1974).

She was also a regular on the Sid and Marty Krofft children's television show *Sigmund and the Sea Monsters* (1973-1975), and the sitcom *Doc* (1975-1976).

She made numerous appearances as a celebrity panelist on the game show *Match Game* (1976-1978). By the 1980s, her appearances in television series such as *M*A*S*H* (1975), *Kolchak: The Night Stalker* (1974), and *Murder, She Wrote* (1985) had made her a widely recognizable character actress.

She was cast as Shirley MacLaine's character's mother in the 1990 film *Postcards from the Edge* and from 1989 to 1991, portrayed Marie Murkin in the television movie and series adaptations of *Father Dowling Mysteries*. She played Sister Mary Lazarus in *Sister Act* (1992) and in the sequel *Sister Act 2: Back in the Habit* (1993). She appeared in the 1994 film version of *Little Women* before she became ill.

Wickes was hospitalized the following year suffering from numerous ailments, including kidney failure, massive gastrointestinal bleeding, severe low blood pressure, ischemic cardiomyopathy, anemia, and breast cancer, which cumulatively resulted in her dying while undergoing surgery on October 22, 1995.

Her final film role, voicing the gargoyle Laverne in Disney's animated feature *The Hunchback of Notre Dame* was released posthumously in 1996. She was interred beside her parents at the Shiloh Valley Cemetery in Shiloh, Illinois.

She never married. Wickes left a large estate and made a $2 million bequest, in memory of her parents, for the Isabella and Frank Wickenhauser Memorial Library Fund for Television, Film, and Theater Arts.

Frank Wilcox

Frank Reppy Wilcox was born March 13, 1907, in DeSoto, Missouri, and was an American character actor in scores of films after substantial stage experience. He was raised in Atchison, Kansas. The son of a railroad worker and law clerk, he wavered between various careers including oil exploration, but found his way after an introduction to the stage with the Atchison Civic Theatre and Kansas City Civic Theatre. He briefly attended the University of Kansas.

He moved from Kansas to California in 1930, where he lived with his grandparents and worked in the lemon groves near Pomona prior to opening a tire-repair shop in that city. He also helped found a theatre company in Pomona. He joined the Pasadena Community Playhouse, where he was spotted by a Warner Brothers talent scout looking for someone with a resemblance to Henry Clay, for the Warners short film *The Monroe Doctrine* (1939).

He signed with Warners as a contract player and was thereafter virtually never without work. He played in an enormous number of films over the next three decades, mostly in small supporting roles. He was equally adept at playing businessmen, attorneys, or historical figures, and was a familiar face on screen and on television for his entire career, though most people would have been unable to identify him by name.

Some of those credits include *Sergeant York* (1941), *Across the Pacific* (1942), *The Fighting Sullivans* (1944), *The Beginning or the End* (1947), as Pat Garrett in *The Kid from Texas* (1950) with Audie Murphy, *Go for Broke!* (1951), *The Greatest Show on Earth* (1952), *The Duel at Silver Creek* (1952) again with Audie Murphy, *Invaders from Mars* (1953), *Waterfront* (1954), *Abbott and Costello Meet the Keystone Kops* (1955), *Earth vs. the Flying Saucers* (1956), *Dance with Me, Henry* (1956) again with Bud & Lou, *Good Day for a Hanging* (1959), *Pete and Gladys* (1961-1962), *The Untouchables* (1959-1963), *Laredo* (1965), *Petticoat Junction* (1968-1969), *The Million Dollar Duck* (1971), and *Kung Fu* (1973).

Perhaps his greatest fame came in the TV role of oil company president John Brewster on *The Beverly Hillbillies* (1962-1966).

During the last years of his life, he was co-owner of a popular restaurant/bar in Encino, California, called The Oak Room. Wilcox died March 3, 1974, at age 66 in Granada Hills, California.

Robert Wilke

Robert Joseph Wilke was born May 18, 1914, in Cincinnati, Ohio. He was a prolific American character actor of primarily villainous roles. The son of German parents, Cincinnati feed-store manager August Wilke and his wife Rose, Robert Joseph Wilke grew up in Cincinnati. He worked as a lifeguard at a Miami, Florida, hotel, where he made contacts in the film business.

He was able to obtain work as a stuntman and continued as such until the mid-1940s, when he began getting actual roles in low-budget westerns and serials. A prominent appearance as one of the heavies in *High Noon* (1952) led to work in higher-quality films. He worked extensively in television as well as movies, and became an enormously familiar face, though a fairly anonymous one to the general public.

Some of his credits included *Buck Privates Come Home* (1947) with Abbott and Costello, *The Kid from Texas* (1950) with Audie Murphy, *The Abbott and Costello Show* (1952), *From Here to Eternity* (1953), *Wichita* (1955), *Night Passage* (1957) again with Audie Murphy, *Never Steal Anything Small* (1959), *Wichita Town* (1959), *The Magnificent Seven* (1960), *The Hallelujah Trail* (1965), *The Fugitive* (1966), *A Gunfight* (1971), *The Boy Who Cried Werewolf* (1973), *How the West Was Won* (1978), *B.J. and the Bear* (1979-1981), and *Stripes* (1981).

His weathered visage made him a perfect western bad guy, but he occasionally played sympathetic parts as well, as in *Days of Heaven* (1978).

An expert golfer, he was said by his friend Claude Akins to have earned more money on the golf course than he ever did in movies.

He died March 28, 1989, at age 74 in Los Angeles, California.

Guy Wilkerson

Guy Wilkerson was born December 21, 1899, in Whitewright, Texas. Lanky, balding character actor, former vaudevillian and burlesque artist, whose dour demeanor lent itself ideally to playing undertakers, hangmen, jurors and stern men of the cloth - when not employed as western sidekicks at PRC or Republic.

A rough count of his movies reveals that sixty-six are westerns, approximately half of the 128 films he made.

Also, he portrayed the character "Panhandle Perkins" in twenty-two PRC westerns from 1942 to 1945. He used the character name "Panhandle" in one other western, a Universal serial called *The Scarlet Horseman* (1946).

Some more of his credits included *Gone with the Wind* (1939), *Sergeant York* (1941), *Dead or Alive* (1944), *Texas, Brooklyn & Heaven* (1948) with Audie Murphy, as Virgil Earp in *Winchester '73* (1950), *The Red Badge of Courage* (1951) again with Audie Murphy, *Ma and Pa Kettle at Home* (1954), *No Name on the Bullet* (1959) a third appearance with Audie Murphy, *Elmer Gantry* (1960), *Seven Ways from Sundown* (1960) film number four with Audie Murphy, *Twilight Zone* (1960), *To Kill a Mockingbird* (1962), *The Fugitive* (1964), *True Grit* (1969), *Adam-12* (1970), and *The Todd Killings* (1971).

He died July 15, 1971, at age 71 in Hollywood, California.

Ellen Willard

Elen Willard, also spelled Ellen Willard was born September 1, 1941 and is an American former actress who appeared on network television between 1960 and 1966.

She is perhaps best remembered for four appearances on the ABC series *Twelve O'Clock High* (1964-1966).

Willard's first appearance in 1960 was as Deidre Waugh in the segment "The Bad Spell" of the short-lived detective series *Markham*. On November 16, 1960, Willard appeared as Belle Bleymier on the episode "The Bleymier Story" of NBC's western series, *Wagon Train*, broadcast just days after the death of series lead Ward Bond. Robert Horton as the scout Flint McCullough struggles to get a wagon train through a Sioux burial ground. Dan Duryea played the mentally unstable Samuel Bleymier, Belle's father, who is obsessed by demons and superstitions. Bleymier opposes the interest shown in Belle by young Justin Claiborne, played by James Drury, two years before NBC launched *The Virginian*. The episode is filmed mostly during heavy rains, high winds, and a cyclone.

In 1961, Willard played Charlotte Laughlin in the episode "The Quest" of NBC's *Whispering Smith*. She was also cast as Mrs. Madera in "Suitable for Framing" on Rod Taylor's *Hong Kong* (1961) series, which aired on ABC opposite *Wagon Train*. Other appearances in 1961 were as Caroline Lord in the episode "The Lords of Darkness" on ABC's western series, *Lawman*. She also appeared as Ione Sykes in the episode "The Grave" of CBS's *The Twilight Zone*.

In 1962, Willard appeared as Althea in "The Hunger" on CBS's *Gunsmoke* and as Anne Farell in "Any Second Now" of ABC's *Combat!*, a World War II drama, and as Joan Prentiss on NBC's *Dr. Kildare* in the episode "The Horn of Plenty." In 1962 and 1963, she made two appearances on Richard Boone's CBS western, *Have Gun, Will Travel*. In 1964, she portrayed Pelas Delcort in "Memory of a Firing squad" on the ABC college drama, *Channing*. Willard's final screen appearance was on December 23, 1966, as Priscilla Worth in the Christmas episode "The Jingle Bells Affair" of the Robert Vaughn NBC series, *The Man from U.N.C.L.E.*

Adam Williams

Adam Williams with Audie Murphy in *Gunfight at Comanche Creek*

Adam Williams was born Adam Berg November 26, 1922, in Wall Lake, Iowa, and was an American film and television actor.

He was a veteran "bad guy" actor of 1950s film and TV who began his career after distinguished WWII military service as a U.S. Navy pilot, being awarded the Navy Cross.

Williams' notable roles included playing Larry, a car bomber, in *The Big Heat* (1953). In 1952, Williams played the lead role as Los Angeles woman killer in *Without Warning!*. Other roles included *The Yellow Tomahawk* (1954), *The Sea Chase* (1955), and *The Oklahoman* (1957).

He had a leading role in the 1958 science fiction movie *The Space Children*. Other notable roles include the psychiatrist in *Fear Strikes Out* (1957) and Valerian in *North by Northwest* (1959).

More roles continued in *The Badlanders* (1958), *Black Saddle* (1959-1960), *Twilight Zone* (1960), *Whispering Smith* (1961) with Audie Murphy, *Combat!* (1962), *Gunfight at Comanche Creek* (1963) again with Audie Murphy, *The Fugitive* (1965), *Custer* (1967), *The Horse in the Gray Flannel Suit* (1968), *Mannix* (1971), *Marcus Welby, M.D.* (1976), *Helter Skelter* (1976), *The Girl Called Hatter Fox* (1977), and *Sword of Justice* (1978).

An accomplished pilot, Williams also worked as an examiner for the FAA.

Adam Williams died from lymphoma in Los Angeles, California, December 4, 2006, at age 84.

Charles Williams

Charles Williams was born September 27, 1898, in Albany, New York and he was an American character actor. He was also the son-in-law of Actress Elisabeth Risdon.

He appeared in 251 films and television programs from 1922 to 1956. Some of those credits include *Blondie of the Follies* (1932), *Dancing Lady* (1933) with The Three Stooges, *The Girl from Missouri* (1934) with Jean Harlow, *The Lone Ranger* (1938), *Primrose Path* (1940), *The Pride of the Yankees* (1942), *Duffy's Tavern* (1945), *It's a Wonderful Life* (1946), *Texas, Brooklyn & Heaven* (1948) with Audie Murphy, *Life with Buster Keaton* (1951), *The Abbott and Costello Show* (1953), *Annie Oakley* (1955), *A Lawless Street* (1955), *Adventures of Superman* (1954-1956), and *Fighting Trouble* (1956).

He died January 3, 1958, at age 59 in Hollywood, California.

Kenny Williams

No biographical information can be found for Kenny Williams, but he did appear as an actor in seventeen films from 1936 to 1959. Some of those credits include *One in a Million* (1936), *Everything's on Ice* (1939), *Sweet Rosie O'Grady* (1943), *Irish Eyes Are Smiling* (1944), *When My Baby Smiles at Me* (1948), *When Willie Comes Marching Home* (1950), *The Pride of St. Louis* (1952), *Night Passage* (1957) with Audie Murphy, and *It Started with a Kiss* (1959).

Rhys Williams

Audie Murphy with Rhys Williams in *Bad Boy*

Rhys Williams was born December 31, 1897, and was a Welsh character actor in movies and television, whose career spanned several decades.

He made his film debut in *How Green Was My Valley* (1941). This movie takes place in rural Wales with a large cast of Welsh characters, but was actually filmed in Hollywood with Canadian, American, Irish, and English actors. Williams, the only genuine Welshman in the cast, was originally hired solely to coach the actors in their Welsh accents; ultimately director John Ford gave Williams a role in the film.

He is recognizable to fans of the TV series *Adventures of Superman* as a sadistic character in an early episode called "The Evil Three" (1952).

His other television and film appearances were *Random Harvest* (1942), *The Bells of St. Mary's* (1945), *The Trouble with Women* (1947), *Bad Boy* (1949), *Million Dollar Pursuit* (1951), *Carbine Williams* (1952), *The Lone Wolf* (1954), *Battle Cry* (1955), *Nightmare* (1956), *The Fastest Gun Alive* (1956), *The Rifleman* (1959-1960), *Wanted: Dead or Alive* (1960-1961), *The Sons of Katie Elder* (1965), *Brigadoon* (1966), *Here Come the Brides* (1969), and *Skullduggery* (1970).

Williams died May 28, 1969, at age 71, and his remains are interred at Forest Lawn-Hollywood Hills, Los Angeles.

Willard Willingham

Audie Murphy with Willard Willingham

William Willingham was born August 20, 1909, in Flagstaff, Arizona. He was an American actor, stuntman, writer, and producer. Some of his acting credits include *Law Comes to Gunsight* (1947), *Red Canyon* (1949), *Riding High* (1950), *Son of Paleface* (1952), *The Savage* (1952), *Pony Express* (1953), *Arrowhead* (1953), *I Led 3 Lives* (1954), *The McConnell Story* (1955), *Santiago* (1956), *Magic Christmas Tree* (1964), and *Deadwood '76* (1965).

He appeared with Audie Murphy in *Joe Butterfly* (1957), *Night Passage* (1957), *Hell Bent for Leather* (1960), two episodes of *Whispering Smith* (1961), *Arizona Raiders* (1965), *40 Guns to Apache Pass* (1967), and *A Time for Dying* (1969).

He was a stuntman on fifteen of Audie Murphy's films from *The Kid from Texas* (1950) to *A Time for Dying* (1969).

He died May 11, 1997, at age 87 in Benton, Kentucky.

Chill Wills

Audie Murphy with Chill Wills in *Tumbleweed*

Chill Wills was born Theodore Childress Wills in Seagoville, Texas, July 18, 1902, and was an American film actor, and a singer in the Avalon Boys Quartet.

He was a performer from early childhood, forming and leading the Avalon Boys singing group in the 1930s. After appearing with them in a few westerns, he disbanded the group in 1938 and struck out on a solo acting career.

He provided the deep voice for Stan Laurel's performance of "The Trail of the Lonesome Pine" in the 1937 movie *Way Out West*.

Other early roles included *Allegheny Uprising* (1939), *Belle Starr* (1941), *See Here, Private Hargrove* (1944), *Tulsa* (1949), *High Lonesome* (1950), *Rio Grande* (1950), *Cattle Drive* (1951), and *Tumbleweed* (1953) with Audie Murphy.

One of his more memorable roles was that of the distinctive voice of Francis the Mule in a series of popular films. Wills' deep, rough voice and Western twang were perfectly matched to the personality of the cynical, sardonic mule. As was customary at the time, Wills was given no billing for his vocal work, though he was featured prominently on-screen as blustery General Ben Kaye in the fourth entry, *Francis Joins the WACS* (1954).

Wills also appeared in numerous serious roles, including that of Uncle Bawley in *Giant*, a 1956 film starring Rock Hudson, Elizabeth Taylor, and James Dean.

Wills was nominated for Best Supporting Actor in 1960 for his role as Davy Crockett's companion "Beekeeper" in the film *The Alamo*.

From 1961–62, Wills starred in the short-run series *Frontier Circus* which aired for only one season on CBS.

He then appeared as Drago in *McLintock!* (1963).

In 1966, Wills was cast in the role of a shady Texas rancher, Jim Ed Love, in the short-lived ABC comedy/western series *The Rounders*, with co-stars Ron Hayes, Patrick Wayne, and Walker Edmiston.

Other roles continued in *Tarzan* (1968), *The Over-the-Hill Gang* (1969), *The Over-the-Hill Gang Rides Again* (1970), *Rod Serling's Night Gallery* (1970), *Alias Smith and Jones* (1972), *Pat Garrett & Billy the Kid* (1973), *Hec Ramsey* (1974), *Mr. Billion* (1977), and *Poco...Little Dog Lost* (1977).

Wills was a poker player and a close friend of Benny Binion, the founder of the World Series of Poker and former owner of the Binion's Horseshoe Casino in Las Vegas. Wills participated in the first World Series, held in 1970, and is seated in the center of the now famous picture with a number of legendary players.

His last role was in 1978 as a janitor in *Stubby Pringle's Christmas*.

Wills died in December 15, 1978, of cancer in Encino, California, at age 76. He is interred in the Grand View Memorial Park Cemetery in Glendale.

Marie Windsor

Marie Windsor was born Emily Marie Bertelson in Marysvale, Piute County, Utah, December 11, 1919, and was an actress known as "The Queen of the Bs" because she appeared in so many B-movies and film noirs.

Windsor, a former Miss Utah, trained for the stage under Maria Ouspenskaya, and after several years as a telephone operator, a stage and radio actress, and a bit and extra player in films, she began playing feature and lead parts in 1947.

The 5'9" actress's first memorable role was opposite John Garfield in *Force of Evil* (1948) playing seductress Edna Tucker. Windsor also had large roles in film noirs including *The Sniper* (1952), *The Narrow Margin* (1952), *City That Never Sleeps* (1953), and Stanley Kubrick's heist movie *The Killing* (1956) playing Elisha Cook, Jr.'s scheming wife.

Other early roles included *The Eddie Cantor Story* (1953), *The Bounty Hunter* (1954), *Abbott and Costello Meet the Mummy* (1955), and *Swamp Women* (1956).

She continued to get juicy roles, appearing on such shows and films as *Maverick* (1957-1962), *Whispering Smith* (1961) with Audie Murphy, *The Day Mars Invaded Earth* (1963), *Destry* (1964), *Chamber of Horrors* (1966), *The*

Good Guys and the Bad Guys (1969), *Support Your Local Gunfighter* (1971), *Hec Ramsey* (1972), *Cahill U.S. Marshal* (1973), *Adam-12* (1971-1973), *Freaky Friday* (1976), *Salem's Lot* (1979), *General Hospital* (1982), *Simon & Simon* (1983-1987), *New Adam 12* (1990), and *Murder, She Wrote* (1987-1991).

She was one of the 500 stars nominated to become one of the fifty greatest American screen legends as part of the American Film Institute's 100 years.

Windsor married twice, first briefly to bandleader Ted Steele, and later to Jack Hupp, a member of the 1936 U.S. Olympic basketball team. Hupp, with whom Windsor had a son, was posthumously inducted into the University of Southern California (USC) Athletic Hall of Fame in 2007.

After her acting career was over, Windsor became a painter and sculptor. She died December 10, 2000, of undisclosed causes on the day before her 81st birthday. She is interred with Hupp in Marysvale, Utah.

Tammy Windsor

Tammy Windsor was born Roberta Lynn Kupcinet March 6, 1941, in Chicago, Illinois, and was an American actress who appeared in nineteen films and television programs from 1957 to 1964. She sometimes went by Tammy Windsor or Karyn Kupcinet.

Kupcinet was born to Irv Kupcinet, a sportswriter for the *Chicago Daily Times*, and his wife, Esther "Essee" Solomon Kupcinet. She acquired the nickname "Cookie" during her childhood. She made her acting debut at age thirteen in the Chicago production of *Anniversary Waltz* and went on to attend Pine Manor College for a semester, eventually studying at the Actor's Studio in New York.

Kupcinet was encouraged into acting by her mother, and was given access to producers through the reputation of her father and his *Kup's Column* in the *Chicago Sun-Times*.

Some of her early roles included *Sheriff of Cochise* (1957), *U.S. Marshal* (1958), *The Wild and the Innocent* (1959) with Audie Murphy, *This Earth Is Mine* (1959), *The Little Shop of Horrors* (1960), and *Hawaiian Eye* (1960-1961).

In 1961, Jerry Lewis offered Kupcinet a role in the film *The Ladies Man*, where she appeared in a bit part as one of dozens of young ladies in a Hollywood boardinghouse. In 1962, she appeared in the role of Annie Sullivan in a Laguna Beach summer theater production of *The Miracle Worker*.

She appeared in guest roles on television including *The Donna Reed Show* (1961), *The Wide Country* (1963), *G.E. True* (1961), and *Going My Way* (1963). In addition to guest spots, Kupcinet had a regular role in the prime time series *Mrs. G. Goes to College* (1961-1962) (retitled *The Gertrude Berg Show* during its short run).

Kupcinet's last onscreen appearance was in an episode of *Perry Mason* entitled, "The Case of the Capering Camera." The episode aired on CBS on January 16, 1964, nearly two months after her death.

By 1961, Kupcinet was living in Hollywood and was getting positive reviews for her acting.

Karyn Kupcinet, was found murdered, strangled in her West Hollywood apartment, on November 28, Thanksgiving Day, 1963, six days after the assassination of President Kennedy. The crime has never been solved.

On September 30, 1999, an episode of *E! True Hollywood Story*, entitled "Death of a Dream: Karyn Kupcinet", detailed Kupcinet's life and theories regarding her death.

Joseph Wiseman

Joseph Wiseman was born May 15, 1918, and was a Canadian theater and film actor, best known for starring as the titular antagonist of the first James Bond film, *Dr. No* (1962), his role as Manny Weisbord on *Crime Story* (1986-1988), and his career on Broadway. He was once called "the spookiest actor in the American theater".

Born in Montreal, Quebec, Canada to Orthodox Jewish parents, Louis and Pearl Rubin (née Ruchwarger), Wiseman grew up in New York. At age sixteen, he began performing in summer stock and became professional, which displeased his parents.

He made his Broadway debut in 1938, playing a small part in Robert E. Sherwood's *Abe Lincoln in Illinois*. Among the many productions he appeared in in a long career in live theatre was the title role in *In the Matter of J. Robert Oppenheimer* on Broadway in 1968, and the role of Father Massieu in the original Broadway production of *Joan of Lorraine*, the Maxwell Anderson play which eventually became the film *Joan of Arc*. His last Broadway appearance was in *Judgment at Nuremberg* in 2001.

He appeared in several films in the 1950s. He made his first major film appearance in 1951's *Detective Story*, where he recreated his performance from Broadway as an unstable small time hood. Soon after he played Marlon Brando's archenemy in *Viva Zapata!* (1952).

Other roles followed like *The Silver Chalice* (1954), *The Prodigal* (1955), *Three Brave Men* (1956), *The Garment Jungle* (1957), and *The Unforgiven* (1960) with Audie Murphy.

More roles continued in television programs and films like *The Untouchables* (1960-1961), *Twilight Zone* (1962), *Wagon Train* (1964), *The Legend of Jesse James* (1966), *The Counterfeit Killer* (1968), *Rod Serling's Night Gallery* (1970), *Lawman* (1971), *O'Hara, U.S. Treasury* (1972), *Murder at the World Series* (1977), *Buck Rogers in the 25th Century* (1979), *Masada* (1981), *The Greatest American Hero* (1981), *The A-Team* (1984), *MacGyver* (1989), and *L.A. Law* (1994).

Wiseman's last appearance on television was the supporting role of Seymour Bergen on a 1996 episode of *Law & Order* titled "Family Business".

Following the death of Charles Gray in 2000, Wiseman was the last surviving main villain of the James Bond films that Sean Connery made for United Artists.

Wiseman died on October 19, 2009, at age 91 at his home in Manhattan, having been in declining health for some time. Wiseman is survived by his daughter, Martha Graham Wiseman, and his sister, Ruth Wiseman.

Although Wiseman is arguably most remembered for his role as the titular character in *Dr. No*, Wiseman, later in his life, would view the film with disdain, wanting to be most remembered for his theater career.

Dave Wolfe

Audie Murphy with Dave Wolfe in *The Cimarron Kid*

David Wolfe was born March 1, 1915, in New York City, New York, and was an American character actor. He appeared in twenty-nine films and television programs from 1949 to 1954.

Some of those credits include *Flaming Fury* (1949), *Tokyo Joe* (1949), *Prisoners in Petticoats* (1950), *Kansas Raiders* (1950) with Audie Murphy, *Appointment with Danger* (1951) with Alan Ladd, *Dangerous Assignment* (1952), *The Cimarron Kid* (1952) again with Audie Murphy, *The Iron Mistress* (1952) again with Alan Ladd, *I'm the Law* (1953), and *Salt of the Earth* (1954). He later became stage manager and lover for Tommy Tune.

He died of AIDS September 23, 1994, at age 79 in New York City, New York.

Frank Wolff

Frank Wolff was born Walter Frank Hermann Wolff May 11, 1928, in San Francisco, California. Frank Wolff started his career by acting in several Roger Corman films.

Some other early American films and television programs included *G.E. True Theater* (1957), *I Mobster* (1958), *Sea Hunt* (1958), *Kathy O'* (1958), *Jefferson Drum* (1958), *The Wild and the Innocent* (1959) with Audie Murphy, *Beast from Haunted Cave* (1959), *The Wasp Woman* (1959), *Ski Troop Attack* (1960), *Twilight Zone* (1960), and *The Four Days of Naples* (1962).

He was finally able to become a well known actor in Italy and Europe with his performance in *Salvatore Giuliano* (1962) and had roles in many European film productions.

Moreover, Wolff became a major star in Spaghetti Westerns. His most famous, but briefest, performance was as Brett McBain, the friendly farmer in Sergio Leone's *Once Upon a Time in the West* (1968). He also brought much needed light relief as the sheriff in Sergio Corbucci's *The Great Silence* (1968).

When the time of "Spaghetti-Westerns" was ending, Wolff had several roles in Italian crime movies. Other memorable performances were in Duccio Tessari's *Giallo La morte risale a ieri sera* (1970) or in one of Wolff's last performances as a police commissioner in Fernando Di Leo's *Caliber 9* (1972).

Sadly, the great actor suffered from depression and killed himself in the Hilton Hotel in Rome in December 12, 1971.

Barbara Woodell

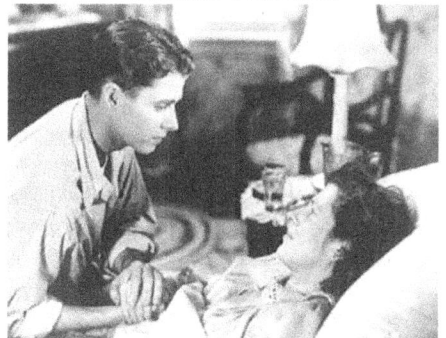

Audie Murphy with Barbara Woodell in *Bad Boy*

Barbara Woodell was born May 25, 1910, in Lewiston, Illinois, and was an American character actress. She appeared in over 100 films and television programs from 1941 to 1964.

Some of those credits include *Mr. & Mrs. Smith* (1941), *The Picture of Dorian Gray* (1945), *Smash-Up: The Story of a Woman* (1947), *The Hal Roach Comedy Carnival* (1947), *Joan of Arc* (1948), as Audie Murphy's mother in *Bad Boy* (1949), *The Stratton Story* (1949), *Little Big Horn* (1951), *And Now Tomorrow* (1952), *The Lone Ranger* (1952-1953), *Seven Angry Men* (1955), *Cavalcade of America* (1953-1957), *Showdown at Boot Hill* (1958), *The Millionaire* (1958-1960), *The Great Impostor* (1961), and *Wagon Train* (1961-1964).

She January 16, 1997, at age 86 in Ojai, California.

Morgan Woodward

Thomas Morgan Woodward was born September 16, 1925, in Fort Worth, Texas. He is probably best known for his recurring role in *Dallas* (1980-1987) as Marvin "Punk" Anderson. He also played the silent, sunglasses-wearing, "man with no eyes", Boss Godfrey (the Walking Boss) in *Cool Hand Luke* (1967) and holds the record for most Guest Appearances on the long-running Western TV series, *Gunsmoke* (1957-1974), with nineteen. He also appeared in the reunion movie *Gunsmoke: To the Last Man* (1992).

Woodward attended the University of Texas at Arlington, then Arlington State College in Arlington, Texas. He graduated from the University of Texas at Austin. Along with two of his four brothers, he has received recognition as a Distinguished Alumnus of the University. He is a member of the Pi Kappa Alpha Fraternity.

He went into active duty with the Air Force during the Korean War. He was sent to Korea and served with the Military Air Transport Command. After being demobilized, he did not return to law school but became an actor instead.

His brother, Lee Woodward, was the weatherman with a lion puppet named "King Lionel" on the television station KOTV in Tulsa, Oklahoma.

One of Woodward's longest TV roles was as the deputy/sidekick "Shotgun" Gibbs in 1955-1961 TV series *The Life and Legend of Wyatt Earp* starring Hugh O'Brian. On that series, Woodward played a tall, cantankerous, shotgun-toting backwoodsman who eventually became the trusted deputy of lawman Wyatt Earp in his days as a Kansas lawman. Though often overshadowed by the cool menace of Douglas Fowley's Doc Holliday, Woodward portrayed Gibbs as a solid, trustworthy, and more pragmatic partner to Earp, making Gibbs a character who, though ostensibly rough around the edges, would gradually come to share many of the qualities demonstrated over the years by another trusted TV deputy, Ken Curtis' world-weary Festus Haggen on *Gunsmoke* (1959-1975).

Some other credits include *Gunsight Ridge* (1957), *Ride a Crooked Trail* (1958) with Audie Murphy, *The Gun Hawk* (1963), *The Sword of Ali Baba* (1965), *Gunpoint* (1966) again with Audie Murphy, *Firecreek* (1968), *Star Trek* (1966-1968), *Death of a Gunfighter* (1969), *Yuma* (1971), *Bonanza* (1960-1971), *Hec Ramsey* (1972), *Planet of the Apes* (1974), *Final Chapter: Walking Tall* (1977), *Logan's Run* (1977-1978), *Starsky and Hutch* (1978), *Centennial* (1978), *The Incredible Hulk* (1979), *The Misadventures of Sheriff Lobo* (1980), *Hill Street Blues* (1982), *The Dukes of Hazzard* (1980-1984), *Murder, She Wrote* (1989), *Renegade* (1993), *The Adventures of Brisco County Jr.* (1994), *The X-Files* (1995), and *Millennium* (1997).

Woodward was a familiar face on the hit television drama *Dallas* from 1980-1989. His recurring role of Marvin "Punk" Anderson, a friend of Jock Ewing's, and a member of the "cartel" of oil barons, became popular with viewers. As the series progressed Woodward's role became that of an advisor to the Ewing boys, and a voice of reason. His character's wife Mavis was played by character actress Alice Hirson. Hirson and Woodward were written out of the show during the 1989 season for budgetary reasons although the characters were mentioned in the following last two seasons of the show.

He appeared in the episode "The Assassin" of *T.J. Hooker* (1985) as Maj. Gen. Robert Selkirk who says in the episode about his efforts in the Korean War "I was a regular Audie Murphy".

In August 1988, he received the prestigious "Golden Boot Award" from the Hollywood Motion Picture and Television Fund.

In 1994, the Texas Arts Council presented Morgan with its Lifetime Achievement in the Arts Award in his hometown of Arlington, Texas. The city also named a prominent street "Morgan Woodward Way".

In 1997 Morgan celebrated fifty years in show business and was given the "International Star Award" in Los Angeles.

Woodward's chief hobby is restoring, rebuilding and flying antique airplanes. In aviation circles, he is recognized as an authority on Early American Aircraft and has received numerous awards for his restoration projects.

He has frequently appeared at Western film and television festivals around the country.

Jane Wyatt

Audie Murphy with Jane Wyatt in *Bad Boy*

Jane Wyatt was born Jane Waddington Wyatt August 12, 1910, and was an American actress perhaps best known for her role as the housewife and mother on the television comedy *Father Knows Best* (1954-1960), and as Amanda Grayson, the human mother of Spock on the science fiction television series *Star Trek* (1967). Wyatt was a three-time Emmy Award-winner.

Jane Wyatt was born in Campgaw (now part of Mahwah, New Jersey), but was raised in New York City. Her father, Christopher Billopp Wyatt, Jr., was a Wall Street investment banker, and her mother, the former Euphemia Van Rensselaer Waddington, was a drama critic for the *Catholic World*. Both of her parents were Roman Catholic converts.

One of her ancestors, Rufus King, was a signer of the U.S. Constitution, a U.S. Senator and ambassador, and the Federalist candidate in the 1816 United States presidential election. She was also a descendant of British Royal Navy captain Christopher Billopp. Through her connection with Captain Billopp she is also related to James Willis. She was a distant cousin of Eleanor Roosevelt and the poet Harry Crosby, through their shared descent from Philip Livingston, also a signer of the Declaration of Independence.

While in New York City, Wyatt attended the Chapin School and later attended two years of Barnard College. After leaving Barnard, she joined the apprentice school of the Berkshire Playhouse at Stockbridge, Massachusetts, where for six months she played a varied assortment of roles.

One of her first jobs on Broadway was as understudy to Rose Hobart in a production of *Trade Winds*–a career move that cost her her listing in the New York Social Register (she later was relisted upon her marriage). Receiving favorable notices on Broadway and celebrated for her understated beauty, Wyatt made the transition from stage to screen and was placed under contract by Universal Pictures.

She made her film debut in 1934's *One More River*. In arguably her most famous role, she co-starred as Ronald Colman's character's love interest in Frank Capra's Columbia Pictures film *Lost Horizon* (1937). Of her experience in *Lost Horizon*, she noted in an article in the *St. Anthony Messenger* newsletter, "During the war, they cut out all the pacifist parts of the film—the High Lama talking about peace in the world. All that was cut because they were trying to inspire those G.I.'s to get out there and go 'bang! bang! bang!' which sort of ruined the film".

Other roles included *None But the Lonely Heart* (1944), *The Bachelor's Daughters* (1946), *Gentleman's Agreement* (1947), *Bad Boy* (1949) with Audie Murphy, *My Blue Heaven* (1950), and *Robert Montgomery Presents* (1950-1953).

For many people, Wyatt is best remembered as Margaret Anderson in the television comedy *Father Knows Best* from 1954 to 1960. She played opposite Robert Young as the devoted wife and mother of the Anderson family in the Midwestern town of Springfield. This role won Wyatt three Emmy Awards for best actress in a comedy series. Billy Gray, Elinor Donahue, and Lauren Chapin played the Anderson children. She reprised the role for the *The Father Knows Best Reunion* (1977) and its sequel *Father Knows Best: Home for Christmas* (1977).

Wyatt also played Amanda Grayson, Spock's mother, in the 1967 episode "Journey to Babel" of the original *Star Trek* series and the 1986 film *Star Trek IV: The Voyage Home*. Wyatt was once quoted as saying her fan mail for these two roles exceeded that of *Lost Horizon*.

She also appeared as Anna, mother of the Virgin Mary, in the 1978 TV film *The Nativity*.

Late in her career, she played Katherine Auschlander, the wife of hospital administrator Dr. Daniel Auschlander (Norman Lloyd), on the medical drama *St. Elsewhere* (1983-1988).

Though one of her early suitors was John D. Rockefeller III, Wyatt was married to investment broker Edgar Bethune Ward from November 9, 1935, until his death on November 8, 2000, just one day short of the couple's 65th wedding anniversary. The couple met in the late 1920s when both were weekend houseguests of Franklin D. Roosevelt, at Hyde Park.

She suffered a mild stroke in the 1990s, but recovered well. She remained in relatively good health for the rest of her life.

Jane Wyatt died on October 20, 2006 of natural causes at her home in Bel-Air, California. She was 96 years old. She is buried in San Fernando Mission Cemetery, next to her husband. Wyatt is survived by her sons Christopher and Michael Ward (according to an obituary in *The Washington Post*, a third son died in infancy in the early 1940s), three grandchildren and five great grandchildren.

Lloyd L. Wyatt

Audie Murphy with Lloyd L. Wyatt in *To Hell and Back*

No biographical information could be found for Lloyd L. Wyatt, but he did appear in only one film. He portrayed Pierce the Tank Commander in *To Hell and Back* (1955) with Audie Murphy.

Keenan Wynn

Keenan Wynn with Audie Murphy in *Joe Butterfly*

Keenan Wynn was born July 27, 1916, and was an American character actor. His bristling mustache and expressive face were his stock in trade, and though he rarely had a lead role, he got prominent billing in most of his film and TV parts. Wynn was born in New York City as Francis Xavier Aloysius James Jeremiah Keenan Wynn, the son of vaudeville comedian Ed Wynn and wife, the former Hilda Keenan. He took his stage name from his maternal grandfather, Frank Keenan, one of the first Broadway actors to star in Hollywood. His father was Jewish and his mother was of Irish Catholic background.

Ed Wynn encouraged his son to become an actor, and the two appeared together in the original *Playhouse 90* television production of Rod Serling's *Requiem for a Heavyweight* (1956). The son was returning the favor: according to radio historian Elizabeth McLeod, it was Keenan who had helped his father overcome professional collapse and a harrowing divorce and nervous breakdown to return to work a decade earlier, and who now helped convince Serling and producer Martin Manulis that the elder Wynn should play the wistful trainer. He also appeared in a subsequent TV drama detailing the problems they had experienced while working on that show called *The Man in the Funny Suit* (1960). In it, the Wynns, Serling, and much of the cast and crew played themselves. Keenan also featured in another Rod Serling production, a *The Twilight Zone* episode entitled, "A World of His Own" (1960) as playwright Gregory West, who uniquely caused the series's creator Rod Serling to disappear.

Wynn appeared in hundreds of films and television shows between 1934 and 1986. His early post-war credits include *Annie Get Your Gun* (1950), *Royal Wedding* (1951), *Kiss Me, Kate* (1953), *The Man in the Gray Flannel*

Suit (1956), *Joe Butterfly* (1957) with Audie Murphy, *A Hole in the Head* (1959), *The Absent-Minded Professor* (1961), *Son of Flubber* (1963), and *Dr. Strangelove* (1964). He had an uncredited role in *Touch of Evil* (1958).

In the 1959-1960 television season, Wynn co-starred with Bob Mathias in NBC's *The Troubleshooters*, an adventure program about unusual events surrounding an international construction company. Wynn played the role of Kodiak, the "troubleshooter", for Mathias's Frank Dugan.

Wynn took a dramatic turn as Yost in the crime drama *Point Blank* (1967) with Lee Marvin. He played Hezakiah in the 1965 comedy *The Great Race* (1965). He was the voice of the Winter Warlock in *Santa Claus Is Comin' to Town* (1970) and was in several Disney films, including *Snowball Express* (1972), *Herbie Rides Again* (1974), and *The Shaggy D.A.* (1976).

He appeared in Francis Coppola's musical *Finian's Rainbow* (1968), Sergio Leone's epic western *Once Upon a Time in the West* (also 1968), and Robert Altman's *Nashville* (1975). During this time his guest television roles included *Alias Smith and Jones* (1971-1972), *Emergency!* (1975), and *The Bionic Woman* (1978).

He also played highly stressed Police Captain Joe 'Mad Dog' Siska trying to keep calm when dealing with Darren McGavin's Carl Kolchak character in *Kolchak: The Night Stalker* (1974-1975) in a couple episodes. His character was unsuccessful in keeping calm.

Wynn became a regular on TV's *Dallas* during 1979 to 1981, playing the part of former Ewing family partner-turned-enemy Willard "Digger" Barnes. David Wayne, a friend of his, was cast for the first season, but was unable to continue owing to his starring role in the *House Calls* (1979-1982) series at the time.

Wynn was initially cast in *Superman* (1978) to play Perry White (the boss of Clark Kent and Lois Lane at the *Daily Planet*) in April 1977. However, by June (production had moved to Pinewood Studios in England), Wynn collapsed from exhaustion and was rushed to the hospital. He was replaced by Jackie Cooper.

In 1983, he guest starred on one of the last episodes of *Taxi*. In 1984 he starred in the television film *Call to Glory*, which later became a weekly television series.

He appeared as 'Butch' in eight episodes of *The Last Precinct* (1986). His last role was as Grandpa in *Hyper Sapien: People from Another Star* (1986).

Wynn was married to former stage actress Eve Lynn Abbott (1914–2004) until their divorce in 1947, whereupon Abbott married actor Van Johnson. One son, actor and writer Ned Wynn (born Edmond Keenan Wynn) wrote the autobiographical memoir *We Will Always Live In Beverly Hills*. His other son, Tracy Keenan Wynn, is a screenwriter whose credits include *The Longest Yard* and *The Autobiography of Miss Jane Pittman* (both 1974). His daughter Hilda was married to Paul Williams. He was uncle by marriage to the Hudson Brothers.

In his later years, Wynn undertook a number of philanthropic endeavors and supported several charity groups. He was a long-standing active member of the Westwood Sertoma service club, in West Los Angeles. During his last few years, Wynn was suffering from pancreatic cancer, from which he died October 14, 1986. He is buried in Glendale's Forest Lawn Memorial Park.

Yossi Yadin

Audie Murphy with Yossi Yadin in *Trunk to Cairo*

Yossi Yadin was born Joseph Sukenik June 7, 1920, in Jerusalem, Palestine, and was an Isreali actor who made numerous films in America.

He served in a British Army musical group during World War II. There he met Hanna Maron, an actress to whom he was married for six years.

He appeared in the films *Four in a Jeep* (1951), *El Dorado* (1963), *Trunk to Cairo* (1966) with Audie Murphy, *The Hero* (1971), *Lies my Father Told Me* (1975), *Mary and Joseph: A Story of Faith* (1979), *Worlds apart* (1980), and *Quick Stop* (2001).

In 1991, Mr. Yadin was awarded the Israel Prize, the country's highest honor. He died May 17, 2001, at age 80 in Tel Aviv, Israel.

Carleton Young

Carleton Scott Young was born October 21, 1905, and was an American character actor born in New York City, New York and known for his deep voice.

Young appeared in 235 American television and film roles with his first being *The Fighting Marines* (1935).

Other films Young was cast in are: *Reefer Madness* (1936) *Navy Blues* (1937), *Dick Tracy* (1937), *Cassidy of Bar 20* (1938), *Billy the Kid Outlawed* (1940), *Billy the Kid in Texas* (1940), *Billy the Kid's Range War* (1941), *Buck Privates* (1941) with Abbott & Costello, *Keep 'Em Flying* (1941) again with Bud & Lou, *Valley of the Sun* (1942), *Thunderhead - Son of Flicka* (1945), *Best of the Badmen* (1951), *Flying Leathernecks* (1951), *The Day the Earth Stood Still* (1951), *Torpedo Alley* (1952), Goldtown Ghost Riders (1953), *From Here to Eternity* (1953), Walt Disney's adaptation of Jules Verne's *20,000 Leagues Under the Sea* (1954) as John Howard, *Battle Cry* (1955), *Battle Hymn* (1957), *The Horse Soldiers* (1959). *Sergeant Rutledge* (1960), *How the West Was Won* (1962), and his big line in *The Man Who Shot Liberty Valance* (1962) was: "This is the West, sir. When the legend becomes fact, print the legend."

Other television programs Young was cast in include: *Schlitz Playhouse of Stars* (1951), *Boston Blackie* (1953), *ABC Album* (1953), *Racket Squad* (1953), *The Whistler* (1954), *The Adventures of Wild Bill Hickok* (1955), twenty-six episodes as Harry Steeger in *The Court of Last Resort* (1957-1958), *The Rebel* (1960), *Whispering Smith* (1961) with Audie Murphy, *Twilight Zone* (1962), *My Three Sons* (1964-1970), *Barnaby Jones* (1973), and he ended his career in the 1973 television series *The Magician* which starred Bill Bixby.

Mr. Young had a few interests beyond acting, forming the Los Angeles Smog Corp. to manufacture cans of "Genuine Los Angeles Smog", which reportedly were sold in the "Fun Shop" at Farmers Market. Hal Tamblin was listed as a vice president of the corporation, according to a 1962 item in The Times, and Art Ryon, author of The Times' "Ham on Ryon" column, claimed to be an executive of the whimsical outfit. Salesman Stan Goodman of Baldwinsville, NY, a longtime friend of Mr. Young and his wife Noel, came up with the idea to sell the city's notoriously polluted air so tourists could take an authentic "slice" of Hollywood back home. Goodman's grandson, attorney Robert C. Goodman of San Francisco, still owns one of the few extant cans of vintage LA smog captured in time by Young's Los Angeles Smog Corp.

Young was married from 1945 until his death in 1994 to Noel Toy (the "Chinese Sally Rand"), an exotic dancer and actress whom he met when he caught her dance act at New York's Latin Quarter and was smitten.

Carleton Yound died in Los Angeles, California, November 7, 1994.

Louis Zito

Louis Zito was born March 15, 1928 in Brooklyn, New York. He was an American actor who appeared in six films and eleven television programs.

His films roles were *The True Story of Jesse James* (1957) as Clell Miller, *Solomon King* (1974), *Drive-In* (1976), *The Executioner* (1978), *Savage Streets* (1984), and *The Big Turnaround (1988)*.

His television roles were in such shows as *Jane Wyman Presents The Fireside Theatre* (1957), *Death Valley Days* (1957), *Suspicion* (1957) as the sanitarium guard in the episode "The Flight" with Audie Murphy, *The Walter Winchell File* (1957), *Tales of Wells Fargo* (1957), *Sergeant Preston of the Yukon* (1957), *Barney Miller* (1977), *Fish* (1978), *Flying High* (1978), *Charlie's Angels* (1981), and *Airwolf* (1985).

He died January 1, 1997, at age 68 in Sherman Oaks, California.

Audie Murphy Filmography

1. A Time for Dying (1969) .... Jesse James
2. 40 Guns to Apache Pass (1967) .... Capt. Bruce Coburn
3. The Texican (1966) .... Jess Carlin
4. Trunk to Cairo (1966) .... Mike Merrick
5. Gunpoint (1966) .... Chad Lucas
6. Arizona Raiders (1965) .... Clint Stewart
7. Apache Rifles (1964) .... Jeff Stanton
8. Bullet for a Badman (1964) .... Logan Keliher
9. The Quick Gun (1964) .... Clint Cooper
10. Gunfight at Comanche Creek (1963) .... Bob 'Gif' Gifford aka Judd Tanner
11. War is Hell (1963) .... Narrator
12. Showdown (1963) .... Chris Foster
13. Six Black Horses (1962) .... Ben Lane
14. Battle at Bloody Beach (1961) .... Craig Benson
15. Posse from Hell (1961) .... Banner Cole
16. Seven Ways from Sundown (1960) .... Seven Ways From Sundown Jones
17. The Unforgiven (1960) .... Cash Zachary
18. Hell Bent for Leather (1960) .... Clay Santell
19. Cast a Long Shadow (1959) .... Matt Brown
20. The Wild and the Innocent (1959) .... Yancy Hawks
21. No Name on the Bullet (1959) .... John Gant
22. The Gun Runners (1958) .... Sam Martin
23. Ride a Crooked Trail (1958) .... Joe Maybe
24. The Quiet American (1958) .... The American
25. Night Passage (1957) .... The Utica Kid
26. Joe Butterfly (1957) .... Pvt. Joe Woodley
27. The Guns of Fort Petticoat (1957) .... Lt. Frank Hewitt
28. Walk the Proud Land (1956) .... John P. Clum
29. World in My Corner (1956) .... Tommy Shea
30. To Hell and Back (1955) .... Audie Murphy
31. Destry (1954) .... Tom Destry
32. Drums Across the River (1954) .... Gary Brannon
33. Ride Clear of Diablo (1954) .... Clay O'Mara
34. Tumbleweed (1953) .... Jim Harvey
35. Column South (1953) .... Lt. Jed Sayre
36. Gunsmoke (1953) .... Reb Kittridge
37. The Duel at Silver Creek (1952) .... Luke Cromwell, The Silver Kid
38. The Cimarron Kid (1952) .... Bill Doolin aka The Cimarron Kid
39. The Red Badge of Courage (1951) .... The Youth
40. Kansas Raiders (1950) .... Jesse James
41. Sierra (1950) .... Ring Hassard
42. The Kid from Texas (1950) .... William Bonney ('Billy the Kid')
43. Bad Boy (1949) .... Danny Lester
44. Beyond Glory (1948) .... Thomas
45. Texas, Brooklyn and Heaven (1948) ....Copy boy

Audie Murphy Television Episodes

1. *Suspicion* (TV anthology series)
   - episode: ''The Flight'' (1957) ... Steve Murray
2. *General Electric Theater* (TV anthology series)
   - episode: "Incident" (1958) ... Tennessee
3. *Startime* (TV anthology series)
   - episode: ''The Man'' (1960) ....Howard Wilton

Whispering Smith (TV series)

1. 08/May/61 The Blind Gun
2. 15/May/61 The Grudge
3. 22/May/61 The Devil's Share
4. 29/May/61 Stakeout
5. 05/Jun/61 Safety Valve
6. 12/Jun/61 Stain of Justice
7. 19/Jun/61 The Deadliest Weapon
8. 26/Jun/61 The Quest
9. 03/Jul/61 Three for One
10. 10/Jul/61 Death at Even Money
11. 17/Jul/61 The Hemp Reeger Case
12. 24/Jul/61 The Mortal Coil
13. 31/Jul/61 Cross Cut
14. 07/Aug/61 Double Edge
15. 14/Aug/61 The Trademark
16. 21/Aug/61 The Jodie Tyler Story
17. 28/Aug/61 Poet and Peasant Case
18. 04/Sep/61 Dark Circle
19. 11/Sep/61 Swift Justice
20. 18/Sep/61 The Idol
21. never aired String of Circumstances
22. never aired The Interpreter
23. never aired The Homeless Wind
24. never aired Trial of the Avengers
25. never aired Prayer of a Chance
26. never aired Hired to Die

Audie Murphy's Co-Stars who attended Audie Murphy Days in Greenville, Texas

June 20, 1996 …………………………..no co-star attended
June 2, 1997…………………………….no co-star attended
May 23, 1998…………………………...no co-star attended
April 9, 10, 11, 1999…………………... no co-star attended
June 23, 24, 25, 2000………………….. no co-star attended
June 22, 23, 2001……………………....Paul Picerni
June 21, 22, 2002……………………....Paul Picerni
June 20, 21, 2003……………………....Paul Picerni & Ben Cooper
June 18, 19, 2004……………………... Paul Picerni & Ben Cooper
June 17, 18, 2005……………………... Paul Picerni, Ben Cooper, & Gregg Palmer
June 16, 17, 2006……………………....Neil Summers (actor/stuntman)
June 15, 16, 2007……………………....no co-star attended
June 27, 28, 2008……………………....Robert Hoy (actor/stuntman)
June 26, 27, 2009……………………....Johnny Western (actor/singer)
June 25, 26, 2010……………………....Paul Picerni
June 24, 25, 2011……………………....Autry & West Ward (actors/stuntmen)
April 20, 21, 2012……………………...Michael Dante
May 17, 18, 2013……………….……...no co-star attended

Audie Murphy Days continues…………………

Alphabetical Index of Co-Stars

A
Aaker, Lee
Acosta, Rudolph
Adams, Lillian
Adams, Mary
Adams, Phil
Adrian, Yvonne
Agar, John
Alaniz, Rico
Albert, Eddie
Alderson, John
Allgood, Sara
Anders, Merry
Anderson, Clinton
Anderson, Herbert
Anderson, James
Anderson, Sara
Andrade, Cisco
Andre, E.J
Ankrim, Morris
Aragon, Art
Archer, John
Arlen, Richard
Armstrong, R.G.
Arness, James
Ates, Roscoe
Athena
Atterbury, Malcolm
Atwater, Barry

B
Backus, Jim
Baird, Jimmy
Baldwin, Walter
Bancroft, Anne
Bane, Holly
Barcroft, Roy
Bardette, Trevor
Barnett, Griff
Barrat, Robert
Barrett, Claudia
Barton, Gregg
Bassett, William
Bates, Florence
Beaumont, Hugh
Beck, James
Beery, Noah
Bell, James
Bender, Russ
Benedict, Val
Best, James
Bettger, Lyle
Bevans, Clem
Bickford, Charles
Birch, Paul
Bissell, Whit
Blanchard, Mari
Blodgett, Michael

Bouchey, Willis
Bradford, Lane
Brady, Scott
Bramley, William
Brandon, Henry
Breck, Peter
Brennan, Walter
Brocco, Peter
Brodie, Kevin
Bromley, Sheila
Bronson, Lillian
Brooks, Rand
Brubaker, Robert
Buchanan, Edgar
Buffington, Sam
Buka, Donald
Burke, James
Burke, Robert Easton
Burkhart, Monte
Burns, Michael
Burton, Robert
Burwick, Viola

C
Cabot, Bruce
Cabot, Susan
Campanella, Joseph
Campbell, Colin
Carey, Harry Jr.
Carey, Olive
Carrizosa, Marty
Carr, Paul
Carter, Jimmy
Caruso, Anthony
Casas, Antonio
Castle, Mary
Castle, Richard
Catron Jack
Chamberlain, Richard
Chambers, Phil
Chandler, George
Chapman Marguerite
Charney, Kim
Chase, Frank
Chase, Stephen
Clark, Fred
Chekhov, Michael
Christy, Ken
Clements, Stanley
Cliff, John
Collier, Don
Collins, Ray
Colon, Miriam
Cook, Tommy
Cooper, Ben
Corby, Ellen
Corcoran, Hugh
Corday, Mara

Coulouris, George
Cowling, Bruce
Crabbe, Buster
Crane, Richard
Crawford, Broderick
Crayne, Dani
Crosby, Gary
Crowley, Kathleen
Crowley, Pat
Curtis, Donald
Curtis, Tony
Cutting, Richard

D
Dalton, Audrey
Dano, Royal
Dante, Michael
Dauphin, Claude
Davis, Jim
Day, Rosemary
Dearing, Edgar
DeCarlo, Suzette
DeCorsia, Ted
Dee, Sandra
Dehner, John
Dekkar, Albert
Delaney, Charles
Del Campo, Oscar
Delevanti, Cyril
Del Ray, Pilar
DeMarney, Terence
Dennis, Nick
Desti, Maria
Devine, Andy
Devon, Richard
DeWilde, Brandon
Diamond, Bobby
Dick, Douglas
Dierkes, John
Dixon, Ivan
Domergue, Faith
Donahue, Vincent
Donovan, King
Donlevy, Brian
Donnell, Jeff
Doran, Ann
Doucette, John
Downs, Johnny
Drake, Charles
Dru, Joanna
Dugan, Tom
Dugay, Yvette
Duncan, Craig
Duncan, Pamela
Dunn, James
Durant, Tim
Duryea, Dan

E
Egan, Richard
Elam, Jack
Eldredge, George
Eliot, Rosemary
Elliott, Ross
Ellis, Steve
Elsom, Isobel
Emerson, Hope
Evans, Charles
Evans, Joan
Erickson, Leif

F
Farr, Felicia
Fawcett, William
Ferguson, Frank
Field, Margaret
Field, Mary
Firestone, Eddie
Fix, Paul
Flavin, James
Flippen, Jay C.
Ford, Paul
Ford, Wallace
Foster, Dianne
Foulger, Rachel
Franz, Arthur
Frawley, William
Freeman, Kathleen
Frichtl, Bruce
Fulton, Rad

G
Gallaudet, John
Gaye, Lisa
Garralaga, Martin
Gebert, Gordon
Geer, Will
Gehring, Ted
Genth, Helga
Gerstle, Frank
Gilbert, Jody
Gish, Lillian
Gleason, James
Glenn, Louise
Goodwin, Harold
Gordon, Leo
Gorman, Annette
Graham, Fred
Grant, Kathryn
Gravers, Steve
Greer, Dabbs
Grey, Virginia
Griffith, James
Gulager, Clu

H

Haggerty, Don
Hale, Jr., Alan
Hall, Gita
Halsey, Brett
Hamilton, Kipp
Hammer, Alvin
Harding, John
Harford, Betty
Harmon, John
Harris, Berkeley
Hart, H. Tommy
Harvey, Harry
Hatton, Raymond
Haworth, Joe
Hayward, Jim
Healey, Myron
Hendrix, Wanda
Henry, Thomas Browne
Hepburn, Audrey
Hickey, William
Hickman, Darryl
Higa, Reiko
Hinton, Ed
Hoey, Dennis
Hogan, Dick
Holman, Rex
Homeier, Skip
Horvath, Charles
Hoy, Robert
Hoyt, John
Hubbard, John
Hudson, John
Hunnicutt, Arthur
Hunter, Henry

I

Iglesias, Eugene
Ingram, Jack
Ishimoto, Dale
Isreal, Victor
Ives, Burl

J

Jaeckel, Richard
Jacques, Ted
Jagger, Dean
Janis, Conrad
Janssen, David
Jara, Maurice
Jarrett, Renne
Johnson, Chubby
Johnson, Russell
Jolley, I. Stanford
Jones, L.Q.
Jordan, Ted
Jory, Victor

K

Karnes, Robert
Karns, Roscoe
Kay, Beatrice
Keefer, Don
Keep, Michael
Kellogg, John
Kelley, DeForest
Kelly, Jack
Kelly, Paul
Kerima
Keymas, George
Keith, Robert
King, Wright
Knowles, Patric
Koch, Marianne
Kohner, Susan
Krone, Fred
Krugman, Lou
Kruschen, Jack

L

Ladd, Alan
Lampert, Zohra
Lancaster, Burt
Lane, Abbe
Lane, Allan
Langton, Paul
Lapp, Richard
La Rue, Walt
Lauter, Harry
Lawrence, Marc
Lawson, Linda
Lee, Alan
Lee, Ruta
Lees, Paul
Leicester, William
Lennon, James
Leonard, Mel
Lewis, Nancy
Light, Pamela
Linn, Jo
Little, Eddie
Livingston, Patricia
Lloyd, Suzanne
Long, Richard
Loo, Richard
Lorys, Diana
Lowery, Robert
Lydon, James
Lynch, Ken
Lynn, Diana
Lynn, Rita

M

MacDonald, Kenneth
Macklin, David
Macready, George
Madison, Guy
Macgill, Moyna
Male, Colin
Maley, Peggy
Marquez, Luz
Martell, Gregg
Martin, Dewey
Martin, Strother
Marvin, Lee
Masak, Ron
Mauldin, Bill
Matthau, Walter
May, Marta
Mayer, Ken
Mazzola, Eugene
McClory, Sean
McClure, Doug
McGavin, Darren
McGovern, John
McGraw, Charles
McIntire, John
McKee, John
McNally, Stephen
McNear, Howard
McVey, Tyler
Medina, Patricia
Meredith, Burgess
Meredith, Charles
Meredith, Madge
Merlin, Jan
Merritt, Arnold
Meyer, Emile
Michaels, Dolores
Middleton, Robert
Milford, John
Millan, Victor
Millay, Diane
Miller, Colleen
Mills, Mort
Mims, William
Mitchell, Belle
Mitchell, George
Mitchell, Guy
Mitchell, Laurie
Mitchell, Thomas
Mitchum, John
Mohr, Gerald
Moll, Georgia
Moody, Ralph
Moore, Joanna
Moore, Terry
Morgan, Read
Morgan, Red
Morris, Barbara
Morrow, Byron
Morrow, Jeff
Morrow, Vic
Moser, Sonia
Mowbray Alan
Murphy, Skip
Murphy, Terry
Murray, Zon

N

Nader, George
Neal, Tom
Nelson, Lori
Nolan, Jeanette
Nolan, Lloyd
Noriego, Felix

O

O'Brian, Hugh
O'Brien, Joan
O'Flynn, Damian
Ojena, Louis
O'Malley, J. Pat
Osterloh, Robert
Overton, Frank
Owen, Beverly
Owens, Patricia

P

Paiva, Nester
Pallais, Dorita
Palmer, Gregg
Paris, Darla
Paris, Jerry
Patrick, Butch
Patterson, Hank
Pendleton, Steve
Peral, Antonio
Perry, Joe
Peters, Ralph
Phillips, John
Picerni, Paul
Pine, Robert
Platt, Edward C.
Pollard, Michael J.
Price, Sherwood
Pryor, Ainslie
Pullen, William
Pyle, Denver

Q

Qualen, John
Qualls, John
Quillan, Eddie

R

Rado, Jorge
Rainey, Ford
Rall, Tommy
Ramsey, Ward
Randall, Anne
Randle, Stuart
Randolph, Donald
Random, Bob
Redford, Robert
Redgrave, Michael
Reed, Donna
Reed, Walter
Reeves, Richard
Reid, Elliott
Rey, Alejandro
Reynolds, William
Richards, Addison

Richards, Frank
Richardson, Jack
Ridgway, Susan
Riguad, Jorge
Risdon, Elisabeth
Ritter, Thelma
Rivas, Carlos
Rober, Richard
Roberto, Freddy
Roberts, J.N.
Roberts, Roy
Roberts, Steven
Robinson, Bartlett
Robinson, Dewey
Rock, Blossom
Roland, Gilbert
Romero, Carlos
Rooney, Teddy
Roth, Gene
Rowland, Betty
Royle, Selena
Rudley, Herbert
Rush, Barbara
Ruskin, Joseph

S
Sadoff, Fred
Saito, Tatsuo
Salmi, Albert
Sambrell, Aldo
Sande, Walter
Sanders, George
Sanders, Hugh
Sanders, Sandy
Sanford, Erskin
Saxon, John
Scala, Gia
Scannell, Frank
Scott, Simon
Scotti, Vito
Seurat, Pilar
Sharman, Della
Shaw, Anabel
Shields, Joanne
Shields, Randy

Sheppard, Jim
Shima Keiko
Shimizaki, Chizo
Shimizaki, Shinpei
Silva, Henry
Silvera, Frank
Silverheels, Jay
Sky, Eddie Little
Sloane, Everett
Smith, K.L.
Sokoloff, Vladimir
Soule, Olan
Staley, Joan
Stander, Lionel
Stapp, Marjorie
Steele, Bob
Stehli, Edgar
Stephens, Laraine
Stephenson, John
Sterling, Robert
Stevens, K.T.
Stevens, Warren
Stevenson, Houseley
Stevenson, Venetia
Stewart, Elaine
Stewart, James
Stewart, Kay
St. John, Howard
Stone, Harold J.
Storm, Gale
Stricklyn, Ray
Stroll, Ed
Strudwick, Sheppard
Stuart, Tina
Sturgess, Olive
Sullivan, Barry
Sullivan, Joseph
Summers, Neil
Swenson, Karl

T
Tackitt, Wesley Marie
Talbot, Gloria
Talbot, Lyle
Talman, William

Tani, Yoko
Tannen, William
Tate, Kevin
Taylor, Forrest
Taylor, Joyce
Teal, Ray
Thomas, Arlette
Thomas, Lyn
Thompson, Marshall
Thurston, Carol
Tibbs, Casey
Tichy, Gerard
Tobey, Kenneth
Tobias, George
Toomey, Regis
Towne, Aline
Travers, Henry
Treen, Mary
Tremayne, Les
Trent, Peter
Trout, Tom
Tucker, Harland
Tumbleweed
Turich, Rosa
Tyler, Beverly
Tzur, Bomba

U
Upton, Julian
Urecal, Minerva

V
Valentine, Nancy
Van Cleef, Lee
Van Rooten, Louis
Van Sickel, Dale
Vejar, Chico
Vermilyea, Harold
Vickers, Martha
Vigran, Herb
Vilanova, Victor
Vitale, Joseph A.

W
Wade, Ernestine
Wade, Russell
Wagenhiem, Charles
Walker, June
Wall, Geraldine
Wallace, George
Warden, Jack
Warwick, Robert
Watts, Charles
Weaver, Dennis
Wessell, Dick
White, Jesse
Whitney, CeCe
Whitney, Peter
Wickes, Mary
Wilcox, Frank
Wilke, Robert
Wilkerson, Guy
Willard, Ellen
Williams, Adam
Williams, Charles
Williams, Kenny
Williams, Rhys
Willingham, Willard
Wills, Chill
Windsor, Marie
Windsor, Tammy
Wiseman, Joseph
Wolfe, Dave
Wolff, Frank
Woodell, Barbara
Woodward, Morgan
Wyatt, Jane
Wyatt, Lloyd L.
Wynn, Keenan

Y
Yadin, Yossi
Young, Carleton

Z
Zito, Louis

About the Author

David Alan Williams became an Audie Murphy fan early in life, as his mother would only let him stay up late when there was an Audie Murphy movie on the late show and she would let him watch it with her. His mother, being a movie fan, named him after David Janssen. His middle name was almost Audie, but Alan Ladd died just before he was born and since his mother was an Alan Ladd fan also, his middle name was Alan instead of Audie.

David has traveled through thirty-three states and has lived in eleven of them, but currently lives with his wife of twenty-four years, four daughters, three cats, and one dog in L.A. (Lower Arkansas). His wife Deborah is a math teacher and yearbook sponsor at their local high school.

www.ingramcontent.com/pod-product-compliance
Lightning Source LLC
Chambersburg PA
CBHW081755300426
44116CB00014B/2125